Victorian Yellowbacks & Paperbacks,
1849–1905

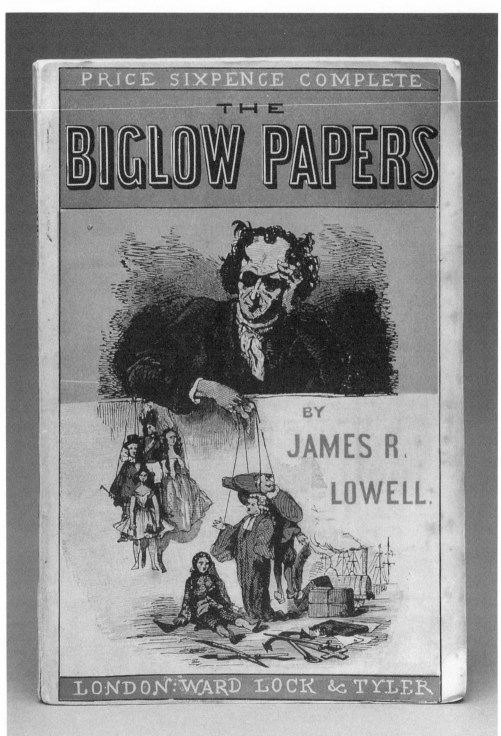

The Biglow Papers. See page 68

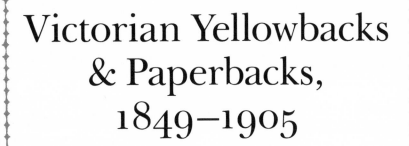

Victorian Yellowbacks & Paperbacks, 1849–1905

VOLUME II
WARD & LOCK

by Dr. Chester W. Topp

HERMITAGE ANTIQUARIAN BOOKSHOP

Denver, Colorado

1995

Published by
The Hermitage Bookshop
290 Fillmore Street
Denver, Colorado 80206-5020
(303) 388-6811

Printed and bound in the United States of America

First edition 1995, limited to 500 copies.
This book was designed by Polly Christensen, edited by Jane Raese,
and photographed by John Youngblut.
Typesetting was done by the patient and impeccable crew of
Wilsted & Taylor, Oakland, California.

∞ The paper used in this publication meets the minimum
requirements of American National Standard for Information
Sciences—Permanence of Paper for Printed Library Materials,
ANSI Z39.48-1984.

International Standard Book Number 0-9633920-1-8
Library of Congress Catalog Card Number: 92-073200

Short Titles and Abbreviations

Acad	*The Academy*
ALG&PC	*American Literary Gazette and Publishers' Circular*
Am Cat	*The American Catalog*
APC&LG	*American Publishers' Circular and Literary Gazette*
Ath	*The Athenaeum*
BAL	*Bibliography of American Literature*
Bks	*The Bookseller* (London)
BM	*The British Library Catalogue*
Eng Cat	*The English Catalogue*
Glover & *Greene*	*Victorian Detective Fiction*
Ind	*The Independent* (New York)
Lit W	*Literary World* (New York and Boston)
PC	*The Publishers' Circular and Booksellers' Record* (London)
PW	*Publishers' Weekly*
Roorbach	*Bibliotheca Americana*
Sat Rev	*The Saturday Review* (London)
Sadleir	Michael Sadleir's *Nineteenth Century Fiction*, 2 Volumes
Spect	*The Spectator*
TLS	*The Times Literary Supplement* (London)
U Cat	*The National Union Catalog*
Wolff	Robert Lee Wolff's *Nineteenth-Century Fiction*, 5 Volumes
Wright	Lyle H. Wright's *American Fiction*, 3 Volumes

Introduction

Ward & Lock was the most prolific publisher of yellowbacks and paperbacks after George Routledge. The company was formed in June 1854 as a partnership between Ebenezer Ward and George Lock. The present compilation consists of virtually all of the yellowbacks and paperbacks issued by Ward & Lock from 1854 through 1905. The change in the style of the imprint is given as it occurred. Each entry gives the date of listing in a British periodical where known and otherwise the date of the title's advertisement or an approximate date obtained from ads, references, and catalogs. In almost every case the first English edition is given and, where there was such, the first American edition. Important later editions are given as well as the first yellowback or paperback edition if different from the Ward & Lock title being noted.

Size is denoted by 32mo, 16mo, Fcp 8vo, 12mo, Cr 8vo, Demy 8vo, 8vo, and 4to as gleaned from ads, references, and catalogs, but the size is given in cm. tall of the bound copies where it is known. A 32mo indicates a book about 12 cm. tall; 16mo, about 15 cm.; Fcp 8vo indicates Sadleir's small format or about 16.8 cm.; 12mo, about 17.5 cm., or Sadleir's large format; Cr 8vo, about 19 cm.; Demy 8vo, about 21 cm.; 8vo, about 23 cm.; and 4to about 30 cm. The number of pages refers to the number of the last page of text. The words "wrappers" and "sewed" refer to paperbacks, and "boards" refers to yellowbacks and other boards issues as described. I have had to omit the type of binding in some cases when not known to me and have merely stated the price of the issue.

For a discussion of early yellowbacks and paperbacks and their precursors, one may refer to a good history and description given by Michael Sadleir in *Collecting Yellowbacks*, (Constable & Co.: London, 1938), a 35-page pamphlet. His pertinent comments in a preliminary note to volume 2 of *XIX Century Fiction* (London: Constable & Co., 1938; Los Angeles: University of California Press, 1951) is of value also.

My collection of yellowbacks numbers approximately 1,700 volumes, and my collection of paperbacks, English and American, numbers about 1,900 volumes. I started acquiring them about twenty years ago after completing my Anthony Trollope collection of first and later editions. The influence of Sadleir thus becomes apparent, as he published a model bibliography of the works of Trollope, and he initiated an interest in yellowback and paperback editions by his volume 2 of *XIX Century Fiction*. The present work makes full reference to appropriate entries in volume 2 and also to entries in the 5-volume issue of *Nineteenth Century Fiction* by Robert L. Wolff (New York and London: Garland Publishing Company, 1981–1986).

In his volume 2 of *XIX Century Fiction*, Sadleir makes the comment that he had a suspicion that Ward & Lock had concealed tie-ups with more than one small publishing firm, perhaps using imprints suited to certain types of books where this seemed prudent. He asks himself what were the ramifications of Ward & Lock and what cover-imprints had they at their disposal? I think his suspicions were correct, and the minor houses involved were Houlston & Wright; C. J. Skeet; W. Kent & Co.; George Vickers; and finally

John Maxwell Co. I think Ward & Lock had substantial interests in, if not outright ownership of, these companies as their joint ads in the periodicals showed.

On November 12 and 19, 1859, Houlston & Wright and Ward & Lock shared an ad in the *Ath* and shared a full-page ad in October 1860. In November 1861 they shared a column ad with Ward & Lock, with notices intermingled; and also in November 1861 a full-page ad was shared by W. Kent and Ward & Lock. In December 1861 a full-page ad was shared by Houlston & Wright and Ward & Lock, and a full-page ad was shared by Houlston & Wright, W. Kent, and Ward & Lock. In September 1862 a two-thirds column ad was shared by Ward & Lock, George Vickers, and Kent. In September and October 1863 a column ad was shared by Ward & Lock, Kent, and John Maxwell; and in November 1863 a column ad was shared by Ward & Lock and John Maxwell. In February and March 1864 a two-thirds column ad was shared by Ward & Lock and John Maxwell with their titles intermingled. In April 1864 Ward & Lock, Maxwell, and Kent shared a column ad; and in April 1865 Ward & Lock and Maxwell shared a full-page ad.

In 1865 Ward & Lock became Ward, Lock & Tyler, and thereafter all ads for Ward, Lock & Tyler, W. Kent & Co., and Houlston & Wright were separate. The last John Maxwell ad was on November 25, 1865, but he surfaced again at intervals from October 1871 to March 1878, as being at 4 Shoe-Lane and for the sole purpose of announcing three-volume novels by Miss Braddon, these probably being the property of Ward, Lock & Tyler and Ward & Lock. These three-volume novels were at times advertised by Ward, Lock & Tyler and by John Maxwell in separate ads for the same novel, but at other times they were advertised with no publisher given. John Maxwell had his first ad announcing novels in the *Ath* on September 5, 1863, his address then being 122 Fleet Street. He started in the novel publishing business by issuing titles that had run in Ward & Lock's *Sixpenny Magazine*. Edward Liveing, in *Adventures in Publishing. The House of Ward, Lock*, thought that Maxwell had been a clerk for Ward & Lock.

A separation of John Maxwell and Ward, Lock & Tyler came in March or April 1878, when a new firm, John and Robert Maxwell, started operations at 4 Shoe-Lane. The issuing of Braddon novels then passed to them from Ward, Lock & Co.

Ward, Lock & Tyler acquired Edward Moxon, Sons & Co. in 1870, and they took over the rights to all of S. O. Beeton's publications and the use of his name about April or May 1866. The last S. O. Beeton ad appeared in the *Ath* on April 28, 1866, and thereafter Beeton titles appeared in Ward, Lock & Tyler ads.

Ward & Lock issued small format yellowbacks well into the 1870s. The *Run and Read Library* from 1865 to 1869, at 2/o boards each, was in small format, and the *Library of Popular Authors*, which ran from September 1863 to June 1870, had all titles in the small format. The first yellowback editions of Miss Braddon's early novels, which appeared from April 1866 until 1877, were in small format; and Gustave Aimard's romances appeared in decorated glazed boards in small format, from December 1860 until 1865.

Flyers of the Hunt and *Stable Secrets*, both by John Mills, were issued in 1865 or 1866 as yellowbacks in large format (18 cm.). Charles Reade's novels were issued in large format yellowbacks and in cloth in 1872 and 1873; and the *Favourite Authors* series, begun in June 1873, was in large format (18.3 cm.). Ward & Lock gave up on yellowbacks in 1896 or 1897, and in 1899 started their *2/o Copyright Novels* series, issued in many-colored lithographed boards with cloth backs.

Ward & Lock issued shilling paperbacks in the year of their founding and continued to issue paperbacks at o/6 and 1/o until well into the 20th century. They issued their *Six-*

penny Lithographed Series of Copyright Novels, starting in 1900, and issued this series until at least 1909, at which time more than 200 titles had been published. These were paperbacks, approximately 21 cm. tall, and had a picture lithographed on the front cover in many colors. They issued occasional paperbacks until at least 1922 when *A Woman's Temptation* by Bertha Clay came out.

Victorian Yellowbacks & Paperbacks,
1849–1905

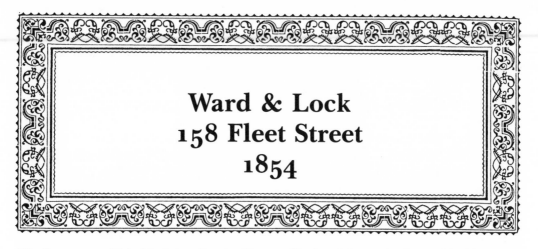

Ward & Lock
158 Fleet Street
1854

The firm was established in June 1854 by Ebenezer Ward and George Lock. Ward had been with Henry Bohn for about 10 years and then took over the management of the book department of Ingram, Cooke and Co. Lock was only 22 years old when the firm was formed. His mother was a member of the Galpin family, and one of her relatives was a partner in Petter & Galpin, the printers with whom Ward & Lock did their printing. The first Ward & Lock book listed in PC *was* Russia, the Land of the Czar, *translated from the German and listed July 15–30, 1854. The first Ward & Lock ad in the* Ath *was for* Zana, *a first edition by Ann S. Stephens, about Sept. 30, 1854.*

Editorial matter in the PC *on Aug. 16 stated that the pretty well recognized protection afforded to foreign authors during the last 18 months was now effectively dispersed by the House of Lords on Aug. 1, defining the law as offering no protection of copyright to foreign authors except if they were residents in England at the time of publication of the works which they claimed.*

1 ANONYMOUS **Russia, the Land of the Czar.** Frontispiece. 1/0 sewed July 29 (*Ath*)

This was the first English edition, 1854, and had an illustrated title page.

2 JOHN MILLS **The Life of a Racehorse.** [New edition]. 1/0 sewed Aug. 15–31 (*PC*)

This is the first edition, the *Field* office; Ward & Lock, 1854, 17.5 cm., 141 pp., illustrated, from the *Field*.
Also 1856, 65, 73, 82, 85

3 NATHANIEL P. WILLIS **Famous Persons and Famous Places.** Fcp 8vo. Frontispiece. 1/6 boards, 2/6 cloth Aug. 15–31 (*PC*)

This is the first English edition, 1854, 16.5 cm., 263 pp. The first American edition was from Charles Scribner, New York, *Famous Persons and Places*, 1854, 19.5 cm., 492 pp., $1.25, advertised in the *New York*

Daily Times on Aug. 19, 1854, as "This day."

4 ANONYMOUS **The Coalition Guide.** 1/0 sewed Sept. 14–30 (*PC*)

The first edition was issued by the *Press* office, London, 1854, from the *Press* newspaper.

5 FANNY FERN (SARAH P. WILLIS, later ELDREDGE, later PARTON) **Fern Leaves from Fanny's Portfolio.** First and second series. 1 vol., 1/6 boards, 2/0, 3/6; 2 vols., 1/0 boards each Sept. 14–30 (*PC*)

The *PC* also listed a new edition of the first series at 1/0 boards, issued by Ward & Lock, Oct. 2–14. The first edition of the first series was issued by Derby & Miller, Auburn, New York, etc., 1853, 20 cm., 400 pp., illustrated, advertised in *Lit World* as "On June 1" and noticed in the *Ind* on June 30 and reviewed on July 7. It was advertised in the *New York Daily Times* on

Sept. 8, 1853, stating that 40,000 copies had been sold in four months. It consisted of pieces from various periodicals and had eight illustrations and sold for $1.25. According to J.C. Derby, 80,000 copies were sold in America within a year, and the two series paid Mrs. Parton over $10,000 within two years of publication. In England the first series was issued by Ingram, Cooke & Co., London, 1853, 18.5 cm., 337 pp., before Oct. 1, noticed in the *British Quarterly Review* for Nov. 1, 1853. It was also issued by Clark, Beeton & Co., London (1853), listed in the *Ath* on Sept. 3. The first edition of the second series was issued by Miller, Orton & Mulligan, Auburn and Buffalo; Sampson Low, London, 1854, 19.5 cm., 400 pp., illustrated, listed in the *Ath* on May 27, 1854, 12mo, 6/0, and noticed there on June 3. It was also issued without the Low imprint, 1854, listed in the *Ind* on June 1. It was advertised in the *New York Daily Times* by J.C. Derby on May 25, 1854, eight illustrations, $1.25, as "This day." Sampson Low, London, advertised it in the *Ath* on Sept. 16, 1854, illustrated, 2/6 cloth, as "Ready." The second series was issued as *Shadows and Sunbeams* by W.S. Orr & Co., London, 1854, 18.5 cm., 295 pp., illustrated, advertised in the *Ath* on Aug. 26, 1854, illustrations, 2/6 cloth, by George Thomas, "Just published."
Also 1855, 56, 58, 73

6 DAVID P. THOMSON **The Stranger's Vade Mecum.** 1/0 sewed   Sept. 14–30 (*PC*)
The *BM* gives Liverpool (1855), and the *U Cat* gives H. Greenwood, Liverpool (Preface, 1854), 16mo, 196 pp., frontispiece.

7 ANN S. STEPHENS **Zana.** Small format. 1/6 boards, 2/0, 2/6 cloth   Sept. 30 (*Ath*)
This is the first edition, 1854, with 286 pp.
Also 1856, 60, 73

8 PERCY B. ST. JOHN **The Book of the War.** 1/0 sewed   Oct. 2–14 (*PC*)
This is the first edition, 1854. It was also listed by *PC* as published Oct. 15–31.
Also 1855

9 ANONYMOUS **William Hogarth's Own Joe Miller.** 1/0 boards, 1/6 cloth Oct. 15–31 (*PC*)
I cannot trace this.

10 ELIZABETH O. SMITH **Bertha and Lily.** 1/6   Oct. 21 (*Ath*)
The first edition was probably Aird & Tunstall, London, 1854, 267 pp., the only English edition given by the *BM*. The first American edition was issued by J.C. Derby, New York; Phillips, Sampson, Boston; etc., 1854, 20 cm., 336 pp., illustrated, advertised in the *New York Daily Times* on Aug. 5, 1854, 12mo, illustrated, $1.25, "On Aug. 10." The third edition was advertised there on Aug. 21, 12mo, $1.00, "Now ready."

11 ROBERT M. BIRD **Nick of the Woods.** 1/6 boards, 2/0, 2/6 cloth   Oct. 28 (*Ath*)
This was 1854, with 316 pp. The first English edition was from Bentley, London, 3 vols., 1837, 20.5 cm., anonymous, 27/0, edited by William H. Ainsworth, listed in the *Ath* on Mar. 13, 1837. The first American edition was issued by Carey, Lea & Blanchard, Philadelphia, etc., 2 vols., 1837, 20 cm., anonymous, reviewed in the *Knickerbocker* for Apr. and thus probably issued in Feb. or Mar. The cost book of Carey & Lea says that 3,000 copies were printed, finished in Mar. 1837.
Also 1856, 59, 60, 72

12 JOHN MILLS **The Old English Gentleman.** Third Edition. Small format. 1/6 boards, 2/0, 2/6 cloth   Oct. 28 (*Ath*)
This appeared in *Tait's Edinburgh Magazine* for Nov. and Dec. 1841. The present edition is 1854, 16.5 cm., 306 pp. The first

edition was issued by Henry Colburn, London, 3 vols., 1841, 20.5 cm., 31/6, listed in the *Ath* on Oct. 2, 1841, and reviewed on Nov. 6.
Also 1856, 58, 62

13 JOHN SCOFFERN *Weapons of War, a History of Projectiles and Explosive Compounds.* Third Edition. Illustrated. 1/6 boards, 2/0 cloth   Nov. 15–30 (*PC*)
This is 1854, 17.5 cm., 213 pp. The first edition was issued by J. Mortimer, London, 1845, 21 cm., with 90 pp. The *BM* gives the second edition as London, 1850, and the *U Cat* gives the second edition as Cooke & Whitely, London, 1852, 17 cm., 213 pp., illustrated. Longmans, London, issued the third edition, revised, 1858, 20 cm., 306 pp., illustrated.

14 MRS. WARREN *Timethrift.* [New edition]. Illustrated. 1/6 boards, 2/0, 2/6 cloth   Nov. 15–30 (*PC*)
This was advertised at the back of my copy of *Sharp-Eye* below as Roy 8vo, 160 pp., 1/6 sewed, 2/0 and 2/6 cloth, the latter with gilt edges, "Now ready." I cannot otherwise trace it.

15 RICHARD B. KIMBALL *Students Abroad.* 1/0 sewed   Nov. 15–30 (*PC*)
This was 1855 (1854), advertised as in the preceding item, Cr 8vo, 128 pp., 1/0 comic wrapper. The first edition was *Romance of Student Life Abroad*, issued by G. P. Putnam, New York, 1853, 19 cm., 261 pp., advertised in the *New York Daily Times* on Nov. 29, 1852, as "This Week" and on Dec. 3 as "On Dec. 3."

16 PERCY B. ST. JOHN *The Trapper's Bride, White Stone Canoe, and The Rose of Ouisconsin.* Small format. 1/0 boards   Dec. 2 (*Ath*)
This is 1855 (1854), with 155 pp. The first edition was issued by John Mortimer, London, 1845, 17 cm., 166 pp., at 3/6

cloth, advertised in the *Ath* on Jan. 25, 1845, as "On Feb. 1" and listed on Feb. 8. It was advertised in the *Spect*, the same, as *The Trapper's Bride with The Rose of Ouisconsin*. It was advertised as in the preceding two items, Fcp 8vo, 160 pp., 1/0 boards. *The White Stone Canoe* was listed in the *Ath* on Oct. 17, 1846, 3/6, published by H. K. Lewis, London, etc., listed in the *Spect* on Oct. 24, 1846. The second edition of the present title was Hayward & Adams, London, 1845, the same as the first edition. In the United States it was issued by E. Ferrett, New York, etc., no date, 48 pp., probably in the 1840s.
Also 1856

17 JAMES WEIR *Sharp-Eye.* Third Edition. 1/0 sewed   Dec. 2 (*Ath*)
This is 1855 (1854), with 122 pp. I have a copy, 1855, with no edition mentioned, probably the first edition, in the original colored white wrappers in red and blue, 18.6 cm., 122 pp., with plain inside covers and with publisher's ads on the back in blue. The first edition was issued by Lippincott, Grambo & Co., Philadelphia, 1852, 19 cm., 195 pp., illustrated, entitled *Simon Kenton*.

18 JOHN LANG *Too Much Alike.* 1/0 sewed   Dec. 23 (*Ath* ad)
This is the first edition, 1855. There was a second edition in 1855.
Also 1858, 70, 82

19 JOHN MILLS *The Wheel of Life.* 1/6 boards, 2/0, 2/6 cloth   Dec. 30 (*Ath*)
This is the first edition, 1855.
Also 1886. See *The Briefless Barrister*, 1857

20 NATHANIEL P. WILLIS *Laughs I Have Put a Pen To.* [Third edition]. 1/0 sewed 1854 (*Eng Cat*)
The first edition was issued by Charles Scribner, New York, 1853, as *Fun-Jottings, or Laughs I Have Put a Pen To*, 19.5 cm., 371

pp., advertised in the *New York Daily Times* on Oct. 5, 1853, 12mo, $1.25, "This day." It was noticed in the *Ind* on Oct. 6 and reviewed there on Oct. 27. The present title was advertised in the *Ath* by Samuel Rowe, London, on Apr. 22, 1854, 1/0, as "Just published" and listed on Apr. 29, Cr 8vo, 1/0 sewed. The second edition was listed on May 27, 1854, p 8vo, 1/0; and a second edition was listed on July 29, 1954, Cr 8vo, 1/0. Rowe advertised the 15th thousand, illustrated, 1/0, as "Now ready" in the *Ath* on July 22, 1854; and advertised the 18th thousand in the *Spect* on Nov. 4, 1854, illustrated, 1/0, as "Now ready."

21 (MARIA S. CUMMINS)
The Lamplighter. 1/6 boards, 2/0, 2/6 cloth 1854?
The first edition was John P. Jewett & Co., Boston, etc., 1854, 12mo, anonymous, 523 pp., advertised in the *Ind* on Feb. 23 as "About Mar. 1" and listed on Apr. 6. It was received by the Library of Congress on Mar. 16 and was reviewed in the *Knickerbocker* for May 1854. By Sept. 1854, there were at least seven reprints in England, including Clarke, Beeton & Co., John Cassell, George Routledge, Thomas Nelson & Sons, and Kent & Co. Clarke, Beeton advertised it in the *Ath* on Apr. 8 for immediate delivery, listed on Apr. 15, 1/6

boards, and listed in *PC* as published Apr. 14–29. It was noticed in the *Ath* on Apr. 29. The Routledge edition was advertised in the *Ath* on Apr. 15 and listed by *PC* as published Apr. 14–29, 1/6 boards. A Nelson edition was listed in the *Ath* on Aug. 12, 1854, p 8vo, illustrated, 3/6; and a Cassell edition was listed there on Aug. 26, Cr 8vo, illustrated, 3/0 cloth. Editions were listed in the *Ath* on May 20, p 8vo, illustrated, 3/6, and on May 27, Fcp 8vo, illustrated, 2/6 cloth, both with no publisher given.
Also 1864, 70,72

22 ANN S. STEPHENS ***Fashion and Famine.*** 1/6 boards, 2/0 cloth 1854?
The first English edition was probably Bentley, London, 1854, 1/6, in their *Railway Library*, listed by *PC* as published Aug. 1–15. A dealer offered a copy with the joint imprint of Kent & Co. and Ward & Lock, 1854, frontispiece, in the original blue cloth. Routledge, London, issued it at 1/6 boards, 2/0 cloth, listed by *PC* as published Aug. 15–31. Kent & Co. issued it at 1/6 in 1854, possibly the joint issue mentioned above. The first American edition was from Bunce & Brother, New York, 1854, 18.5 cm., 426 pp., listed in the *Ind* on June 29, and noticed in *Harper's New Monthly Magazine* for July 1854.

Ward & Lock
1855

23 P. T. BARNUM *The Autobiography of P. T. Barnum.* [New edition]. 1/o sewed Jan. 1–15 (*PC*)

This is 1855, 18.5 cm., 160 pp. The *U Cat* also gives a fifth edition from Ward & Lock, 1855, the same. It was issued simultaneously in London and New York on Dec. 20, 1854. The American edition was issued by J. S. Redfield, New York, 1855, 19.5 cm., 404 pp., frontispiece (portrait), illustrated, *The Life of P. T. Barnum, Written by Himself*, listed in the *Ind* on Dec. 21, 1854. The listing in the *Knickerbocker* for Dec. 1854 stated that 90-odd thousand copies had been reached. The first English edition was issued by Sampson Low, London, 1855, author's edition, identical to the Redfield edition with a different title page, 2/6 boards, 7/6 in red cloth, and with 11 pp. of ads at the back dated Jan. 1, 1855. It was listed in the *Ath* on Dec. 23, 1854, and listed by *PC* as published Dec. 15–30. Willoughby & Co., London, also issued it with the same title in 1855, 332 pp. Clarke, Beeton & Co., London, issued it as *Barnum, the Yankee Showman*, no date, 16.6 cm., 171 pp., listed by *PC* as published Jan 15–31, 1855, 1/o boards. It was advertised by Low in the *Spect* on Dec. 16, 1854, Fcp 8vo, 2/6, "On Dec. 20." The Clarke, Beeton issue was slightly abridged. It was also issued by L. T. Holt, London (1855), as *Barnum, or, the Life of a Humbug.*
See 1882, 89

24 ANONYMOUS *Shillingsworth of Nonsense.* [New edition]. Illustrated. 1/o sewed Jan. 1–15 (*PC*)

This is probably the first edition reissued. It has 50 illustrations.

25 PERCY B. ST. JOHN & EDWARD COPPING *Lobster Salad Mixed.* Illustrated. 1/o sewed Jan. 15–31 (*PC*)

This is the first edition, 1855, 120 pp.

26 PRIAM (CHARLES J. COLLINS) *Dick Diminy.* New and Revised Edition. Illustrated. 1/6 boards, 2/6 cloth Mar. 3 (*Ath*)

This has no date, 256 pp. The *U Cat* gives the fourth edition (1855?), 17 cm., 256 pp., illustrated. The first edition was *The Life and Adventures of Dick Diminy, the Jockey*, issued by Collins & Ponsford, London (1854), 18 cm., 420 pp., illustrated, advertised in the *Ath* on May 20, 1854, 7/o, "On May 22," by C. J. Collins. It was noticed there on June 3, 1854.
Also 1869, 75

27 EMMA D. E. SOUTHWORTH *The Lost Heiress.* 1/6 boards, 2/6 cloth Mar. 31 (*Ath*)

This is the first English edition, 1855, with 202 pp. The first edition was issued by T. B Peterson, Philadelphia (1854), 19 cm., 502 pp., portrait, listed in the *Ind* on Oct. 19, 1854, and advertised in the *New York Daily Times* by Bunce & Brother, New York, on Oct. 13, 1854, 12mo, portrait,

$1.00 paper, $1.25 cloth, "Just received for sale this day."
Also 1856

28 PERCY B. ST. JOHN *Our Holiday: A Week in Paris.* [New edition]. Illustrated. 1/0 sewed   Apr. 14–30 *(PC)*

This was advertised on the back of my copy of *Sharp-Eye* (see Dec. 2, 1854) as Cr 8vo, 1/0 sewed, "Just ready." The first edition was issued by Edward Tinsley, London, 1854, 12mo, 120 pp., frontispiece, listed by *PC* as published Oct. 2–14, and listed by the *Spect* on Oct. 14, 1/0. It was bound in glazed yellow wrappers, cut flush, and printed on the back and front with an elaborate design.

29 JOHN LANG *The Forger's Wife.* 1/0 sewed   Apr. 28 *(Ath)*

This is the first edition, 1855. The second edition was listed by *PC* as published June 1–14.
Also 1858, 70, 82

30 AZEL S. ROE *A Long Look Ahead.* 1/6 boards   May 14–31 *(PC)*

The first English edition was probably an import by Trübner & Co., London, Cr 8vo, 7/0, listed in the *Ath* on Apr. 28, 1855, no publisher given, and listed in the *Spect* on Apr. 14, as issued by Trübner and reviewed on Apr. 21. It was issued by Simpkin, Marshall, London; etc., 1855, 1/6 boards, in the *Run and Read Library*, listed in the *Ath* on Aug. 4. The first American edition was issued by J.C. Derby, New York, etc., 1855, 18.5 cm., 441 pp., advertised in the *New York Daily Times* on Mar. 10, 1855, 12mo, $1.25, as "Today." A new edition was advertised there on Mar. 31, $1.25; and the fourth thousand was advertised there on May 17 as "Now ready."

31 ANONYMOUS *Hodge-Podge for Railway Travellers.* 1/0 sewed May 14–31 *(PC)*

This is the first edition, 1855.

32 FANNY FERN (SARAH P. WILLIS, later PARTON) *Fern Leaves from Fanny's Portfolio.* [Second edition]. First and second series. 1/6 boards   June 1–14 *(PC)*

Also 1854, 56, 58, 73

33 PERCY B. ST. JOHN *The Book of the War.* [Third edition]. 1/0 sewed June 1–14 *(PC)*

The *BM* gives London, 1855, second edition, small format; and the second edition (10th thousand) was advertised on the back of my copy of *Sharp-Eye* (see Dec. 2, 1854) as 1/0, revised and continued to the battle of Inkermann.
Also 1854

34 RICHARD B. KIMBALL *The Saint Leger Family.* 1/6 boards   July 14 *(Ath)*

This is 1855, in yellow, paper-covered boards, decorated and lettered in black, with ads on the endpapers. Kimball was an American author, and the first edition was *Saint Leger*, issued by G.P. Putnam, New York, 1850, 20 cm., 384 pp. It first appeared in the *Knickerbocker* in 1849. The first English edition was issued by Bentley, London, 1850, anonymous, the same as the American edition.

35 PERCY B. ST. JOHN *Keetsea.* 1/0 sewed July 14–30 *(PC)*

This is the first edition, 1855, 125 pp. It was issued by DeWitt, New York, no date, 16 cm., 100 pp.
See *Indian Tales* below

36 OLIVER GOLDSMITH *The Vicar of Wakefield.* 1/0 boards   Aug. 1–14 *(PC)*

The first authorized edition was printed by B. Collins, Salisbury, for F. Newbery, London, 2 vols., 1766, anonymous, 17.4 cm. The first Dublin edition was issued by W. & W. Smith, etc., Dublin, 2 vols., 1766, anonymous, 16.3 cm. It was also issued by Eugene Swiney, Corke (i.e., London), 2

vols., 1766, 17 cm., anonymous, a pirated edition that may have preceded the authorized edition. The first American edition was issued by William Mintz, Philadelphia, 2-vols.-in-1, 1772, 16.6 cm., anonymous, 180 pp. There is some evidence of a Boston printed edition of 1767 but apparently no copy is known.
Also 1864, 86

37 WATTS PHILLIPS **The Wild Tribes of London.** Illustrated. 1/0 sewed
Aug. 14–30 (*PC*)
This is the first edition, 1855, 120 pp.
Also 1856, 66

38 HARRY GRINGO (HENRY A. WISE) **Tales for the Marines.** 1/6 boards
Aug. 14–30 (*PC*)
This is the first edition, 1855, 256 pp. It was in Sadleir's collection, small format, in yellow pictorial boards, printed in black, with ads on the endpapers. The first American edition was issued by Phillips, Sampson, Boston; etc., 1855, 19.5 cm., 436 pp., frontispiece, and an added illustrated title page. It was advertised in the *New York Daily Times* on Nov. 15, 1855, at $1.25, as "Recent" and advertised there on May 1, 1855, 12mo, illustrated, portrait, $1.25, "On May 10."

39 CUTHBERT BEDE (EDWARD BRADLEY) **Love's Provocations.** 12mo. Illustrated. 1/0 sewed   Sept. 14–29 (*PC*)
This is the first edition, my copy, 1855, 18.1 cm., 104 pp., frontispiece, and many textual illustrations. It is bound in white wrappers, pictorially printed in red and green, identically on the front and back covers, with publisher's ads on the endpapers. *See color photo section*

40 MARGARET CASSON **Cross Purposes.** Small format. 1/6 boards, 2/6 cloth
Sept. 22 (*Ath*) *See color photo section*
This is the first edition, my copy, 1855, 16.7 cm., 245 pp., in glazed yellow boards,

pictorially printed in black, identically on the front and back, with ads on the endpapers, and a leaf of ads at the back.

41 (CALVIN W. PHILLEO) **Twice Married.** 1/0 boards   Oct. 13 (*Ath*)
This is the first edition, 1855. The first American edition was issued by Dix & Edwards, New York, 1855, 12mo, 264 pp.

42 STEPHEN W. FULLOM **The Daughter of Night.** New Edition. 1/6 boards, 2/6 cloth
Oct. 13–31 (*PC*)
This is dated 1855. The first edition was issued by Henry Colburn, London, 3 vols., 1851, p 8vo, 31/6, advertised in the *Ath* on Jan. 11, 1851, as "Just ready" and listed in the *Spect* on Feb. 1, 1851. The first American edition was from Harper & Bros., New York, 1851, 22.5 cm., 124 pp., noticed in *Harper's New Monthly Magazine* for Aug. 1851, and thus probably issued in May or June.
Also 1856

43 ALICE SOMERTON **Oeland.** 1/0 boards
Dec. 1 (*Ath*)
This is the first edition, 1856 (1855).

44 PERCY B. ST. JOHN **Indian Tales.** Boards   1855
This is a known copy, 1855, 16.8 cm., 156 pp., in decorated boards, with four pp. of ads. The *BM* gives *Indian Tales: Keetsea, The Trapper's Bride, etc.*, London (1863).
Also 1870. See *Keetsea* above

45 EMILIE CARLÉN (EMILIE FLYGARE, later CARLÉN) **The Events of a Year.** 1/6   1855
The first edition was *Ett År*, Stockholm, 1846. The first English edition was issued by T. C. Newby, London, 3 vols., 1853, Cr 8vo, 31/6, listed in the *Spect* on Apr. 9, 1853. Clarke & Beeton, London, issued it in 1853 at 1/0 boards, as *Twelve Months of*

Matrimony, listed by *PC* as published Nov. 1–14, 1853. They reissued it in 1854 and also in the *Parlour Library* in 1860. The first American edition was issued by Charles Scribner, New York, 1853, as *One Year*, translated by Alexander Krause and Albert Perce, $.50 paper, $.75 cloth, listed by *Lit World* as published May 9–June 11. It was advertised by Scribner in the *New York Daily Times* on May 14, 1853, as "This day" and advertised again, the third edition, the same, "Just issued," on July 30. It was also issued in London by Eli Charles Eginton & Co., as *One Year*, Fcp 8vo, 1/0 cloth, in their *Pocket Library*, listed in the *Ath* on July 2, 1853.

See *Twelve Months of Matrimony*, 1882

46 FANNY FERN (SARAH P. WILLIS, later ELDREDGE, later PARTON) ***Ruth Hall.***
1/0   1855 (*Eng Cat*)

The first edition was issued by Mason Bros., New York, 1855, 18 cm., 400 pp. It was reviewed in the *Knickerbocker* for Jan. 1855, and thus probably issued in Dec. 1854. It was advertised in the *Ind* on Feb. 22, 1855, as published two months ago. J. C. Derby stated that it sold 75,000 copies in the United States. In England it was issued by George Routledge, London, 1855, 1/0 boards, listed by *PC* as published Feb. 1–14; and by Houlston & Stoneman, London, 1855; and by Knight & Son, London (1855).

Also 1856

Ward & Lock
1856

47 MINA MACGOWAN **The Heir of Dunspringmore; and The Moorswamp Wedding.** 1/0 boards   Jan. 5 (*Ath*)

This is the first edition, 1856. The *BM* gives it as London, 1856, 6 parts, 12mo.

48 ANONYMOUS **The Queen's Visit to Paris.** 1/0 sewed   Jan. 14–30 (*PC*)

The only other reference to this that I've been able to uncover is the *BM* listing *The Queen's Visit to France* (a song) (London, 1855), a single 4to sheet. This may not be the present title.

49 ANONYMOUS **How to Dress with Taste.** [Second edition]. Sq 16mo. 0/6 sewed   Mar. 1–14 (*PC*)

In a book of Sept. 1855 this was advertised as "Just published," 0/6 sewed.

50 ANONYMOUS **How to Speak with Propriety.** Sq 16mo. 0/6 sewed   Mar. 1–14 (*PC*)

I cannot trace this.

51 JOHN MILLS **The Old English Gentleman.** Fourth Edition. 1/6 boards   Mar. 14–31 (*PC*)

This is 1856, 17 cm., 306 pp.
Also 1854, 58, 62

52 JAMES J. MORIER **The Maid of Kars, "Ayesha."** Small format. 2/0 boards   Mar. 14–31 (*PC*)

This is Sadleir's copy, 1856, in yellow pictorial boards printed in black, with the *Bentley Standard Novels* engraved frontispiece, given on the title page and cover as by Miss Morier! It was bought at an auction of *Bentley's Standard Novels* at Hodson's Rooms in Feb. 1856, when the copyrights were sold. The first edition was issued by Bentley, London, 3 vols., 1834, p 8vo, anonymous, 31/6, as *Ayesha, the Maid of Kars*, listed and reviewed in the *Spect* on May 31, 1834. The Bentley private catalog states that it was published on May 30. Bentley issued it as *Standard Novels* No. 100, 1846. The first American edition was issued by Carey, Lea & Blanchard, Philadelphia, 2 vols., 1834, 21 cm., anonymous. The cost book of Carey & Lea states that 1,000 copies were finished on July 23, 1834, with the first edition title.

53 FANNY FERN (MRS. PARTON) **Fern Leaves from Fanny's Portfolio.** 1/6 boards   Apr. 1–14 (*PC*)

Also 1854, 55, 58, 73

54 WATTS PHILLIPS **The Wild Tribes of London.** [Third edition]. 1/0 sewed   Apr. 1–14 (*PC*)

Also 1855, 66

55 JAMES J. MORIER **The Adventures of Hajii Baba of Ispahan.** [New edition]. 1/6 boards   Apr. 14–30 (*PC*)

This was probably in the small format. The copyright was purchased at an auction of *Bentley's Standard Novels* copyrights in Feb. 1856. The first edition was issued by John Murray, London, 3 vols., 1824,

18.5 cm., anonymous, listed by the *Edinburgh Review* as published Jan.–Mar. 1824, 21/0. Bentley issued it as *Standard Novels* No. 44 in Jan 1835. The first American edition was issued by A. Small, Philadelphia, 2 vols., 19 cm., 1824.
Also 1878 *See color photo section*

56 FREDERICK CHAMIER **Ben Brace.**
Fifth Edition, Revised and Corrected.
2/0 boards, 2/6 cloth   Apr. 14–30 (*PC*)
Standard Novels. This is 1856, 419 pp. The copyright was purchased for £199 at the auction of *Bentley Standard Novels* copyrights in Feb. 1856. The copyright and stereo plates were sold at a Southgate & Barrett auction in May 1859. The first edition was issued by Bentley, London, 3 vols., 1836, p 8vo, 31/6, on Feb. 16 according to the Bentley private catalog. Bentley issued it as *Standard Novels* No. 77, 1840 (Dec. 1839). The first American edition was Carey, Lea & Blanchard, Philadelphia, 2 vols., 1836, 20.5 cm.

57 FRANCES TROLLOPE **The Widow Barnaby.** New Edition. Small format.
2/0 boards, 2/6 cloth   Apr. 14–30 (*PC*)
Standard Novels. This is Sadleir's copy, 1856, 494 pp., in pictorial boards with dark yellow printed endpapers. This and *The Vicar of Wrexhill* were purchased at the auction of *Bentley Standard Novels* copyrights at Hodgson's Rooms in Feb. 1856, for £172. The copyright and stereo plates were sold at a Southgate & Barrett auction in May 1859. The first edition was issued by Bentley, London, 3 vols., 1839, 20.5 cm., 24/0, published Dec. 26, 1838, according to the Bentley private catalog. He issued it as *Standard Novels* No. 81 in Oct. 1840, with 494 pp.
Also 1865

58 FREDERICK CHAMIER **The Life of a Sailor.** New Edition. Small format.
2/0 boards, 2/6 cloth   May 1–14 (*PC*)
Standard Novels. This is Sadleir's copy, 1856, 394 pp., in yellow pictorial boards.

The copyright of this and *Ben Brace* were purchased at the sale of *Bentley Standard Novels* copyrights for £199. The first English edition was issued by Bentley, London, 3 vols., 1832, 19.5 cm., 31/6, by a captain in the navy, listed in the *Edinburgh Review* as published Oct. 1832–Jan. 1833. In the United States it was issued by J. & J. Harper, New York, 2 vols., 1833, 21 cm.; and by Key & Biddle, Philadelphia, 2 vols., 1833, 19 cm., both by a captain in the navy. Bentley advertised it in the *Spect* on Dec. 15, 1832, as "Just published," and issued it in *Bentley's Standard Library* at 6/0, advertised there on July 6, 1839.

59 STEPHEN W. FULLOM **The Daughter of Night.** [New edition]. 1/6 boards
May 14–31 (*PC*)
Also 1855

60 THOMAS MEDWIN **Rhymes and Chimes.** 1/0 sewed   May 14–31 (*PC*)
This is possibly the title given by the *U Cat* as issued by J. S. Wolff, Heidelberg, 1853, with 240 pp. They issued the second edition, the same, 1854, 15 cm., 259 pp.

61 ANONYMOUS **Illustrated and Unabridged Edition of the Times Report of the Trial of Richard Palmer.** 8vo.
Frontispiece. Illustrated. 1/0 sewed,
1/6 brown cloth   May 14–31 (*PC*)
This is 1856, 184 pp., with a folding frontispiece. There were many other accounts of the trial issued in 1856, including *The Illustrated Life, Career and Trial of William Palmer . . . with a Verbatim Report of His Trial . . .* issued by Ward & Lock, 1856, new edition, 136 pp., advertised in the *Spect* on Aug. 30, 1856, as "On Sept. 4." There were accounts issued by Henry Lea, London; John Lofts, London; Longmans, London; and others.

62 JOHN BANIM **The Smuggler.**
New Edition. 2/0 boards   May 31 (*Ath*)
Standard Novels. This is 1856, 490 pp. The first edition was issued by Colburn &

Bentley, London, 3 vols., 1831, 19.5 cm., anonymous, published Sept. 24 according to the Bentley private catalog, and listed and reviewed in the *Spect* on Oct. 1, 31/6 boards. It was issued as *Standard Novels* No. 29 in June 1833, 490 pp., with a new preface. Ward & Lock issued it also at 2/6 cloth about June 28, 1856. The first American edition was issued by J. & J. Harper, New York, 2 vols., 1832, listed as "Recent" in the *New-England Magazine* (Boston) for Mar. 1832.

Also 1857, 62

63 MADAME DE STAËL (ANNE DE STAËL-HOLSTEIN) *Corinne; or, Italy.* 2/0 boards, 2/6 cloth   May 31–June 12 (*PC*)

Standard Novels. This was purchased at the auction of *Bentley's Standard Novels* copyrights in Feb. 1856. The first edition was *Corinne; ou, d'Italie*, Paris, 2 vols., 1807, 17 cm. In England it was issued by Henry Colburn, London, 5 vols., 1807, listed by the *Edinburgh Review* as published Apr.–July 1807, translated by D. Lawler. It was also issued by Tipper, London, 3 vols., 1807, at 20/0, in July, a different translation, listed by the *Edinburgh Review* as published July–Oct. 1807. Both of these English editions were entitled *Corinna*. Bentley issued it as *Standard Novels* No. 24, in Jan. 1833, 392 pp., expressly translated for that edition by Isabel Hill. In the United States it was issued by Ferrand, Mallory & Co., Boston, 2 vols., 1808, 18 cm.; and by D. Longworth, etc., New York, 1808, 12mo, 422 pp.; and by Fry & Krammerer, Philadelphia, 2 vols., 1808, 18 cm., all having the title *Corinna; or, Italy*.

Also 1859

64 THOMAS L. PEACOCK *Headlong Hall, and Nightmare Abbey.* Small format. 1/0 boards   June 7 (*Ath*)

This was 1856, 171 pp., Sadleir's copy in yellow pictorial boards. It was purchased at the Feb. 1856 sale of *Bentley Standard Novels* copyrights. The first edition of the

first title was issued by T. Hookham, Jr., London, 1816, 19 cm., anonymous, 216 pp., 6/0. The first American edition was issued by M. Carey, Philadelphia, 1816, 15 cm., 196 pp. The first edition of the second title was issued by T. Hookham, Jr., 1818, 17 cm., anonymous, 218 pp., at 6/6 boards, in Dec. 1818. The first American edition was M. Carey & Son, Philadelphia, 1819, 14.5 cm., 222 pp. These two titles along with *Maid Marian* and *Crotchet Castle* were issued by Bentley as *Standard Novels* No. 57 in 1837, anonymous.

Also 1858

65 ALICE CARY *Married, Not Mated.* 1/6 boards   June 28 (*Ath*)

Standard Novels. This is 1856, 253 pp. The first edition was issued by Derby & Jackson, New York; etc., 1856, 19 cm., 425 pp., $1.00, advertised in the *New York Daily Times* on Apr. 17, 12mo, "Now ready," and listed in the *Ind* on Apr. 24 and in *APC&LG* on Apr. 26. A new edition was advertised in the *New York Daily Times* on Feb. 26, 1859, seventh thousand, 12mo, $1.00, "On Mar. 1." The present edition was the first English edition.

66 ANN S. STEPHENS *Zana.* [Second edition]. 1/6 boards   July 1–15 (*PC*)

Also 1854, 60, 73

67 JAMES J. MORIER *Zohrab.* New Edition. Small format. 2/0 boards, 2/6 cloth   July 12 (*Ath*)

Standard Novels. This is Sadleir's copy, 1856, in yellow pictorial boards. The first edition was issued by Bentley, London, 3 vols., 19.5 cm., anonymous, 31/6 boards, listed in the *Ath* on Sept. 22, 1832. The second edition was advertised by Bentley in the *Spect* on Nov. 24, 1832, 3 vols., Fcp 8vo, 21/0, as "On Nov. 29"; and the third edition in 3 vols. was issued by Bentley, 1833. He issued it as *Standard Novels* No. 54, 1836, 471 pp., in Aug. The copyright was purchased at the sale of the *Standard Novels* copyrights at an auction in Feb. 1856. The first American edition was issued by J. & J. Harper, New York, 2 vols., 18.5 cm., anonymous. Both first editions had the title *Zohrab the Hostage*.

68 MARY J. PIERCY **Deeds of Genius.** 1/o boards   July 15–31 (*PC*)

This is 1856, a duplicate with a new title page of *Popular Tales*, issued by J. M. Stark, Hull, 1854, 205 pp.

69 MATTHEW G. LEWIS & HORACE WALPOLE **The Bravo of Venice and The Castle of Otranto.** Small format. 1/6 boards   July 15–31 (*PC*)

This was probably in the *Standard Novels* series. It is 1856, 16.5 cm., 240 pp. It along with *Vathek* was probably purchased at the Bentley sale of *Standard Novels* copyrights in Feb. 1856. The first edition of the first title was issued by J. F. Hughes, London, 1805, 19 cm., 340 pp., 6/o, in Dec. 1804, translated by Lewis (an adaptation of J. H. D. Zschokke's *Abellino*). *Abellino* was issued by Warner & Hanna, Baltimore, 1809, the first American edition from the fifth London edition, 16.5 cm., 299 pp., translated by Lewis. The first edition of the second title was probably T. Lownds, London, 1765, 200 pp., with the conceit that it was translated from the Italian of Onuphrio Muralto. It was also issued by J. Hoey, etc., Dublin, 1765, 17 cm., 146 pp., by Muralto. In the United States it was issued by The Shakespeare-Gallery, New York, 1801, 18 cm., 216 pp., containing also *Lothaire* by Harriet Lee. Both the present titles along with *Vathek* by William Beckford were issued as *Standard Novels* No. 41 in June 1834, by Bentley.

70 FANNY FERN (MRS. PARTON) **Ruth Hall.** 1/o boards   Aug. 1–15 (*PC*) Also 1855

71 FRANCES TROLLOPE **The Vicar of Wrexhill.** New Edition, Revised. Small format. 2/o boards, 2/6 cloth   Aug. 16 (*Ath*)

This is 1856, 16.5 cm., 436 pp. The copyright was purchased at the auction of the *Bentley Standard Novels* copyrights in Feb. 1856, at which £172 were paid for it and *The Widow Barnaby*. The first edition was issued by Bentley, London, 3 vols., 1837, 19 cm., illustrated, 31/6, on Sept. 6 according to the Bentley private catalog. It was noticed in the *Spect* on Sept. 9; and the second edition in 3 vols. was advertised there on Feb. 24, 1838. Bentley issued it as *Standard Novels* No. 78 in Feb. 1840.

72 THOMAS H. SEALY **Broad Grins from China.** [New edition]. 1/o boards Aug. 15–30 (*PC*)

This, entitled *Chinese Legends*, was sold by Bentley to Ward & Lock at an auction by Southgate & Barrett on July 14, 1856. The first edition was *The Porcelain Tower* by T. T. T., Bentley, London, 1841, 21 cm., 299 pp., illustrated, published on Aug. 30 in an edition of 750 copies according to the Bentley private catalog. It was listed in the *Ath* on Sept. 4, 10/6, and reviewed on Sept. 25. It was illustrated by Leech, and Bentley reissued it, 1848 and 1849, 18 cm., 180 pp., illustrated. The first American edition was issued by Lea & Blanchard, Philadelphia, 1842, by T. T. T., 18.5 cm., 322 pp., illustrated by Leech.

73 CATHERINE G. F. GORE **Sketches of English Character.** 2/o boards   Aug. 15–30 (*PC*)

The first edition was issued by Bentley, London, 2 vols., 1846, 21 cm., 21/o, listed in the *Ath* on Apr. 11, 1846. He issued it, 1852, new edition, revised and corrected, 12mo, 159 pp., in his *Shilling Series* at 1/o boards, listed in the *Ath* on Sept. 4, 1852. It was sold by Bentley to Ward & Lock at a Southgate & Barrett auction on July 14, 1856, for £26.

74 ANONYMOUS **The Rival Lovers.**
1/6 boards   Aug. 15–30 (*PC*)
I cannot trace this.

75 HORACE MAYHEW **Wonderful People.**
[New edition]. Illustrated. 1/0 boards
Aug. 15–30 (*PC*)
I suspect that this contains *Model Men*; *Model Women and Children*; and *Change for a Shilling*. The first edition of the first title was issued by David Bogue, London, 1848, 13.5 cm., 88 pp., illustrated, listed in the *Spect* on Oct. 7, 1/0; and a new edition was advertised there on Oct. 28, 1/0. I have a copy, *Comic Library* No. 2, issued by W. Kent & Co., London, o/6, in orange pictorial wrappers, issued about Feb. 19, 1859. It has Kent on the cover and David Bogue, 1848, on the title page, with Bogue ads at the back dated July 1848. It was issued in the United States by Harper & Bros., New York, illustrated, noticed in *Godey's Lady's Book* for Feb. 1849. The first edition of the second title was issued by David Bogue, London (1848), 13.5 cm., 90 pp., listed in the *Spect* on Nov. 4, 1848, 1/0. Kent reissued it in 1859. It was issued in the United States by Harper & Bros., New York, illustrated, reprinted from *Punch*, listed in *Lit World* as published Dec. 23–30, 1848. The first edition of the third title was issued by David Bogue (1848), 13.5 cm., 120 pp., illustrated, 1/0 sewed. The second edition was advertised in the *Spect* on Sept. 3, 1848, illustrated, 1/0. I have a copy of the Kent reissue, no date, o/6, in orange pictorial wrappers, with Kent on the front cover and title page, *Comic Library* No. 5.
See 1872, 73, 75

76 HENRY COCKTON **Stanley Thorn.**
[New edition]. 2/0 boards, 2/6 cloth
Aug. 15–30 (*PC*)
Standard Novels. The first edition was issued by Bentley, London, 3 vols., 1841, 20.5 cm., illustrated by Cruikshank,

Leech, and Crowquill, 31/6, listed in the *Ath* on Oct. 2, 1841. He issued it in the *Railway Library*, 1854, 17 cm., 373 pp., 2/0 sewed, in Dec. 1853. It was sold to Ward & Lock at a Southgate & Barrett auction in July 1856. The copyright and stereo plates were sold again there in May 1859, to Henry Lea, London, who issued it (1860), 312 pp., illustrated, in Sept. The first American edition was issued by Lea & Blanchard, Philadelphia, 1841, 8vo, 363 pp., frontispiece, engraved title page, and 10 plates by Cruikshank et al. It was bound in gray-green cloth. It was also issued by Colyer, New York, 1841, with 296 pp.

77 ANGUS B. REACH **Men of the Hour.**
[New edition]. Illustrated. 2/0 boards
Aug. 15–30 (*PC*)
This has no date and contains *The Natural History of "Bores," The Natural History of Tuft Hunters and Toadies*, and *The Bal Masqué*, the first two by Reach and the third by Count Chicard (pseudonym). The first edition of the first title was issued by David Bogue, London, 1847, my copy, 13.3 cm., 112 pp., illustrated, in drab wrappers printed on the front with a vignette in black, and printed on the back with a publisher's ad with vignette in black. There is a 16-page catalog at the back, plain white endpapers, 1/0. It was noticed in the *Ath* on Aug. 2, 1847, and the second edition was listed in the *Spect* on Aug. 7. The third edition was advertised on Dec. 18. Kent & Co., London, reissued it in 1859. The first edition of the second title was issued by Bogue in 1847, 13.3 cm., 112 pp., illustrated, 1/0 sewed, listed in the *Ath* on Nov. 27, 1847. The first edition of the third title was issued by Bogue, 1848, my copy, 13.3 cm., 136 pp., in wrappers in a rainbow coloring, printed and with a vignette in black on the front, with a publisher's ad in black on the back, plain inside covers, and with a 16-page catalog at the back. I have another copy issued by W. Kent & Co.,

London, no date, 13.3 cm., o/6, in orange pictorial wrappers, with commercial ads on the inside covers and on the back cover, *Comic Library* No. 4, issued in 1859. The Bogue issue was listed in the *Ath* on Jan. 8, 1848.

78   ALBERT SMITH   *Sketches of the Day.*
Illustrated. 2/o boards   Sept. 1–15 (*PC*)
The *Bks* and *PC* give this as the first and second series in 1 vol., and the *Eng Cat* gives first and second series in 2 vols., 2/o each. The *U Cat* gives the second series, Ward & Lock (1856), 3-parts-in-1 vol., 13.5 cm., illustrated, with the 3 parts being *The Gent*, *The Ballet Girl*, and *The Idler Upon Town*. I suspect that there were 2 vols. and that the other volume contained *The Natural History of "Stuck-up" People*, *The Natural History of the Flirt*, and *The Natural History of Evening Parties*. Five of these were first issued by David Bogue, London, 13.6 cm., illustrated, 1/o sewed each, in white wrappers printed and with a vignette in black or in blue and black for *Evening Parties*. *The Natural History of "Stuck-up" People* was listed in the *Ath* on Sept. 4, 1847, and the fourth edition was advertised in the *Ath* on Dec. 18, 1847. I have a copy, 1847, 112 pp., with plain inside covers, a publisher's ad on the back, and a 16-page catalog at the back. *The Natural History of the Flirt* was advertised in the *Ath* on Apr. 1, 1848, as "Now ready," and the second edition was listed in the *Spect* on Apr. 8, 1848. *The Natural History of Evening Parties* was in *Punch* in 1842 and was reprinted in *The Wassail Bowl* in 1843. Bentley issued it, 1846, new edition, 17.5 cm., 71 pp., illustrated by Leech, listed in the *Spect* on Apr. 11, with additions and corrections. Bogue issued it, 1849, 119 pp., and he issued a new edition, listed in the *Spect* on Jan. 6, 1849, both illustrated by Leech. *The Natural History of the Gent* was listed in the *Ath* on Apr. 3, 1847, and the sixth edition was advertised in the *Ath* on Dec. 18, 1847. It was in *Bentley's Miscellany*

for Mar. 1846 and was issued in the United States by D. Appleton & Co., New York, listed in the *United States Magazine* (monthly) for July 1847. *The Natural History of the Ballet Girl* was listed in the *Ath* on June 5, 1847, and the fourth edition was advertised there in the *United States Magazine* for Oct. 1847. *The Natural History of the Idler Upon Town* was listed in the *Ath* on Mar. 4, 1848. W. Kent & Co., London, reissued them in 1858 and 1859 at o/6 sewed each, from the Bogue plates. I have a copy of *"Stuck-up" People*, W. Kent & Co., no date, in orange pictorial wrappers, *Comic Library* No. 6, with commercial ads on the inside covers and on the back. I have a copy of *Evening Parties*, W. Kent & Co., no date, in orange pictorial wrappers, *Comic Library* No. 3, with 8 pp. of ads at the back, and with commercial ads on the inside covers and on the back. I have a copy of *The Gent*, David Bogue, London, 1847, 104 pp., with plain inside covers, and with a publisher's ad on the back. I have a copy of the *Flirt*, W. Kent & Co., no date, in orange pictorial wrappers, *Comic Library* No. 1, with 8 pp. of ads at the back, and ads on the inside covers and on the back.
See 1872, 75

79   EMMA D. E. SOUTHWORTH   *The Lost Heiress.* [Third edition]. 1/6 boards
Sept. 1–15 (*PC*)
Also 1855

80   ALEXANDRE DUMAS, THE YOUNGER
The Lady of the Camelias. 1/6   Sept. 13 (*Ath*)
This was advertised by Ward & Lock in the *Ath* on Aug. 30, 1856, and listed on Sept. 13. It was translated unabridged from the eighth Paris edition. The *BM* gives George Vickers, London, 1856, 208 pp., and it was advertised by Vickers in the *Spect* on Sept. 13, 1856, 1/6 boards, as "This day." The first edition was *La Dame aux Camélias*, Paris, 2 vols., 1848, 22.5 cm.

It was issued in the United States by DeWitt & Davenport, New York, advertised in the *New York Daily Times* on Jan. 13, 1855, *La Dame aux Camélias*, $.37½. It was also issued by E. J. Hincken, Philadelphia, 1857, 19.5 cm., 249 pp.

81 THOMAS L. PEACOCK *Maid Marian and Crotchet Castle*. New Edition.
1/o boards　Sept. 13 (*Ath*)
This is 1856, 16.5 cm., 228 pp. The first edition of the first title was issued by T. Hookham, etc., London, 1822, 18 cm., anonymous, 262 pp., 7/o, listed by the *Quarterly Review* as published Jan.–Mar. 1822. The first edition of the second title was issued by T. Hookham, London, 1831, listed in the *Spect* on Mar. 12, 300 pp., 7/6. These two titles along with *Headlong Hall* and *Nightmare Abbey* were issued by Bentley as *Standard Novels* No. 57, anonymous, in 1837. Ward & Lock purchased the copyright at the auction in Feb. 1856.

82 L. E. L. (LETITIA E. LANDON, later MACLEAN) *Romance and Reality*. 2/o boards, 2/6 cloth　Sept. 15–30 (*PC*)
Standard Novels. This is 1856, 495 pp. The first edition was issued by Colburn & Bentley, London, 3 vols., 1831, 19 cm., 31/6, by L. E. L., published in Nov. Bentley issued it as *Standard Novels* No. 111, 1848. Ward & Lock purchased the copyright at the Hodgson auction in Feb. 1856. The first American edition was issued by J. & J. Harper, New York, 2 vols., 1832, by L. E. L.

83 ANONYMOUS *Father and Daughter*.
1/6 boards　Sept. 15–30 (*PC*)
This was probably the first edition. The *BM* gives only The Society for Promoting Christian Knowledge, London (1866), which may not be the same work.
Also 1857

84 ROSE E. HENDRICKS, later TEMPLE *A Woman's Struggles*. 1/6 boards
Sept. 15–30 (*PC*)
I cannot trace this.

85 ANNA M. HOWITT, later WATTS *The School of Life*. 1/o sewed
Sept. 15–30 (*PC*)
This is the only edition given by the *BM*, but I hesitate to call it a first edition since it was issued by Ticknor & Fields, Boston, 1855, 19 cm., 266 pp., in an edition of 2,539 copies, selling for $.75, and for which they paid $30 for early sheets. It was noticed in *Putnam's Monthly* for July 1855, Ticknor & Fields. Presumably they got the early sheets from an English publisher!

86 JOHN MILLS *The Life of a Race-Horse*. [Fifth edition]. 1/o sewed　Sept. 15–30 (*PC*)
Ward & Lock also issued this, 1861, 112 pp., illustrated.
Also 1854, 65, 73, 82, 85

87 ROBERT M. BIRD *Nick of the Woods*. Fourth Edition. Frontispiece. Boards
Sept. 27 (*Ath*)
This is 1856, 17 cm., 316 pp.
Also 1854, 59, 60, 72

88 JAMES J. MORIER *The Adventures of Hajii Baba of Ispahan*. 2/o boards
Sept. 27 (*Ath*)
Also Apr. above and 1878

89 ANONYMOUS *Mary Ellis*. 2/6 boards
Sept. 30–Oct. 14 (*PC*)
This is 1856. The first edition was issued by Hope, London, 3 vols., 1854, p 8vo, 31/6.

90 ANONYMOUS *The Unhappy Queen*.
1/6 boards　Sept. 30–Oct. 14 (*PC*)
I cannot trace this.

91 EMILIE CARLÉN (EMILIE FLYGARE, later CARLÉN) *A Brilliant Marriage.* [New edition]. 1/6 Sept. 30–Oct. 14 (*PC*)

This has no date, 16.5 cm., 195 pp., a duplicate of the first English edition of Bentley with a new title page. The Bentley edition was 1852, 195 pp., 1/o boards, in his *Shilling Series.* The *BM* gives the incomprehensible description: From the German (a domestic tragedy from the French of Samuel H. Berthould, Quentin Metzis, A. Dumas)! This was purchased at a Southgate & Barrett auction of Bentley *Railway Library* titles in July 1856.
Also 1865

92 ROBERT M. BIRD *The Hawks of Hawk Hollow.* 1/6 boards Oct. 4 (*Ath*)

This is 1856, 17.5 cm., 256 pp. The first edition was issued by Carey, Lea & Blanchard, Philadelphia, 2 vols., 1835, 19 cm. The cost book of Carey & Lea states that 3,000 copies were finished on Sept. 25, 1835, bound in purple cloth, with a publisher's catalog at the front of vol. 2. The first English edition was issued by A. K. Newman & Co., London, 3 vols., 1837, 27/o, listed in the *Ath* on Feb. 18.

93 FREDERICK HARDMAN, ed. *Sigismund; or, Hidden Treasures.* [New edition]. 1/6 boards Oct. 14–30 (*PC*)

This is a duplicate of the first edition with a new title page. The first edition was *Hidden Treasures,* London, 1853 (1852), 12mo, 4/6.

94 JAMES F. COOPER, ed. *Ned Myers.* 1/o boards Oct. 14–30 (*PC*)

The first American edition was issued by Lea & Blanchard, Philadelphia, 1843, 19.5 cm., 232 pp., narrated by Myers, and written down by Cooper. It was reviewed in the *Southern Literary Messenger* for Dec. 1843 and published after Nov. 4, according to Brussel. The first English edition

was issued by Bentley, London, 2 vols., 1843, 19.5 cm., published on Nov. 6, according to Brussel. It was listed in the *Ath* on Nov. 11, 2 vols., 18/o, and reviewed on Nov. 25. Bentley issued it in his *Railway Library,* 1853, 192 pp., 1/o sewed, about Nov. 26; it was sold at the Southgate & Barrett auction in July 1856.

95 JONATHAN F. SLINGSBY (JOHN F. WALLER) *The Dead Bridal.* 1/6 boards Oct. 25 (*Ath*)

This is the first edition, 1856.

96 JOHN LANG *Captain Macdonald.* 1/6 boards Nov. 1 (*Ath*)

This is the first edition, 1856, 248 pp. Also 1858, 60, 70, 82, 85

97 SAMUEL G. GOODRICH *Sketches of Paris and the Parisians.* Small format. Illustrated. 2/o boards Nov. 1–14 (*PC*)

This is the first edition, 1856, 368 pp., frontispiece and illustrations, with an extra illustrated title page.

98 ELIZABETH INCHBALD *A Simple Story and Nature and Art.* [New edition]. 2/o boards, 2/6 cloth Nov. 14–29 (*PC*)

Standard Novels. The first edition of the first title was issued by G. G. & J. Robinson, London, 4 vols., 1791, 16.5 cm. It was also issued by W. Weldon, Dublin, 2 vols., 1791, 17 cm. The first American edition was issued by Robert Campbell, Philadelphia, 2-vols.-in-1, 1793, 17 cm. The first edition of the second title was issued by the same London publishers, 2 vols., 1796, 17 cm.; the first American edition was issued by H. & P. Rice, Philadelphia, 2-vols.-in-1, 1796, 18 cm. Bentley issued both titles in 1 vol. as *Standard Novels* No. 26 in Mar. 1833.

99 A WORKING BEE *To Commercial Travellers. Honey Gathered in Commercial Rooms.* 1/o Nov. 14–29 (*PC*)

This is the first edition, 1856.

100 A. MACFARLANE *Railway Scrip.*
Small format. 1/o sewed   Dec. 1–15 (*PC*)
This is the first edition, 1856, 135 pp.

101 ANONYMOUS *Aldershottana.*
2/6 boards   Dec. 1–15 (*PC*)
This is the first edition, 1856, 228 pp.
Ward & Lock issued the second edition,
1859, 324 pp.

102 WILDWOOD NEVILLE *The Life and
Exploits of Robin Hood.* 1/o boards
Dec. 1–15 (*PC*)
This was probably issued jointly with D.
Green, Leeds, as the latter issued the first
edition (1855), 188 pp., frontispiece.

103 HENRY MOSES *An Englishman's Life
in India.* 2/o boards   Dec. 13–31 (*PC*)
The first edition was issued by Binns &
Goodwin, London; etc., 1853, 17.5 cm.,
342 pp., colored frontispiece, 6/o.

104 ANGUS REACH, JAMES HANNAY, &
ALBERT SMITH *Christmas Cheer in Three
Courses.* 18mo. Illustrated. 1/o boards
Dec. 13–31 (*PC*)
This is in 3 parts, 13.5 cm. I think part 1
by Reach was either *The Natural History of
Humbugs* or *A Romance of a Mince Pie.* The
first edition of the first one was David
Bogue, London, 1847, 13.5 cm., 126 pp.,
illustrated, listed in the *Spect* on Nov. 6,
and a second edition was advertised in the
Ath on Dec. 18, 1847. The first edition of
the second one was Bogue, 1848, 13.5
cm., 104 pp., illustrated, 1/o sewed, listed
in both the *Spect* and the *Ath* on Dec. 25,
1847. Part 2 is *Hearts Are Trumps* by Hannay, first issued by Bogue, 1849, my copy,
in white wrappers pictorially printed in
red and black, 13.5 cm., 93 pp., with a
publisher's ad on the back in black and
red, and with their ads on the inside back
cover and on 14 pp. at the back. It was illustrated by "Phiz" and listed in the *Spect*
on Dec. 9, 1848. I have another copy, W.

Kent & Co., London (1858), 13.3 cm.,
from the Bogue plates, in orange wrappers, illustrated and printed in red and
black. There are commercial ads on the
back and on the inside covers and a page
of George Vickers ads, 2 pp. of Ward &
Lock ads, and 1 p. of Houlston & Wright
ads at the back. The words "Comic Library" do not appear. Part 3 is *A Bowl of
Punch* by Albert Smith, first issued by
Bogue, 1848, 13.5 cm., 125 pp., illustrated, 1/o sewed, in red wrappers cut
flush and decorated and lettered in white.
It was listed in the *Spect* on Feb. 5, 1848.

105 WILLIAM BECKFORD *Vathek.*
1/o boards   Dec. 27 (*Ath*)
This is 1856, 150 pp. The first continental
edition was either at Lusanne, 1787 (Dec.
1786), 19.4 cm., anonymous, 204 pp., illustrated; or Paris, 1787. The first English
edition was issued by J. Johnson, London,
1786, 20.5 cm., anonymous, 339 pp., entitled *An Arabian Tale.* The first American
edition was issued by Matthew Carey, Philadelphia, 1816, from the third London
edition, revised and corrected, 15 cm.,
234 pp.

106 ANONYMOUS *Joe Miller's Jest Book.*
1/o   1856 (*Eng Cat*)
The first edition was issued by T. Read,
London, 1739, 19.5 cm., 70 pp.
Also 1872, 91

107 ANONYMOUS *The Railway and
Parlour Song-Book.* 1/o   1856 (*Eng Cat*)
This is 1856, 16.5 cm., 192 pp., with a
frontispiece (portrait). The *BM* gives London, 1855.

108 SAMUEL SIDNEY *Gallops and
Gossips in the Bush of Australia.* 1/o
1856 (*Eng Cat*)
The first edition was issued by Longman,
London, 1854, 17 cm., 227 pp., frontis-
piece.

109 ROSE E. HENDRICKS, later TEMPLE
Real and Ideal. 1/6   1856 (*Eng Cat*)
I cannot trace this.

110 JOHN BIRD, ed. ***The Autobiography
of the Blind James Wilson.*** Cr 8vo.
Frontispiece. 2/0   1856 (*Eng Cat*)
This is 1856, 18.5 cm., 108 pp. The first
edition was issued at Limerick, 1825, as
The Life of James Wilson, 17 cm., 72 pp. It
was reissued by J. W. Showell, Birming-
ham, 1842, 12mo, 108 pp.

111 MARY DOIG ***Stories About Stars and
Star-Gazers.*** 2/0   1856 (*Eng Cat*)
The *BM* gives London, printed in Mussel-
burgh, 1856.

112 JAMES J. MORIER ***The Adventures of
Hajii Baba, of Ispahan, in England.*** New
Edition. Small format. 2/0 boards   1856
This is my copy, 1856, 16.8 cm., 291 pp.,
in yellow pictorial boards with publisher's
ads on the endpapers in blue and on the

back in black. The author's name appears
only on the front cover, and the title page
states, "Revised, corrected, and illustrated
with notes by the author." The first English edition was issued by John Murray,
London, 2 vols., 1828, 17 cm., anonymous, 15/0 boards, listed in the *Monthly
Review* for June 1828, and listed in the
Quarterly Review as published Apr.–June
1828. It was issued by Bentley as *Standard
Novels* No. 45 in 1835. The first American
edition was issued by J. & J. Harper, New
York; etc., 2 vols., 1828, 20.5 cm.

113 PERCY B. ST. JOHN ***The Trapper's
Bride and White Stone Canoe, etc.*** Third
Edition. Small format   1856 (*U Cat*)
This is 1856, 155 pp., and contains also
The Rose of Ouisconsin.
Also 1854

114 ANONYMOUS ***Everyday Cookery for
Every Family.*** 1/0   1856?
This is the first edition, no date.

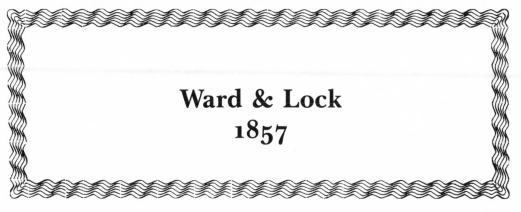

Ward & Lock
1857

115 ONE OF THEM (ANNIE TURNER, later TINSELY **Women as They Are.** Reduced to 2/o boards   Jan. 1–14 (*PC*)

The first edition was issued by Bentley, London, 2 vols., 1854, 17 cm., anonymous.

116 MARIANNE FINCH **An Englishwoman's Experience in America.** [New edition]. 2/o boards   Jan. 1–14 (*PC*)

The first edition was issued by Bentley, London, 1853, 20.5 cm., 386 pp.

117 CHARLES L. KENNEY **The Gates of the East.** 8vo. Illustrated. Maps. 1/o sewed Jan. 1–14 (*PC*)

This is the first edition, 1857, 22 cm., 72 pp., with 4 plates (one folding), and 2 folding maps.

118 JOHN BENWELL **An Englishman's Travels in America.** Small format. 1/o boards   Jan. 1–14 (*PC*)

This has no date, 16.5 cm., 231 pp. The first edition was issued by Binns & Goodwin, London; etc. (1853), 17 cm., 231 pp., with a colored frontispiece.

119 ANONYMOUS **How to Be Healthy.** Sq 16mo. o/6 sewed   Jan. 1–14 (*PC*)

I cannot trace this.

120 (PERCIVAL LEIGH) **The Comic English Grammar.** [New edition]. 1/o boards Jan. 14–31 (*PC*)

A dealer offered a copy, 1856, new edition, small format, anonymous, illustrated

by Leech, 1/o, with a publisher's ad on the back cover. The first edition was issued by Bentley, London, 1840, 19.5 cm., anonymous, 228 pp., illustrated by John Leech, 8/o, listed in the *Ath* on Dec. 5, 1840, and noticed on Dec. 26. Bentley issued it in his *Shilling Series*, 1851, illustrated by Leech, listed in the *PC* as published Oct. 13–29, 1851, and listed in the *Spect* on Jan. 24, 1852, the latter possibly a reissue. It was sold at a Southgate & Barrett auction in July 1856. It was issued in the United States by Wilson, New York, 1845, 144 pp., illustrated; and by Dick & Fitzgerald, New York, no date, illustrated.
Also 1864

121 EMILIE CARLÉN (EMILIE FLYGARE, later CARLÉN) **John.** 2/o   Jan. 14–31 (*PC*)

The first English edition was issued by Bentley, London, 2 vols., 1853, 21 cm., 8/o, noticed in the *Gentleman's Magazine* (monthly) for Feb. 1854, 2 vols., thus probably issued Oct.–Dec. 1853. It was the third novel issued by Bentley in a new pricing experiment. The first American edition was issued by D. Appleton & Co., New York, 1854, 23.5 cm., 110 pp., in double columns, reprinted from the English translation. It was also issued by Garrett, Dick & Fitzgerald, New York, listed in *APC&LG* on May 2, 1857.

122 HANS C. ANDERSEN **The Improvisatore.** Small format. 2/o boards, 2/6 cloth   Jan. 31 (*Ath*)

This is 1857, 16.5 cm., 340 pp., translated by Mary Howitt. The first edition was is-

sued in Copenhagen in 2 parts, 1837, *Improistoren*. The first English edition was issued by Bentley, London, 2 vols., 1845, 20 cm., translated by Howitt and published Feb. 14 according to the Bentley private catalog. It was listed in the *Ath* on Feb. 15, 2 vols., 21/0, and reviewed on Mar. 8 and 15. Bentley issued it as *Standard Novels* No. 110 in Nov. 1847, and it was probably sold to Ward & Lock at the auction in Feb. 1856. The first American edition was issued by Harper & Bros., New York, 1845, 23 cm., 124 pp., translated by Howitt, and noticed in the *Southern Literary Messenger* for May 1845.
Also 1863, 73, 89

123 ANONYMOUS *The Comic Cocker.* Illustrated. 1/0 boards   Feb. 1–16 (*PC*)
The first edition was issued by Bentley, London, in 1843, p 8vo, 7/0. It probably refers to Edward Cocker's *Arithmetic*.

124 JOHN W. W. TYNDALE, ed.
Adventures and Anecdotes of the South Army of the Emperor of Austria. 2/0 boards   Feb. 1–16 (*PC*)
The first edition was issued by Bentley, London, 1850, 19.5 cm., 340 pp., 10/6.

125 WILLIAM HOOKER *Physician and Patient.* 2/0 boards   Feb. 1–16 (*PC*)
The first edition was Bentley, London, 1850, 303 pp., 7/6, edited by Edward Bentley.

126 (ERSKINE NEALE) *Dark Deeds.* 1/6 boards   Feb. 16–28 (*PC*)
The first edition was issued by George Vickers, London, no date, anonymous, in 1856, 256 pp., at 1/6. It was advertised by Vickers in *PC* on Jan. 16, 1857, but it was listed in *PC* as I've given it, by Ward & Lock. The *U Cat* gives Vickers, no date, anonymous; the *Eng Cat* gives Vickers, 1856, at 1/6; and the *BM* gives London, 1857, anonymous. I think Ward & Lock

had a substantial interest in if not outright ownership of Vickers.

127 (JANE E. HORNBLOWER) *Vara.* [New edition]. 1/0 boards   Feb. 16–28 (*PC*)
The first edition was issued by Robert Carter & Bros., New York, 1854, 20 cm., anonymous, 316 pp., frontispiece, advertised in the *New York Daily Times* on Apr. 21, 1854, as "Just published." The first English edition was issued by Nisbet, London, 1854, at 2/6.

128 STEPHEN W. FULLOM *The King and the Countess.* 1/6 boards   Feb. 28 (*Ath*)
The first edition was issued by Henry Colburn, London, 3 vols., 1849, anonymous, advertised in the *Ath* on July 7 as a new publication, listed in the *Spect* on July 21, and reviewed on July 28.

129 JOHN MILLS *The Briefless Barrister; or, The Wheel of Life.* Third edition. 1/6 boards   Mar. 14–31 (*PC*)
The *U Cat* gives this as the third edition, 1856, 259 pp.; and the *Eng Cat* gives it as issued in 1859. It was advertised in a book of 1857 as the third edition, at 1/6 boards. Sadleir had a copy, no date, Ward & Lock, small format, a 2/0 yellowback, in the *Library of Popular Authors*, which he gave as (after 1871), but I think it was after 1868.
Also 1854, 86

130 "CUJUS" *Divorce in 1857: The Talbot Case.* 1/6 boards   Apr. 1–14 (*PC*)
This is the first edition, 1857, 17 cm., 228 pp., a series of letters, the first four of which appeared in the *Standard* of London.

131 FRANCES TROLLOPE *Lynch Law.* New Edition. Small format. 2/0 boards May 2 (*Ath*)
Standard Novels. This has no date. The first edition was *The Life and Adventures of Jonathan Jefferson Whitlaw*, issued by Bentley,

London, 3 vols., 1836, 19 cm., illustrated, 31/6 boards, published June 26 according to the Bentley private catalog. It was listed and reviewed in the *Spect* on July 2, p 8vo, with 15 illustrations. The second edition in 3 vols. was advertised by Bentley in the *Spect* on Aug. 27, 1836.

132 TIMOTHY TEMPLETON (CHARLES ADAMS) *Adventures of My Cousin Smooth.* 1/6 boards   June 1–14 (*PC*)

This has no date. The first edition was probably in 1855 as it was listed by the *Spect* on Oct. 27, 1855, no publisher given. The first American edition was issued by Miller, Orton & Mulligan, New York and Auburn; etc., 1856, 19.5 cm., 236 pp., listed in the *Ind* on Feb. 21, reviewed on Mar. 27, and listed in *APC&LG* on Feb. 23, $.50 paper, $.75 cloth.

133 HENRY P. WRIGHT *Recollections of a Crimean Chaplain.* 1/o boards June 16–30 (*PC*)

This is the first edition, 1857, 141 pp.

134 CATHERINE G. F. GORE *Castles in the Air.* 2/o boards   June 30–July 14 (*PC*)
Standard Novels. This is 1857. The first edition was issued by Bentley, London, 3 vols., 1847, p 8vo, 31/6, listed in the *Ath* on June 12, 1847, and noticed on June 19. The first American edition was issued by H. Long & Brother, New York, 1848, noticed in *Godey's Lady's Book* for Jan. 1849.

135 IK MARVEL (DONALD G. MITCHELL) *Dream Life.* 1/o boards   July 16–31 (*PC*)
The first edition was issued by Charles Scribner, New York, 1851, 19.5 cm., 286 pp., frontispiece, listed in *Lit World* as published Dec. 17–27 and advertised on Dec. 13 and 20 as "This week." It was noticed in the *Ind* on Dec. 25 and reviewed on Jan. 8, 1852. It was issued in England by Thomas Nelson & Sons, London and Edinburgh, 1853, 17.5 cm., 250 pp., frontispiece, il-

lustrated. It was also issued jointly by Edward Howell, Liverpool, and George Routledge, London, as *Howell's Select Book-Case* No. 3, 1/o boards, 1/6 cloth, in Apr. 1853, with 1853 on the title page and the initials "D. G. M." on the dedication page.

136 JOSEPH TURNLEY *The Language of the Eye.* [New edition]. Illustrated. 1/o sewed   July 16–31 (*PC*)
The first edition was issued by Partridge & Co., London, 1856, 21.5 cm., 118 pp.

137 (JOSEPH T. J. HEWLETT) *Parsons and Widows.* Small format. 2/o boards
Aug. 1 (*Ath*)
This is 1857, 16.5 cm., 352 pp. The first edition was issued by Henry Colburn, London, 1844, 3 vols., 19 cm., anonymous, 31/6, listed in the *Ath* on Aug. 10 and reviewed on Sept. 28.
Also 1858, 66

138 JOHN BANIM *The Smuggler.* [New edition]. 2/o boards   Aug. 1–15 (*PC*)
Also 1856, 62

139 JABEZ HOGG *The Domestic Medical and Surgical Guide.* Fourth Edition. Illustrated. 1/o boards   Aug. 15–31 (*PC*)
This is 1857, 156 pp. The first edition was issued by Ingram, Cooke & Co., London, 1853, 19 cm., 156 pp., illustrated. Ward & Lock issued the fifth edition (1860), Fcp 8vo, 2/6.

140 JULIA S. H. PARDOE *The Romance of the Harem.* 2/o boards   Aug. 28 (*Ath*)
Standard Novels. This is 1857, purchased at a sale of Colburn copyrights on May 26, 1857, for 40 guineas. The first edition was issued by Henry Colburn, London, 1839, 3 vols., 20 cm., 31/6, listed in the *Ath* on Feb. 2. The first American edition was issued by Carey & Hart, Philadelphia, 1839, 2 vols., 19 cm., listed in the *New York Review* (quarterly) for Apr. 1839, 12 mo.

141 THEOPHILUS OPER *Across the Channel.* 1/0 sewed   Sept. 1–15 (*PC*)
This is the first edition, 1857.

142 (HARRIETTE SMYTHIES) (MRS. GORDON SMYTHIES) *The Matchmaker.* 2/0 boards   Sept. 15–30 (*PC*)
This was purchased at the Colburn sale on May 26, 1857, for 36 guineas. The first edition was issued by Henry Colburn, 1842, 3 vols., 20.5 cm., anonymous, 31/6, advertised in the *Spect* on Oct. 16, 1841, by (Theodore Hook) as "Just ready." This was edited by Hook. In the United States it was issued by H. Long & Brother, New York, anonymous, listed in *Godey's Lady's Book* for Apr. 1850, in their *Library of Select Novels*.

143 JOSEPH TURNLEY *Priest and Woman.* Illustrated. 1/0 sewed   Sept. 15–30 (*PC*)
This is the first edition, 1857.

144 HUGH JAMESON *Remarkable Adventures of Don Viquete.* 2/0 boards Oct. 1–15 (*PC*)
This is 1857, 171 pp. The first edition was *Don Viquete de los Montes*, issued by Wilson, London, illustrated, 7/6.

145 COUNTESS OF BLESSINGTON (MARGUERITE GARDINER) *The Lottery of Life.* 2/0 boards   Oct. 3 (*Ath*)
This has no date, 348 pp., purchased at the Colburn sale of copyrights in May 1857 for 36 guineas. The first edition was issued by Henry Colburn, London, 1842, 3 vols., 18.5 cm., 31/6, listed in the *Ath* on May 28, 1842, and reviewed on June 11. The first American edition was issued by J. Winchester, New York, 1842, 40 cm., 24 pp., from the London edition, *The New World*, dated June 29, 1842.
Also 1859

146 (EDWARD G. HOWARD) *The Buccaneer, Sir Henry Morgan.* 2/0 boards   Oct. 24 (*Ath*)
Standard Novels. This has no date, 339 pp. It was purchased at the sale of Colburn copyrights in May 1857 for 61 guineas. The first edition was *Sir Henry Morgan, the Buccaneer*, issued by Henry Colburn, London, 1842, 3 vols., p8vo, anonymous, frontispiece (portrait), 31/6, listed in the *Ath* on Feb. 19 and reviewed on Mar. 12. The first American edition was issued by Lea & Blanchard, Philadelphia, 1842, 2 vols., *Sir Henry Morgan*, listed in *Godey's Lady's Book* for Sept. 1842.

147 C. WATERS (WILLIAM RUSSELL) *The Game of Life.* Illustrated. 2/0 boards Nov. 28 (*Ath*)
This is the first edition, no date, 272 pp. Also 1858 and as *Leonard Harlowe*, 1862, 69

148 ANONYMOUS *Christian Melville.* Reduced to 1/6 boards   Dec. 1–14 (*PC*)
The first edition was issued by David Bogue, London, 1856, anonymous.

149 CHARLES E. ARMSTRONG *A Tar of the Last War: Being the Services and Anecdotes of Sir Charles Richardson.* Reduced to 2/0 boards   Dec. 14–31 (*PC*)
The first edition was issued by Longmans, London, 1855, 19.5 cm., 228 pp., illustrated.

150 (JOSEPH TURNLEY) *The Voice of Beauty.* Cr 8vo. Illustrated. 1/0 sewed 1857
This is my copy, 1857, the first edition, 18.8 cm., 76 pp., in white pictorial wrappers in red and blue, with an ad on the back in red and blue, and with plain inside wrappers. There are 16 pp. of ads at the back.

151 (ERSKINE NEALE) *Experiences of a Gaol Chaplain.* 2/0 boards   1857 (*Eng Cat*)
Standard Novels. The first edition was issued by Bentley, London, 1847, 3 vols., anonymous, advertised in the *Ath* on May

29 as "Just published." He issued it as *Standard Novels* No. 115, 1849, 422 pp., with a new preface and with additions. The first edition was listed in both the *Ath* and the *Spect* on Feb. 6, p 8vo, 31/6.

152 ANONYMOUS *Fable of the Seasons.*
1/0   1857 (*Eng Cat*)
I cannot trace this.

153 ANONYMOUS *Father and Daughter.*
1/6   1857 (*Eng Cat*)
Also 1856

154 D. L. MACKENZIE *A Practical Dictionary of English Synonyms.* 2/0 cloth 1857 (*Eng Cat*)
This is 1857, 216 pp. The first edition was issued by Willis, London, 1854, 15.5 cm.

155 JAMES G. MACWALTER *Tales of Ireland and the Irish.* 1/6   1857 (*Eng Cat*)
The first edition was issued by J. F. Shaw, London, 1854, 17.5 cm., 224 pp., frontispiece. It contains three tales.

156 MARIA J. M'INTOSH *Violet; or the Cross and the Crown.* Small format.
2/0 linen   1857
This is my copy, 1857, 16.6 cm., 380 pp., in orange linen boards, lettered and with a vignette in black on the front, and a publisher's ad on the back. There are publisher's ads in blue on the endpapers and an inserted yellow half sheet in front advertising *Stanley Thorn* at 2/0 boards. The front cover has the words, "Author's un-

abridged edition." The first edition was issued by J. P. Jewett & Co., Boston, 1856, 21 cm., 448 pp., listed in the *Ind* on Dec. 11, 1856, and in *APC&LG* on Nov. 22. The first English edition was probably issued by George Routledge, London, at 1/6 boards, 2/0 cloth, listed in *PC* as published Jan. 1–14, 1857, and given by the *BM* as 1856, 305 pp. The *BM* also gives J. Nisbet & Co., London, 1857, 380 pp.; and the *Eng Cat* gives Nisbet, issued in 1856 at 2/6!

157 ÉMILE SOUVESTRE *Man and Money; or, The Two Rivals.* 1/6 boards   1857?
This was advertised in *Violet* above and has a preface dated 1854, 16.5 cm., 252 pp., frontispiece. It is from the French work, *L'Homme et L'Argent.* It was issued by E. Howell, Liverpool, 1854; and by C. H. Clarke, London, the latter at 1/6 boards, in Aug. 1854. In the United States it was issued by T. R. Dawley, New York (1869), 80 pp., as *The Two Rivals.*

158 HORACE MAYHEW, ed. *Letters Left at the Pastry Cook's.* Cr 8vo. Illustrated. Ornamental wrapper   1857?
This was advertised in *Violet* above, illustrated by "Phiz." It had a date 185_ but the last digit was cut off in the *U Cat.* The first edition was issued by Ingram, Cooke, London, 1853, 18.5 cm., 119 pp., at 1/0, in white pictorial wrappers. The ninth edition was issued by Nathaniel Cooke, London, 1854, both having the illustrations by "Phiz."

Ward & Lock
1858

159 (CATHERINE SPENCE) *Clara Morison.*
Reduced to 2/0 boards Jan. 1–14 (*PC*)
The first edition was issued by J. W. Parker, London, 1854, 2 vols., 18 cm., anonymous, 9/0.

160 C. WATERS (WILLIAM RUSSELL)
The Game of Life. [Second edition].
Illustrated. 2/0 boards Jan. 2 (*Ath*)
Also 1857 and as *Leonard Harlowe*, 1862,
69

161 ANONYMOUS *Jesuit Executorship.*
2-vols.-in-1. Reduced to 2/0 boards
Jan. 14–30 (*PC*)
The first edition was issued by John W.
Parker & Son, London, 1853, 2 vols., 20.5
cm., 18/0, advertised in *Notes & Queries* on
Dec. 25, 1852, as "This day." In the United
States it was issued by DeWitt & Daven-
port, New York, as I surmise, as it was ad-
vertised by them as for sale in the *New York
Daily Times* for Nov. 22, 1853, as *Helen
Mulgrave*, anonymous, $.50 paper, $.75
cloth.

162 ANONYMOUS *Valentines.* 1/0 boards
Jan. 14–30 (*PC*)
The *BM* gives London, no date (1856?), a
series of 43 valentines.

163 (HENRY MAYHEW) *The Mormons.*
Illustrated. 2/0 boards Jan. 30 (*Ath*)
Ward & Lock issued the fourth edition,
revised and corrected, 19.5 cm., 308 pp.,
illustrated, 3/6, edited by Charles McKay

(1856), advertised in the *Spect* on Dec. 6,
1856, a new edition, Cr 8vo, 3/6. The first
edition was issued by Ingram, Cooke &
Co., London (1851), 19 cm., anonymous,
326 pp., in their *National Illustrated Library*.
They issued the third edition, 1852, Cr
8vo, anonymous, 320 pp., 2/6, edited by
McKay. The first American edition was
probably Derby & Miller, Auburn, 1853,
399 pp., as they issued the second thousand then, *History of the Mormons*.

164 (THOMAS CARTER) *Memoirs of a
Working Man.* 1/6 boards Jan. 30–
Feb. 13 (*PC*)
The first edition was issued by C. Knight
& Co., London, 1845, 15 cm., 234 pp.,
Knight's Weekly Volume No. 34. Cox, Lon-
don, issued it at 3/0 in 1848.

165 THOMAS MILLER *Godfrey Malvern.*
[New edition]. 2/0 boards Jan. 30–
Feb. 15 (*PC*)
A known copy has no date, 23 cm., 400
pp., illustrated, in red cloth. It was first issued by Thomas Miller, London, in 15
monthly parts, illustrated by "Phiz," 1/0
each, No. 1 issuing on Mar. 31, 1842, and
Nos. 1–8 forming vol. 1. Vol. 1 was listed
in the *Ath* on Nov. 5, 1842, 8vo, 8/6, and
was reviewed on Dec. 10. No. 9 was issued
in Jan. 1843; and vol. 2 was listed May 13,
1843, and noticed on June 17. The 2 vols.
sold for 14/0. Miller reissued it, 1843, 22
cm., 400 pp., illustrated, with an extra illustrated title page. H. G. Bohn, London,
issued it at 13/0 in 1847; and C. H. Clarke,

London, issued it at 2/0 boards, listed in *PC* as published Mar. 14–31, 1857. In the United States it was issued in 15 monthly parts by William A. LeBlanc, New York, part 1 listed in *Godey's Lady's Book* for Oct. 1842. Harper & Bros., New York, issued it, 1851, 23.5 cm., 193 pp., illustrated, listed by *Lit World* as published July 12–26. The *U Cat* gives it as 1850!

166 ANONYMOUS *How to Make a Home and Feed a Family.* Illustrated. 2/0 boards Feb. 1 (*Ath*)

This is probably the first edition. It is also given by the *Eng Cat*, but otherwise I cannot trace it.
Also 1859

167 JOHN BENNETT *Night and Day.* Illustrated. 2/0 boards Feb. 6 (*Ath*)

This is the first edition, no date, 2 parts, 293 pp. It was issued by George Vickers, London (1859), as *The Worst in the World.*

168 ESTHER BAKEWELL *Glenwood Manor House.* [New edition]. 1/6 boards Feb. 27–Mar. 13 (*PC*)

The first edition was issued by Arthur Hall, Virtue, London, 1857, 249 pp.

169 CHARLES NEILL *The Soldier's Wife.* 2/0 boards Mar. 13–31 (*PC*)

The first edition was issued by the author, Edinburgh, 1856, 4/6, as *Ellen of Ayr; or, The Soldier's Wife.*

170 KINAHAN CORNWALLIS *Yarra Yarra.* Fifth Edition, Enlarged. 2/0 boards Apr. 1–14 (*PC*)

This was 1858. A new edition, enlarged, was issued by Hamilton, Adams, London, 1857, 188 pp., a poetical narrative in 11 books, listed in the *Spect* on Oct. 17.

171 ANONYMOUS *Experiences of a Clergyman.* Reduced to 1/6 boards Apr. 14–30 (*PC*)

I cannot trace this.

172 THOMAS MILLER *The Poacher, and Other Pictures of Country Life.* 2/0 boards, 3/6 cloth June 26 (*Ath*)

This has no date, and the cloth edition, at least, has 30 illustrations. The first edition was *Pictures of Country Life and Rambles in Green and Shady Places*, issued by David Bogue, London, 1847, 363 pp., illustrated, listed in the *Ath* on Oct. 31, 1846, at 10/6, and reviewed on Nov. 28.

173 JOHN LANG *The Forger's Wife.* [Fifth edition]. 1/0 sewed July 15–31 (*PC*)
Also 1855, 70, 82

174 JOHN LANG *Too Much Alike.* [Fifth edition]. 1/0 sewed July 15–31 (*PC*)
Also 1854, 70, 82

175 JOHN LANG *Captain Macdonald's Haps and Mishaps.* 1/6 boards July 15–31 (*PC*)
Also 1856, 60, 70, 82, 85

176 ANONYMOUS *The Best Method of Doing Common Things.* [Fourth edition]. Fcp 8vo. 1/0 cloth boards Aug. 1–14 (*PC*)

This has 90 pp. It was advertised in one of my Ward & Lock titles as I've given it, but it was given as 1/0 sewed by the *PC*. The *Eng Cat* gives the fourth edition, 12mo, 1/0, as published by Ward & Lock in 1860. The *BM* gives London (1854), 16mo, and London (1860), fourth edition, 12mo.

177 THOMAS L. PEACOCK *Headlong Hall and Nightmare Abbey.* [New edition]. 1/6 boards Aug. 7 (*Ath*)
Also 1856

178 FREDERICK TAYLOR *Telfer's System of Horse Training.* 1/0 sewed Sept. 1–14 (*PC*)

This has no date, 110 pp., probably the first edition.

179 ANONYMOUS *The Railway Anecdote Book.* [New edition]. 8vo. Illustrated. 1/0 sewed, 2/0 cloth   Sept. 1–14 (*PC*)

I think this had no date, 23 cm., 160 pp., with portraits. Ingram, Cooke & Co., London, issued it, no date, new edition, 8vo, 192 pp., 1/0 sewed, 1/6 cloth, with portraits and an illustrated title page, listed by *PC* as published Oct. 15–30, 1852. The *BM* gives London (1850?), but otherwise I cannot trace the first edition.

180 ALEXANDRE DUMAS, THE ELDER *The Count of Monte Cristo.* 2 vols. 3/0 boards   Oct. 1–14 (*PC*)

The first edition was *Le Comte de Monte-Cristo*, Paris, 18 vols., 1844–45. In England it was issued by Chapman & Hall, London, 2 vols., 1846, 8vo, illustrated, 24/0, listed in the *Ath* on May 23, 1846. They issued it in parts, ten 2/0 numbers, illustrated, part 1 advertised in the *Ath* on Feb. 28, 1846, as "This day." It was also issued by Simms & McIntyre; Belfast, etc., as *Parlour Novelist* No. 3, *The Chateau D'If*, 2/0 sewed, 2/6 cloth, advertised in the *Ath* on Mar. 28, 1846, as "This day" and listed on Apr. 4; and *Parlour Novelist* Nos. 8 and 9, *The Count of Monte Cristo*, 2/0 sewed, 2/6 cloth each, listed in the *Ath* on Sept. 5, 1846, translated by Emma Hardy. It was also issued by them as extra volumes of the *Parlour Library*, 3 vols.: vol. 1 being issued on Dec. 1, 1847; and vol. 2 on Feb. 1, 1848, according to Sadleir in vol. 2, p. 149. George Peirce, London, issued *The Prisoner of d'If* (1846), 406 pp. Routledge, London, issued the 2 vol. edition of Chapman & Hall, 8vo, illustrated, 10/6, in 1852 or 1853 and later in 1 vol., illustrated, 8/6, listed in the *Ath* on June 24, 1854. They issued it as *Railway Library* No. 181, 1858, Fcp 8vo, 754 pp., at 2/6 boards, listed in the *Ath* on Nov. 13, 1858. In the United States it was issued by Burgess & Stringer, New York, 1846, 2-vols.-in-1, illustrated; and by H. L. Williams, New York, 1846, 25 cm., 422 pp., illustrated. It ran in *Ains-*

worth's Magazine (Chapman & Hall) in 1845–46, chapters 18–26 appearing in the Mar. 1846 issue. Dumas received 50,000 francs ($10,000) for the right to publish it in the *Journal des Debats*, and he retained all other rights.
Also 1885, 88

181 STEPHEN W. FULLOM *The King and the Countess.* 2/0 boards   Oct. 2 (*Ath*)
Standard Novels.
Also 1857, 80

182 JOHN MILLS *The Old English Gentleman.* [Fourth edition]. 2/0 boards Oct. 2 (*Ath*)
Standard Novels.
Also 1854, 56, 62

183 E. WARMINGTON *Railroad Management.* 1/0 sewed   Oct. 14–31 (*PC*)
This is the first edition, no date.

184 FANNY FERN (SARAH PARTON) *Fern Leaves from Fanny's Portfolio.* [Second edition]. First and second series. 1 vol. 2/0 boards   Oct. 16 (*Ath*)
Standard Novels.
Also 1854, 55, 56, 73

185 STEPHEN W. FULLOM *The Man of the World.* [Third edition]. 2/0 boards Oct. (*Bks*)

The first edition was issued by Charles J. Skeet, London, 3 vols., 1856, 20 cm., illustrated, 31/6, listed in the *Ath* on June 28. The third edition was listed by *PC* as published Nov. 15–29, 1856, 12mo, 460 pp., 5/0, by Ward & Lock.

186 FRANCES TROLLOPE *Adventures of the Barnabys in America.* Small format. 2/0 boards   Nov. 20 (*Ath*)

This has no date, 344 pp., a pictorial yellowback. It was sold at the auction of Colburn copyrights in May 1857 for 59 guineas. The first edition was *The Barnabys in America; or, The Widow Wedded*, issued by Henry Colburn, London, 3 vols., 1843, 20.5 cm., illustrated by Leech, 31/6, and listed in the *Ath* on July 29.

187 WILLIAM A. BUTLER *"Two Millions"; and "Nothing to Wear."* 1/o boards
Nov. 27 (*Ath*)

This is 1858, 88 pp., two poems. Ward & Lock issued a new edition, 1858, listed by *PC* as published Dec. 14–31. Sampson Low, London, issued a new edition, 1858, 16.6 cm., 109 pp., at 1/o, pink glazed pictorial boards in red and black, my copy, with a 12-page catalog (Nov. 1858), listed by *PC* as published Nov. 30–Dec. 14. The first English edition of the first title was Low (1858), 16.5 cm., 96 pp., 1/o sewed, listed in the *Spect* on Aug. 21. The first English edition of the second title was Low, 1857, 16.5 cm., anonymous, 58 pp., 1/o, listed in the *Ath* on Oct. 17 and by *PC* as published Oct. 15–31. Low issued the fifth edition, 1858, 1/o, advertised in *PC* on Apr. 1, 1858; and Low advertised it in the *Ath* on Aug. 21, 1858, 16.5 cm., anonymous, 58 pp., illustrated, 1/o sewed. The first American edition of the first title was issued by D. Appleton & Co., New York, 1858, 17 cm., 93 pp., $.50, listed in the *Ind* on Aug. 12, and reviewed in the *Knickerbocker* for Sept. 1858. The first American edition of the second title was issued by Rudd & Carleton, New York, 1857, 16.5 cm., anonymous, 68 pp., illustrated, $.50 cloth, from *Harper's Weekly*, advertised in the *New York Daily Times* on June 20, and noticed in the *Knickerbocker* for July 1857. The *U Cat* gives also G. P. Putnam, New York (1857), 14 cm., 85 pp., illustrated.

188 (HENRY CLAPP) *Husband v. Wife.*
Illustrated. o/6 sewed   Dec. 1–14 (*PC*)

This is the first English edition, 1859, 31 pp., reprinted from the *Weekly Novelist*, in verse. The first edition was issued by

Rudd & Carleton, New York, 1858, 18 cm., 44 pp., illustrated.
See 1859, 60

189 ANONYMOUS *Adventures of a Volunteer.* 2/o   1858 (*Eng Cat*)
I cannot trace this.

190 (ARABELLA J. SULLIVAN) *Tales of a Chaperone.* 2/o   1858 (*Eng Cat*)

The first edition was *Recollections of a Chaperone*, issued by Bentley, London, 3 vols., 1833, five tales, edited by Mrs. Sullivan's mother, Lady Dacre (Barbarina Wilmot, later Brand). It was advertised in the *Spect* on Dec. 29, 1832, as "On Jan. 2" and listed in the *Ath* on Jan. 5, 1833, at 31/6. Bentley issued it as *Standard Novels* No. 114, 1849, 428 pp. The first American edition was issued by J. & J. Harper, New York, 1833, 2 vols., 21 cm.

191 JOSEPH T. J. HEWLETT *Parsons and Widows.* 2/o   1858 (*Eng Cat*)
Also 1857, 66

192 (EDWARD J. TRELAWNY) *The Younger Son.* 1/o   1858 (*Eng Cat*)

The first edition was *Adventures of a Younger Son*, issued by Colburn & Bentley, London, 3 vols., 1831, anonymous. Bentley issued it as *Standard Novels* No. 48, in Sept. 1835. In the United States it was issued by J. & J. Harper, New York, 2 vols., 1832, 18 cm., anonymous.

193 ANONYMOUS *Revelations from the Cloister.* 2/o   1858 (*Eng Cat*)
I cannot trace this.

194 LOLA MONTEZ (MARIE GILBERT, COUNTESS VON LANDSFELD) *Lectures of Lola Montez Including Her Autobiography.*
Small format. 1/6 boards   1858

This was Sadleir's copy, 1858, 16.6 cm., 192 pp., in yellow pictorial boards, with "Lectures and Life of Lola Montez" (with an inverted z) and "Gilbert's Edition" on the front cover. My copy is identical except the imprint is Gilbert, London, 1858. The *BM* states that it was written by C. C. Burr. It was issued by James Blackwood, London, no date, 202 pp., frontispiece, 1/6 boards, 2/6 cloth, listed by *PC* as published July 15–31, 1858, *Autobiography and Lectures of Lola Montez*. He issued it at 1/0 boards also, listed by *PC* as published Aug. 14–31, 1858. In the United States it was issued by Rudd & Carleton, New York, 1858, 292 pp., frontispiece (portrait), advertised in *Harper's Weekly* on June 19 as "Just out," and listed in *APC&LG* on June 26. It was also issued by T. B. Peterson & Bros., Philadelphia, 18.5 cm., 292 pp., frontispiece (portrait), *The Life of Lola Montez. With a Full and Complete Autobiography of Her Life.* It was listed in *Godey's Lady's Book* for Mar. 1860, $1.00 paper, $1.25 cloth. The Rudd & Carleton issue was in muslin at $1.00. The *U Cat* gives the Peterson issue as (1858), but I have found no confirmation of this.

Ward & Lock
1859

Houlston & Wright, London, shared ads with Ward & Lock from Nov. 1859 to Dec. 1861.

195 ROBERT M. BIRD *Nick of the Woods.* [New edition]. 2/0 boards   Jan. 8 (*Ath*)
Also 1854, 56, 60, 72

196 ANONYMOUS *Valentines, Serious and Satirical, Sublime and Ridiculous.* 1/0 boards   Jan.?
Also 1858

197 ANONYMOUS *How to Make a Home and Feed a Family.* Illustrated. 2/0 boards
Feb. 1–14 (*PC*)
Also 1858

198 CHARLES DICKENS, ed. *The Pic-Nic Papers, Part 1.* Cr 8vo. 1/0 sewed   Apr. 1–14 (*PC*)

This was issued in 5 parts and 1 vol., the latter at 5/0 illustrated. Part 5 was listed by *PC* as published July 15–30. These papers contain items by Dickens, Ainsworth, Horace Smith, W. H. Maxwell, Leitch Ritchie, et al. My copy of part 3 has no date, 18.2 cm., pp. 191–285, in yellow pictorial wrappers, with a publisher's ad on the back cover advertising the 5 parts as "Just published," and with a half-page yellow slip inserted at the front advertising *The Hawks of Hawk-Hollow.* My copy of part 4 is the same, pp. 287–381, with publisher's ads on the inside covers and on the endpapers, those in front being upside down! The other parts had no frontispieces. The copyright was purchased at a Colburn sale in May 1857 for 200 guineas. The first

edition was issued by Henry Colburn, London, 3 vols., 1841, illustrated by Cruikshank, "Phiz," et al., with an 8-page catalog (May 1841) at the back of vol. 2. Colburn paid £500 for it, and it was listed in the *Ath* on Aug. 14, 1841, edited by Dickens, illustrated, 31/6. In the United States the first 2 vols. were issued by Lea & Blanchard, Philadelphia, 1841, 12mo, by various hands, in drab boards with pink cloth spines and paper labels. The third volume was not issued as it contained matter copyrighted in the United States by Mr. Neal.
Also 1862, 65, 70, 82

199 HORACE GREELEY *Aunt Sally, Come Up!* 1/0 boards   June 4 (*Ath*)
This is the first book edition, reprinted from the *New York Tribune.*

200 JOHN LANG *My Friend's Wife.* 1/0 sewed   June 18 (*Ath*)
This is the first edition, no date, 88 pp.
Also 1870, 82

201 JOHN LANG *The Secret Police.* 1/0 sewed   July 2 (*Ath*)
This is the first edition, no date.
Also 1870, 82, 83

202 (THOMAS OAKLEIGH) (pseudonym) *The Shooter's Hand-Book.* 1/0 boards
July 15–30 (*PC*)
The first edition was issued jointly by an Edinburgh publisher and Simpkin, Marshall, London, 1842, p 8vo, 6/0.

203 (EDWARD T. TURNERELLI) *A Night in a Haunted House.* 1/0 sewed   July 30 (*Ath*)

This is the first edition, no date.

204 MADAME DE STAËL (ANNE DE STAËL-HOLSTEIN) *Corinne; or, Italy.* 2/0   July?

Also 1856

205 EMMA D. E. SOUTHWORTH *The Hidden Hand.* 2/0   Aug. 13 (*Ath*)

An ad in the *New-York Times* on Jan. 21, 1859, said that this would begin in the *New York Ledger* "Next week." It ran there again in 1868, weekly, beginning Aug. 24. Also 1861

206 ANONYMOUS *True Love versus Fashion. Also Brown's Daughter, and Husband and Wife.* Illustrated. 1/0 boards   Aug. 13 (*Ath*)

This has no date and was received by the *BM* on Aug. 18, 1859.
Also 1860. See *Husband and Wife*, 1858

207 JOHN C. WILSON *Jonathan Oldaker.* Small format. 2/0 boards   Oct. 8 (*Ath*)

Standard Novels. This is 1859, 270 pp. The first edition was issued by Bentley, London, 1856, p 8vo, 10/6.

208 SAMUEL R. T. MAYER *Amy Fairfax.* 1/0 sewed   Dec. 14–31 (*PC*)

This is the first edition, 1859.

209 ANONYMOUS *Amusing Stories for Boys and Girls.* 8vo. Colored illustrations. 2/6 boards   Dec. (*Bks*)

This is also given by the *Eng Cat*, but otherwise I cannot trace it.

210 COUNTESS OF BLESSINGTON (MARGUERITE GARDINER) *The Lottery of Life.* 2/0 boards   1859 (*Eng Cat*)

Standard Novels.
Also 1857

211 ARMAND F. L. DE WAILLY *Stella and Vanessa.* [New edition]. 1/6   1859 (*Eng Cat*)

There was a 2 vol. edition, Bruxelles, 1846, 16.5 cm., possibly the first edition. The first English edition was issued by Bentley, London, 2 vols., 1850, translated from the French by Lady Duff Gordon, whose name alone appears on the title pages and spines. He published it on July 30 according to the Bentley private catalog. It was listed in the *Spect* on Aug. 10, p 8vo, 21/0. A second edition was listed by *PC* as published Nov. 30–Dec. 14, 1850, the same. He issued it in his *Railway Library*, 1853, at 2/0 sewed, listed in the *Ath* on Nov. 12.

212 (THOMAS C. HALIBURTON) *The Attaché; or, Sam Slick in England.* Fcp 8vo. 2/0 linen   1859?

This is my copy, no date, 17 cm., 395 pp., in yellow linen, printed on the front in black. It has Ward & Lock on the front cover and spine, and has their ads on the back and the endpapers—but with David Bryce, London; W. P. Nimmo, Edinburgh, on the title page. I date it from the ads, which is a dangerous thing to do. This contains both series. The copyright of Bryce was sold at a Hodgson auction on June 8, 1858, for £80, and the entire stock in quires and in binding of Bryce was sold at auction on June 2–5, 1858. George Routledge, London, issued it about Sept. 4, 1858, both series in 1 vol., 395 pp., 2/0 boards, 2/6 cloth. He again issued it, 1859, 2/0 boards (my copy). The first edition of the first series was Bentley, London, 2 vols., 1843, 19.5 cm., anonymous, 21/0, listed and reviewed in the *Ath* on July 8, 1843. The first edition of the second series was the same, 1844, listed and reviewed in the *Ath* on Oct. 26. In the United States the two series were issued by Lea & Blanchard, Philadelphia, 1843, 1844, respectively, anonymous. The second series was also issued by William H.

Colyer, New York, 1844, anonymous, 68 pp.

213 DALTON INGOLDSBY (RICHARD H. BARHAM) **The Rubber of Life.** Fcp 8vo. 1/o boards 1859?
This was advertised in *The Attaché* above. The *Eng Cat* ascribes it to Ward & Lock in 1854, which is incorrect. It was issued by Bentley, London, in his *Railway Library* about June 3, 1854, at 1/o. It was adver-tised in the *New York Daily Times* on June 30, 1854, to start in the *Sunday Courier* (New York), *The Rubber of Life*, on July 2, anonymous. The first edition was in *Some Account of My Cousin Nicholas by Thomas Ingoldsby to Which Is Added the Rubber of Life by Dalton Ingoldsby*, Bentley, 3 vols., 1841, 20 cm., 31/6, listed in the *Ath* on Mar. 27, 1841, and reviewed on Apr. 17. The second story begins in vol. 2 and takes up all of vol. 3.

Ward & Lock
1860

214 CORPORAL BIGSBY *The Adventures of Corporal Brown.* o/6 sewed   Jan. (*Bks*)
I cannot trace this.

215 ANONYMOUS *Wit and Wisdom.*
p 8vo. 2/o sewed   Mar. 15–31 (*PC*)
This is probably the first edition, 1860. Five hundred copies were remaindered at a Hodgson auction in Nov. 1861.

216 HENRY CURLING *Love at First Sight, and Stories of the Barrack and Battlefield.*
2/o boards   Mar. 17 (*Ath*)
This is the first edition, no date, 286 pp. It was issued in the United States by T. B. Peterson & Bros., Philadelphia, no date, 132 pp.

217 ALBANY FONBLANQUE, JR.
Tom Rocket. 2/o boards   Apr. 21 (*Ath*)
This is the first edition, 1860. Glover and Greene describe it. At a Hodgson auction in Jan. 1861, 1,000 copies were remaindered.

218 (H. BUTCHER) *Sir Gilbert.* Reduced to 2/o boards   Apr. (*Bks*)
The first edition was issued by Bentley, London, 1859, 6/o.

219 CHARLES MARTEL, ed. (THOMAS DELF) *The Detective's Note-Book.* Small format. 2/o boards   May 5 (*Ath*)
This is the first edition, 1860, 312 pp., in yellow pictorial boards. Glover and Greene and Sadleir both had copies. At a

Hodgson auction in July 1861, 2,000 copies were remaindered; and 2,500 copies were put up for remaindering at a Hodgson auction in Oct. 1861. The *U Cat* gives Published for the Proprietors, London, 1863, 16.5 cm., 312 pp. Sadleir thought this imprint was used for some of the more sensational Ward & Lock titles. A new edition of the present title was listed by *PC* as published July 16–31, the same.

220 ALEXANDRE DUMAS, THE ELDER
Roland de Montrevel; or, The Companions of Jehu. 2/o boards   May 12 (*Ath*)
This is the first English edition, 1860, 286 pp. The first edition was *Les Compagnons de Jehu*, Paris, 2 vols., 1859.

221 JOHN LANG *Captain Macdonald.*
Advanced to 2/o boards   May 19 (*Ath*)
Also 1856, 58, 70, 82, 85

222 ANN S. STEPHENS *Zana.* [Third edition]. 2/o boards   May 19 (*Ath*)
Standard Novels.
Also 1854, 56, 73

223 ANONYMOUS *The Illustrated Life and Career of Garibaldi.* p 8vo. Illustrated.
1/o sewed   June 1–14 (*PC*)
This is the first edition, no date, with a portrait of Garibaldi on the cover.
Also 1861

224 ROBERT M. BIRD *Nick of the Woods.*
[New edition]. 2/o boards   June 1–14 (*PC*)
Also 1854, 56, 59, 72

225 ANONYMOUS **Yankee Humour, and Uncle Sam's Fun.** [New edition]. 12mo. Illustrated. 1/o sewed June 1–14 (*PC*)

This had an introduction by W. Jerdan. The first edition was issued by Ingram, Cooke & Co., London, 1853, 17.5 cm., 115 pp., illustrated, listed in the *Spect* on Aug. 20. They issued a second edition, listed by *PC* as published Oct. 14–31, 1853; and they issued the third edition, 1853, in wrappers, with the introduction by Jerdan, a known copy. The first edition was at 1/o sewed, 1/6 cloth. Also 1865, 82

226 JAMES E. RICHIE **Here and There in London.** [New edition]. 2/o boards June 26–July 26 (*Bks*)

W. Tweedie, London, issued the first edition in 1859, 17 cm., 228 pp., 3/6.

227 (PERCIVAL LEIGH) **The Comic Latin Grammar.** [New edition]. Illustrated. 1/6 boards July 1–16 (*PC*)

The first edition was issued by Charles Tilt, London, 1840, 19.5 cm., anonymous, 163 pp., illustrated, listed in the *Ath* on Nov. 23, 1839. He advertised the second edition in the *Spect* on June 13, 1840, anonymous, portrait, 8/o; and it was advertised the same by Tilt & Bogue, London, on Sept. 12, 1840. It was reissued by Tilt & Bogue, 1843, new edition, the same; and again by David Bogue, London, 1848, new edition, 5/o, the same. At a Hodgson auction in Nov. 1861, 300 copies were for sale.

228 JAMES GRANT **Sketches in London.** New Edition. 2/o boards July 1–16 (*PC*)

This has no date, 376 pp. The first edition was issued by William Orr & Co., London, 1838, 8vo, 408 pp., illustrated by "Phiz" et al., 13/o, listed in the *Ath* on Oct. 13. Wolff's copy was bound from the parts. The author was editor of the *Morning Advertiser*. It was reviewed in the *Knicker-*

bocker for Nov. 1838, and the imprint was given as W. S. Orr, London; Wiley & Putnam, New York. Thomas Tegg, London, issued the second and third editions, the same, in 1840 and 1850, respectively. *Sketches of London*, with subject matter differing from the London edition, was issued by Carey & Hart, Philadelphia, 1839, 2 vols., 19 cm., anonymous.

229 WILLIAM JONES **How to Make Home Happy.** Fcp 8vo. 2/o boards, 2/6 cloth July 1–16 (*PC*)

The first edition was issued by David Bogue, London, 1857, 4/6. The present edition was advertised in a book of 1860 as "Just published," 320 pp., 2/o linen boards, 2/6 cloth. Ward & Lock reissued it (1862), new edition, 3/6, as *Household Hints; or, How to Make Home Happy*. Also 1880

230 THOMAS H. KAVANAGH **How I Won the Victoria Cross.** Frontispiece. 2/o boards July 13–31 (*PC*)

This is the first edition, 1860, reviewed in *Chambers' Journal* for Oct. 20, 1860.

231 JOHN SCOFFERN **The National Rifle-Shooting Match; the Royal Rifle-Match on Wimbledon Common.** 1/o July 14 (*Spect*)

This is the first edition, 1860, 96 pp., advertised in the *Spect* on July 14 as "This day."

232 ANONYMOUS **True Love Versus Fashion, etc.** [Second edition]. 1/o boards July 16–31 (*PC*)

Also 1859. See *Husband v. Wife*, 1858

233 FRANCES TROLLOPE **The Widow Married.** 2/o boards July 21 (*Ath*)

The first edition was issued by Henry Colburn, London, 3 vols., 1840, 20 cm., illustrated, 31/6, listed in the *Ath* on Mar. 7, 1840, and reviewed on Apr. 4. The copyright was sold at auction in May 1857 for

83 guineas to Ward & Lock. The latter issued it, 1857, 19 cm., 382 pp., 5/o cloth, listed in the *Ath* on Aug. 15, 1857; and reissued it, the same, listed in the *Ath* on Oct. 17, 1857.

234 (EDWARD WILSON) *Rambles at the Antipodes.* 12mo. 2/o boards July 26–Aug. 27 (*PC*)

The first edition was issued by W. H. Smith & Son, London, 1859, 17.5 cm., 219 pp., with 2 folding maps and 12 illustrations, 3/6, partly colored.

235 ROBERT B. BROUGH *Marston Lynch.* Small format. Frontispiece. 1/o boards July 28 (*Ath*)

This is the first edition, 1860, my copy, 16.5 cm., 354 pp., with a memoir of the author by George Sala, dated July 20, 1860, and with a frontispiece (portrait). It is in yellow pictorial boards, with plain endpapers, a publisher's ad on the back, and a 4-page insert at the front for W. H. Smith's Library, dated June 1862. At a Hodgson auction in Jan. 1861, 1,000 copies were for sale.

236 ALBERT R. SMITH *Mont Blanc.* Small format. Illustrated. 2/o boards July 28 (*Ath*)

This has no date, 299 pp., frontispiece and illustrations, and a memoir of the author by Edmund Yates. The first edition was issued by David Bogue, London, 1853, 19.5 cm., 219 pp., colored frontispiece, illustrated, 10/6, *The Story of Mont Blanc.* It had previously been printed for private circulation, London, 1852, 88 pp., portrait, in blue paper covers, as *Mont Blanc.* The first edition from Bogue was listed in the *Spect* on Aug. 6, 1853, p 8vo, illustrated by Birket Foster, 10/6. The first American edition was issued by G. P. Putnam & Co., New York, 1853, 19.5 cm., 208 pp., frontispiece, illustrated, advertised in the *New York Daily Times* on Sept. 2 as "On

Sept. 3," 12mo, illustrated, $.50 cloth, quoting an *Ath* review. It was reviewed in the *Knickerbocker* for Oct. 1853, *The Story of Mount Blanc.*
Also 1876

237 OCTAVE FEUILLET *The Disguised Nobleman.* [New edition]. Fcp 8vo. 2/o boards Aug. 11 (*Ath*)

The first edition was *Le Roman d'un Jeune Homme Pauvre,* Paris, 1858, 352 pp., in wrappers. The present edition is 1860. It was issued as *The Marquis d'Hautterive* by Cassell, Petter & Galpin, London, 1860, p 8vo, 5/o. In the United States it was issued by Rudd & Carleton, New York, 1859, 19 cm., as *The Romance of a Poor Young Man.*

238 ANONYMOUS *A Book for Every Household.* p 8vo. 2/o boards Aug. 14–31 (*PC*)

This is also given by the *Eng Cat,* but otherwise I cannot trace it.

239 HENRY R. ADDISON *Diary of a Judge.* 2/o boards Aug. 18 (*Ath*)

This is the first edition, 1860, 312 pp. The second edition was advertised in the *Ath* on Oct. 6 as "Recently published." At a Hodgson auction in Jan. 1861, 5,000 copies were for sale; 2,000, the same, in July 1861; and 1,000, the same, in Oct. 1863.

240 HONORÉ DE BALZAC *Daddy Goriot.* 2/o boards Aug. 25 (*Ath*)

This is the first English edition, no date, 232 pp. The first editions had the title *Le Père Goriot* and were issued in 2 vols., 1835, in Paris and Bruxelles. It was issued in the United States by J. Winchester, New York, no date, 104 pp.
Also 1875 as *Unrequited Affection*

241 JOHN F. SMITH *The Prelate.* 2/o boards Sept. 1 (*Ath*)

This is the first edition, no date.
Also 1863 as *Ambition*

242 ROBERT B. BROUGH *Miss Brown a Romance; and Other Tales in Prose and Verse.* Small format. Illustrated. 2/0 boards Sept. 8 (*Ath*)

This is the first edition, my copy, 1860, 16.6 cm., 331 pp., illustrated, in yellow pictorial boards and plain white endpapers, with a publisher's ad on the back cover. It is reprinted from the *Welcome Guest.* At a Hodgson auction in Jan. 1861, 2,100 copies were for sale.

243 JOHN HORSELEYDOWN (pseudonym) *John Horseleydown; or, the Confessions of a Thief.* Small format. 2/0 boards Sept. 8 (*Ath*)

This is the first edition, 1860, 312 pp., revised by Thomas L. Holt. At a Hodgson auction in Jan. 1861, 2,000 copies were for sale.

244 ANDREW HALLIDAY (ANDREW H. DUFF) *The Adventures of Mr. Wilderspin.* Illustrated. 2/0 boards Sept. 8 (*Ath*)

Ward & Lock reissued this at 2/0 in Nov. The first edition was issued by Houlston & Wright, London 1860 (1859), large 8vo, 205 pp., with hundreds of illustrations by M'Connell, 7/6, listed in the *Ath* on Nov. 5, 1859. The *BM* gives a new edition, London, 1861. At a Hodgson auction in Jan. 1861, 1,000 copies were for sale; 2,000 copies, the same, in July 1861. Also 1868, 73

245 ROBERT B. BROUGH *Ulf the Minstrel.* Small format. Illustrated. 1/0 boards Sept. 8 (*Ath*)

This is 1860, 103 pp., illustrated by "Phiz." The first edition was issued by Houlston & Wright, London (1859), 103 pp., illustrated, 3/6, listed by *PC* as published Nov. 30–Dec. 14, 1859.

246 GEORGE A. SALA *Make Your Game.* Small format. Illustrated. 2/0 boards Oct. 6 (*Ath*)

This is the first edition, 1860, 266 pp., illustrated by "Phiz," A. Mayhew, et al., with a folding frontispiece, and 32 pp. of ads at the back. Ward & Lock reissued it, 1861, the same. It was first published in the *Welcome Guest* of Vizetelly, Jan. 8–Sept. 17, 1859. At a Hodgson auction in Jan. 1861, 2,700 copies were for sale; and 2,000 copies, the same, in Oct. 1861. Also 1864, 69

247 MRS. H. C. ELLIS *The Mother's Mistake.* [New edition]. Illustrated. 1/6 boards Oct. 6 (*Ath*)

The first edition was issued by Houlston & Wright, London, in 1857, Cr 8vo, illustrated by Anelay, 3/6. Both it and the present edition are in the *Eng Cat*, but otherwise I cannot trace them.

248 WILKIE COLLINS *Antonina.* 2/0 boards Oct. 10?

I am doubtful of this entry although it was advertised by Ward & Lock in both the *Ath* and the *Sat Rev* as "On Oct. 10." I have not seen it listed anywhere as published by them, and it would, indeed, be a strange title for them to issue as the following publishing history will show. The first edition was issued by Bentley, London, in 3 vols., 1850, p 8vo, 31/6, listed by *PC* as published Feb. 27–Mar. 14 and listed in the *Ath* on Mar. 2. He issued a second edition, 3 vols., revised and corrected, 1850, advertised in the *Spect* as "On July 30." Sampson Low issued a new edition, 1861, 18.5 cm., 420 pp., in cloth; and issued it at 2/6 boards, 1865, 420 pp., listed in the *Reader* on May 13. He issued it at 5/0, with 1 illustration by John Gilbert, advertised in the *Spect* on May 16, 1863, as "This day." He sold the copyright and probably sheets and covers to Smith, Elder, London, in 1865, and the latter firm issued it at 2/6 boards, also in 1865, about May 6. Low sold three Collins titles to Smith, Elder in 1865, and copies have turned up with Low covers and a Smith, Elder title page. Smith, Elder issued it as a 2/0 yellowback, 1871, in July; and reissued it, the same,

1872, my copy. The first American edition was issued by Harper & Bros., New York, 1850, in their *Library of Select Novels* as No. 141, listed by *Lit World* as published Apr. 27–May 11. It had a short review in *Harper's New Monthly Magazine* for July 1850, 8vo, 160 pp.

249 GEORGE A. SALA ET AL. *The Wedding Rings*. Fcp 8vo. 2/o boards   Oct.?

This was advertised in the back of *Miss Brown* above as "This day," but I can find no evidence that Ward & Lock ever published it! It appeared in the Christmas number of the *Welcome Guest* for 1858, *The Wedding Rings of Shrimpington-Super-Mare*, by Sala, Edmund Yates, John Lang, Augustus Mayhew, et al. The only entry given by the *Eng Cat* and by the *BM* is *The Wedding Rings*, issued by James Blackwood, 1855, 16.8 cm., anonymous, 155 pp., frontispiece, 1/o boards, listed by *PC* as published May 1–14, 1855. I think this was not the same work as the present title.

250 ANONYMOUS *Memoirs of a Sheriff's Officer*. 2/o boards   Nov. 1 (*Ath*)

This was advertised in the *Ath* on Oct . 6 as "On Nov. 1," but I cannot trace it.

251 CHARLES MARTEL, ed. *Diary of an Ex-Detective*. Small format. 2/o boards Nov. 3 (*Ath*) *See color photo section*

This is the first edition, my copy, 1860, 16.6 cm., 315 pp., in yellow pictorial boards with plain white endpapers, a page of publisher's ads at the back, and a publisher's ad on the back cover. It has a W. H. Smith & Son ad on an insert before the front free endpaper. At a Hodgson auction in Jan. 1861, 1,500 copies were for sale.

252 WATTS PHILLIPS *The Hooded Snake*. 2/o boards   Nov. 17 (*Ath*)

This is the first edition, no date. At a Hodgson auction in Jan. 1861, 1,024 cop-

ies were for sale; and 2,000 copies were for sale at a Southgate and Barrett auction in Apr. 1868.

253 W. G. WINDHAM *Up Among the Arabs in 1860*. p 8vo. Illustrated. 1/o sewed Nov. (*Bks*)

This is the first edition, my copy, 1860, 18 cm., 96 pp., in yellow pictorial wrappers cut flush, with publisher's ads in blue on the endpapers and back cover. It has a 4-page leaflet of publisher's ads inserted before the front free endpaper, 15.7 cm. in size. It was listed in the *British Quarterly Review* for Jan. 1861.

254 GUSTAVE AIMARD (OLIVER GLOUX) *The Tiger Slayer*. Small format. 2/o boards, 3/o cloth   Dec. 8 (*Ath*)

This is the first English edition, 1860, 16.6 cm., 339 pp., with a foreword by Sir Lascelles Wraxall. This was the first title in Ward & Lock's long series of Aimard's tales of Indian life, edited by Wraxall. They were in brightly colored boards, decoratively lettered in two contrasting colors with a Ward & Lock emblem on the front cover bearing the words "Aimard's Tales of Indian Life," and these words were repeated on the spines. Six titles were advertised in the *Reader* on Nov. 28, 1863, in an illustrated edition at 3/6 each as "Now ready." The present title was included, 1863, 16.5 cm., 339 pp., with the illustrations and an added illustrated title page. There is a known copy of this illustrated edition bearing the imprint of Ward, Lock & Tyler, which style was assumed in Feb. 1865. At a Hodgson auction on Oct. 31 and Nov. 1 and 2, 1865, 15,000 copies in some form were for sale, and they were probably purchased by J. A. Berger, London, who issued the whole series in yellowback form in 1866–68. The first edition was *La Grande Flibuste*, Paris, 1860, 414 pp. The first American edition was *The Tiger Slayer*, issued by E. D. Long & Co., New York (1861), 8vo, $.50, listed

in *APC&LG* on Mar. 16. It was also issued by T. B. Peterson & Bros., Philadelphia (1863), 23 cm., 164 pp., a complete and unabridged edition, noticed in *APC&LG* on Aug. 1.
Also 1876, 80

255 GUSTAVE AIMARD **The Gold-Seekers.** Small format. 2/o boards, 3/o cloth
Dec. 22 (*Ath*)

This is the first English edition, 1861, 16.6 cm., 310 pp. The first edition was *La Fièvre d'Or*, Paris, 1860, 332 pp. In the United States it was issued by E. D. Long & Co., New York, no date, 23 cm., 130 pp.; and by T. B. Peterson & Bros., Philadelphia (1863), 22 cm., 148 pp., at $.50 in wrappers, complete and unabridged, listed in *APC&LG* on Oct. 15, 1863, and advertised in the *New-York Times* on Sept. 26, 1863, as "This day," $.50.
Also 1880

256 FREDERICK CHAMIER **The Spitfire.** 2/o boards   Dec. 29 (*Ath*)

This has no date, 364 pp. The first edition was from Henry Colburn, London, 3 vols., 1840, 19.5 cm., 31/6, listed in the *Ath* on Dec. 21, 1839. The first American edition was issued by Carey & Hart, Philadelphia, 1840, 2 vols. (or possibly 2-vols.-in-1), 18 cm., noticed in *Godey's Lady's Book* for Jan. 1840.

257 ANONYMOUS **Hints and Helps for Every-Day Emergencies.** 1/o sewed
Dec. (*Bks*)

This is the first edition, no date.
Also 1880

258 ANONYMOUS **The Illustrated Book of Pastimes.** 1/o sewed   Dec. (*Bks*)
I cannot trace this.

259 ANONYMOUS **A Guide to Charade Acting.** o/6 sewed   Dec. (*Bks.*)
I cannot trace this.

260 ANONYMOUS **Adventures of an Attorney in Search of Practice.** [Second edition]. 2/o   1860 (*Eng Cat*)

The first edition was issued by Saunders & Otley, London, 1839, p 8vo, anonymous, 407 pp., 10/6, listed in the *Ath* on July 6 and reviewed on Aug. 17. The supposed author has been given as both George Stephen and Samuel Warren.

261 FRANCESCO D. GUERRAZZI **Beatrice Cenci.** [New edition]. 2/o   1860 (*Eng Cat*)

The first edition was at Pisa, 1854, 606 pp. In England it was issued by Ward & Lock, 1858, 9/o; and by Bosworth, London, translated by C. H. Scott. The latter was noticed in the *British Quarterly Review* for Jan. 1859. Some edition was listed in the *Spect* on Aug. 28, 1858, and reviewed on Sept. 25, no publisher given. In the United States it was issued by Mason Bros., New York, 2 vols., 1858, 20 cm., $1.00 paper, $1.50 cloth. They issued it in 4 weekly parts, part 1 advertised in the *New-York Times* on Feb. 4, 1858, $.38, translated by Mrs. Watts Sherman, "To-day." Part 2 was advertised on Feb. 10 as "This day," the ad stating that their edition was the only unmutilated and unabridged edition. It was also issued by Rudd & Carleton, New York, 2-vols.-in-1, 1858, 19 cm., frontispiece, translated by Luigi Monti, advertised in the *New-York Times* on Jan. 30, 1858, 12mo, portrait, $1.25 cloth as "This day." They advertised the fifth edition on Feb. 13, as "Now ready" in which they cast aspersions on the Mason Bros. for issuing it, calling it a lack of courtesy! Mason Bros. answered on Mar. 6, listing the omissions in the Rudd & Carleton issue!

262 ANONYMOUS **Exiles of Italy.** 2/o   1860 (*Eng Cat*)

The first edition was issued by Hamilton, Adams, London, in 1857. Aside from the *Eng Cat* I cannot trace this.

263 ANONYMOUS **Garibaldi, Miraculous Escapes.** 2/0   1860 (*Eng Cat*)

I cannot trace this.

264 BREWIN GRANT **A New Beginning for New Beginners.** 2/0   1860 (*Eng Cat*)

The *BM* gives London, Sheffield (printed) (1860), five inaugural discoveries.

265 ANONYMOUS **The Master of the Situation.** 1/0   1860 (*Eng Cat*)

This has no date, edited by "Who comes there."

266 LLEWELLYNN F. W. JEWITT **Rifles and Volunteer Rifle Corps.** 1/0   1860 (*Eng Cat*)

This is the first edition, 1860, 8vo, 97 pp., with 1 plate.

Ward & Lock
1861

In Nov. 1861, Kent & Co., London, shared a full-page ad in the Ath with Ward & Lock. There were shared ads also in Dec. 1861, Sept. 1862, Oct. 1863, and Apr. 1864. Beginning in 1865 all Kent ads were separate.

267 W. B. BROOKE *Out with Garibaldi.*
2/o boards Jan. 26 (*Ath*)

This is the first edition, no date, 338 pp. At a Hodgson auction in July 1861, 1,000 copies were for sale.

268 GUSTAVE AIMARD *The Indian Chief.*
Small format. 2/o boards, 3/o cloth
Feb. 2 (*Ath*)

This is the first English edition, 1861, 16.6 cm., 324 pp. Ward & Lock issued the illustrated edition at 3/6 cloth, advertised in the *Reader* on Nov. 28, 1863, as "Now ready." The first edition was *Curumilla*, Paris, 1860, 17.5 cm., 336 pp. The first American edition was issued by T. B. Peterson & Bros., Philadelphia (1864), complete and unabridged edition, advertised in the *New-York Times* on Jan. 30, 1864, $.50, as "This day," listed in the *Ind* on Feb. 11 and in *APC&LG* on Feb. 15. It was 8vo in size and had 164 pp.
Also 1876, 80

269 MARY E. BRADDON *The Trail of the Serpent.* 2/o boards Feb. 23 (*Ath*)

This is 1861, 380 pp., containing various revisions of the first edition text with about 10,000 words cut out. The first edition was *Three Times Dead*, issued by W. M. Clark, Beverley; C. H. Empson, Toll-Gavel (1860), 218 pp., in yellow, paper-covered boards. It was issued in 27 parts, parts 1–26 with 8 pp. each, and part 27 with 16 pp. Braddon said that it was her first novel and that it appeared in a newspaper in Beverley. At a Hodgson auction in July 1861, 1,000 copies of the Ward & Lock issue were for sale. In the United States it was issued by Dick & Fitzgerald, New York, $.50 paper, $.75 cloth, advertised in the *New-York Times* on Dec. 17, 1863, as "Just published," *Three Times Dead*. It was noticed in *Godey's Lady's Book* for Mar. 1864. It was advertised in the *New-York Times* by the *Sunday Mercury* on Sept. 19, 1863, anonymous, to start tomorrow morning.
Also 1867

270 GUSTAVE AIMARD *The Trail Hunter.*
Small format. 2/o boards, 3/o cloth
Mar. 2 (*Ath*)

This is the first English edition, 1861, 16.6 cm., 392 pp. Ward & Lock issued the illustrated edition at 3/6 cloth, advertised in the *Reader* on Dec. 5, 1863, as ready. The first edition was *Le Chercheur de Pistes*, Paris, 1858, 450 pp. The first American edition was issued by T. B. Peterson & Bros., Philadelphia (1862), complete and unabridged edition, 24 cm., 175 pp., $.50 paper, $.75 cloth, advertised in the *New-York Times* on July 26, 1862, as "This day," and listed in the *Ind* on Aug. 28 and in *APC&LG* (monthly) on Sept. 1.

271 WILLIAM H. HILLYARD **Recollections of a Physician.** 2/0 boards   Mar. 2 (*Ath*)

This is the first edition, 1861, 371 pp. At a Hodgson auction on July 9, 1861, 2,000 copies were for sale.

272 FREDERICK TAYLOR **Recollections of a Horse Dealer.** 2/0 boards   Mar. 30 (*Ath*)

This is the first edition, 1861, in yellow printed boards, the last half of the book covering the selection and training of horses. At a Hodgson auction on Oct. 9–11, 1861, 1,000 copies were for sale.

273 ANONYMOUS **The Wonder Book of Nature's Transformation.** 8vo. 2/0   Mar. (*Bks*)

This is also given by the *Eng Cat*, but otherwise I cannot trace it.

274 GUSTAVE AIMARD **The Pirates of the Prairies.** Small format. 2/0 boards, 3/0 cloth   May 4 (*Ath*)

This is the first English edition, 1861, 16.6 cm., 320 pp. Ward & Lock issued the illustrated edition at 3/6 cloth, advertised in the *Reader* on Dec. 5, 1863, as ready. The first edition was *Les Pirates des Prairies*, Paris, 1858, 374 pp. The first American edition was issued by T. B. Peterson & Bros., Philadelphia (1862), complete and unabridged edition, 8vo, 152 pp., $.50 paper, listed in *Godey's Lady's Book* for Feb. 1863 and thus probably issued in Nov. or Dec. 1862.
Also 1878, 80

275 ANONYMOUS **Marine Botany and Sea-Side Objects.** Illustrated. 1/0 boards   May 11 (*Sat Rev*)

Indispensable Handy-Books No. 1. This is the first edition, 1861, 128 pp. The *Bks* lists it as both May and June.
Also 1869, 80

276 ANONYMOUS **British Ferns and Mosses.** Illustrated. 1/0 boards   May 11 (*Sat Rev*)

Indispensable Handy-Books No. 2. This is the first edition, 1861, 136 pp. The *Bks* lists it as both May and June.
Also 1869, 80

277 ROBERT CURTIS **The Irish Police Officer.** Small format. 2/0 boards   May 11 (*Ath*)

This is the first edition, my copy, 1861, 16.6 cm., 216 pp., with a preface dated 1861. It is in yellow pictorial boards, with a publisher's ad on the back in black and on the endpapers in blue. There is a half-page slip with publisher's ads and a 4-page W. H. Smith ad inserted before the free front endpaper.

278 CHARLES MILLS **Two Historical Essays.** 1/6 sewed   May (*Bks*)

This is the first edition, no date. It contains *The German and Swiss Reformation* and *Cromwell and the Commonwealth.*

279 GUSTAVE AIMARD **The Prairie Flower.** Small format. 2/0 boards, 3/0 cloth   June 1 (*Ath*)

This is 1861, 16.6 cm., 360 pp. Ward & Lock issued the illustrated edition at 3/6 cloth, advertised in the *Reader* on Dec. 5, 1863, as ready. The first edition was *Balle-Franche*, Paris, 1861, 432 pp. The first American edition was issued by T. B. Peterson & Bros., Philadelphia (1862), *The Flower of the Prairie*, 8vo, 165 pp., $.50 paper, $.75 cloth, listed in *APC&LG* (monthly) on Mar. 1, and noticed in the *Knickerbocker* for Apr. 1862.

280 ANONYMOUS **Gardening and Monthly Calendar of Operations.** 1/0 boards   June 15 (*Sat Rev*)

Indispensable Handy-Books. This is the first edition, 1861.
Also 1881. See 1890, 92

281 ANONYMOUS *Wild Flowers.* 1/0
boards   June 15 (*Sat Rev*)
Indispensable Handy-Books. This is the first
edition, 1861.
Also 1869, 80

282 FREDERICK C. L. WRAXALL *Only a
Woman.* New Edition. Small format.
2/0 boards   June 22 (*Ath*)
This is 1861, 440 pp. The first edition was
issued by Hurst & Blackett, London, 3
vols., 1860, 19 cm., 31/6.

283 GUSTAVE AIMARD *The Trapper's
Daughter.* Small format. 2/0 boards,
3/0 cloth   June 22 (*Ath*)
This is the first English edition, 1861, 381
pp. The first edition was *Le Loi de Lynch*,
the second edition of which was issued at
Paris, 1859, 18 cm., 464 pp. It was issued
in the United States by E. J. Long & Co.,
New York, as *Lynch Law*, 120 pp., translated by Henry Williams, *Dime Romances*
No. 3. The *BM* gives it as (1860). It was
also issued by T. B. Peterson & Bros., Philadelphia (1863), 25 cm., 176 pp., in double columns, a complete and unabridged
edition. It was advertised in the *New-York
Times* on Mar. 21, 1863, $.50 paper, as
"This day," listed in *APC&LG* (fortnightly) on May 1, and listed by the *Knickerbocker* as published Mar. 12–Apr. 11.

284 (W. H. HILLYARD) *Tales in the Cabin.*
Small format. 2/0 boards   June 29 (*Ath*)
This is the first edition, Sadleir's copy,
1861, 380 pp., in pale blue boards designed and lettered in dark blue, by "a
Ship's Surgeon." Sadleir had another
copy, "Published for the Proprietors,"
London, 1863, in yellow pictorial boards
with the collation as for the first edition
and with Ward & Lock ads on the back
cover. He thought that Ward & Lock di-
verted some of their more sensational titles with spicier covers into this channel.

At a Hodgson auction in Oct. 1863, 1,000
copies were for sale.
Also 1864, 68

285 GUSTAVE AIMARD *The Indian Scout.*
Small format. 2/0 boards, 3/0 cloth
July 6 (*Ath*)
This is the first English edition, 1861, 16.6
cm., 429 pp. Ward & Lock issued the illustrated edition at 3/6 cloth, advertised in
the *Reader* on Dec. 5, 1863, as ready. The
first edition was *L'Eclaireur*, Paris, 1859,
460 pp. The first American edition was issued by T. B. Peterson & Bros., Philadelphia (1862), 23 cm., 202 pp., called a complete and unabridged edition, listed in
APC&LG (monthly) on May 1, and listed
by the *Atlantic Monthly* for Aug. 1862 as recent, $.50 paper, $.75 cloth, in double
columns.
Also 1878, 80

286 GUSTAVE AIMARD *The Border Rifles.*
Small format. 2/0 boards, 3/0 cloth
July 20 (*Ath*)
This is the first English edition, 1861, 16.6
cm., 311 pp. Ward & Lock issued the illustrated edition at 3/6, in Nov. 1863. The
first edition was *Les Rodeurs de Frontieres*,
Paris, 1861, 360 pp. The first American
edition was issued by T. B. Peterson &
Bros., Philadelphia (1866), a complete
and unabridged edition, 24 cm., 172 pp.,
probably at $.50 paper and $.75 cloth, advertised in the *New-York Times* on Apr. 11,
at $.75, as "On Apr. 14" and as if ready on
Apr. 14. It was listed in *ALG&PC*
(monthly) on May 15.
Also 1878, 80

287 GUSTAVE AIMARD *The Freebooters.*
Small format. 2/0 boards, 3/0 cloth
Aug. 17 (*Ath*)
This was the first English edition, 1861,
16.6 cm., 380 pp., reissued in the illustrated edition at 3/6 cloth, advertised in
the *Reader* on Nov. 28, 1863, as ready. The

first edition was *Les Franc Tireurs*, Paris, 1861, 18 cm., 450 pp. The first American edition was issued by T. B. Peterson & Bros., Philadelphia (1868), a complete and unabridged edition, 25 cm., 162 pp., $.50 paper, advertised in the *New-York Times* on Apr. 18, 1868, as "This day." Also 1878, 80

288 ALBANY FONBLANQUE, JR. *Hector Mainwaring.* Small format. 2/o boards Aug. 24 (*Ath*)

The *BM* gives London (1860), and the *Eng Cat* calls this a new edition. Also 1880

289 EDWARD P. ROWSELL, ed. (FRANCIS W. ROWSELL) *The Autobiography of a Joint-Stock Company.* 1/6 boards Aug. (*Bks*)

This is the first edition, 1861.

290 GUSTAVE AIMARD *The White Scalper.* Small format. 2/o boards, 3/o cloth Sept. 7 (*Ath*)

This is the first English edition, my copy, 1861, 16.6 cm., 352 pp., in yellow boards with decorative lettering on the front in red and yellow on a very dark green ground, with a circular emblem of Ward & Lock surrounded by "Aimard's Tales of Indian Life," with these words also on the spine. There is a 3-page advertisement in the front as part of the collation and a publisher's ad on the back cover. It was reissued in the illustrated edition at 3/6 cloth, advertised in the *Reader* on Dec. 5, 1863, as ready. The first edition was *Les Scalpeurs Blancs*, Paris. The first American edition was T. B. Peterson & Bros., Philadelphia (1868), 154 pp., advertised in the *New-York Times* on Oct. 17, 1868, $.50, "This day," and listed in the *Nation* on Oct. 22, $.50 sewed. Also 1878, 80

291 MARCHIONESS M. F. OSSOLI (SARAH FULLER, later OSSOLI) *Summer on the Lakes with Autobiography.* Fcp 8vo. 1/o boards Sept. (*Bks*)

British Library. This is 1861, 360 pp., with a memoir by Ralph W. Emerson et al. It inaugurates a new series, touted on the back of the preceding title with grandiose puffery in a new series to be issued monthly, the present title being No. 1 and now ready. The series was abortive as I've found no further titles in it. The first edition was issued by Little & Brown, Boston; etc., 1844, 20.5 cm., 256 pp., illustrated, as *Summer on the Lakes in 1843*.

292 WESTLAND MARSTON (JOHN W. MARSTON) *The Family Credit, and Other Tales.* Small format. 1/o sewed Nov. 23 (*Ath*)

Shilling Volume Library No. 1. This is 1862, 261 pp. It is the first edition of the title story with the other tales reprinted from various periodicals. In Oct. 1864, 5,000 copies of this series were for sale at a Hodgson auction, and 5,000 copies were still for sale at the auction in May 1865. Also 1869

293 (EMMA ROBINSON) *Which Wins, Love or Money?* Small format. 1/o sewed Nov. 23 (*Ath*)

Shilling Volume Library No. 2. This is the first edition, 1862 (1861), with 262 pp. It has Louis Ulbach as author on the front cover! Also 1869

294 EDWARD P. ROWSELL *Recollections of a Relieving Officer.* Small format. 1/o sewed Nov. 23 (*Ath*)

Shilling Volume Library No. 3. This is the first edition, 1861. A duplicate with a new title page was issued by John & Robert Maxwell, London, 1866 (1865), 251 pp., a large-size yellowback.

295 MARY E. BRADDON **The Lady Lisle.** Small format. 1/0 sewed   Nov. 30 (*Ath*)

Shilling Volume Library No. 4. This is the first edition, 1862, 268 pp. Sadleir describes it as in greenish-blue wrappers, printed in black with uncut edges. Strangely enough, he also had a copy in cloth, 1862. Ward, Lock & Tyler issued it, 1867, 6/0, advertised in the *Spect* on Dec. 8, 1866, as revised and partly rewritten, "In Dec." The first American edition was issued by Dick & Fitzgerald, New York, 1863, 8vo, $.50 paper, $.75 muslin, advertised in the *New-York Times* on Feb. 6, 1863, as "Tomorrow" and on Feb. 8 as "This day." It was listed in *APC&LG* on Feb. 20 and listed by the *Knickerbocker* as published Jan. 1–Feb. 10.
Also 1868

296 EDMOND F. V. ABOUT **The Round of Wrong.** Small format. 1/0 sewed   Nov. 30 (*Ath*)

Shilling Volume Library No. 5. This is the first English edition, 1862 (1861), 253 pp. The first edition was issued by Germaine, Paris, 1857, 318 pp. The present edition was translated by Lascelles Wraxall.
Also 1869

297 MRS. FENTON AYLMER **Memoirs of a Lady in Waiting.** Small format. 1/0 sewed   Nov. 30 (*Ath*)

Shilling Volume Library No. 6. This is 1862 (1861), 247 pp. The first edition was issued by Saunders & Otley, London, 2 vols., 1860, 21 cm., 18/0, by J. D. Fenton.
Also 1869

298 EMMA SOUTHWORTH **The Hidden Hand.** [New edition]. 2/0 boards   Nov. (*Bks*)
Also 1859

299 (ERSKINE NEALE) **Scenes Where the Tempter Has Triumphed.** Small format. 1/0 sewed   Dec. 15 (*Ath*)

Shilling Volume Library No. 8. This is 1862. The first edition was issued by Bentley, London, 1849, p 8vo, anonymous, 316 pp., 10/6, listed in the *Spect* on June 30. It was listed by *PC* as published Dec. 30, 1854–Jan. 15, 1855, p 8vo, anonymous, reduced to 6/0, Bentley. The first American edition was issued by Harper & Bros., New York, 1849, anonymous, 277 pp., listed in *Lit World* as published Aug. 18–Sept. 1, and reviewed in the *Ind* on Oct. 18. The present title was advertised in the *Ath* on Dec. 7 as "On Dec. 15."

300 ROBERT WARNEFORD (WILLIAM RUSSELL) **The Cruise of the Blue Jacket and Other Sea Stories.** Small format. 1/0 sewed   Dec. 21 (*Ath*)

Shilling Volume Library No. 7. This is the first edition, 1862.
Also 1869

301 PERCY H. FITZGERALD **The Night Mail.** Small format. 1/0 sewed   Dec. 28 (*Ath*)

Shilling Volume Library. This is the first edition, 1862. It was reissued by John & Robert Maxwell, London (1883), 247 pp., a large-size yellowback.
Also 1869

302 ROBERT W. BUCHANAN & CHARLES GIBBON **Storm-Beaten.** Small format. 2/0 boards   Dec. 28 (*Ath*)

Shilling Volume Library. This is the first edition, 1862, 248 pp.
Also 1869

303 WATTS PHILLIPS **Amos Clark.** Small format. 2/0 boards   Dec. 28 (*Ath*)

This is the first edition, my copy, 1862, 16.6 cm., 348 pp., in purple boards, decoratively lettered and with a vignette in black on the front, and a publisher's ad on the back. It has new endpapers. At a Hodgson auction in Oct. 1863, 657 copies were for sale; and 2,000 copies were for sale at a Southgate & Barrett auction in Apr. 1868.

304, 305, 306 ANONYMOUS *A Handy Book to the Sky, Air, Earth and Waters. A Handy Book to the Vegetable Kingdom. A Handy Book to the Animal Kingdom.* 3 vols., 1/0 sewed each. Illustrated Dec. (*Bks*)

The *BM* gives these in 1 vol., 3 parts, 338 pp., illustrated.

307 ANONYMOUS *The Illustrated Life and Career of Garibaldi.* 1/0 sewed   1861 (*Eng Cat*)

Also 1860

308 (SIR JOHN W. KAYE) *Long Engagements.* 2/0   1861 (*Eng Cat*)

The first edition was issued by Chapman & Hall, London, 1846, p 8vo, 320 pp., 9/0.

309 ELIZA WARREN *The Economical Cookery Book.* 1/0   1861 (*Eng Cat*)

The *BM* gives London (1858). Also 1875, 80

310 BLANCHARD JERROLD (WILLIAM B. JERROLD) *Chronicles of the Crutch.* Fcp 8vo. 1/6 boards   1861

This is my copy, 1861, 17 cm., 261 pp., in yellow pictorial boards, with an ad for the *Select Library of Fiction* (Chapman & Hall) on the back cover, and a 4-page W. H. Smith insert before the free front endpaper. It has plain white endpapers. Most of the pieces were reprints from *Household Words*, and the remainder here for the first time. The preface is dated Oct. 1860. The first edition was issued by William Tinsley, London, 1860, 19.5 cm., 264 pp., 5/0, listed in the *Spect* on Nov. 10, 1860.

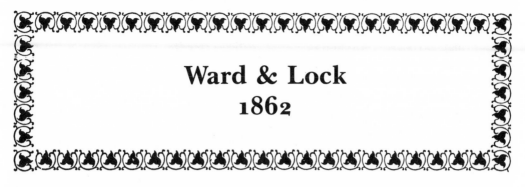

Ward & Lock
1862

George Vickers shared an ad with Ward & Lock and Kent & Co. in the Ath *in Sept. 1862.*

311 WATTS PHILLIPS *Canary Bird.* Small format. 2/o boards   Jan. 18 (*Ath*)

This is the first edition, 1862, a sequel to *Amos Clark.* At a Hodgson auction in Oct. 1863, 693 copies were for sale; and 2,000 copies were for sale at a Southgate & Barrett auction in Apr. 1868.

312 ROBERT CURTIS *Curiosities of Detection.* Small format. 2/o boards Jan. 18 (*Ath*)

This is the first edition, 1862, 320 pp.

313 EDMOND F. V. ABOUT *The King of the Mountains.* Small format. Illustrated. 1/o sewed   Jan. (*Bks*)

Sixpenny Volume Library No. ? This is the first English edition, 1862, 252 pp., illustrated by Doré and translated by Wraxall. It was reissued by J. & R. Maxwell, London (1881), 18.5 cm., 2/o boards, 2/6 cloth, as *The Greek Brigand.* The first edition was *Le Roi des Montagnes*, Paris, 1857, 17 cm., 301 pp. The first edition in English was issued by J. E. Tilton & Co., Boston, 1861, 18.5 cm., 300 pp., translated by Mary L. Booth, and listed in *APC&LG* on Oct. 27, 1860, at $1.00. It was advertised in the *New-York Times* on Nov. 17, 1860, new edition, $1.00, "Ready to-day," with an introduction by Sargent. It was reissued by Tilton, the same, listed in *Godey's Lady's Book* for Sept. 1862, where it was stated that it had had six translations into English.

Also 1869 as *The Greek Brigand*

314 J. HAIN FRISWELL *The Young Couple and Miscellanies.* Small format. 1/o sewed Jan. (*Bks*)

Shilling Volume Library. This is 1862, 248 pp. The preface states that the *Miscellanies*, pp. 56–248, are now collected for the first time and implies that the title story had been previously issued. The preface is dated July 1861, and Kent & Co., London, advertised the title story on Aug. 16, 1861, as "On Sept. 1."

315 WATERS (WILLIAM RUSSELL) *Leonard Harlowe; or, The Game of Life.* Small format. 1/o sewed   Feb. (*Bks*)

Shilling Volume Library. This is 1862.

Also 1857, 58, 69

316 MARY E. BRADDON *The Captain of the Vulture.* Small format. 1/o sewed Feb. (*Bks*)

This is the first edition, 1862, 252 pp. It was advertised in the *Ath* in June 1862, and I think Sadleir was probably wrong in stating this to be dated 1863. It was reissued by Ward, Lock & Tyler, 1867, frontispiece, 6/o, revised and in part rewritten, about 20,000 words longer than the first edition. The first American edition was issued by Dick & Fitzgerald, New York, as *Darrell Markham*, 1863, $.50, listed in the *Knickerbocker* for June 1863, and noticed in *APC&LG* on May 1.

Also 1868

317 GUSTAVE AIMARD **The Red Track.**
Small format. 2/o boards, 3/o cloth
Mar. 15 (*Ath*)

This is the first English edition, 1862, 16.6 cm., 344 pp., in green-tinted boards, decorated and titled in lighter green, black, and red. The first edition was *Valentin Guillois*, Paris, 1862, 354 pp. The first American edition was issued by T. B. Peterson & Bros., Philadelphia (1864), complete and unabridged edition, 23 cm., 157 pp., $.50 paper, advertised in the *New-York Times* on Apr. 6, 1864, as "Tomorrow," and on Apr. 7 as "This day." It was listed in the *Ind* on Apr. 14, 1864, and in *APC&LG* on Apr. 15.
Also 1878, 80

318 W. S. HAYWARD **Hunted to Death.**
Small format. 1/o sewed   Apr. 12 (*Ath*)

Shilling Volume Library No. 16. This is the first edition, 1862. The first American edition was issued by A. K. Loring, Boston (1865), 22 cm., 170 pp., listed in *ALG&PC* on July 1.
Also 1869, 73, 74

319 GUSTAVE AIMARD **Last of the Incas.**
Small format. 2/o boards   Apr. 15 (*Ath*)

This is 1862, 16.6 cm., 317 pp. The first edition was *L'Araucan*, Paris, 12mo, 313 pp.
Also 1878, 80 *See color photo section*

320 WILLIAM CARLETON **The Silver Acre, and Other Tales.** Small format. 1/o sewed
Apr. (*Bks*)

Shilling Volume Library No. 15. This is the first edition, 1862, 238 pp., in pale blue wrappers, printed in black. It was first issued serially in the *Illustrated London Magazine* in 1853–54, illustrated by "Phiz."

321 JOHN MILLS **The Old English Gentleman.** [Fifth edition]. 2/o boards
Apr. (*Bks*)
Also 1854, 56, 58

322 ANONYMOUS **The Flower Garden and Kitchen Garden.** 1/o sewed   Apr. (*Bks*)

Useful Hand-Books. This has no date, and the two parts have separate pagination. It appears that they were issued separately at a prior date, and the *Bks* gives the present issue as a new edition. The *BM* gives only the two parts in 1 volume, with no indication of edition.

323 JOHN BANIM **The Smuggler.**
[New edition]. Small format. 2/o boards
May 3 (*Ath*)

This was listed in the *Bks* for both May and June.
Also 1856, 57

324 GEORGE A. SALA **The Ship Chandler and Other Tales.** Small format. 1/o sewed
May 3 (*Ath*)

Shilling Volume Library No. 17. This is the first edition, 1862, 219 pp., containing five tales. It was advertised in the *Ath* also on Feb. 20, 1864, 1/o, as "Just out."
Also 1869

325 MAYNE REID **The Wild Huntress.**
[Third edition]. Small format. 2/o boards
May 24 (*Ath*)

Ward & Lock issued this, second edition, Cr 8vo, at 5/o, listed in the *Ath* on Dec. 7, 1861. The first edition was issued by Bentley, London, 3 vols., 1861, 20 cm., published on Jan. 26, 1861, according to the Bentley private catalog. The first American edition was issued by R. M. DeWitt, New York, no date, 19 cm., 466 pp., frontispiece and six full-page illustrations, with the copyright notice on the verso of the title page dated 1861.
Also 1875

326 MARY E. BRADDON **Ralph the Bailiff and Other Tales.** Small format. 1/o sewed
May 31 (*Ath*)

Shilling Volume Library No. 18. This is the first edition, containing eight stories. In

1867 Ward, Lock & Tyler issued a revised edition at 6/o with four more stories, advertised as thoroughly revised and in parts rewritten.
Also 1869

327 MRS. FENTON AYLMER, ed. ***Bush Life.*** Small format. 1/o sewed   May 31 (*Ath*)
Shilling Volume Library No. 19. This is 1862, 204 pp. The second edition was *Adventures of Mrs. Colonel Somerset in Caffraria, During the War*, edited (or rather written) by I. D. Fenton, issued by J. F. Hope, London, 1858, 309 pp.

328 JAMES PAYN ***Rough and Ready.*** 2/o boards   May (*Bks*)
Other than this listing in the *Bks* I have never seen a reference to this title!

329 HUGO REID ***The American Crisis; or, Sketches in North America.*** 2/o boards May (*Bks*)
The first edition was *Sketches in North America*, issued by Longmans, London, 1861, 16.5 cm., 320 pp., at 5/6.

330 ANONYMOUS ***The Horse.*** New Edition. 1/o sewed   May (*Bks*)
Useful Hand-Books. This has no date. The *BM* gives only this new edition.

331 GUSTAVE AIMARD ***The Queen of the Savannah.*** Small format. 2/o boards June 14 (*Ath*)
This is the first English edition, 1862, 16.6 cm., 456 pp. The first French edition was *L'Eau-Qui-Court*, Paris, 1863.
Also 1878, 80

332 (EMMA ROBINSON) ***Cynthia Thorold.*** Small format. 1/o sewed   June 21 (*Ath*)
Shilling Volume Library No. 20. This is the first edition, 1862.
Also 1869

333 VANE I. ST. JOHN ***The Chain of Destiny.*** Small format. 1/o sewed June 21 (*Ath*)
Shilling Volume Library No. 21. This is the first edition, 1862.
Also 1869

334 S. G. FINNEY ***Hints on Agriculture, for Landlords and Tenants.*** 1/o sewed June (*Bks*)
This is 1862, Guildford printed. The first edition was *Hints to Landlords, Tenants, and Labourers*, London, Guildford printed, 1860.

335 WATERS, ed. (WILLIAM RUSSELL) ***Experiences of a Real Detective.*** Small format. 1/o sewed   July 5 (*Ath*)
Shilling Volume Library No. 22. This is the first edition, 1862, 252 pp., by Inspector F.
Also 1869

336 PIERRE A. PONSON DU TERRAIL ***The King's Page.*** Small format. 1/o sewed   July 5 (*Ath*)
Shilling Volume Library No. 23. This is the first edition in England, 1862, 252 pp., translated by Wraxall.

337 CHARLES DICKENS ***The Pic-Nic Papers.*** [New edition]. Small format. 2/o boards   July 5 (*Ath*)
Also 1859, 65, 70, 82

338 LOUIS CANLER ***Autobiography of a French Detective from 1818 to 1858.*** Small format. 2/o boards   Aug. 9 (*Ath*)
This is the first English edition, 1862, Sadleir's copy, 315 pp., yellow boards, designed and lettered on the front in scarlet and black. It was translated by Lascelles Wraxall, and his preface states that the work was suppressed in France. The second edition was listed in the *Ath* on Sept. 6. At a Hodgson auction in Oct. 1863, 1,000 copies were for sale.
Also 1869

339 HENRY R. ADDISON *Recollections of an Irish Police Magistrate, and Other Reminiscences of the South of Ireland.* Small format. 2/o boards   Sept. 6 (*Ath*)

This is the first edition, 1862, Sadleir's copy, 305 pp., bright green boards, designed and lettered in scarlet and black. It was reissued by J. & R. Maxwell, London, no date, 12mo, 2/o boards, 2/6 cloth, in Mar. 1883. At a Hodgson auction in Oct. 1863, 868 copies were for sale.
Also 1869

340 WATERS (WILLIAM RUSSELL) *Undiscovered Crimes.* Small format. 2/o boards   Sept. 6 (*Ath*)

This is the first edition, 1862, Sadleir's copy, 316 pp., yellow boards, designed and lettered in scarlet and dark green. At a Hodgson auction in Oct. 1863, 874 copies were for sale.
Also 1869

341 THOMAS ARCHER *Madame Prudence, and Other Tales.* Small format. 1/o sewed Sept. 13 (*Ath*)

Shilling Volume Library No. 24. This is the first edition, 1862, 247 pp.

342 AUGUSTUS MAYHEW, ed. *Blow Hot— Blow Cold.* Small format. 1/o sewed Oct. 1 (*Ath* ad)

Shilling Volume Library No. 25. This is the first edition, 1862.
Also 1869

343 JOSEPH VEREY *Roland the Painter.* Small format. 1/o sewed   Oct. 4 (*Ath*)

Shilling Volume Library No. 26. This is the first edition, 1862, 16.3 cm., 251 pp. It is my copy, with Ward & Lock on the title page, Ward, Lock & Tyler on the front cover, and with their ads on the endpapers and back cover; thus it is probably a reissue of 1865. It is in yellow wrappers, designed and lettered in black and red,

cut flush, with top edges trimmed and the others cut. *See color photo section*

344 J. C. AYRTON (MARY F. CHAPMAN) *Lord Bridgenorth's Niece.* Small format. 1/o sewed   Oct. 4 (*Ath*)

Shilling Volume Library No. 27. This is the first edition, 1862, 251 pp.

345 ALBANY FONBLANQUE, JR. *The Filibuster: A Story of American Life and Other Tales.* Small format. 1/o sewed   Nov. 1 (*Ath*)

Shilling Volume Library No. 28. This is the first edition, 1862, containing six tales.
Also 1869

346 ANONYMOUS *The Funny Fellow.* Fcp 8vo. Illustrated. 1/o sewed   Nov. 10 (*Ath*)

This is the first edition, 1862.
Also 1869

347 ANONYMOUS *Something to Laugh At.* Fcp 8vo. Illustrated. 1/o sewed   Nov. 29 (*Ath*)

This is 1862, uniform with the preceding title. The first edition was issued by Piper, London, 1855, 4to, 2/6.
Also 1869.

348 JOHN BENNETT, ed. *Revelations of a Sly Parrot.* Small format. Illustrated. 2/o boards   Dec. 6 (*Ath*)

This is the first edition, no date, Sadleir's copy, 312 pp., yellow pictorial boards. At a Hodgson auction in Oct. 1863, 1,300 copies were for sale.

349 EDMUND KIRKE (JAMES R. GILMORE) *Life in Dixie's Land.* 2/o boards   Dec. (*Bks*)

This is 1863 (1862). Ward & Lock issued the third edition, 1863, 18 cm., 282 pp., frontispiece. The *Eng Cat* gives this as *Among the Pines*. The first edition was issued by J. R. Gilmore, etc., New York, 1862, 18.5 cm., 310 pp., *Among the Pines*, reviewed in the *New Englander* (quarterly) for July 1862. It ran in the *Continental Monthly* from Feb. 1862 through at least June 1862. The third Gilmore edition was noticed in the *Knickerbocker* for Aug. 1862. Charles T. Evans, New York, advertised it in the *New-York Times* on June 21, 1862, 12mo, $1.00 cloth, as "On June 25"; he advertised a new edition, the ninth thousand, $.50 paper, $.75 cloth, on July 29, as to be issued "about Aug. 1." The Tribune Co., New York, then assumed publication and advertised it in the *New-York Times* on Aug. 1, 1862, 12mo, 310 pp., $.50 paper, $.75 cloth, as "Now ready." Charles T. Evans advertised a new edition, the 30th thousand, 12mo, $.50 paper, $.75 cloth, in the *New-York Times* on Nov. 11, 1862, as "Now ready." Carleton, New York, assumed publication and advertised it in the *New-York Times* on Dec. 13, 1862, $.75 paper, $1.00 cloth.

350 EDMUND YATES *After Office Hours.* [New edition]. Small format. 1/o sewed Jan. 3, 1863 (*Ath*)

Shilling Volume Library No. 29. This is 1863 (1862), a collection of 22 papers previously published in magazines. The first edition was issued by W. Kent & Co., London (1861), small format, 312 pp., 2/o, bright green boards, with the series title on the front cover and spine, *First Class Library* No. 1.

351 ANONYMOUS *Health: How to Gain and How to Keep It.* 1/o 1862 (*Eng Cat*)

Useful Hand-Books. This is the first edition, no date, 96 pp.

352 JAMES PAYN *The Bateman Household.* 2/o boards 1862 (*Eng Cat*)

I doubt whether this was ever issued by Ward & Lock, as I've found no reference to it in any Ward & Lock ads, nor anywhere else. The first edition was issued by Arthur Hall, Virtue, London, 1860, 19 cm., 305 pp., at 5/o.

353 ANONYMOUS *Practical Family Cookery Book.* 1/o 1862 (*Eng Cat*)

Useful Hand-Books. This is the first edition, no date.

354 ANONYMOUS *The Practical Letter Writer.* 1/o 1862 (*Eng Cat*)

Useful Hand-Books. This is the first edition, no date.
Also 1865

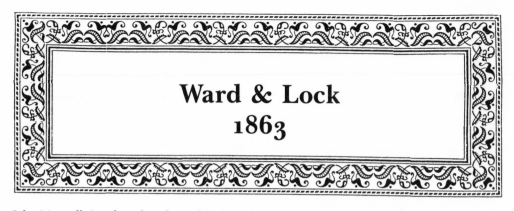

Ward & Lock
1863

John Maxwell, London, shared an ad in the Ath *with Ward & Lock and W. Kent & Co., London, in Sept. 1863; and Maxwell and Ward & Lock shared ads in Nov. 1863, Mar. 1864, and Apr. 1865. The last Maxwell ad was on Nov. 25, 1865, but he surfaced again at intervals, from premises at 4 Shoe-Lane, from Oct. 1871 to Mar. 1878, solely to announce the three volume titles of Braddon's novels. These latter were issued by Ward, Lock & Tyler, although they were at times advertised by both firms in separate ads and at times with no publisher given. In Mar. or Apr. 1878, a new firm, John & Robert Maxwell, was formed, operating from 4 Shoe-Lane, and Braddon's novels passed to this firm. Mary Braddon was John Maxwell's wife. John Maxwell & Co. announced their first novels in the* Ath *on Sept. 5, 1863, starting up by issuing stories that had run in Ward & Lock's* Sixpenny Magazine. *John Maxwell, I think, had been a clerk for Ward & Lock.*

355 ROBERT WARNEFORD (WILLIAM RUSSELL) *Running the Blockade.* Small format. 2/o boards   Jan. 10 (*Ath*)

This is the first edition, 1863, 16.6 cm., 315 pp. At a Hodgson auction in Oct. 1863, 1,200 copies were for sale.

Also 1875

356 GUSTAVE AIMARD *The Adventurers.* Small format. 2/o boards   Feb. 21 (*Ath*)

This is the first English edition, 1863, 16.6 cm., 346 pp. The first French edition was *Les Aventuriers*, Paris, 1863, 422 pp.

Also 1876, 80

357 GUSTAVE AIMARD *The Pearl of the Andes.* Small format. 2/o boards Mar. 31 (*Ath*)

This is the first English edition, 1863, 373 pp. It was listed by the *Ath* on Apr. 25 also. The first edition was *Le Grand Chef des Aucas*, Paris, 2 vols., 1858.

Also 1877, 80

358 JOHN M. WILSON *Tales of the Borders.* 20 vols. Vol. 1. Small format. 1/o sewed each   Apr. 25 (*Ath*)

Vols. 1–9 were issued monthly, Apr. through Dec. and vols. 10–20 were issued in 1864. They were issued jointly with J. Ainsworth, Manchester. The first edition was *Wilson's Historical, Traditionary, and Imaginative Tales of the Borders*, issued by John Sutherland, Edinburgh; etc., 6 vols., 1835–40, yearly, in Oct., 28.5 cm., at 8/0 each. He advertised a reissue in 6 vols. in the *Ath* on Oct. 30, 1841, at 8/0 each. This latter issue was also published in weekly numbers at 1.5 d each and in monthly parts at o/6 each. J. Ainsworth, Manchester, issued 20 vols., 1857–59, revised by A. Leighton, 17 cm. Five vols. were issued in the United States, 1847–50, 24.5 cm., illustrated. Vol. 1 of this American issue was published by R. T. Shannon, New York, and vols. 2–5 by Robert Martin, New York. It was also issued in parts in the United States by Martin, as part XI, containing Nos. 17 and 18, was listed by *Lit World* as published by him Aug. 26–Sept. 2, 1848.

359 CHARLES J. COLLINS **Matilda the Dane.** Small format. 1/0 sewed May 9 (*Ath*)

Shilling Volume Library No. 30. This is the first edition, 1863, 215 pp.

360 HANS C. ANDERSEN **The Improvisatore.** New Edition. 2/0 boards May 23 (*Reader*)

This has no date, 340 pp.

Also 1857, 73, 89

361 PAUL FÉVAL **The Duke's Motto.** Small format. 2/0 boards May 23 (*Reader*)

This is the first English edition, my copy, 1863, 16.6 cm., 360 pp., translated from the French *Le Bossu* by Bertha Browne. It is in green boards, decorated and lettered on the front in red, green, and black. It has plain white endpapers and a publisher's ad on the back cover. The first American edition was R. M. DeWitt, New York (1863), "*I Am Here!*", the Duke's Motto, 96 pp., translated by H. L. Williams. It was *DeWitt's Twenty-Five Cent Novels* No. 25, listed in *ALG&PC* on Sept. 15. At a Hodgson auction in Oct. 1864, 1,000 copies were for sale.

362 DANIEL DEFOE **Robinson Crusoe.** 1/0 boards June 20 (*Reader*)

The first edition was issued by W. Taylor, London, 3 vols., anonymous, vol. 1 being *The Life and Strange Surprizing Adventures of Robinson Crusoe*, in Apr. 1719; vol. 2, *The Farther Adventures of Robinson Crusoe*, in Aug. 1719; vol. 3, *Serious Reflections During the Life and Surprising Adventures of Robinson Crusoe*, in Aug. 1720. The first American edition was printed for Peter Stewart, Philadelphia, 1 vol., 3 parts, 1789.

Also 1864, 68, 79, 85

363 F. STRAUSS **The Englishman's Illustrated Pocket Guide to Paris . . .** Fcp 8vo. 1/0 boards June 20 (*Reader*)

This has 100 pp.

364 JOHN F. SMITH **Ambition.** [New edition]. 2/0 boards July 4 (*Reader*)

This has 254 pp.

Also 1860 as *The Prelate*

365 ANONYMOUS **The American Mail-Bag.** 2/0 boards July 11 (*Ath*)

This is the first edition, 1863, 348 pp. At a Hodgson auction on Dec. 14, 1863, 500 copies were for sale.

366 ANDREW FORRESTER, JR. **The Revelations of a Private Detective.** Small format. 2/0 boards July 11 (*Ath*)

This is the first edition, 1863, Sadleir's copy, 360 pp., yellow pictorial boards, with "The Private Detective" on the front cover, and a pink paper tipped onto the front fly-leaf with an ad for W. H. Smith's Library.

Also 1868

367 PERCY B. ST. JOHN **The Indian Maiden.** 2/0 boards July 11 (*Ath*)

This is the first edition, 1863.

368 ANONYMOUS **Etiquette, Politeness, and Good Breeding.** Fcp 8vo. 1/0 boards Aug. 29 (*Reader*)

Useful Hand-Books. This is the first edition, no date.

369 PERCY B. ST. JOHN **The Red Queen.** 2/0 boards Sept. 12 (*Ath*)

This is the first edition, no date.

370 WILLIAM H. C. NATION **Trifles.** Fcp 8vo. 2/0 boards Sept. 12 (*Reader*)

This is the first edition, 1863, 145 pp., a collection of original tales, rhymes, and sketches.

371 (ANNIE EDWARDES) **The Morals of May Fair.** [New edition]. 2/0 boards Sept. 19 (*Reader*)

Library of Popular Authors No. 1. This began the long series of pictorial yellow-

backs, 16.4 cm., with the series title on the spine. The present title has no date, 320 pp. The first edition was issued by Hurst & Blackett, London, 3 vols., p 8vo, anonymous, 31/6, advertised in the *Ath* on Jan. 16, 1858, as "Next week," and listed Jan. 23. It was reissued by J. & R. Maxwell, London, no date, in 1878, 12mo, 320 pp., at 2/0 boards, 2/6 cloth. The first American edition was issued by the American News Co., New York, 1866, as *Philip Earnscliffe*, listed in the *ALG&PC* on Sept. 1.
Also 1869, 70, 74

372 JOSEPH STAPLES *The Diary of a London Physician*. 2/0 boards   Oct. 3 (*Ath*)
This is the first edition, 1863.

373 MARTIN F. TUPPER *Stephan Langton*. [New edition revised]. 2/0 boards   Oct. 3 (*Ath*)
This was Sadleir's copy, 1863, 244 pp., in pictorial boards. The first edition was issued by Hurst & Blackett, London, 2 vols. (1858), 21 cm., illustrated, 21/0, advertised as "This day" and listed in the *Ath* on Dec. 4, 1858.
Also 1875

374 ANNIE THOMAS (MRS. PENDER CUDLIP) *Lady Lorne and the Dream and the Waking*. Small format. 1/0 sewed Oct. 17 (*Ath*)
Shilling Volume Library. This is the first edition, 1863.
Also 1869

375 PAUL FÉVAL *Bel Demonio*. Small format. 2/0 boards   Nov. 14 (*Ath*)
This is the first English edition, my copy, 1863, 16.5 cm., 395 pp., with the words "Never before printed" on the title page. It is bound in yellow pictorial boards with plain white endpapers and has a publisher's ad on the back cover. It was translated

from the French by Bertha Browne. At a Hodgson auction in Oct. 1864, 1,000 copies were for sale.

376 GEORGE A. SALA *Accepted Addresses*. Small format. 1/0 sewed   Nov. 28 (*Ath*)
Shilling Volume Library. This is 1863. The first edition was issued by Tinsley Bros., London, 1862, 18.5 cm., 307 pp., advertised in the *Ath* on July 5 as "On July 10" and listed on July 12 at 7/6.

377 GEORGE A. SALA *The Perfidy of Captain Slyboots, and Other Tales*. Small format. 1/0 sewed   Nov. 28 (*Ath*)
Shilling Volume Library. This is the first edition, 1863, Sadleir's copy, 219 pp., violet wrappers printed in dark purple and green, with the series title on the front. It was a contribution to the *Welcome Guest* for May 8, 1858.
Also 1869

378 ANONYMOUS *Dalziel's Illustrated Arabian Nights' Entertainments*. Penny weekly numbers. No. 1   Dec. 16 (*Spect*)
This was also issued simultaneously in monthly parts at 0/6 each. The text was revised by H. W. Dulcken and illustrated by A. B. Houghton, J. D. Watson, Sir John Tenniel, Thomas Dalziel, et al. It was issued also in four divisions, and Division 1, 28 cm., 200 pp., 2/6, was advertised in the *Spect* on July 30, 1864, as "On July 28." It was also issued in two vols., vol. 1, 28 cm., 7/6, advertised in the *Spect* on Sept. 24, 1864, as "This day." A *Spect* notice stated that this edition suppressed a few words.
Also 1882, 89. See 1886

379 F. C. ARMSTRONG (FRANCIS C. ARMSTRONG) *The Cruise of the Daring*. Small format. 2/0 boards   Dec. (*Bks*)
Library of Popular Authors No. 2. This has no date, Sadleir's copy, 315 pp., yellow boards. The first edition was *The Cruize of*

the Daring [sic], issued by T.C. Newby, London, 3 vols., 1860, 20.5 cm.
Also 1873, 90

380 F.C. ARMSTRONG **The Sailor Hero.** Small format. 2/o boards Dec. (*Bks*)

Library of Popular Authors No. 3. This has no date, Sadleir's copy, 319 pp., yellow pictorial boards. The first edition was *The Frigate and the Lugger*, issued by T.C. Newby, London, 3 vols., 1861, 21 cm.
Also 1873, 87

381 ANDREW FORRESTER, JR. **Secret Service, or Recollections of a City Detective.** Small format. 2/o boards Dec. (*Bks*)

This is the first edition, 1864, Sadleir's copy, 316 pp., yellow pictorial boards, with a slip of blue paper tipped onto the front fly-leaf advertising a Chapman & Hall book and with the words "Never before published" on the title page. At a Hodgson auction in Oct. 1864, 1,000 copies were for sale.

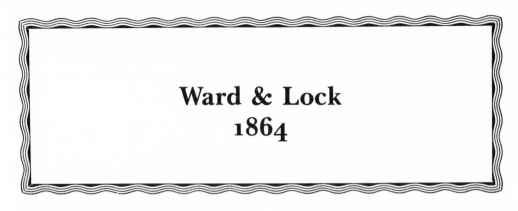

Ward & Lock
1864

382 (PERCIVAL LEIGH) *The Comic English Grammar.* [New edition]. Small format. Illustrated. 1/0 sewed   Jan. 16 (*Reader*)
Shilling Volume Library.
Also 1857

383 GEORGE A. SALA *Make Your Game.* Small format. Illustrated. 1/0 sewed Jan. 16 (*Ath*)
Shilling Volume Library.
Also 1860, 69

384 RICHARD COBBOLD *The History of Margaret Catchpole: A Suffolk Girl.* New Edition, Enlarged and Improved. Small format. 2/0 boards   Jan. 30 (*Reader*)
Library of Popular Authors No. 4. This is my copy, no date, 16.4 cm., 368 pp., with a supplement (Oct. 21, 1858) on pp. 369–378, and a second supplement (Jan. 18, 1862) on pp. 379 and 380. It is in yellow pictorial boards with the series title on the spine and publisher's ads on the back cover and the endpapers, those at the back being upside down! There is a buff slip tipped onto the front fly-leaf with Ward & Lock ads. The first edition was issued by Henry Colburn, London, 3 vols., 1845, 20.5 cm., anonymous, illustrated, 31/6. The (third edition) was advertised in the *Spect* on Jan. 10, 1846, illustrated, 10/6. Sadleir's copy of the first edition had an inscribed date (Apr. 19, 1845) and a 24-page catalog (1845) at the back of vol. 3. It was listed in the *Ath* on Mar. 1, 1845; and a new edition was issued in two vols., Fcp 8vo, 12/0, listed in the *Ath* on May 3,

1845. It was issued as *Parlour Library* No. 74, 1852, 368 pp.; and Simpkin, Marshall, London; etc., issued it in the *Run and Read Library* (1858), a new edition, enlarged and improved, 378 pp., 2/0 boards, listed in the *Spect* on Dec. 11, 1858. The first American edition was issued by D. Appleton & Co., New York, 1846, 167 pp., illustrated, noticed in the *Southern Quarterly Review* for Apr. 1846.
Also 1867, 73, 77, 87

385 JOHN M. WILSON *Tales of the Borders.* Vols. 10–20. Vol. 10. 1/0 sewed   Jan. (*Bks*)
These were issued monthly, Jan.–Nov. See 1863 for vols. 1–9

386 OLIVER GOLDSMITH *Dalziel's Illustrated Goldsmith. The Vicar of Wakefield.* Weekly parts. No. 1. Illustrated. 0/1 each   Mar. 5
This was simultaneously issued in monthly parts at 0/6 each, the first monthly part being ready on Mar. 26. It was illustrated by G. J. Pinwill. It was completed in two divisions in one vol., Division 1 of 200 pp., at 2/6, advertised in the *Spect* on July 30, 1864, as "On July 28." One vol., 4to, 7/6, with a life of Goldsmith, was advertised in the *Spect* on Sept. 3 as "Now ready."
Also 1855, 86

387 GUSTAVE AIMARD (OLIVER GLOUX)
The Trappers of the Arkansas. Small
format. 2/o boards   Mar. 12 (*Reader*)

The first edition was *Les Trappeurs de l'Arkansas*, Paris, 1858, 18 cm., 455 pp. The
first English edition was *The Loyal Heart;
or, The Trappers*, issued by George Routledge, London, 1858, 294 pp., at 1/6
boards, issued about Oct. 16. The first
American edition was probably T. R. Dawley, New York, 1858, 337 pp. At a Hodgson auction in Dec. 1863, 300 copies were
for sale.
Also 1876, 80

388 GUSTAVE AIMARD **The Buccaneer
Chief.** Small format. 2/o boards   Mar. 12
(*Reader*)

This is the first English edition, 1864, 16.6
cm., 384 pp. The first edition was *La
Grande Flibuste*, Paris, 1860, 414 pp.
Also 1878, 80

389 HENRY R. ADDISON **"All at Sea."**
2/o boards   Mar. 12 (*Reader*)

This is the first edition, 1864, 312 pp. At a
Hodgson auction in Oct. 1864, 750 copies
were for sale.

390 ANONYMOUS **Leah, the Jewish
Maiden.** Small format. 2/o boards
Apr. 16 (*Ath*)

This is the first edition, 1864, 316 pp., yellow pictorial boards, with the words
"Never before published" on the title
page.
Also 1870, 73, 90

391 EDGAR ALLAN POE **Tales of Mystery,
Imagination and Humour; and Poems.**
Illustrated. 2/o boards   Apr. 23 (*Reader*)

Tales of the Grotesque and Arabesque was issued by Lea & Blanchard, Philadelphia, 2
vols., 1840, 20 cm., with none of the better
known tales. *Tales* was issued by Wiley &
Putnam, New York, 1845, 18.5 cm., 228
pp., containing many of the best known

tales. It was imported into England and issued by Wiley & Putnam, London, 1845,
with a cancel title page. Vizetelly, London,
issued it with this Ward & Lock title about
Feb. 20, 1852, as *Readable Books* No. 1, 256
pp., illustrated, 1/o boards. Series 2 was issued by Clarke, Beeton, London; etc.,
about Feb. 5, 1853, as *Readable Books* No.
9, 1/o boards. I have a copy of series 1,
Henry Vizetelly; Clarke & Co., London,
1852, 20th thousand, 17.5 cm., 256 pp.;
and I have a copy of series 2, Clarke, Beeton & Co., London, no date, 16.7 cm., 252
pp. These are in salmon boards, series 1
decorated in tan, and series 2 with the
same decoration in white, both printed in
black. *Tales and Sketches; to Which Is Added
the Raven* was issued by George Routledge, London, the first half of Mar. 1852,
1/o boards, 1/6 cloth. Ward & Lock issued
the present title again in Nov., the same,
and probably put it in the *Library of Popular Authors* at that time.
Also 1873, 80

The following four titles were listed in the
Bks for May, and the first two were also
listed by the *Reader* on May 7. All are illustrated and were 1/o sewed each:

392 **Country Pursuits and Amusements**
393 **Games and Amusements**
394 **The Boy's Handy Book**
395 **The Boy's Manual of Seaside and
Holiday Pursuits**

I give here what light I've been able to
throw on the publishing history of these
titles. Ward & Lock advertised *The Boy's
Handy Book of Games, Sports, Pastimes and
Amusements*, illustrated, 5/o, in a book of
1856, as a new book. The *U Cat* gives the
same as (1863) and (1881), 374 pp., illustrated. Both of these dates are suspect because the entries give the wrong style in
the imprint. The *U Cat* gives the same text
and illustrations for the *Boy's Manual of
Seaside and Holiday Pursuits*, issued by
Cameron & Ferguson, Glasgow (1863),
Sixpenny Volume Library, with the running

head "The Boy's Handy Book." The *Eng Cat* gives *The Boy's Handy Book of Cricket, Football, etc.*, 12mo, 1/0, issued by Ward & Lock in 1864. The *U Cat* gives *Games & Amusements*, no date, 140 pp., consisting of round games, table games, cards, billiards, charades, etc. It gives *Country Pursuits and Amusements*, Cameron & Ferguson, Glasgow, no date, 289 and 374 pp., illustrated, in the *Sixpenny Volume Library*, with the running head "The Boy's Handy Book." The *Eng Cat* gives *The Boy's Manual of Seaside and Holiday Pursuits*, 12mo, 1/0, issued by Ward & Lock in 1864; and the *U Cat* gives the same title, Cameron & Ferguson, no date, 19 cm., pp. 97–200, illustrated.

396 SAMUEL GUY *The Doctor's Note-Book.* 2/0 boards   May 21 (*Ath*)

This is the first edition, 1864. At a Hodgson auction on Oct. 18, 1864, 1,000 copies were for sale.

397 HARRIET B. STOWE *Uncle Tom's Cabin.* Illustrated. 2/0 boards   May 28 (*Reader*)

The first edition was issued by John P. Jewett, Boston; Jewett, Proctor & Worthington, Cleveland, 2 vols., 1852, noticed in the *Ind* on Mar. 25 and reviewed on Apr. 8, and it was probably issued on Mar. 20. It ran in the *National Era* in 1851–52. The first English edition was issued by Henry Vizetelly; Clarke & Co., London, 1852, 19 cm., 329 pp., ten illustrations, 2/6 cloth, in an edition of 2,500, with a preface by "G." It was reprinted verbatim from the 10th American edition and advertised in the *Ath* on Apr. 24, 1852, as "On Apr. 30," and advertised the same on May 1. At least 12 different editions (not reissues) were issued by English houses from this until the end of 1852, and 40 editions were issued by English houses within a year of the first edition. I give here all the ads for it in the *Ath* through

Oct. 23, 1852, in addition to the two given above.

May 15. Clarke & Co., 360 pp., 2/6 cloth, "Now ready."

Aug. 7. Clarke & Co., Part 1, Demy 8vo, illustrated edition, 0/6. To be issued in six monthly parts, each part with 64 pp. and 8 to 10 illustrations.

Aug. 14. Clarke & Co.; Menzies, Edinburgh; M'Glashan, Dublin, Demy 8vo, illustrated edition, 40 illustrations, 7/6, "This day."

Aug. 14. Same imprint, the People's Edition, weekly penny numbers and monthly sixpenny parts, illustrated.

Aug. 14. Same imprint, 10th thousand of the original edition, Cr 8vo, 2/6, "Now ready."

Aug. 21. Thomas Bosworth, London, author's edition, Cr 8vo, 3/6, a preface by Mrs. Stowe, "This day." Bosworth claimed in his ads that he had permission from Mrs. Stowe to state that she had not authorized nor had an interest in any English edition except his! (Editorial matter in the *Ath* on Feb. 13, 1904, announcing the death of C. H. Clarke, said that he had printed, bound, and delivered 1.25 million copies within a 12-month period and that in the fall of 1853 he had sent his clerk, S. O. Beeton, to America with 1,000 guineas for Mrs. Stowe!)

Sept. 11. Ingram, Cooke, London, an illustrated edition, Cr 8vo, 8 illustrations, 2/6, "In a few days," and 8 illustrations, 2/0 sewed, 2/6 cloth, "Now ready" in a Sept. 18 ad.

Sept. 11. Clarke & Co., illustrated edition, fifth thousand, 40 illustrations, 7/6. The ninth thousand was in an ad on Oct. 23.

Sept. 11. George Routledge, London, original edition, 30th thousand, p 8vo, 2/6, now reprinted in large type.

Sept. 11. Routledge, railway edition, 95th thousand. I cannot explain this ad, as the first evidence I've found for a 1/0 Routledge issue was at 1/0 boards, listed in the *Ath* on Oct. 9, 1852, and listed by *PC* as published Sept. 29–Oct. 14; and Routledge advertised the 19th thousand in the *Ath* on Oct. 16, 1852, illustrated, 2/6, 3/6 cloth, and 1/o boards. William Talbot in the *American Book Collector*, 1933, says the Routledge 1/o issue sold 145,900 copies by Sept. 1852!

Sept. 11. Clarke & Co., People's Illustrated Edition, 25th thousand, in penny numbers and sixpenny parts.

Sept. 11. The Publisher's Trade Edition, pocket size, 188 pp., o/6 sewed. Piper Bros. & Co., London, have the disposal of this issue. It was shortly advertised by Piper as the Sixpenny Pocket Edition.

Sept. 18. Simms & M'Intyre, *Parlour Library*, 1/o, "In a few days."

Sept. 18. Partridge & Oakey, London, People's Shilling Edition, Cr 8vo, in double columns, 1/o boards, with an illustrated title page and cover.

Sept. 25. Bentley, London, *Standard Novels*, 3/6, "On Sept. 29."

Sept. 25. Henry G. Bohn, London, three editions: 2/6; 3/6 illustrated; 1/o green boards. (An ad by Bohn in *Notes and Queries* on Sept. 18, 1852, gave p 8vo, in an unabridged edition, 2/6 green cloth; and an illustrated edition, p 8vo, 3/6 green cloth, illustrated by Leech, Gilbert, and Hinchliffe. The ad on Oct. 9, 1852, was for the 1/o green boards edition, Fcp 8vo, with an introduction by James Sherman. The 2/6 was noticed on Oct. 9, "The most readable edition we have yet seen.")

Oct. 16. George Routledge, London, the Family Edition, 2 illustrations, 2/6 cloth; the Drawing-Room Table Edition, p 8vo, 12 illustrations, 3/6; the Railway Shilling Edition, 18oth thousand, 1/o boards, all with a preface by the Earl of Carlisle.

Oct. 23. John Lofts, London, 1/o, engraved title page and frontispiece, 6 illustrations; 1/6, 2/o cloth, 2/6 gilt edges, 6 illustrations.

Oct. 23. C. H. Clarke & Co., London,

the People's Illustrated Edition, Demy 8vo, 50 illustrations, 4/o.

Routledge issued an edition jointly with C. H. Clarke, 1852, 20.5 cm., 351 pp., illustrated, with a preface signed "G." Vizetelly; Clarke & Co., London, issued a new edition, 12mo, illustrated, 1/o boards, 1/6 cloth, listed by *PC* as published July 15–31, in the *Select Family Series*. They issued the author's edition, with the Clarke imprint, 1/o sewed, listed by *PC* as published Sept. 14–25. There is a known copy of the Routledge, 1852, edition, 8vo, 351 pp., 8 illustrations, 16 pp. of ads, in blind-stamped green cloth with yellow coated endpapers. John Cassell, London, issued it, 1852, 27 illustrations by Cruikshank, 1/o boards, listed by *PC* as published Sept. 29–Oct. 14, and listed in the *Ath* on Oct. 9, 1852.

Also 1873, 78

398 ANDREW FORRESTER, JR., ed. ***The Female Detective.*** Small format. 2/o boards   June 4 (*Reader*)
This is the first edition, Sadleir's copy, 1864, 316 pp., in yellow pictorial boards. At a Hodgson auction on Oct. 18, 1864, 1,000 copies were for sale.
Also 1868

399 DANIEL DEFOE   ***Robinson Crusoe.*** [New edition]. Illustrated. 2/o boards June 25 (*Reader*)
Also 1863, 68, 79, 85

400 ANNE MARSH, later MARSH-CALDWELL ***Emilia Wyndham.*** Small format. 2/o boards   July 2 (*Reader*)
Library of Popular Authors. The first edition was issued by Henry Colburn, London, 3 vols., 1846, 19.5 cm., anonymous, 31/6, listed in the *Ath* on Mar. 28 and reviewed on Apr. 25. Sadleir's copy had an inscribed date of Aug. 14, 1846. It was issued as *Parlour Library* No. 14, 1848, 352 pp., my copy. The first American edition

was issued by Harper & Bros., New York, 1846, 8vo, anonymous, 165 pp., *Library of Select Novels* No. 81. It was noticed in the *Southern Literary Messenger* for July.
Also 1882

401 HARRIETTE SMYTHIES (MRS. GORDON SMYTHIES) *The Life of a Beauty.* Small format. 2/o boards   July 2 (*Reader*)
Library of Popular Authors. The first edition was issued by T. C. Newby, London, 3 vols., p 8vo, anonymous, 31/6, dated 1846, listed in the *Ath* on June 27 and reviewed on Aug. 1.
Also 1870

402   W. H. WATTS *London Life at the Police Courts.* Small format. 2/o boards July 2 (*Reader*)
This is the first edition, 1864, Sadleir's copy, 316 pp., in yellow pictorial boards. At a Hodgson auction on Oct. 18, 1864, 1,000 copies were for sale.

403   MARIA S. CUMMINS *The Lamplighter.* [New edition]. 2/o boards   July 23 (*Reader*)
Run and Read Library. This started a long series of reissues of this series. The copyrights, stereo plates, and stocks of the series (nearly 100 vols.), the property of J. M. Burton of Ipswitch, were for sale at a Southgate & Barrett auction on Nov. 16 and 17, 1863. Apparently many if not all were purchased by Ward & Lock. The present title was first issued in this series as No. 7 by Clarke, Beeton & Co., London, in 1854, at 1/6 boards; and reissued in the series by Simpkin, Marshall, London; J. M. Burton, Ipswitch, in 1861, at 1/6 boards, my copy.
Also 1854, 70, 72

404   (FRANCIS CARR) *Archimago.* Demy 8vo. 2/6 wrappers   July (*Bks*)
This was advertised in the *Spect* on July 23 as "This day." It has no date, 119 pp., a narrative purporting to be written in the latter half of the 20th century. It is given by the *U Cat*, but the *Eng Cat* gives only Saunders & Otley, London, in 1864, 8vo, anonymous, at 2/6. A known copy is imprinted Ward & Lock, London; D. H. Wilson, Newcastle, with no date, in brown wrappers printed in black.

405   PAUL H. C. FÉVAL *The Woman of Mystery.* Small format. 1/o sewed Aug. 6 (*Reader*)
Shilling Volume Library. This is the first English edition, 1864, translated from the French by J. Stebbing.

406   (WILLIAM S. HAYWARD) *The Woman in Red.* 2/o boards   Aug. 6 (*Reader*)
This is the first edition, 1864. It was issued by T. B. Peterson & Bros., Philadelphia, no date, probably in 1864, complete and unabridged edition, anonymous, 121 pp.

407   GUSTAVE AIMARD *Stronghand.* Small format. 1/o boards   Aug. 6 (*Reader*)
This is 1864, 402 pp. The first edition was *La Main-Ferme*, Paris, 1862, 520 pp. The first English edition was issued by John Maxwell & Co., London, 2 vols., 1863, 20 cm., 21/o, advertised in the *Ath* on Sept. 5 as "On Sept. 15" and on Sept. 19 as "Just out."
Also 1877, 80

408   AZEL S. ROE *The Star and the Cloud.* 2/o boards   Aug. 20 (*Reader*)
Run and Read Library. The first American edition was issued by Derby & Jackson, New York; Sampson Low, London, 1857, 19 cm., 410 pp., advertised in the *Ind* on Feb. 12, $1.25, "Now ready," listed Mar. 19 and reviewed May 14. It was listed in *APC&LG* on Feb. 14. The first English edition was Simpkin, Marshall, London; J. M. Burton, Ipswitch, as *Run and Read Library* No. 25, 1/6 boards, listed by *PC* as published Jan. 14–31, 1857.
Also 1876

409 GUSTAVE AIMARD *The Smuggler Chief.* Small format. 2/0 boards Sept. 10 (*Reader*)

This is 1864, 357 pp. The first French edition was *Les Fils de la Tortue*, Paris (1864), 342 pp. The first English edition was *The Smuggler Hero*, issued by John Maxwell & Co., London, 2 vols., 1864, 19 cm., 21/0, translated by Lascelles Wraxall, and advertised in the *Ath* on Jan. 9, 1864, as "On Jan. 15" and listed Jan. 23. It had just finished its run in Ward & Lock's *Sixpenny Magazine*.

Also 1878, 80

410 MARY M. SHERWOOD (M. M. BUTT, later SHERWOOD) *The Monk.* Fcp 8vo. 2/0 boards Oct. 8 (*Reader*)

Run and Read Library. This is a reissue of the Simpkin, Marshall; etc., issue in this series as No. 17 (1855), a new and improved edition, 360 pp., probably issued in Nov. It was listed in the *Spect* on Mar. 8, 1858, and Sadleir had a copy, the 129th thousand, no date, in bright green boards, with 16 pp. of ads at the back. It had a frontispiece and an added illustrated title page. The first edition was *The Monk of Cimies*, issued by Darton & Son, London, no date, 17 cm., 428 pp., listed and reviewed in the *Spect* on Feb. 11, 1837. *The Monk of Cimies and Other Tales*, vol. 14 of Mrs. Sherwood's works, was issued by Harper & Bros., New York, listed by the *New York Review* (quarterly) for Apr. 1838, as published Jan. 1–Mar. 15, 1838.

411 CATHERINE SINCLAIR *The Mysterious Marriage.* 2/0 boards Oct. 15 (*Reader*)

Run and Read Library. This is a reissue of No. 5 in this series, issued by Clarke & Beeton, London, in 1854. Simpkin, Marshall, London, issued it as *Cheap Library* No. 2, 1/0 boards, about May 1, 1860. The first edition was issued by Longmans, London, as *Sir Edward Graham*, 3 vols., 1849, listed in the *Spect* on Oct. 27, 1849, p

8vo, 3 vols. The first American edition was issued by Harper & Bros., New York, 1850, with the Longmans title, listed in *Lit World* as published Jan. 19–Feb. 2, 1850.

Also 1875

412 MARY M. SHERWOOD *The Nun.* 2/0 boards Nov. 5 (*Reader*)

Run and Read Library. This was a reissue of No. 56 in this series, issued by Simpkin, Marshall, London; etc., in 1859, at 1/6 boards, 2/6 cloth, about Dec. 14. The first edition was issued by Seeley, London, 1833, anonymous, 326 pp., at 6/0 boards, listed in the *Ath* on Dec. 7, 1833. It was listed in the *Edinburgh Review* as published Oct. 1838–Jan. 1839, a new edition, 18mo, at 4/6.

Also 1869, 76, 85

413 RICHARD COBBOLD *Mary Anne Wellington.* 2/0 boards Dec. 3 (*Reader*)

Run and Read Library. This was a reissue of No. 6 in this series issued by Clarke, Beeton, London, in Dec. 1854; reissued in the series by Simpkin, Marshall, London; etc., the 17th thousand, 1/6 boards, about Apr. 9, 1859. Clarke, Beeton issued it, 1853, a new and improved edition, 322 pp., 1/6 boards, in royal blue glazed boards printed in black, with a frontispiece and an added illustrated title page. The first edition was issued by Henry Colburn, London, 3 vols., 1846, 20 cm., illustrated, 31/6, listed in the *Ath* on Sept. 16, 1846. He issued it in 1 vol., illustrated, 10/6, advertised in the *Illustrated London News* on June 19, 1847, as "Now ready."

Also 1875

414 MARY LANGDON (MARY H. PIKE) *Ida May.* 2/0 boards Dec. 3 (*Reader*)

Run and Read Library. This is a reissue of No. 32 in this series, issued by Simpkin, Marshall, London; etc., at 1/6 boards, about June 6, 1857. The first edition was issued by Sampson Low, London, 1854,

edited by an English clergyman, 323 pp., at 1/6 boards, in an edition of 10,000 copies. It was listed in *PC* as published Sept. 1–14 and advertised in the *Ath* on Sept. 16 as "This day." The first American edition was issued by Phillips, Sampson, Boston; etc., 1854, 19 cm., 478 pp., listed in the *Ind* on Nov. 16, and advertised in the *New York Daily Times* on Nov. 4 as "On Nov. 15," but an ad on Nov. 14 announced an unavoidable delay with publication postponed until Nov. 22. The 20th thousand at $1.25 was issued before the end of the year.
Also 1870, 72

415 (JANE E. HORNBLOWER) *Nellie of Truro.* 2/0 boards   Dec. 3 (*Reader*)
Run and Read Library. This is a reissue of No. 30 in this series, issued by Simpkin, Marshall, London; etc., anonymous, at 1/6 boards, about May 30, 1857. The first edition was issued by Robert Carter & Bros., New York, 1856, 19 cm., anonymous, 432 pp., with an added illustrated title page. It was listed in the *Ind* on Nov. 22, 1855, at $1.00, and in *APC&LG* on Nov. 24. The first English edition was issued by Sampson Low, London, 1856, at 2/0 cloth, from American proof sheets, listed by *PC* as published Dec. 15–31, 1855, and listed in the *Ath* on Dec. 15.
Also 1876, 85

416 GUSTAVE AIMARD *The Rebel Chief.* Small format. 2/0 boards   Dec. 24 (*Reader*)
This is the first English edition, 1865 (1864), 416 pp. The first French edition was *Les Nuits Mexicaines*, Paris, 1864, 480 pp. The first American edition was issued by T. B. Peterson & Bros., Philadelphia (1867), complete and unabridged edition, 24.5 cm., 203 pp., in double columns, at $.75, listed in the *Ind* on July 25, and advertised in the *New-York Times* on July 20, 1867, 8vo, $.75, as if ready.
Also 1877, 80

417 M. J. H. (JOSEPHINE HANNON) *Gertrude Waynflete.* 1/0 boards   Dec. 24 (*Reader*)
This is the first edition (1864).

418 (RICHARD COBBOLD), ed. *John H. Steggall.* Small format. 2/0 boards   1864
Library of Popular Authors. This is my copy, no date, enlarged edition, Narrated by Himself, 16.5 cm., 320 pp., yellow pictorial boards, with "Cobbold" on the front cover and spine. There is a dedication by Steggall (Aug.1856) and an introduction by Cobbold (Aug. 1857). The series title is on the spine, and there are publisher's ads in blue on the endpapers and in black on the back cover. The first edition was issued by Simpkin, Marshall, London, 1857, 19.5 cm., 312 pp., 7/6, with a frontispiece and vignette title, edited by (Cobbold), and listed in the *Ath* on Sept. 12. It was reissued as *Run and Read Library* No. 49, 1859, enlarged edition, 320 pp., at 2/0 boards, listed by *PC* as published Apr. 14–30, 1859.
Also 1875

419 (ANNE MARSH) *Father Darcy.* Small format. 2/0 boards   1864
Library of Popular Authors. This is my copy, 1864, 16.6 cm., 408 pp., in green pictorial boards, with the series title on the spine and half-title, and with the author's name on the front cover and the spine. The title page imprint and the imprints on the front cover and for the ad on the back cover are Ward & Lock, but the imprint on the blue ads on the endpapers is Ward, Lock & Tyler, thus dating them as after Apr. 10, 1866. The first edition was issued by Chapman & Hall, London, issued in four parts, May–Aug. 1846, anonymous, 3/0 each; and in two vols., 1846, anonymous, 14/0, as Nos. 9 and 10 in their *Monthly Series*. Vol. 1 was listed in the *Ath* on June 6, 1846, and vol. 2 on Aug. 1, 7/0 each. There was no evidence in the *Ath* of

a four part issue. The first American edition was issued by Harper & Bros., New York, 1846, 8vo, anonymous, reviewed in the *Harbinger* (weekly) on Sept. 12, and listed as new book of the month in the *United States Magazine* (monthly) for Oct. Also 1882

420 W. H. HILLYARD *Tales in the Cabin.* o/6 sewed   1864 (*Eng Cat*)

Also 1861, 68

421 ANNA M. HALL (MRS. S. C. HALL) *Marian.* Small format. 2/o boards   1864 (*Eng Cat*)

Library of Popular Authors. The first edition was issued by Henry Colburn, London, 1840, 3 vols., p 8vo, 31/6. The second edition was issued by Simms & M'Intyre, London and Belfast, 1847, *Parlour Library* No. 9, with a dedication (Apr. 3, 1847). The first American edition was issued by Harper & Bros., New York, 1840, 2 vols., 19.5 cm.

422 FRANCES TROLLOPE *The Attractive Man.* Small format. 2/o boards   1864 (*Eng Cat*)

Library of Popular Authors. This has no date, 415 pp. The first edition was issued by Henry Colburn, London, 1846, 3 vols., 20 cm., 31/6, listed in the *Ath* on Oct. 11, 1845. It was issued by J. & C. Brown, London (1857), copyright edition, 17 cm., 415 pp., at 2/o boards, listed by *PC* as published July 16–31.

423 HARRIETTE SMYTHIES *The Jilt.* Small format. 2/o boards   1864 (*Eng Cat*)

Library of Popular Authors. The first edition was issued by Bentley, London, 1844, 3 vols., 20 cm., anonymous, 31/6. It was advertised in the *Spect* on Aug. 3 as "Just published." It was issued as *Parlour Library* No. 269 by Darton & Hodge, London (1862), anonymous.

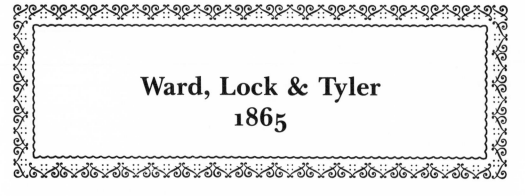

Ward, Lock & Tyler
1865

On Feb. 28, 1865, Ward & Lock announced in the Bks *the change of style to Ward, Lock & Tyler, 158 Fleet Street and 107 Dorset Street, Salisbury Square.*

424 THEODORE HOOK **Jack Brag.** Small format. 2/o boards   Mar. 18 (*Ath* ad)

The ad gave this and the following five titles as "Just published."

Library of Popular Authors. The first edition was issued by Bentley, 1837, 3 vols., p 8vo, anonymous, 31/6, in an edition of 2,000 copies, published Mar. 16 according to the Bentley private catalog. It was listed in the *Ath* on Mar. 18, illustrated. He issued it as *Standard Novels* No. 75, 1839, revised by the author, anonymous, 441 pp. Six Hook titles were purchased by David Bryce, London, at a Hodgson auction in Feb. 1856, for £478, and the present title was included; and it was issued by Bryce at 2/o boards in July 1856, new edition, no date, revised by the author, 441 pp. The copyright and stereo plates were sold at a Hodgson auction in June 1858, for £46. It was issued as *Parlour Library* No. 276? (1863), by Darton & Hodge, London. The first American edition was issued by Carey, Lea & Blanchard, Philadelphia, 1837, 2-vols.-in-1, 18 cm., anonymous. The cost book of Carey & Lea gives 2 vols., anonymous, 1,500 copies, finished in Apr. 1837, for which Hook was paid $100.
Also 1892

425 SAMUEL LOVER **He Would Be a Gentleman.** Small format. 2/o boards Mar. 18 (*Ath* ad)

Library of Popular Authors. The first edition was *Treasure Trove,* issued by Frederick Lover, London, 1844, 8vo, 411 pp., illustrated, 14/o, listed in the *Ath* on Jan. 4, 1844. It was previously issued in parts as *£.S.D.; Treasure Trove,* at 1/o monthly, part 1 listed in the *Spect* on Jan. 6, 1843, and part 10 on Oct. 14, 1843. Henry G. Bohn, London, issued it, 1845, the same as the first edition, at 9/o; and it was issued by David Bryce, London (1854), a new edition, as *He Would Be a Gentleman,* small format, 2/o, in bright green boards printed in black, published in May. It was sold at a Hodgson auction in June 1858, for £75. It was issued as *Parlour Library* No. 275 by Darton & Hodge, London (1862). It was issued in the United States by D. Appleton & Co., New York; etc., 1844, 23.5 cm., 173 pp., illustrated; and by J. Winchester, New York, 1844, 29 cm., 80 pp., *The New World* extra series, Jan. 1844, with a caption title, *£.S.D.*
Also 1892

426 ELIZABETH C. GREY **The Daughters.** Small format. 2/o boards   Mar. 18 (*Ath* ad)

Library of Popular Authors. The first edition was issued by T.C. Newby, London, 3 vols., 1847, 20 cm., anonymous, 31/6, listed in the *Ath* on May 29 and noticed on July 17. It was issued as *Parlour Library* No. 233 by C.H. Clarke, London, in 1861, a new edition, at 2/o boards.
Also 1884

427 SAMUEL LOVER *Legends and Stories of Ireland.* Small format. 2/o boards Mar. 18 (*Ath* ad)

Library of Popular Authors. The first edition of the first series was issued by W. F. Wakeman, Dublin, 1831, 19.5 cm., 227 pp., illustrated, listed and reviewed in the *Spect* on Mar. 5, 1831, at 7/o. The first edition of the second series was issued by Baldwin & Craddock, London, 1834, 18 cm., 324 pp., 7/6, listed in the *Ath* on June 21. David Bryce, London, issued it at 2/o boards, listed by *PC* as published Dec. 1–15, 1854, and Mar. 15–31, 1860. It was sold at a Hodgson auction in June 1858 for £80. C. H. Clarke, London, issued it in Sept. 1858, at 2/o boards, and reissued it as *Parlour Library* No. 243 (1861), a new edition, at 2/o boards, containing both series. The first American edition was issued by Carey & Hart, Philadelphia, 2 vols., 1835, containing both series. Lea & Blanchard, Philadelphia, issued it at $.50 paper, illustrated, from the last revised London edition, for Christmas 1846.

428 CHARLES LEVER *Maurice Tiernay.* Small format. 2/o boards Mar. 18 (*Ath* ad)

Library of Popular Authors. The first edition was *Parlour Library* No. 119 (1855), issued by Thomas Hodgson, London, 496 pp. It ran in the *Dublin University Magazine* beginning in Apr. 1850 through Dec. 1851. It was issued as *Select Library of Fiction* No. 54 by Chapman & Hall, London, 2/o boards, at the end of 1864 or early 1865, and was reissued by them in 1868, 1875, and 1876. I cannot explain this Ward & Lock issue, but I have found several titles advertised by Ward & Lock as in this series and issued about the same time by Chapman & Hall! The present title ran in *Harper's New Monthly Magazine* almost monthly from June 1850 to Feb. 1852, from the *Dublin University Magazine.* A notice in the magazine for June 1851, stated that it had been issued in Harper's *Library of Select*

Novels, which was obviously not the case. They issued it, 1852, 24 cm., 202 pp., double columns, in the *Library of Select Novels,* advertised in *Lit World* on Feb. 14, and listed in the Apr. number of *Godey's Lady's Book.*

429 ANNE MARSH, later MARSH-CALDWELL *Time the Avenger.* Small format. 2/o boards Mar. 18 (*Ath* ad)

Library of Popular Authors. The first edition was issued by Henry Colburn, London, 3 vols., 1851, 20 cm., anonymous, advertised in the *Ath* on Jan. 4, 1851, as "Just ready," and listed in the *Spect* on Jan. 18. It was issued as *Parlour Library* No. 96, 1853, 381 pp. The first American edition was issued by Harper & Bros., New York, 1851, anonymous, 140 pp., *Library of Select Novels* No. 153. It was listed in *Lit World* as published Mar. 8–22.

430 CHARLES DICKENS, ed. *The Pic-Nic Papers.* Small format. 2/o boards Mar. (*Bks*)

Library of Popular Authors. Also 1859, 62, 70, 82

431 AZEL S. ROE *True to the Last.* 2/o boards Apr. 8 (*Reader*)

Run and Read Library. The first English edition was in this series as No. 46, issued by Simpkin, Marshall, London; etc. (1858), 1/6 boards, listed in the *Spect* on Nov. 13, 1858. The first edition was issued by Derby & Jackson, New York, 1858, 18.5 cm., 384 pp., $1.25, listed in the *Ind* on Sept. 16 and by *APC&LG* on Sept. 11. The third edition was advertised as "Now ready" in the *New-York Times* on Oct. 4, 1858, $1.25.
Also 1866

432 CATHERINE SINCLAIR *Holiday House.* 2/o boards Apr. 8 (*Reader*)

Run and Read Library. This is a reissue of No. 19 in the series, issued by Simpkin,

Marshall, London; etc., at 2/o boards, about Mar. 1, 1856. The first edition was issued by William Whyte, Edinburgh; Longmans, London, 1839, 5/6, advertised in the *Ath* on Jan. 26, 1839, as "This day." They issued it, 1844, the fourth thousand, 17.5 cm., 356 pp., frontispiece, 5/6. The first American edition was issued by Robert Carter, New York, 1839, listed in the quarterly list of new publications in the *New York Review* for July 1839, 12mo, 252 pp.
Also 1872, 85

433 SIR FREDERICK C. L. WRAXALL
Wild Oats. Small format. 2/o boards
Apr. 15 (*Reader*)
Library of Popular Authors. This has no date. The first edition was issued by J. & C. Brown, London (1858), my copy, 17 cm., 370 pp., 2/o boards in yellow linen, with a pictorial cover in red and black, and with a specially designed spine, the whole binding in imitation of a yellowback. It has pale yellow endpapers and a publisher's ad on the back cover. It was listed by *PC* as published Mar. 1–13, 1858.

434 GUSTAVE AIMARD *The Bee Hunters.* Small format. 2/o boards Apr. 22 (*Reader*)
This has no date, 16.6 cm., 336 pp. The first edition was *Les Chasseurs d'Abeilles*, Paris, 1864, 393 pp. The first English edition was issued by John Maxwell & Co., London, 3 vols., 1864, p 8vo, 31/6, advertised in the *Ath* on Sept. 24 as "On Sept. 28" and listed Oct. 1.
Also 1878, 80

435 GUSTAVE AIMARD *Stoneheart.* Small format. 2/o boards Apr. 22 (*Reader*)
This is the first English edition, no date, 16.6 cm., 322 pp. The first French edition was *Le Coeur de Pierre*, Paris, 1864, 12mo, 371 pp.
Also 1878, 80

436 BLANCHARD JERROLD (WILLIAM BLANCHARD JERROLD) *The Disgrace to the Family.* Small format. 2/o boards
Apr. 22 (*Reader*)
The first edition was in six monthly parts, illustrated, 1/o each, issued by Darton & Co., London. Part 1 was advertised in the *Illustrated London News* on May 8, 1847, as "On June 1." They issued it in book form, 1848, p 8vo, 282 pp., illustrated by "Phiz," listed in the *Ath* on Dec. 18, 1847, at 7/o. They issued it as *Parlour Library* No. 187 (1859), 348 pp. The first American edition was issued in parts by Carey & Hart, Philadelphia, part 1 noticed in *Godey's Lady's Book* for Sept. 1847, illustrated by "Phiz." No. 2 was noticed in the Oct. 1847 issue. They issued it in book form, 1848, advertised in *Lit World* on Feb. 26, 1848, as "Recently published."

437 SALLIE R. FORD *Mary Bunyan.* 2/o boards May 6 (*Reader*)
Run and Read Library. The first English edition was as No. 65 of this series, issued by Simpkin, Marshall, London; etc. (1860), at 1/6 boards, about Aug. 27. The first American edition was issued by Sheldon & Co., New York, 1860, 19 cm., 488 pp., illustrated, with Gould & Lincoln, Boston, or T. J. Starke, Richmond, also in the imprint.
Also 1875

438 ANNIE WEBB, later WEBB-PEPLOE
The Five-Pound Note: An Autobiography. 2/o boards June 3 (*Reader*)
Run and Read Library. The first edition was as No. 2 in this series, issued by Clarke, Beeton, London; etc., 1853, 17.3 cm., 277 pp., about Oct. 29, noticed in the *Ath* on Dec. 31, 1853, *The Autobiography of a Five-Pound Note.*
Also 1875, 85

439   EMILIE CARLÉN (EMILIE FLYGARE, later CARLÉN) *A Brilliant Marriage.*
1/0 sewed   June 3 (*Reader*)

This has no date, a duplicate of the first English edition issued by Bentley, London, 1852, with a new title page.
Also 1856

440   RICHARD COBBOLD   *Freston Tower.*
2/0 boards   June 24 (*Reader*)

Run and Read Library. This is a reissue of No. 18 in this series, issued by Simpkin, Marshall, London; etc. (1856), 303 pp., 1/6 boards, with a preface dated Jan. 15, 1856, the same as the preface in the first edition with four lines added. This first *Run and Read* issue was published about Jan. 30, 1856. The first edition was issued by Henry Colburn, London, 1850, 3 vols., illustrated, 31/6, advertised in the *Spect* on May 4, six illustrations, "Just ready," and listed by *PC* as published May 14–29, p 8vo. Wolff's copy has a dedication (May 1850). An edition was listed in the *Spect* on Mar. 8, 1856, no details given. See Sadleir's copy of the first *Run and Read* edition.

441   CATHERINE SINCLAIR   *Jane Bouverie.*
2/0 boards   June 24 (*Reader*)

Run and Read Library. This was issued as No. 15 in this series by Simpkin, Marshall, London; etc., 1855, 1/6 salmon pink pictorial boards, with an engraved frontispiece and title page. It was issued about Sept. 22 and had 16 pp. of series ads, a page of the author's works, and endpaper ads of the series. They issued it at 2/0 cloth, listed by *PC* as published Dec. 15–31, 1855, 12mo, 332 pp. They reissued it as *Cheap Series* No. 4, at 2/0 boards, about June 30, 1860. In the United States it was issued by Harper & Bros., New York, 1851, listed by *Lit World* as published Feb. 22–Mar. 8. It was noticed in *Harper's New Monthly Magazine* for Mar. and in *Godey's Lady's Book* for May. It was also issued by

H. Hooker, Philadelphia, 1851. The first edition was issued by William Whyte, Edinburgh, 1846.
Also 1876

442   CATHERINE SINCLAIR   *The Journey of Life.* [Eleventh edition]. 2/0 boards
June 24 (*Reader*)

Run and Read Library. This was issued as No. 63 in this series by Simpkin, Marshall, London; etc., 1860, the ninth edition, 2/0 boards, with a portrait, about June 26. They issued in at 3/6 cloth about July 28, 1860; and reissued it as *Cheap Library* No. 12, 12mo, 1/6 boards, about Mar. 23, 1861. The first edition was issued by Longmans, London, 1847, Fcp 8vo, 5/0, listed in the *Ath* on July 17. They issued the second edition at 5/0, 1848; and Sadleir had a copy of the third edition, with additions and corrections, issued by Longmans, 1848.

443   MAJOR SKUNKS (pseudonym)
The Great Battle of Patchump.
1/0 picture wrapper   June?

This is the first edition, no date, 130 pp.

444   RACHEL MCCRINDELL   *The Convent.*
Small format. 2/0 boards   July 1 (*Reader*)

Run and Read Library. This is my copy, no date, 16.3 cm., 272 pp., yellow pictorial boards, with the series title on the spine, and publisher's ads on the endpapers and back cover. The first English edition was Aylott & Jones, London, 1848, listed in the *Ath* on Dec. 18, 1847, and noticed on Jan. 29, 1848. They issued a new edition at 5/0 in 1853. It was issued in the present series as No. 27 by Simpkin, Marshall, London; etc. (1857), 1/6 boards, listed in the *Spect* on Apr. 18, 1857. They reissued it in 1861. The first American edition was issued by B. Perkins & Co., Boston, listed by *Lit World* as published May 27–June 3, 1848. It was also issued by Robert Carter,

New York, 1848, 16 cm., 317 pp., listed by *Lit World* as published Oct. 14–21, 1848. Also 1870

445 (ELIZABETH HARDY) **The Confessor.** Small format. 2/o boards   July 8 (*Reader*) *Run and Read Library.* This is my copy, no date, 16.3 cm., 298 pp., yellow pictorial boards in red and blue, with the series title on the spine, and publisher's ads on the endpapers, back cover, and on a white slip tipped onto the front flyleaf. There is a preface by C. B. Tayler. The first edition was as No. 3 in this series, issued by Clarke, Beeton & Co., London; etc., 1854, my copy, with the Tayler preface (Dec. 1852), 17.3 cm., 299 pp., green boards, issued about Dec. 24, 1853, at 1/6 boards, 2/o cloth. The present title is not to be confused with the three vol. Bentley issue of 1851 by (Ellen Walker). *See color photo section*

446 EDWARD YARDLEY, JR. **Fantastic Stories.** 1/o boards   Sept. 23 (*Reader*) This is 1865, a duplicate of the first edition with a new title page. The first edition was issued by Longmans, London, 1864, 150 pp., at 3/6.

Sixpenny Volume Library. 14 vols. o/6 sewed each   Oct. 7 (*Reader*) The following titles began this long series.

447 (M. H. HORSBURGH) **Henry Morgan.** The *BM* gives this as 1863 only.

448 ANONYMOUS **The Rover's Daughter.** This is 1865.

449 ANONYMOUS **The Maniac's Secret.** This is 1865.

450 (MAY A. FLEMING) **The Midnight Queen.** This is 1865 and was first issued as *La Masque* by Cousin May Carleton in the *New York Mercury* as a serial beginning July 16, 1862. It is a story of London during the great plague of 1666. It was issued by Frank Starr & Co., New York, about May 6, 1870, as *Frank Starr's Fifteen Cent Illustrated Novels* No. 7, 21.5 cm., in buff wrappers.

451 (J. H. ROBINSON) **The Cotton Planter's Daughter.** This is 1865, 128 pp. It ran as a serial, *Milrose the Heiress*, in the *New York Mercury* beginning Mar. 29, 1862, and was issued as *Melrose* by J. H. Robinson, by F. A. Brady, New York (1862), 24 cm., 110 pp., illustrated. It was issued by Frank Starr & Co., New York, about Apr. 14, 1871, as *Frank Starr's Fifteen Cent Illustrated Novels* No. 19, 21.4 cm., in buff wrappers.

452 (BRUIN ADAMS, i.e., JAMES F. C. ADAMS) **Nick Whiffles Among the Modocs.** The *BM* gives this as *Nick Whiffles*, London, 1868, anonymous, *Sixpenny Volume Library.* The *Eng Cat* gives Ward, Lock & Tyler, London, 1865, anonymous, o/6, with the title as I've given it. It was issued by Beadle & Adams, New York, about June 17, 1873, as *The Young Spy*, by James F. C. Adams, *Beadle's Dime Novels* No. 284, 16.2 cm., in orange wrappers.

453 (JOSEPH E. BADGER) **Mountain Outlaw.** The *Eng Cat* gives this as issued in 1865, o/6. It was issued by Frank Starr & Co., New York, about Sept. 2, 1873, by Ralph Roy (Joseph E. Badger, Jr.), 16.5 cm., *Frank Starr's American Novels* No. 125, in yellow wrappers, *Rattling Dick, the Mountain Outlaw.*

454 (NED BUNTLINE, i.e., EDWARD Z. C. JUDSON) **The War-Eagle or the Scourge of the Mohawks.** This is 1865 and first appeared as a serial in the *New York Mercury* as *Thayendanegea, the Scourge*, beginning Nov. 27, 1858. It was issued by F. A. Brady, New York (copyright 1858), 24.5 cm., 77 pp., illustrated, by Ned Buntline. It was issued by Beadle & Co., London, about May 1, 1862, as *Beadle's Sixpenny Tales* No. 3, 16.4 cm.

455 ANONYMOUS **The Smuggler's Mystery (The Fatal Cliff).** This is 1865, 128 pp.

456 (MRS. HENRY J. THOMAS) **The Niche in the Wall (The Prairie Bride).** This is 1865. It was issued by Beadle & Co., New York, about May 25, 1869, *The Prairie*

Bride, as *Beadle's Dime Novels* No. 178, 16.4 cm., in orange wrappers.

457 NED BUNTLINE (EDWARD Z.C. JUDSON) *The Fire-Demon.*   This is 1865. It was issued by F. A. Brady, New York, in 1861 or 1862, as *Ella Adams*, 24.5 cm., 84 pp., illustrated, *Mercury Stories.*

458 (NED BUNTLINE, i.e., EDWARD Z.C. JUDSON) *The Ocean Love-Chase.*   This is 1865. It appeared as a serial in the *New York Mercury*, beginning on Aug. 11, 1860, as *The Shell-Hunter*, and was issued with this title by F. A. Brady, New York, no date, 24.5 cm., 78 pp., illustrated, by Ned Buntline, which the *U Cat* and Wright give as (1858). It was issued as *The Shell-Hunter* by Beadle & Co., New York, about Oct. 24, 1871, 21 cm., in wrappers with a pictorial cover in black, as *American Tales* No. 87.

459 *The Black Monk's Curse.* This is 1865.

460 *The Border Hunters.* This is 1865, 128 pp. It could possibly be *The Border Huntress* by William J. Hamilton, issued by Beadle & Co., New York, about Aug. 27, 1872, as *Dime Novels* No. 263, 16.2 cm., in orange wrappers, with a pictorial cover in black.

461 PAMPHILIUS *Economy of Life.* o/6 boards   Nov. 4 (*Reader*)

My Library No. 1. It was advertised in the *Spect* on Oct. 21 as "Now ready," and it is given by the *Eng Cat*. It is probably a first edition.

462 PAMPHILIUS *Patient Boys.* o/6 boards   Nov. 4 (*Reader*)

My Library No. 2. This was advertised in the *Spect* on Oct. 21 as "Now ready," and it is given by the *Eng Cat*. Both this title and the preceding one were issued in 1 vol., at 2/6 cloth, gilt edges, advertised in the *Spect* on Dec. 23, 1865.

463 ARTEMUS WARD (CHARLES F. BROWNE) *Artemus Ward: His Travels.* o/6 sewed   Nov. 11 (*Reader*)

Sixpenny Volume Library. This is 1865, 121 pp., with an introduction by George A. Sala. The first edition was issued by J. C. Hotten, London, illustrated, at 3/6, listed in the *Ath* on Sept. 23, 1865. He reissued it, 1865, 16.3 cm., 192 pp., 1/0 sewed, edited by E. P. Hingston, *Artemus Ward (His Travels) Among the Mormons. Part I—On the Rampage. Part II—Perlite Litteratoor*, about Nov. 11, 1865. It was issued by Carleton, New York; Sampson Low, London, 1865, 231 pp., illustrated, as *Artemus Ward—His Travels. Part I, Miscellaneous; Part II, Among the Mormons*, noticed in the *Ind* on Nov. 2, and listed in *ALG&PC* (fortnightly) on Oct. 2. In England the Low edition was listed in *PC* on Nov. 1. Strangely enough, the sheets or plates of this Ward, Lock edition were used by George Routledge, London, who issued it in 1867 at o/6. Also 1874

464 OLIVER W. HOLMES *The Autocrat of the Breakfast Table.* o/6 sewed   Nov. 11 (*Reader*)

Sixpenny Volume Library. This is 1865, 18.1 cm., 123 pp., with an introduction by George A. Sala, white pictorial wrappers cut flush. It has plain inside covers and a publisher's ad on the back cover. The *U Cat* gives a reissue, 1866. The first American edition was issued by Phillips, Sampson, Boston; Sampson Low, London, 1858, 19 cm., 373 pp., illustrated, with an added illustrated title page. It was advertised as "This day" and listed in the *Ind* on Nov. 25, 1858, at $1.00, and listed in *APC&LG* (weekly) on Nov. 20. It was imported by Low and issued with both names in the imprint but in reverse order and without the illustrated title page. It was advertised in the *Ath* on Dec. 11, 1858, Fcp 8vo, 6/0, as "New American books just received." The first English edition entirely set up and printed in Britain was is-

sued by Alexander Strahan, Edinburgh; etc., 1859 (1858), advertised in the *Ath* on Nov. 20, 1858, Fcp 8vo, 3/6, as "On Nov. 24" and listed there on Nov. 27.
Also 1870, 83

465 PETROLEUM V. NASBY *The Nasby Papers.* Original Stereotyped Edition. 12mo. o/6 sewed   Nov. 11 (*Reader*)
Sixpenny Volume Library. This is my copy, 1865, 18 cm., 88 pp., with an introduction by George A. Sala (Oct. 1865), and a dedication (Aug. 1, 1864). It is in white pictorial wrappers cut flush, with plain inside covers, and a publisher's ad on the back cover. The first edition was issued by C. O. Perrine & Co., Indianapolis, 1864, 19.5 cm., 64 pp., listed in *ALG&PC* (fortnightly) on Nov. 1, 1864. It was issued by S. O. Beeton, London, 1865, 16 cm., 124 pp., 1/o, in Sept., with a preface signed S. O. B. At a Southgate & Co. auction in Apr. 1867, 555 copies were for sale.
Also 1866   *See color photo section*

466 JAMES R. LOWELL   *The Biglow Papers.* (First series). 12mo. o/6 sewed   Nov. 15 (*Reader*)
Sixpenny Volume Library. This is my copy, 1865, 18 cm., 96 pp., reprinted from the original, with an introduction by George A. Sala (Oct. 1865). It is in white pictorial wrappers cut flush, with plain inside covers, and a publisher's ad on the back cover. It was reissued, 1867. At a Southgate & Co. auction in Apr. 1867, 800 copies were for sale. The first edition, by Homer Wilbur, had three different imprints, all 1848: George Nichols, Cambridge, 1,500 copies, noticed in the *Daily Evening Transcript*, Boston, on Nov. 20, 1848, and listed by *Lit World* as published Nov. 18–25; George Nichols, Cambridge; G. P. Putnam's American Literary Agency, John Chapman, London, 100 copies; and George Nichols, Cambridge; G. P. Putnam, New York, 500 copies. Trübner & Co., London, issued it, 1859, Cr 8vo, 140

pp., reprinted from the fourth American edition, newly edited with a preface by (Thomas Highes). It was priced at 3/6 and advertised in the *Ath* on Nov. 5, 1859, as "This day" and listed Nov. 5. It was also issued by J. C. Hotten, London, 1859, 198 pp., frontispiece, 3/6, advertised in the *Ath* on Nov. 5 as "Now ready," and listed also on Nov. 5.
Also 1873

467 ANONYMOUS   *The Queen of the Rangers.* 12mo. o/6 sewed   Nov. 25 (*Reader*)
Sixpenny Volume Library. This is my copy, no date, 18.2 cm., 128 pp., white pictorial wrappers cut flush, with the series title on the front cover. It has plain white inside covers and a publisher's ad on the back cover. The *BM* gives this as 1866.

468 MARGARET BLOUNT (MARY O'FRANCIS) *A Broken Life.* 12mo. o/6 sewed   Nov. 25 (*Reader*)
Sixpenny Volume Library. This is 1866 (1865), 127 pp. It was issued as a serial, *Kitty Atherton*, in the *New York Mercury*, beginning Oct. 4, 1862, and was later issued in book form by F. A. Brady, New York (1863?), 25 cm., 64 pp., with six illustrations, the *Mercury Stories*. It was later issued under various titles in Beadle publications.

469 ANONYMOUS   *The Foundlings.* 12mo. o/6 sewed   Nov. 25 (*Reader*)
Sixpenny Volume Library. This is 1865.

470 ARTEMUS WARD   *Artemus Ward: His Book.* 12mo. o/6 sewed   Dec. 2 (*Reader*)
Sixpenny Volume Library. This is my copy, 1865, 18 cm., 96 pp., reprinted from the original, with an introduction by George A. Sala. It is in white pictorial wrappers cut flush, with plain inside covers, and a publisher's ad on the back cover. The first

edition was issued by Carleton, New York,
1862, 19 cm., 262 pp., illustrated, $1.00,
listed in *APC&LG* (monthly) on May 1,
and advertised in the *Ind* on May 15 as
"New Books." The first English edition
probably came from J. C. Hotten, London, 1865, 19 cm., 210 pp., author's edition, now printed for the first time with
additional chapters and extra sketches,
with notes and a preface by (Hotten). It
was listed in *Notes & Queries* on Mar. 25,
1865, 3/6. The last sketch is spurious. He
issued it at 1/0 sewed about July 1, 1865,
the fourth English edition, 182 pp. The *U
Cat* gives Hotten, 1865, 20 cm., 167 pp.,
with an introduction signed by Hotten. It
was also issued by S. O. Beeton, London,
1865, 16 cm., 168 pp.
Also 1867, 72, 85

471 C. F. ARMSTRONG (F. C. ARMSTRONG)
Perils by Sea and by Land. Small format.
2/0 boards   Dec. 2 (*Ath*)
Library of Popular Authors. This is my copy,
no date, 16.2 cm., 320 pp., yellow pictorial
boards in red and blue, with the series title
on the spine, and publisher's ads on the
endpapers and back cover. The first edition was *The Neapolitan Commander*, issued
by T. C. Newby, London, 3 vols., 1863.

472 C. F. ARMSTRONG *The Pirates of the
Foam.* Small format. 2/0 boards   Dec. 2
(*Ath*)
Library of Popular Authors. This has no
date, 319 pp. The first edition was issued
by T. C. Newby, London, 3 vols., 1863, 21
cm., advertised in the *Reader* on Oct. 17,
1863, as "Just published."

473 CHARLES H. ROSS, ed. *The Great
Gun.* 8vo. Illustrated. 1/0 sewed   Dec. 30
(*Ath*)
This is the first edition, no date, 21 cm., 96
pp., by Boswell Butt, Esq., edited (or
rather written) and illustrated by C. H.
Ross.
Also 1870

474 (ROBERT H. NEWELL) *The Orpheus C.
Kerr Papers.* 12mo. 0/6 sewed   1865
Sixpenny Volume Library. This is my copy,
1865, 18.1 cm., 127 pp., double columns,
reprinted from the original, with an introduction by George A. Sala (Oct. 1865). It
is clothed in white pictorial wrappers cut
flush, with plain inside covers, and a publisher's ad on the back cover. I think this
was just the first series. J. C. Hotten, London, issued the first series at 1/0 sewed,
listed in the *Reader* on Oct. 28, 1865. The
first edition was in 3 vols., series 1–3, illustrated: vol. 1 from Blakeman & Mason,
New York, 1862, 19 cm., 382 pp., $1.00,
advertised in *Harper's Weekly* on Aug. 30 as
"Just published," and listed in *APC&LG*
(monthly) on Sept. 1; vol. 2 was issued by
Carleton, New York, 1863, 367 pp., $1.25,
advertised in the *Ind* on Feb. 12 as "This
week," and listed in *APC&LG* (fortnightly) on Feb. 20; vol. 3 was issued by
Carleton, 1865, advertised in *Harper's
Weekly* on June 17, and listed in *ALG&PC*
(fortnightly) on June 15.
Also 1873, 86   *See color photo section*

475 CHARLES MARTEL (THOMAS DELF),
ed. *Love-Letters of Eminent Persons.*
Fcp 8vo. 1/0 sewed   1865 (*Eng Cat*)
I have a copy, probably a reissue of 1867
judging by the endpaper ads. It has no
date, with an unusual shape, 17 × 10.2
cm., 184 pp., yellow wrappers cut flush,
designed and lettered on the front in red,
yellow, and dark green. There are publisher's ads on the endpapers and the back
cover. The first edition was issued by William Lay, London, 1859, Fcp 8vo, 1/6
boards, advertised in the *Spect* on Apr. 16
at 3/6 and 1/6 fancy boards as "Just ready."
It was in books received in *Notes and Queries* for May 14.

476 JAMES A. MAITLAND *The Watchman.*
2/0 boards   1865 (*Eng Cat*)
Run and Read Library. The first edition was
probably H. Long & Brother, New York

(1855), 19.5 cm., anonymous, 400 pp., $1.00, advertised in the *New York Daily Times* on June 9 as if ready, quoting American reviews. Another edition was advertised on June 10, 5,000 copies, as "This day"; a June 14 ad said 13,000 copies in two weeks. The first English edition was issued by Routledge, London, 1855, my copy, 16.7 cm., 304 pp., 1/6 boards, yellow boards pictorially printed in black, with ads on the endpapers, back cover, and on pp. (1)–8 at the back, the latter dated Sept. 1855. Routledge issued the 18th thousand, 1855. C. H. Clarke, London, issued it at 1/0 boards, listed by *PC* as published Oct. 13–31, 1855, and reissued it as the 33rd thousand at 1/0 in 1861. It was also issued by T. B. Peterson, Philadelphia, listed in *APC&LG* on May 23, 1857.

477 JOHN MILLS *Flyers of the Hunt.* 12mo. 2/0 boards 1865 (*Eng Cat*)

This is my copy, no date, 18 cm., 115 pp., frontispiece and three plates by John Leech, with publisher's ads on the endpapers and back cover, these indicating an 1866 issue. It is in yellow pictorial boards printed in red and black. The first edition was issued by the "Field" office; Ward & Lock, London, 1859, 19 cm., 114 pp., with a colored frontispiece and five colored plates by Leech. Sadleir states that it was also issued with uncolored plates. It was in red cloth at 3/6. The *BM* gives the first edition as described here and also gives a duplicate with a new title page, 1865.
Also 1873, 82

478 JOHN MILLS *Stable Secrets.* 12mo. 2/0 boards 1865 (*Eng Cat*)

This is my copy, no date, 18 cm., 112 pp., frontispiece and three plates, yellow pictorial boards in red, purple, and black. It has publisher's ads on the endpapers and back cover. The first edition was issued by Ward & Lock, London, 1863, 19.5 cm., 112 pp., illustrated, in violet or green cloth, with a picture on the front as for the present edition. It was listed in the *Reader* on Mar. 14 at 2/6. Wolff's copy has an inscribed date of Mar. 1863, and he says that it has a frontispiece and only two illustrations! The ads in my copy indicate an 1866 issue, and a copy was offered for sale with 1865 on the title page.
Also 1873, 82, 85

479 JOHN MILLS *The Life of a Racehorse.* 2/0 boards 1865 (*Eng Cat*)
Also 1854, 56, 73, 82, 85

480 ANONYMOUS *The Practical Letter Writer.* 1/0 1865 (*Eng Cat*)
Also 1862

481 ANONYMOUS *Yankee Humour and Uncle Sam's Fun.* 12mo. 1/0 1865 (*Eng Cat*)

This has no date, 18 cm., 111 pp., illustrated, with an introduction by W. Jerdan.
Also 1860, 82

482 CATHERINE SINCLAIR *Modern Flirtations.* 2/0 boards 1864–66 (*Eng Cat*)

Run and Read Library. This was first issued as No. 8 in this series by Clarke, Beeton & Co., London, 1854, at 1/6 boards, listed in the *Spect* on Sept. 9. *PC* listed a new edition, 12mo, at 4/6 cloth, published Nov. 30–Dec. 15, 1855, J. M. Burton, Ipswitch; Simpkin, Marshall, London. Simpkin, Marshall issued it as *Cheap Series* No. 10, at 1/0 boards, about Jan. 12, 1861. The first edition was issued by William Whyte & Co., Edinburgh; Longmans, London, 3 vols., 1841, listed in the *Ath* on Nov. 13 and noticed on Nov. 20. A second edition was issued in 3 vols. at 21/0 cloth, listed by the *Edinburgh Review* as published Oct.–Dec. 1842. The earliest American edition I've found was issued by Stringer & Townsend, New York, in 1853, $.50 paper, $.75 cloth, *Standard Library of Novels* No. 1, issued monthly. It was listed by *Lit World* as

published May 9–June 11, and noticed in the *Ind* on June 9. They issued a third edition, illustrated, at $.75 cloth, advertised in the *New York Daily Times* on June 27, 1853, as "Now ready."
Also 1875

483 CATHERINE SINCLAIR *Modern Accomplishments.* 2/o boards 1864–66 (*Eng Cat*)

Run and Read Library. This was first issued in this series as No. 20 by Simpkin, Marshall, London; etc., at 2/o boards, about Apr. 12, 1856. They had previously issued it at 4/6 about Dec. 8, 1855, and reissued it as *Cheap Series* No. 1, at 1/6 boards, about Apr. 2, 1860. Ward & Lock issued a new edition, 12mo, at 3/6 cloth, listed by *PC* as published July 16–Aug. 1, 1872. The first edition was issued by Waugh & Innes, Edinburgh; J. Nisbet, London, 1836, Cr 8vo, 7/6, listed in the *Ath* on Feb. 20. The seventh thousand at 7/o was advertised in the *Spect* on Oct. 26, 1839, by William Whyte & Co., Edinburgh; Longmans, London; and the eighth thousand was issued by them, 1841, Sadleir's copy. The first American edition was issued by Robert Carter, New York, 1836.
Also 1876, 78

484 CATHERINE SINCLAIR *Modern Society.* 2/o boards 1864–66 (*Eng Cat*)

Run and Read Library. This was first issued as No. 22 in this series by Simpkin, Marshall, London; etc., at 2/o boards, about July 21, 1856, and reissued in 1859. They issued a new edition, Cr 8vo, 468 pp., at 4/6 cloth, listed by *PC* as published Dec. 15–30, 1855. They issued it as *Cheap Series* No. 3 at 1/6 boards, about June 2, 1860. The first edition was in 1 vol., 1837, issued in London by J. Nisbet (with Waugh & Innes, Edinburgh?), listed by the *Edinburgh Review*, p 8vo, 7/o, published Jan.–Apr. The fifth thousand was advertised by William Whyte & Co., Edinburgh; Longmans, London, at 7/o, in the *Spect* on Oct. 26, 1839; and they issued the ninth thousand, 1847, Sadleir's copy. The first American edition was issued by Robert Carter, New York, 1837.

485 JULIA PARDOE *The Confessions of a Pretty Woman.* Small format. 2/o boards 1865?

Library of Popular Authors. This has no date, with ads on the endpapers in purple, and a back cover ad for the series. The first edition was issued by Henry Colburn, London, advertised in the *Illustrated London News* on Mar. 7, 1846, 3 vols., as "Just ready." The first American edition was issued by Harper & Bros., New York, as *Library of Select Novels* No. 84, listed as new books of the month in the *United States Magazine* (monthly) for July 1846. It was issued by W. P. Fetridge & Co., New York, 8vo, $.50 paper, advertised in the *New York Daily Times* on Dec. 19, 1855, as "Just published."

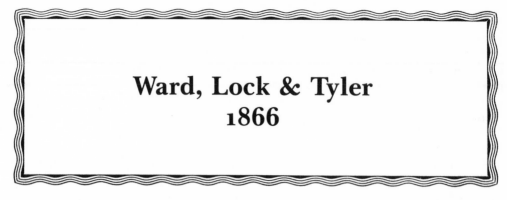

Ward, Lock & Tyler
1866

The last S. O. Beeton & Co. ad in the Ath *appeared on Apr. 28, 1866, and Beeton publications thereafter appeared in Ward, Lock & Tyler ads, as they took over the rights to his titles and the use of his name. In the May 26, 1866, issue of the* Ath, *Beeton announced the postponement of several titles due to his premises in the Strand being required for the new law courts! This was his last gasp. He stayed on with Ward & Lock as an editorial adviser until 1870.*

On Apr. 10, 1866, Ward, Lock & Tyler moved from 158 Fleet Street to Warwick House, Salisbury Square. The Warwick House address was better known as No. 1 Amen Corner, Paternoster Row.

486 F. C. ARMSTRONG **The Sunny South.** Small format. 2/o boards   Jan. 20 (*Ath*)
Library of Popular Authors. This is my copy, no date, 16.8 cm., 320 pp., yellow pictorial boards in red and blue, with the series title on the spine. It has publisher's ads on the endpapers and back cover. The first edition was *The Battle of the Bosphorus,* issued by T. C. Newby, London, 3 vols., 1855. Also 1880, 90   *See color photo section*

487 AZEL S. ROE **Looking Round.** Small format. 2/o boards   Jan. 20 (*Ath*)
Run and Read Library. This has no date, the first English edition. The first edition was issued by Carleton, New York, 1865, 12mo, 312 pp., $1.50, *Looking Around,* listed in *ALG&PC* (fortnightly) on June 15, and advertised in the *New-York Times* on June 6 as "Next week" and as if ready in a June 9 ad.
Also 1872

488 EDGAR ALLAN POE **The Complete Poetical Works of Edgar Allan Poe with a Selection of His Sketches and Reviews.** Small format. Illustrated. 2/o boards Feb. 3 (*Reader*)
Library of Popular Authors. This is my copy, no date, 16.4 cm., 280 pp., with a frontis-piece and many textual illustrations. It is in yellow pictorial boards in red, green, and black, with a vignette title page, and publisher's ads on the endpapers and back cover, and the series title on the spine. It has a life of Poe on pp. (ix)–xl, and there is a white slip tipped onto the front fly-leaf advertising *The Great Gun* (see above). Various editions of the poems (in various states of completeness) were issued, from *Poems,* issued by E. Bliss, New York, 1831, to *Poems, Complete,* issued by W. J. Widdleton, New York, 1863. The Bliss edition had a second edition, 1831, 15.5 cm. page size, 124 pp., in olive green or tan linen with orange, yellow, or white endpapers, and a presentation copy is known (Dec. 1831). Wiley & Putnam, New York, issued *The Raven and Other Poems,* 1845, 91 pp., *Library of American Books* No. 8, reviewed in the *Knickerbocker* for Jan. 1846. They issued it in London, 1846, using American sheets, with a green cloth binding, listed in the *Spect* on Jan. 24, 1846, at 2/6. J. S. Redfield, New York, issued vol. 2 of a four vol. set, *Poems and Miscellanies,* 1850, 19 cm. page size, deposited Jan. 11, 1850, and listed by *Lit World* on Jan. 19, 1850. It was imported by Chap-

man, London, and advertised in the *Ath* on Jan. 11, 1851. Addey & Co., London, issued *The Poetical Works of Edgar Allen Poe*, 1853, 144 pp., the first English edition printed in England and possibly the first illustrated edition, although the *U Cat* gives J. & C. Brown, London, with the same title (1852), 18.5 cm., 185 pp., illustrated, a complete edition, bound in bright red or purple cloth, with a notice of the life by James Hannay. It was twice reissued, the same, probably in 1853 and 1855.

Also 1876

489 ANONYMOUS *Friend Eli's Daughter, and Other Tales.* Small format. 2/o boards
Mar. 3 (*Ath*)

Library of Popular Authors. This is the first edition, no date.
Also 1868

490 ANONYMOUS *Major Jack Downing of the Downingville Militia.* 12mo.
o/6 sewed   Mar. 17 (*Reader*)

Sixpenny Volume Library. This has no date and has an introduction by George A. Sala. It is probably a reissue of *Letters of Major Jack Downing of the Downingville Militia*, issued by Bromley & Co.; J. F. Feeks, New York, 1864, 19.5 cm., 254 pp., illustrated, listed in *ALG&PC* (fortnightly) on Sept. 15. It is not by either of the earlier authors, Seba Smith or Charles Davis. Warne, London, issued it in 1865, with 286 pp., listed in the *Ath* on Aug. 12. The Jack Downing writings were first issued in the *Portland Courier* of Portland, Maine, 1830–33, written by (Seba Smith), and were issued for the publisher, Philadelphia, 1834, 17.5 cm., 212 pp., frontispiece, *The Select Letters of Major Jack Downing of the Downingville Militia, etc.* The *Life and Writings of Major Jack Downing of Downingville, etc.*, was issued by Lilly, Wait, Colman & Holden, Boston, 1833, 260 pp., illustrated, listed in the *American Monthly Magazine*, New York, for Jan. 1834. This latter issue was imported into England by Kennett, London, and listed in the *Ath* on Mar. 15, 1834. Harper & Bros., New York, issued *The Letters, etc.*, 1834, 19.5 cm., 240 pp., illustrated, by (C. A. Davis), which was probably the text used by Murray, London, 1835, 14 cm., 223 pp., 207–215 pp., which the *BM* calls the second English edition.
Also 1875

491 PETROLEM V. NASBY (DAVID R. LOCKE) *The Nasby Papers.* o/6 sewed
Mar. 17 (*Reader*)

This is a reissue in the *Sixpenny Volume Library.*
Also 1865

492 WATTS PHILLIPS *The Wild Tribes of London.* Illustrated. 1/o sewed   Mar. 17 (*Reader*)

Also 1855, 56

493 MARY E. BRADDON *Lady Audley's Secret.* Small format. 2/o boards
Apr. 21 (*Ath*)

This is the first yellowback edition and began the series of reissues of Braddon's novels in this form. Ward, Lock & Tyler advertised in the *Spect* on Apr. 7, 1866, that they had concluded arrangements for the future publication of the Braddon novels. It ran serially in the *Sixpenny Magazine* of Ward & Lock from Jan. 1862 to Dec. 1862, and ran in *Robin Goodfellow*, chapters 1–18 only, from July 6, 1861, to Sept. 28, 1861, and ran in the *London Journal*, a weekly, from Mar. 21, 1863, to Aug. 15, 1863. It was advertised as thoroughly revised for the present edition. The first edition was issued by Tinsley Bros., London, 3 vols., 1862, Cr 8vo, 31/6, by Braddon, advertised in the *Ath* as "On Oct. 1" and listed Oct. 4. William Tinsley, in his recollections, says they paid £250 for it, but the Wolff collection has a letter from Edward Tinsley of Mar. 3, 1863, enclosing

£500! The second edition was advertised in the *Spect* on Oct. 11, 1862, 3 vols., as "Ready this day"; the third edition, 3 vols., 31/6, was advertised there on May 28, 1864, as "Now ready"; the fourth edition in 3 vols., 31/6, was advertised on June 4, 1864, as "This day"; the fifth edition was advertised by John Maxwell & Co., London, in the *Reader* on Sept. 3, 1864, as "This day." A cheap edition was advertised by Maxwell in the *Spect* on Apr. 15, 1865, anonymous, frontispiece, vignette title page, at 6/o. The first American edition was issued by Dick & Fitzgerald, New York, 1863, 8vo, $.50 paper and $.75 muslin, listed in *APC&LG* (fortnightly) on Feb. 2, and reviewed in the *Ind* on Feb. 5. It was advertised in the *New-York Times* on Jan. 24, 1863, and another edition was advertised on Jan. 26 as "On Jan. 27."

494 (MARY E. BRADDON) *Henry Dunbar.* Stereotyped Edition. Small format. 2/o boards   May 12 (*Ath*)

This was the first yellowback edition, my copy, no date, 16.6 cm., 351 pp., yellow pictorial boards in red, green, and black, with the author's name on the spine only, and publisher's ads on the endpapers and back cover. The last 6/o Braddon title on the back cover is *Rupert Godwin* (In the press). My copy is a reissue of 1867, judging by the ads on the endpapers. Wolff also had a later yellowback, no date, with the last title on the back cover being *Run to Earth*. Ward & Lock issued it, Cr 8vo, anonymous, 3/6, listed in the *Spect* on July 11, 1868. The first edition was issued by John Maxwell & Co., London, 3 vols., 1864, p 8vo, anonymous, 31/6, advertised in the *Ath* on May 7 as "On May 10" and listed on May 14. This was the first Braddon novel issued by Maxwell, with whom Braddon had been living since 1861, his wife being in an insane asylum. Tinsley Bros. refused to pay £2,000 for it as they had for the two previous novels, according to Wolff.

495 ISABELLA M. BEETON *How to Manage House and Servants.* Cr 8vo. Illustrated. 1/o printed cloth wrappers   June 20 (*Reader*)

Beeton's House and Home Books No. 1. This is the first edition, no date, 19 cm., 120 pp. It and No. 2 were issued in 1 vol. (1871).

496 (MARY E. BRADDON) *Eleanor's Victory.* Stereotyped Edition. Small format. 2/o boards   June 23 (*Reader*)

This was the first yellowback edition, my copy, no date, 16.3 cm., 400 pp., yellow pictorial boards, with the author's name on the spine only, and publisher's ads on the endpapers and back cover. The ads indicate an 1867 reissue. Wolff's copy had no date, a reissue of 1873. This ran in *Once a Week*, beginning on Mar. 7, 1863, anonymous. The first book edition was issued by Tinsley Bros., London, 3 vols., 1863, advertised in the *Ath* on Sept. 5 as "On Sept. 9" and listed on Sept. 12. According to Wolff they paid £2,000 for the rights for two years. The second edition in 3 vols. was advertised in the *Spect* on Oct. 24, 1863, as "This day" by Tinsley. He advertised a new edition there on Apr. 2, 1864, Cr 8vo, anonymous, 503 pp., one illustration, 6/o, as "This day." It was listed in the *Spect* on Aug. 1, 1868, Cr 8vo, anonymous, 3/6, Ward & Lock. The first American edition was issued by Harper & Bros., New York, 1863, 8vo, illustrated, $.50 paper, advertised in the *New-York Times* on Sept. 29, 1863, as "This day," *Library of Select Novels* No. 236, by Braddon.

497 ISABELLA M. BEETON *The Management of Children in Health and Sickness.* Cr 8vo. Illustrated. 1/o printed cloth wrappers   July 14 (*Ath*)

Beeton's House and Home Books No. 2. This is the first edition, no date, 19 cm., 92 pp. This and No. 1 were issued in 1 vol. (1871).

498 (MARY E. BRADDON) *Aurora Floyd.*
Small format. 2/0 boards   July 21 (*Ath*)

This is the first yellowback edition, 487 pp. The Wolff copy was a reissue of 1875. It ran in the *Temple Bar Magazine*, Jan. 1862–June 1863. The first book edition was issued by Tinsley Bros., London, 3 vols., 1863, p 8vo, 31/6, advertised in the *Ath* on Jan. 10, 1863, as "On Jan. 20" and listed Jan. 17. According to Wolff, Tinsley paid £1,000 for the rights for two years. A second edition in 3 vols., Cr 8vo, 31/6, was issued by Tinsley, listed in the *Reader* on Jan. 31, 1863, and the fifth edition in 3 vols. was advertised in the *Spect* Apr. 11, 1863, as "Now ready." A cheap edition was advertised by Tinsley at 6/0 on Aug. 29, 1863, as "Now ready." In the United States it was issued by Harper & Bros., New York, 1863, 8vo, $.25 paper, advertised in the *New-York Times* on Jan. 16, 1863, as "This day," and advertised in *Harper's Weekly* on Jan. 31 as "Just published." It was also issued by T. B. Peterson & Bros., Philadelphia, 1863, listed in *APC&LG* (fortnightly) on Feb. 2, from advanced sheets, and reviewed in the *Ind* on Feb. 5. It was listed by the *Knickerbocker* as published Jan. 1–Feb. 10, 1863, 8vo, 270 pp., $.25 paper covers. It was listed in the *Atlantic Monthly*, 8vo, 270 pp., $.50 paper, and advertised in the *New-York Times* on Jan. 15 as from *Temple Bar*, 309 pp., double columns, $.75 paper, $1.00 cloth, "This day." Frank Leslie, New York, advertised it in the *New-York Times* on Jan. 16, 1863, 375 pp., $.50 paper, as "Just published." The *English Catalogue* gives a reissue of the present edition in 1868.

499 ISABELLA M. BEETON *How to Dine; Dinners and Dining, etc.* Cr 8vo.
Illustrated. 1/0 printed cloth wrappers July 21 (*Ath*)

Beeton's House and Home Books No. 3. This is the first edition, 18.5 cm., 138 pp.

500 HARRIETTE SMYTHIES (MRS. GORDON SMYTHIES) *Guilty; or, Not Guilty.* Small format. 2/0 boards   Aug. 18 (*Reader*)

Library of Popular Authors. This has no date. The first edition was issued by Hurst & Blackett, London, 3 vols., 1864, 19.5 cm., anonymous, 31/6, advertised in the *Ath* on July 30 as "On Aug. 4" and listed Aug. 6. The *U Cat* gives W. B. Cordier, Montreal; American News Co., New York (1867?), 17 cm., 286 pp.
Also 1885

501 PERCY B. ST. JOHN *The Countess Miranda.* Small format. 2/0 boards Sept. 1 (*Reader*)

Library of Popular Authors. The first edition was issued by C. H. Clarke, London (1861), about Mar. 20, at 2/0 boards, as *Parlour Library* No. 231.

502 (MARY E. BRADDON) *John Marchmont's Legacy.* Revised Edition. Small format. 2/0 boards   Sept. 1 (*Reader*)

This is the first yellowback edition, no date, 413 pp. The *U Cat* and Sadleir both give it as a revised edition, but Wolff's copy, a reissue of 1876, was not so called. It ran in *Temple Bar*, Dec. 1862–Jan. 1864. The first book edition was issued by Tinsley Bros., London, 3 vols., 1863, p 8vo, 31/6, advertised in the *Ath* on Nov. 21 as "On Dec. 1" and listed on Dec. 5, 1863. According to Wolff, Tinsley paid £2,000 for the rights for two years. Tinsley issued the second edition in 3 vols., anonymous, advertised in the *Spect* on Dec. 12, 1863, as "This day"; and issued the third edition, the same, advertised on Feb. 13, 1864, as "This day." The fourth edition, the first one-vol. edition, was issued by Tinsley, 1864, Cr 8vo, 614 pp., 6/0 in blue cloth, advertised in the *Spect* on June 18, 1864, as "On June 24," and advertised on June 25 as "This day." Ward, Lock & Tyler, London, issued a Library Edition, Cr 8vo, with a frontispiece and a vignette title page, 6/o, advertised in the *Spect* on May 5, 1866, as "This day"; and issued it Cr 8vo, anonymous, at 3/6, listed in the *Spect* on Sept. 12, 1868. The first American edition was issued by Harper & Bros., New York, 1863, *Library of Select Novels*, 8vo, $.50 paper, advertised in the *New-York Times* on Dec. 14, 1863, as "Just published," and noticed and listed in the *APC&LG* (fortnightly) on Jan. 1, 1864. T. B. Peterson & Bros., Philadelphia, issued it in 12 numbers, No. 1 listed in *Godey's Lady's Book* for Mar. 1863.

503 ANNE MARSH, later MARSH-CALDWELL *The Wilmingtons.* Small format. 2/o boards   Sept. 1 (*Reader*)

Library of Popular Authors. The first English edition was issued by Henry Colburn, London, 3 vols., 1850, 19 cm., anonymous, advertised in the *Illustrated London News* on Dec. 29, 1849, as "Now ready." It was issued by Simms & M'Intyre, London and Belfast, 1852, as *Parlour Library* No. 79, 368 pp.; and reissued in the *Parlour Library* by C. H. Clarke, London, anonymous, at 2/o boards, about Jan. 11, 1862. The first American edition was issued by Harper & Bros., New York, 1850, *Library of Select Novels* No. 137, 24 cm., anonymous, 136 pp., listed in *Lit World* as published Mar. 16–23.

504 AZEL S. ROE *True to the Last.* Small format. 2/o boards   Sept. 8 (*Reader*)

This was a reissue in the *Run and Read Library.*

Also 1865

505 AZEL S. ROE *A Long Look Ahead.* Small format. 2/o boards   Sept. 8 (*Reader*)

Run and Read Library.

Also 1855

506 ELIZABETH C. GREY *The Old Dower House.* Small format. 2/o boards   Sept. 8 (*Reader*)

Library of Popular Authors. The first edition was issued by T.C. Newby, London, 3 vols., 1844, p 8vo, anonymous, 31/6, listed in the *Ath* on Mar. 2, 1844. It was issued by J. & C. Brown, London (1857), 463 pp., at 2/o boards, listed by *PC* as published Aug. 15–31. The first American edition was issued by T. B. Peterson, Philadelphia (1848), 115 pp., listed by *Lit World* as published Dec. 23–30, 1848.

507 CHARLES H. ROSS *The Eldest Miss Simpson.* p 8vo. Illustrated. 1/o sewed Sept. 15 (*Ath*)

This is the first edition, no date, 18.4 cm., 125 pp., with an extra illustrated title page.

Also 1882

508 MARION HARLAND *Alone.* Small format. 2/o boards   Sept. 15 (*Reader*)

Run and Read Library. This was first issued in this series as No. 33 by Simpkin, Marshall, London; etc., at 1/6 boards, about June 27, 1857. The first edition was issued by A. Morris, Richmond, Virginia, 1854, 19.5 cm., 499 pp. He issued the 15th edition, 1855, 19.5 cm., 384 pp. J. C. Derby, New York, issued the 19th thousand about Jan. 24, 1856; and he claimed that more than 100,000 copies had been sold in the United States by 1884. The first English edition was issued by Sampson Low, London, 1854, Fcp 8vo, 2/o boards, listed in the *Ath* on Oct. 28, and by *PC* as published Oct. 15–31, from advanced sheets by international arrangement.

Also 1871

509 CATHERINE SINCLAIR *Beatrice.* Small format. 2/o boards   Sept. 22 (*Reader*)

Run and Read Library. This was issued in this series by Simpkin, Marshall, London;

etc., 1855, as No. 12, 492 pp., 2/0 boards, listed in the *Spect* on May 19. They issued it at 3/6 cloth, 12mo, 526 pp., listed by *PC* as published May 31–June 14, 1856; and reissued it as *Cheap Series* No. 11 at 1/6 boards, about Feb. 9, 1861. The present edition has no date and 492 pp. The first edition was issued by Bentley, London, 3 vols., 1852, 19.5 cm., listed in the *Spect* on Oct. 2. The first American edition was issued by DeWitt & Davenport, New York, 1853, 19.5 cm., 384 pp., noticed in the *Ind* on Jan. 20, 1853, and advertised in the *New York Daily Times* on Feb. 25, $.50 paper, $.75 cloth, as "Next week." This went through at least 15 editions from DeWitt & Davenport.

510 CAPTAIN STEWART **Harry Hamilton; or, Adventures Afloat and Ashore.** Small format. 2/0 boards   Sept. 22 (*Reader*)
Library of Popular Authors. The first edition was issued by T. Hodgson, London, 1857, as *Parlour Library* No. 171, 311 pp., listed in the *Spect* on Sept. 26. It was issued by C. H. Clarke, London, as *Shilling Readable Novels* No. 3, Fcp 8vo, at 1/0 sewed, about Nov. 1, 1862.

511 ANONYMOUS **The Royal Highwayman.** 12 mo. 0/6 sewed   Sept. 29 (*Reader*)
Sixpenny Volume Library. This has no date.

512 MRS. KEMP **Rachel Cohen, the Usurer's Daughter.** Small format. 2/0 boards   Nov. 3 (*Reader*)
Run and Read Library. This was first issued in this series as No. 60 by Simpkin, Marshall, London; etc. (1860), at 1/6 boards, about June 7, and at 2/6 cloth, about July 28. The first edition was issued by Birns & Goodwin, Bath; etc. (1850), 16mo, 272 pp., in rose cloth, with a frontispiece, an added illustrated title page, and a preface dated Dec. 14, 1849.

513 FRANCIS C. BURNAND **No Secret at All.** 1/0 sewed   Nov. 20 (*Ath*)
This is Beeton's Christmas Annual, seventh season, and the first issue over the Ward, Lock & Tyler imprint.

514 ANONYMOUS **The Book of Animals.** 4to. Colored illustrations. 0/6 sewed, 1/0 cloth   1866 (*BM*) (*U Cat*)
This probably has no date, 24 cm., 68 pp., illustrated by Harrison Weir. The sewed edition is in yellow paper, pictorially printed in blue, red, and black with a cow and her calf on the front cover. A copy with inscribed date of 1874 is shown in Ruari McLean's *Victorian Publishers' Book-Bindings in Paper.* The *Eng Cat* gives *The Pleasure-Book of Domestic Animals*, 4to, illustrated by Weir, 3/6, as issued by Ward & Lock in 1864.

515 (JOSEPH T. J. HEWLETT) **Parsons and Widows.** Small format. 2/0 boards   1866?
Library of Popular Authors. This is given in this series as to follow *The Old Dower House* in publisher's lists.
Also 1857, 58

516 GEORGE CUPPLES **A Country Ghost Story.** Small format. 2/0 boards   1866?
Library of Popular Authors. This was given in publisher's lists of this series as to follow *Parsons and Widows.* Wolff's copy is entitled *Hinchbridge Haunted: A Country Story*, issued by William P. Nimmo, Edinburgh; etc., 1859, 21 cm., 422 pp., with a frontispiece and vignette title preceding the printed title page. It is bound in brown cloth. It was issued by James Blackwood, London, as *Hinchbridge Haunted; A Country Ghost Story*, in May 1881, anonymous, 338 pp., illustrated, at 2/0.

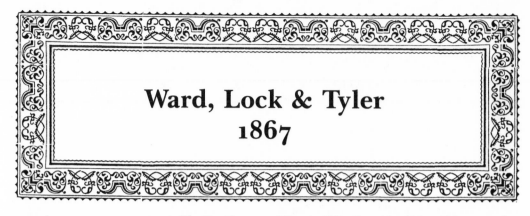

Ward, Lock & Tyler
1867

517 (EDWARD Z. C. JUDSON) *The Death Mystery.* 12mo. o/6 sewed   Jan. (*Bks*)

Sixpenny Volume Library. This has no date and 128 pp. It first appeared as a serial in the *New York Mercury* beginning Apr. 20, 1861, and was issued as *Frank Starr's Fifteen Cent Illustrated Novels* No. 20, about May 12, 1871, with the title *The Secret Vow*, by Ned Buntline.

518 ANONYMOUS *The Secret Revealed.* 12mo. o/6 sewed   Jan. (*Bks*)

Sixpenny Volume Library. This has no date.

519 EDWARD SKELTON *Dictionary of Every-Day Difficulties in Reading, Writing, and Speaking.* 2/o boards   Jan. (*Bks*)

The first edition was probably issued by Ward & Lock, as it was noticed in the *Spect* on Oct. 11, 1862, issued by them. The *U Cat* gives an edition, no date, 18.5 cm., 364 pp., no author given, which was issued after 1882 according to the imprint.

520 RICHARD COBBOLD *The History of Margaret Catchpole.* 2/o boards. Jan. (*Bks*)

Sadleir had a copy, which he thought might be 1870, the 20th thousand, with a frontispiece, bound in bright blue cloth, with an inscribed date (Dec. 15, 1870). Also 1864, 73, 77, 87

521 ANNA M. THORESEN *Signe's History.* 1/o sewed   Jan. (*Bks*)

The first edition was issued in Copenhagen, 1864, 19 cm., 271 pp., as *Signes Historie.* The first English edition was issued by Chapman & Hall, London, 1865, p 8vo, 9/o, translated by M. R. Barnard, titled *Signe's History.*

522 RACHEL MCCRINDELL *The English Governess.* Small format. 2/o boards   Feb. (*Bks*)

Run and Read Library. This first appeared in this series as No. 43 (1858), issued by Simpkin, Marshall, London; etc., at 1/6 boards, 2/6 cloth, about Aug. 14. It was listed in the *Spect* on Nov. 13, 1858, probably a reissue. The first edition was issued by W. H. Darton, London, 1844, 18 cm., 300 pp., and reissued by him in 1848 at 5/o. The Darton first edition was listed in the *Ath* on Oct. 21, 1843, at 5/o.

523 (MARY E. BRADDON) *The Doctor's Wife.* Small format. 2/o boards   Feb. (*Bks*)

Wolff had a copy, no date, of 1875, a yellowback. The first edition was issued by John Maxwell, London, 3 vols., 1864, p 8vo, 31/6, advertised in the *Ath* on Oct. 1 as "On Oct. 10" and listed on Oct. 15, anonymous. It ran in *Temple Bar* (Jan.–Dec. 1864). The fourth edition in 3 vols., 31/6, was advertised in the *Reader* on Nov. 5, 1864, as "Just ready"; and the fifth edition was advertised on Nov. 26 as "Ready." Ward, Lock & Tyler issued it in 1868, Cr 8vo, at 3/6, listed in the *Spect* on July 11. The first American edition was issued by Dick & Fitzgerald, New York, 1864, $.75, advertised in the *New-York*

Times on Oct. 18 as "Just published," from advance sheets, to be issued simultaneously in England and America. They claimed to have paid $2,000 for the advance sheets. It was listed in the *Ind* on Nov. 24 and noticed in *ALG&PC* (fortnightly) on Nov. 1.

524 (MARY E. BRADDON) *Only a Clod.* Stereotyped Edition. Small format. 2/0 boards   Mar. 30 (*Ath*)

This is the first yellowback edition, no date, with the author's name on the spine. Wolff had a copy, no date, in green cloth. The first edition was issued by John Maxwell, London, 3 vols., 1865, anonymous, 31/6, advertised in the *Ath* on Apr. 29 as "On May 10" and listed May 20. It ran in *St. James Magazine* during 1865. The second edition in 3 vols. was advertised in the *Spect* on May 20, 1865, as "Now ready." Ward, Lock & Tyler issued it in 1868, Cr 8vo, at 3/6, listed in the *Spect* on Aug. 1. The first American edition was issued by Dick & Fitzgerald, New York, 1865, advertised in the *New-York Times* on June 6, 224 pp., $.75, as "Just published," and noticed and listed in *ALG&PC* (fortnightly) on June 15.

525 ISABELLA M. BEETON *Meats.* p 8vo. 1/0 printed cloth wrappers   Apr. (*Bks*)

Beeton's House and Home Books. This is the first edition, no date, 189 pp.

526 (ADELINE D. T. WHITNEY) *A Summer in Leslie Goldthwaite's Life.* 1/0 sewed, 1/6, 2/0 cloth   May (*Bks*)

Lily Series No. 1. The first three titles in this series were issued in 1867, and No. 4 didn't appear until 1870! The first edition of the present title was issued by Ticknor & Fields, Boston, 1866, 19 cm., 230 pp., illustrated, $1.75 in morocco cloth, advertised in the *New-York Times* on Dec. 1, and listed in the *Ind* on Dec. 13. It was issued by Sampson Low, London, 1867, 18 cm.,

anonymous, 300 pp., illustrated, advertised in the *Spect* on Nov. 10, 1866.

527 (ADELINE D. T. WHITNEY) *Faith Gartney's Girlhood.* 1/0 sewed   May (*Bks*)

Lily Series No. 3. The first edition was issued by A. K. Loring, Boston, 1863, 19 cm., anonymous, 348 pp., listed in *APC&LG* (fortnightly) on July 1 with F. Leypoldt, Philadelphia, also in the imprint. The first English edition was probably issued by Sampson Low, London, 1865, anonymous, 2/6 boards, listed in the *Ath* on Sept. 23, and in the *Reader* on Oct. 7. He also issued it, 1866 (1865), new edition, by A. D. T. W., 355 pp., at 1/6 boards, advertised in the *Ath* on Nov. 25, 1865, and listed in the *Reader* on Dec. 23. I have a copy issued by Low, 1871, 355 pp., at 1/6, in brown boards decorated in yellow, in *Low's Copyright Series of American Authors.* I think Beeton, London, also issued it in 1865, at 1/0.

528 MAYNE REID *The Mountain Marriage.* Small format. 2/0 boards May (*Bks*)

Library of Popular Authors. This has no date. It first appeared in *Saturday Night,* published by Davis & Elverson, Philadelphia, advertised in the *New-York Times* on Apr. 28, 1866, "Bandolero," to begin in this week's number. The first book edition was issued by Bentley, London, 1866, 20.5 cm., 308 pp., illustrated, 6/0, advertised in the *Ath* on Aug. 25 as "On Aug. 27," and listed on Sept. 8. It was listed in the *Spect* on Sept. 8. It is in green cloth with the title of *Bandolero.*
Also 1876

529 (ADELINE D. T. WHITNEY) *The Gayworthys.* 1/0 sewed   May?

Lily Series No. 2. The first edition was issued by A. K. Loring, Boston, 1865, 19.5 cm., anonymous, 399 pp., listed in *ALG&PC* (fortnightly) on June 15. There

was also a fourth edition, Loring, Boston;
Sampson Low, London (copyright 1865),
the same. Low issued it in 2 vols., 1865, by
A. D. T. W., at 16/0, advertised in the *Ath*
on June 17, as "On June 22" and listed
June 24. He also issued it at 3/6 in 1865
and at 1/6 boards, new edition, 1866
(1865), my copy, about Nov. 11, 1865. The
latter is in white pictorial boards, printed
in red, yellow, blue, and black, 17.5 cm.,
400 pp., with a preface signed A. D. T. W.,
but otherwise anonymous. It has plain
white endpapers and a publisher's ad on
the back. Beeton, London, also issued it,
1866, 17 cm., anonymous, 359 pp.
Also 1870

530 CHARLES H. ROSS *The Extraordinary
Adventures of a Young Lady's Wedding
Bonnet.* p 8vo. Illustrated. 1/0 sewed
June 22 (*Ath*)

This is the first edition, no date, 18 cm.,
125 pp.

531 ISABELLA M. BEETON *Fish and Soups.*
p 8vo. 1/0 printed cloth wrappers   June
(*Bks*)

Beeton's House and Home Books. This is the
first edition, no date, with 130 pp.
Also 1869

532 ISABELLA M. BEETON *Poultry and
Game.* p 8vo. 1/0 printed cloth wrappers
June (*Bks*)

Beeton's House and Home Books.

533 ISABELLA M. BEETON *Puddings and
Pastry.* p 8vo. 1/0 printed cloth wrappers
June (*Bks*)

Beeton's House and Home Books.

534 ISABELLA M. BEETON *Preserves and
Confectionery.* p 8vo. 1/0 printed cloth
wrappers   June (*Bks*)

Beeton's House and Home Books.

535 ISABELLA M. BEETON *Vegetables.*
p 8vo. 1/0 printed cloth wrappers   July
(*Bks*)

Beeton's House and Home Books.

536 (MARY E. BRADDON) *Sir Jasper's
Tenant.* Stereotyped Edition. Small
format. 2/0 boards   July (*Bks*)

This has no date and 457 pp. Ward, Lock
& Tyler issued it in 1868, Cr 8vo, 3/6,
listed in the *Spect* on Nov. 21; and issued it
in cloth, 1866, the sixth edition, 457 pp.,
with a frontispiece. Wolff's copy of the yellowback had no date, a reissue of 1869.
The first edition was issued by John Maxwell, London, 3 vols., in 1865, anonymous, 31/6, advertised in the *Ath* on Sept.
30 as "This day" and listed Oct. 7. He issued the second edition in 3 vols., advertised in the *Spect* on Oct. 7, 1865, as "This
day." The first American edition was issued by Dick & Fitzgerald, New York,
1865, at $.75, from advance sheets, no-
ticed and listed in *ALG&PC* in Nov. 1865,
and advertised in the *New-York Times* on
Nov. 3 as "On Nov. 4." The present edition
was the first yellowback edition.

537 (MARY E. BRADDON) *The Lady's Mile.*
Stereotyped Edition. Small format. 2/0
boards   Sept. 21 (*Ath*)

This is the first yellowback edition, no
date, 16.3 cm., 364 pp., in yellow pictorial
boards with the publisher's ads on the
endpapers and back cover, and with the
author's name on the spine only. My copy
is probably a reissue of 1868. This first appeared in *St. James Magazine.* The first
book edition was issued by Ward, Lock &
Tyler, London, 1866, 3 vols., p 8vo, 31/6,
advertised in the *Ath* on Apr. 14 as "On
Apr. 18" and listed on Apr. 21. With this
novel Ward & Lock became Braddon's
publisher for five years. They issued the
fourth edition in 3 vols. in 1866, advertised in the *Spect* on May 19 as "This day";

and issued it in 1868, at 3/6 cloth, listed in the *Spect* on Sept. 12. The first American edition was issued by Dick & Fitzgerald, New York, in 1866, from advance sheets, at $.75, advertised in the *New-York Times* on May 2 as "On May 4," and as "This day" on May 4.

538 MARY E. BRADDON *The Trail of the Serpent.* Small format. 2/o boards Oct. 20 (*Ath*)

Ward, Lock & Tyler issued this in 1866, 6/o, thoroughly revised and in part rewritten, listed and reviewed in the *Spect* on Aug. 11, the text being the same as for the 1861 issue. Ward, Lock & Tyler advertised it in 1868 at 3/6, Cr 8vo, listed in the *Spect* on Nov. 21.
Also 1861

539 ISABELLA M. BEETON *The Englishwoman's Cookery Book.* New Edition. Illustrated. 1/o Oct. (*Bks*)

This has no date and 208 pp. The first edition was issued by Beeton, London, 1863 (1862), 208 pp., illustrated. There was a reissue by Ward, Lock & Tyler as *Mrs. Beeton's Shilling Cookery Book*, and it was advertised by Ward, Lock & Tyler in the *Times Weekly Edition* (London), on Feb. 9, 1877, 1/o cloth and 1/6 with colored plates. It was reissued around 1880, a new and improved edition, 176 pp., diagrams and colored plates.

540 MRS. M. A. BIRD *Cozynook.* 12mo. 2/o boards Nov. 9 (*Ath*)

This is the first edition, 1867, with 298 pp.

541 MARY E. BRADDON, ed. *Belgravia Annual.* Illustrated. 1/o sewed Nov. 25 (*Ath*)

Ward, Lock & Tyler started this periodical with Braddon as editor in Oct. 1866, the first number appearing on Oct. 24. Another *Belgravia* periodical was started about the same time with offices at 9 St.

Bride's Avenue, Fleet-Street, which office also published *London Society*; the publisher was probably John Maxwell. The Ward, Lock *Belgravia* passed into the hands of Chatto & Windus, London, in Mar. 1876.

542 LYULPH (HENRY R. LUMLEY) *Snow: A Christmas Story.* 8vo. o/6 sewed Nov. (*Bks*)

This is the first edition.

543 ANONYMOUS *Nine of Us.* 1/o sewed Nov. (*Bks*)

This is Beeton's Christmas Annual, the eighth season.

544 (AMELIA BRISTOW) *Emma de Lissau.* Small format. 2/o boards 1867 (*Eng Cat*)

Run and Read Library. This first appeared in this series as No. 44, issued by Simpkin, Marshall, London; etc., no date, 2/o boards, about Sept. 14, 1858. It was listed in the *Spect* on Nov. 13, 1858, a new edition, anonymous, no publisher or price given. The first edition was issued by T. Gardiner & Son, London, 2 vols., 1828, anonymous, 12/o boards, in June. A new edition was advertised by Tilt & Bogue, London, in the *Spect* on Feb. 6, 1841, anonymous, illustrated, 7/6 cloth, 10/6 morocco. David Bogue, London, issued the sixth edition, 1847, 368 pp., illustrated. The first American edition was issued by H. Hooker, Philadelphia, 1855, anonymous, 286 pp., from the sixth London edition.

545 HONORÉ DE BALZAC *Money and Misery.* Small format. 2/o boards 1867?

Library of Popular Authors. I cannot trace this title; it may be a reissue of *Daddy Goriot* (see 1860). In lists of this series given by the publishers, it followed *The Mountain Marriage* (see above).

546 ARTEMUS WARD (CHARLES F. BROWNE) ***Artemus Ward, His Book.*** Small format. 1/o sewed   1867?

This is my copy, no date, 16.1 cm., 168 pp., yellow pictorial wrappers cut flush, with publisher's ads on the endpapers and back cover, and with "Unmutilated edition" on the front cover. I date this from the ads, one of which gives *Sir Jasper's Tenant*, 2/o boards, as "This day." Pages (153)–168 are taken up with *Miscellaneous*.

Also 1865, 72, 85

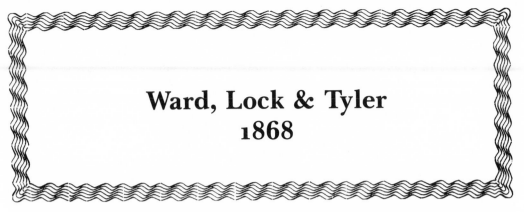

Ward, Lock & Tyler
1868

547 MARY E. BRADDON *Lady Lisle.*
Small format. 2/o boards   Jan. 11 (*Ath*)

This was also issued by Ward, Lock & Tyler in 1866, at 6/o, listed in the *Spect* on Dec. 8, anonymous.
Also 1861

548 BRACEBRIDGE HEMYNG *The Danger Signal, and Other Tales.* 1/o sewed
Feb. 8 (*Spect*)

This is the first edition, 1868, Cr 8vo, 107 pp.

549 A RAILWAY GUARD *On the Line.*
1/o sewed   Feb. (*Bks*)

This was also issued by David Bryce, London, 1866, at 1/o, listed in the *Ath* on May 26.

550 (JOHN T. TROWBRIDGE) *The Three Scouts and Cudjo's Cave.* Small format.
2/o boards   Mar. 14 (*Spect*)

Library of Popular Authors. BAL says this was listed in the *Ath* on Nov. 9, 1867, and in *PC* on Dec. 10, issued by Ward, Lock & Tyler. See the separate title below.

551 ANDREW FORRESTER *The Female Detective.* 12mo. o/6 sewed   Apr. (*Bks*)

Sixpenny Volume Library. This has no date.
Also 1864

552 ANDREW FORRESTER *Revelations of a Detective.* 12mo. o/6 sewed   Apr. (*Bks*)

Sixpenny Volume Library. This has no date.
Also 1863

553 W. H. HILLYARD *Tales in the Cabin.*
12mo. o/6 sewed   Apr. (*Bks*)

Sixpenny Volume Library. This has no date.
Also 1861, 64

554 ANDREW FORRESTER, ed. *Tales by a French Detective.* 12mo. o/6 sewed   Apr. (*Bks*)

Sixpenny Volume Library. This is the first edition, no date.

555 ANDREW HALLIDAY (ANDREW H. DUFF) *The Adventures of Mr. Wilderspin.*
Small format. 2/o boards   Apr. (*Bks*)

Library of Popular Authors. The *Bks* listing gives this as the fourth edition.
Also 1860, 73

556 EMMA J. WORBOISE, later GUYTON *Helen Bury.* Small format. 2/o boards
May 2 (*Spect*)

Run and Read Library. This is my copy, no date, 16.6 cm., 258 pp., with the series title on the spine, yellow pictorial boards. There are publisher's ads on the endpapers and back cover and a leaf of ads at the back. This was first issued in this series as No. 61 by Simpkin, Marshall, London; etc. (1860), at 1/6 boards, about June 14, and at 2/6 cloth about July 28. The first edition was issued by Binns & Goodwin, Bath; etc., in 1850, 12mo, 380 pp., 4/6, listed by *PC* as published July 29–Aug. 14, 1850.

557 OLIVER W. HOLMES *The Guardian Angel.* Small format. 2/o boards   May 2 (*Spect*)

Library of Popular Authors. This was also listed by the *Bks* as issued in May. It ran in the *Atlantic Monthly*, Jan.–Dec. 1867, and ran in the *Weekly Tribune*, New York, advertised as running in the *New-York Times* on Dec. 4, 1867. The first American book edition was issued by Ticknor & Fields, Boston, 1867, 12mo, 420 pp., at $2.00 in morocco green cloth, listed in the *Ind* on Nov. 7, and in *ALG&PC* (fortnightly) on Nov. 15, and advertised in the *New-York Times* on Nov. 5 as "This day." The first English edition was issued by Sampson Low, London, 2 vols., 1867, 19.5 cm., 16/o, listed in the *Ath* on Nov. 2, and in *PC* on Nov. 1. He issued the second edition in 2 vols., Cr 8vo, 16/o, listed in the *Spect* on Feb. 22, 1868. He issued a new edition, 1869, with 301 pp., at 1/6 orange printed boards and 2/o cloth, listed in the *Ath* on Dec. 5, 1868, and in the *Spect* on Nov. 28. He reissued it in his *Rose Library*, 1876. Low went to the Court of Chancery to get an injunction against this Ward, Lock issue. The last six chapters had been published first in Montreal, and the court felt that it could not grant an injunction against the last six chapters. But the vice-chancellor did do so, and thus Ward, Lock were prohibited from publishing the last six chapters. Apparently this caused them to abandon the enterprise, as I've never seen it in any list of ads.

558 ANONYMOUS *The Abyssinian War . . .* 12mo. 1/o boards   May 2 (*Spect*)

This is given by the *Eng Cat*, but otherwise I cannot trace it.

559 MARY E. BRADDON *The Captain of the Vulture.* Small format. 2/o boards May 23 (*Ath*)

Wolff's copy of the yellowback had no date, probably issued in 1876. Ward, Lock

& Tyler issued a revised edition, 1867, Cr 8vo, frontispiece, 6/o, about 20,000 words longer than the first edition of 1862, listed in the *Spect* on Oct. 26, 1867. They issued it, 12mo, 3/6, listed in the *Spect* on Aug. 7, 1869.
Also 1862

560 ANGUS B. REACH & C. W. SHIRLEY BROOKS *A Story with a Vengeance.* Illustrated. 1/o sewed   June (*Bks*)

The *U Cat* gives printed by Robson, etc., London (1852), 19 cm., 119 pp., illustrated; and the same but with only 90 pp. Actually, it was issued by Ingram, Cooke, London (1852), a second edition, revised, 19 cm., illustrated, 1/o sewed, listed by *PC* as published Mar. 13–30. It was printed in red and blue, with a hideous idol on the front, smoke issuing from its nostrils. Nathaniel Cooke reissued it, listed by *PC* as published Dec. 14–31, 1853. The *Bks* calls the present edition the fifth. Ward & Lock issued the third edition, revised, 1856, 128 pp., illustrated.
Also 1882

561 CHARLES DICKENS, ed. *Household Words.* Parts 1–3. 3 vols. o/6 each; quarterly vol. 1, 2/6 sewed   July 11 (*Ath* ad)

This was issued in monthly parts and quarterly vols. Parts 4–6 were advertised in the *Ath* on Sept. 26, and vol. 2 was listed on Oct. 1. Part 1, 120 pp., o/6, was advertised in the *Spect* on Apr. 18, 1868, as "On May 1." The *BM* gives a cheap edition, Mar. 30, 1850–May 28, 1859, 19 vols., London (1868–73). The *Eng Cat* gives a reissue, vols. 1–9, Roy 8vo, 2/6, 3/6 each, and vols. 10–13, 3/6 each, issued by Ward, Lock & Tyler, 1868–71.

562 FRANCIS DERRICK (FRANCES E. M. NOTLEY) *Mildred's Wedding.* Small format. 2/o boards   July 11 (*Spect*)

Library of Popular Authors. This has no date, 336 pp. The first edition was issued by Frederick Warne, London, 3 vols., in 1865, p 8vo, 31/6, listed by the *Reader* on Oct. 7, and noticed in the *Spect* on Nov. 4. The first American edition was issued by Bunce & Huntington, New York, 1866, 8vo, 176 pp., $.75 paper, advertised in the *New-York Times* on Jan. 25, 1866, as "This day," quoting reviews from the *Ath*. It was listed in the *Nation* on Feb. 1, 1866.

563 (MARY E. BRADDON) ***Birds of Prey.*** Stereotyped Edition. Small format. 2/0 boards   Aug. 22 (*Ath*)

This is the first yellowback edition, no date, 352 pp. It first appeared in the first number of *Belgravia*, a periodical of John Maxwell's and edited by Braddon. It ran from Nov. 1866 to Oct. 1867. The first book edition was in 3 vols., issued by Ward, Lock & Tyler, 1867, 19.5 cm., anonymous, 31/6, advertised in the *Ath* on Sept. 14 as "Ready" and listed on Sept. 21. They issued the fourth edition, the same, 1867. They issued the first one-vol. edition in 1868, Cr 8vo, frontispiece and vignette title page, 6/0, listed in the *Spect* on Mar. 14. The illustration on the title page served as the basis for the covers of the yellowback editions. They issued it, 12mo, at 3/6, listed in the *Spect* on Aug. 6, 1869. The first American edition was from Harper & Bros., New York, 1867, 8vo, illustrated, $.75 paper, advertised in the *New-York Times* on Oct. 11 as "This day," and advertised in *Harper's Weekly* on Oct. 19.

564 HENRY J. BYRON ***Paid in Full.*** Small format. 2/0 boards   Aug. 29 (*Ath*)

Library of Popular Authors. This has 460 pp. The first edition was issued by John Maxwell, London, 3 vols., 19 cm., 31/6, advertised in the *Ath* on Jan. 7, 1865, as "On Jan. 16" and listed on Jan. 21. The second edition was issued by him in 3 vols., 31/6, advertised in the *Spect* on Mar. 18, 1865, as "Ready." He issued it in 1 vol., 1865, Cr 8vo, 460 pp., at 6/0, listed in the *Reader* on Aug. 12.

Also 1881, 84   *See color photo section*

565 WILLIAM RUSSELL ***Eccentric Personages.*** Small format. 2/0 boards   Aug. 29 (*Ath*)

Library of Popular Authors. This has no date. The first edition was issued by John Maxwell & Co., London, 2 vols., 1864, p 8vo, 21/0, advertised and listed in the *Ath* on Sept. 24. He issued it in 1 vol., 1865, Cr 8vo, 6/0. It was issued in the United States by the American News Co., New York, 1866, 12mo, 418 pp., $1.75, listed in the *Nation* on Mar. 22, and advertised in the *New-York Times* on Mar. 26 as "Recent."

566 (JOHN T. TROWBRIDGE) ***Cudjo's Cave.*** 1/0 sewed   Sept. 5 (*Ath*)

This has no date and 220 pp. The first edition was issued by J. E. Tilton & Co., Boston, 1864, 12mo, 504 pp., $1.50, listed in the *Ind* on Feb. 11, and in *APC&LG* (fortnightly) on Feb. 15. The Tilton issue also bore the imprint of Trübner, London, and the Trübner was listed in the *Spect* on Mar. 19, 1864. The Tilton issue had severe birth pangs, as delays were announced in the *New-York Times* several times, and according to the Tilton ads there, it was in the third edition before it was ever published! See above

567 MADAME GOUBAUD ***Madame Goubaud's Crochet Instructions.*** Illustrated. 1/0 sewed   Sept. 12 (*Spect*)

This has no date, 16 pp., and 24 illustrations. Also 1871

568 MADAME GOUBAUD ***Madame Goubaud's Berlin Work Instructions.*** Illustrated. 1/0 sewed   Sept. 12 (*Spect*)

This has no date, 15 pp. Also 1870

569 MADAME GOUBAUD ***Madame Goubaud's Embroidery Instructions.*** Illustrated. 1/0 sewed   Sept. 12 (*Spect*)

This has no date, 24 pp., and 65 illustrations. Also 1871

570 ANONYMOUS *Beeton's Book of Acting Charades.* 1/o sewed Sept. 26 (*Ath* ad)
This is a new edition with new wrappers. The first edition was issued by S.O. Beeton, London (1866), 149 pp.

571 ANONYMOUS *Beeton's Riddle Book.* 1/o sewed Sept. 26 (*Ath* ad)
This is a new edition with new wrappers. The first edition was issued by S.O. Beeton, London, 1865, 152 pp., illustrated, and listed by the *Spect* as books received on Jan. 27, 1866, issued by Frederick Warne, London!

572 WILLIAM BROUGH & F.C. BURNAND *Beeton's Book of Burlesques.* 1/o sewed Sept. 26 (*Ath* ad)
This is a new edition with new wrappers. The first edition was issued by S.O. Beeton, London, 1865, 156 pp., illustrated, and was listed as books received in the *Spect* on Jan. 27, 1866, published by Frederick Warne, London! This and the two preceding titles, including copyrights, stereo plates, and remainders of stock, were for sale at a Southgate and Barrett auction, Dec. 10–14, 1866.

573 ROBERT GREENE *The Confidential Advisor.* Cr 8vo. 1/o sewed Sept. (*Bks*)
This is the first edition (1868).

574 ANONYMOUS *Friend Eli's Daughter, and Other Tales.* Fcp 8vo. o/6 sewed Sept. (*Bks*)
Sixpenny Volume Library. This is my copy, no date, 16.8 cm., 169 pp., white wrappers cut flush, with a pictorial front cover in red and green. It has the series title on the front, a publisher's ad of the series on the back, and plain white inside covers. It contains five tales.
Also 1866

575 ANONYMOUS *The Real Experiences of an Emigrant.* p 8vo. 1/o sewed Oct. (*Bks*)
This is the first edition, no date, 19 cm., 128 pp.

576 RACHEL MCCRINDELL *The School Girl in France.* Small format. 2/o boards Oct. (*Bks*)
Run and Read Library. This was first issued in this series as No. 50 by Simpkin, Marshall, London; etc. (1859), at 1/6 boards, a new edition, about June 14, and reissued in 1862. Ward & Lock issued a new edition in 1864, Fcp 8vo, 284 pp., illustrated, at 3/6, listed in the *Reader* on June 18. The first edition was issued by R.B. Seeley & Burnside, London, 1840, Fcp 8vo, anonymous, 6/o, listed in the *Ath* on May 2. They issued the second edition, by McCrindell, 1842, 16.5 cm., 363 pp. The *BM* gives Philadelphia, 1845, anonymous, the first American edition from the last London edition. J.K. Wellman, New York, issued it, 1845, second edition, 17 cm., with the cover reading "Fourth edition"; and reissued it, 1846, fourth edition, 248 pp. H. Hooker, Philadelphia; etc., issued it, 1846, 16 cm., anonymous, 280 pp., as *The Protestant Girl in a French Nunnery*, called the fourth edition from the last London edition.

577 LYULPH (HENRY R. LUMLEY) *Something Like a Nugget.* 8vo. o/6 sewed Nov. 9 (*Ath*)
This is a Christmas story, probably the first edition. It has no date and 48 pp. The *BM* gives London (1868); and also London, 1868, a drama in four acts (and in prose); and London, 1868, another edition, abridged.

578 MADAME GOUBAUD *Madame Goubaud's Embroidery Book.* 1/o sewed Nov. 14 (*Ath*)
This has no date and contains 85 patterns.

579 (JOHN T. TROWBRIDGE) *The Three Scouts.* 8vo. 1/o sewed Nov. 14 (*Ath*)
This has no date, 21.5 cm., 174 pp., with a Beeton device on the title page. The first edition was issued by J.E. Tilton & Co.,

Boston, 1865, 18 cm., 381 pp., $1.75, advertised in the *New-York Times* on Jan. 21 as "This morning," and listed in *ALG&PC* (fortnightly) on Feb. 1.

Also above and 1885

580 CHARLES DICKENS ET AL. *Household Words Christmas Stories. 1855–58.* 8vo.
1/0 sewed   Nov. 14 (*Ath*)

This has no date, 22.2 cm., in a colored wrapper. It is uniform with the 1869 issue (which see). Ward, Lock & Tyler advertised in the *Spect* on Nov. 12, 1870, both series (the present vol. and the 1869 vol.) at 1/0 sewed each, and both in 1 vol. at 2/0 sewed, 3/6 cloth. The extra Christmas numbers for 1850–58 were issued by Chapman & Hall, London; All the Year Round Office (1859), nine parts, Roy 8vo, 2/6 cloth, listed by *PC* as published Dec. 14–31, 1859. The present edition contains four of them.

See 1869

581 ANONYMOUS *Money Lent.* 1/0 sewed
Nov. 14 (*Ath*)

This is Beeton's Christmas Annual, ninth season.

582 MARY E. BRADDON, ed. *Belgravia Annual.* 1/0 sewed   Nov. 18 (*Ath*)

583 DANIEL DEFOE *Robinson Crusoe.*
Square. Illustrated. 0/6 sewed   Nov. or Dec. (*Bks*)

Also 1863, 64, 79, 85

ANONYMOUS *Beeton's Country Books.*
8 vols. Illustrated. 1/0 sewed each
Nov. or Dec. (*Bks*)

These each had one or more colored plates. They were extracted from *The Book of Home Pets*, issued by S. O. Beeton, London (1861, 1862), 18.5 cm., 832 pp., illustrated, colored plates, advertised in a Ward, Lock & Tyler catalog of 1873 at 7/6

half-bound, with 11 colored plates. *Beeton's Book of Poultry and Domestic Animals* was also extracted (pp. 353–832) and issued in 1870, 18.5 cm., illustrated, and with 5 colored plates, at 3/6 cloth. The *BM* gives the titles below as issued by Bickers & Bush, London (1862). The pages given for the titles below are from *The Book of Home Pets*.

584 *Poultry and Pigeons,* pp. 353–480.
585 *British Song and Talking Birds*
586 *British Song Birds*
587 *The Parrot Book*
588 *Birds' Nests and Eggs.* Also 1877
589 *Rabbits ... with Chapters on ... Squirrels, Mice, etc.,* pp. 481–544 and 673–704.
590 *Bees, Silkworms, and Inhabitants of the Aquarium,* pp. 705–832.
591 *Dogs ... with a Chapter on ... Cats,* pp. 545–672.

592 MADAME GOUBAUD *Madame Goubaud's Crochet Book.* 1/0 sewed
Dec. 1 (*Ath*)

This has no date and contains 48 patterns.

593 FANNY MAYNE *Jane Rutherford.*
Small format. 2/0 boards   1868 (*Eng Cat*)
Run and Read Library. The first edition was the issue in this series by Clarke, Beeton & Co., London; etc., 1854, as No. 4, 17.3 cm., illustrated, 1/6 boards, about Mar. 25, by "a Friend of the People."

594 AZEL S. ROE *Time and Tide.* Small format. 2/0 boards   1868 (*Eng Cat*)
Run and Read Library. The first English edition was the issue in this series by Simpkin, Marshall, London; etc., 1860, as No. 55, 1/6 boards, about Dec. 24, 1859. The first edition was issued by D. Appleton & Co., New York, 1852, 243 pp., $.50 paper, $.75 cloth, advertised in the *New-York Times* on July 7 as "On July 8," and listed by *Lit World* as published July 1–12.

Ward, Lock & Tyler
1869

595 (MARY E. BRADDON) *Charlotte's Inheritance.* Stereotyped Edition. Small format. 2/0 boards   Jan. 30 (*Ath*)

This is the first yellowback edition, my copy, no date, 16.6 cm., 336 pp., with the author's name on the spine only, yellow pictorial boards. There are publisher's ads on the endpapers, back cover, and a leaf of ads at the back. I have another copy, the same except for variant printing on the front cover, a different publisher's ad on the back cover, and having plain endpapers. It was issued in 1872. This story is the conclusion of *Birds of Prey*. The first edition was issued by Ward, Lock & Tyler, London, 3 vols., 1868, Cr 8vo, 31/6, advertised in the *Ath* on Feb. 15 as "This day" and listed on Feb. 22. They issued the fifth edition in 3 vols., advertised in the *Spect* on Feb. 29, 1868, and issued it in 1 vol., Cr 8vo, anonymous, 6/0, listed in the *Spect* on Sept. 12, 1868. The first American edition was issued by Harper & Bros., New York, 1868, 8vo, 145 pp., $.50 paper, *Library of Select Novels* No. 30. It was advertised in the *New-York Times* on Apr. 10 as "This day," and listed in *ALG&PC* (fortnightly) on Apr. 15.

596 ANONYMOUS *The Gambler's Last Throw.* 1/0 sewed   Feb. 6 (*Ath*)

This is the first edition, no date, by the author of *On the Line* (see 1868).

597 ANONYMOUS *The Great Convent Case.* 8vo. 1/0 sewed   Feb. 27 (*Spect*)

This is my copy, no date, 21.5 cm., 174 pp., with a preface by James Grant. It is bound in white wrappers cut flush and printed on the front in red and aquamarine, with plain inside covers, a leaf of publisher's ads at the back, and a commercial ad on the back cover. The preface is dated Feb. 25, 1869. The front cover has "The Great Nunnery Trial" and "Saurin v. Star and Kennedy" and "Sole unabridged and Authentic Report." There were many accounts of this trial including *Extraordinary Trial by a Sister of Mercy*, issued by E. Griffiths, London (1869), 22 cm., 192 pp., with portraits. There was also an account from the *Times* issued by Diprose & Bateman, London (1869), 22 cm., 264 pp., portrait.

598 (MARY E. BRADDON) *Rupert Godwin.* Stereotyped Edition. Small format. 2/0 boards   May 1 (*Ath*)

This is the first yellowback edition, no date, 315 pp. Wolff's copy had an inscribed date of Jan. 24, 1870. The second installment in the *Sunday Mercury* (New York) was advertised in the *New-York Times* on Dec. 9, 1865, as "Tomorrow." The first book edition was issued by Ward, Lock & Tyler, 3 vols., 1867, p 8vo, 31/6, advertised in the *Ath* on July 6 as "This day" and listed on July 13. Wolff states that this first appeared in the *Halfpenny Journal* as *The Banker's Secret*, running from Nov. 21, 1864, to June 5, 1865. It was then translated into French and then retranslated back into English to run in the *New York Mercury*. Ward, Lock & Tyler issued the third edition in 3 vols. in 1867, advertised in the *Spect* on July 13; and they issued the fourth edition in 3 vols., advertised in the *Spect* on July 27, 1867, as "Now ready." The first American edition was issued by Dick & Fitzgerald, New York, 1867, 8vo, 231 pp., $.75, advertised in the *New-York Times* on Oct. 3, by Braddon, as "This day," and listed in *ALG&PC* (fortnightly) on Oct. 15.

The Parlour Library. 7 vols. o/6 sewed each May 29 (*Ath*)

An ad in the *Ath* stated that Ward, Lock were again issuing the *Parlour Library*, some at o/6, some at 1/o, and some at 2/o. This was not strictly true, as they had merely acquired the right to use the name in issuing the titles given passim below. Neither Sadleir nor I have ever found a 2/o title. The only title in the o/6 series that Sadleir had seen was in paper wrappers cut flush, printed in black, green, and yellow.

599 **The Child's Own Book of Tales.** The *BM* gives only *The Child's Own Book of Pictures, Tales and Poetry* (1870), illustrated. The *Eng Cat* gives *The Child's Own Book of Tales, The Silver Acre,* issued in 1869, o/6. Actually *The Silver Acre* by William Carleton was listed in this bunch of 7 vols., and it with other tales was issued in the *Shilling Volume Library* (see 1862).

600 **The Boy's Own Book of Tales.** This is probably the first edition, no date, 125 pp.

601 ANNIE THOMAS **Lady Lorne.** See the *Shilling Volume Library,* 1863

602 WILLIAM CARLETON **The Fair of Emyvale and The Master and Scholar.** This is probably the first edition. *The Fair of Emyvale* ran in the *Illustrated London Magazine* July–Sept. 1853, illustrated.

603 **The Book of Moral Tales.** I cannot trace this.

604 WILLIAM CARLETON **The Silver Acre.** See the *Shilling Volume Library,* 1862

605 ANNIE THOMAS **The Dream and the Waking.** This has no date. See the *Shilling Volume Library,* 1863

The Parlour Library. 7 vols. 1/o sewed each May 29 (*Ath*)

The only title Sadleir had was in white wrappers cut flush, pictorially printed in black, scarlet, and yellow with the series title on the front and spine, and with a publisher's ad on the back cover.

606 LADY SARAH GOODCHILD (pseudonym). **Lady Goodchild's Fairy Ring.** This has no date. The first edition was issued by Houlston & Wright, London (1860), 19 cm., 376 pp., illustrated, 5/o.

607 HENRY R. ADDISON **Recollections of an Irish Police Magistrate.** Also 1862

608 LOUIS CANLER **Autobiography of a French Detective.** Also 1862

609 CHARLES J. COLLINS **Dick Diminy, the Jockey.** Also 1855, 75

610 EDMOND F. V. ABOUT **The Greek Brigand.** This has no date, illustrated by Doré. Also 1862 as *The King of the Mountain*

611 MRS. FENTON AYLMER **Memoirs of a Lady in Waiting.** This has no date. Also *Shilling Volume Library,* 1861

612 **Clever Jack.** *Clever Jack and Other Tales* was issued by James Miller, New York, 1864, by Anne Bowman, but I suspect it was not the present title. The full title of the present issue is *Clever Jack; or, The Adventures of a Donkey, by Himself,* and is given by the *Eng Cat* as issued by Ward, Lock in 1869, 12mo, anonymous, 1/o. It was issued by J. B. Lippincott & Co., Philadelphia, 1871, advertised in the *New-York Times* on Dec. 3, 1870, 16mo, anonymous, illustrated, $1.00, as "Just issued."

613 ISABELLA M. BEETON **Fish and Soups.** 1/o May?

Also 1867

The Parlour Library. 5 vols. June (*Bks*)

614 **The Young Lady's Book of Tales.** This is probably the first edition, no date, illustrated, o/6 sewed.

615 ROBERT WARNEFORD (WILLIAM RUSSELL) **The Cruise of the Blue Jacket.** This has no date, o/6 sewed. Also in the *Shilling Volume Library*, 1861

616 WATERS (WILLIAM RUSSELL) **Undiscovered Crimes.** This has no date, o/6 sewed. Also 1862

617 EDMOND ABOUT **The Round of Wrong.** 12mo, 1/o sewed. Also *Shilling Volume Library*, 1861

618 **The Funny Fellow.** 12mo, illustrated, 1/o sewed. Also 1862. This title was listed in the *Spect* on June 19, and the preceding title was listed on June 12.

619 (MARY E. BRADDON) **Run to Earth.** Small format. 2/o boards July 17 (*Spect*) This is the first yellowback edition. According to Wolff, this first appeared as *Diavola* in the *London Journal*, Oct. 27, 1863–July 20, 1867, anonymous. The *New York Sunday Mercury* bought sheets from John Maxwell and issued it as *Nobody's Daughter*, by Braddon, probably in 1866. The first English edition was issued by Ward, Lock & Tyler, London, 3 vols., 1868, Cr 8vo, 31/6, advertised in the *Ath* on Sept. 26 as "On Oct. 3" and listed Oct. 3. They issued the second edition in 3 vols., advertised in the *Spect* on Oct. 24, 1868; and they issued the fourth edition in 3 vols., 1868. In the United States it was issued as *Diavola; or, Nobody's Daughter*, from advanced sheets, 8vo, 270 pp., $.75, advertised in the *New-York Times* on July 10, 1867, as "This day," by Dick & Fitzgerald, New York.

The Parlour Library. 5 vols. July (*Bks*)

620 ALBANY FONBLANQUE, JR. **The Filibuster.** o/6 sewed. Also in the *Shilling Volume Library*, 1862

621 (EMMA ROBINSON) **Cynthia Thorold.** 1/o sewed. Also in the *Shilling Volume Library*, 1862

622 AUGUSTUS MAYHEW, ed. **Blow Hot— Blow Cold.** This has no date, 1/o sewed. Also in the *Shilling Volume Library*, 1862

623 (EMMA ROBINSON) **Which Wins, Love or Money?** 1/o sewed. Also in the *Shilling Volume Library*, 1861

624 PERCY H. FITZGERALD **The Night Mail.** 1/o sewed. Also in the *Shilling Volume Library*, 1861

The Parlour Library. 12 vols. Aug. (*Bks*)

625 GEORGE A. SALA. **The Ship Chandler.** o/6 sewed. Also in the *Shilling Volume Library*, 1862

626 J. W. MARSTON **The Family Credit.** o/6 sewed. Also in the *Shilling Volume Library*, 1861

627 ALBANY FONBLANQUE, JR. **Give a Dog a Bad Name and —. With Other Tales.** This is the first edition, no date, o/6 sewed.

628 J. W. MARSTON **The Wife's Portrait; and Other Tales.** This is the first edition, no date, o/6 sewed.

629 INSPECTOR F. **Mrs. Waldegrave's Will and Other Tales.** edited by Waters (William Russell). This is the first edition, no date, o/6 sewed.

630 WATERS, ed. **Experiences of a Real Detective.** o/6 sewed. Also *Shilling Volume Library*, 1862

631 GEORGE A. SALA **The Late Mr. D—, and Other Tales.** This is the first edition, no date, o/6 sewed.

632 **The Little Red Man and Other Tales.** o/6 sewed, illustrated. This is the first edition, no date, illustrated by "Phiz" et al.

633 WATERS **Leonard Harlowe.** 1/o sewed. Also as *The Game of Life*, 1857, 58, and as *Leonard Harlowe*, 1862, in the *Shilling Volume Library*

634 GEORGE A. SALA **Make Your Game.** 1/o sewed. Also 1860 and as *Shilling Volume Library*, 1864

635 W.S. HAYWARD **Hunted to Death.**
1/0 sewed. Also 1873, 74 and *Shilling Volume Library,* 1862

636 VANE I. ST. JOHN **The Chain of Destiny.** 1/0 sewed. Also in the *Shilling Volume Library,* 1862

637 WILLIAM JOHNSTON **Nightshade.** Small format. 2/0 boards   Sept. 11 (*Spect*)

Run and Read Library. This first appeared in this series as No. 41, issued by Simpkin, Marshall, London; etc. (1858), 1/6 boards, a new and corrected edition, listed in the *Spect* on July 31, 1858. The first edition was issued by Bentley, London, 1857, p 8vo, 5/0, advertised in the *Ath* on Apr. 11 as "Just Ready."

638 (ANNIE EDWARDES) **The Morals of Mayfair.** 12mo. 2/0 boards   Sept. 18 (*Ath*)

Also 1863, 70, 74

639 GEORGE A. SALA **The Perfidy of Captain Slyboots.** 0/6 sewed   Sept. (*Bks*)
Parlour Library.
Also *Shilling Volume Library,* 1863

640 ANONYMOUS **Something to Laugh At.** 1/0 sewed   Sept. (*Bks*)
Parlour Library.
Also 1862

641 (PERCY H. FITZGERALD) **The Reverend Alfred Hoblush and His Curacies.** 12mo. 1/0 sewed   Oct. 30 (*Spect*)

Parlour Library. The first edition was issued by John Maxwell & Co., London, 1863, p 8vo, 309 pp., 10/6, advertised and listed in the *Ath* on Sept. 19. He reissued it at 2/0 boards about Sept. 24, 1864, both editions being anonymous.

642 MARTINGALE (JAMES WHITE) **Turf Characters.** 0/6 sewed   Oct. (*Bks*)
Parlour Library. The first edition was issued by Bentley, London, 1851, at 1/0

boards, as *Shilling Series* No. 3, about Dec. 6, 1851. He reissued it, 1852 (Sadleir's copy).

643 ROBERT BUCHANAN & CHARLES GIBBON **Storm-Beaten.** 1/0 sewed   Oct. (*Bks*)

Parlour Library. This was Sadleir's copy, no date, in white paper wrappers, pictorially printed in black, scarlet, and yellow, with the series title on the front cover and spine.
Also *Shilling Volume Library,* 1861

644 (MARY E. BRADDON) **Dead Sea Fruit.** Stereotyped Edition. Small format. 2/0 boards   Nov. 6 (*Ath*)

This has no date, 348 pp., the first yellowback edition. The first edition was issued by Ward, Lock & Tyler, 3 vols., 1868, Cr 8vo, anonymous, 31/6, advertised in the *Ath* on May 23 as "On May 20" and listed May 23. The first American edition was issued by Harper & Bros., New York, 1868, 8vo, illustrated, $.50 paper, advertised in the *New-York Times* on July 3 as "This day," and listed in *ALG&PC* (fortnightly) on July 15.

645 CHARLES DICKENS ET AL. **Household Words Christmas Stories.** 8vo. 1/0 sewed Nov. (*Bks*)

This is my copy, no date, 22.2 cm., various pagination, white wrappers cut flush, decorated and printed on the front in red, green, blue, and black. There is no title page, the front cover acting as such. It contains four Christmas stories, 1851–54 with separate caption titles and pagination, double columns. There are ads on the back cover, inside covers, on pp. (1)–8 in front, and on pp. 9–12 plus 6 pp. at the back. The Christmas stories for 1851–58 were issued at 2/6 sewed, 3/6 cloth, about Oct. 29, 1870.
See 1868

646 **This Way Out.** Illustrated. 1/o sewed
Nov.
Beeton's Christmas Annual, tenth season.

647 MARY E. BRADDON, ed.
Belgravia Annual. 1/o sewed
Nov. (*Bks*)

648 S. O. BEETON **Beeton's British
Gazetteer.** 1/o sewed, 1/6, 2/o cloth
Dec. 11 (*Spect*)
This is the first edition, no date, 18 cm.,
284 pp.

649 (MARY E. BRADDON) **Ralph the
Bailiff, and Other Stories.** Stereotyped
Edition. Small format. 2/o boards
Dec. 25 (*Ath*)
This has no date, 350 pp., and contains an
added story beyond the 12 in the 1867
edition. It was reissued, Cr 8vo, at 6/o,
listed in the *Spect* on Dec. 12, 1868.
Also 1862

650 MADAME GOUBAUD **Madame
Goubaud's Book of Monograms and
Initials.** 16mo. 1/o sewed   Dec. 25 (*Spect*)
This is the first edition, no date, 18 cm.,
284 pp.

651 ANONYMOUS **British Ferns and
Mosses.** Illustrated. 1/o   1869 (*Eng Cat*)
This has no date.
Also 1861, 80

652 ANONYMOUS **Marine Botany and
Sea-Side Objects.** Illustrated. 1/o   1869
(*Eng Cat*)
This has no date.
Also 1861, 80

653 MARY M. SHERWOOD (M. M. BUTT,
later SHERWOOD) **The Nun.** 2/o boards
1869 (*Eng Cat*)
Also 1864, 76, 85

654 ANONYMOUS **Wild Flowers.**
Illustrated. 1/o   1869 (*Eng Cat*)
Also 1861, 80

655 WATERS (WILLIAM RUSSELL)
The Valazy Family. o/6 sewed
1869 (*Eng Cat*)
Parlour Library. This is the first edition, no
date.

656 LT. WARNEFORD (WILLIAM RUSSELL)
Mutiny of the Saturn. o/6 sewed   1869?
Parlour Library. This is probably the first
edition, no date. Sadleir gives it in his list
of the *Parlour Library.* I cannot trace it, although there is a known copy.

Ward, Lock & Tyler
1870

Ward, Lock & Tyler acquired Edward Moxon, Son & Co. in 1870.

657 ELIZABETH S. PHELPS, later
WARD **The Gates Ajar.** 12mo. 1/0 sewed
Jan. 29 (*Spect*)

Lily Series No. 4. This has no date, 155 pp.
This was listed by the *Bks* as 1/0 in Jan. and
1/6 in Apr. 1870. Ward, Lock & Tyler issued the 20th thousand, no date, 1/0, in
glazed emblematic colored wrappers in
brown and green, with 30 pp. of ads, and
ads on the endpapers. The first edition
was issued by Fields, Osgood & Co., Boston, 1869, 18 cm., 248 pp., advertised in
the *Ind* on Feb. 25 as "New books"; it was
given a short review in *Harper's New
Monthly Magazine* for Mar. 1869. It was issued by E. A. Taylor & Co., London, On-
tario, 1869, 12mo, 190 pp. The first English edition was issued by Sampson Low,
London (1869), 32mo, 1/0 cloth, advertised in the *Ath* on May 22 as "Ready." He
advertised it at 14/0, illustrated, on Jan. 8,
1870. George Routledge, London, issued
it at 0/4 sewed, and in cloth at 0/6, 1/0, 2/0,
and 3/6, all advertised in the *Ath* on May
14, 1870; the 2/0 was listed in the *Spect* on
June 11; and the 3/6 was listed there on
Mar. 5, 1870, and in the *Ath* on Mar. 15.
Other publishers also issued it in 1869
and 1870.

658 MADAME GOUBAUD **Madame
Goubaud's Knitting and Netting Book.**
1/0 Jan. (*Ath*)

This is the first edition, no date, with 64
patterns.

659 BRACEBRIDGE HEMYNG **The Man of
the Period.** 12mo. 1/0 sewed Feb. 26
(*Ath*)

Everybody's Library No. 1. This is the first
edition, no date. It was also listed by the
Spect on Feb. 26 and by the *Bks* as published in Mar. I think Sadleir must have
been mistaken in stating that the first edition was from C. H. Clarke, London.
They indeed issued it at 1/0 sewed, no
date, but about June 22, 1872!

660 BRACEBRIDGE HEMYNG **The Season
at Brighton.** 12mo. 1/0 sewed Feb. 26
(*Ath*)

Everybody's Library No. 2. This is the first
edition, no date. It was issued by C. H.
Clarke & Co., London, in 1872, as *Alma
Maitland*, 12mo, 1/0 sewed.

661 OLIVER W. HOLMES **The Autocrat
of the Breakfast Table.** 1/0 Feb. (*Bks*)

This is a reissue with the Sala introduction.
Also 1865, 83

662 MADAME GOUBAUD **Madame
Goubaud's Point Lace Book, Instructions
and Patterns.** 16mo. Illustrated.
1/0 sewed Mar. 12 (*Spect*)

This is the first edition. The 32nd thousand was issued in 1878, with 56 pp.

663 MICHAEL & JOHN BANIM **The Peep
O'Day.** 12mo. 2/0 Apr. 9 (*Spect*)

This has been frequently issued as *John
Doe*. The first edition was issued by W.

Simpkin & R. Marshall, London, 3 vols., 1825, anonymous, *Tales by the O'Hara Family*, containing *Crohoore of the Bill-Hook*; *The Fetches*; and *John Doe*. Part 3, containing *John Doe* and *Peter of the Castle*, was issued by Simms & M'Intyre, Belfast; etc., in Nov. 1846, as *Parlour Novelist* No. 11, listed in the *Ath* on Nov. 7, 1846, Fcp 8vo, 2/6 cloth. *John Doe* was issued as *Parlour Library* No. 88, 1853. In the United States it was issued by H. C. Carey & I. Lea, Philadelphia, 2 vols., 1827, 18 cm., 500 copies, finished Feb. 8, 1827, according to the Carey & Lea cost book. *The Peep O'Day* was issued by the Petersen Publishing Co., New York, no date, 17 cm., 102 pp.

664 (HERBERT B. HALL) *The Pigskins Abroad.* Cr 8vo. 1/0   Apr. 23 (*Ath*)
This is the first edition, no date, 124 pp.

665 CHARLES DICKENS, ed. *The Pic-Nic Papers. Part 1.* 12mo. 1/0 sewed   Apr. 23 (*Spect*)
Part 2 was listed in the *Spect* on June 11, and parts 3 and 4 were listed by the *Bks* as published in July and listed in the *Spect* on July 2.
Also 1859, 62, 65, 82

666 BRACEBRIDGE HEMYNG *Eton School Days.* 12mo. 2/0   May 7 (*Ath*)
This has no date, 316 pp. The first edition was issued by John Maxwell & Co., London, 1864, by An Old Etonian, p 8vo, 10/6, advertised and listed in the *Ath* on Nov. 28, 1863. He issued it at 2/0 boards, 1864, about Oct. 8. At a Hodgson auction of Oct. 31, Nov. 1, 2, 1865, 840 copies were for sale.

667 JANE PORTER *The Scottish Chiefs.* 12mo. 2/0 boards   May 7 (*Spect*)
This has no date. The first edition was issued by Longmans, London, 5 vols., 1810, 19 cm., listed by the *Edinburgh Review* as published Feb.–May 1810, at 25/0. It was

issued as *Bentley's Standard Novels* Nos. 7 and 8, 1831. Routledge, London, issued it at 2/0 boards, 2/6 cloth, in Oct. 1853.
Also 1873

668 ANONYMOUS *Bits About Babies.* 8vo. Illustrated. 1/0   May 28 (*Spect*)
This is the first edition, 1870, 59 pp. It was listed in the *Bks* for both May and June.

669 A BETTING MAN *Out of the Ring.* 12mo. 1/0 sewed   May 28 (*Spect*)
Everybody's Library No. 3. This is probably the first edition, no date.

670 CHARLES H. ROSS, ed. *The Great Mr. Gun.* 8vo. Illustrated. 1/0 sewed   May 28 (*Spect*)
Also 1865

671 MADAME GOUBAUD *Madame Goubaud's Book of Guipure d'Art.* Illustrated. 1/0 sewed   May (*Bks*)
This has 64 pp. It is possibly the same as *The Book of Guipure d'Art*, Fcp 4to, 2/0, issued by Ward, Lock & Tyler in 1869, listed in the *Ath* and the *Spect* on Apr. 24.

672 RICHARD COBBOLD *Freston Tower.* 2/0 boards   May (*Bks*)
Also 1865, 75, 80

JOHN LANG Novels. 7 vols. 1/0 sewed each May (*Bks*)
673 *Captain Macdonald.* Also 1856, 58, 60, 82, 85
674 *Clever Criminals.* This was issued by W. Tegg, London, 1859, as *Botany Bay*, with 238 pp. The present edition has no date and 188 pp. The *U Cat* gives *Botany Bay*, New South Wales Bookstall Co., Sydney (185-?), 188 pp. Also 1871, 82
675 *The Forger's Wife.* This has no date. Also 1855, 58, 82
676 *My Friend's Wife.* This has no date. Also 1859, 82
677 *The Secret Police.* Also 1859, 82, 83

678 **Too Much Alike**. This has no date.
Also 1854, 58, 82

679 **Too Clever by Half**. This has no date.
The first edition was issued by Nathaniel
Cooke, London, 1853, by The Mofussi-
lite, 19 cm., 126 pp., illustrated. In the
United States it was issued by Bangs,
Bros. & Co., anonymous, noticed in the
July 1854 issue of the *Southern Quarterly
Review*. Also 1882

680 ANONYMOUS **Leah, the Jewish
Maiden**. Small format. 2/o boards
May (*Bks*)
Library of Popular Authors. This has no
date, 316 pp.
Also 1864, 73, 90

681 RACHEL MCCRINDELL **The Covent**.
2/o boards May (*Bks*)
Also 1865

682 MAYNE REID **The Fatal Chord**.
1/o sewed May (*Bks*)
This has no date. The first edition was issued by C. Brown, London, in 1869,
12mo, 1/o, listed in the *Spect* on Aug. 7.
The Fatal Chord: and The Falcon Rover was
issued by C. H. Clarke, London (1872),
12mo, 2/o boards; and Routledge, London, issued the same title in the *Railway
Library* (1878), 307 pp., 2/o boards, 3/6
cloth, about June 1, the second title taking
up pp. 172–307.

683 MAYNE REID **The White Squaw**.
1/o sewed May (*Bks*)
This has no date. The first English edition
was issued by C. Brown, London, in 1869,
12mo, 1/o, listed in the *Spect* on Aug. 7. It
ran in *Boys of England* beginning in 1867.
The first book edition was issued by Beadle & Co., New York, *Dime Novel* No. 155,
published about July 24, 1868. The present title together with the next title was issued in one vol. by C. H. Clarke, London
(1871), 12mo, 154 pp., 148 pp., 2/o
boards, about July 22.

684 MAYNE REID **The Yellow Chief**.
1/o sewed May (*Bks*)
This is the first English edition, no date.
The first American edition was issued by
Beadle & Co., New York, *Dime Novel* No.
189, published about Oct. 26, 1869, and
listed in *ALG&PC* (fortnightly) on Dec. 1,
1869. See the preceding entry for the issue by C. H. Clarke.

685 CAROLINE E. S. NORTON **Stuart of
Dunleath**. 2/o boards June 4 (*Ath*)
The first edition was issued by Henry Col-
burn, London, 3 vols., 1851, 20.5 cm.,
31/6, listed in the *Spect* and in the *Ath* on
May 3. It was issued by Simms & M'Intyre,
London and Belfast, 1853, *Parlour Library*
No. 90, 384 pp., about Feb. 1. Darton,
London, issued it (1860), in a 2/o yellow-
back, 384 pp. A one-vol. edition was listed
in the *Spect* on Jan. 31, 1857, with no pub-
lisher or other details given. The first
American edition was issued by Harper &
Bros., New York, 1851, noticed in the
Southern Literary Messenger (Richmond), a
monthly, in Sept. 1851, and thus probably
issued in July or Aug. It was noticed in
Harper's New Monthly Magazine for July
1851.

686 ANONYMOUS **Brought to Light**. Small
format. 2/o boards June 25 (*Ath*)
Library of Popular Authors. This is the first
edition, no date.

687 ELIZABETH C. GREY **The Gambler's
Wife**. 2/o boards June (*Bks*)
The first edition was issued by T. C.
Newby, London, 3 vols., 1844, 20.5 cm.,
anonymous, 31/6, listed in the *Ath* on Nov.
2 and noticed on Nov. 9. The second edition in 3 vols. was listed in the *Spect* on Feb.
8, 1845. It was issued by Clarke, Beeton &
Co., London (1853), 17.3 cm., 415 pp.,
with a frontispiece, 1/6 boards, 2/o cloth,
my copy, listed in the *Ath* on June 25. It
was reissued in May 1854 at 1/6 boards,

and reissued as *Parlour Library* No. 252 in 1861 at 2/0 boards. It was issued by David Bryce, London, in 1855 at 1/6 boards, 2/0 cloth, advertised in the *Ath* on Jan. 27; reissued in 1857 at 1/6 boards, advertised in the *Ath* on Sept. 26; reissued in 1858 at 2/0 boards, listed by *PC* as published Feb. 27–Mar. 13; reissued in 1860 at 2/0 boards, listed by *PC* as published Jan. 14–31. According to the *Ath* it was sold at Hodgson's Rooms, both copyright and stereo plates, on June 8, 1858, for £46. This does not harmonize with the above publishing history! The first American edition was issued by Harper & Bros., New York, 1845, *Library of Select Novels* No. 50, 23 cm., anonymous, 155 pp., noticed in the *Southern Messenger* for June 1845, and listed in the *Knickerbocker* for July 1845, anonymous.

688 S. O. BEETON **Beeton's British Biography.** 1/0 sewed, 1/6, 2/0 cloth
July 2 (*Spect*)

This is the first edition, no date, 252 pp. It and *Modern Men and Women* (below) were issued in one vol. also about this time, no date.

689 JAMES GREENWOOD **Escaped at Last.** Cr 8vo. 2/0 boards   July 9 (*Ath*)

Everybody's Library. This is probably the first edition. It is given also by the *Eng Cat*, but otherwise I cannot trace it.

690 A LIGHT DRAGOON **Wheels and Woes.** p 8vo. Illustrated. 1/0 sewed   July 23 (*Spect*)

This is the first edition, no date, 18 cm., 90 pp.

691 MARY LANGDON (MARY H. PIKE) **Ida May.** 2/0 boards   July (*Bks*)
Also 1854, 64, 72

692 MARIA S. CUMMINS **The Lamplighter.** 2/0 boards   July (*Bks*)
Also 1854, 64, 72

693 MADAME GOUBAUD **Madame Goubaud's Berlin Work Instructions.** 0/6 sewed   Aug. (*Bks*)
Also 1868

694 (ADELINE D. T. WHITNEY) **The Gayworthys.** 2/0 boards
Aug. (*Bks*)
Also 1867

695 ELIZABETH C. GREY **The Opera-Singer's Wife.** 2/0 boards   Aug. (*Bks*)

The first edition was issued by C. H. Clarke & Co., London (1860), *Parlour Library* No. 223, 2/0 boards, issued about Oct. 27.
Also 1885

696 HARRIETTE SMYTHIES **The Life of a Beauty.** 2/0 boards   Aug. (*Bks*)
Also 1864

697 (ANNIE EDWARDES) **The Morals of Mayfair.** 2/0 boards   Aug. (*Bks*)
Also 1863, 69, 74

698 AZEL S. ROE **How Could He Help It?** 2/0 boards   Aug. (*Bks*)

The first edition was issued by Derby & Jackson, New York, 1860, 18.5 cm., 443 pp., $1.25, listed in the *Ind* on Dec. 29, 1859, and in *APC&LG* (weekly) on Dec. 24. It was issued by Simpkin, Marshall, London; etc., the first English edition (1860), *Run and Read Library* No. 57, 1/6 boards, listed in the *Spect* on Jan. 3, 1860.

699 PERCY B. ST. JOHN **Indian Tales.** 2/0 boards   Aug. (*Bks*)
Also 1855

700 PERCY B. ST. JOHN **Amy Moss.** 2/0 boards   Aug. (*Bks*)

The first edition was probably David Bryce, London, at 2/0 boards, listed in *PC* as published Feb. 1–14, 1860, and by the

Bks as published Jan. 24–Feb. 24. It was listed by the *Bks* as issued in a new edition at 2/o boards, Mar. 26–Apr. 26, 1860, given as Cassell, Petter, & Galpin, London, which I believe is highly unlikely! It was issued by C. H. Clarke & Co., London, as *Parlour Library* No. 240 (1861), 2/o boards, probably in July.

701 S. O. BEETON *Beeton's Guide to Investing Money with Safety and Profit.* 1/o linen Oct. 15 (*Ath*)

This is the first edition, no date, 64 pp. *Beeton's Guide to Investing Money* was listed in the *Spect* on Mar. 16, 1872, 12mo, 2/6, Ward & Lock.

702 S. O. BEETON *Beeton's Guide Book to the Stock Exchange and Money Market.* 1/o linen Oct. 15 (*Ath*)

This is the first edition, no date, 96 pp.

703 S. O. BEETON *Beeton's Modern Men and Women.* 12mo. 1/o sewed, 1/6, 2/o cloth Oct. 29 (*Ath*)

This is the first edition, no date, 17.5 cm., 260 pp. See *Beeton's British Biography* above.
Also 1876

704 (ALFRED W. DRAYSON) *The Young Dragoon.* 2/o boards Nov. 12 (*Spect*)

This has no date. The first edition was issued by S. O. Beeton, London, 1866, small 8vo, illustrated, in blue cloth with all edges gilt.
Also 1874

705 ANONYMOUS *Beeton's Englishwoman's Almanac.* 1/o Nov. 12 (*Spect*)

This was the second year for this almanac. See 1876

706 LYULPH (HENRY R. LUMLEY) *An Ancient Mariner.* o/6 Nov. (*Ath*)

This is the first edition, no date, a Christmas story.

707 MARY E. BRADDON, ed. *Belgravia Annual.* 1/o sewed Nov. (*Ath*)

708 S. O. BEETON *Beeton's Bible Dictionary.* 12mo. 1/o sewed, 1/6, 2/o cloth Dec. 3 (*Spect*)

This is the first edition, no date, 252 pp. Also 1876

709 ÉMILE ERCKMANN & PIERRE CHATRIAN *The Great Invasion of 1813–14.* Small format. 1/o sewed Dec. 31 (*Spect*)

An edition at 3/6, illustrated, was also issued by Ward, Lock & Tyler, listed in the *Spect* on Dec. 10, 1870. It had 284 pp. and no date, as did this 1/o issue. The first edition was *L'Invasion, ou le Fou Yégof*, Paris, 1862. *The Invasion of France in 1814* was issued by Smith, Elder & Co., London, 1871, 12mo, illustrated, 1/o boards, listed in the *Spect* on Dec. 24, 1870, 276 pp. Smith, Elder issued it at 3/6, 12mo, illustrated, listed in the *Ath* and the *Spect* on Feb. 4, 1871. In the United States it was issued by Charles Scribner & Co., New York, 1871, with the Smith, Elder title, 18 cm., 369 pp., illustrated, listed in the *Ind* on Nov. 23, 1871, and advertised in the *New-York Times* on Nov. 18, 1871, 12mo, four illustrations, $.50 paper, $.90 cloth, as "Just published." This Ward, Lock edition began the long series of *Beeton's Erckmann-Chatrian Library*.

Ward, Lock & Tyler
1871

After the copyrights of Moxon & Son had passed into the hands of Ward, Lock & Tyler, Arthur Moxon, the son, continued the superintendence of the commercial portion of the business, and the literary management was placed under the control of S. O. Beeton. The imprint of Moxon & Son was still used with their old address but with the Ward, Lock & Tyler address added. This form of imprint continued through Jan. 1873. Thereafter, through 1878, the only address on Moxon ads was that of Ward, Lock & Tyler, and the Moxon name was abandoned. Arthur Moxon began his own company in late 1878 or early 1879 at 12 Tavistock Street.

710 LOUISA M. ALCOTT **Little Women.**
1/o sewed, 1/6, 2/o cloth Feb. 4 (*Ath*)

Lily Series No. 5. This has no date, 283 pp. It was also listed in the *Spect* on Oct. 7 at 1/6 cloth, whereas the *Ath* listing given here was for a 1/o sewed issue. The first edition was issued by Roberts Bros., Boston, 1868, 16mo, illustrated, $1.50, deposited Oct. 3, and listed in *ALG&PC* (fortnightly) on Oct. 15; in the *Nation* on Oct. 8; and advertised in the *New-York Times* on Sept. 30 as "Just published." The first English edition was issued by Sampson Low, London, 1869 (1868), 17 cm., 341 pp., illustrated, 3/6 brown cloth, listed in the *Ath* on Dec. 12, 1868. Roberts Bros. issued *Little Women* in two parts, both entitled *Little Women*. Ward, Lock & Tyler called part 2 *Good Wives*, and Low called part 2 *Little Women Wedded*.

711 LOUISA M. ALCOTT **An Old-Fashioned Girl.** 12mo. 1/o Feb. 4 (*Spect*)

This first appeared in *Merry's Museum* (Horace B. Fuller), a monthly, beginning in July 1869 and ending in 1870. The first book edition was issued by Roberts Bros., Boston, 1870, 17 cm., 378 pp., illustrated with a double frontispiece and two en-

gravings, $1.50 cloth. It was advertised in the *New-York Times* on Mar. 19, 1870, 10,000 copies, "On Apr. 1," and advertised on Apr. 2 as "This day"; the 30th thousand was advertised on May 26. *BAL* noted a copy with an inscribed date of Mar. 1870. It was deposited on Apr. 20 and listed in *ALG&PC* (fortnightly) on Apr. 15. The first English edition was issued by Sampson Low, London, 1870, 16 cm., 314 pp., 3/6 cloth, advertised in the *Ath* on Apr. 2 as "This day" and listed then also. An ad in *Notes & Queries* for July 2, 1870, gave it at 2/o flexible cloth in addition to the 3/6 cloth. A Low notice in *PC* for Feb. 15, 1871, stated that the Ward, Lock & Tyler edition had been withdrawn, being an infringement of copyright. *BAL* states that no listing or ads for the Ward, Lock edition had ever been found. I have found this one!

712 LOUISA M. ALCOTT **Good Wives.**
1/o sewed, 1/6, 2/o cloth Mar. 11 (*Ath*)

Lily Series No. 6. The *Ath* (and also the *Spect*) listing was for a 1/o edition. The first edition was part two of *Little Women*, issued by Roberts Bros., Boston, 1869, illustrated, $1.50, listed in *ALG&PC* (fortnightly) on May 1, and noticed in the *Ind* on May 6. They issued both parts in one vol., 12mo, 350 pp., illustrated, dated 1869, and listed in the *New Englander* (New Haven), a quarterly, for Oct. 1869. The first English edition was issued by Sampson Low, London, 1869, as *Little Women Wedded*, 16mo, illustrated, 3/6 cloth, advertised in the *Ath* on May 22 as "Ready" and listed June 12. Low issued both parts in one vol., 12mo, 3/6, listed in the *Spect* on Sept. 17, 1870; and he issued the second edition of this one-vol. issue, 1871, 464 pp. Ward, Lock & Tyler issued both parts in one vol., 12mo, 3/6, listed by the *Spect* on Oct. 7, 1871.

713 ÉMILE ERCKMANN & PIERRE CHATRIAN *Madame Thérèse.* Small format. 1/o sewed Mar. 11 (*Ath*)

This is 16.2 cm., with 210 pp. Ward, Lock & Tyler issued it at 3/6 cloth, 12mo, 210 pp., listed in the *Spect* on June 1, 1872. The first edition was in Paris in 1862; and the eighth edition was issued there in 1863, 19.5 cm., 377 pp. The first English edition was issued by W. Hunt & Co., London, 1869, 271 pp., at 3/6. Ward, Lock & Tyler issued it at 3/6, illustrated, listed in the *Spect* on Mar. 25, 1871. The first American edition was issued by Charles Scribner & Co., New York, 1869, 12mo, 289 pp., with 10 full-page illustrations, $1.50 cloth, advertised in the *New-York Times* on Nov. 12, 1868, as "On Nov. 19"; and the fourth thousand was advertised on Nov. 28 as "Now ready." It was listed in the *Nation* on Nov. 26, 1868.

714 S. O. BEETON *Beeton's Book of the War.* 8vo. 1/o Mar. 11 (*Spect*)

This is the first edition, no date, 120 pp., illustrated.

715 ANONYMOUS *Women, Children, and Registration.* 12mo. 1/o linen Apr. 1 (*Spect*)

Beeton's Law Books.

716 ANONYMOUS *Property.* 12mo. 1/o linen Apr. 1 (*Spect*)

Beeton's Law Books.

717 JOHN LANG *Clever Criminals.* 1/o sewed Apr. 15 (*Spect*)

Also 1870, 82

718 ÉMILE ERCKMANN & PIERRE CHATRIAN *The Conscript.* Small format. 1/o sewed Apr.?

This had no date, 256 pp., translated by H. W. Dulcken. It was also listed by *PC* as published Dec. 18–31, 1872, 12mo, 1/o sewed, by Ward, Lock & Tyler. They issued it at 3/6 cloth also. The first edition was *Histoire d'un Conscrit de 1813*, Paris (1864), 310 pp. The first English edition was issued by Smith, Elder & Co., London, 1865, 288 pp., at 6/o, about May 13; they reissued it at 2/6 boards, about Dec. 22, 1866; and reissued it, 1870, 12mo, illustrated, 1/o sewed, about Dec. 10, 1870 (my copy). Hotten, London, issued it (1871), 220 pp., 1/o sewed, 1/6 cloth, translated by T. Taylor, listed in the *Spect* on Dec. 17, 1870, at 1/o. An ad in the *Ath* on Feb. 11, 1871, called it the only unabridged English edition issued in England. The first American edition was issued by Charles Scribner & Co., New York, 1869, 18.5 cm., 330 pp., eight full-page illustrations, $1.50, advertised in the *New-York Times* on Dec. 2, 1868, as "Immediately," and advertised on Jan. 9, 1879, as "This day." It was a translation of the 20th French edition. It was listed in *ALG&PC* (fortnightly) on Jan. 15, 1879. Also 1875

719 ANONYMOUS *Divorce and Matrimonial Causes.* 12mo. 1/o linen May 13 (*Spect*)

Beeton's Law Books.

720 ANONYMOUS *Wills, Executors, and Trustees.* 12mo. 1/o linen June 17 (*Spect*)

Beeton's Law Books.

721 ÉMILE ERCKMANN & PIERRE
CHATRIAN *The Story of a Peasant;
(1789). Part 1.* Small format. 1/0 sewed
June 17 (*Ath*)

This has no date and 274 pp. It was issued
also, 12mo, illustrated, 3/6 cloth, listed in
the *Spect* on June 24. Bentley issued *The
Outbreak of the Great French Revolution*, 3
vols., 1871, a translation of parts 1 and 2,
by Mrs. Cashel Hoey. The first edition was
Histoire d'un Paysan, 4 vols., Paris (1868–
70), the four vols. being: *1879. Les Etats
Generaux; 1792. La Patrie en Danger; 1793.
L'An I de la Republique; 1794 au 1815. Le
Citoyen Bonaparte.*
Also 1875 as *The States General and The
Country in Danger*
Also 1884 as *The States General*

722 (MARY E. BRADDON) *Fenton's Quest.*
Stereotyped Edition. Small format. 2/0
boards   June 24 (*Ath*)

This has no date, 364 pp., the first yellowback edition. It was reissued (1875). The
first edition was issued by Ward, Lock &
Tyler, 3 vols., 1871, Cr 8vo, anonymous,
31/6, advertised in the *Ath* on Jan. 14,
1871, as "Ready" and listed on Jan. 21.
The first American edition was issued by
Harper & Bros., New York, 1871, 8vo,
161 pp., $.50 paper, *Library of Select Novels*
No. 358, listed in the *Nation* on Apr. 13,
and in the *Ind* on Apr. 15. It was advertised in the *New-York Times* on Apr. 8 as
"This day."

723 S. O. BEETON *Beeton's Classical
Dictionary.* 12mo. 1/0 sewed, 1/6 cloth,
2/0 half-bound   July 15 (*Spect*)

This is the first edition, no date, 17.5 cm.,
with 254 pp.

724 MARY E. BRADDON, ed. *The Summer
Tourist.* 8vo. 1/0 sewed   July 22 (*Ath*)

This is the first edition, 1871, 128 pp.,
white wrappers decorated with holiday
scenes in many colors on the front, and

with ads on the inside covers. Only the
first article is signed by Braddon (Wolff's
copy).

725 S. O. BEETON *Beeton's Ready
Reckoner.* 1/0 cloth boards   July 29
(*Spect*)

This is the first edition, no date, 17.5 cm.,
240 pp. There was a third edition, the
same. An extract was issued at 0/6, no
date, with 96 pp., given by the *Eng Cat* as
issued in 1871.

726 ANONYMOUS *Transactions in Trade,
Securities, and Sureties.* 12mo. 1/0 linen
July?
Beeton's Law Books.

727 S. O. BEETON *Beeton's Book of the
Laundry.* 12mo. 1/0 sewed   Aug. 5 (*Ath*)

This is the first edition, no date, with 64
pp.

728 ANONYMOUS *Partnership and
Joint-Stock Companies.* 12mo. 1/0 linen
Aug. 19 (*Spect*)
Beeton's Law Books.

729 ÉMILE ERCKMANN & PIERRE
CHATRIAN *The Story of a Peasant. Part 2.*
Small format. 1/0 sewed   Aug. 26 (*Ath*)

This has no date, 253 pp. (See part 1
above.) It was issued at 3/6 cloth, advertised in the *Ath* on Sept. 23; and it was issued at 2/0 linen, both parts in 1 vol.,
listed in the *Ath* on Oct. 7. This linen edition is my copy, no date, 16.5 cm., 274 pp.,
253 pp., printed and decorated on the
front in red and dark blue. It has publisher's ads on the endpapers, on pp. (1)–5 at
the back, and has a publisher's ad on the
back cover.
See 1875

730 ANONYMOUS *Landlord and Tenant,
Lodgers, Rates and Taxes.* 12mo. 1/0 linen
Oct. 7 (*Spect*)
Beeton's Law Books.

731 S. O. BEETON *Beeton's Medical Dictionary.* 12mo. 1/0 sewed, 1/6 cloth, 2/0 half-bound   Oct. 29 (*Spect*)

This is the first edition, no date, 292 pp. Also 1876

732 MARION HARLAND (MARY HAWES, later TERHUNE) *Alone.* 1/0 sewed, 1/6 cloth, 2/0 cloth   Oct. (*Bks*)

Lily Series No. 7.
Also 1866

733 AZEL S. ROE *I've Been Thinking.* 1/0 sewed, 1/6 cloth, 2/0 cloth   Oct. (*Bks*)

Lily Series No. 8. This has no date and is edited by C. B. Tayler. Ward, Lock issued it at 3/6 cloth, Fcp 8vo, 306 pp., illustrated, listed in the *Reader* on July 9, 1864. The first edition was *James Montjoy*, issued by D. Appleton & Co., New York, 1850, 19.5 cm., 327 pp., listed in *Lit World* as published Jan. 19–Feb. 2, and it was reviewed in the *Ind* on Mar. 7. The first English edition was with the present title, issued by Clarke, Beeton & Co., London; etc., 1853, as *Run and Read Library* No. 1, 12mo, frontispiece, 1/6 boards, 2/0 cloth, edited by Tayler, listed in the *Spect* on Aug. 27.

734 ÉMILE ERCKMANN & PIERRE CHATRIAN *The Blockade.* Small format. 1/0 sewed   Oct.?

This has no date, 239 pp., advertised in the *Ath* on Sept. 23 as "In press" but not listed as the Erckmann-Chatrian books in press in Nov. It was also issued at 3/6, but without illustrations, listed in the *Spect* on May 25, 1872. It was listed in *PC* as pub-

lished Dec. 18–31, 1872, 12mo, 240 pp., 1/0 sewed. The first edition was *Le Blocus*, Paris (1867), 18 cm., 335 pp. The first English edition was issued by Smith, Elder & Co., London, 1869, 17.5 cm., 246 pp., illustrated, 7/6, about Nov. 20, as *The Blockade*. They issued it as *The Blockade of Phalsburg*, illustrated, 2/0 sewed, about Dec. 10, 1870. The first American edition was *The Blockade of Phalsburg*, issued by Charles Scribner & Co., New York, 1871, 17.5 cm., 308 pp., advertised in the *Ind* on May 11 as "Just published," and advertised in the *New-York Times* on May 20, $.50 stiff paper wrappers, $.90 cloth, illustrated, as "Next week," and on May 27 as "This day."

735 ANONYMOUS *Masters, Apprentices, Servants and Working Contracts.* 12mo. 1/0 linen   Nov. 11 (*Spect*)

Beeton's Law Books.

736 ANONYMOUS *Beeton's Christmas Annual.* 1/0 sewed   Nov. 18 (*Ath*)

This was the twelfth season for this annual. *See color photo section*

737 MARY E. BRADDON, ed. *Belgravia Annual.* 1/0 sewed   Nov.

738 MADAME GOUBAUD *Madame Goubaud's Embroidery Instructions.* Illustrated. 0/6 sewed   1871 (*Eng Cat*)

Also 1868

739 MADAME GOUBAUD *Madame Goubaud's Crochet Instructions.* Illustrated. 1/0 sewed   1871 (*Eng Cat*)

Also 1868

Ward, Lock & Tyler
1872

740 ANONYMOUS *Law Relating to Conveyance, Travellers, and Innkeepers.* 12mo. 1/0 linen   Jan. 20 (*Spect*)
Beeton's Law Books. This has 108 pp.

741 BRET HARTE *Poems and Prose of Bret Harte.* Small format. 1/0 sewed   Feb. 3 (*Spect*)
Beeton's Humorous Books No. 1. This began this long series. It is my copy, no date, 16.3 cm., 246 pp., white wrappers cut flush, pictorially printed on the front in red, blue, and black, with the series title on the front and on the title page. There are publisher's ads on the endpapers, back cover, and on one leaf at the back. The front cover depicts the heathen Chinee. *Poems* was issued by Fields, Osgood, Boston; etc., 1871, 18 cm., 152 pp., listed in the *Nation* on Dec. 29, 1870, and in *ALG&PC* (fortnightly) on Jan. 2, 1871. It was probably imported by Trübner & Co., London, and issued in Jan. 1871. Routledge issued *Prose and Poetry* (1872), 144 pp., 2/0 boards, in Apr.; and issued *The Poetical Works of Bret Harte*, complete edition (1872), 19 cm., 248 pp., illustrated, 3/6 cloth, in June; and at 1/0 sewed in Aug. The present edition was reissued in Apr. 1872.
Also 1880

742 ÉMILE ERCKMANN & PIERRE CHATRIAN *The Illustrious Doctor Mathéus.* Small format. 1/0 sewed   Feb. 17 (*Ath*)
This was probably the first English edition, no date, 200 pp., and with "Erckmann-Chatrian Library, Volume 8" on the verso of the title page. It ran in *Temple Bar* where chapters 10 and 11 appeared in the July 1871 issue, and it was still running in the Sept. issue. The first edition was *L'Illustre Docteur Mathéus*, Paris, 1858, 18.5 cm., 305 pp.
Also 1875

743 C. D. A. FRIEDLEIN *Building Societies and Borrowers and the Commission.* p 8vo. 1/0 sewed   Mar. 2 (*Spect*)
This is the first edition, 1872. It is listed in *PC* as published May 1–15, which possibly was a reissue.

744 ANONYMOUS *Law Relating to Auctions, Valuations, etc.* Mar. 9 (*Spect*)
Beeton's Law Books. 82 pp.

745 ÉMILE ERCKMANN & PIERRE CHATRIAN *Popular Tales and Romances.* Small format. 1/0 sewed   Mar. 16 (*Ath*)
This was also issued at 3/6. Both issues had no date and 176 pp. It consists of stories selected from the authors' works. The first edition was *Contes et Romans Populaires*, Paris, 6 parts, 1867, illustrated, but this could not possibly be wholly reproduced here, as the catalog of the Librairie Française gives it as 1867, 4to, illustrated, containing *Maître Daniel Rock*; *L'Illustre Docteur Mathéus*; *Contes des Bords du Rhin*; *L'Ami Fritz*, et al.

746 ANONYMOUS *Law of Arbitrations, Legal Documents, etc.* 12mo. 1/0 linen   Mar. 23 (*Spect*)
Beeton's Law Books. This has 98 pp.

747 ANONYMOUS *Law Relating to Debtors, Creditors, Compositions, etc.*
Mar. 23 (*Spect*)

Beeton's Law Books. This has 82 pp. *Beeton's Law Book* was advertised in the *Spect* on Apr. 13, 1872, at 10/6 half-roan as "In a few days." *Beeton's Legal Handbooks*, 18 vols., were advertised in the *Times Weekly Edition* (London) on Mar. 6, 1891, Cr 8vo, 1/o cloth each, the first eight as given above in 1871, and the next four as given here. Both these issues were from Ward & Lock.

748 ANN & JANE TAYLOR ET AL.
The Original Ongar Poems for Children.
[New edition]. 18mo. o/9 sewed, 1/o, 1/6 cloth   Mar. 23 (*Spect*)

Beeton's Good-Aim Series No. 1. This is a selection, no date, with 150 pp. The *PC* lists this as published Mar. 16–30 at 1/o cloth, and lists it as published Dec. 18–31 at 1/6 cloth. The *Spect* listing is for 1/o cloth. The first edition was *Original Poems for Infant Minds*, by several young persons (Ann Taylor Gilbert, Jane Taylor, Isaac Taylor, et al.). It was listed in the *Edinburgh Review*, 2 vols., as published July 6–Oct. 10, 1805. The *U Cat* and a copy in the Osborne collection give Darton & Harvey, London, 2 vols., 1805, 13.4 cm., with frontispieces dated Aug. 22, 1805. F. J. Darton Harvey gives 1804; Percy Muir gives 1804–05; and Eric Quayle in *Early Children's Books* gives 1894–05! A new and revised edition was issued by Arthur Hall, Virtue, London, 2 vols., 1854–56, 14 cm., anonymous. It was issued in the United States by Saxton & Miles, New York, portrait, from the 12th London edition, noticed in *Godey's Lady's Book* for June 1844.

749 (ELIZABETH S. PHELPS) *Trotty's Book.*
18mo. o/9 sewed, 1/o, 1/6 cloth   Mar. 23 (*Spect*)

Beeton's Good-Aim Series No. 2. This has no date. This listing in the *Spect* is for the 1/o

issue. It was listed on May 18 at 1/6. The first edition was *The Trotty Book*, issued by Fields, Osgood, Boston, 1870, 18 cm., 118 pp., illustrated, $1.50, in purple, blue, red, or green cloth, with brown endpapers. It was listed in the *Nation* on Dec. 9, 1869, and in *ALG&PC* (fortnightly) on Jan. 1, 1870. It was advertised in the *New-York Times* on Dec. 2, 1869, as "This day." Also 1881

750 CATHERINE SINCLAIR
Holiday House. [New Edition].
2/o boards   Mar. (*Bks*)

This has 356 pp.
Also 1865, 85

751 ANONYMOUS *Beeton's Date-Book.*
12mo. 1/o sewed, 1/6 cloth, 2/o half-bound
Apr. 13 (*Spect*)

This is the first edition, no date, with 238 pp.
Also 1876

752 (MARY E. BRADDON) *The Lovels of Arden.* Stereotyped Edition.
Small format. 2/o boards, 2/6 cloth
Apr. 20 (*Ath*)

This has no date, 399 pp., the first yellowback edition. The first edition was John Maxwell & Co., London, 3 vols., 1871, Cr 8vo, anonymous, 31/6, advertised in the *Ath* on Oct. 7 as "Ready" and listed on Oct. 14. This was the first Braddon novel issued by Maxwell after the Ward, Lock period. The first American edition was issued by Harper & Bros., New York, 1872, 8vo, illustrated, $.75 paper, as *Library of Select Novels* No. 369, listed in *PW* on Feb. 22, and by *Lit World* as published in Feb.
Also 1875

753 ÉMILE ERCKMANN & PIERRE CHATRIAN *Waterloo.* [New edition].
Small format. 1/o sewed   Apr. 27 (*Spect*)

This has no date, 307 pp., translated by H. W. Dulcken. This was also listed by *PC*

as published May 1–15 and also Dec. 18–31, both at 1/0 sewed. It was also issued at 3/6 cloth, probably about the same time. The first edition was Paris (1865). The first English edition was issued by Smith, Elder & Co., London, 1865, 314 pp., 6/0, listed in the *Ath* on Oct. 21. They reissued it at 3/6, illustrated, listed in the *Spect* on Sept. 24, 1870; and issued it, 1870, 12mo, illustrated, 1/0 sewed, listed in the *Spect* on Dec. 10, 1870. It was issued by John C. Hotten, London (1871), 12mo, 265 pp., 1/0 sewed, 1/6 cloth, translated by Theodore Taylor, listed in the *Ath* on Jan. 21, 1871, advertised as the only unabridged English edition issued in England! The first American edition was issued by Charles Scribner & Co., New York, 1869, 18.5 cm., 368 pp., with six full-page illustrations, $1.50 cloth, listed in the *Nation* on June 3, and advertised in the *New-York Times* on May 22 as "On May 29," and on May 29 as "This day."
Also 1884. See 1875

754 MARY LANGDON (MARY H. PIKE)
Ida May. 12mo. 1/0 sewed, 1/6, 2/0 cloth
May 4 (*Ath*)

Lily Series No. 9. This has 320 pp. It was reissued in 1882, Cr 8vo, 3/6, listed in the *Spect* on Aug. 12, 1882, Ward & Lock.
Also 1864, 70

755 CHARLES READE **It Is Never Too Late to Mend.** New Edition. p 8vo. 2/6 boards, 3/6 cloth   May 25 (*Ath*)

This has no date, 18 cm., 462 pp. It begins a reissue of Reade's novels. The first edition was issued by Bentley, London, 3 vols., 19.5 cm., in drab boards or red cloth, published Aug. 1 according to the Bentley private catalog, and advertised in the *Ath* on July 26 as "On July 29," and on Aug. 2 as "Ready." He issued the second edition, 3 vols., 31/6 boards, listed by *PC* as published Sept. 15–31, 1856. He issued it, Cr 8vo, 274 pp., illustrated, 5/0 cloth, listed in the *Spect* on Jan. 31, 1857; reis-

sued, the same, the eighth thousand, advertised in the *Spect* on Apr. 4, 1857; reissued, the same, the 11th thousand, advertised there on May 23, 1857. He issued it, 1857, a new edition, 19 cm., 274 pp., at 2/0 boards, 3/0 cloth, advertised in *Notes & Queries* on June 29, 1857, as "This day." Bradbury & Evans, London, issued a new edition, Cr 8vo, 5/0, listed in the *Spect* on Oct. 10, 1868. The story is derived from *Gold!*, a drama in five acts by Reade, issued by T. H. Lacy, London (1853), with 48 pp., salmon-pink wrappers, and first performed on Jan. 10, 1853. The first American edition was issued by Ticknor & Fields, Boston, 2 vols., 1856, author's edition, 19 cm., $1.75, in olive cloth, with an Aug. 1856 catalog (also in maroon cloth with an Oct. 1856 catalog). It was listed in *APC&LG* (weekly) on Sept. 13 and advertised in the *New York Daily Times* on Sept. 10, 1856, from the author's MS, "On Sept. 10." From the cost books of Ticknor & Fields, it is stated that the first printing was 4,000 copies with royalties to Reade of $372; a second edition printing of 2,000 copies with royalties of $350; and 500 copies in May 1857, to sell at $1.50, with royalties of $322.
Also 1881

756 ANONYMOUS **Joe Miller's Jest Book.**
Small format. 1/0 sewed   June 15 (*Spect*)

Beeton's Humorous Books No. 8. This is my copy, no date, 16.2 cm., 160 pp., white wrappers cut flush, pictorially printed on the front in red, blue, and black, with the series title on the front and on the title page. There are publisher's ads on the back cover, on 4 pp. at the back, and there are ads on the endpapers.
Also 1856, 91

757 CHARLES READE **Christie Johnstone.**
[New edition]. p 8vo. 2/0 boards, 3/6 cloth
June 29 (*Ath*)

This has no date and 262 pp. The first edition was issued by Bentley, London,

1853, 20.5 cm., 334 pp., 10/6, in maroon cloth or gray boards, issued Aug. 25 according to the Bentley private catalog, and listed in the *Ath* on Aug. 20. Bentley issued a new edition, 1857, 19.5 cm., with a frontispiece and music, without Reade's consent, causing a hassle. The third edition, one illustration, 3/6 cloth was listed in the *Spect* on Mar. 28, 1857. A new edition was issued by Bradbury & Evans, London, in 1868, Cr 8vo, illustrated, 3/6, listed in the *Spect* on Sept. 5. This story is based on a failed play, *Fish, Flesh, and Good Red Herring*, written before 1851 (see Parrish). The first American edition was issued by Ticknor & Fields, Boston, 1855, 16mo, 309 pp., $.75, in an edition of 2,500 copies, listed in the *Ind* on June 28 and published on June 9 according to Bentley. It was advertised in the *New York Daily Times* on June 9, 1855, as "Now ready"; and a new edition, the same, was advertised on July 23, as "Now ready." The second edition printing was 1,000 copies to sell at $.75; and the third edition printing was 1,000 copies to sell at $.75. After the issue of Peg Woffington (below) Reade was paid £20 in royalties for the two novels. I think the 3/6 issue of the present edition of Ward, Lock was issued somewhat later than the 2/0 boards issue. It was listed in the *Spect* on July 13.

758 ARTEMUS WARD (CHARLES F. BROWNE) *Artemus Ward, His Book.* [New edition]. Small format. 1/0 sewed July 13 (*Spect*)

Beeton's Humorous Books No. 2. This was also listed in the *Bks* for Dec. 3 and by *PC* as published Nov. 1–15. My copy is (1877), 16.2 cm., 168 pp., white wrappers cut flush, pictorially printed on the front in red, blue, and black, with the series title on the front. There are ads on the back cover, the endpapers, and publisher's ads on pp. (1)–16 at the back.
Also 1865, 67, 85

759 (AGLEN A. DOWTY) *Connubial Bliss.* Small format. 1/0 sewed   Aug. 3 (*Spect*)
Beeton's Humorous Books No. 9. This is the first edition, no date, with 176 pp.
Also 1855

760 CHARLES READE *Hard Cash.* p 8vo. 2/6 boards, 3/6 cloth   Aug. 10 (*Ath*)
This has no date, 18 cm., 474 pp. The 3/6 issue was illustrated. The first English edition was issued by Sampson Low, London, 3 vols., 1863, 21 cm., 31/6, green cloth, with publisher's ads at the back of vol. 3 dated Dec. 10, 1863. It was advertised in the *Ath* on Dec. 5 as "On Dec. 10" and listed on Dec. 19. The story had run in *All the Year Round* as *Very Hard Cash*, Mar. 28–Dec. 26, 1863. The first American edition was issued by Harper & Bros., New York, 1864, as *Very Hard Cash*, deposited on Dec. 21, 1863. It was 23.2 cm., 258 pp., illustrated, double columns, in black cloth and in tan wrappers. It was advertised in the *New-York Times* on Jan. 4, 1864, at $.75 paper and $1.00 cloth, as "This day"; and a new edition was advertised there on Feb. 13, 1869, 8vo, illustrated, $.35 paper, as "Just published." It ran in *Harper's Weekly*, Apr. 4, 1863–Jan. 9, 1864. Low issued a new edition, advertised in the *Spect* on Feb. 27, 1864, as "This day," 3 vols.; and a second edition in 3 vols., 24/0, was listed in the *Reader* on Mar. 19, 1864. A new and cheaper edition was issued by Low at 6/0, Cr 8vo, 480 pp., listed in the *Reader* on Mar. 25, 1865. Bradbury & Evans, London, issued a new edition, Cr 8vo, illustrated, 5/0, listed in the *Spect* on Sept. 5, 1868, all these new editions having the title, *Hard Cash*.

761 CHARLES READE *Peg Woffington.* p 8vo. 2/0 boards, 3/6 cloth   Aug. 31 (*Ath*)
This has no date and 255 pp. The 3/6 issue had a plate. The first edition was issued by Bentley, London, 1853, 20 cm.,

331 pp., 10/6, in bright blue cloth, with a dedication (Dec. 15, 1852). It was listed in the *Ath* on Dec. 18, 1852. Bentley issued a new edition, 1857, Cr 8vo, 255 pp., frontispiece, 3/6, listed in the *Spect* on Mar. 28. A new edition was issued by Bradbury & Evans, London, in 1868, Cr 8vo, illustrated, 3/6, listed in the *Spect* on Sept. 5, 1868. The first American edition was issued by Ticknor & Fields, Boston, 1855, 19 cm., 303 pp., $.75 cloth, in an edition of 2,500 copies. It was published on June 6 according to the publisher, and it was listed in the *Ind* on June 21, and advertised in the *New-York Times* on June 9, 16mo, as "Now ready." A new edition, the same, was advertised there on July 23, as "now ready." Wolff states that the first American edition was in green cloth with an undated catalog, and Parrish gives it as in maroon cloth with a catalog (Apr. 18, 1856). The second through fourth editions were issued in June and July 1855, in runs of 1,000 each, to sell at $.75 each.

762 (MARY E. BRADDON)
Robert Ainsleigh. Stereotyped Edition. Small format. 2/o boards, 2/6 cloth Sept. 21 (*Ath*)

This had no date and 412 pp. The first edition was issued by John Maxwell & Co., London, 3 vols., 1872, Cr 8vo, 31/6, advertised in the *Ath* on Mar. 23 as "Ready" and listed on Apr. 6. The story had run in *Belgravia* as *Bound to John Company* (July 1868–Oct. 1869), but due to Braddon's ill health, it was finished by a stranger's hand. For book issue Braddon wrote an entirely new third vol. The first American edition was issued by the J. B. Lippincott Co., Philadelphia, 2 vols., 1872, listed in *PW* and the *Nation* on Sept. 25.

763 MARIA S. CUMMINS *The Lamplighter.*
12mo. 1/o sewed, 1/6, 2/o cloth Sept. 21 (*Ath*)

Lily Series No. 10. This has 378 pp.
Also 1854, 64, 70

764 ANONYMOUS *Little Alfred's Visit to Wombwell's Menagerie.* 4to. 1/o sewed Sept. 21 (*Spect*)

This is the first edition. It was also listed as published Dec. 2–17 by *PC*.

765 ELIZABETH S. PHELPS, later WARD *Gypsy Breynton.* 12mo. 1/o sewed, 1/6, 2/o cloth Sept. 21 (*Ath*)

Lily Series No. 12. This is the first English edition, 186 pp. It was listed by *PC* as published also Nov. 16–30, at 1/6 cloth. The *PC* listed it at 1/o sewed, published Oct. 1–15. The present edition has no date. The first edition was issued by Graves & Young, Boston, 1866, 17.5 cm., 276 pp., with an added illustrated title page. It was deposited on May 25, listed in the *Ind* on June 7, and in *ALG&PC* (fortnightly) on June 15. It was in purple or blue cloth with yellow endpapers. Strahan, London, issued it in 1873, Fcp 8vo, 1/6 cloth, listed in the *Spect* on May 3.
Also 1874

766 S. O. BEETON & RONALD M. SMITH *Livingstone and Stanley.* 8vo. Illustrated. 1/o sewed Sept. 28 (*Ath*)

This is the first edition, 1872, with 96 pp. The second edition was advertised on Nov. 2 as "Just ready." It was issued in the United States by Adams, Victor & Co., New York, 1872, 19.5 cm., 292 pp., frontispiece (portrait), map, from the English edition but with the title *Livingstone and His African Exploration, etc.*

767 ELIZABETH PRENTISS *Aunt Jane's Hero.* 12mo. 1/o sewed, 1/6, 2/o cloth Oct. 12 (*Ath*)

Lily Series No. 13. This is the first English edition, 188 pp. George Routledge, London, issued it at 2/6 cloth, listed in the *Spect* on Sept. 27, 1873; and issued it at 1/o sewed, 1/6, 2/o cloth, listed in the *Ath* on July 25, 1874. The first edition was issued by A. D. F. Randolph, New York (1871),

19.5 cm., 292 pp., advertised in the *Nation* and the *Ind* as "On Oct. 20," and listed by *ALG&PC* (fortnightly) on Nov. 1.

768 AZEL S. ROE *Looking Round.* [New Edition]. 12mo. 1/0 sewed, 1/6, 2/0 cloth Oct. 12 (*Ath*)

Lily Series No. 16. This has 320 pp. Also 1866

769 (ELIZABETH PRENTISS) *Stepping Heavenward.* 12mo. 1/0 sewed, 1/6, 2/0 cloth Oct. 19 (*Spect*)

Lily Series No. 11. This has 230 pp. It originally appeared in *The Advance*, and the first English edition was issued by James Nisbet & Co., London, 1870, colored illustrations, 3/6, in the *Golden Ladder Series*, listed in the *Ath* on Dec. 11, 1869. Nisbet issued the fourth edition, 12mo, 280 pp., at 2/6 cloth, listed by *PC* as published Jan. 1–15, 1872. George Routledge, London, issued it, 1873, 12mo, 2/6 cloth, listed in the *Spect* on Sept. 27; and issued it at 1/0 sewed, 1/6, 2/0 cloth, listed in the *Spect* on Aug. 29, 1874. Ward, Lock issued the present title and *Aunt Jane's Hero* above in one vol. in 1873, at 3/6 cloth, listed in the *Spect* on Jan. 25. The first edition in America was issued by A. D. F. Randolph, New York, 1870, 19.5 cm., 426 pp., listed in *ALG&PC* (fortnightly) on Nov. 1, and in the *Nation* on Nov. 4, 1869.

770 JAMES HANNAY & HORACE MAYHEW *Hearts Are Trumps and Change for a Shilling.* 16mo. 1/0 sewed Oct. 26 (*Ath*)

Beeton's Humorous Books No. 15. This has 218 pp., the first title by Hannay and the second by Mayhew. These were issued by Kent & Co., London, in the *Comic Library*, illustrated, 0/6, advertised in the *Ath* on Feb. 19, 1859. I have a copy of the Kent issue, no date, *Hearts Are Trumps*, 13.3 cm., 93 pp., illustrated, in orange wrappers cut flush and pictorially printed on the front in red and black, and with ads on the in-

side covers, the back cover, and on four pp. at the back.

Also 1875. See *Christmas Cheer*, 1856, and *Wonderful People*, 1856

771 ALBERT SMITH *The Idler Upon Town and The Ballet Girl.* [New edition]. 16mo. 1/0 sewed Oct. 26 (*Ath*)

Beeton's Humorous Books No. 13. Kent & Co. issued these two titles as in the preceding item. I have a copy of the Kent issue of *The Idler Upon Town*, no date, 13.4 cm., 120 pp., in orange wrappers cut flush, pictorially printed on the front in red and black, with "Comic Library No. 7" on the front. It has ads on the inside covers and the back cover and is illustrated. I have a copy of the Kent issue of *The Ballet Girl*, no date, 13.2 cm., 103 pp., illustrated, with "Comic Library No. 8" on the front, wrappers as for the preceding title and with ads the same.

Also 1875. See *Sketches of the Day*, 1856

772 ALBERT SMITH *The Gent and The Natural History of Stuck-Up People.* [New edition]. 16mo. 1/0 sewed Oct. 26 (*Ath*)

Beeton's Humorous Books No. 12. These titles were issued by Kent & Co. as in the previous titles. I have a Kent issue of each of these titles, no dates, 13.2 cm., 104 pp., and 112 pp., respectively, pictorially printed on the front covers in red and black, orange wrappers cut flush, with "Comic Library No. 9" and "Comic Library No. 6," respectively, on the front covers. They are illustrated and have ads on the inside covers and on the back covers.

Also 1875. See *Sketches of the Day*, 1856

773 ANGUS B. REACH *The Natural History of Humbugs and Mince Pies.* [New edition]. 16mo. 1/0 sewed Nov. 9 (*Ath*)

Beeton's Humorous Books No. 14. These titles were issued by Kent & Co. as for the

preceding issues. The first edition of the first title was issued by David Bogue, London, 1847, 13.5 cm., 126 pp., illustrated, listed in the *Ath* on Oct. 30 and reviewed on Nov. 13. The first edition of the second title was as *A Romance of a Mince Pie*, issued by Bogue, 1848, 13.5 cm., 104 pp., illustrated, 1/o sewed, listed in the *Ath* on Dec. 25, 1847.
Also 1873, 75

774 CHARLES READE *Griffith Gaunt.* [New edition]. p 8vo. 2/6 boards, 3/6 cloth Nov. 9 (*Ath*)

This has no date and 410 pp. It first appeared in the *Argosy* (Strahan), Dec. 1865–Nov. 1866, illustrated. The first English edition was issued by Chapman & Hall, London, 3 vols., p 8vo, 31/6, dated 1866, advertised in the *Ath* on Oct. 13 as "On Oct. 15" and listed Oct. 20. It was in purple cloth with a 16-page catalog (Oct. 1866) at the back of vol. 3. The second edition, 3 vols., was advertised by Chapman & Hall in the *Spect* on Nov. 10, 1866; and the third edition in 3 vols. was advertised on Mar. 16, 1867, as "This day." The fifth edition, 1868, a new edition, was issued as *Select Library of Fiction* No. 124 at 2/o boards, by Chapman and Hall, about July 25; and Chapman & Hall issued it at 6/o, Cr 8vo, six illustrations, advertised in the *Spect* on July 27, 1867, as "Next week." Bradbury & Evans, London, issued it at 5/o, Cr 8vo, with a frontispiece and an illustrated title page, listed in the *Spect* on Mar. 20, 1869. The first American edition was issued by Ticknor & Fields, Boston, 1866, author's edition, 23.5 cm., 214 pp., illustrated, double columns, $1.00 paper, $1.50 cloth, bound in purple cloth. It was listed in *ALG&PC* (fortnightly) on Oct. 15 and advertised in the *New-York Times* on Oct. 6 as "This day." It ran in the *Atlantic Monthly* from Dec. 1865 to Nov. 1866. It got a bad review in the *Round Table*, which stated that it was not fit for an American lady to read. This aroused Reade's ire

(very easily done), and he replied in *The Prurient Prude*, a pamphlet, in 1866 (see Parrish). It was also issued by Hilton & Co., New York, 1866, 8vo, 165 pp., double columns. Harper & Bros., New York, issued it in 1869, 8vo, illustrated, $.30 paper, advertised in the *New-York Times* on Mar. 12 as "This day."

775 HORACE MAYHEW *Model Men and Model Women and Children.* [New edition]. 16mo. 1/o sewed Nov. 16 (*Ath*)

Beeton's Humorous Books No. 10. These titles were also issued by Kent & Co. as for the titles above. The present title was also listed by the *Spect* on Dec. 28.
Also 1873, 75. See *Wonderful People*, 1856

776 ALBERT SMITH *The Flirt and Evening Parties.* [New edition]. 16 mo. 1/o sewed Nov. 16 (*Ath*)

Beeton's Humorous Books No. 11. These titles were also issued by Kent & Co. as for the above titles. The present edition is illustrated and was also listed in the *Spect* on Dec. 28.
Also 1875. See *Sketches of the Day*, 1856

777 CHARLES READE *The Double Marriage; or, White Lies.* [New edition]. p 8vo. 2/6 boards, 3/6 cloth Nov. 16 (*Ath*)

This has no date and 370 pp. It first appeared in the *London Journal* where it ran from July 11 to Dec. 5, 1857, illustrated. The first English book edition was issued by Trübner & Co., London, 3 vols., 1857, p 8vo, 21/o, in green or purple cloth, with a preface (Nov. 28, 1857). It was advertised in the *Ath* on Nov. 21 as "On Dec. 1," on Dec. 5 as "Just out," and listed Nov. 21 with the title, *White Lies*. It was issued by Bradbury & Evans, London, 1868, as *Double Marriage*, a new edition, 19.5 cm., 366 pp., 4/o, in three-quarters watered cloth, listed in the *Spect* on Dec. 5. The first American edition was issued by Ticknor &

Fields, Boston, in four parts at $.25 each, in buff wrappers, listed in *APC&LG* (weekly) on Aug. 15, Sept. 12, Oct. 10, and Dec. 19, 1857, respectively, as *White Lies*. The parts were printed in editions of 2,000 copies each and Reade received $180 for them. They issued it in one vol., 1857, 18.5 cm., 586 pp., $1.25 cloth, in dark brown cloth, with a catalog (Dec. 1857). It had a printing of 2,000 copies, for which Reade received $238. It was reviewed in the *Ind* on Jan. 7, 1858. There were editions two through five, issued Jan., Jan., Mar., and Sept. 1858, respectively, also selling at $1.25, for which Reade received $427.

778 ANONYMOUS *The Coming K———*. 8vo. Illustrated. 1/o sewed   Nov. 16–30 (*PC*)

This was Beeton's Christmas Annual, the 13th season. It is my copy, no date, 24.3 cm., 47 pp. of the title poem, plus pp. (48)–75, plus 10 pp. of illustrations and 2 pp. of text interspersed with ads at the back. It is printed in double columns and clothed in white wrappers cut flush with scenes and decorative printing on the front in red, blue, and black. There are ads on the inside covers, the back cover, on 6 pp. and verso of the title page at the front, and 9 pp. at the back interspersed with illustrations and text. There is an 8-page and a 4-page insert at the front. This was issued by Samuel Miller, London, 1873, 17.5 cm., 245 pp., at 5/o, advertised in the *Saturday Review* on Jan. 18, 1873. The *BM* thinks the title poem was by S. O. Beeton, A. A. Dowty, and S. R. Emerson.

779 MARY E. BRADDON, ed. *Belgravia Annual*. 1/o sewed   Nov. (*Bks*)

780 ÉMILE ERCKMANN & PIERRE CHATRIAN *The Alsacian Schoolmaster*. Small format. 1/o sewed, 3/6 cloth Dec. 7 (*Ath*)

This has no date and 148 pp. It was also issued at 2/6 cloth, listed in the *Spect* on Apr.

12, 1873. The first edition was *Histoire d'un Sous-Maître*, Paris, 1871, 19 cm., 283 pp., reviewed in the *British Quarterly Review* for Jan. 1872, and in the *Atlantic Monthly* for Feb. 1872, as "Recent." Also 1875, 87

781 ELIZABETH S. PHELPS *Ellen's Idol*. 18mo. Frontispiece. o/9 sewed, 1/o, 1/6 cloth   Dec. 7 (*Ath*)

Beeton's Good-Aim Series No. 3. This is the first English edition, no date, 15.5 cm., 156 pp. The first edition was issued by the Massachusetts Sabbath School Society, Boston (1864), 16 cm., anonymous, 230 pp., bound in lavender cloth with yellow endpapers. It was listed in *APC&LG* on Nov. 15, 1864.

782 JOHANN C. VON SCHMID *The Basket of Flowers*. 18mo. o/9 sewed, 1/o, 1/6 cloth   Dec. 18–31 (*PC*)

Beeton's Good-Aim Series No. 4. This has no date and 157 pp., and is translated by G. T. Bedell from a French version. The first edition was issued at Landshut, 1823, as *Das Blumenkörbchen*. There was an English edition listed in the *Edinburgh Review*, *The Flower Basket*, Fcp 8vo, 3/6, as published July–Oct. 1839 and the same by Christopher Schmidt was listed in the *Spect* on June 29, 1839, translated by Samuel Jackson. It was issued by Thomas Nelson, London and Edinburgh, 1853, 192 pp. George Routledge, London, issued it (1862), a new edition, 16mo, 128 pp., translated by Bedell; and Frederick Warne, London, issued it, 18mo, with colored illustrations, 1/o cloth, advertised in the *Ath* on Dec. 9, 1865, with no date. Eric Quayle, in *Early Children's Books*, thinks that the Warne issue was the first direct translation from the German into English, the other earlier issues always being from the French version, translated by Bedell. In the United States it was issued by H. Perkins, Philadelphia; etc., 1833,

15.5 cm., 144 pp., illustrated, in the Bedell translation.
Also 1885

783 ANONYMOUS ***Beeton's Dictionary of Commerce.*** 1/o sewed, 1/6 cloth, 2/o half-bound   1872 (*Eng Cat*)
This has no date, edited by (R. M. Smith). It was also listed in the *Spect* on Oct. 11, 1873, and on June 17, 1876, 1/o. *Beeton's Dictionary of Industries and Commerce* was issued in the 8os, 25 cm., 338 pp., illustrated.

784 ROBERT W. BIRD ***Nick of the Woods.*** 2/o boards   1872 (*Eng Cat*)
Also 1854, 56, 59, 60

Ward, Lock & Tyler
1873

785 (MARTHA D. TOLMAN) *Fabrics.*
12mo. 1/0 sewed, 1/6, 2/0 cloth
Jan. 11 (*Ath*)

Lily Series No. 17. The first edition was issued by A. D. F. Randolph, New York (copyright 1871), anonymous, 380 pp.

786 CHARLES D. WARNER *Pusley.*
Fcp 8vo. 1/0 sewed   Jan. 25 (*Ath*)

Beeton's Humorous Books No. 16. The first edition was issued by Fields, Osgood, Boston, 1871, 19 cm., 183 pp., $1.00, in green, purple, or terra-cotta cloth with brown endpapers. By Nov. 23, 1870, 1,540 copies were bound; and 1,020 copies were bound Dec. 20–23, 1870, with the title *My Summer in a Garden.* It was listed in *Lit World* as published in Nov. 1870, and listed by the *Nation* on Dec. 1. The first English edition was issued by Sampson Low, London, 1871, 16 cm., 249 pp., 1/6 boards, 2/0 cloth, with the American title, and an introduction by Henry W. Beecher, advertised in the *Ath* on July 22 as "This day" and listed on Aug. 5. In a letter to the *Ath* on June 7, 1873, Low said that they had issued this title some 18 months ago and that it was not protected by copyright, although they had paid the author; and now Ward, Lock & Tyler issued it as *Pusley* after it had been well-promoted by Low. The first Canadian edition was issued by Adam, Stevenson & Co., Toronto, 1871, 18 cm., 86 pp., with the American title, reprinted from the third American edition. It was probably in paper wrappers.
Also 1875

787 MARY R. MITFORD *Our Village. Tales.*
12mo. 1/0 sewed, 1/6, 2/0 cloth   Feb. 8
(*Ath*)

Lily Series No. 18. This has no date, 278 pp. The first edition was issued in London, 5 vols., 1824–32, with the imprint of G. & W. B. Whittaker on vol. 1; G. B. Whittaker on vols. 2 and 3; and Whittaker & Treacher on vols. 4 and 5. Vol. 1 was listed in the *Edinburgh Review* as published Apr.–July 1824, at 7/6 boards. Vol. 2 was listed by the *Quarterly Review* as published Oct.–Dec. 1826, p 8vo, 311 pp., at 8/6 boards. Vol. 3 was listed by the *Quarterly Review* as published Apr.–June 1828, p 8vo, 315 pp., 9/0 boards. Vol. 4 was listed by the *Edinburgh Review* as published Apr.–July 1830, p 8vo, 10/6 boards, with "Fourth series" on the title page. Vol. 5 was advertised in the *Spect* on Sept. 29, 1832, as "This day," 362 pp., 10/6 boards. There was a new edition in 3 vols., p 8vo, 25/0, advertised in the *Spect* on May 16, 1829. There was another new edition in 4 vols., p 8vo, 35/6, advertised there on Feb. 26, 1831. Elam Bliss, New York, issued the fourth series, 1830, 20 cm., 275 pp., and probably issued the whole work as Roorbach gives 3 vols., no date.
See 1875 for further sketches

788 CHARLES READE *Love Me Little, Love Me Long.* New Edition. p 8vo. 2/6 boards, 3/6 cloth   Feb. 8 (*Ath*)

This has no date and 336 pp. The 3/6 edition has a frontispiece. The first edition was issued by Trübner & Co., London, 2 vols., 1859, 19.5 cm., 21/0, in green cloth, advertised in the *Ath* on Apr. 2 as "Immediately" and listed on Apr. 9. Bradbury & Evans, London, issued it, 1868, Cr 8vo, 4/0, listed in the *Spect* on Nov. 21. The first American edition was issued by Harper & Bros., New York, 1859, 12mo, 435 pp., $.65 paper and $.75 muslin, black or red. It was listed in the *Ind* on Apr. 28, and by *APC&LG* (weekly) on Apr. 30. It was advertised in the *New-York Times* on Apr. 23, 1859, as "This day."

789 ROSE PORTER *The Winter Fire.*
12mo. 1/0 sewed, 1/6, 2/0 cloth
Feb. 15 (*Ath*)
Lily Series No. 19. This is the first English edition and possibly the first edition. The *U Cat* gives only A. D. F. Randolph, New York (copyright 1874), 18 cm., 231 pp.

790 ÉMILE ERCKMANN & PIERRE CHATRIAN *Friend Fritz.* Small format.
1/0 sewed   Feb. 15 (*Ath*)
This is my copy, no date, 16.2 cm., 274 pp., white wrappers cut flush, with a pictorial front cover in red, blue, and black, with "Beeton's Erckmann-Chatrian Library" on the front. There are ads on the endpapers, the versos of the half-title and title pages, the back cover, and 18 pp. at the back. The 2/6 edition was listed in the *Spect* on Mar. 8, 1873, and the 3/6 edition was listed on July 4, 1874. The first edition was *L'Ami Fritz*, Paris, 1864, 341 pp. The first American edition was issued by Charles Scribner & Co., New York, 1869, 12mo, 289 pp. Scribner, Armstrong & Co., New York, issued it in 1877, 12mo, at $1.25 in cloth, advertised in the *New-York Times* on Feb. 17 as "This day." There was a short review in *Scribner's Monthly* for Apr. 1877.
See 1875

791 ELIZABETH WETHERELL (SUSAN WARNER) *The Wide, Wide World.* 12mo. 1/0 sewed, 1/6, 2/0 cloth   Feb. (*Bks*)
Lily Series No. 14. This has no date. Ward, Lock issued it, Fcp 8vo, illustrated, at 3/6 cloth, listed in the *Reader* on June 18, 1864. The first edition was issued by G. P. Putnam, New York, 2 vols., 1851, 19 cm., deposited in New York on Dec. 5, 1850, and in Washington on Dec. 14. It was reviewed in *Lit World* on Dec. 28. The first English edition was issued by Sampson Low, London, 2 vols., 1851, Fcp 8vo, anonymous, 12/0, edited by a clergyman of the Church of England. It was advertised in *Notes & Queries* on Mar. 13, 1852, quoting reviews. It was listed in the *Ath* on Dec. 27, 1851. Putnam issued the fifth edition, 2 vols., 12mo, advertised in the *New York Daily Times* on Sept. 18, 1851; and issued the 13th edition in 2 vols. at $1.50 cloth, advertised there on Apr. 26, 1852. John Chapman, London, imported it and issued it in 2 vols., Cr 8vo, 7/0, advertised in the *Ath* on Feb. 14, 1852. It was issued by James Nisbet; Sampson Low; Hamilton, Adams, London, with a preface by Anna Warner, 2 vols., Cr 8vo, listed in the *Ath* on Aug. 7, 1852, and by *PC* on Aug. 15. They issued it in 2 vols., also in a second edition. They issued the third edition (the author's edition), in 1852, 20 cm., 657 pp., 5/0, dated 1852, and listed in the *Ath* on Oct. 30. They issued it in 2 vols., carefully revised by the author, with added material and a preface by Anna Warner, illustrated, 6/0, listed in the *Ath* on Jan. 29, 1853, and in *PC* on Feb. 16. George Routledge, London, issued it at 2/0 boards, 1853, listed by *PC* as published Nov. 30–Dec. 15, 1852, and listed in the *Ath* on Nov. 13, 1852. He reissued it at least nine times before 1885. It was issued by H. G. Bohn, London, p 8vo, 3/6 in blue cloth, listed in the *Ath* on Dec. 4, 1852; and issued it in blue cloth, p 8vo, illustrated, 9/0 cloth with gilt edges, advertised in *Notes &*

Queries on Feb. 5, 1853, as "This day." Thomas Nelson, London, issued it at 4/0, listed in the *Ath* on Nov. 6, 1852, and in *PC* on Dec. 3. It was issued by Clarke, Beeton, London, 12mo, illustrated, 1/6 boards, 2/0 cloth, listed by *PC* as published Dec. 15–30, 1852, and listed in the *Ath* on Dec. 11. It was also issued by Eginton, London, and Farrington, London, in 1853.
Also 1875

792 CHARLES D. WARNER *Back-Log Studies.* Fcp 8vo. 1/0 sewed, 1/6 cloth Mar. 8 (*Ath*)

Beeton's Humorous Books No. 17. This has no date. It was first issued in book form simultaneously by J. R. Osgood, Boston, and Sampson Low, London. The Osgood issue was 1873, 18 cm., 281 pp., illustrated, $3.00, listed by *PW* on Dec. 12, 1872, and advertised in the *New-York Times* on Dec. 19 as "This day." It was bound in terra-cotta, green, blue, or orange cloth with bevelled covers and with brown or blue endpapers. From Dec. 17, 1872–Jan. 11, 1873, 3,000 copies were bound. There was a second printing of 1,000 copies on Jan. 5, 1873. They issued a new edition, illustrated, $1.50, advertised in the *New-York Times* on Nov. 17, 1877. It first appeared in *Scribner's Monthly* in July 1871 and Feb.–July 1872. The Low edition was 1872, 16mo, at 1/6 boards, 2/0 cloth, listed in the *Ath* on Dec. 7. In a letter to the *Ath* by the author on May 10, 1873, he stated that this was published at the same time in Boston and by Low in England and that Low paid the author for it. He said that it consisted of eleven papers and that he had now received a book published by Ward, Lock & Tyler with the same title and his name as author but that it was not the same book, containing only seven of the papers (the other four being protected by copyright) and having an added portion of the author's address delivered at a college anniversary and which had no connection with the volume whatsoever.

He expressed his appreciation for the delicacy Ward, Lock must have felt in preparing the vol. Actually it was prepared by S. O. Beeton and reprints the seven items from *Scribner's Monthly* and a slightly abridged address, "A Summary of Culture," delivered at Hamilton College on June 26, 1872!
Also 1875

793 (MARY E. BRADDON) *To the Bitter End.* Stereotyped Edition. Small format. 2/0 boards, 2/6 cloth   Mar. 15 (*Ath*)

This was 1873, 380 pp., the first yellowback edition. Wolff's yellowback had no date, issued in 1874. The first edition was issued by John Maxwell & Co., London, 3 vols., 1872, Cr 8vo, 31/6, listed in the *Spect* on Sept. 21, and listed by *PC* as published Sept. 17–30. A panel ad in the *Ath* on Sept. 14 and 21, 1872, gave no publisher; a panel ad on Sept. 28, Oct. 5 and 12 gave Maxwell as the publisher; and an ad in the *Saturday Review* on Sept. 14 and 21 was by Ward, Lock & Tyler. It was also advertised there on Sept. 28 and Oct. 5 and 12 by Maxwell. No further Maxwell ads of any kind appeared for at least eight months! The first American edition was issued by Harper & Bros., New York, 1873, 8vo, illustrated, $.75 paper, listed in *PW* on Mar. 29, and in the *Ind* on Mar. 27.

794 ELIZABETH PRENTISS *The Flower of the Family.* 12mo. 1/0 sewed, 1/6, 2/0 cloth   Mar. 22 (*Ath*)

Lily Series No. 20. The first edition was issued by A. D. F. Randolph & Co., New York (copyright 1853), 16mo, anonymous, 385 pp., $.75, advertised in the *New-York Times* on Nov. 23, 1853, as "On Nov. 25." It was issued in England in 1854 by Sampson Low, London, listed in the *Ath* on June 17, 1854, Fcp 8vo, anonymous, 2/0 cloth; and by Thomas Nelson & Sons, London and Edinburgh, Fcp 8vo, 1/0 fancy boards, listed in the *Spect* on Sept. 23; and by W. Collins, London, anonymous. It was issued as *Run and Read Library* No. 26 by Simpkin, Marshall, London; etc., no date, 1/6 boards, about Jan. 31, 1857.

795 CHARLES READE *The Course of True Love Never Did Run Smooth*. New Edition. 2/0 boards, 3/6 cloth   Mar. 29 (*Ath*)

This has no date. The first edition was issued in England by Bentley, London, 1857, advertised in *Notes & Queries* on Sept. 26, Cr 8vo, 2/0 boards, 3/0 cloth, as "On Sept. 28," a *Popular New Series*, noticed on Oct. 24. It was listed and reviewed in the *Ath* on Sept. 26. It was in pink pictorial boards or blue cloth. It contains *The Bloomer*; *Art: A Dramatic Tale*; and *Clouds and Sunshine*. In the United States Ticknor & Fields, Boston, issued *Clouds and Sunshine* and *Art: A Dramatic Tale*, 1855, 18.4 cm., 288 pp., $.75, published on Sept. 11 according to the publisher, and listed in the *Knickerbocker* for Oct. It was printed in an edition of 3,800 copies, and Reade was told in Mar. 1857 that the book had as yet hardly paid expenses, although the second edition of 2,000 copies, to sell at $.75, was issued in Sept. 1855. Reade replied that the agreement was for him to get 10 percent of the gross receipts. The publisher's books show no payment to him. Ticknor & Fields issued *Propria Quae Maribus . . .* (The Bloomer); *and The Box Tunnel, a Fact*, 1857, 108 pp., $.20, with an author's note (Sept. 1857), and a catalog (Oct. 1857). It was published in Oct. according to the publisher, listed in *APC&LG* (weekly) on Oct. 3, and advertised in the *New-York Times* on Sept. 28 as "On Oct. 1." It had a printing of 3,000 copies, and the race was to beat the Bentley issue, accomplished by Reade sending the MS to Ticknor. After much haggling, Reade got £30 for it. The English issue of the present title was issued by Bradbury & Evans, London, in 1868, Cr 8vo, 3/6, listed in the *Spect* on Oct. 24. *Clouds and Sunshine* ran in *Bentley's Miscellany*, Jan.–

Aug. 1854, and *The Box Tunnel* first appeared in *Bentley's Miscellany* in Nov. 1853. The copyright and stereo plates of the first Bentley issue of the present title were for sale at a Southgate & Barrett auction on Oct. 25, 1858.

796 HORACE MAYHEW *Model Men and Model Women and Children*. 1/0 sewed Mar. (*Bks*)

Also 1872. See 1856, 75

797 ANGUS REACH *The Natural History of Humbugs and Mince Pies*. 1/0 sewed Mar. (*Bks*)

Also 1872, 75

798 CHARLES READE *The Cloister and the Hearth*. New Edition. 2/6 boards, 3/6 cloth   Apr. 5 (*Ath*)

Wolff had a copy of the 2/6 yellowback. The first edition was issued by Trübner & Co., London, 4 vols., 1861, 19 cm., 31/6, listed in the *Ath* on Sept. 28, and by *PC* as published Oct. 1–14. They issued the second edition, 1862, 4 vols., advertised on Nov. 2, 1861, as "Just out." It is based on *A Good Fight*, which ran in *Once a Week*, July 2–Oct. 1, 1859, and ran in *Harper's Weekly*, July 23–Oct. 15, 1859. Harper & Bros., New York, issued *A Good Fight, and Other Tales*, 1859, illustrated, $.75, in black or green cloth, containing *Jack of All Trades* and *The Autobiography of a Thief*. The present title was issued by Bradbury & Evans, London, in 1868, Cr 8vo, 5/0, listed in the *Spect* on Dec. 5, 1868. The first American edition of the present title was issued by Rudd & Carleton, New York; Trübner & Co., London, 1861, 24 cm., 256 pp., double columns, bound in green cloth, and selling for $.75 and $1.25. It was deposited on Oct. 24 and listed in *APC&LG* (monthly) on Nov. 15. It was also issued by Harper & Bros., New York, 1861, $1.25, reviewed briefly in *Godey's Lady's Book* for Jan. 1862, and thus probably issued in

Oct. or Nov. 1861. The Harper issue of *A Good Fight, and Other Tales* was advertised in the *New-York Times* on Oct. 29, 1859, 12mo, illustrated, $.75 muslin, as "Just ready." *A Good Fight* ran also in the *Semi-Weekly Times*, starting with the July 25 issue in 1859. The eighth printing of the Rudd & Carleton was advertised on Nov. 16, 1861.

799 HENRY HALLAM *View of the State of Europe During the Middle Ages.* Reprint of the Fourth Edition as Revised and Corrected. 2/6 boards   Apr. 26 (*Spect*)

This has no date, with 720 pp. The first edition was issued by John Murray, London, 2 vols., 1818, 29 cm., 63/0 boards, listed in the *Edinburgh Review* as published Feb.–June 1818. It was issued in the United States by T. Dobson & Son, Philadelphia, 4 vols., 1821, 22 cm. Ward, Lock reissued several times in cloth.

800 ELIZABETH WETHERELL *Queechy.* 12mo. 1/0 sewed, 1/6, 2/0 cloth   May 3 (*Ath*)

Lily Series No. 15. This has no date. The first American edition was issued by George Putnam, New York, 2 vols., 1852, 19.5 cm., $1.75 in cloth, listed in *Lit World* as published Apr. 10–May 15, and deposited Apr. 23. The ads said it was delayed in order to secure English copyright. There are 8 or 10 pp. of ads in vol. 1, and it is bound in purple, brown, black, or blue cloth with yellow or buff endpapers. There is a known copy inscribed Apr. 27, 1852. 7,000 copies were printed, and a new edition was advertised in *Lit World* on May 8, 1852, and listed May 15; and the 13th thousand was issued in 2 vols. in July 1852. The first English edition was issued by James Nisbet & Co., etc., London, 2 vols., 1852, 18 cm., 12/0, in decorated blue cloth, advertised in the *Ath* on Apr. 24 as "This day," and listed in *PC* on May 1. It had a preface (Mar. 24, 1852), not in the American edition. It had no illustra-

tions due to the hurry to get it out. There was a new edition listed in the *Ath* on Nov. 27, 1852; and a new edition in 2 vols., at 12/0, listed on Mar. 12, 1853. The first English illustrated edition was issued by George Routledge, London, 1853, with a pictorial title page and a frontispiece, 2/0 boards, 2/6 cloth, listed by *PC* as published Mar. 30–Apr. 14. Mumby in *The House of Routledge* says that Routledge made an agreement with Nisbet to issue a 2/0 edition and to pay 0/2 per copy, but after the House of Lords decision declaring no copyright in American works, the 0/2 per copy was never paid.

Also 1875

801 ADELINE D. T. WHITNEY *Patience Strong's Outings.* 12mo. 1/0 sewed, 1/6, 2/0 cloth   May 3 (*Ath*)

Lily Series No. 22. This has no date. The first edition was issued by A. K. Loring, Boston, 1869, 19 cm., 233 pp., listed in *ALG&PC* (fortnightly) on Jan. 1, 1869. The first English edition was issued by George Routledge, London (1870), anonymous, illustrated, in cloth, entitled *Patience Strong*. He reissued it at 2/0 boards, illustrated, about Apr. 11, 1874.

802 JOHN TILLOTSON *Sermons on the Walls.* 18mo. 0/9 sewed, 1/0, 1/6 cloth   May 3 (*Spect*)

Beeton's Good-Aim Series No. 5. This is the first edition.

803 CHARLES READE & DION BOUCICAULT *Foul Play.* New Edition. p 8vo. 2/6 boards, 3/6 cloth   May 10 (*Ath*)

This has no date and 414 pp. The 3/6 issue was illustrated. It ran in *Once a Week* (Jan. 4–June 20, 1868), illustrated by Du Maurier. The first edition was issued by Bradbury & Evans, London, 3 vols., 1868, 19.5 cm., 31/6, in red cloth, with a map in vol. 2. It was listed in the *Ath* on May 23. They issued it in 1869, Cr 8vo, with a frontispiece and illustrated title page, 5/o, listed in the *Spect* on Mar. 20. In the United States it ran in Ticknor & Field's *Every Saturday*, beginning on Jan. 4, 1868, from advanced sheets. They issued it, 1868, 25.5 cm., 136 pp., double columns, illustrated by Du Maurier, $.75 paper, pink wrappers. It was deposited on June 1, listed in *ALG&PC* (fortnightly) on June 15, and advertised in the *New-York Times* on June 8, 1868, author's copyright edition, from advanced sheets, as ready. John Lovell, Montreal, issued it, 1868, with 175 pp.

804 LOUISA M. ALCOTT *Something to Do.* 12mo. 1/o sewed, 1/6, 2/o cloth   May 31 (*Ath*)

Lily Series No. 23. This has no date and 250 pp., the first English edition. The first edition was issued by J. R. Osgood & Co., Boston, 1871, 8vo, anonymous, $.75 paper and $1.00 cloth, listed in the *Nation* on Apr. 13, in *ALG&PC* (fortnightly) on Apr. 15, and advertised in the *New-York Times* on Apr. 8 as "This day."

805 MARY JEFFERIS *Gertrude's Trial.* 12mo. 1/o sewed, 1/6, 2/o cloth May 31 (*Ath*)

Lily Series No. 24. This is the first edition.

806 MARY DENSEL *Goldy and Goldy's Friends.* 18mo. o/9 sewed, 1/o, 1/6 cloth May 31 (*Spect*)

Beeton's Good-Aim Series No. 6. This is the first English edition, with no date and 128 pp. The first edition was issued by E. P. Dutton & Co., New York, 1872, 18mo, 139 pp., illustrated.

807 ANONYMOUS *Beeton's Book of Cottage Management.* 18mo. o/6 boards   May (*Bks*)

This is in four parts and has no date, probably the first edition.

808 BRET HARTE *Sandy Bar: With Other Stories, Sketches, Legends and Tales.* Fcp 8vo. 1/o sewed   June 7 (*Ath*)

Beeton's Humorous Books No. 18. This has no date, 16.5 cm., 227 pp., apparently a first edition. *BAL* gives also a later binding with an ad for Fry's Cocoa on the back cover with a reference to an 1878 medal. Also 1885

809 ANONYMOUS *Leah; or, the Jewish Maiden.* p 8vo. 2/o boards   June 7 (*Spect*)

Library of Favourite Authors No. 3. Also 1864, 70, 90

810 RICHARD COBBOLD *The History of Margaret Catchpole.* p 8vo. 2/o boards June 7 (*Spect*)

Library of Favourite Authors No. 4. Also 1864, 67, 77, 87

811 JANE PORTER *The Scottish Chiefs.* p 8vo. 2/o boards   June 7?

Library of Favourite Authors No. 2. This has 520 pp. It was also listed at 2/o boards as published Dec. 2–17, 1872, by *PC*. Also 1870

812 W. STARBUCK MAYO *Never Again.* p 8vo. 2/o boards   June 14 (*Ath*)

Library of Favourite Authors No. 1. This begins a new and long series. It has no date and 396 pp. The series title probably appears at the head of the spine. The first edition was issued by G. P. Putnam & Sons, New York, 1873, 19 cm., anonymous, 714 pp., illustrated, $2.00, advertised in the *New-York Times* on Nov. 28, 1872, as "In a few days," and reviewed in *Lit World* on Jan. 1, 1873, and in the *Ind* on Jan. 9. The first English edition was issued by Sampson Low, London, 2 vols., 1873, Cr 8vo, 21/o, listed in the *Ath* on Jan. 11, 1873. Low issued it, 1873, Cr 8vo, 484 pp., 5/o, listed in the *Spect* on Mar. 8.

813 ELIZABETH S. PHELPS
Mercy Gliddon's Work. 12mo.
1/o sewed, 1/6, 2/o cloth   June 21 (*Ath*)
Lily Series No. 21. This is the first English edition. The first edition was issued by Henry Hoyt, Boston (copyright 1865), 17.5 cm., 311 pp., frontispiece and added illustrated title page, bound in green or purple cloth, with yellow endpapers, listed in *ALG&PC* on Mar. 1, 1866.

814 MARION HARLAND (MARY V. HAWES, later TERHUNE) *The Hidden Path.* 12mo.
1/o sewed, 1/6, 2/o cloth   June 21 (*Spect*)
Lily Series No. 25. The first American edition was issued by J. C. Derby, New York; etc., 1855, 19.5 cm., 434 pp., $1.25, listed in the *Ind* on Aug. 23, and advertised in *APC&LG* (weekly) on Sept. 1 as "Recently published." The 14th thousand was advertised in the *New-York Times* on Oct. 3, 1855, $1.25, as "This day," and the first edition was advertised there on Aug. 23, 1855. It was supposed to be issued simultaneously in New York and by Sampson Low in London. Low issued it, 1855, 2/o boards, listed in the *Ath* on Sept. 24 and listed by *PC* as published Sept. 14–29. He issued a new edition at 2/6 cloth, 12mo, 344 pp., listed by *PC* as published Feb. 29–Mar. 14, 1856. It was also issued by George Routledge, London, in 1855, at 2/o boards, listed in the *Ath* on Sept. 29, and he issued the 12th thousand, 1855. It was issued as *Run and Read Library* No. 31, about May 30, 1857, by Simpkin, Marshall, London; etc., another copy of the Low issue with a frontispiece and an added illustrated title page.

815 CHARLES READE *Autobiography of a Thief; and Jack of All Trades.* p. 8vo.
2/o boards, 3/6 cloth   June 28 (*Ath*)
This has no date and is a new edition of *Cream*, the latter issued by Trübner & Co., London, 1858, 20.5 cm., 270 pp., 10/o, bound in blue cloth, listed in the *Ath* on

Mar. 13. *Jack of All Trades* ran in *Harper's New Monthly Magazine*, Dec. 1857–Mar. 1858. *A Good Fight, and Other Tales* containing both the stories of *Cream* was issued by Harper & Bros., New York, 1859, 19.2 cm., 341 pp., in black or green cloth, noticed in *De Bow's Magazine* (monthly) for Jan. 1860 and thus probably issued in Nov. or Dec. 1859. Harper's issued *Jack of All Trades* in 1884, 16mo, 49 pp., listed in *Harper's New Monthly Magazine* for June.

816 ANN S. STEPHENS *Zana, the Gipsy.*
p 8vo. 2/o boards   June 28 (*Spect*)
Library of Favourite Authors No. 5.
Also 1854, 56, 60

817 LUCY AIKEN *Memoirs of the Court of Elizabeth.* Reprint of the Sixth Edition, Revised and Corrected. Cr 8vo. 2/o boards   June 28 (*Spect*)
The first edition was issued by Longmans, London, 2 vols., 1818, at 25/o. The present edition is a reissue of the edition issued by A. Murray & Son, London, 1869, 532 pp., itself a reprint of the sixth edition, revised and corrected.
Also 1875

818 JOHN MILLS *Stable Secrets.*
1/o sewed   June (*Bks*)
Also 1865, 82, 85

819 JOHN MILLS *Flyers of the Hunt.*
1/o sewed   June (*Bks*)
Also 1865, 82

820 JOHN MILLS *The Life of a Racehorse.*
1/o sewed   June (*Bks*)
Also 1854, 56, 65, 82, 85

821 (MARY E. BRADDON) *Milly Darrell, and Other Tales.* Stereotyped Edition. Small format. 2/o boards, 2/6 cloth
July 12 (*Ath*)
This has no date, 348 pp., with the list of Braddon yellowbacks on the back cover

ending with *To the Bitter End*. This is the first yellowback edition. The first edition was issued by John Maxwell & Co., London, 3 vols., 1873, Cr 8vo, 31/6, listed in the *Ath* on Feb. 15. It was advertised in the *Saturday Review* for several weeks beginning on Feb. 8, but with no publisher given, and finally on Mar. 8 it was advertised by Ward, Lock & Tyler! It was issued in the United States by G. W. Carleton & Co., New York, at $1.00 paper and $1.50 cloth, advertised in the *New-York Times* on Apr. 21, 1877.

822 HERBERT BYNG HALL *The Queen's Messenger.* 2/0 boards, 3/6 cloth   July 12 (*Spect*)

The first edition was issued by John Maxwell & Co., London, 1865, 19.5 cm., 404 pp., at 16/0, listed in the *Ath* on Sept. 23. Ward, Lock & Tyler issued it (1870), 18.5 cm., 407 pp., at 6/0, listed in the *Spect* on Apr. 9.
Also 1874

823 W. S. HAYWARD *Hunted to Death.* [New and enlarged edition]. 2/0 boards   July 19 (*Spect*)
Also 1862, 69, 74

824 (LOUISA M. ALCOTT) *Fireside and Camp Stories.* 12mo. 1/0 sewed, 1/6, 2/0 cloth   July 19 (*Spect*)

Lily Series No. 27. This has no date and 251 pp. It was also listed in the *Bks* on Sept. 2. *Hospital Sketches* was issued by James Redpath, Boston, 1863 (revised and enlarged), 102 pp.; and a second edition was advertised in the *New-York Times* on Oct. 22, 1863, at $.50 cloth, as "Just published." The first American edition of the present title was issued by Roberts Bros., Boston, 1869, 16mo, 379 pp., illustrated, $1.50, *Hospital Sketches and Camp and Fireside Stories*. It contained the pieces from the Redpath issue plus six sketches (from the *Commonwealth*, May 22 and 29,

June 12 and 26, 1863) and eight camp and fireside stories from various periodicals. It was advertised in the *New-York Times* on Aug. 7, 1869, as "On Aug. 9," and listed in *ALG&PC* (fortnightly) on Aug. 16. A duplicate of the American edition was issued in England by Sampson Low, London, 1870, 12mo, 3/6, listed in the *Spect* on Apr. 16, *Hospital Sketches*.

825 ELIZABETH S. PHELPS *I Don't Know How.* 18mo. 0/9 sewed, 1/0, 1/6 cloth   July 19 (*Spect*)

Beeton's Good-Aim Series No. 8. This is the first English edition. It was issued by the Massachusetts Sabbath Society, Boston, in 1867, 15 cm., 272 pp., frontispiece, listed in *ALG&PC* (fortnightly) on July 15. *BAL* gives this as dated 1868! The *U Cat* gives H. A. Young & Co., Boston (copyright 1866), 15.5 cm., 272 pp., illustrated; and gives the same (1867).

826 HARRIET B. STOWE *Uncle Tom's Cabin.* 12mo. 1/0 sewed, 1/6, 2/0 cloth   July?
Lily Series No. 26.
Also 1864, 78

827 C. F. ARMSTRONG *The Sailor Hero.* p 8vo. 2/0 boards   July?
Library of Favourite Authors No. 6.
Also 1863, 87

828 ÉMILE ERCKMANN & PIERRE CHATRIAN *The Polish Jew, and Other Tales.* 12mo. 1/0 sewed   Aug. 2 (*Ath*)

This is my copy, no date, 17.3 cm., 229 pp., in white wrappers cut flush, with a pictorial front cover in red, blue, and black. It has the words "Beeton's Erckmann-Chatrian Library" on the front cover and has publisher's ads on the inside covers. The title piece is a drama in three acts and occupies the first 65 pp., followed by 10 other pieces. The *BM* gives *The Bells* (1873), issued by Ward, Lock & Tyler, 4to,

65 pp. This was a play adapted from *The Polish Jew* and was issued as *The Bells* by Tinsley Bros., London, 1872, 12mo, 127 pp., 1/o, listed in the *Ath* on Mar. 20. *The Bells* was also issued by R. M. DeWitt, New York, 1872, translated by H. L. Williams, 19 cm., 33 pp.; and by H. L. Hinton, New York, 1873, 12mo, 115 pp., in Mar. The first edition was *Le Juif Polonaise*, Paris, 1869, and first appeared in *Contes et Romans Populaires*, Paris, 1867, 4to, illustrated. John C. Hotten, London, issued *The Polish Jew*, translated by H. L. Williams, 156 pp., 1/o sewed, about Feb. 10, 1872. The present edition was listed in the *Spect* on Aug. 14, 1875, at 2/6.

829 ANONYMOUS *The One Thing Needful.* 18mo. o/9 sewed, 1/o, 1/6 cloth   Aug. 16 (*Spect*)

Beeton's Good-Aim Series No. 7. This is the first edition, no date.

830 EDGAR ALLAN POE *Tales of Mystery, Imagination, and Humour.* p 8vo. Illustrated. 2/o boards   Aug. 16 (*Spect*)

Library of Favourite Authors No. 7. This has no date, 395 pp., and many textual illustrations.
Also 1880. See 1864

831 (MARTHA S. HUBBELL) *The Shady Side.* 12mo. 1/o sewed, 1/6, 2/o cloth Sept. 20 (*Ath*)

Lily Series No. 28. The first American edition was issued by J. P. Jewett, Boston; etc., 1853, 18.5 cm., 348 pp., by a pastor's wife, noticed in the *Ind* on Mar. 24, and listed by *Lit World* as published Apr. 9–May 7. The first English edition was issued by Sampson Low, London, 1853, 12mo, 5/6, listed in the *Ath* on Apr. 23. It was also listed on May 14 at 3/6; and the second edition was issued by Low, 1853, Fcp 8vo, anonymous, portrait, 3/6, listed on May 28. The 36th thousand was issued with the joint imprint of Fields, Osgood and Sampson

Low, 1854, 19 cm., 348 pp. Low reissued it, anonymous, at 1/o sewed, jointly with Constable, Edinburgh, listed in the *Spect* on Aug. 26, 1854. Low reissued it in Sept. 1857; and issued it with *The Sunny Side* (see below) in 1 vol., Cr 8vo, anonymous, 3/6, by two country ministers' wives, listed in the *Spect* on Feb. 22, 1868.

832 WILLIAM STARBUCK MAYO *The Berber; or, The Mountaineer of the Atlas.* p 8vo. 2/o boards   Sept. 20

Library of Favourite Authors No. 10. The first edition was issued by G. P. Putnam, New York; etc., 1850, 19 cm., 454 pp., advertised in *Lit World* on Aug. 17 as "This week," and noticed in the *Southern Quarterly Review* in Sept. Putnam advertised the third edition in the *New York Daily Times* on Apr. 15, 1852, 12mo, $1.25, as "Ready." This was supposed to be issued simultaneously by Putnam and Bentley in London. Bentley issued it, 1850, listed in the *Spect* on Sept. 14. The Bentley issue was probably printed in New York. It was also issued by H. G. Bohn, London, 1850, at 1/o, listed by *PC* as published Sept. 28–Oct. 14; and by George Routledge, London, 1850, 1/o boards, 1/6 cloth, listed in the *Ath* on Sept. 28, and listed in the *Spect* on Nov. 2, 1850.

833 SUSAN COOLIDGE (SARAH C. WOOLSEY) *What Katy Did.* 12mo. 1/o sewed, 1/6, 2/o cloth   Sept. 27 (*Ath*)

Lily Series No. 30. This is the first English edition, no date, with 238 pp. Frederick Warne, London, issued it in late 1873, illustrated, 2/o cloth, reviewed in the *Ath* on Jan. 31, 1874. The first edition was issued by Roberts Bros., Boston, 1873 (1872), 18 cm., 274 pp., illustrated, $1.50 cloth, deposited on Jan. 7, 1873, listed in *PW* on Nov. 28, 1872, and in the *Ind* on Dec. 12. It was advertised in the *New-York Times* on Dec. 21, 1872.

834 ANONYMOUS ***Beeton's Complete Letter-Writer for Ladies and Gentlemen.***
1/0   Sept. 27 (*Spect*)

This is the first edition, no date. It was also issued for ladies and for gentlemen separately, each at 0/6. These were all advertised as "Just ready" in *The Siliad* below.

835   BRET HARTE   ***The Heathen Chinee, with East and West Poems and Parodies.***
Fcp 8vo. 1/0 sewed   Sept. (*Bks*)

Beeton's Humorous Books No. 20. This has no date and 150 pp., with the series title on the front and at the head of the title page. The first edition of *The Heathen Chinee* was on nine cards in an envelope, issued by the Western News Co., Chicago, 1870, deposited on Nov. 22. It appeared in *The Piccadilly Annual* in Dec. 1870, issued by John C. Hotten, London, 24.5 cm., illustrated, 1/0 sewed. He issued *That Heathen Chinee and Other Poems, Mostly Humorous* (1871), my copy, 16.3 cm., 141 pp., 1/6 stiff wrappers in white, with a pictorial front cover in black, the picture duplicating that of the frontispiece, and with a 20-page catalog at the back. This Hotten edition was also issued at 2/6 cloth, both issues coming out in Mar. *That Heathen Chinee* was issued by James R. Osgood & Co., Boston, 1871, small 8vo, 19 pp. plus publisher's ads, illustrated, orange pictorial wrappers printed in black. It was listed in the *Nation* on May 11 and in *ALG&PC* (fortnightly) on May 15. *The Heathen Chinee* first appeared in the *Overland Monthly*, San Francisco, in Sept. 1870 as *Plain Language from Truthful James*. The first edition of *East and West Poems* was issued by James R. Osgood & Co., Boston, 1871, 18 cm., 171 pp., in terra-cotta or purple cloth, listed in *ALG&PC* (fortnightly) on Nov. 1, and noticed in the *Nation* on Nov. 2. John C. Hotten, London, issued *East and West*, probably the first edition set up in England (1871), 17.5 cm., 140 pp., 1/0 sewed, 1/6 cloth, with a preface dated 1871. It was listed in the *Ath* on Dec. 23,

1871, and by *PC* as published Dec. 15–30. It was imported, probably by Trübner & Co., London, listed in the *Bks* for Dec. 1871, and by *PC* on Dec. 8.
Also 1884

836   BRET HARTE   ***Roaring Camp, and Other Sketches, Stories, and Bohemian Papers.*** Fcp 8vo. 1/0 sewed   Sept.?

Beeton's Humorous Books No. 19. This has no date and has the series title at the head of the title page, received by the *BM* on Sept. 11, 1873. It probably had 245 pp., although the *U Cat* gives an issue (1873?), pp. 69–245, and an issue (187–?), 245 pp., both from Ward, Lock & Tyler. The first edition was *The Luck of Roaring Camp and Other Sketches*, issued by Fields, Osgood & Co., Boston, 1870, 19 cm., 239 pp., deposited Apr. 15, and listed in *ALG&PC* (fortnightly) on May 2. John C. Hotten, London, issued it with the same title (1870), 17.5 cm., 216 pp., 1/0 sewed, 3/6 cloth, received by the *BM* on Nov. 15, and listed by *PC* as published Nov. 1–15. After the American edition came out, Hotten wasted no time in advertising it on May 7, 1870, as "This day"! Routledge, London, issued *The Luck of Roaring Camp and Other Stories* in 1872, 1/0 sewed, listed in the *Spect* on Jan. 20, 1872.
Also 1875

837   FRANCIS C. ARMSTRONG   ***The Cruise of the Daring.*** p 8vo. 2/0 boards   Sept.?

Library of Favourite Authors No. 8. Sadleir had a copy of a yellowback issued by Ward, Lock & Co. in the *Select Library of Fiction*, which he thought was issued in 1881, but this couldn't be correct as Ward, Lock didn't start issuing titles in this series until 1882.
Also 1863, 90

838   ANDREW HALLIDAY   ***The Adventures of Mr. Wilderspin.*** p 8vo. 2/0 boards   Sept.?

Library of Favourite Authors No. 9.
Also 1860, 68

839 H. TRUSTA (ELIZABETH S. PHELPS)
The Sunny Side. 12mo. 1/0 sewed, 1/6,
2/0 cloth   Oct. 11 (*Ath*)

Lily Series No. 29. Trusta is an anagram for
Stuart, the author's maiden name. This
has no date and 183 pp. I have a cloth
copy, issued about 1883, 18 cm., in
smooth olive cloth, elaborately decorated
on the front and spine in gold, silver,
green, and black, with plain white endpapers. It has all edges cut and has the series
title on the front and spine. The first edition was issued by the American Sunday-
School Union, Philadelphia, etc., 1851,
15.5 cm., 198 pp., illustrated, noticed in
the *Ind* on July 31. A revised edition was
issued in Mar. 1852. In England it was issued by Eli Charles Eginton, London, Fcp
8vo, 1/0 cloth, in their *Pocket Library*, listed
in the *Ath* on Dec. 3, 1853; and by Clarke,
Beeton & Co., London (1853), who issued
it in *The Sunny Side; and a Peep at "Number
Five,"* 1/0 boards, 1/6 cloth, listed by *PC* as
published Feb. 15–28. The first title was
listed in the *Ath* on Sept. 24, 1853, p 8vo,
2/6 cloth, and on Oct. 22, 1853, third edition, Fcp 8vo, 1/0 boards, both with no
publisher given. The joint title was listed
on Feb. 4, 1854, p 8vo, illustrated, 3/6.

840 LOUISE C. REYNOLDS (MRS.
ADOLPHUS BELL) *The Walton Mystery.*
2/0 boards   Nov. 1 (*Ath*)

This has no date. The first edition was issued by Ward, Lock & Tyler (1872), Cr
8vo, 5/0, listed in the *Spect* on Dec. 7, 1872.

841 JOHN B. SMITH *The Sayings and
Doings of Children.* 18mo. 0/9 sewed,
1/0, 1/6 cloth   Nov. 1 (*Spect*)

Beeton's Good-Aim Series No. 9. This was issued in New York by U. D. Ward, 1873, 16
cm., 169 pp., illustrated.

842 FANNY FERN (SARAH P. WILLIS,
later PARTON) *Fern Leaves from Fanny's
Portfolio.* 12mo. 1/0 sewed, 1/6, 2/0 cloth
Nov. 8 (*Spect*)

Lily Series No. 31.
Also 1854, 55, 56, 58

843 FANNY FERN *Shadows and Sunbeams.*
12mo. 1/0 sewed, 1/6, 2/0 cloth   Nov. 8
(*Spect*)

Lily Series No. 32. This has no date and
174 pp.
Also 1854, 55, 56, 58

844 THOMAS HOOD, THE ELDER
Whims in Prose and Verse. Fcp 8vo.
1/0 sewed   Nov. 15 (*Spect*)

Beeton's Humorous Books No. 22. The first
edition of *Whims and Oddities in Prose and
Verse* was issued by Lupton, Relfe, London, 1826, 19 cm., 146 pp., with 40 designs, 10/6, listed in the *Edinburgh Review*
(quarterly) as published Sept.–Dec. 1826.
The first edition of the second series was
issued by Charles Tilt, London, 1827,
19.5 cm., 150 pp., with 40 designs, 10/6,
issued in Nov. 1827. The first American
edition was issued by Carey, Lea & Carey,
Philadelphia, 1828, *Whims and Oddities*, 18
cm., 146 pp. On Apr. 24, 700 copies were
finished. Charles Tilt issued the fourth
edition of the first series, illustrated, at
10/6, advertised in the *Spect* on Jan. 16,
1830; and he advertised both series in 1
vol. in the *Spect* on Mar. 10, 1832, a new
edition, 12/6, with a new preface and additions, "This day." Tilt & Bogue, London, advertised it in the *Spect* on Dec. 17,
1842, a new and cheaper edition, Fcp 8vo,
illustrated, 6/0, "Now ready."
See 1885

845 THOMAS HOOD, THE ELDER *Oddities
in Prose and Verse.* Fcp 8vo. 1/0 sewed
Nov. 15 (*Spect*)

Beeton's Humorous Books No. 23. See the
preceding item.
See 1885

846 MARY E. BRADDON, ed. ***Belgravia Annual.*** Illustrated. 1/0 sewed   Nov. 29 (*Ath*)

847 HANS C. ANDERSEN
The Improvisatore.
New and Corrected Edition.
2/0 boards   Nov. 29 (*Spect*)
This has no date and 340 pp., translated by Mary Howitt.
Also 1857, 63, 89

848 ANONYMOUS   ***The Siliad.*** 8vo.
Illustrated. 1/0 sewed   Nov. (*Ath*)
This is *Beeton's Christmas Annual*, the 14th season, my copy, no date, 24.7 cm., 97 pp., in white wrappers cut flush, pictorially decorated on the front in red, blue, and black. There are ads on the back cover, the inside covers, and the verso of the title page. At the front there is an orange insert, then ads, pp. i–viii, then the title page, then two pp. from The Coming K—, then two inserts, then ads paged (1)–4, and finally a fold-out frontispiece. At the back there are 3 pp. of ads, ads and portraits paged xvii–xxxii, and ads paged ix–xvi. The text is in verse and double columns. It was listed in the *Spect*, a new edition, Fcp 8vo, 1/0 in colored wrappers, on Jan. 31, 1874. This new edition was *Beeton's Humorous Books* No. 27, no date, 16.2 cm., 236 pp., in white wrappers cut flush, with a decorated front cover in red, blue, and black, the series title on the front cover, and publisher's ads on the front endpapers and the back cover.

849 ORPHEUS C. KERR (ROBERT H. NEWELL) ***The Orpheus C. Kerr Papers.***
Fcp 8vo. 1/0 sewed   Nov.?
Beeton's Humorous Books No.?
Also 1865, 86

850 JAMES R. LOWELL ***The Biglow Papers.***
First series. Fcp 8vo. 1/0 sewed   Dec. 8 (*PC*)
Beeton's Humorous Books No. 6. This is a reissue of the 1865 edition, no date.
Also 1865

851 DOUGLAS W. JERROLD ***Jokes and Wit.***
Fcp 8vo. 1/0 sewed   Dec. 13 (*Ath*)
Beeton's Humorous Books No. 26. This has no date and was probably the first edition thus.

852 MARK TWAIN (SAMUEL L. CLEMENS)
The New Pilgrim's Progress. Fcp 8vo.
1/0 sewed   Dec. 13 (*Spect*)
Beeton's Humorous Books No. 25. This has no date and 307 pp., an unauthorized edition. It is the second half of *Innocents Abroad*, the first edition of which was issued by the American Publishing Co., Hartford; etc., 1869, deposited July 28, listed in the *ALG&PC* (fortnightly) on Oct. 1, and in the *Nation* on Aug. 12, 8vo, 651 pp., $3.50 by subscription, in brown cloth. A variant imprint had H. H. Bancroft & Co., San Francisco; American Publishing Co., Hartford, 1869. It was imported by Trübner & Co., London, and advertised in the *Bks* on Mar. 1, 1870. The first English edition was issued by John C. Hotten, London, 2 vols., 1/0 sewed, 3/6 cloth each. The first vol. was *The Innocents Abroad. The Voyage Out*, listed in the *Spect* on May 14, 1870; and the second vol. was *The New Pilgrim's Progress. The Journey Home*, listed in the *Ath* on Oct. 22, 1870. These had no dates, pirated editions, the first with 256 pp., and the second with 259 pp. In a letter to the *Spect*, Twain complained of Hotten's piracies, asking "How would that sinful aborigine feel if I were to call him John Camden Hottentot?" He said that he wanted to take a broom straw and go and smash that man's brains out. The first authorized edition set up in England was issued by George Routledge, London, 2 vols. (1872), Fcp 8vo, 1/0 sewed each. *The Innocents Abroad* had 246 pp. I have a copy of vol. 2, *The New Pilgrim's Progress* (1872), 255 pp., with a statement on the title page by Twain, "Messrs. George Routledge & Sons are my only authorized London publishers." These

Routledge vols. were listed in the *Ath* on Aug. 24, 1872.

Also 1875, 86. See 1874

853 MARK TWAIN *The Innocents Abroad.* Fcp 8vo. 1/0 sewed   Dec. 20 (*Spect*)

Beeton's Humorous Books No. 24. This has no date and 291 pp., an unauthorized edition. This is the first half of *The Innocents Abroad.* See the preceding item. I have a copy of this, no date, but judging by the ads it was issued in the spring of 1874, 16 cm., 289 pp., in white wrappers cut flush, with a pictorial front cover in red, brown, and black. It has the series title on the front, the words "Beeton's Humorous Series" at the head of the title page, and "Unauthorised edition" on the title page. There are 4 pp. of ads at the front, 16 pp. at the back, and there are ads on both sides of the back cover. The list of the series on the verso of the title page gives titles through No. 24, *The Siliad* (see above). The list of the *Erckmann-Chatrian Library* on the back cover gives *Year One of the Republic. 1793*, as No. 15 (see 1874) and *Citizen Bonaparte. 1794–1815*, as No. 16 (see 1874). I give it as having 291 pp. above, in accordance with the *BM* entry, but my copy has only 289 pp.

Also 1875, 79, 84. See 1874

854 (MARY E. BRADDON) *Strangers and Pilgrims.* Stereotyped Edition. Small format. 2/0 boards, 2/6 cloth   Dec. 20 (*Spect*)

This is my copy, no date, 16.4 cm., 396 pp., the first yellowback edition, having the author's name on the spine only. It is a pictorial yellowback with the front cover printed in red, blue, and black. It has an inscribed date (Aug. 1874), plain white endpapers, and a list of Braddon yellowbacks on the back cover ending with *Milly Darrell.* The imprint on the front cover is Ward, Lock & Tyler, but it is Ward & Lock on the title page, a fact that I'm at a loss to explain. The first edition was issued by

John Maxwell & Co., London, 3 vols., 1873, Cr 8vo, 31/6, listed in the *Ath* on July 12. The first American edition was issued by Harper & Bros., New York, 1873, 8vo, illustrated, $.75 paper, advertised in the *New-York Times* on Sept. 6 as "On Sept. 8" and as "This day" in the Sept. 8 ad. It was listed in *PW* on Sept. 13.

855 FRANÇOIS P. G. GUIZOT *Monk.* 12mo. 2/0 boards   1873   *See color photo section*

This is my copy, no date, 17.5 cm., 256 pp., translated by Andrew R. Scoble, with the translator's preface dated Oct. 1850. It is in yellow boards with a portrait and decoration on the front cover in red, green, and black. It has a commercial ad on the back cover and publisher's ads on the endpapers. This translation was issued by Henry C. Bohn, London, 1851, 18.5 cm., 256 pp., in *Bohn's Shilling Series*; it was reissued by Bell & Daldy, London, 1866. The first edition was issued either at Bruxelles, 1851, 18 cm., 328 pp., or at Paris, 1851, 400 pp., illustrated.

856 NATHANIEL P. WILLIS *Hurry-Graphs.* 12mo. 2/0 boards   1873

This is my copy, no date, 17.4 cm., 234 pp., uniform with the preceding item except it has a building instead of a portrait on the front cover. It has a commercial ad on the back cover, publisher's ads on the endpapers, and a 32-page catalog at the back. It has a preface (Mar. 1851) and consists of items from the *Home Journal*. The first English edition was issued by Henry G. Bohn, London, 1851, 18.5 cm., 234 pp., 1/6, in *Bohn's Cheap Series*, listed in the *Ath* on May 17. The first American edition was issued by Alden & Beardsley, Auburn & Rochester, 1851, 21 cm., 364 pp. Charles Scribner, New York, issued it, 1851, second edition, 19 cm., 364 pp., and it was given a short review in *Harper's New Monthly Magazine* for June 1851.

857 JOHN G. SAXE **Saxe's Poems.**
Fcp 8vo. 1/0 sewed   1873 (*BM*)
Beeton's Humorous Books No. 7. This has no date and 260 pp., with a preface (1849). Beeton issued it as *The Times, the Telegraph, and Other Poems*, 1866, with 260 pp. The first edition was issued by Ticknor, Reed & Fields, Boston, 1850, 18.5 cm., 130 pp., late in 1849, in an edition of 1,000 copies, entitled *Poems*, listed in the *Massachusetts Quarterly Review* for Mar. 1850. The second edition of 1,000 copies was published on Mar. 9, 1850, with 140 pp.; and the fifth edition, enlarged, was issued by the same publishers, 1854, noticed in the *Southern Literary Messenger* for Jan. 1854.

858   THOMAS HOOD, THE ELDER **Poems of Wit and Humour.** Nineteenth Edition.
Fcp 8vo. 1/0 sewed   1873
Beeton's Humorous Books No. 21. The first edition was issued by Edward Moxon, London, 1847, with 282 pp. Moxon issued the 16th edition, 1866, with 282 pp.; and issued *The Comic Poems of Thomas Hood*, edited by Samuel Lucas with a preface by Thomas Hood, the younger, listed in *Notes & Queries* on May 4, 1867. *Humorous Poems of Thomas Hood*, edited by Epes Sargent, with 476 pp., was issued by Phillips, Sampson & Co., Boston, reviewed in the *Knickerbocker* for May 1856.

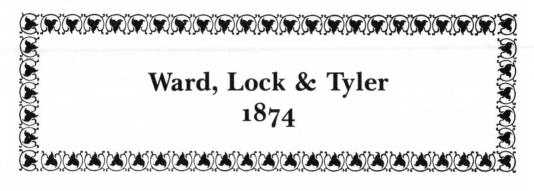

Ward, Lock & Tyler
1874

859 (HENRY G. JEBB) *Out of the Depths.*
Cr 8vo. 2/6 boards   Jan. 3 (*Ath*)

This has no date and 316 pp. It is a story
of a prostitute. The first edition was issued by Macmillan & Co., Cambridge and
London, 1859, Cr 8vo, anonymous, 381
pp., at 10/6, with a 24-page catalog (Apr.
15, 1859). It was listed in the *Ath* on May
21. The first American edition was issued
by W. A. Townsend & Co., New York,
1860, 19.5 cm., anonymous, 370 pp., at
$1.00. It was listed in the *Ind* on Sept. 29,
1859, and again on Oct. 13, the latter giving 1860 on the title page. It was listed as
"Recent" in the *Atlantic Monthly* for Nov.
1859, and advertised in the *New-York Times*
on Sept. 19, 1859, as "On Sept. 20." The
fourth thousand was advertised on Nov.
3, at $1.00.
Also 1876

860 ÉMILE ERCKMANN & PIERRE
CHATRIAN *Year One of the Republic.*
1793. The Story of a Peasant. Small
format. 1/o sewed   Jan. 17 (*Ath*)

This has no date and 305 pp. It was also issued at 3/6 cloth with illustrations. It is a
translation of part 3, *L'An I de la Republique*, of *Histoire d'un Paysan*. See *The Story of
a Peasant*, 1871.
Also 1875

861 NATHANIEL P. WILLIS *Pencillings by
the Way.* 12mo. 2/o boards   Jan. 17 (*Ath*)

The first edition was issued by J. Macrone,
London, 3 vols., 1835, 19 cm., 31/6, listed
in the *Ath* on Nov. 28. He issued the second edition with a new preface and with
added letters, advertised in the *Spect* on
Mar. 19, 1836, as "This day." He issued a
new edition, greatly enlarged, advertised
there on Sept. 30, 1837, as "Just published"; and issued a new edition, Fcp 8vo,
illustrated, 6/o, listed there on Apr. 6,
1839. Virtue, London, issued it, a new
edition, Fcp 8vo, illustrated, 6/o, advertised in the *Spect* on June 11, 1842, as "Just
ready." The first American edition was issued by Carey, Lea & Blanchard, Philadelphia; etc., 2 vols., 1836, 19 cm., 1,500 copies being finished in Mar. 1836. It was
deposited on Feb. 25 and reviewed in the
Knickerbocker for Apr.

862 FRANÇOIS P. G. GUIZOT *The English
Revolution.* 12mo. 1/o sewed   Jan. 17
(*Spect*)

This is my copy, no date, 17.5 cm., 195
pp., translated by A. R. Scoble, with a
preface (Mar. 1851), and a translator's
preface (July 1851). It is in yellow wrappers cut flush with front and back as for
Monk (1873 above). There are publisher's
ads on the endpapers, and it has a running title, *Monk's Contemporaries*. It was issued by Henry G. Bohn, London, 1851,
19.5 cm., 195 pp., at 1/6, as *Lives of Monk's
Contemporaries*. *Histoire de la Revolution de
l'Angleterre*, part 1, 2 vols., was issued at
Paris, 1826, 1827, 22 cm. *History of the English Revolution* was issued by D. A. Tal-
boys, Oxford and London, 2 vols., 1838,
22 cm.; and it was issued in the United
States by D. Appleton & Co., New York;
etc., 1846, 19.5 cm., 515 pp.

863 KATHERINE S. MACQUOID **Wild as a Hawk.** New Edition. p 8vo. 2/o boards Jan. 24 (*Spect*)

Library of Favourite Authors No. 12. This has no date. The first edition was issued by Tinsley Bros., London, 3 vols., 1868, Cr 8vo, 31/6, listed in the *Ath* on Aug. 1. It was issued by George Carleton, New York, 1874, as *A Charming Widow*, advertised in the *New-York Times* on Aug. 1, 12mo, $1.75 cloth, and listed by *Lit World* as published in Aug. Harpers issued it as *Marjorie* in 1886.

864 THOMAS B. MACAULAY **Reviews and Essays from The Edinburgh.** 1/o sewed, 1/6, 2/o cloth   Feb. 7 (*Spect*)

Books for All Time No. 1. This was a first se-Fies, no date. See 1875 for the second series and 1881 for the third series. Longmans, London, issued *Critical and Historical Essays*, from the *Edinburgh Review*, 3 vols., 8vo, 36/o, listed in the *Ath* on Mar. 18, 1843; and they issued them in 1 vol., square Cr 8vo, portrait, 21/o, advertised in *Notes & Queries* on Jan. 12, 1850.

865 SUSAN COOLIDGE **What Katy Did at School.** 12mo. 1/o sewed, 1/6, 2/o cloth Feb. 28 (*Ath*)

Lily Series No. 33. This is the first English edition, no date and 236 pp. The first edition was issued by Roberts Bros., Boston, 1874, 17 cm., 278 pp., illustrated, listed in *PW* on Nov. 1, 1873, and in the *Ind* on Nov. 27.

866 ÉMILE ERCKMANN & PIERRE CHATRIAN **Citizen Bonaparte. 1794–1815. The Story of a Peasant.** Small format. 1/o sewed   Mar. 7 (*Ath*)

This has no date and 288 pp., and was also issued at 3/6 illustrated. It is a translation of part 4 of *Histoire d'un Paysan*, with the title *1794 au 1815; Le Citoyen Bonaparte*. See *The Story of a Peasant*, 1871. See also 1875

867 ANONYMOUS **Beeton's Gardening Book.** 12mo. 1/o   Mar. 7 (*Spect*)

This has no date, 252 pp., illustrated.

868 ANONYMOUS **The Tichborne Trial.** 2/o   Mar. 7 (*Spect*)

This contained the summing-up by the Lord Chief Justice of England and the addresses of the judges, etc., 1874, 302 pp., with 2 pp. of ads. There were many accounts of this famous trial, all issued in 1874, including ones from the *Times* office, Samuel Tinsley, Diprose & Bateman, etc. The same title was advertised by Scribner, Welford & Armstrong, New York, in the *New-York Times* on Mar. 28, 1874, 8vo, 318 pp., $1.00 paper.

869 JOSIAH G. HOLLAND **Arthur Bonnicastle.** p 8vo. 2/o boards Mar. 7 (*Spect*)

Library of Favourite Authors No. 13. This has no date and 341 pp. The last chapter is by another hand, and it has a preface by S.O. Beeton on the law of copyright, 1874, probably to help justify this piracy. The last chapter was first published in England to give George Routledge the copyright, and hence Ward, Lock had to improvise a final chapter! George Routledge issued it (1873), illustrated, 5/o, listed in the *Ath* on Aug. 23, paying the author royalties—the first he had received from any of his books in England. In a letter to the *Ath* on Apr. 4, 1874, Holland stated that this Ward, Lock edition left out nearly 100 pp., and added in their place 2 pp. by another hand. Routledge issued a new edition, Fcp 8vo, at 2/o boards, listed in the *Spect* on Mar. 14, 1874. The first American edition was issued by Scribner, Armstrong & Co., New York, 1873, 19.5 cm., 401 pp., illustrated, listed in *PW* on Sept. 6, and in the *Nation* on Sept. 18. It was advertised in the *New-York Times* on Aug. 23, 12mo, 12 illustrations, $1.75, "On Sept. 6"; advertised on Sept. 5 as postponed until Sept. 11; and advertised on Sept. 11 as "This day." The 13th thousand was advertised on Sept. 20, the same, as "This morning." It ran serially in *Scribner's Monthly*, Nov. 1872–Oct. 1873, illustrated.

870 ELIZABETH S. PHELPS, later WARD
Gypsy's Sowing and Reaping. 12mo. 1/0 sewed, 1/6, 2/0 cloth   Mar. 21 (*Ath*)

Lily Series No. 36. This has no date, 17 cm., 180 pp. The first edition was issued by Graves & Young, Boston, 1866, 17 cm., 302 pp., illustrated, deposited on Oct. 27. It was listed in *ALG&PC* (fortnightly) and in the *Ind* on Nov. 1, 1866. Strahan & Co., London, issued it in 1873, Fcp 8vo, 1/6 lavender cloth with cream endpapers, listed in the *Spect* on May 3. George Routledge, London, issued it (1874), 17 cm., 192 pp., 1/0 sewed, 1/6, 2/0 cloth, in Oct. 1874.

871 ELIZABETH S. PHELPS, later WARD
Tiny. 18mo. 0/9 sewed, 1/0, 1/6 cloth
Mar. 21 (*Spect*)

Beeton's Good-Aim Series No. 10. This is the first English edition, no date, with 155 pp. The first edition was issued by the Massachusetts Sabbath School Society, Boston, 1866, 15.5 cm., 198 pp., illustrated, deposited Jan. 27, 1866, and listed in *APC&LG* on Mar. 15, bound in purple cloth with yellow endpapers.

872 ELIZABETH S. PHELPS, later WARD
Tiny's Sunday Nights. 18mo. 0/9 sewed, 1/0, 1/6 cloth   Apr. 4 (*Spect*)

Beeton's Good-Aim Series No. 11. This is the first English edition. The first edition was issued by the Massachusetts Sabbath School Society, Boston (copyright 1866), 15.5 cm., 217 pp., 4 illustrations, in green cloth with cream endpapers, or in red cloth with 3 illustrations, listed in *ALG&PC* on Apr. 15, 1866. The *U Cat* also gives Henry A. Young, Boston, 1866, 15.5 cm., 217 pp., illustrated.

873 THOMAS MILLER *Royston Gower.*
2/0 boards   Apr. 4 (*Spect*)

This has no date. The first edition was issued by Henry Colburn, London, 3 vols., 1838, 19 cm., 31/6, listed in the *Ath* on Jan. 27, 1838. It was issued in London in 1858 at 3/6, probably by David Bryce, as Bryce issued it at 2/0 in Sept. 1860. It was issued in the United States by Carey, Lea & Blanchard, Philadelphia, 2 vols., 1838, 18 cm. Also 1886

874 ELIZABETH PRENTISS *The Percys.*
12mo. 1/0 sewed, 1/6, 2/0 cloth   Apr. 4 (*Ath*)

Lily Series No. 35. This is the first English edition. The first edition was issued by A. D. F. Randolph, New York (1870), 17 cm., 341 pp., frontispiece, listed in *ALG&PC* on Jan. 2, 1871, and in the *Christian Union* on Jan. 4.

875 WATERS (WILLIAM RUSSELL)
The Privateer Captain. 2/0 boards
Apr. 4 (*Spect*)

This has no date. The first edition was issued by Knight & Son, London (1858), as *Kirke Webb, the Privateer Captain*, 12mo, 260 pp., at 1/6, in yellow pictorial boards, with the endpapers printed in blue with Knight ads. There is an 8-page catalog of J. & C. Brown, London, at the end. It was issued by C. H. Clarke, London (1861), Fcp 8vo, at 2/0 boards, in the *Naval and Military Library*, in Apr.
Also 1886

876 W. M. L. JAY (JULIA L. M. WOODRUFF)
Shiloh. 12mo. 1/0 sewed, 1/6, 2/0 cloth
Apr. 25 (*Ath*)

Lily Series No. 34. The *U Cat* gives this as (1875), 19 cm., 518 pp., partly colored illustrations. The first English edition was issued by James Nisbet, London, 1871, 12mo, 3/6, listed in the *Ath* on Apr. 29. Griffith & Farran, London, issued it in 1883. The first edition was issued by E. P.

Dutton & Co., New York; etc., 1870, 18.5 cm., 488 pp., at $2.00, advertised in the *New-York Times* on Dec. 15, 1870, listed in the *Nation* on Dec. 1, and in *ALG&PC* (fortnightly) on Jan. 2, 1871.
Also 1882

877 ELIZABETH S. PHELPS, later WARD *Gypsy's Cousin Joy.* 12mo. 1/0 sewed, 1/6, 2/0 cloth   Apr. 25 (*Ath*)

Lily Series No. 37. This was issued by Strahan, London, in 1873, listed in the *Spect* on Apr. 26, Fcp 8vo, 1/6 in cloth; and by George Routledge, London, in 1874, at 1/0 sewed, 1/6, 2/0 cloth, in Oct. The first edition was issued by Graves & Young, Boston, 1866, 17 cm., 282 pp., illustrated, with 6 pp. of ads, in purple, blue, or brown cloth with cream endpapers. It was deposited Sept. 24 and listed in *ALG&PC* (fortnightly) on Oct. 1.

878 (MARY E. BRADDON) *Lucius Davoren.* Stereotyped Edition. Small format. 2/0 boards, 2/6 cloth   May 2 (*Spect*)

This is the first yellowback edition. My copy has no date and was issued in 1876 or early 1877, 16.8 cm., 448 pp., with the author's name on the spine only, and with the list of Braddon yellowbacks on the back cover ending with *Dead Men's Shoes.* It is in yellow pictorial boards, printed in red, blue, and black, and has plain white endpapers. The first edition was issued by John Maxwell & Co., London, 3 vols., 1873, 31/6, advertised in the *Ath* on Nov. 1 as "Now ready," and listed in the *Spect* on Jan. 17, 1874. I suspect this latter listing was for a new edition, as it was reviewed in the *Ath* on Nov. 1, 1873. It ran as *Publicans and Sinners* in the *Sunday Mercury* (New York) beginning on June 1, 1873, from advance sheets, and it was the first Braddon novel serialized in the Tillotson newspapers. The first American edition was as *Publicans and Sinners,* issued by Harper & Bros., New York, 1874, 23.5 cm., 190 pp., $.75 paper, *Library of Select Novels* No. 408.

It was listed in *PW* on Feb. 7 and in the *Ind* on Feb. 12.

879 W. S. HAYWARD *Eulalie.* 12mo. 2/6 boards   May 23 (*Ath*)

Household and Railway Books No. 1. This is the first edition, no date.
Also 1890

880 THE BROTHERS MAYHEW (HENRY & AUGUSTUS) *The Image of His Father.* Small format. 2/0 boards   May 23 (*Ath*)

Household and Railway Books No. 3. My copy has no date, a reissue of 1876, 16.5 cm., 288 pp., yellow pictorial boards printed in red, green, and black, with an extra illustrated title page and illustrations by "Phiz." There are ads on the endpapers, the back cover, and the verso of the title page, and there is a 28-page catalog at the back. The first edition was in six monthly parts, 1/0 each, No. 1 advertised in the *Ath* on Mar. 25, 1848, by H. Hurst, London, as "On Mar. 31." He issued it in 1 vol., 1848, 288 pp., illustrated by "Phiz," listed in the *Illustrated London News* on Sept. 23. Henry G. Bohn, London, reissued it, 1851 and 1859, 288 pp., with the illustrations, the 1859 edition being advertised in *Notes & Queries* on Feb. 19, 1859, *Cheap Series* for Feb., p 8vo, 12 illustrations by "Phiz," 2/0. In the United States it was issued by Carey & Hart, Philadelphia, part 1 noticed in *Godey's Lady's Book* for June 1858, and in 1 vol., complete, listed Dec. 1848. It was also issued by Harper & Bros., New York, in 2 parts, 18mo, listed in *Godey's Lady's Book* for Dec. 1848.

881 ANNE MARSH, later MARSH-CALDWELL *The Previsions of Lady Evelyn.* 2/0 boards   May 23 (*Spect*)

This is one of the three stories in *The Triumphs of Time,* issued by Bentley, London, 3 vols., 1844, 19 cm., anonymous; and issued in the United States by Harper

& Bros., New York, 1844, anonymous. It was issued with the present title by Simms & M'Intyre, London and Belfast, 1849, as *Parlour Library* No. 26; and reissued in that series by C. H. Clarke, London, in 1860, at 2/o boards.

882 ÉMILE ERCKMANN & PIERRE CHATRIAN *Confessions of a Clarionet Player, and Other Stories.* Small format. 1/o sewed   May 30 (*Ath*)

This has no date and 271 pp., the first English edition. It was also issued at 3/6 illustrated. *Le Joueur de Clarinette* with two other stories was issued in Paris, 1863; and *Confidences d'un Joueur de Clarinette* was issued in Paris, 1865.

883 ELIZABETH S. PHELPS, later WARD *Gypsy's Year at the Golden Crescent.* 12mo. 1/o sewed, 1/6, 2/o cloth   May 30 (*Ath*)

Lily Series No. 38. The first edition was issued by Graves & Young, Boston, 1867, 17 cm., 261 pp., illustrated, $1.25, in blue, green, or purple cloth with cream endpapers. It was deposited Sept. 27, 1867, listed in *ALG&PC* (fortnightly) on Oct. 15, and in the *Ind* on Nov. 7. Strahan & Co., London, issued it in 1873, Fcp 8vo, at 1/6 cloth, listed in the *Spect* on Apr. 26. George Routledge, London, issued it (1874), 17 cm., 209 pp., at 1/o sewed, 1/6, 2/o cloth, in Oct.

884 ALFRED T. TURPIN *Spring Blossoms.* 2/o   May 30 (*Spect*)

This is the first edition, no date, a poem.

885 ANONYMOUS *How to Live on a Hundred a Year.* Fcp 8vo. 1/o May 30 (*Spect*)

This is also given by the *Eng Cat*, but otherwise I cannot trace it.

886 ALFRED W. DRAYSON *The Young Dragoon.* Illustrated. 2/o boards May 30 (*Spect*)

Household and Railway Books No. 2. This has no date.
Also 1870

887 MARK TWAIN (SAMUEL L. CLEMENS) *The Innocents Abroad and The New Pilgrim's Progress.* Fcp 8vo. 2/o boards May 30 (*Spect*)

Household and Railway Books No. 4.
Also 1873, 75, 79, 84

888 MAX ADELER (CHARLES H. CLARK) *Out of the Hurly-Burly.* 12mo. Illustrated. 2/o boards   June (*Bks*)

This has no date, 17.8 cm., 398 pp. It was issued at 6/o, 18.5 cm., 398 pp., illustrated, author's edition, listed in the *Spect* on May 30, 1874; and reissued at 3/6, the same, listed in the *Spect* on June 13, 1874. It was issued as *Household and Railway Books* No. 6, 17.8 cm., 398 pp., illustrated, at 2/o boards, advertised in the *Ath* on Sept. 5, 1874. Routledge, London, issued it at 1/o sewed, in June, probably about the 13th. The first American edition was probably the To-Day Publishing Co., Philadelphia, etc., 1874, 19.5 cm., 398 pp., illustrated, listed in the *Ind* on May 7, and in the *Nation* on May 14. It is given by Wright, who also gives G. Maclean, Philadelphia, 1874, the same; and Thompson, St. Louis, 1874, the same. The *U Cat* gives also David M'Kay, Philadelphia (1874), the same.
Also 1878, 82, 83, 1900

889 TIMOTHY TITCOMB (JOSIAH G. HOLLAND) *Letters to Young People.* Cr 8vo. 1/o sewed, 1/6, 2/o   July 18 (*Spect*)

Friendly Counsel Series No. 1. This has no date and 208 pp., rewritten by an English editor after Titcomb. It first appeared in the *Springfield Republican*, and the first edition was issued by Charles Scribner, New York, 1858, 19 cm., 251 pp., $1.00, listed in the *Ind* on Aug. 5, and in *APC&LG* (weekly) on July 31. The fourth edition was reviewed in the *Southern Literary Messenger* (monthly) for Oct. 1858, and the 25th edition was advertised in the *New-York Times* as 12mo, $1.00, on Oct. 25,

1860. The book sold over 100,000 copies in the United States. It was distributed in England by Sampson Low, London, listed in the *Ath* on Aug. 28, 1858. The first edition title was *Timothy Titcomb's Letters to Young People, Single and Married.*
Also 1875

890 ANONYMOUS **Beeton's Modern European Celebrities.** 1/0 sewed, 1/6 cloth, 2/0 half bound   July 25 (*Spect*)
This is the first edition, no date, 18.5 cm., 263 pp.

891 JOSEPH H. INGRAHAM **The Prince of the House of David.** 12mo. 1/0 sewed, 1/6, 2/0 cloth   Aug. 1 (*Ath*)
Lily Series No. 41. Ward, Lock issued it at 3/6, Cr 8vo, listed in the *Spect* on Mar. 13, 1875. The first edition was issued by Pudney & Russell, New York, 1855, 19.5 cm., 456 pp., frontispiece, $1.25 cloth, listed in *APC&LG* (weekly) on Nov. 26. A new and revised edition with new illustrations and many changes was advertised in the *New York Times* on Jan. 17, 1859, 12mo, 472 pp., $1.25. The first English edition was issued by Arthur Hall, Virtue & Co., London, in 1859, listed in the *Ath* on Mar. 12, Fcp 8vo, illustrated, 5/0. A new edition was listed in the *Reader* on Apr. 22, 1865, Fcp 8vo, 360 pp., illustrated, 3/6. It was issued by Strahan, London, in June 1869; and George Routledge, London, purchased the copyright from Strahan and issued it, revised by H. W. Dulcken, illustrated, at 5/0 cloth, listed in the *Spect* on Aug. 28, 1869. Routledge issued it at 3/6, illustrated, about Aug. 27, 1870; and issued it at 1/0 sewed, 1/6, 2/0 cloth, my copy in yellow wrappers, listed in the *Spect* on Aug. 8, 1874. Routledge stated that they had purchased it from Strahan and were issuing it as the only English publisher. That this was not so the present issue testifies.

892 SYLVESTER JUDD **Margaret.**
p 8vo. 2/0 boards   Aug. 1 (*Spect*)
Library of Favourite Authors No. 14. This has no date. The first edition was issued by Jordan & Wiley, Boston, 1845, 20.5 cm., anonymous, 460 pp. This edition was probably imported by Chapman, London, who advertised it in the *Spect* on Jan. 27, 1849, 12mo, at 9/6 cloth. A revised edition was issued by Phillips, Sampson, Boston, 1851, 2 vols., 19 cm., anonymous, listed in *Lit World* as published Sept. 27–Oct. 18. This edition was imported by J. Chapman, London, who issued it in 2 vols., in 1851, p 8vo, 14/0. It was issued by Stringer & Townsend, New York, in 1854, anonymous, illustrated, at $.50 paper and $.75 cloth, advertised in the *New-York Times* on Mar. 31 as "Now ready." They issued a second edition, the same, advertised there on Apr. 27 as "Just published." It was also issued by Roberts Bros., Boston, in 1870, by Judd, 12mo, 401 pp., at $1.50, advertised in the *New-York Times* on Oct. 17 as "This day."
Also 1881

893 MENRA HOPEWELL **Legends of the Missouri and Mississippi.** Small format. 2/0 boards   Aug. 15 (*Spect*)
This has no date, 16.5 cm., 506 pp. Ward, Lock & Tyler also issued it at 3/6, listed in the *Spect* on Aug. 22, and they advertised it in the *Spect* on July 25 at 3/0, 5/0 cloth! The first edition was issued by the London branch of Beadle & Co., 3 vols., Nos. 9–11 of *Beadle's Sixpenny Tales*, on Oct. 15, 1862, and Mar. 2, and July 1, 1863. Many of the legends first appeared in *Legends of the Missouri* in the *Missouri Republican*, starting on Apr. 12, 1858.
Also 1875

894 TIMOTHY S. ARTHUR **Anna Lee.**
12mo. 1/0 sewed, 1/6, 2/0 cloth
Aug. 15 (*Spect*)
Lily Series No. 42. This has no date and 254 pp. The first edition was issued by A.

Hislop & Co., Edinburgh, 1869, with 228 pp. It was probably issued by Ward, Lock & Tyler at 3/6 in 1875, 305 pp.; and reissued at 2/6, the latter listed in the *Spect* on July 27, 1878.

895 MARIA EDGEWORTH *Moral Tales.*
12mo. 1/0 sewed, 1/6, 2/0 cloth
Aug. 15 (*Spect*)

Lily Series No. 39. This has no date and 320 pp. I have a copy in cloth (1882), 17.3 cm., 320 pp., in brown cloth, elaborately blocked in gold, silver, and black on the front and spine, with pale yellow endpapers. It has 8 pp. of ads at the back and has a printer's date of Aug. 1882. The first edition was *Moral Tales for Young People*, issued by J. Johnson, London, 5 vols., 1801, 12mo, at 3/0 each. In the United States it was issued by Johnson & Warner, Philadelphia, 3 vols., 1810, 14 cm. George Routledge, London, issued it at 3/6, 4/0, Fcp 8vo, illustrated, in Oct. 1856; and advertised a new edition in the *Ath* on Oct. 5, 1872, with colored illustrations, 3/6. He issued it 1/0 sewed, 1/6, 2/0 cloth, listed in the *Spect* on Aug. 8, 1874.

896 MARIA EDGEWORTH *Popular Tales.*
12mo. 1/0 sewed, 1/6, 2/0   Aug. 15
(*Spect*)

Lily Series No. 40. This has no date and 361 pp. The first edition was issued by J. Johnson, 3 vols., 1804, 18 cm., at 15/0 boards, listed in the *Edinburgh Review* as published Apr. 18–July 7, 1804. The first American edition was issued by James Humphreys, Philadelphia, 2 vols., 1804, 18 cm. All the Routledge issues were as in the preceding item.

897 THOMAS DE QUINCEY *Confessions of an English Opium-Eater and Essays.* 1/0 sewed, 1/6, 2/0 cloth   Aug. 15 (*Spect*)

Books for All Time No. 3. This has no date and 244 pp. The first edition was issued by Taylor & Hessey, London, 1822, 12mo,

anonymous, 206 pp., 5/0 boards, just the *Confessions*, listed by the *Quarterly Review* as published Apr.–June 1822. There is a known copy with appendix dated Sept. 30, 1822. It was first published in the *London Magazine* in 2 parts. They issued the second edition, 1823, 12mo, 206 pp. It was issued in the United States by Littell, Philadelphia; etc., 1823, 16 cm., 183 pp., just the *Confessions*.
See 1886

898 ÉMILE ERCKMANN & PIERRE CHATRIAN *The Story of a Campaign in Kabylia . . . and Other Tales.*
12mo. 1/0 sewed   Aug. 15 (*Ath*)

This is the first English edition, my copy, no date, 17.2 cm., 242 pp., white pictorial wrappers in red, blue, and black, with "Beeton's Erckmann-Chatrian Library" on the front and spine. There are ads (mostly publisher's) on the back, the inside covers, 2 pp. in front, and 4 pp. at the back, plus a 16-page publisher's catalog at the back. This was also issued at 3/6. The first edition was *Une Campagne en Kabylie*, Paris, 1874. The title story began in *Cassell's Magazine* in Sept. 1873 and probably concluded in Nov.
Also 1875   *See color photo section*

899 BRET HARTE *Stories, Sketches and Bohemian Papers. Complete with a Memoir.* 2/0 boards, 2/6   Aug. 15 (*Spect*)

Household and Railway Books No. 5. This has no date and is in 2 parts, 245 pp., 227 pp.
Also 1878

900 SYDNEY SMITH *Essays, Social and Political, 1802–1825.* 1/0 sewed, 1/6, 2/0 cloth   Aug. 15 (*Spect*)

Books for All Time No. 2. This is the first series, no date, 254 pp. *Sydney Smith's Works*, people's edition, complete in 2 vols., was advertised by Longmans, London, in *Notes & Queries* on Nov. 5, 1859, seven 1/0 parts or 2 vols. at 8/o, "Recent or preparing." For the second series see 1878

901 MADAME D'ARBLAY (FRANCES BURNEY, later D'ARBLAY) *Evelina.* 2/o boards   Aug. 22 (*Ath*)

Library of Favourite Authors No. 15. This has no date and 379 pp. The first edition was issued by T. Lowndes, London, 3 vols., 1778, 17.5 cm., anonymous. In the United States it was issued by Benjamin Johnson, Philadelphia, 2 vols., 1792, 16.5 cm., anonymous; and by Mordecai Jones, Philadelphia, 2 vols., 1792, 17 cm., anonymous.
Also 1881

902 ANONYMOUS *The Orphan Boy.* 18mo. o/9 sewed, 1/o, 1/6 cloth Aug. 22 (*Spect*)

Beeton's Good-Aim Series No. 12. This is also given by the *Eng Cat*, but otherwise I cannot trace it.

903 ANONYMOUS *Child's First Book of Natural History.* 12mo. 1/o   Sept. 5 (*Spect*)

This is the first edition, no date, 93 pp., illustrated.

904 ANNIE EDWARDES *The Morals of Mayfair.* 2/o boards   Sept. 12 (*Spect*)
Also 1863, 69, 70

905 AMELIA EDWARDS *Hand and Glove.* [New edition]. p 8vo. 2/o boards Sept. 12 (*Spect*)

This was also listed in the *Spect* on Oct. 17 at 2/o. Sadleir gives the first edition as issued by Darton & Co., London (1859), as *Parlour Library* No. 191, with 421 pp., whereas the *Eng Cat* gives it as issued at 2/6 in 1858. John Maxwell & Co., London, issued a new edition, 1865, p 8vo, 421 pp., 6/o, listed in the *Reader* and in the *Spect* on Sept. 2. The *U Cat* gives J. & C. Brown, London, no date, 421 pp. The first Amer-

ican edition was issued by Harper & Bros., New York, 1866, 23.5 cm., 122 pp., $.50 paper, advertised in the *New-York Times* on June 2 as "This day," and listed in *ALG&PC* on June 15.

906 HERBERT BYNG HALL *The Queen's Messenger.* 2/o boards   Sept. 12 (*Spect*)
Also 1873

907 JOSEPH H. INGRAHAM *The Pillar of Fire.* 12mo. 1/o sewed, 1/6, 2/o cloth Sept. 19 (*Spect*)

Lily Series No. 44. Ward, Lock & Tyler also issued this at 3/6, listed in the *Spect* on May 15, 1875; and issued it again at 3/6, 22 cm., 495 pp., illustrated, in Dec. 1878. The first edition was issued by Pudney & Russell, New York; etc., 1859, 20 cm., 600 pp., $1.25, advertised in the *New-York Times* on Apr. 11 as "Just published," in *Harper's Weekly* on Mar. 26 as "On Apr. 11," and listed in the *Ind* on Apr. 14. It was also issued by Sheldon & Co., New York, 12mo, $1.25, advertised in the *New-York Times* on Apr. 2, 1859, as "On Apr. 11," and advertised in *Harper's Weekly* on May 14 as "Just published." It was also issued by Evans, Philadelphia, reviewed in *De Bow's Review* (monthly) for Mar. 1860, and thus probably issued in Dec. 1859 or earlier. The first English edition was issued by Virtue Bros., London, 1865, Fcp 8vo, illustrated, 5/o, advertised in the *Spect* on Oct. 7 as "now ready." George Routledge, London, issued it at 5/o cloth, illustrated, in 1869; and at 3/6, illustrated, revised by H. W. Dulcken, in Aug. 1870; and issued it at 1/o sewed, 1/6, 2/o cloth, listed in the *Spect* on Aug. 8, 1874.

908 THOMAS B. ALDRICH *Prudence Palfrey.* 12mo. 1/o sewed, 1/6, 2/o Sept. 19 (*Spect*)

Lily Series No. 45. This has no date and 216 pp. The first English edition was issued by George Routledge, London

(1874), 383 pp., 2/o boards, 2/6 cloth, listed in the *Spect* on June 13, 1874. The first American edition was issued by James R. Osgood & Co., Boston, 1874, 18 cm., 311 pp., frontispiece, listed in the *Nation* on June 4, in *PW* on June 6, and advertised in the *Ind* on June 4. It ran in the *Atlantic Monthly*, Jan.–June 1874.

909 (MARY E. BRADDON) *Taken at the Flood.* Stereotyped Edition. Small format. 2/o boards, 2/6 cloth   Sept. 26 (*Ath*)

This has no date, 16.9 cm., 416 pp., the first yellowback edition. The list of Braddon yellowbacks on the back cover ends with *Lucius Davoren.* The first edition was issued by John Maxwell & Co., London, 3 vols., 1874, Cr 8vo, 31/6, listed in the *Ath* on May 9. The first American edition was issued by Harper & Bros., New York, 1874, 8vo, $.75 paper, *Library of Select Novels* No. 412, listed in *PW* on June 27, and in the *Ind* on July 2.

910 JOSEPH H. INGRAHAM *The Throne of David.* 12mo. 1/o sewed, 1/6, 2/o cloth Sept. 26 (*Spect*)

Lily Series No. 43. Ward, Lock & Tyler issued it also, 3/6, listed in the *Spect* on May 15, 1875. The first edition was issued by George G. Evans, Philadelphia, 1860, 19 cm., 603 pp., illustrated, $1.25, advertised in the *Ind* on May 10 as "Now ready," and listed in *APC&LG* on May 5. The first English edition was issued by Virtue, London, in 1866, Fcp 8vo, eight illustrations, 5/o cloth, listed in the *Spect* on Sept. 29. It was issued by Strahan, London, in 1869 at 3/6; and George Routledge, London, issued it in Aug. 1869 at 5/o, illustrated, revised by H. W. Dulcken; and issued it in Aug. 1870 at 3/6, illustrated. He issued it at 1/o sewed, 1/6, 2/o cloth, listed in the *Spect* on Aug. 8, 1874. Also 1882

911 ANONYMOUS *Tom, Tom, the Printer's Son.* 18mo. o/9 sewed, 1/o, 1/6 cloth Oct. 3 (*Spect*)

Beeton's Good-Aim Series No. 13. This is the first edition.

912 FRANCIS BACON *The Proficience and Advancement of Learning. With His Essays.* 1/o sewed, 1/6, 2/o cloth   Oct. 24 (*Spect*)

Books for All Time No. 4. This has no date. The first edition of the first title was issued by Henrie Tomes, London, 1605, in two books. The *Essays* . . . were issued by Samuel Smith & Benjamin Watford, London, 1701, one of four simultaneous issues. Also 1886. For the second series see 1877

913 H. TRUSTA (ELIZABETH S. PHELPS) *A Peep at "Number Five."* 12mo. 1/o sewed, 1/6, 2/o cloth   Oct. 31 (*Ath*)

Lily Series No. 46. This is the first English edition. The first edition was issued by Phillips, Sampson & Co., Boston, 1852, 16 cm., 296 pp., frontispiece, listed by *Lit World* as published May 15–June 1, listed in the *Ind* on May 27; and it was advertised in the *New York Daily Times* on May 24, 1852, by George P. Putnam, New York, 12mo, cloth, as "This day." Either Putnam was only advertising it for sale or he issued it jointly with Phillips, Sampson. *Sunnyside and a Peep at Number Five* was listed in the *Ath* on Feb. 4, 1854, 1 vol., p 8vo, anonymous, 3/6, no publisher given.

914 W. S. HAYWARD *The Perils of a Pretty Girl.* 2/o boards   Nov. 7 (*Spect*)

This is probably the first edition. The *BM* gives only London, 1875; and the *Eng Cat* gives C. H. Clarke, London, 2/o, issued between 1872 and 1879, for which I can find no evidence!

915 W. S. HAYWARD *Hunted to Death.* 2/o boards   Nov. 7 (*Ath*)

Also 1862, 69, 73

916 ARTEMUS WARD (CHARLES F. BROWNE) *Artemus Ward in London.* Fcp 8vo. 1/o sewed   Nov. 14 (*Spect*)

Beeton's Humorous Books No. 30. This has no date. I think the title on the cover was *Letters to "Punch."* The first edition was issued by G. W. Carleton, New York; Sampson Low, London, 1867, 19 cm., 229 pp., illustrated, $1.50, *Artemus Ward in London, and Other Papers*. It was advertised in the *New-York Times* on July 2, 1867, but a July 13 ad stated that it was postponed until this week, and an Aug. 17 ad said "Recent." It was listed in *Godey's Lady's Book* for Sept. and thus probably issued in July. The first English edition was issued by John C. Hotten, London (1870), 15.6 cm., 195 pp., 1/6 stiff wrappers, 2/o cloth, edited by E. P. H. (Edward P. Hingston), *Artemus Ward in London Comprising the Letters to "Punch" and Other Humorous Papers*. It was listed in the *Ath* on Oct. 15. It is my copy and is the first edition issued in England that was set up in England, in wrappers with a portrait on the front cover, which is printed in red and black. Hotten reissued it as *Letters to "Punch," Among the Witches and Other Humorous Papers*, Fcp 8vo, 1/o sewed, listed in the *Ath* on Oct. 25, 1873. It was issued in Canada by C. R. Chisholm, Montreal, 1868, 24 cm., 108 pp., illustrated, from the American edition, with the Carleton title.

Also 1884

917 THOMAS B. ALDRICH *Marjorie Daw and Other People.* Fcp 8vo. 1/o sewed Nov. 21 (*Ath*)

Beeton's Humorous Books No. 28. This has no date and 195 pp. The first American edition was issued by James R. Osgood & Co., Boston, 1873, 18 cm., 272 pp., listed in *PW* on Sept. 27, and in the *Nation* on Oct. 2. It was issued in England at the same time by George Routledge, London (1873), 19 cm., 365 pp., frontispiece, 5/o, listed in the *Spect* on Sept. 27. Routledge issued it in 1876, Fcp 8vo, 365 pp., at 2/o boards, listed in the *Spect* on Apr. 8.

918 LYULPH (HENRY R. LUMLEY) *As You Like It.* 8vo. 1/o sewed Nov. 28 (*Spect*)

This is the first edition, no date, a Christmas story.

919 MARY E. BRADDON, ed. *Belgravia Annual for 1875.* 1/o sewed   Nov.

920 MARK TWAIN *The Jumping Frog and Other Stories and Sketches.* Small format. 1/o sewed   Nov. (*Bks*)

Beeton's Humorous Books No. 29. This has no date, 16.2 cm., 135 pp., in pictorial wrappers cut flush, with the words, "From the original edition" on the title page. The first edition was issued by C. H. Webb, New York (American News Co., Agent), 1867, 17.5 cm., 198 pp., *The Celebrated Jumping Frog of Calaveras County, and Other Sketches*. It was edited by John Paul (Charles H. Webb) and bound in variously colored cloths including dark brown, lavender, or purple, these having a golden frog on the lower left front cover and in blind on the back; and in blue cloth with the frog in the center of the front cover. It was advertised in the *New-York Times* on Apr. 22, at $1.50, as "On Apr. 24," and on Apr. 25 as "Today." It was listed in the *Ind* on May 9. A railway edition was advertised in the former on May 2, $1.00 paper, "On May 4." The first English edition was issued by George Routledge, London, 1867, 16.5 cm., 187 pp., 1/o sewed, in illustrated yellow wrappers, listed in the *Ath* on Aug. 31. He issued it about Apr. 16, 1870, at 1/o sewed, with a new copyrighted chapter. John C. Hotten, London, issued it in 1871, Fcp 8vo, 1/o sewed, listed in *PC* as published Dec. 15–30.

Also 1876, 84. See *American Drolleries*, 1875

921 ARTEMUS WARD (CHARLES F. BROWNE) *Artemus Ward Among the Mormons.* 1/o sewed   Nov. (*Bks*)

Beeton's Humorous Books No. 31. See 1865

922 ANONYMOUS *The Fijiad.* 8vo. Illustrated. 1/o sewed   Nov.

This is Beeton's Christmas Annual, 15th season. It is the first edition, my copy, no date, 24.7 cm., 96 pp., double columns, white wrappers cut flush, pictorially decorated on the front in red, blue, and black, with ads on the inside front and both sides of the back cover. In front there is Beeton's Christmas Annual Advertiser, paged i–viii (including the decision in Chancery against S. O. Beeton). Beeton's Christmas Annual Advertiser, paged 97–120 occurs at the back. An ad in the *Ath* for Nov. 21, 1874, by S. O. Beeton, stated that Beeton's Christmas Annual had no participation on his part and that his annual was *Jon Duan*, to be issued by Weldon & Co., London, and not by Ward, Lock, for reasons not pertinent here to mention. In an ad for Dec. 5, Ward, Lock quoted the Chancery decision in *Ward & Lock v. S. O. Beeton* to the effect that the vice-chancellor has this day (Nov. 15) ordered the defendant (Beeton) to stop advertising that he has a Christmas annual, to stop advertising that he has terminated his connection with Ward & Lock, and to stop advertising that Ward & Lock's use of the name, "Beeton's Christmas Annual" is improper or unauthorized. In an ad of Dec. 12, Weldon published a long article from the *Times* of Nov. 26 about the court case, their reason, they said, was to assure the trade that their annual would be published. The upper half of the full-page ad was for the *New Annual for the Season*, and Beeton's name is nowhere mentioned!

923 THE BROTHERS OWEN *Biggles's Wharf.* Illustrated. 1/o sewed   Dec. 26 (*Spect*)

This is the first edition, no date, a Christmas story.

924 ANONYMOUS *Naughty Jemima.* Fcp 8vo. Illustrated. 1/o sewed Dec. (*Bks*)

Beeton's Humorous Books No. 32. This is also given by the *Eng Cat*, but otherwise I cannot trace it.

925 LOUISE C. REYNOLDS, later BELL *Barbara.* 2/o boards   1874 (*Eng Cat*)

This has no date. The first edition was issued by Ward, Lock & Tyler in 1874, Cr 8vo, illustrated, 5/o, listed in the *Ath* on May 9. Also 1875

926 ELIZABETH S. PHELPS, later WARD *Gypsy Breyton.* 12mo. 1/o sewed, 1/6, 2/o cloth   1874 (*Eng Cat*)

This is a reissue in the *Lily Series*. Also 1872

927 P. SMYTH *The Great Pyramid and the Royal Society.* o/6   1874 (*Eng Cat*)

I cannot trace this.

928 C. P. MORGAN *The Phantom Cruiser.* Small format. 2/o boards   1874?

Household and Railway Books No. 8. This has no date, 233 pp., edited by Lt. Warneford (William Russell). The first English edition was issued by John Maxwell & Co., London 1865 (1864), small format, 236 pp., 1/o sewed, in yellow wrappers cut flush, printed in dark green with fancy lettering, and with Ward & Lock ads, listed in the *Ath* on Dec. 17, 1864. The *American Catalog* gives F. Gleason, Boston, 1864.

929 EMILIE CARLÉN **The Brilliant Marriage.** 2/o boards 1874?

Household and Railway Books No. 9. Also 1856, 65

930 JAMES F. COOPER **Mark's Reef.** 2/o boards 1874?

Household and Railway Books No. 10. The first edition was issued by Bentley, London, 3 vols., 1847, 20.5 cm., anonymous, 31/6, listed in the *Ath* on Sept. 25 and reviewed on Oct. 9, and listed in *PC* on Oct. 1. Thomas Hodgson, London, issued it as *Parlour Library* No. 117 (1854), 359 pp. The first American edition was issued by Burgess, Stringer & Co., New York, 2 vols., 1847, 18.5 cm., anonymous, in wrappers, listed in *Lit World* on Oct. 16 and deposited on Nov. 16. Spiller & Blackburn give it as 2-vols.-in-1, 1847, 18.5 cm., in boards, issued on Oct. 12.

931 WATERS (WILLIAM RUSSELL) **The Heir-at-Law, and Other Tales.** 2/o boards 1874?

Household and Railway Books No. 11. The first edition was issued by Henry Lea, London (1861), Fcp 8vo, 351 pp., at 2/o boards, in June.

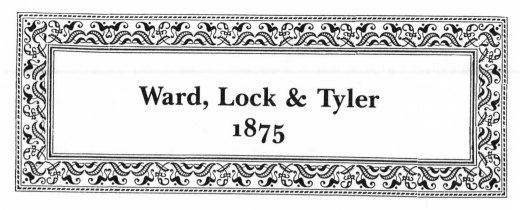

Ward, Lock & Tyler
1875

932 ANNIE WEBB, later WEBB-PEPLOE
The Five-Pound Note: An Autobiography.
Fcp 8vo. 1/0 sewed, 1/6, 2/0 Jan. 2
(*Spect*)

Rose Library No. 1.
Also 1865, 85

933 JAMES F. COOPER **The Sea Lions.**
2/0 boards Jan. 9 (*Spect*)

Household and Railway Books No. 13. The
first American edition was issued by
Stringer & Townsend, New York, 2 vols.,
1849, 20 cm., anonymous, listed by *Lit
World* as published Mar. 31–Apr. 14, and
given by Spiller & Blackburn as issued on
Apr. 10. The first English edition was issued by Bentley, London, 3 vols., 1849,
20.5 cm., anonymous, 31/6, advertised in
the *Ath* on Mar. 24 as "On Mar. 28," and
listed on Mar. 31. Brussel says it was issued on Mar. 29. Thomas Hodgson, London, issued it as *Parlour Library* No. 116
(1854), 351 pp., the plates of which were
used for the present edition. George
Routledge, London, issued it, Fcp 8vo,
339 pp., 1/6 boards, listed by *PC* as published Aug. 15–31, 1854.

934 RICHARD COBBOLD **Zenon the
Martyr.** Fcp 8vo. 1/0 sewed, 1/6, 2/0
Jan. 9 (*Spect*)

Rose Library No. 2. This has no date and
332 pp. The first edition was issued by
Henry Colburn, London, 3 vols., 1847,
20.5 cm., 31/6, listed in the *Ath* on May 29.
The second edition was advertised in the
Illustrated London News on Sept. 25, 1847, 3

vols., p 8vo, 21/0 [sic!]. It was issued as
Run and Read Library No. 10 by J. M. Burton, Ipswitch; Simpkin, Marshall, London, 1855, a new edition, 1/6 boards,
listed by *PC* as published Feb. 1–14, and
according to Sadleir it had Clarke, Beeton, London, on the title page.

935 RICHARD COBBOLD **Mary Anne
Wellington.** Fcp 8vo. 1/0 sewed, 1/6, 2/0
Jan. 9 (*Spect*)

Rose Library No. 4. The 2/0 issue was listed
in the *Spect* on Feb. 20.
Also 1864

936 M. R. LAING MEASON **Three Months
After Date and Other Tales.** 2/0 boards
Jan. 16 (*Spect*)

This is the first edition, no date, 321 pp.

937 W. S. HAYWARD **Love Against the
World.** 2/0 boards, 2/6 cloth Jan. 16
(*Ath*)

This is 1875, the only edition given by the
U Cat and the *BM*.

938 THE OLD SAILOR (MATTHEW H.
BARKER) **Nights at Sea.** Small format.
2/0 boards Jan. 30 (*Ath*)

Household and Railway Books No. 14. The
first edition was issued by N. C. Nafis, New
York, 1840, 19 cm., 159 pp. The first English edition was issued by Bentley, London, in 1850, p 8vo, anonymous, 310 pp.,
10/6, listed by *PC* as published Feb. 14–27.
He issued it in his *Shilling Series*, 1852, 148
pp., listed in the *Ath* on Jan. 31, 1852. He

sold the copyright to Henry Lea, London, at a Southgate & Barrett auction on July 14, 1856; and Lea issued it at 1/0 boards in July 1858, and reissued it at 1/6 boards in Aug. The pieces had appeared in *Bentley's Miscellany* No. 4 in Aug. 1837; No. 8 in Apr. 1838; and another in Dec. 1838.

939 MAYNE REID *The Cliff-Climbers.*
2/0 boards   Feb. 13 (*Spect*)

This was also issued at 3/6 cloth, listed in the *Spect* on June 5, 1875. The first edition was issued by Ward & Lock (1864), Fcp 8vo, 408 pp., illustrated, 3/6 cloth, listed in the *Ath* on Mar. 26. It was issued by C. H. Clarke, London (1864), 408 pp., 2/0 boards, 3/6 cloth, about June 18; and reissued (1872), my copy, 17.7 cm., 408 pp., frontispiece, a 2/0 yellowback, with *Clarke's Standard Novel Library* on the spine and title page. The front cover is in red, blue, and black and there are commercial ads on the front endpapers and on the back cover and Chapman & Hall ads on the back endpapers. The first American edition was issued by Ticknor & Fields, Boston, 1864, 18 cm., 304 pp. illustrated, $1.25 cloth, listed in *ALG&PC* (fortnightly) on Sept. 1, and advertised in the *New-York Times* on Sept. 3, *Books of Adventure for Boys* No. 12, "This day." It was listed and reviewed in the *Atlantic Monthly* for Sept.

940 JEANNIE T. GOULD, later LINCOLN
Marjorie's Quest. 12mo. 1/0 sewed, 1/6, 2/0 cloth   Feb. 13 (*Spect*)

Lily Series No. 47. This and the Routledge issue were the first English editions. George Routledge, London, issued it (1875), at 1/0 sewed, 1/6, 2/0 cloth, listed in the *Spect* on Feb. 20 and in the *Ath* on Feb. 13. The first edition was issued by James R. Osgood & Co., Boston, 1872, 18.5 cm., 356 pp., illustrated, listed in the *Ind* on Oct. 10 and by *Lit World* as published in Oct.

941 MAYNE REID *The Boy Slaves.*
2/0 boards   Feb. 13 (*Spect*)

This was also issued at 3/6 cloth, listed in the *Spect* on Apr. 3. It first appeared in the *Boy's Journal* for 1864. The first book edition was issued by Ticknor & Fields, Boston, 1865, 18.5 cm., 321 pp., illustrated, $1.50 cloth, from advance proof sheets, in blue sand-grained cloth with yellow endpapers. It was listed in *ALG&PC* (fortnightly) on Jan. 16, 1865, and advertised in the *New-York Times* on Dec. 31, 1864, as "This day." The first English edition was issued by C. H. Clarke, London (1865), 12mo, 2/0 boards, 3/6 cloth, listed in the *Ath* on June 17. They reissued it (1872), at 2/0 boards.

942 WATERS (WILLIAM RUSSELL)
Recollections of a Detective Police-Officer.
2/0 boards, 2/6 cloth   Feb. 20 (*Spect*)

This contains both series, no date, with a preface signed C. Waters. The first edition of the first series was issued by Cornish, Lamport & Co., New York, 1852, 12mo, $.75 muslin, as *Recollections of a Policeman*, advertised in the *New York Daily Times* on Feb. 25 as "Just published." Roorbach gives also an issue by Sheldon, Lamport & Blakeman, New York, as issued Oct. 1852–May 1855. The first English edition of the first series was issued by J. & C. Brown, London, 1856, 17 cm., frontispiece, 1/6, with a preface signed C. Waters, and listed in *PC* as published July 15–31. The first English edition of the second series was issued by Kent, London, 1859, 262 pp., with the signed preface. It was listed by *PC*, 1/6 boards, as published Sept. 14–30. Both series were issued by Darton & Hodge, London (1863), as *Parlour Library* No. 278, Fcp 8vo, 489 pp., 2/0 boards, about Apr. 25.

943 MARY R. MITFORD *Our Village.*
Country Pictures. 12mo. 1/0 sewed, 1/6, 2/0 cloth   Feb. 20 (*Spect*)

Lily Series No. 48. This has no date and 291 pp. For *Tales* see 1873.

944 JOSH BILLINGS (HENRY W. SHAW)
Josh Billings, His Sayings. Fcp 8vo. 1/0
sewed   Feb. 27 (*Spect*)

Beeton's Humorous Books No. 39. This has
no date and 200 pp., with an introduction
by E. P. Hingston. The first American edition was issued by G. W. Carleton, New
York, 1866, 19 cm., 232 pp., frontispiece,
11 illustrations, all on yellow paper. It was
bound in purple, brown, or blue cloth
with blue endpapers. It was advertised in
the *New-York Times* on June 1 as "This
week" and was listed in *ALG&PC* (fortnightly) on June 1. The title was *Josh Billings, Hiz Sayings.* Beadle & Co., New York,
included three of the Carleton pieces in
their *Beadle's Dime Book of Fun* No. 3
(1866), on pp. 4–16, entitled *Josh Billings:
His Writins, His Sayins, an His Doins.* It was
deposited on Apr. 19 and advertised in
the *New York Tribune* on Apr. 21, as "Ready
this morning." The first English edition
was issued by John C. Hotten, London
(1866), as *Josh Billings: His Book of Sayings,*
at 1/0 sewed, 3/6 cloth, with the Hingston
preface. It was a reprint of the Carleton issue with one addition and one omission
and was advertised in *PC* on June 1 as
"Just appeared" and listed in the *Ath* on
June 23. He reissued it in 1869, edited by
Hingston, probably with 200 pp.

945 (MARY E. BRADDON) ***Lost for Love.***
Stereotyped Edition. Small format. 2/0
boards, 2/6 cloth   Feb. 27 (*Ath*)

This has no date and 374 pp., the first yellowback edition. Wolff's copy of the yellowback was a reissue of late 1876 or early
1877, with the list of Braddon yellowbacks
on the back cover ending with *Dead Men's
Shoes.* The first edition was issued by
Chatto & Windus, London, 3 vols., 1874,
Cr 8vo, anonymous, 31/6, listed in the *Ath*
on Sept. 19. It was the only Braddon novel
issued by this firm! The first American
edition was issued by Harper & Bros.,
New York, in 1874, 8vo, $.75 paper, as *Li-
brary of Select Novels* No. 423. It was listed

in the *Ind* on Dec. 24, 1874, and in *PW* on
Dec. 26.

946 HENRY W. BEECHER ***Lectures to
Young Men.*** Cr 8vo. 1/0 sewed, 1/6,
2/0 cloth   Feb. 27 (*Ath*)

Friendly Counsel Series No. 2. This has no
date and 226 pp. The first edition was issued by J. P. Jewett & Co., Salem, 1845, 19
cm., 249 pp. The first English edition was
issued by Ward & Co., London, 1851, 208
pp., at 2/6. Ticknor & Fields, Boston, issued a new edition, with added lectures,
1868, with 287 pp. Clarke, Beeton & Co.,
London, issued it as *The Vices* (1853), 19
cm., 213 pp., at 2/6 cloth and later at 1/0.

947 ÉMILE ERCKMANN & PIERRE
CHATRIAN ***Stories of the Rhine.***
1/0 sewed   Mar. 13 (*Ath*)

This has no date and 217 pp. It was also is-
sued at 3/6 cloth. The first edition was
Contes des Bords du Rhin, Paris, 1862.
See *Popular Tales and Romances,* 1872

948 ANNIE WEBB, later WEBB-PEPLOE
The Pilgrims of New England. Fcp 8vo.
1/0 sewed, 1/6, 2/0 cloth   Mar. 13 (*Ath*)

Rose Library No. 3. The first edition was issued by Simpkin, Marshall, London, 1853
(1852), 17.5 cm., 496 pp., frontispiece,
listed in the *Spect* on Oct. 30, 1852. They
reissued it as *Run and Read Library* No. 13,
17 cm., 295 pp., frontispiece, at 1/6
boards, about June 14, dated 1855.
Also 1885

949 ELIZABETH PRENTISS ***Only a
Dandelion and Other Stories.*** 18mo.
0/9 sewed, 1/0, 1/6 cloth   Mar. 20
(*Spect*)

Beeton's Good-Aim Series No. 14. This has no
date, 159 pp., abridged. The first edition
was issued by A. D. F. Randolph, New
York, 1854, 17.5 cm., anonymous, 308
pp., illustrated, $.75 cloth, advertised in

the *New York Daily Times* on Nov. 18, "On Nov. 20."
Also 1885, 88

950 (ELIZABETH PRENTISS) *"Follow Me," and Other Stories.* 18mo. 0/9 sewed, 1/0, 1/6 cloth   Mar. 20 (*Spect*)
Beeton's Good-Aim Series No. 15. This is the first edition.
Also 1885

951 MARY C. HAY *Old Myddleton's Money.* 2/0 boards, 2/6 cloth   Mar. 20 (*Spect*)
This is 1875. The first edition was issued by Hurst & Blackett, London, 3 vols., 1874, Cr 8vo, 31/6, listed in the *Ath* on Sept. 5. The first American edition was issued by Harper & Bros., New York, 1875, 23.5 cm., 135 pp., as *Library of Select Novels* No. 430. It was listed in the *Ind* on Feb. 4 and in *PW* on Feb. 6, $.50 paper.

952 W. S. HAYWARD *Ethel Grey.* 2/0 boards, 2/6 cloth   Mar. 20 (*Ath*)
This is the first edition, 1875.

953 MAYNE REID, ed. *Lost Lenore.* 2/0 boards, 3/6 cloth   Mar. 20 (*Spect*)
The 3/6 edition was listed in the *Spect* on May 22, 1875. This was written by Charles Beach and largely reworked by Reid. The first edition was issued by C. J. Skeet, London, 3 vols., p 8vo, 31/6, listed in the *Ath* on Feb. 20, 1864, dated 1864. It was issued by C. H. Clarke, London (1865), 392 pp., at 2/0 boards, listed in the *Ath* on Feb. 4, and at 3/6 cloth, illustrated, listed in the *Reader* on Apr. 22, 1865. He reissued it (1872), 392 pp., frontispiece, 2/0 boards. The first American edition was issued by R. M. DeWitt, New York (1866), 19 cm., 382 pp., illustrated.

954 CATHERINE SINCLAIR *Beatrice.* 12mo. 2/0 boards   Mar. 20 (*Spect*)
Lily Series, a double volume.
Also 1866

955 ANONYMOUS *Moody and Sankey; Their Lives and Labours.* 1/0 sewed
Mar. 27 (*Ath*)
This is the first edition, 2 parts, no date. It was listed at 2/0 in the *Spect* on Apr. 24. In the United States it was issued by John C. Hall, New York; etc., as *The American Evangelists D. L. Moody and Ira D. Sankey.* It was received by the *Atlantic Monthly* for Sept. 1875.

956 CHARLES W. VINCENT, ed. *The Year-Book of Facts in Science and Art for 1874.* 2/0 boards, 3/6 cloth   Apr. 10 (*Ath*)
This is the first issue of this serial edited by Vincent and, in fact, he edited only this issue and the Year-Book for 1875, the latter listed in the *Spect* on Feb. 19, 1876. The issues for 1876–79 were edited by James Mason, issued by Ward, Lock & Tyler and Ward, Lock & Co., 2/0 boards, 3/6 cloth each. The last issue was for 1879–80, edited by Mason, and noticed in the *Spect* on Apr. 30, 1881. The first issue with the present name was a continuation of *Arcana of Science*, and was listed in the *Spect* on Mar. 9, 1839, portrait, 5/0, issued by Simpkin, Marshall, London. The issue for 1840 was published by Charles Tilt, London, Fcp 8vo, 5/0, edited by John Timbs. The succeeding issues were always issued at 5/0, illustrated, those for 1841–43 by Tilt & Bogue, London; those for 1844–57 by David Bogue; those for 1858–61 by Kent & Co., London; and those for 1862–74 by Lockwood & Co., London. All these were at 5/0 and were edited by John Timbs. Lockwood issued a year-book for 1874, listed in the *Spect* on Mar. 25, 1874; and Ward, Lock & Tyler issued the number for 1874, the present title! A. Hart, Philadelphia, issued it in 1851, edited by Timbs, listed in *Godey's Lady's Book* for Aug., and issued it again in 1852 and 1853, edited by Timbs, both given in the same, for July 1852, 1853.

957 ÉMILE ERCKMANN & PIERRE CHATRIAN *The States General and the Country in Danger.* 12mo. 2/0 boards Apr. 10 (*Spect*)

This is my copy, no date, 17.5 cm., 274 pp., 253 pp., in white boards, decorated on the front in red, green, and black, with "Beeton's Erckmann-Chatrian Library" on the front and spine. There are ads on the endpapers, a 22-page catalog at the back, and a commercial ad on the back cover.

See 1871, 84

958 SIR WILLIAM MATHEWS *Getting on in the World.* First series. Cr 8vo. 1/0 sewed, 1/6, 2/0 cloth Apr. 17 (*Spect*)

Friendly Counsel Series No. 3. The first English edition was issued by Sampson Low, London, 1873, at 6/0. The first American edition was issued by S. C. Griggs & Co., Chicago, 1873, 26 cm., 365 pp., listed by *Lit World* as published in Dec. 1872, and reviewed in the Jan. 1, 1873, issue. They issued the 10th thousand, 1874, advertised in the *Ind* on Nov. 20, 1873.

For the second series see 1877

959 ÉMILE ERCKMANN & PIERRE CHATRIAN *The Mysterious Doctor.* 1/0 boards Apr. 24 (*Spect*)

I'm not sure of the title, as it was listed in the *Spect* as *The Illustrious Doctor Mathéus and Friend Fritz.*

See 1872, 73

960 SALLIE R. FORD *Mary Bunyan.* 2/0 boards Apr.?

Household and Railway Books No. 15. Also 1865

961 MAYNE REID *The Headless Horseman.* 2/6 boards, 3/6 cloth Apr.?

This was first issued in 20 sixpenny parts in wrappers: parts 1–17 by Chapman & Hall, London; and parts 18–20 by Bent-

ley, London, both monthly, from Mar. 1, 1865, to Oct. 1, 1866. The first book edition was in 2 vols.: vol. 1 by Chapman & Hall, London (1865), illustrated, 6/0, advertised in the *Ath* on Dec. 16, 1865, as "Now ready," and listed on Dec. 23; vol. 2 by Bentley (1866), illustrated, 6/0, listed in the *Ath* on Oct. 27. These two vols. had continuous pagination and both had Chapman & Hall on the spines. I think Bentley reissued vol. 1 with his vol. 2; and he issued it in 1 vol., 1866, in red cloth, about Jan. 5, 1867. An issue was listed in the *Ath* on Sept. 18, 1869, 8vo, illustrated, 7/6, with no publisher given. Neither publisher ever advertised vol. 2 in the *Ath*! The first American edition was issued by R. M. DeWitt, New York; etc. (1867), 19 cm., 408 pp., listed in *ALG&PC* (fortnightly) on Nov. 15, 1867. G. W. Carleton, New York, issued it in 1868 at $1.75 cloth, advertised in the *New-York Times* on May 29 as "This morning."

962 HENRY KINGSLEY *Reginald Hetherege.* 2/0 boards May 1 (*Ath*)

Library of Favourite Authors No. 17. This has 355 pp. The first edition was issued by Bentley, London, 3 vols., 1874, 19 cm., 31/6, advertised in the *Ath* as "On June 4," and listed on June 13.

Also 1882

963 ANONYMOUS *Won by a Neck . . . to Which Is Added, Turf Characters.* 2/0 boards, 2/6 cloth May 1 (*Spect*)

This is the first edition, 2 parts, 1875.

964 CHARLES J. COLLINS *Dick Diminy, the Jockey.* 2/0 boards, 2/6 cloth May 8 (*Ath*)

This had no date and 297 pp. Also 1855, 69

965 ÉMILE ERCKMANN & PIERRE
CHATRIAN *The Story of a Peasant,
1793–1815*. 2/0 boards   May 8
(*Spect*)
This contains *Year One of the Republic* and
Citizen Bonaparte.
Also 1874 and below

966 ÉMILE ERCKMANN & PIERRE
CHATRIAN *Two Years a Soldier.*
2/0 boards   May 15 (*Spect*)
This contains *The Conscript* and *Waterloo.*
See 1871, 72, 84, and below

967 S. O. BEETON *Beeton's Book of
Anecdotes, Wit and Humour.* Demy
8vo. 1/0 sewed, 2/6   May 22 (*Spect*)
Comic Holiday Books No. 1. This has 140
pp. The first edition was issued by Beeton,
London, 1864, 21 cm., 140 pp., at 1/0,
listed in the *Reader* on Feb. 13. He issued
the third edition, 1865. This and the following title were issued as *Beeton's Book of
Anecdotes, Jokes, and Jests* (1866), 21 cm.,
279 pp., at 3/0, by Beeton, listed in the
Reader on May 19.
See 1887

968 S. O. BEETON *Beeton's Book of Jokes
and Jests.* Demy 8vo. 1/0 sewed   May 22
(*Spect*)
Comic Holiday Books No. 2. The first edition was probably the Frederick Warne,
London, issue 1866 (1865), 8vo, 140 pp.,
1/0 sewed, listed in the *Reader* on Nov. 11,
1865. See the preceding item.
See 1887

969 ANONYMOUS *Love Lyrics and
Valentine Verses.* 1/0 sewed   May 22
(*Spect*)
This is the first edition of the first series.
The second series, satirical, was listed in
the *Ath* and in the *Spect* on July 3 at 1/0.
The third series, names and birthdays,
was listed in the *Spect* on Aug. 14 at 1/0.
There was probably a fourth series, as it

was issued in 1 vol. with four parts (1875),
12mo, 479 pp., at 5/0, *Love Lyrics and Valentine Verses for Young and Old*, listed in the
Spect on Oct. 9.
See 1877

970 W. S. HAYWARD *Maude Luton.*
2/0 boards, 2/6 cloth   June 5 (*Spect*)
This is probably the first edition, 1875,
with 368 pp., although the *Eng Cat* gives
an edition at 2/0, 2/6, issued by Ward &
Lock between 1873 and 1879, possibly the
present issue.

971 ANNE MARSH, later MARSH-
CALDWELL *Norman's Bridge.*
2/0 boards, 2/6 cloth   June 5
(*Spect*)
The first edition was issued by Bentley,
London, 3 vols., 1847, anonymous, in a
printing of 1,000 copies. It was divided
into two editions, the first listed in the *Ath*
on June 26 at 31/6, and the second issued
in the fall of 1847. Bentley issued a new
edition in 1850, small 8vo, anonymous,
448 pp., at 3/6 cloth, listed in the *Spect* on
Jan. 19, 1850. The first American edition
was issued by Harper & Bros., New York,
1847, 23 cm., anonymous, 144 pp., double columns, noticed in *Godey's Lady's Book*
for Nov. 1847.

972 ANNE MARSH *Two Old Men's Tales.*
2/0 boards, 2/6 cloth   June 19 (*Spect*)
The first edition was issued by Saunders &
Otley, London, 2 vols., 1834, p 8vo, anonymous, 21/0, listed in the *Ath* on May 3.
Bentley, London, issued it as *Standard Novels* No. 94, 1844, 364 pp., in May. It was issued by Simms & M'Intyre, London and
Belfast, as *Parlour Library* No. 43, 1850,
287 pp., in May. The first American edition was issued by Harper & Bros., New
York, 2 vols., 1834, 20 cm., reviewed in the
Knickerbocker for Sept.

973   ELIZABETH PRENTISS *Nidworth, and His Three Magic Wands.* Fcp 8vo. 1/o sewed, 1/6, 2/o cloth   June 19 (*Ath*)

Rose Library No. 7. The first edition was issued by Roberts Bros., Boston, 1870, 17 cm., 279 pp., frontispiece, $1.25, listed in the *Nation* on Oct. 21, and advertised in the *New-York Times* on Oct. 11 as "On Oct. 15," and as "This day" on Oct. 15. The first English edition was issued by James Nisbet, London, in 1873, at 2/o, 2/6. Also 1885

974   HENRY VIZETELLY *The Wines of the World.* Cr 8vo. 1/o sewed, 1/6 cloth   June 19 (*Ath*)

This is the first edition, 1875, 19 cm., 202 pp.

975   AZEL S. ROE *Woman Our Angel.* 12mo. 1/o sewed, 1/6, 2/o   June 19 (*Ath*)

Lily Series No. 49. The first edition was issued by Carleton, New York; Sampson Low, London, 1866, 19.5 cm., 312 pp., $1.50, advertised in the *New-York Times* on Oct. 6 as "This morning."

976   MENRA HOPEWELL *Legends of the Missouri and the Mississippi.* 2/o boards June 19 (*Spect*)

Also 1874

977   M. CAROLL (MARTHA BROOKS) *How Marjory Helped.* 12mo. 1/o sewed, 1/6, 2/o June 26 (*Spect*)

Lily Series No. 50. This has no date and 189 pp. It was also issued by George Routledge, London, in 1875, no date, Fcp 8vo, 245 pp., listed in the *Ath* and in the *Spect* on Jan. 9, 1875. It is a prize story selected by the Ladies Commission on Sunday School Books. The first edition was issued by Lee & Shepard, Boston; etc., 1874, 17 cm., 315 pp., illustrated, listed in the *Ind* on July 16, and listed by *Lit World* as published in June. They reissued it in 1882 at

$1.25, advertised in the *New-York Times* on Dec. 6.

978   (SUSAN WARNER) *Sceptres and Crowns.* Fcp 8vo. 1/o sewed, 1/6, 2/o cloth   June 26 (*Spect*)

Rose Library No. 6. This was issued with *The Flag of Truce* (below) in 1 vol. at 3/6, listed in the *Spect* on July 14, 1877. George Routledge issued both in 1 vol. at 2/6 cloth, listed in *PC* on Dec. 18, 1875. The first edition was issued by Carter & Bros., New York, 1875, 17.5 cm., anonymous, 427 pp., $1.25 cloth, listed in *PW* on Sept. 26, 1874, and in the *Ind* on Oct. 1. It was bound in green, orange, or brown cloth with yellow, cream, or pink endpapers. It was given a long scathing review in *Scribner's Monthly* for July 1875. George Routledge issued it in his *Ruby Series* at 1/o sewed, 1/6, 2/o cloth, listed in the *Ath* on Nov. 7, 1874, and in the *Spect* on Dec. 5. Warne, London, issued it at 1/o sewed, 1/6 cloth, listed in *PC* on May 1, 1875, jointly with *The Flag of Truce*. James Nisbet, London, issued the present title in his *Golden Ladder Series* in 1875; and he issued it with *The Flag of Truce* in 1874, anonymous, 3/6, listed in *PC* on Dec. 18, 1874. A joint issue was listed in the *Spect* on Jan. 9, 1875, 12mo, 3/7, issued by Frederick Warne, London. The *Ath* listed an edition of the present title on Oct. 17, 1874, 12mo, 3/6, with no publisher given.

979   SUSAN COOLIDGE (SARAH C. WOOLSEY) *The New Year's Bargain.* 18mo. o/9 sewed, 1/o, 1/6 cloth June 26 (*Spect*)

Beeton's Good-Aim Series No. 16. The first edition was issued by Roberts Bros., Boston, 1872, 19 cm., 231 pp., illustrated, listed in *ALG&PC* (fortnightly) on Jan. 1, 1872, and in *Scribner's Monthly* for Dec. 1871. It was issued in England by Seeley, Jackson, & Halliday, London, 1873, 222 pp., with the same illustrations as were in the Boston edition, at 3/6. It was listed in the *British Quarterly Review* for Jan. 1873, and thus probably issued between Sept. and Dec. 1872. Frederick Warne, London, issued it in 1873, 182 pp., illustrated, 1/o sewed, 1/6 cloth, with no date. The present edition also has no date.

980 ÉMILE ERCKMANN & PIERRE CHATRIAN *The Old Schoolmaster.* 2/o boards June 26 (*Spect*)

This contains *The Alsatian Schoolmaster* and *The Story of a Campaign in Kabylia.*
For the first title see 1872, 75, 87, and below. For the second title see 1874

981 HONORÉ DE BALZAC *Unrequited Affection.* 2/o boards July 3 (*Ath*)

Library of Favourite Authors No. 18. This is a reissue of the edition of 1860, no date, a translation of *Père Goriot.*
Also 1860

982 RICHARD COBBOLD, ed. *The Suffolk Gypsy.* 2/o boards July 3 (*Ath*)

Library of Favourite Authors No. 19. This is a reissue of *John Steggall* of 1864.
Also 1864

983 LOUISE C. REYNOLDS, later BELL *Barbara.* 2/o boards July 10 (*Spect*)
Also 1874

984 ANNE MARSH, later MARSH-CALDWELL *Castle Avon.* 2/o boards, 2/6 cloth July 10 (*Spect*)

The first edition was issued by Henry Colburn, London, anonymous, listed in the *Spect* on Nov. 27, 1852, dated 1852, in 3 vols. It was issued by Thomas Hodgson, London, as *Parlour Library* No. 122 (1855), anonymous, with 352 pp. The first American edition was issued by Harper & Bros., New York, 1853, 8vo, anonymous, $.37½, advertised in *Lit World* on Jan. 22, 1853, as "Recently published," and advertised in the *New York Daily Times* on Feb. 19 as "Now ready."

985 MARY M. SHERWOOD (M. M. BUTT, later SHERWOOD) *The History of the Fairchild Family.* Fcp 8vo. 1/o sewed, 1/6, 2/o cloth July 17 (*Spect*)

Rose Library No. 5. This has no date and 213 pp., a reissue of part 1, with an account of the authoress by J. M. It was also issued about this time, no date, 300 pp., with a colored frontispiece. The first edition was issued by J. Hatchard, London, 3 parts: part 1, 1818, 12mo, 5/o, in Apr.; part 2, 1842, 12mo, 5/o, listed in the *Spect* on Jan. 15, 1842; part 3, 1847, by Mrs. Sherwood and her daughter, listed in the *Spect* on July 17. The first part was 18 cm., 302 pp., with a frontispiece. The first part was issued by W. Burgess, Jr., New York, 2 vols., 1828, 15.5 cm., the first American from the ninth London edition.

986 RICHARD COBBOLD *Freston Tower.* Fcp 8vo, 1/o sewed, 1/6, 2/o cloth July 17 (*Ath*)
Rose Library No. 8.
Also 1865, 70, 80

987 WILLIAM COBBETT *Advice to Young Men, and, Incidentally, to Young Women.* Cr 8vo. 1/o sewed, 1/6, 2/o cloth July 17 (*Ath*)

Friendly Counsel Series No. 4. My copy has the imprint of Ward, Lock & Co., London and New York, no date, a reissue of 1882, with the same imprint on the front cover but with Ward, Lock & Tyler ads on the endpapers. It is 18.1 cm., with 232 pp., in white wrappers cut flush and decorated on the front in pale blue and black. It has the series title on the front and spine and has a printer's date of Sept. 1882. There is a 22-page catalog with the Ward, Lock & Co. imprint at the back. There is a life of the author signed J. M. and an unsigned introduction, and the last page of text is signed by the author and dated Aug. 25, 1830. There is a commercial ad on the back cover. The first edition was issued by the author, London, 1829, 18 cm., 382 pp. Anne Cobbett, London, issued it, 1837, with 334 pp.; and the *U Cat* gives Charles Griffin, London (1830), with 335 pp. In the United States it was issued by J. Doyle, New York, 1831, 16.5 cm., with 268 pp. Also 1886

988 OLIVER W. HOLMES *Wit and Humour: Poems.* Fcp 8vo. 1/o sewed July 31 (*Spect*)

Beeton's Humorous Books No. 38. This has no date and 192 pp. The first edition was issued by Ticknor & Fields, Boston, in 1865, *Companion Poets for the People*, entitled *Humorous Poems*. It was listed in the *Nation* (New York) on Dec. 7, 1865, and noticed on Dec. 14. They reissued it, 1867, 16 cm., 100 pp., illustrated. The first English edition was issued by John C. Hotten, London, 1867, 19.5 cm., 192 pp., 3/6, with an introduction by Hotten. It was advertised in the *Ath* on May 5, 1866, with the title as for the present edition. It was listed in the *Ath* on Dec. 1, 1866. He reissued it in Dec. 1869, Fcp 8vo, at 1/o sewed. Also 1886

989 MARK TWAIN (SAMUEL L. CLEMENS) *Eye Openers.* Fcp 8vo. 1/o sewed July 31 (*Spect*)

Beeton's Humorous Books No. 33. This has no date, 17 cm., and 173 pp., with a title vignette. The first book edition was issued by John C. Hotten, London (1871), 16 cm., 173 pp., illustrated, 1/o sewed, 2/6 cloth, listed in the *Ath* on Aug. 26. It was a piracy. The 1/o was in light yellow wrappers printed in black with 16 pp. of ads at the back (1871). It contained the first book edition of *Journalism in Tennessee* and had pieces by a Carl Byng, which Twain disavowed. It also had reprints of *Memoranda*, which had appeared in the *Galaxy* from May 1870 to Feb. 1871. *Memoranda from the Galaxy* was issued by the Canadian News & Publishing Co., Toronto, 1871, unauthorized, listed in the

Canada Bookseller for Apr. 1871 as "Already published." Also 1885

990 RETLAW SPRING (pseudonym) *Hedged with Thorns.* Cr 8vo. o/6 sewed July (*Bks*)

Violet Series No. 1. This is the first edition, no date. Also 1891

991 MARK TWAIN (SAMUEL L. CLEMENS) *The New Pilgrim's Progress.* 1/o sewed July (*Bks*)

Also 1873, 86. See 1874

992 HORACE MAYHEW *Model Men.* o/6 sewed July (*Bks*)

Beeton's Comic Library. See 1856, 72, 73

993 HORACE MAYHEW *Model Women and Children.* o/6 sewed July (*Bks*)

Beeton's Comic Library. See 1856, 72, 73

994 ANGUS B. REACH *A Romance of a Mince Pie.* o/6 sewed July (*Bks*)

Beeton's Comic Library. See 1872, 73

995 ALBERT SMITH *The Natural History of "Stuck-up" People.* o/6 sewed July (*Bks*)

Beeton's Comic Library. See 1856, 72

996 ELIZABETH PRENTISS *Christians in Council.* Cr 8vo. 1/o sewed, 1/6, 2/o cloth Aug. 14 (*Ath*)

Friendly Counsel Series No. 5. This is the first edition.

997 MARK TWAIN (SAMUEL L. CLEMENS) *Screamers.* Fcp 8vo. 1/o sewed Aug. 14 (*Spect*)

Beeton's Humorous Books No. 35. This has no date and is a reissue of the Hotten edi-

tion. The first book issue was from John C. Hotten, London (1871), 16.5 cm., 172 pp., illustrated, 1/o sewed, 2/6 cloth. The 1/o issue was listed in the *Ath* on Dec. 30, 1871, and in *PC* on Dec. 8, and the 2/6 issue was listed in *PC* on Dec. 30. *BAL* says that it was the first book appearance of five sketches, three of which Twain disavowed, and most of the items were reprinted from the *Galaxy* (Sheldon & Co.) (see *Eye Openers* above). The 1/o issue has 18 pp. of ads (1871) and was in yellow wrappers printed in black. Another issue in wrappers had 166 pp. and had ads (1872). These were piracies.
See *American Drolleries* below

998 MARY C. HAY *Victor and Vanquished.*
2/o boards, 2/6 cloth   Aug. 21 (*Ath*)

This is 1875. The first edition was issued by Hurst & Blackett, London, 3 vols., 1874, Cr 8vo, 31/6, listed in the *Ath* on Jan. 17, 1874. The first American edition was issued by Harper & Bros., New York, 1876, 8vo, 145 pp., $.50 paper, in *Library of Select Novels*. It was listed in *PW* on Jan. 22, 1876, and in the *Ind* on Jan. 17.

999 ANNE MARSH, later MARSH-CALDWELL *Aubrey.* 2/o boards, 2/6 cloth   Aug. 21 (*Ath*)

This has no date. The first English edition was issued by Hurst & Blackett, London, 3 vols., 1854, 19 cm., anonymous, listed in the *Spect* on Apr. 29. Sadleir's copy had a presentation date of Oct. 28, 1854. It was issued by Thomas Hodgson as *Parlour Library* No. 155 (1857), anonymous, with 411 pp.; and reissued by C. H. Clarke, London, at 2/o boards, in 1860. The first American edition was issued by Harper and Bros., New York, 1854, 24 cm., anonymous, 168 pp., at $.50 paper, as *Library of Select Novels* No. 190. It was advertised in the *New York Daily Times* on June 22 as "This morning," and listed in *Harper's New Monthly Magazine* for July.

1000 W. S. HAYWARD *Caroline.*
2/o boards, 2/6 cloth   Aug. 21 (*Ath*)

This is the first edition, 1875, with 367 pp. Also 1879

1001 (MARY E. BRADDON) *A Strange World.* Stereotyped Edition. 2/o boards, 2/6 cloth   Sept. 4 (*Ath*)

This is the first yellowback edition, no date, with 384 pp. There is a known copy issued by J. & R. Maxwell (1882), with the Braddon yellowback titles on the back cover ending with No. 37, *Just as I Am.* The first English edition was issued by John Maxwell & Co., London, 3 vols., 1875, 19 cm., anonymous, 31/6, advertised in the *Ath* on Feb. 6 as ready, and reviewed on Feb. 13. The first American edition was issued by Harper & Bros., New York, 1875, 8vo, $.75 paper, as *Library of Select Novels* No. 432. It was advertised in the *New-York Times* on Feb. 12, 1875, as "This day," listed in the *Ind* on Feb. 18, and in *PW* on Feb. 20.

1002 THOMAS B. MACAULAY *Reviews, Essays and Poems.* Second series. 1/6 sewed, 2/o, 2/6 cloth   Sept. 4 (*Spect*)
Books for All Times No. 5. This has no date. It was also listed in the *Spect* on Oct. 9, Cr 8vo, 3/6.

For the first series see 1874; for the third series see 1881

1003 MARK TWAIN (SAMUEL L. CLEMENS) *The Innocents Abroad.* 1/o sewed   Sept. (*Bks*)

This is a reissue in *Beeton's Humorous Books.* Also 1873, 84. See 1874, 79

1004 (SUSAN WARNER) *The Flag of Truce.* o/6 sewed   Oct. 6 (*Bks* ad)

Violet Series No. 2. This has no date. It was, in some form, deposited by Ward & Lock at the *BM* on Aug. 11, 1875, and Ward & Lock advertised it in some form in the *Bks*

on June 3, 1875. The first edition was issued by Robert Carter & Bros., New York,
1875, 17.5 cm., anonymous, 397 pp., illustrated, listed in the *Ind* on Nov. 26, 1874,
and in *PW* on Nov. 21. It was clothed in
lavender or brown cloth and had pink
endpapers. The first English edition was
issued by George Routledge, London
(1875), in his *Ruby Series*, at 1/o sewed, 1/6,
2/o cloth, listed in the *Ath* on Jan. 16,
1875, and deposited at the *BM* in May
1875.
See *Sceptres and Crowns* above

1005 JULES VERNE **A Journey into the
Interior of the Earth.** 12mo. 1/o sewed,
1/6, 2/o cloth   Oct. 9 (*Spect*)
Youth's Library of Wonders and Adventures
No. 1. This has no date, 17.8 cm., the 1/o
issue in yellow wrappers cut flush, elaborately decorated on the front in green,
red, and black, with a small illustration in
black, and "The Jules Verne Library" on
the front and spine. There is a commercial ad on the back cover and there are 267
pp. The first edition was *Voyage au Centre
de la Terre*, Paris (1864). The first English
edition was issued by Griffith & Farran,
London, 1872 (1871), 18 cm., 384 pp.,
6/o, *A Journey to the Centre of the Earth*, listed
in the *Ath* on Oct. 28, 1871; and reissued,
the same, about Oct. 11, 1873, at 6/o. The
first American edition was issued by Scribner & Welford, New York, 1871, 12mo, illustrated, $2.50 cloth, with the English ti-
tle. It was advertised in the *New-York Times*
on Dec. 9, 1871, and in the *Nation* on
Dec. 14. Scribner, Armstrong & Co., New
York, advertised a new edition in the *New-
York Times* on Sept. 20, 1873, 12mo, illustrated, $2.00, as "This day," and adver-
tised a popular edition on June 5, 1874,
authorized edition, 12mo, illustrated,
$.25 paper, $.75 cloth.
Also 1887. See 1877

1006 JULES VERNE **The English at the
North Pole.** 12mo. 1/o sewed, 1/6, 2/o
cloth   Oct. 9 (*Spect*)
Youth's Library of Wonders and Adventures
No. 2. This is uniform with the preceding
title and has 248 pp. It has "Voyages and
Adventures of Captain Hatteras" at the
head of the title page. The first edition
was *Les Anglais au Pôle Nord. Aventures du
Capitaine Hatteras*, Hetzel, Paris (1866). It
appeared in the *Magasin d'Education et de
Récréation* from Mar. 20, 1864, to Feb. 20,
1865. The first English edition was issued
by George Routledge, London, in 1874,
Cr 8vo, 314 pp., illustrated, 6/o, in blue
cloth, listed in the *Spect* on Oct. 17. It was
possibly dated 1875, as there is a known
copy thus dated, *A Journey to the North Pole*,
illustrated, in green pictorial cloth, and
also a copy in red cloth. The *U Cat* gives
George Routledge, London; E. P. Dutton,
New York (1875), 18 cm., 254 pp., frontispiece. This last item is puzzling as George
Routledge, New York, advertised it in the
New-York Times on Dec. 16, 1874, 12mo, illustrated, $1.50 cloth. Routledge issued
this title and the following in 1 vol., 1875,
The Adventures of Captain Hatteras, Cr 8vo,
illustrated, 10/6, listed in the *Spect* on Oct.
16, 1875. In the United States it was issued by James R. Osgood & Co., Boston,
with the following title, in 1 vol., in 1874,
advertised in *Lit World* on Nov. 1, 1874, as
"New books." *The Voyages and Adventures of
Captain Hatteras* was issued by Osgood,
1875, 12mo, illustrated, $3.00, listed in
PW on Oct. 16, and advertised in the *New-
York Times* on Oct. 10, the latter stating
that it had never before been translated
into English! It is possible that the new
book advertised by Osgood in Nov. 1874
was, indeed, the Oct. 1875 issue. *At the
North Pole* was issued by Porter & Coates,
Philadelphia (1874) (copyright by James
R. Osgood), 8vo, 231 pp., illustrated,

bound in pictorial green cloth with brown endpapers.

Also 1876

1007 JULES VERNE **The Ice Desert.** 12mo. 1/0 sewed, 1/6, 2/0 cloth   Oct. 9 (*Spect*)

Youth's Library of Wonders and Adventures No. 3. This is my copy, no date, 17.9 cm., 223 pp., in stiff yellow paper wrappers, illustrated and decorated on the front in green, red, and black, with "The Jules Verne Library" on the front and spine, publisher's ads on the endpapers, and a 16-page catalog at the back. The first book edition was *Le Désert de Glace. Aventures de Capitaine Hatteras*, Hetzel, Paris (1866). It ran in the *Magasin d'Education et de Récréation*, Mar.–Dec. 1865. The present edition is the first English edition. Routledge, London, issued it as *The Field of Ice*, 1876, Cr 8vo, 269 pp., illustrated, 6/0, listed in the *Ath* and in the *Spect* on Oct. 30, 1875. He issued it at 1/0 sewed, 1/6, 2/0 cloth, listed in the *Ath* on Nov. 20, 1875. George Routledge, New York, advertised it in the *New-York Times* on Dec. 16, 1874, 12mo, illustrated, $1.50 cloth. Porter & Coates, Philadelphia, issued *The Desert of Ice*, 1874 (copyright by James R. Osgood & Co.). For other American editions see the preceding item.

Also 1886. See 1876

1008 JULES VERNE **Five Weeks in a Balloon.** 12mo. 1/0 sewed, 1/6, 2/0 cloth   Oct. 9 (*Spect*)   *See color photo section*

Youth's Library of Wonders and Adventures No. 4. This is my copy, no date, uniform with the preceding title, with a different illustration on the front, 268 pp., and a 20-page catalog at the back. It was translated by F. A. Malleson. The first edition was *Cinq Semaines en Ballon, Voyage de Decouverte en Afrique par Trois Anglais*, Paris (1863), 354 pp. The first English edition was issued by Chapman & Hall, London, 1870, illustrated, 7/6, listed in the *Ath* on May 14. Sampson, Low, London, issued a

second edition, 1874, Sq Cr 8vo, illustrated, 7/6, listed in the *Ath* on Apr. 11. Low issued the author's illustrated edition, 12mo, at 1/0 in limp, pictorial gray boards cut flush, with an illustration in black and white on the lower three-fifths of the front cover, and with "Low's Authorised and Illustrated Edition" on the cover, listed in the *Academy* on Feb. 5, 1876. By July 1 Low was advertising it at 2/0 cloth, illustrated. George Routledge, London, issued it, 1876, 249 pp., at 2/0 sewed, 1/6, 2/0 cloth, listed in the *Spect* on Dec. 25, 1875. The first edition in English was issued by D. Appleton & Co., New York, 1869, 12mo, 345 pp., $1.00 paper, $1.50 cloth, translated by William Lackland, advertised in the *New-York Times* on Feb. 20 as "This day." A second edition was advertised, the same, on Mar. 6 as "This day." The Low, Ward & Lock, and Routledge editions had different translations.

See 1877, 87

1009 MICHAEL SCOTT **Tom Cringle's Log.** 2/0 boards   Oct. 9 (*Spect*)

Library of Favourite Authors No. 20. This has no date and 436 pp. The first English edition was issued by William Blackwood, Edinburgh; etc., 2 vols., 1833, Fcp 8vo, anonymous, 12/0, reprinted from *Blackwood's Magazine*, with additions and corrections. It was listed in the *Ath* on Nov. 2. In the United States it was issued by Carey & Hart, Philadelphia; etc., 3 vols., 1833, 8vo, anonymous, with considerably different contents from the English edition (probably without the additions and corrections). This was also issued jointly with Lilly, Wait & Co., Boston, in 2 vols., 20.5 cm., and with Allen & Ticknor, Boston, 2 vols., both 1833, and both 20.5 cm., anonymous. Blackwood issued a second edition, 1834, 2 vols., Fcp 8vo, 12/0, in dark green cloth, advertised in the *Spect* on Nov. 1, 1834.

1010 ANONYMOUS *Beeton's Complete Etiquette for Gentlemen.* 1/0   Oct. 9 (*Ath*)

This has no date and 124 pp.

1011 ANONYMOUS *Beeton's Complete Etiquette for Ladies.* 1/0   Oct. 9 (*Ath*)

This has no date and 124 pp.
Also 1883

1012 ANONYMOUS *Beeton's Complete Family Etiquette.* Oct. 9 (*Ath*)

I cannot trace this.

1013 DWIGHT L. MOODY *Saviour and Sinner.* 1/0 sewed   Oct. 9 (*Spect*)

This is the first edition, no date, consisting of sermons and addresses. It was also listed in the *Spect* on Dec. 11, Fcp 8vo, 1/0.

1014 CHARLES GIBBON *Dangerous Connexions.* 2/0 boards, 2/6 cloth
Oct. 30 (*Ath*)

This is 1875 with 402 pp. The first edition was issued by John Maxwell & Co., London, 3 vols., 1864, p 8vo, 31/6, advertised in the *Ath* on July 9 as "On July 12" and on July 16 as "This day."

1015 ANNE MARSH, later MARSH-CALDWELL *Angela.* 2/0 boards, 2/6 cloth   Oct. 30 (*Ath*)

The first edition was from Henry Colburn, London, 3 vols., 1848, anonymous, 31/6, listed in the *Ath* on Feb. 19. Colburn issued it in 1850, 12mo, anonymous, 576 pp., at 3/6 cloth, listed by *PC* as published Oct. 30–Nov. 14. It was issued by W. Tegg, London, 1850, 17 cm., anonymous, 568 pp., illustrated; and by Thomas Hodgson, London (1855), as *Parlour Library* No. 126, anonymous, 462 pp. The first American edition was issued by Harper & Bros., New York, 1848, 19 cm., anonymous, 498 pp., listed by *Lit World* as published June 10–17.

1016 TOM HOOD *Tom Hood's Comic Annual, 1876.* 4to. 1/0 sewed   Oct. 30 (*Ath*)

This was issued in London (1867–75) except there was no issue for 1869, and it was continued as *Hood's Comic Annual*, for 1877–95, annually, issued in London (1876–94), 4to.

1017 PERCY B. ST. JOHN *The Arctic Crusoe.* 2/0 boards   Oct. 30 (*Ath* ad)

This is 1875. Ward, Lock & Tyler also issued it at 3/6, illustrated. The first edition was issued by Clarke & Beeton, London (1854), 12mo, 197 pp., illustrated, 2/6 boards, listed by *PC* as published Aug. 1–15. It was listed in the *Ath* on Sept. 16, 1854, Cr 8vo, 3/6 cloth, with no publisher given. David Bryce, London, issued it in 1856, reduced to 2/0 boards, listed by *PC* as published June 14–30. In the United States it was issued by Mayhew & Baker, Boston, as *The Sea of Ice*, illustrated, $.75, noticed in *Godey's Lady's Book* for Jan. 1860, and thus probably issued in Oct. or Nov. 1859. It was issued by Lee & Shepard, Boston, 1863, 17.5 cm., 243 pp., illustrated.

1018 MARK TWAIN & OLIVER W. HOLMES *Funny Stories and Humorous Poems.* 2/0 boards   Oct.?

Household and Railway Books No. 18. This has no date, and two parts, the first part being *Eye Openers* (above) and the second part being, I suspect, *Wit and Humour: Poems* (above). The pages are 173 and 192, and part two has the preface by John C. Hotten.
See 1885, 86, and above.

1019 MARTIN F. TUPPER *Stephan Langton.* New Edition, Revised.
2/0   Nov. 6 (*Spect*)

The *U Cat* gives this as 1875, 244 pp., illustrated.
Also 1863

1020 MARY E. BRADDON, ed. *Belgravia Annual for 1876.* 1/o sewed   Nov. 13 (*Ath* ad)

The ad said "On Nov. 15." Shortly after this, *Belgravia* was taken over by Chatto & Windus, London.

1021 MARY E. S. LEATHLEY *Conquerors and Captives.* 18mo. o/9 sewed, 1/o, 1/6 cloth   Nov. 13 (*Spect*)

Beeton's Good-Aim Series No. 18. This is the first edition.

1022 MARY E. S. LEATHLEY *The Star of Promise.* 18mo. o/9 sewed, 1/o, 1/6 cloth Nov. 13 (*Spect*)

Beeton's Good-Aim Series No. 19. This is the first edition.

1023 CATHERINE SINCLAIR *The Mysterious Marriage.* Fcp 8vo. 1/o sewed, 1/6, 2/o cloth Nov. 20 (*Ath*)

Rose Library No. 9. Also 1864

1024 ELIZABETH LYNN, later LINTON *The Mad Willoughbys and Other Tales.* 1/o sewed, 2/o cloth   Nov. 20 (*Ath*)

Country House Library No. 1. This is the first book edition, no date. It appeared complete in Ward & Lock's *New Quarterly Magazine* for Jan. 1875. Also 1880

1025 ANONYMOUS *Faust and 'Phisto.* 8vo. Illustrated. 1/o sewed   Nov. 27 (*Ath*)

This is Beeton's Christmas Annual, 16th season. It is my copy, the first edition, no date, 24.5 cm., 96 pp., in white wrappers cut flush, decorated on the front in red, blue, and black, with ads on the inside covers and on the back cover. At the front is Beeton's Christmas Annual Advertiser, paged (i)–viii, followed by a yellow full-page insert with a commercial ad, then 4

pp. of Cassell & Co. ads, (a three-quarter page size insert), then a small gray inserted slip for the Queen Insurance Co. The 96 pp. of text includes poetry and 5 pp. of music, the text in double columns. At the back is Beeton's Christmas Annual Advertiser paged 97–114.

1026 ELIZABETH WETHERELL (SUSAN WARNER) *The Wide, Wide World.* 1/o sewed   Nov. (*Bks*)

This is a reissue of *Lily Series* No. 14, advertised as the only complete edition at 1/o. Also 1873

1027 ELIZA WARREN *The Sixpenny Economical Cookery Book.* o/6 linen Nov. (*Bks*)

This has no date, another edition of *The Economical Cookery Book* of 1861. Also 1861. See 1888

1028 ELIZABETH WETHERELL (SUSAN WARNER) *Queechy.* 1/o sewed   Nov.?

This is a reissue in the *Lily Series*. It was advertised as the only complete edition at 1/o. Also 1873

1029 BRET HARTE *Sensation Novels Condensed.* Fcp 8vo. Frontispiece. 1/o sewed   Nov./Dec. (*Bks*)

Beeton's Humorous Books No. 44. This is my copy, no date, 16.5 cm., 215 pp., with a vignette title page, and with a preface signed J.C.H. (John C. Hotten) and dated Feb. 6, 1871. It is in white wrappers cut flush, decorated on the front in red and black with four stylized small illustrations, and with the series title at the head of the title page. There are ads on the inside covers, on the back cover, and on the verso of the title page. The first edition was issued by G. W. Carleton, New York, as *Condensed Novels; and Other Papers,* with

the joint imprint with Sampson Low, London, 1867, illustrated, listed in *ALG&PC* on Oct. 15. It was issued as *Condensed Novels* by James R. Osgood & Co., Boston, 1871, a new and enlarged edition, 18.5 cm., 212 pp., in green or purple cloth, and it contained two new pieces. It was listed in the *Nation* on May 18 and advertised in the *New-York Times* on May 15, $1.50, as "This day." John C. Hotten, London, issued it, with the present title (1871), 16.5 cm., 215 pp., 1/6 sewed, 2/o cloth, with a frontispiece and an introduction by Hotten (Feb. 6, 1871). The 1/6 edition has 32 pp. of ads and was uncut in pictorial wrappers. It was deposited at the *BM* on May 30. George Routledge, London, issued it, 1873, 16.5 cm., 176 pp., at 1/o boards, listed in the *Ath* on Apr. 12.
Also 1885

1030 FRANCES P. COBBE *False Beasts and True.* 1/o sewed, 2/o cloth   Dec. 4 (*Ath*)
Country House Library No. 2. This is the first edition, no date, 218 pp.
Also 1888

1031 GEORGE C. EGGLESTON *How to Make a Living.* Cr 8vo. 1/o sewed, 1/6, 2/o cloth   Dec. 11 (*Spect*)
Friendly Counsel Series No. 6. This is the first English edition. The first edition was issued by G. P. Putnam's Sons, New York, 1875, 19 cm., 127 pp., listed by *Lit World* as published in Apr.

1032 MARY E. S. LEATHLEY *The Story of Stories for Little Ones.* 18mo. Frontispiece. o/9 sewed, 1/o, 1/6 cloth Dec. 11 (*Spect*)
Beeton's Good-Aim Series No. 17. This has no date, 16 cm., 223 pp. The first edition was issued by Ward, Lock & Tyler in 1875 at 3/6, listed in the *Spect* on Oct. 9.

1033 CATHERINE SINCLAIR *Modern Flirtations.* Fcp 8vo. 1/o sewed, 1/6, 2/o cloth   Dec. 11 (*Spect*)
Rose Library No. 11.
Also 1865

1034 (SUSAN WARNER) *Melbourne House.* 12mo. 1/o sewed, 1/6, 2/o cloth   Dec. 18 (*Spect*)
Lily Series No. 52. This has no date and 431 pp. The first American edition was issued by Robert Carter & Bros., New York, 2 vols., 1864, 20 cm., anonymous, illustrated, $3.50, in pink or brown cloth with yellow or cream endpapers. They issued a new edition in 1 vol. at $2.00, advertised in the *New-York Times* on Dec. 20, 1865, as "Just published." The first Carter edition was listed in *ALG&PC* (fortnightly) on Nov. 15 and in the *Ind* on Nov. 24, 1864. The first English edition was issued by James Nisbet, London, in the *Golden Ladder Series*, in 1864, small Cr 8vo, 553 pp., with 8 colored plates, 3/6 cloth. It was advertised in the *Ath* on Nov. 26 as "This day" and listed also on Nov. 26 and listed in *PC* on Dec. 15 as published Dec. 1–15. Nisbet issued a second edition, Fcp 8vo, 553 pp., illustrated, 3/6 cloth, listed in the *Reader* on Feb. 11, 1865. He issued a third edition at 2/o boards, listed there on May 27, 1865. George Routledge, London, issued it, 1865 (1864), anonymous, 2/o boards, 2/6 cloth, listed in the *Ath* on Dec. 10, 1864, and listed by *PC* as published Dec. 1–15.

1035 W. S. HAYWARD *The Diamond Cross.* 2/o boards   Dec. 18 (*Spect*)
Household and Railway Books No. 25. I cannot give the history of this title with any certainty. The *BM* gives London (1868); the *Eng Cat* gives Ward & Lock, 2/6, 2/o, as issued between 1873 and 1879; and the *U Cat* gives an edition of 353 pp., with a caption title. It was listed in *ALG&PC* (fort-

nightly) on Mar. 15, 1867, as issued by Hilton & Co., New York, and the author was given as W. B. Phillips!
Also 1885

1036 JULES VERNE *The Mysterious Document.* 12mo. 1/o sewed, 1/6, 2/o cloth   Dec. 25 (*Ath*)
Youth's Library of Wonders and Adventures No. 5. This is the first English edition. The *BM* gives two copies of the wrappered edition, the second with "New edition with colored pictures" on the front cover. The first edition was part 1 of *Les Enfants du Capitaine Grant. Voyage Autour du Monde. Amérique de Sud.* Part 2 was *Australie* and part 3 was *Océan Pacifique.* The 3 parts first appeared in the *Magasin d'Education et de Récréation* from Dec. 20, 1865, to Dec. 5, 1867. The first book edition of part 1 was issued by Hetzel, Paris, 1867. George Routledge, London, issued *A Voyage Round the World. South America*, 1876, Cr 8vo, 312 pp, illustrated, 6/o, in green pictorial cloth, listed in the *Ath* and in the *Spect* on Mar. 18, 1876. He issued it at 1/o sewed, 1/6, 2/o cloth, 1877, listed in the *Ath* on Mar. 24. The 2/o had gilt edges, 312 pp., in green pictorial cloth, and had a 32-page catalog at the back. Since it has been supposed by some that the Routledge was the first English edition, I mention that the present edition was not only listed in the *Ath* on Dec. 25, 1875, but also in the *Spect*, the same, and was advertised in the *Ath* on Dec. 25 as "Now ready." J. B. Lippincott, Philadelphia, issued *A Voyage Round the World*, 1873, given by the *U Cat* (which also gives *In Search of the Castaways, etc.*), Lippincott, 1873. The latter title was noticed in *Harper's New Monthly Magazine* for Sept. 1873, illustrated.

1037 BRET HARTE *Roaring Camp, and Other Sketches, Stories and Bohemian Papers.* 1/o sewed   Dec. 31 (*PC*)
Also 1873

1038 ANONYMOUS *Major Jack Downing of the Downingville Militia.* o/6 sewed? Dec. 31 (*PC*)
This is a reissue.
Also 1866

1039 ANGUS B. REACH *The Natural History of Humbugs.* o/6 sewed   1875
Beeton's Comic Library.
Also see 1872, 73

1040 HORACE MAYHEW *Change for a Shilling.* o/6 sewed   1875
Beeton's Comic Library.
Also 1872

1041 JAMES HANNAY *Hearts Are Trumps.* o/6 sewed   1875
Beeton's Comic Library.
See 1856, 72

1042 ALBERT SMITH *The Natural History of the Ballet Girl.* o/6 sewed   1875
Beeton's Comic Library.
See 1856, 72

1043 ALBERT SMITH *The Natural History of the Gent.* o/6 sewed   1875
Beeton's Comic Library.
See 1856, 72

1044 ALBERT SMITH *The Natural History of the Flirt.* o/6 sewed   1875
Beeton's Comic Library.
See 1856, 72

1045 ALBERT SMITH *The Natural History of the Idler upon Town.* o/6 sewed   1875
Beeton's Comic Library.
Also 1856, 72

1046 ALBERT SMITH *The Natural History of Evening Parties.* o/6 sewed   1875
Beeton's Comic Library.
See 1856, 72

1047 LUCY AIKEN *Memoirs of the Court of Elizabeth.* 2/o 1875 (*Eng Cat*)

This is a reissue of the (1873) edition, no date.

Also 1873

1048 TIMOTHY TITCOMB (JOSIAH G. HOLLAND) *Letters to Young People.* 1/o sewed, 1/6, 2/o cloth 1875 (*Eng Cat*)

This is a reissue in the *Friendly Counsel Series* No. 1, with a new title page, no date.

Also 1874

1049 CHARLES D. WARNER *Backlog Studies and My Summer in a Garden.* 2/o boards 1875 (*Eng Cat*)

Household and Railway Books No. 16. This has no date, an issue in 1 vol. of the two titles of 1873.

See 1873

1050 MAYNE REID *Afloat in the Forest.* 2/o boards, 3/6 illustrated 1875 (*Eng Cat*)

Ward, Lock & Tyler issued this at 3/6, illustrated, listed in the *Spect* on June 26, 1875. The first edition was issued by C. H. Clarke, London (1866), 17 cm., 382 pp., 2/o boards, 3/6 illustrated, listed in the *Ath* on Apr. 28. It ran in *The Boy's Journal* in 1865 and in *Our Young Folk's Magazine* in 1866. The first American edition was issued by Ticknor & Fields, Boston, 1867, 19 cm., 292 pp., illustrated, $1.75, advertised in the *New-York Times* on Nov. 24, 1866, as if ready, and listed in *ALG&PC* (fortnightly) on Dec. 1, and in the *Ind* on Dec. 6. George Routledge issued it at 2/o boards, 3/6 cloth, in the latter part of 1877.

1051 MAYNE REID *The Giraffe Hunters.* 2/o boards, 3/6 illustrated 1875 (*Eng Cat*)

The 3/6 was listed in the *Spect* on June 12, 1875. The first edition was issued by Ticknor & Fields, Boston, 1867, 18.5 cm., 298 pp., illustrated, $1.75, advertised in the *New-York Times* on Dec. 22, 1866, and advertised in the *Ind* on Jan. 3, 1867, as "This day." The first English edition was issued by Hurst & Blackett, London, 3 vols., 1867, listed in the *Ath* on Sept. 14.

1052 MAYNE REID *The Half-Blood.* 2/o boards, 3/6 illustrated 1875 (*Eng Cat*)

The 3/6 edition was listed in the *Spect* on June 26, 1875. The first edition was issued by R. M. DeWitt, New York (1858), 19 cm., 454 pp., illustrated, $1.25, listed in *APC&LG* (weekly) on July 3. The first English edition was issued by Hurst & Blackett, London, 3 vols., 1859, 19.5 cm., frontispieces and title vignettes, 31/6, *Oçeola*, listed in the *Ath* on Jan. 29, 1859. The DeWitt issue had been entitled *Osceola*. It appeared in *Chambers' Journal*, Jan. 2– June 26, 1858. Henry Lea, London, issued it as *Osceola* in 1859, 16.9 cm., 438 pp., at 2/o boards, 3/6 illustrated, listed in the *Ath* on Dec. 3, 1859. Chapman & Hall, London, issued it (1861) as *The Half-Blood*, 18 cm., 438 pp., reviewed in the *Spect* on Feb. 5, 1861. It was issued by C. H. Clarke, London, as *Parlour Library* No. 239 (1861), 438 pp., at 2/o boards, as *The Half-Blood*, probably in July.

1053 MAYNE REID *The Hunter's Feast.* 2/o boards, 3/6 illustrated 1875 (*Eng Cat*)

The 3/6 edition was listed in the *Spect* on Apr. 17, 1875. This has no date and 336 pp. Wolff thought the first edition was issued by David Bogue, London, 1854, citing Mrs. Reid, but I've found no evidence for this. I think the first edition was issued by Thomas Hodgson, London (1855), as *Parlour Library* No. 120, 336 pp., at 1/6 in white pictorial boards as well as in the usual green glazed boards. It was listed in the *Ath* on Dec. 30, 1854. The first American edition was issued by DeWitt & Davenport, New York, 1856, 19 cm., 364 pp., illustrated, $1.25, advertised in the *New*

York Daily Times on Jan. 25, 1856, as "This day." They issued the eighth thousand, advertised there on Feb. 16. It was listed in *APC&LG* (weekly) on Jan. 12, 1856, as received since Jan. 5. Wolff's copy has an inscribed date (Feb. 20, 1856). The first illustrated edition in England was issued by C. H. Clarke, London, 1860, Fcp 8vo, 336 pp., at 3/6 cloth, listed in the *Ath* on June 30. The illustrations were not the same as for the American edition. Clarke reissued it with just a frontispiece and with a new title page, at 2/0 boards, listed in the *Ath* on Sept. 2, 1871.

1054 MAYNE REID **The Maroon.** 2/0 boards, 3/6 illustrated   1875 (*Eng Cat*)

The 3/6 edition was listed in the *Spect* on June 5, 1875. The first edition was issued by Hurst & Blackett, London, 3 vols., 1862, 19.5 cm., 31/6, listed in the *Ath* on Sept. 13. Wolff had a presentation copy inscribed Sept. 1862. Cassell, Petter, and Galpin, London, advertised in the *Ath* on Jan. 4, 1862, that it was to start in *Cassell's Family Paper*. It was issued in the United States by R. M. DeWitt, New York, listed in *ALG&PC* (fortnightly) on Jan. 2, 1865. It was also issued by G. W. Carleton, New York, though I cannot date it, but Carleton eventually owned the copyright. It was issued by C. H. Clarke, London (1864), with 491 pp., at 2/0 in yellow pictorial boards, and at 3/6 illustrated in cloth, listed in the *Ath* on June 4. Sadleir had a copy, C. H. Clarke, no date, a yellowback with "The Mayne Reid Library" on the spine and with endpaper ads for Ward & Lock's *Mayne Reid Library*, possibly the present edition. It was issued by Chapman & Hall, London, at 2/0 boards, listed in the *Spect* on Aug. 9, 1873.

1055 MAYNE REID **The Ocean Waifs.** 2/0 boards, 3/6 illustrated   1875 (*Eng Cat*)

The 3/6 edition was listed in the *Spect* on June 5, 1875. The first edition was issued by David Bryce, London, 1864, illus-

trated, 2/0 boards, listed in the *Ath* on Aug. 6. The first 63 chapters ran in the *Boy's Journal* of Henry Vickers, London, in 1863, according to Wolff. The first American edition was issued by Ticknor & Fields, Boston, 1865, 12mo, 366 pp., illustrated, $1.50, advertised in the *New-York Times* on Oct. 15, 1864, as "This day," and listed and noticed in *ALG&PC* (fortnightly) on Nov. 1, 1864. C. H. Clarke, London, issued it in 1871, no date, 328 pp., at 2/0 boards and 3/6 cloth, listed in the *Spect* on Aug. 19.

1056 MAYNE REID **The Scalp Hunters.** 2/0 boards, 3/6 illustrated   1875 (*Eng Cat*)

The 3/6 edition was listed in the *Spect* on June 26. The first edition was issued by Charles J. Skeet, London, 3 vols., 1851, 20.5 cm., listed in the *Ath* on June 28. The first American edition was issued by Lippincott, Grambo & Co., Philadelphia, 1851, 23.5 cm., 204 pp., $.50, advertised in *Lit World* on Aug. 30 as "This day," and listed as published Sept. 13–27. Simms & M'Intyre, London and Belfast, issued it as *Parlour Library* No. 77, 384 pp., in May 1852. It was issued in the 1850s by Henry Lea, London, no date, 27 cm., 264 pp., illustrated, and was previously issued by him in 31 parts with the original preface (June 1851) but with the first words of the text changed from "About a year ago" to "Some years ago." It was also issued in the 1850s by J. & C. Brown, London, no date, 16.7 cm., 448 pp., with the Lea illustrations, at 3/6 in crimson cloth. It was also issued in the 1850s by Darton & Hodge, London, no date, 18 cm., 448 pp., with the same illustrations, in magenta cloth. The copyright and stereo plates of the Brown edition were for sale at a Hodgson auction in Nov. 1858; and C. H. Clarke, London, purchased the entire stock of Brown about Jan. 1860. Clarke issued the present title in 1861, 448 pp., at 2/0 boards, 3/6 cloth. Beadle & Adams, New York, issued it as *Dime Novel* No. 150 on May 19,

1868, a double number with 208 pp. It was advertised in the *New York Weekly* on June 18, and the ad immediately below was for the care of the scalp and hair!

1057 MAYNE REID *The Tiger-Hunter.* 2/o boards, 3/6 illustrated   1875 *(Eng Cat)*

The 3/6 edition was listed in the *Spect* on Apr. 24. The 2/o edition has no date, and this title is given as No. 10 in a list of 17 Reid titles on the endpapers and back cover. The first edition was *Costal l'Indien*, by Gabriel Ferry (Louis F. G. de Belle-mare), Paris, 1852, 18 cm., 491 pp. The first English edition was issued by James Blackwood, London, 1857, Fcp 8vo, 378 pp., at 1/6 boards, entitled *Costal, the Indian Zapotec*, by Ferry. It was *Blackwood's London Library* Vol. X and was reviewed in the *Ath* on July 18. The first English edition in a free translation by Mayne Reid was issued by Hurst & Blackett, London, 3 vols., 1861, 31/6, as *A Hero in Spite of Himself*, advertised in the *Spect* on Aug. 17 as "Next week," and listed in the *Ath* on Aug. 24. *The Tiger-Hunter* was issued by Darton & Hodge, London (1862), as *Parlour Library* No. 271, Fcp 8vo, 373 pp., at 2/o boards, in the Reid translation. It was also issued by C. H. Clarke, London (1862), Fcp 8vo, 373 pp., 2/o boards, and in an illustrated edition at 3/6, listed in the *Ath* on Aug. 30, in the Reid translation. The first American edition was *The Tiger-Hunter*, issued by R. M. DeWitt, New York (1865), 19 cm., 369 pp., illustrated.

1058 MAYNE REID *The Wild Huntress.* 2/o boards, 3/6 illustrated   1875 *(Eng Cat)*

The 3/6 edition was listed in the *Spect* on July 3.
Also 1862

1059 MAYNE REID *The Wood-Rangers.* 2/o boards, 3/6 illustrated   1875 *(Eng Cat)*

The 3/6 edition was listed in the *Spect* on May 29. The first edition was *Le Coureue*

des Bois, Paris, 1850, by Gabriel Ferry (Louis de Bellemare). The first English edition was issued by Hurst & Blackett, London, with the present title, 3 vols., 1860, frontispieces, 31/6, a translation by Mayne Reid, in purple cloth, listed in the *Ath* on Jan. 14, 1860. It was issued by Henry Lea, London, 1860, 18 cm., 340 pp., illustrated, 2/o boards, and I suspect it was also issued in a 3/6 illustrated edition. It was issued by C. H. Clarke, London, 1861, as *Parlour Library* No. 241, Fcp 8vo, 340 pp., 2/o boards, and at 3/6 in an illustrated edition in crimson cloth. The first American edition was issued by Robert M. DeWitt, New York (1860), 19.5 cm., 456 pp., listed in *APC&LG* (weekly) on Aug. 4, 1860, Wolff's copy. A notice on the verso of the title page and repeated in a publisher's preface states that portions of the work are now first published by express arrangement with the author in order to protect copyright in the United States and that advance sheets were secured at considerable expense. Poor Bellemare is not mentioned. I have copies of both the first English and the first American edition.

1060 ÉMILE ERCKMANN & PIERRE CHATRIAN *The Conscript.* 1/o sewed 1875?
This is a reissue.
Also 1871 and above

1061 ÉMILE ERCKMANN & PIERRE CHATRIAN *The Alsatian Schoolmaster.* 1/o sewed   1875?
This is a reissue.
Also 1872, 87, and above

1062 ÉMILE ERCKMANN & PIERRE CHATRIAN *Year One of the Republic.* 1/o sewed   1875?
This is a reissue.
Also 1874 and above

1063 LT. ROBERT WARNEFORD *Running the Blockade.* 2/0 boards 1875?
Household and Railway Books No. 12.
Also 1863

1064 MARK TWAIN (SAMUEL L. CLEMENS) *American Drolleries.* 2/0 boards 1875?
Household and Railway Books No. 17. This is my copy, containing *The Jumping Frog, etc.*, and *Screamers.* It has no date and is 16.7 cm., 135 pp., 166 pp., with a half-title for *Screamers.* It is in yellow pictorial boards in red, blue, and black, with the series title at the head of the spine. There are commercial ads on the back cover, publisher's ads on the endpapers, and a 4-page insert on smaller paper at the front giving Chapman & Hall titles.
For the first title see 1874, and for the second title see above

1065 MAYNE REID *The Rifle Rangers.* 2/0 boards, 3/6 illustrated 1875?
This has no date, 18 cm., 448 pp. The first edition was issued by W. Shoberl, London, 2 vols., 1850, 19 cm., illustrated, advertised in the *Ath* on Jan. 18, 1851, as "Now ready." I have a copy of this in red cloth. It was issued as *Parlour Library* No. 98 by Simms & M'Intyre, London and Belfast, 1853, 384 pp., about June 25, greatly enlarged by the author, and rewritten with new scenes and adventures (see Wolff). It was reissued by Thomas Hodgson, London, 1854. Darton & Hodge, London, issued the new enlarged edition, probably about 1856, 448 pp., illustrated, in red cloth, Wolff's copy. It was issued by W. Kent, London, no date, 333 pp.; and by C. H. Clarke, London, in 1861, at 2/0 boards, 3/6 cloth. It was issued by J. & C. Brown, London, before Nov. 1858, 16.7 cm., 498 pp., illustrated. See the previous item for the disposal of the Brown stock. The first American edition was issued by DeWitt & Davenport, New York (1852),

24 cm., 196 pp., illustrated, advertised in *Lit World* on Sept. 6, 1851, as "In Oct." Roorbach gives 1852.

1066 MAYNE REID *The White Chief.* 2/0 boards, 3/6 illustrated 1875?
The first edition was issued by David Bogue, London, 3 vols., 19.5 cm., 31/6, my copy in claret cloth. It was listed in the *Ath* on Dec. 1, 1855. It was issued by J. & C. Brown, London, in 1857, no date, 16.7 cm., 444 pp., a 2/0 yellowback, and a 3/6 illustrated edition, listed in the *Ath* on Apr. 18, 1857. Darton & Hodge, London, issued it (1859), as *Parlour Library* No. 198; and C. H. Clarke, London, issued it in 1861, 444 pp., at 2/0 boards, 3/6. The first American edition was issued by DeWitt & Davenport, New York, no date, 19 cm., 401 pp., illustrated, noticed in *Godey's Lady's Book* for Sept. 1856.

1067 MAYNE REID *The White Gauntlet.* 2/0 boards, 3/6 illustrated 1875?
The first edition was issued by Charles J. Skeet, London, 3 vols., 1865 (1864), p 8vo, frontispiece, 31/6, in blue cloth, listed in the *Ath* on Oct. 29, 1864. It ran in the *National Magazine* (Tweedie, London) beginning in May 1863, and it concluded in the May 1864 issue. Tweedie advertised in the *Ath* on Apr. 2, 1864, that a 2-vols.-in-1 issue at 10/6 would be published on Apr. 21. However, there were no further ads, and it was never listed so probably it was a ghost. It was issued in Paris in 2 vols., 1865, *Le Gantelet Blanc.* It was issued by C. H. Clarke, London (1865), 12mo, 451 pp., at 2/0 boards, and at 3/6 illustrated, listed in the *Reader* on June 3, 1865. The first American edition was issued by G. W. Carleton, New York, 1868, 19 cm., 405 pp., illustrated, $1.75 cloth, listed in *ALG&PC* (fortnightly) on Oct. 15, and in the *Ind* on Oct. 22.

Ward, Lock & Tyler
1876

1068 MARY C. HAY *Hidden Perils.*
2/o boards, 2/6 cloth   Jan. 15 (*Spect*)

The first edition was issued by Hurst & Blackett, London, 3 vols., 1873, Cr 8vo, 31/6, advertised and listed in the *Ath* on Mar. 1. The first American edition was issued by Harper & Bros., New York, 1876, my copy, 23 cm., 164 pp., double columns, in buff wrappers, *Library of Select Novels* No. 463. It has publisher's ads on pp. 1–6 at the back, on pp. 1–4 at the front, and has ads on the inside covers and on the back cover. It was listed in the *Ind* on June 29 and in *PW* on July 8.

1069 ANNE MARSH, later MARSH-CALDWELL *Lettice Arnold.* 2/o boards, 2/6 cloth   Jan. 15 (*Spect*)

This has no date. The first edition was issued by Henry Colburn, London, 2 vols., 1850, 19 cm., anonymous, 21/o boards, listed in *PC* as published Oct. 14–30. Thomas Hodgson, London, issued it as *Parlour Library* No. 145 (1856), anonymous. It was also issued by C. H. Clarke, London, in 1860, at 1/6 boards. It ran in the *Ladies' Companion* (Bradbury & Evans), a weekly, beginning Mar. 9, 1850. Chapter 8 was in May; Chapter 10 on May 25; and it was no longer in the Aug. 17 issue. In the United States it was issued by Harper & Bros., New York, 1850, 23/5 cm., anonymous, 67 pp., double columns; and by E. Littell & Co., Boston (1850), 23 cm., 83 pp., along with *Lizzie Wilson*. Both of these American editions were listed in *Lit World* as published June 22–July 20.

1070 EDGAR ALLAN POE *The Complete Poetical Works of Edgar Allan Poe.*
2/o boards   Jan. 15 (*Spect*)
Household and Railway Books No. 26. Also 1866

1071 FRANCES CASHEL HOEY *The Blossoming of an Aloe.* 1/o sewed, 2/o   Jan. 22 (*Spect*)
Country House Library No. 3. This is probably the second book appearance of this title. It ran in *Chambers's Journal* from Sept. 1874 to Dec. 1874. The first edition was issued by Hurst & Blackett, London, 3 vols., 1875, Cr 8vo, 31/6, *The Blossoming of an Aloe and The Queen's Token*. It was listed in the *Ath* on Dec. 19, 1874. The second story began on p. 89 of vol. 3. The first American edition was issued by Harper & Bros., New York, 1875, 23 cm., 117 pp., double columns, at $.50 paper, *Library of Select Novels* No. 435. It was listed in *PW* on Mar. 13 and in the *Ind* on Mar. 18. Also 1880, 86

1072 (MARIA S. CUMMINS) *Mabel Vaughan.* 12mo. 2/o sewed, 1/6, 2/o cloth   Jan. 22 (*Spect*)
Lily Series No. 51. This has no date and 437 pp. It was also issued at 3/6, Cr 8vo, anonymous, listed in the *Spect* on July 8. The first American edition was issued by J. P. Jewett & Co., Boston; etc.; Sampson Low, London, 1857, anonymous, 508 pp., listed in *APC&LG* (weekly) on Sept. 26 and in the *Ind* on Oct. 8. It was also issued by Crosby & Nichols, Boston, who an-

nounced a new edition, anonymous, at
$1.00, in an ad in the *Ind* on Oct. 29, 1857,
"Now ready," stating that the first edition
of 15,000 copies had been exhausted and
the former publisher being embarrassed
and not able to continue, new arrangements had been made with the authoress.
It was listed in *Godey's Lady's Book* for Jan.
1858, and thus was probably issued in
Oct. or Nov. of 1857. The first English
edition was issued by Sampson Low, London, 1857, anonymous, 459 pp., with a
frontispiece, 3/6 cloth, and as a yellowback
at 1/6 boards, with 310 pp., both edited by
Mrs. Gaskell. Both were advertised in the
Ath on Sept. 5 as "On Sept. 20," and the
yellowback was listed on Sept. 19. The latter was pictorially printed on the front in
red and black, Sadleir's copy, with ads on
the back in red, and with pale yellow endpapers with ads (Sept. 19, 1857). George
Routledge, London, issued it, 1857, Fcp
8vo, 369 pp., at 1/6 boards, listed by *PC* as
published Nov. 14–30.

1073 JULES VERNE *On the Track.* 12mo.
1/0 sewed, 1/6, 2/0 cloth   Jan. 22 (*Spect*)
Youth's Library of Wonders and Adventures
No. 6. It has no date. The 1/0 edition is in
pictorial stiff wrappers. For details see *The
Mysterious Document*, 1875, the present ti-
tle being part 2 of *Les Enfants de Capitaine
Grant. Australie.*
Also 1886

1074 CHARLES W. VINCENT, ed. *The Year-
Book of Facts in Science and the Arts for
1875.* 2/0 boards, 3/6   Feb. 12 (*Ath*)
See 1875 for details.

1075 JOHN LATOUCHE (OSWALD
CRAWFURD) *Country House Essays.*
1/0 sewed, 2/0 cloth   Feb. 19 (*Spect*)
Country House Library No. 4. This is the
first edition, with a preface (1876), 19 cm.,
235 pp.

1076 GRACE KENNEDY *Father Clement.*
12mo. 1/0 sewed, 1/6, 2/0 cloth   Feb. 19
(*Spect*)
Lily Series No. 53. This was also issued at
3/6 cloth, Cr 8vo, listed in the *Spect* on
Aug. 12. The first edition was issued by
William Oliphant, Edinburgh, 1823, 15.5
cm., anonymous, 370 pp., with a frontispiece. The *U Cat* gives T. B. Peterson, Philadelphia (1825), 19 cm., anonymous, 155
pp.; and Crocker & Brewster, Boston;
etc., 1827, 15.5 cm., anonymous, 252 pp.
It was also issued by Bliss & White, New
York, 1827, 246 pp., from the fourth
Edinburgh edition; and by E. Duyckinck,
New York, 1827, 15 cm., anonymous, 246
pp., from the sixth Edinburgh edition.

1077 (JANE E. HORNBLOWER) *Nellie of
Truro.* Fcp 8vo. 1/0 sewed, 1/6, 2/0 cloth
Feb. 19 (*Spect*)
Rose Library No. 13.
Also 1864, 85

1078 (MARY E. BRADDON) *Hostages to
Fortune.* Stereotyped Edition. 2/0 boards,
2/6 cloth   Feb. 26 (*Ath*)
This is the first yellowback edition, no
date, 354 pp. The first edition was issued
by John Maxwell & Co., London, 1875, 3
vols., Cr 8vo, anonymous, 31/6, listed in
the *Ath* on Sept. 11. The first American
edition was issued by Harper & Bros.,
New York, 1875, 8vo, $.75 paper, *Library
of Select Novels* No. 448, with the ad for the
series ending with No. 448. It was listed in
PW on Nov. 20 and in the *Nation* on Dec. 2,
1875. It was reviewed in *Harper's New
Monthly Magazine* for Dec. 1875.

1079 CATHERINE SINCLAIR
Jane Bouverie. Fcp 8vo. 1/0 sewed,
1/6, 2/0 cloth   Mar. 11 (*Spect*)
Rose Library No. 10.
Also 1865

1080 JULES VERNE **Among the Cannibals.**
12mo. 1/0 sewed, 1/6, 2/0 cloth   Mar. 11
(*Spect*)
Youth's Library of Wonders and Adventures
No. 7. The 1/0 edition is in pictorial stiff
wrappers. The first edition was as part 3
of *Les Enfants du Capitaine Grant. Océan Pa-*
cifique. For details see *The Mysterious Docu-*
ment in 1875.

1081 CAPTAIN FLACK **The Redskins.**
2/0 boards   Mar. 18 (*Spect*)
Household and Railway Books No. 27. This is
also given by the *Eng Cat*, but otherwise I
cannot trace it.

1082 ALBERT SMITH **Mont Blanc.**
2/0 boards   Mar. 18 (*Spect*)
Household and Railway Books No. 28.
Also 1860

1083 CATHERINE SINCLAIR
Modern Accomplishments. 2/0 boards
Mar. 18 (*Spect*)
Also 1865, 78

1084 EDWARD P. ROE **From Jest to**
Earnest. 12mo. 1/0 sewed, 1/6, 2/0 cloth
Apr. 8 (*Spect*)
Lily Series No. 55. This has no date. It was
also issued at 3/6 cloth, no date, with colored illustrations, listed in the *Spect* on
July 13, 1878. The first American edition
was issued by Dodd, Mead & Co., New
York (1875), 19 cm., 548 pp., $1.75, ad-
vertised in the *Ind* on Sept. 28 as "On Sept.
25" and listed on Oct. 7, and listed in *PW*
on Sept. 25, and in the *Nation* on Oct. 14.
It is in terra-cotta cloth with yellow endpapers. The 10th thousand was advertised in the *New-York Times* on Oct. 23,
1875, as "Now ready," probably with a revised preface. The first English edition
was issued by Frederick Warne, London
(1875), 16mo, 312 pp., 1/0 sewed, advertised in the *Ath* on Oct. 16 as copyright in
Great Britain and issued simultaneously

in England and America. It was listed in
PC on Nov. 2. They issued it at 1/6 cloth,
listed in the *Spect* on May 13.
Also 1883, 86, 92

1085 AZEL S. ROE **The Star and the Cloud.**
Fcp 8vo. 1/0 sewed, 1/6, 2/0 cloth   Apr. 8
(*Spect*)
Rose Library No. 12.
Also 1864

1086 WILLIAM CARLETON **The Squanders**
of Castle Squander. Cr 8vo. 2/0 boards
Apr. 15 (*Ath*)
Library of Favourite Authors No. 21. This
has no date, 18 cm., 414 pp., with 32 pp.
of ads, ads on the endpapers, and a commercial ad on the back cover. The first edition was issued by the Office of the Illustrated London Library (Ingram, Cook &
Co.), London, 2 vols., 1852, 19 cm., illustrated, 5/0. It was listed in the *Spect* on
June 26 and reviewed on July 3. The *Eng*
Cat gives an edition by Henry Lea, London, in 1852, but this is hard to believe as
Nathaniel Cooke, London, reissued it,
probably in 1853, and I've found no evidence for the Lea issue. It was advertised
for sale by a New York bookstore in the
New York Daily Times for May 26, 1854, 2
vols., no publisher, of course, being given.
Also 1891

1087 BRET HARTE **The Pagan Child**
and Other Sketches. Fcp 8vo. 1/0 sewed
Apr. 29 (*Spect*)
Beeton's Humorous Books. This has no date,
16.5 cm., 185 pp., in pictorial wrappers. It
contains *Wan Lee, the Pagan, The Fool of Five*
Forks, the title story, and four others.
Routledge issued *Wan Lee, the Pagan, and*
Other Sketches, about Jan. 22, 1876, at 1/0
boards, the first separate edition, containing six stories reprinted from *Tales of the*
Argonauts and Other Stories and Sketches, issued by James Osgood & Co., Boston,
listed in *Lit World* as published in Oct.

1875, and listed in the *Ind* on Nov. 4. It contained *The Rose of Tuolume* (*The Pagan Child*); *Wan Lee, the Pagan*; *The Fool of Five Forks*; *An Episode of Fiddletown*; and four others. *Wan Lee, the Pagan* appeared in *Scribner's Monthly* for Sept. 1874. Routledge, London, issued *The Fool of Five Forks* about Jan. 2, 1875, at 1/0 boards, the first edition of the title story in that work.
Also 1878, 85

1088　GRACE KENNEDY　*Dunallan.* 12mo. 1/0 sewed, 1/6, 2/0 cloth　May 6 (*Spect*)
Lily Series No. 54. This was also issued at 3/6 cloth, Cr 8vo, illustrated, listed in the *Spect* on Aug. 5. The first edition was issued by William Oliphant, Edinburgh; etc., 3 vols., 1825, 19 cm., anonymous, listed by the *Edinburgh Review* as published Oct. 1824–Jan. 1825, at 18/0. The sixth edition, 12mo, at 7/0, was listed there as published May–July 1841. Frederick Warne, London, issued it at 1/0 sewed, 1/6 cloth, advertised in the *Ath* on Apr. 10, 1875, as "On Apr. 14," and on Apr. 17 as "Now ready." Warne issued it at 3/6 cloth, 12mo, listed in the *Spect* on May 22, 1875. Warne took it over from James Nisbet, London, who had issued it in his *Golden Ladder Series*. The first American edition was issued by Charles Ewer, etc., Boston; etc., 2 vols., 1827, 19 cm., anonymous.

1089　MARION HARLAND (MARY V. HAWES, later TERHUNE) *Jessamine.* 12mo. 1/0 sewed, 1/6, 2/0 cloth　May 6 (*Spect*)
Lily Series No. 56. The first edition was issued by G. W. Carleton, New York; Sampson Low, London, 1873, 18.5 cm., 387 pp., $1.50, listed in the *Nation* on Oct. 30, in *PW* on Nov. 1, and in the *Ind* on Nov. 6. I cannot discover that Low issued it!

1090　(HENRY G. JEBB) *Out of the Depths.* 12mo. 2/6 boards　May 6 (*Spect*)
This is my copy, no date, 17.8 cm., 316 pp., in yellow pictorial boards printed in red, green, and black. There is a commercial ad on the back cover, publisher's ads on the endpapers, and a catalog paged 1–16 at the back.
Also 1874

1091　(ADA BUISSON) *Put to the Test.* 2/0 boards　May 6 (*Spect*)
This is 1876, 392 pp., edited by Mary E. Braddon. The first edition was issued by John Maxwell & Co., London, 3 vols., Cr 8vo, anonymous, 31/6, not edited by Braddon. It was advertised in the *Ath* on Jan. 1, 1865, as "On Jan. 16" and listed on Jan. 21.

1092　ANNE MARSH, later MARSH-CALDWELL　*The Heiress of Haughton.* 2/0 boards, 2/0 cloth　May 6 (*Spect*)
The first edition was issued by Hurst & Blackett, London, 3 vols., 1855, 19.5 cm., anonymous, 31/6, listed in the *Ath* on Apr. 28. It was issued as *Parlour Library* No. 180 by Thomas Hodgson, London (1858), anonymous, 380 pp.; and reissued by C. H. Clarke, London, at 2/0 boards, in 1860. The first American edition was issued by Harper & Bros., New York, 1855, 8vo, anonymous, 142 pp., $.37½ paper, as *Library of Select Novels* No. 199. It was listed in *APC&LG* on Sept. 1, and advertised in the *New York Daily Times* on July 25 as "Tomorrow morning." It is a sequel to *Aubrey* and was issued from advanced sheets.

1093　W. S. HAYWARD　*The Three Red Men.* 2/0 boards, 2/6 cloth　May 6 (*Spect*)
This is the first edition, 1876, probably with 367 pp.

1094　MAYNE REID　*The Mountain Marriage.* 2/0 boards　May 13 (*Spect*)
Library of Favourite Authors No. 23.
Also 1867

1095 GUSTAVE AIMARD (OLIVER GLOUX)
The Tiger Slayer. 12mo. 1/0 sewed
May 13 (*Spect*)
Also 1860, 80

1096 JULES VERNE *Twenty Thousand Leagues Under the Sea.* Vol. 1. 1/0 sewed, 1/6, 2/0 cloth   May 13 (*Acad*)
Youth's Library of Wonders and Adventures No. 8. Vol. 2, No. 9 in the series, was listed in the *Spect* on June 24, 1876. It was also issued at 2/0 in 1 vol., listed in the *Spect* on Aug. 5, 1876. It first appeared in the *Magasin d'Education et de Récréation* (Mar. 20, 1869–June 20, 1870) in Paris. The first book edition was *Vingt Mille Lieues sous les Mers*, issued by Hetzel, Paris (1869, 1870), 18.5 cm., illustrated. The first edition in English was issued by Sampson Low, London, 1873, 19.5 cm., 303 pp., illustrated, 10/6, in green pictorial cloth, listed in the *Ath* on Oct. 19, 1872, and in the *PC* as published Nov. 1–15, 1872. Low reissued this many times at 10/6, the fifth edition being about July 11, 1874; and another reissue listed in the *Spect* on Apr. 22, 1876. Low issued it in 2 vols., 1876, author's edition, my copy, illustrated, 1/0 stiff wrappers each, vol. 1 with a 16-page catalog (Jan. 1876) at the back, listed in the *Acad* on Feb. 5. The Low editions were translated by Louis Mercier. George Routledge, London, issued it in 2 vols., 1876, complete edition, 1/0 sewed, 1/6, 2/0 cloth each, translated by Henry Frith, listed in the *Spect* on Feb. 26. The first American edition was issued by James R. Osgood & Co., Boston; etc., 20.5 cm., 303 pp., illustrated, from the Low plates, advertised in *Lit World* on Dec. 1, 1872, and listed in *PW* on Dec. 5. The *BM* gives a strange entry, giving another copy of the 1/0 sewed, Ward & Lock issue with "New edition, coloured plates" on the wrappers. This may be so, but the 2/0, 2-vols.-in-1 edition issued by Ward & Lock in Aug. was in boards with three colored illustrations.
Also 1886

1097 FRANCES CASHEL HOEY *No Sign, and Other Tales.* 1/0 sewed, 2/0   May 20 (*Spect*)
Country House Library No. 5. This is the first book edition. *No Sign* appeared in Ward, Lock & Tyler's *New Quarterly Magazine*, complete, advertised in *Notes & Queries* on Oct. 9, 1875, "Now ready."
Also 1880

1098 CONTESS JEANNE DE LA MOTTE
The Diamond Necklace. 2/0 boards
May 20 (*Spect*)
Household and Railway Books No. 29. This has no date. I cannot be sure of where or when this derives. C. H. Clarke, London, issued it, 12mo, 2/0 boards, listed in the *Ath* on Sept. 21, 1867. *The Story of the Diamond Necklace* by Henry Vizetelly was issued by Tinsley Bros., London, 2 vols., 1867, p 8vo, illustrated, 25/0; and Vizetelly & Co., London, reissued it, 1881 (1880), the third edition with 414 pp.; and also the third edition revised, 1887, 20.5 cm., 414 pp. This revised third edition was issued by Scribner & Welford, New York, 1881, 20 cm., 414 pp., frontispiece. *Vie de Jeanne de St.-Remy*, written by herself, was translated and issued by J. Bew, London, 2 vols., 1791. *Histoire de Collier* was issued in Paris, 1786, with 63 pp., and also with 45 pp. *Mémoire pour Dame Jeanne de Saint-Remy de Valois* was issued in Paris, 1785, 22.5 cm., 46 pp.

1099 CHRISTOPH W. VON HUFELAND
The Art of Prolonging Life. Cr 8vo. 1/0 sewed, 1/6, 2/0   June 3 (*Spect*)
Friendly Counsel Series No. 7. *Die Kunst des Menschliche Leben zu Verlängerern* was issued in Wien and Prag, 2-vols.-in-1, 1797, 21 cm.; and in Jena, 2 vols., 1798, 20 cm. *The Art of Prolonging Life* was issued by J. Bell, London, 2 vols., 1797, 22 cm. It was issued by J. Churchill, London, 1853, 16 cm., 271 pp., edited by Erasmus Wilson. He issued the second edition, listed in the

Spect on Apr. 30, 1859, and issued the sixth thousand, advertised in the *Spect* on Jan. 28, 1860, Fcp 8vo, 2/6. In the United States it was issued by Ticknor, Reed & Fields, Boston, 1854, 18.5 cm., 328 pp., $.75, in an edition of 1,500 copies, on Nov. 6, 1853.
Also 1885

1100 JOHN DANGERFIELD (OSWALD CRAWFURD) *Grace Tolmar.* 1/0 sewed, 2/0 cloth   June 10 (*Spect*)
Country House Library No. 6. This has no date. The first edition was issued by Smith, Elder, London, 1872, p 8vo, 304 pp., 7/0, listed in the *Spect* on Dec. 21, 1872. Sadleir was incorrect in thinking this Ward, Lock edition was the first.
Also 1883

1101 J. T. Y. *The People's Housekeeper.* 1/0 linen   June 10 (*Spect*)
House and Home Books No. 9. This is the first edition, 1876.

1102 S. O. BEETON *Beeton's Modern Men and Women.* 1/0 sewed, 1/6, 2/0   June 17 (*Spect*)
Also 1870

1103 ANONYMOUS *Beeton's Dictionary of Commerce.* 1/0 cloth   June 17 (*Spect*)
Also 1872

1104 FRANCES E. M. NOTLEY *The Kiddle-a-Wink.* 2/0 boards   June 24 (*Spect*)
Library of Favourite Authors No. 25. This first appeared in Beeton's Christmas Annual for 1863, fourth season, by Francis Derrick, 1/0 sewed, frontispiece, advertised in the *Reader* on Dec. 12, 1863, as "Now ready." Beeton issued it in book form, 1864, 8vo, 146 pp., 1/0 sewed, listed in the *Reader* on Feb. 13, 1864.

1105 (FRANCES E. M. NOTLEY) *Forgotten Lives.* 2/0 boards   July 1 (*Acad*)
Library of Favourite Authors No. 22. This has no date and 475 pp. The first edition was issued by Tinsley Bros., London, 3 vols., 1875, 19 cm., anonymous, reviewed in the *Ath* on Aug. 7.

1106 CAPTAIN FLACK *The Castaways of the Prairie.* 2/0 boards   July 1 (*Spect*)
Household and Railway Books No. 30. This has no date, a duplicate, with a new title page and table of contents, of a copy that the *BM* gives as London (1868).

1107 ANONYMOUS *Beeton's Date Book.* 1/0 cloth, 1/6, 2/0   July 1 (*Spect*)
This was reissued, 1892, a new edition with 282 pp., brought down to the end of 1891.
Also 1872

1108 GUSTAV FREYTAG *Debit and Credit.* 2/0 boards   July 1 (*Spect*)
Library of Favourite Authors No. 24. This has 503 pp. The first edition was *Soll und Haben*, Leipzig, 3 vols., 1855, 18 cm. The first English edition was issued by Bentley, London, 1857, Cr 8vo, 500 pp., 6/0, translated by Mrs. Malcolm with her name on the spine. It was listed in the *Ath* on Oct. 31, advertised by Bentley as unabridged and the only copyright edition. He issued the second thousand, the same, advertised in the *Spect* on Nov. 21, 1857, as "This day." It was issued in 2 vols. by Thomas Constable & Co., Edinburgh; etc., 1857, 17.5 cm., at 12/0, with many omissions, listed in the *Ath* on Oct. 24, translated by L. C. C. (Lucy C. Cummings). It was given a short review in *Notes & Queries* on Nov. 7. It was also issued by James Blackwood, London, as *Debtor and Creditor*, in 1857, Fcp 8vo, 2/0 boards, 3/6 cloth, listed in the *Ath* on Oct. 31. The first American edition was issued by Harper & Bros., New York, 1858, 19 cm., 564 pp., $1.00 muslin, as *Debit and Credit*, translated by L. C. C. It was listed in *APC&LG* (weekly) on Jan. 23, 1858, and in the *Ind* on Jan. 28. It was advertised in the *New-York Times* on Feb. 12 as "Just ready."

1109 JOHN FOSTER *Decision of Character and Other Essays.* Cr 8vo. 1/o sewed, 1/6, 2/o cloth   July 1 (*Spect*)

Friendly Counsel Series No. 8. This has no date and 270 pp., edited by J. M., with a life of Foster. The first edition was *Essays in a Series of Letters to a Friend*, issued by Longmans, London, 2 vols., 1805. They issued the third edition, 2 vols., 1806. The first American edition was issued by Lincoln & Gleason, Hartford, 2-vols.-in-1, 1807, 18 cm., from the third London edition.

1110 JULES VERNE *The Adventures of Captain Hatteras.* Colored illustrations. 2/o boards, 2/6   July 9 (*Spect*)

This has no date and three colored illustrations. It contains *The English at the North Pole* and *The Ice Desert*. The *BM* gives another copy without the illustrations, and I suspect it is the 2/o boards edition of the present title.
Also 1875. See 1886

1111 VICTOR HUGO *Les Misérables (Jean Valjean).* 2/o boards   July 15 (*Spect*)

Library of Favourite Authors No. 26. The first edition was in Paris, 10 vols., 1862, the complete work, and it was also issued in Bruxelles and in Leipzig in 10 vols., in 1862. Part 1 of the Bruxelles edition was reviewed in the *Ath* on Apr. 5, 1862; parts 2 and 3, 4 vols., were reviewed May 24; parts 4 and 5, 4 vols., were reviewed on July 5. An authorized English edition was issued by Hurst & Blackett, London, 3 vols., 1862, 20 cm., 31/6, listed in the *Ath* on Oct. 18. It was translated by Lascelles Wraxall. They issued a second edition in 3 vols., advertised in the *Spect* on Nov. 1, 1862; and issued a third edition in 3 vols. at 31/6, advertised on Jan. 24, 1863, as "On Jan. 29"; and they issued a cheap edition at 5/o, illustrated by Millais, advertised on Apr. 23, 1864.

In the United States it was issued by W. I. Pooley, New York; Hurst & Blackett, London, in 1 vol., advertised in the *New-York Times* on Nov. 14, 1862, as complete, large 8vo, $1.00 paper, $1.50 cloth, "On Nov. 15." They claimed it was translated at Hugo's request by Wraxall and M. Esquiros, and was the only translation legally published in Great Britain, France, Italy, and Germany, and the only one rightfully published in the United States. G. W. Carleton, New York, advertised in the *New-York Times* on Nov. 20, 1862, that the Pooley edition was abridged with over 100 pp. omitted and that it was a wretched translation!

It was also issued by G. W. Carleton & Co., New York, in 5 vols., 8vo, $.50 paper, $1.00 cloth each, translated by E. Wilbour, 1862. The 5 parts were advertised in the *New-York Times* as follows: part 1 on May 28, 1862, as "This morning"; a new edition of part 1 on June 14, as "This morning"; part 2 on July 2 as "On July 5"; part 3 on Aug. 9 as "This morning"; part 4 on Sept. 12 as "This morning"; part 5 on Oct. 11 as "Today." The paper issues were in printed blue wrappers. Part 1 had 171 pp.; part 2, 164 pp.; part 4, 184 pp.; part 5, 165 pp. Parts 1 and 2 were listed in *APC&LG* (monthly) on June 1, 1862; part 3 on Sept. 1; part 4 advertised in the *Ind* on Sept. 11 as "Just ready"; part 5 advertised there on Oct. 9 as "Just published." Carleton issued a new library edition in 5 vols., 12mo, at $1.00 per vol., part 1 advertised in the *New-York Times* on Jan. 8, 1863, as "This day." He advertised a cheap edition in 1 vol. at $1.00 paper, $1.50 cloth, on Nov. 29, 1862.

Fantine was issued by F. W. Christern, New York, reviewed in the *Atlantic Monthly* for July 1862. Two vols., by Christern, were listed in Aug. 1862, 8vo, 355 pp., 376 pp., at $3.00. I don't know just what these 2 vols. contained.

Chatto & Windus, London, issued *Saint Denis and Jean Valjean* as a 2/6 yellowback, listed in the *Ath* on Aug. 22, 1874.

1112 EDWARD P. ROE *What Can She Do?*
2/0 boards, 2/6 cloth   Aug. 12 (*Spect*)

The *Eng Cat* gives this as I've given it, but the *Spect* and the *Acad* list it at 1/0. Ward & Lock issued it at 3/6 cloth, listed in the *Spect* on July 13, 1878. The first edition was issued by Dodd & Mead, New York (1873), 19 cm., 509 pp., $1.75, in green, brown, or terra-cotta cloth with yellow endpapers. It was advertised in the *Ind* on Oct. 23 as "About Oct. 20," and listed in *PW* on Oct. 25. Five thousand copies were issued. The first British edition was Edmonston & Douglas, Edinburgh; etc., 1874, Cr 8vo, 10/6, listed in the *Ath* on Apr. 11 and in *PC* on May 16. George Routledge, London, issued it also in 1874, at 3/6, listed in the *Spect* on Nov. 28.
Also 1886

1113 MARY M. SHERWOOD *The Nun.*
Fcp 8vo. 1/0 sewed, 1/6, 2/0 cloth
Aug. 19 (*Spect*)

Rose Library No. 14. This has no date and 278 pp.
Also 1864, 69, 85

1114 MATTHEW WEBB *The Art of Swimming.* 1/0   Aug. 19 (*Spect*)

The first edition was issued by Ward, Lock & Tyler (1875), 18.5 cm., 111 pp., with a colored frontispiece, and edited by A. G. Payne, at 2/6 in gold-stamped cloth. It was listed in the *Spect* on Nov. 6, 1875.

1115 (MARY E. BRADDON) *Dead Men's Shoes.* Small format. 2/0 boards, 2/6 cloth
Aug. 26 (*Ath*)

This is 1876, 384 pp., the first yellowback edition, with the list of Braddon yellowbacks on the back of the boards issue ending with this title. The first edition was issued by John Maxwell & Co., London, 3 vols., 1876, anonymous, 31/6, listed in the *Ath* on Feb. 26. Tillotson paid £450 for the serial rights for his papers. This title is not to be confused with the Lippincott issue of

1872 by Jeannette Walworth. The first American edition was issued by Harper & Bros., New York, 1876, 8vo, $.75 paper, as *Library of Select Novels* No. 461. It was listed in *PW* on Apr. 8 and in the *Ind* on Apr. 13.

1116 RICHARD H. DANA, JR. *Two Years Before the Mast.* 12mo. 1/0 sewed, 1/6, 2/0 cloth   Aug. 26 (*Spect*)

Youth's Library of Wonders and Adventures No. 10. This has no date and 284 pp. The first edition was issued by Harper & Bros., New York, 1840, 16 cm., anonymous, 483 pp., the first chapter signed R. H. D. Jr. It was *Harper's Family Library* No. 106, reviewed in the *Knickerbocker* for Oct. and noticed in *Dial* (quarterly) for Oct. The first English edition was issued by Edward Moxon, London, 1841, 24 cm., anonymous, 124 pp., 3/6 cloth, advertised in the *Ath* on Feb. 6 and reviewed on Feb. 13. There is also a known copy in wrappers (pictorial yellow), large 8vo, with 124 pp., double columns. There is another known copy of the wrappers issue, 1841, denoted as the second English edition. It was issued by George Routledge, London, 1853, at 1/0 boards, 1/6 cloth, listed in the *Ath* on Dec. 4, 1852, and by *PC* as published Dec. 15–30.

1117 ANONYMOUS *Impudent Imposters and Celebrated Claimants.* 12mo. 2/0 boards   Aug. 26 (*Spect*)

Household and Railway Books No. 31. This is my copy, no date, 17.7 cm., 311 pp., in yellow pictorial boards with the series title on the spine. There is a commercial ad on the back cover, publisher's ads on the endpapers and on the verso of the title page, and a catalog paged 1–8 at the back. "Imposters" is spelled as given on the title page but "Impostors" on the front cover. The claimant, Arthur Orton, is dealt with on pp. 255–311. The first edition was issued by Chatto & Windus, London (1873), *Celebrated Claimants, Ancient and Modern,* 2/0 boards, listed in the *Spect* on

Dec. 13, 1873. Both the *U Cat* and the *BM* give it as having 255 pp., but it was advertised in the *Ath* from Nov. 1, 1873, to Feb. 7, 1874, as having 330 pp. The catalog of the publisher for Sept. 1874 gives 350 pp.! Chatto & Windus issued a second edition, 1874, 15.5 cm., 311 pp., at 2/o boards, advertised in the *Ath* on June 27 and listed by the *Bks* as published in Aug.

1118 JOSIAH G. HOLLAND *Miss Gilbert's Career.* 12mo. 1/o sewed, 1/6, 2/o cloth
Sept. 2 (*Spect*)
Lily Series No. 57. The first edition was issued by Charles Scribner, New York; Sampson Low, London, 1860, 18.5 cm., 476 pp., $1.25, the Scribner listed in *APC&LG* (weekly) on Oct. 13, and it was reviewed in the *Ind* on Oct. 18. The ninth thousand was advertised in the *New-York Times* on Oct. 25, 1860, as "This day," and the 15th edition was advertised there on Feb. 5, 1862, $1.25, as "Now ready." The Low edition was listed in *PC* on Dec. 15, 1860.

1119 MARY SABILLA NOVELLO
Bluebeard's Widow and Her Sister Anne.
Illustrated. 2/6 sewed   Sept. 2 (*Ath*)
This is the first edition, no date, and 53 pp.
See 1878

1120 JULES VERNE *From the Earth to the Moon.* 12mo. 1/o sewed, 1/6, 2/o cloth
Sept. 9 (*Ath* ad)
Youth's Library of Wonders and Adventures No. 11. This has no date. One of the cloth editions was in purple cloth decorated in black, and I think both the cloth issues were illustrated, and in fact the *BM* gives it as a new edition with colored pictures. The first edition was issued by Hetzel, Paris (1865), 18 cm., 302 pp. It had appeared, *De la Terra a la Lune, Trajet Direct en 97 Heures,* in the *Journal des Debats Politiques et Litteraires* from Sept. 14 to Oct. 14,

1865. The first edition in English was *From the Earth to the Moon,* issued by the Newark Printing & Publishing Co., Newark, 1869, 8vo, 84 pp., with a frontispiece. The first English edition was issued by Sampson Low, London, 1873, as *From the Earth to the Moon . . . ; and a Trip Round It,* Cr 8vo, 10/6, translated by Louis Mercier and Eleanor King. It was listed in the *Ath* on Oct. 11. Low issued the third edition, 1874, Cr 8vo, 10/6, listed in the *Ath* on May 9, and in the *Spect* on May 2. The same was issued by Scribner, Armstrong & Co., New York, 1873, 12mo, 8 illustrations, $3.00, advertised in the *New-York Times* on Nov. 29, 1873, as "Next week," and as "This day" on Dec. 4. They issued a new edition, the same, reduced from $3.00 to $1.50, advertised in the *New-York Times* on Oct. 13, 1877, as "Now ready." The first Scribner issue was listed in *PW* on Nov. 22 and in the *Nation* on Jan. 8, 1874. Low issued the present title, 1876, author's illustrated edition, my copy, 12mo, at 1/o in stiff wrappers, about Jan. 29, 1876; and issued it at 2/o cloth, illustrated, by July 1, 1876. *The American Gun Club* was issued by Scribner, listed in *PW* on June 13, 1874; and *The Baltimore Gun Club* was issued by King & Baird, Philadelphia, listed in *PW* on June 13, 1874.
Also 1877

1121 GUSTAVE AIMARD (OLIVER GLOUX)
The Trappers of Arkansas. 12mo. 1/o sewed   Sept. 16 (*Spect*)
This is 17.8 cm. in pale pink pictorial wrappers, cut flush.
Also 1864, 80

1122 EDMUND YATES, ed. *For Better, for Worse.* 2/o boards   Sept. 16 (*Ath*)
This has no date and 360 pp. The first edition was issued by John Maxwell & Co., London, 2 vols., 1864, p 8vo, 21/o, advertised in the *Ath* on Dec. 5, 1863, as "Now ready," and listed on Dec. 12.

1123 GUSTAVE AIMARD (OLIVER GLOUX)
The Indian Chief. 12mo. 1/0 sewed
Sept. 23 (*Spect*)
This is in pale pink pictorial wrappers, cut
flush, 17.8 cm.
Also 1861, 80

1124 CHARLES W. ALCOCK, ed.
The Foothill Annual. 1/0   Sept. 23 (*Spect*)

1125 VICTOR HUGO **Cosette and Marius.**
2/0 boards   Sept.?
Library of Favourite Authors No. 27. This is
part of *Les Misérables* (see *Jean Valjean*
above). The Carleton issue of *Cosette* was
listed in the *Knickerbocker* for Sept. 1862,
and their issue of *Marius* was noticed there
in Nov. 1862. The first title was listed in
APC&LG (monthly) on June 1, 1862, and
the second title on Sept. 1. Chatto & Windus, London, issued the present title,
1874, my copy, 12mo, 2/0 boards, about
May 16. It has a 40-page catalog at the
back (Sept. 1874).
Also 1882. See 1887

1126 VICTOR HUGO **Fantine.** 2/0 boards
Sept.?
Library of Favourite Authors No. 28. This is
part of *Les Misérables* (see *Jean Valjean*
above). It formed vol. 1 of the Carleton issue, advertised in the *Ind* on June 5, 1862,
as "This day." It was also vol. 1 of a new library edition issued by Carleton in 5 vols.,
12mo, $1.00 muslin each, published Jan.
1–Feb. 10, 1863. The present title was issued by Chatto & Windus, London, no
date, my copy, 12mo, 2/0 boards, about
Mar. 14, 1874, with an inscribed date
(May 1, 1874). It has a 48-page catalog at
the back (Apr. 1874). Chatto & Windus
listed it in their catalogs as now published
in an English translation, complete and
unabridged with the exception of a few
advisable omissions!

1127 VICTOR HUGO **By the King's
Command.** 2/0 boards   Sept.?
Library of Favourite Authors No. 29. The
first edition was issued in Paris, 4 vols.,
1869, *L'Homme qui Rit*, 22 cm. It ran in *Appleton's Journal* beginning with the first is-
sue on Mar. 27, 1869; and the first edition
in English was issued by D. Appleton &
Co., New York, 23 cm., in 2 parts, in both
French and English, and in 1 vol. in both.
Part 1, *La Mer et la Nuit* (*The Sea and the
Night*) had 95 pp., with a portrait, at $.50
paper, advertised in the *New-York Times* on
Apr. 27, 1869, and listed in *ALG&PC*
(fortnightly) on May 15. Part 2, *Par Ordre
du Roi* (*By Order of the King*), was issued in
English at $.75 paper, advertised in the
New-York Times on Aug. 21, 1869, as "This
day," and listed in *ALG&PC* (fortnightly)
on Sept. 1. Part 2 in French at $1.00 was
advertised in the *New-York Times* on May
14, 1869, as "This day." The 1-vol. issue
had 352 pp., sold at $1.25 paper and
$1.75 cloth, with a portrait, advertised in
the *New-York Times* on Aug. 21, 1869, as
"This day." It had the title, *The Man Who
Laughs* and was translated by William
Young.
    It was advertised in the *Ath* on Apr. 17,
1869, by David Nutt, London, 4 vols., in
French, 8vo, 30/0, as "This day"; and by
Hachette & Co., London, 4 vols., 30 Fr, as
"Just out." *By Order of the King* ran in the
Gentleman's Magazine (Chatto & Windus)
during 1869–70, beginning in May 1869,
illustrated. The first English edition was
By Order of the King, issued by Bradbury &
Evans, London, 3 vols., 1870, 20.5 cm., illustrated, 31/6, an authorized English
translation by (Mrs. A. C. Steele), the illus-
trator being S. L. Fildes. It was listed in the
Ath on June 25. They issued it at 5/0, Cr
8vo, listed in the *Spect* on July 15, 1871. It
was issued by Chatto & Windus, London,
as *By the King's Command*, 1875, 528 pp.,
2/6 boards, listed in the *Spect* on Apr. 10.

The present edition is a reissue of the Chatto & Windus, no date, 528 pp.

1128 SYLVIA *How to Dress Well on a Shilling a Day.* 1/o sewed   Oct. 7 (*Acad*)
Sylvia's Home Help Series No. 1. This is the first edition, no date, with diagrams.
Also 1877

1129 C. M. CORNWALL (MARY A. ROE) *Forging Their Own Chains.* 1/o sewed, 1/6, 2/o   Oct. 14 (*Acad*)
Lily Series No. 59. This is the first English edition, no date, and 378 pp. The first American edition was issued by Dodd, Mead & Co., New York (copyright 1876), 19.5 cm., 378 pp., with the title, *Free, Yet Forging Their Own Chains.*

1130 ÉMILE ERCKMANN & PIERRE CHATRIAN *The Man-Wolf and Other Tales.* 1/o sewed, 1/6, 2/o   Oct. 14 (*Acad*)
This has no date and 252 pp., translated by F. A. M. (F. A. Malleson). The cloth issues were illustrated. It contained seven stories, three of which are from *Contes de la Montagne* and two of which are from *Contes des Bords de Rhin.*

1131 MARY C. HAY *The Squire's Legacy.* 2/o boards, 2/6 cloth   Oct.?
This is 1876. The first edition was issued by Hurst & Blackett, London, 3 vols., 1875, Cr 8vo, 31/6, listed in the *Ath* on Oct. 16. The first American edition was issued by Harper & Bros., New York, 1876, as *Library of Select Novels* No. 455, listed in the *Ind* on Mar. 9 and in *PW* on Mar. 11.

1132 ANONYMOUS *The Mystery.* 8vo. Illustrated. 1/o sewed   Nov. 25 (*Ath* ad)
This is Beeton's Christmas Annual, 17th season, my copy. It has no date, 24.5 cm., in white wrappers decorated on the front in red, blue, and black, with commercial ads on the back and inside covers. It is in double columns with many textual illustrations and proceeds as follows: Beeton's Christmas Annual Advertiser, pp. i–viii, frontispiece, a 4-page insert for Pear's soap, a 4-page insert for the Cassell Publishing Co., a 4-page pale pink publisher's insert, a slip advertising wines, 32 pp. of text, an 8-page publisher's insert, text on pp. 33–80, ads on pp. 81–84, and finally Beeton's Christmas Annual Advertiser on pp. 85–96.

1133 HENRY VIZETELLY *Facts About Sherry.* Illustrated. 1/o sewed, 1/6 cloth   Dec. 9 (*Ath*)
This is the first edition, 19 cm., 108 pp., which the *U Cat* gives as (1876), and which the *BM* gives as 1876, and which the *Eng Cat* gives as published in 1877!

1134 MAX ADELER (CHARLES H. CLARK) *Elbow-Room.* Illustrated. 2/o boards, 2/6 cloth   Dec. 9 (*Ath*)   *See color photo section*
Household and Railway Books No. 32. This is the first English edition, 1876, with 384 pp. George Routledge, London, issued it (1877), with 320 pp., at 1/o boards, advertised on Feb. 3, 1877. The first American edition was issued by J. M. Stoddart, Philadelphia (copyright 1876), 19 cm., 284 pp., illustrated, listed in the *Ind* on Nov. 30, 1876.
Also 1882, 83, 1902

1135 ANONYMOUS *The Englishwoman's Annual and Illustrated Almanack for 1877.* 2/o   Dec. (*Ath*)
See 1870

1136 ANONYMOUS *Beeton's Bible Dictionary.* 1/o cloth   1876 (*Eng Cat*)
Also 1870

1137 ANONYMOUS *Beeton's British Biography.* 1/o cloth   1876 (*Eng Cat*)
Also 1870

1138 ANONYMOUS *Beeton's British Gazetteer.* 1/o cloth   1876 (*Eng Cat*)
Also 1869

1139 ANONYMOUS *Beeton's Medical Dictionary.* 1/o cloth   1876 (*Eng Cat*)
Also 1871

1140 ANONYMOUS *Beeton's Modern European Celebrities.* 1/o cloth   1876 (*Eng Cat*)
Also 1874

1141 WILLIAM A. CLOUSTON, ed. *Wine and Walnuts.* 2/o boards   1876 (*Eng Cat*)
Household and Railway Books No. 33. This has no date with 296 pp. It is a reprint with a new title page of the first edition, which was *Literary Curiosities and Eccentricities,* issued by Ward, Lock & Tyler (1875), 19 cm., 296 pp., at 3/6 cloth.

1142 RAWDON CRAWLEY (GEORGE F. PARDON) *Chess. Its Theory and Practice. To Which Is Added a Chapter on Draughts.* Illustrated. 1/o sewed, 2/o cloth   1876 (*Eng Cat*)
Captain Crawley's Shilling Handbooks No. 3. This is the 10th edition, revised, no date, with 188 pp. It has a preface (1876) and a cover title, *Chess and Draughts.* Ward, Lock issued the 13th edition, revised, about 1880, with 188 pp. The first edition was issued by C. H. Clarke, London (1858), 24mo, 180 pp., illustrated; and they issued the third edition, no date, 24mo, 180 pp., illustrated, at 2/6, in Mar. 1859. S. O. Beeton, London, issued it as the eighth edition (1863), 191 pp.

1143 MARK TWAIN (SAMUEL L. CLEMENS) *The Jumping Frog and Other Humorous Sketches.* From the Original Edition. Small format. 1/o sewed   1876 (*Eng Cat*)
This is my copy, no date, 16.2 cm., 135 pp., in white wrappers cut flush, with a pictorial front cover in red, green, and black. There are ads on the back cover, on the endpapers, and on the versos of the title page and dedication page, and there is a catalog paged (1)–32 at the back and a 4-page insert at the front for *Chapman & Hall's Select Library of Fiction.*
Also 1874, 84. See *American Drolleries,* 1875

1144 (SUSAN WARNER) *The Old Helmet.* 12mo. 1/o sewed, 1/6, 2/o cloth   1876 (*Eng Cat*)
Lily Series No. 58. This has no date and 434 pp. The first American edition was issued by Robert Carter & Bros., New York, 2 vols., 1864, 18 cm., anonymous, listed in the *Ind* on Dec. 24, 1863, and listed in *APC&LG* (fortnightly) on Dec. 15. It had a long scathing review in the *Knickerbocker* for Mar. 1864. The first English edition was issued by James Nisbet, London, 2 vols., 1864 (1863), p 8vo, anonymous, at 12/o, listed in the *Ath* on Dec. 12, 1863. Routledge, Warne & Routledge, London, issued it in their *Railway Library,* 1864, anonymous, 437 pp., at 2/o boards, listed in the *Ath* on Jan. 30, 1864.

1145 SARAH TRIMMER *The History of the Robins.* 18mo. o/9 sewed, 1/o, 1/6 cloth 1876 (*Eng Cat*)
Beeton's Good-Aim Series No. 20. This has no date and has some account of the author by J. M. The first edition was *Fabulous Histories. Designed for the Instruction of Children, etc.,* issued by Longmans, 1786, 17.5 cm., 203 pp., with a dedication (Nov. 3, 1785). Mrs. Trimmer had 12 children and so was probably highly motivated to write children's books. The first American edition was probably issued by William Gibbons, Philadelphia, 1794, 214 pp., *Fabulous Histories, Designed for the Amusement and Instruction of Young Persons.* Frederick Warne, London; Scribner, Welford, New York, issued *The Story of the Robins* in 1870, 160 pp., with colored illustrations, at 3/6 cloth; and Warne issued it with the colored illus-

trations at 2/o cloth, listed in the *Ath* on Oct. 23, 1875. George Routledge, London, issued it in 1867, 18mo, at 1/6, listed in the *Spect* on Oct. 26.

1146 RICHARD WHITEING *Mr. Sprouts, His Opinions.* Fcp 8vo. 1/o sewed   1876 (*Eng Cat*)

Beeton's Humorous Books No. 46. The first edition was issued by John C. Hotten, London, 1867, 19 cm., 200 pp., at 3/6 cloth, listed in the *Spect* on Nov. 23. It first appeared in the *Evening Star*. He issued the second edition, 1868, Cr 8vo, 200 pp., at 3/6, in blue cloth, with 16 pp. of ads, listed in the *Spect* on Feb. 8. He reissued it at 1/o sewed, listed in the *Ath* on May 30, 1868.

1147 (SUSAN WARNER) *Daisy.* 12mo. 1/o sewed, 1/6, 2/o cloth   Late 1876 or early 1877

Lily Series No. 60. This has no date and 284 pp. The first American edition was issued by J. B. Lippincott & Co., Philadelphia, 1868, 18 cm., anonymous, 435 pp., with 8 pp. of ads, bound in slate-purple, purple, or blue cloth with yellow endpapers. It was deposited in June 3 and noticed in the *Ind* on June 18, and in *ALG&PC* (fortnightly) on June 15, and advertised in the *Nation* on June 11, $2.00 cloth, as "Just published." The first English edition was issued by James Nisbet, London, 1868, anonymous, 344 pp., in the *Golden Ladder Series*, listed in the *Ath* on June 6, in *PC* on June 15, and deposited at the *BM* on July 2.

1148 GUSTAVE AIMARD (OLIVER GLOUX) *The Adventurers.* 12mo. 1/o sewed 1876?

This is in pale pink wrappers cut flush, with a pictorial cover.
Also 1863, 80

1149 CAPTAIN RAWDON CRAWLEY (G. F. PARDON) *Billiards with a Chapter on Bagatelle.* Fcp 8vo. 1/o sewed, 2/o cloth   1876?

Captain Crawley's Shilling Handbooks. This and the following three titles were advertised in *The Mystery* of Nov. 1876 (see above). *The Handy Book of Games for Gentlemen* is given by the *BM* as Bickers, London (1860), 563 pp., containing articles on billiards, backgammon, chess, and whist. The *U Cat* gives it as issued by C. H. Clarke, London (1859), 4 parts in 1 vol,. illustrated; and also gives it as issued by Ward, Lock & Tyler (1876), 640 pp. This book is by Crawley. The present edition had a preface (1876) and is the 11th edition, thoroughly revised, 154 pp. The *BM* gives also the 10th edition, thoroughly revised (1876). It was issued at 2/6, Cr 8vo, listed in the *Spect* on July 8, 1871. C. H. Clarke, London, issued the third edition, with diagrams, at 2/6, in the late 1850s; and George Routledge, London, issued *A Handbook of Billiards*, by G. F. Pardon, 1862, 14 cm., 96 pp., illustrated, at 0/6 boards, in Mar.

1150 CAPTAIN RAWDON CRAWLEY *Whist . . . with Chapters on Loo and Cribbage.* Fcp 8vo. 1/o sewed, 2/o cloth   1876?

Captain Crawley's Shilling Handbooks. This is (1876), the 10th edition, revised. See the preceding title. *Whist* was issued by Bell & Wood, London, 1843, 17 cm., anonymous, 99 pp., illustrated; and reissued by David Bogue, London, 1844, a new edition, anonymous, 99 pp., illustrated. C. H. Clarke, London, issued the third edition, by Crawley (1859), 15 cm., 170 pp., with chapters on loo and cribbage. Routledge, Warne & Routledge, London, issued *A Handbook of Whist*, by Pardon, 1861, 13 cm., 94 pp.; and reissued it, 1863 and 1865. It was advertised in the *Ath* on Jan. 5, 1861, at 0/6 boards.

1151 CAPTAIN RAWDON CRAWLEY
**Backgammon. To Which Is Added a
Chapter on Solitaire.** Fcp 8vo. 1/o sewed,
2/o cloth   1876?

Captain Crawley's Shilling Handbooks. This is
(1876), the 10th edition, illustrated (see
Billiards above). *Backgammon* was issued by
David Bogue, London, 1844, 17 cm.,
anonymous, 79 pp., illustrated; and was
issued by C. H. Clarke, London, with a
preface (1860), 15 cm., 111 pp., by Crawley, illustrated, 2/6. *A Handbook of Draughts*
with a Chapter on Backgammon was issued by
Routledge, Warne & Routledge, London,
1862, 24mo, by Pardon, 95 pp., illustrated, at 0/6 boards, in Apr.

1152 CAPTAIN RAWDON CRAWLEY
Bezique, Euchre, Ecarté, etc. Fcp 8vo.
1/o sewed, 2/o cloth   1876?

Captain Crawley's Shilling Handbooks. This is
(1876).
See the title on billiards above

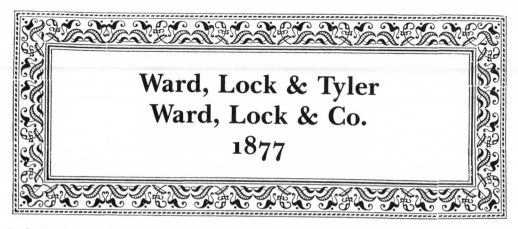

Ward, Lock & Tyler
Ward, Lock & Co.
1877

In the Bookseller *for Sept. 4, 1877, and in* Publisher's Circular *for Sept. 1, 1877, it was stated that the company had removed to the Dorset Buildings, Salisbury Square and Dorset Street. The style of the company was changed to Ward, Lock & Co. at the same time. An ad in the* Ath *of Aug. 25 had the imprint of Ward, Lock & Tyler, and an ad on Sept. 8 had Ward, Lock & Co.*

1153 (JOHN HABBERTON) *Helen's Babies.*
1/o sewed   Jan. 6 (*Ath* ad)

The *Ath* ad said "Just ready." This was later, circa 1881, put in the publisher's *Popular Sixpenny Books* as No. 51. The first edition was issued by A. K. Loring, Boston (1876), 17.5 cm., anonymous, 206 pp., $.50, listed in both the *Ind* and the *Nation* on July 27, *Tales of the Day.* At least 12 houses in England issued it in 1876 or 1877. Sampson Low, London, issued it at 1/o sewed, 2/6 cloth, as *Rose Library* No. 30, 16mo, advertised in the *Ath* on Dec. 9, 1876, as "Now ready." He claimed that it was the only English edition with the sanction of the author and in which he participated financially. It was also issued by William Mullan & Son, London, 1877, anonymous, in pink cloth, listed in the *British Quarterly Review* for Apr. 1877. It was also issued by Frederick Warne & Co., London, 2/o boards, listed in the *Ath* on Dec. 30, 1876; and by George Routledge, London, 1/o boards, 160 pp., my copy, advertised in the *Ath* on Feb. 3, 1877.
Also 1897. See below

1154   E. MASE (ELIZA M. A. SAVAGE) *Art-Needlework.* 4to. Illustrated. 1/o sewed
Jan. 6 (*Ath* ad)

Sylvia's Home Help Series No. 2. This is the first edition, no date, 28.5 cm., 78 pp.,

probably issued at the end of 1876. It was later issued with colored designs, with 104 pp., probably in the early 1880s. It was issued in the United States by S. M. Tilton & Co., Boston, 1879, 21.5 cm., 67 pp., illustrated, reprinted with corrections from the English edition.

1155 JAMES MASON, ed. *The Year Book of Facts in Science and the Arts. For 1876.*
2/6 boards, 3/6 cloth   Jan. 20 (*Spect*)
See 1875 for publishing details

1156 RICHARD COBBOLD *The History of Margaret Catchpole.* 2/o boards, 2/6 cloth
Jan. 20?

This is a reissue in *Favourite Authors*, advertised on Jan. 20. The 2/6 edition may have been illustrated, as the *BM* gives (1878), 380 pp., illustrated. My copy is a reissue of (1879), 17.2 cm., 378 pp., plus a supplement No. 2 of 2 pp., a reissue of *Favourite Authors* with the series title on the spine. It is in pictorial yellow boards, with ads on the endpapers, back cover, and verso of the title page. There is a 16-page catalog at the back.
Also 1864, 67, 73, 87

1157 (JOHN HABBERTON) **The Barton Experiment.** Fcp 8vo. 1/0 sewed   Feb. 3 (*Ath* ad)

Ward & Lock's Humorous Books. This has no date and 162 pp. The first edition was issued by G. P. Putnam's Sons, New York, 1877, 18 cm., anonymous, 202 pp., $.50 paper, $1.00 cloth, listed in *PW* on Dec. 2, 1876, in the *Ind* on Dec. 14, and in the *Nation* on Jan. 4, 1877. It was advertised in the *New-York Times* on Dec. 8 as "This day," and the 20th thousand was advertised on Dec. 20 as "Ready today"; the 30th thousand was advertised on June 9, 1877, all the same as the first edition. At least four English houses issued it in 1877. Sampson Low, London, issued it, 1877, 18mo, anonymous, 126 pp., at 1/0 sewed, 2/6 cloth, listed in the *Spect* on Feb. 3, 1877, by arrangement with the author. It was issued by George Routledge, London (1877), 12mo, anonymous, 157 pp., at 1/0 boards, advertised on Feb. 3, 1877, in the *Ath*. It was also issued by William Mullan, London, 1877.

1158 JULES VERNE **The Wonderful Travellers.** 2/0 boards, 2/6, 3/6 cloth Feb. 3 (*Ath* ad)

This is a double vol. containing *A Journey into the Interior of the Earth* and *Five Weeks in a Balloon*. It has no date, and the cloth copies at least had colored illustrations. Also 1875, 87

1159 JULES VERNE **Round the Moon.** 1/0 sewed, 1/6, 2/0 cloth   1877 (*Eng Cat*)

Youth's Library of Wonders and Adventures No. 12. This has no date. The first edition was *Autour de la Lune*, Paris (1870), 27.5 cm., 180 pp., illustrated. Sampson Low, London, issued *Round the Moon*, 1876, 12mo, 192 pp., illustrated, in stiff wrappers at 1/0. This is my copy, with a 16-page catalog (Jan. 1876) at the back. It is illustrated by Louis Mercier and Eleanor King, and was listed in the *Acad* on Feb. 5.

By July 1 Low had issued it at 2/0 cloth, illustrated. It was issued in the United States by the Catholic Publication Society, New York, 1876, *All Around the Moon*, listed in *PW* on June 3 and in the *Nation* on June 15. See *From the Earth to the Moon*, 1876, for other details and see also the next item.
Also 1887

1160 JULES VERNE **The Moon Voyage.** Illustrated. 2/0 boards, 2/6, 3/6 cloth Feb. 3 (*Ath* ad)

This has no date and contains *From the Earth to the Moon* and the preceding title, with separate pagination, with the cloth copies in dark blue cloth, and they at least have colored illustrations.
See the preceding item and 1876

1161 SIR WILLIAM MATHEWS **Getting on in the World.** Second series. Cr 8vo. 1/0 sewed, 1/6, 2/0 cloth   1877 (*Eng Cat*)

Friendly Counsel Series No. 9. This has no date. The first edition was probably issued by Sampson Low, London, 1876, Cr 8vo, 2/6 cloth, listed in the *Spect* on Mar. 25, 1876.
For the first series see 1875

1162 JAMES MASON **How to Excel in Business.** Cr 8vo. 1/0 sewed, 1/6, 2/0 cloth Feb. 3 (*Ath* ad)

Friendly Counsel Series No. 10. This is the first edition.

1163 WILLIAM G. WILLS **The Wife's Evidence.** 2/0 boards, 2/6 cloth   Feb. 24 (*Spect*)

The first edition was issued by Hurst & Blackett, London, 3 vols., 1864, p 8vo, 31/6, advertised in the *Ath* on Nov. 14, 1863, as "Ready," and listed on Nov. 21. The first American edition was issued by Harper & Bros., New York, 1864, 22 cm., 155 pp., at $.50 paper, as *Library of Select Novels* No. 240, listed in *APC&LG* (fortnightly) on Mar. 15, and advertised in the *New-York Times* on Mar. 4 as "This day."

1164 (MARY E. BRADDON)
Joshua Haggard. Small format.
2/o boards, 2/6 cloth   Mar. 10 (*Ath*)
This is 1877, with 353 pp., and with 4 pp. of *Select Library of Fiction* ads (Chapman & Hall) inserted. The list of Braddon yellowbacks on the back cover ends with this title. It ran in *Belgravia* during 1876, concluding in Dec. The first edition was *Joshua Haggard's Daughter*, issued by John Maxwell & Co., London, 3 vols., 1876, Cr 8vo, anonymous, at 31/6, listed in the *Ath* on Oct. 21. The first American edition was issued by Harper & Bros., New York, 1877, as *Library of Select Novels* No. 477, 8vo, illustrated, $.75 paper, listed in *PW* on Dec. 23, 1876, in the *Ind* on Dec. 28, and advertised in the *New-York Times* on Dec. 22 as "This day."

1165 MARK TWAIN (SAMUEL L. CLEMENS)
The Mississippi Pilot. Fcp 8vo. 1/o sewed Mar. 16 (*PC*)
Ward & Lock's Humorous Books. This has no date, in pictorial wrappers. It is a reprint of *Old Times on the Mississippi*, issued by Belford Bros., Toronto, 1876, a pirated edition in wrappers and cloth. It ran with the Belford title in the *Atlantic Monthly* from Jan. to July 1875. *The Mississippi Pilot* by Twain and *Two Men from Sandy Bar* by Harte was issued in 1 vol. by G. Cozens & Co., London, with no date (after 1877), small 8vo, with 142 pp., 162 pp., in blue gray cloth, pirated. The first authorized edition was *Life on the Mississippi*, issued by Chatto & Windus, London, 1883, at 7/6, about May 12. In the United States it was issued by James R. Osgood & Co., Boston, 1883, deposited May 17, and listed in *PW* on July 7, and in the *Nation* on July 5.
Also 1886

1166 ANONYMOUS *The Lover's Poetic Companion and Valentine Writer*.
Illustrated. 2/o boards   Mar.?
Household and Railway Books No. 34.
See 1875

1167 ANONYMOUS *The Lover's Birthday Book and Valentine Verses*. Illustrated.
2/o boards   Mar.?
Household and Railway Books No. 35.
See 1875

1168 RAWDON CRAWLEY (GEORGE F. PARDON) *The Card Players' Manual*.
2/o boards, 2/6 cloth   Apr. 14 (*Spect*)
Household and Railway Books No. 36. The Apr. 14 listing in the *Spect* was for a 2/o issue, and a 2/6 cloth issue was listed on Dec. 2, 1876. This latter was the first edition with a preface (1876), 18 cm., 242 pp.

1169 MARY C. HAY *The Arundel Motto*.
2/o boards, 2/6 cloth   June 23 (*Ath*)
This is the first English edition, 1877. The first edition was from Harper & Bros., New York, 1877, 23.5 cm., 167 pp., *Library of Select Novels* No. 472, listed in the *Ind* on Nov. 30, 1876, and in *PW* on Dec. 2.

1170 WILLIAM G. WILLS *David Chantrey*.
2/o boards, 2/6 cloth   June 23 (*Ath*)
This is the first yellowback edition, 1877. The first edition was issued by John Maxwell & Co., London, 3 vols., 1865, p. 8vo, at 31/6, listed in the *Ath* on Sept. 16.

1171 FRANCES H. BURNETT *That Lass o' Lowrie's*. 12mo. 1/o sewed, 1/6, 2/o cloth July 10?
Lily Series No. 62. This has no date, 18 cm., 181 pp. The first American edition was issued by Scribner, Armstrong & Co., New York, 1877, 12mo, with 4 illustrations, in red decorated cloth, $1.50, listed in *PW* on Apr. 7, in the *Nation* on Apr. 12, and advertised in the *New-York Times* on Apr. 7 as "This day." The third edition was ad-

vertised there on Apr. 14, the same, as "Just published," and it was advertised there on Aug. 2 at $.90 paper, "Now ready." It ran in *Scribner's Monthly* from Aug. 1876 to May 1877. The authoress, in a note in *Surly Tim, and Other Stories* (issued by Scribner, Armstrong & Co. in Oct. 1877), stated that that title and the present title were the only works with the author's name which were prepared and corrected for publication in book form under her supervision. The first English edition was issued by Frederick Warne, London (1877), Fcp 8vo, 207 pp., at 1/0 sewed, listed in *PC* on May 1 as published Apr. 15–30.

Also 1889

1172 ELIZABETH S. PHELPS
That Dreadful Boy Trotty. Fcp 8vo.
1/0 sewed   July 14 (*Spect*)

Ward & Lock's Humorous Books. This is a reissue of *Trotty's Book* and has no date and 123 pp.

Also 1883. See 1872

1173 (MARY E. BRADDON) *Weavers and Weft and Other Tales.* Stereotyped Edition. Small format. 2/0 boards, 2/6 cloth   Sept. 8 (*Ath*)

This is the first yellowback edition, 1877, 16.8 cm., 367 pp. The list of Braddon yellowbacks on the back cover ends with this title. This was the last Braddon novel issued by Ward, Lock & Co., although they continued to reissue previous titles. The first edition was issued by Harper & Bros., New York, 1877, 8vo, at $.25 paper, as *Library of Select Novels* No. 482, with the list of the series in an ad ending with No. 479. It was listed in the *Ind* on Feb. 15 and in *PW* on Feb. 17. The first English edition was issued by John Maxwell & Co., London, 3 vols., 1877, Cr 8vo, at 31/6, advertised by Ward, Lock & Tyler in the *Spect* on Mar. 3 and Mar. 17 as "Ready," but listed by Maxwell on Mar. 17. It was listed in the *Ath* on Mar. 10. This helps to confirm the impres-

sion that Ward, Lock controlled John Maxwell & Co. Tillotson paid £300 for the serial rights for his newspapers according to Wolff. The Harper title was *Weavers and Weft* and contained only this story.

1174 JOHN W. KIRTON, ed. *Standard Temperance Reciter.* 1/0 boards, 1/6 cloth Sept. 8 (*Ath* ad)

This is the first edition, no date.
See 1888

1175 CHARLES G. LELAND
Hans Breitmann's Barty and Other Ballads. Fcp 8vo. 1/0 sewed   Sept.

Ward & Lock's Humorous Books. This has no date and 160 pp. It contains, in addition to the title poem, *Hans Breitmann's Christmas* and *Hans Breitmann in Politics*. I have a copy, no date, but after 1882, in white pictorial boards, printed in red, blue, and black with the number 58 on the front (presumably the number in the series), 16.8 cm., 160 pp., at 1/0. It has commercial ads on the endpapers, back cover, and on the verso of the half-title. The Table of Contents is given for the first part only, but the pagination is continuous. The title poem was first issued by T. B. Peterson & Bros., Philadelphia (1868), 21.5 cm., anonymous, 32 pp., listed in *ALG&PC* (fortnightly) on July 15. It was imported by Trübner, London, and issued in Aug. 1868. Trübner issued the eighth edition, enlarged, 1869, 14 cm., 72 pp., probably containing all three titles, as such a 1-vol. edition was reviewed in the *British Quarterly Review* for July 1869. John C. Hotten, London, issued the title poem, 81 pp., at 0/6 sewed, in Mar. 1869. The first American edition of *Hans Breitmann in Politics* was issued by J. B. Lippincott, Philadelphia, 1869, 22.5 cm., 13 pp., with a frontispiece, listed in *ALG&PC* (fortnightly) on May 15. It was issued by Hotten, 1869, 16 cm., 54 pp., at 0/6 sewed, in Mar., containing only the first three sections, the other five being copyrighted by Trübner.

Trübner issued it as *Hans Breitmann as a Politician*, 1869, at 1/0 sewed, listed in the *Ath* on Mar. 27. Hotten issued a complete edition, 1869, with both the title poem and *Hans Breitmann in Politics*, 2 parts, 81 pp., 54 pp., at 1/0 sewed, 1/6 cloth, about Mar. 20. Trübner issued *Hans Breitmann's Christmas with Other Ballads*, 1869, at 1/0 sewed, listed in the *Ath* on Mar. 27. Hotten issued *Hans Breitmann's Christmas and in Politics and Other Ballads*, 1869, at 0/6 sewed, in May. In a letter dated Sept. 29, 1877, to the *Ath*, Leland complained about this edition of the present title by Ward, Lock, being advertised as "The complete book from the author's revised edition." "In fact," he said, "it contains only nine ballads and parts of two others, while in the only complete (Trübner) edition, there are forty-six, and the statement that they are revised by me is utterly untrue. It may be an edition corrupted and mutilated, taken from one that I did revise, but it is, in fact, simply an edition published by Hotten, reprinted, the errors of which were fully exposed when it first appeared." He stated that the text had been falsified, altered, and garbled; and its meaning was distorted by absurd footnotes, perverting the meaning. Ward, Lock answered in the *Ath* of Oct. 13 with an apology and stated that they took the copy for their ad from a catalog of Chatto & Windus from whom they had purchased the stereo plates. They further stated that in the future the objectionable part of the ad would not appear. In fact, the word "complete" did not appear either on the title page of their edition or on the cover. Chatto & Windus, of course, used the Hotten plates.
Also 1885

1176 OUR FUNNY FELLOW **The Comic Holiday Annual.** Demy 8vo. 1/0 sewed Sept.?
Comic Holiday Books No. 3. This is the first edition, no date.

1177 W. L. M. JAY (JULIA L. M. WOODRUFF) **Holden with the Cords.** 2/0 Oct. 13 (*Spect*)
This was listed in the *Spect* on Sept. 16, 1876, Cr 8vo, 3/6. The first edition was issued by E. P. Dutton & Co., New York, 1874, 19 cm., 517 pp., at $2.00, listed in the *Nation* on Sept. 17 and in *PW* on Sept. 19. The first English edition was issued by James Nisbet, London, 1874, Cr 8vo, 7/6, listed in the *Ath* and in the *Spect* on Oct. 31. Nisbet issued it at 3/6 cloth, 12mo, listed in the *Spect* on Oct. 9, 1875. The present edition probably has 384 pp., the same as their cloth issue (1883). It was issued by Griffith & Farran, London, in 1883, noticed in the *British Quarterly Review* for Oct. 1883. Weldon, London, issued it in their *Daisy Books* at 0/9, listed in the *Spect* on Sept. 25, 1875.
Also 1890

1178 (ROSE PORTER) **The Years That Are Told.** 12mo. 1/0 sewed, 1/6, 2/0 cloth Oct. 13 (*Spect*)
Lily Series No. 63. The first edition was issued by A. D. F. Randolph & Co., New York (copyright 1875), 18 cm., 233 pp.

1179 ANONYMOUS **Children's Forget-Me-Not.** 4to. 2/6 sewed Oct. 13 (*Spect*)

1180 BRET HARTE **Two Men of Sandy Bar (a drama) and New Poems.** Fcp 8vo. 1/0 sewed Nov. 16 (*PC*)
Ward & Lock's Humorous Books. This has no date, 16.5 cm., 161 pp., bound in pictorial wrappers. It was received by the *BM* on Nov. 26, and is probably the first English edition. The drama is essentially a dramatization of *Thompson's Prodigal*, which was in *Mrs. Skaggs's Husbands*, Boston, 1873. The first edition of the drama was issued by James R. Osgood & Co., Boston, 1876, 15 cm., 151 pp., $1.00, listed in *PW* on Nov. 11, 1876, and deposited in Boston on Nov. 9; but for some reason it was with-

drawn, and *PW* noted on Apr. 14, 1877, that it was now publishing, the obstacle being removed. It was again listed in *PW* on Apr. 14, 1877, and deposited Apr. 18. It was listed for the first time in the *Ind* on Apr. 26, 1877, and was advertised in the *New-York Times* on Apr. 14, 1877, as "This day."
Also 1882

1181 ALFRED V. DE VIGNY
The Conspirators. 2/0 boards
Nov. 17 (*Spect*)

Library of Favourite Authors No. 31. The first edition was issued in Paris, 2 vols., 1826, 19.8 cm., *Cinq-Mars*. The first English edition was issued by David Bogue, London, 1847, 18.5 cm., 397 pp., with a frontispiece (portrait), at 3/6 cloth, from the ninth Paris edition. It was advertised in the *Ath* on Jan. 2, 1847, as "Now ready." It was reissued by Henry G. Bohn, London, 1860, at 2/0. George Routledge, London, issued *Cinq-Mars* about Nov. 2, 1850, at 1/0 boards, 1/6 cloth; and reissued it in the *Railway Library* at 1/0 sewed, about Oct. 31, 1863, and again in Apr. 1877.

1182 ANONYMOUS **Beeton's Christmas Annual. Sixes and Sevens.** Illustrated.
1/0 sewed   Nov. 28

This was the 18th season for this annual. It was advertised in the *Ath* as "On Nov. 28." It contains three stories or sketches by Mark Twain: *The Echo That Didn't Answer*; *A Story of Haunting Horror*; and *Punch, Brothers, Punch!* and other Twain items and items by Burnand.

1183 ANONYMOUS **Sylvia's Annual and Englishwoman's Almanac for 1878.**
Illustrated. 1/0 sewed   Nov.?

This has no date and was advertised in the *Ath* on Oct. 20 as "Shortly," and the *Eng Cat* gives it as issued in 1877.

1184 GEORGE M. F. GLENNY
Glenny's Illustrated Garden Almanack.
1/0 sewed   Nov.?

This was advertised in the *Ath* on Oct. 20 as "Shortly," and it is the almanack for 1878. It was issued as *Glenny's Garden Almanac and Florist's Directory* by George Glenny, the elder, for the years 1847–74 (1846–73). It was continued as *Glenny's Illustrated Garden Almanack* for the years 1875–—(1874–—), by George M. F. Glenny.

1185 HENRY JAMES, JR. **The American.**
Cr 8vo. 2/0 boards   Dec. 8 (*Spect*)

Library of Favourite Authors No. 30. This is the first English edition, no date, with 435 pp., with the series title on the spine. There is a known copy in the original brown cloth, no date, with a 12-page catalog at the back containing a date indicating 1880. It is said to be in this series of *Favourite Authors*, but I've found no evidence for a cloth issue in this series. This ran in the *Atlantic Monthly* from June 1876 to May 1877. The first American edition was issued by James R. Osgood & Co., Boston, 1877, 19 cm., 473 pp., at $2.00, listed in *PW* on May 12, and in the *Ind* on May 17. It was issued by Macmillan & Co., London, 1879, 19.5 cm., 350 pp., at 6/0 in decorated dark blue cloth in an edition of 1,250 copies. There should be a catalog at the back (Nov. 1878), but there is a known copy with the catalog (May 1882). This was probably the first authorized and the first complete English edition. James described the Ward & Lock edition as "vilely printed" and with "whole paragraphs omitted." The Macmillan was listed in the *Ath* on Mar. 8. Macmillan reissued it at 1/0 sewed, 1/6 cloth, listed in the *Ath* on Nov. 10, 1883. Ward, Lock, Bowden & Co. issued it at 3/6 cloth in their *Royal Library* in the 1890s, with 435 pp.

1186 FRANCES E. M. NOTLEY *Love's Bitterness.* 2/0 boards Dec. 22 (*Ath*)

Library of Favourite Authors No. 33. This is 1877, with 384 pp. The first edition was issued by Tinsley Bros., London, 3 vols., 1870, anonymous, entitled *Patience Caerhydon*.

1187 JAMES MASON, ed. ***The Year-Book of Facts in Science and the Arts, for 1877.*** Cr 8vo. Frontispiece. 2/6 boards, 3/6 cloth Dec.

This is my copy, 1877, with an inscribed date (Jan. 1878) and a preface signed and dated (Dec. 1, 1877). It is 19.9 cm., 280 pp., double columns. It is the cheaper issue in aquamarine boards, decorated and with a small picture on the front in black and tan, the picture repeated on the title page, and with yellow endpapers. There are ads on the endpapers, on the back cover, and on 2 pp. at the front, with a catalog of the publishers at the back, paged (1)–29, and with ads of Edward Moxon & Co., London, paged 30–32.
See 1875 for publishing details

1188 ANONYMOUS ***Babbleton's Baby.*** Fcp 8vo. 1/0 sewed 1877 (*Eng Cat*)

Ward & Lock's Humorous Books. I cannot trace this.

1189 JAMES M. BAILEY ***The Danbury Newsman.*** Fcp 8vo. 1/0 sewed 1877 (*Eng Cat*)

Ward & Lock's Humorous Books. This is (1877), with 182 pp., a reissue of the Hotten issue of 1873; and since the imprint is Ward, Lock & Tyler, it was issued before Sept. 1. Ward, Lock acquired most of the Hotten humorous books of 1871–73 from Chatto & Windus, the successor to Hotten. The first edition was issued by Shepard & Gill, Boston, 1873, as *Life in Danbury*, 17.5 cm., 303 pp., with a frontispiece (portrait). It was advertised in *Lit World* on June 1 as "Ready June 5," and listed in the

Ind on June 26. George Routledge, London, issued *Life in Danbury*, 1873, with 188 pp., at 1/0 boards, listed in the *Ath* on July 12. It was also issued as *The Danbury Newsman* by John C. Hotten, London, with no date, 182 pp., at 1/0 sewed, listed in the *Spect* on July 19, 1873. In Canada it was issued by W. Warwick, Toronto, 1873, with 192 pp., as *The Danbury Newsman and His Friends*.

1190 JAMES M. BAILEY ***Folks in Danbury.*** Fcp 8vo. 1/0 sewed 1877 (*Eng Cat*)

Ward & Lock's Humorous Books. This has no date and 224 pp. The first American edition was *They All Do It*, issued by Lee & Shepard, Boston; C. T. Dillingham, New York, 1877, 18 cm., 313 pp., illustrated. It was advertised in the *New-York Times* on Sept. 19, $.50 paper, $1.00 cloth, with eight illustrations, as "This day." It was issued by George Routledge, London, as *Mr. Miggs of Danbury*, Fcp 8vo, at 2/0 boards, listed in the *Ath* and in the *Spect* on Sept. 15, 1877.

1191 ANONYMOUS ***Birds' Nests and Eggs, and Bird-Stuffing.*** 12mo. Colored plates. 1/0 sewed 1877 (*Eng Cat*)

Beeton's Country Books. This has no date and is 18 cm. tall, with pages numbered 289–352, and with the series title on the cover.
Also 1868

1192 (HENRY PETERSON) ***Bessie's Six Lovers.*** Fcp 8vo. 1/0 sewed 1877 (*Eng Cat*)

Ward & Lock's Humorous Books. This has no date and 159 pp. It was issued in the United States by T. B. Peterson & Bros., Philadelphia (1877), 12mo, anonymous, with 240 pp.

1193 CHARLES DICKENS ***Sketches and Tales of London Life.*** 0/6 sewed 1877 (*Eng Cat*)

I suspect this is part or all of *Sketches by "Boz,"* which was issued as *Popular Sixpenny Books* No. 55, circa 1881.

1194 NEIL FOREST (CORNELIA FLOYD) **Some Other Babies.** Fcp 8vo. 1/0 sewed 1877 (*Eng Cat*)

Ward & Lock's Humorous Books. This has no date and 188 pp. It was also issued as *Mice at Play* by John S. Marr & Sons, Glasgow (1877), jointly with Simpkin, Marshall & Co., London, at 1/0 and 2/0. The first edition was *Mice at Play*, issued by Roberts Bros., Boston, 1876, 271 pp., illustrated, listed by *Lit World* as published in Jan. 1877.

1195 HENRY FRITH **My Wife's Relations.** Fcp 8vo. 1/0 sewed 1877 (*Eng Cat*)

Ward & Lock's Humorous Books. This is the first edition.

1196 JOHN HABBERTON **Grown-up Babies.** Fcp 8vo. Illustrated. 1/0 sewed 1877 (*Eng Cat*)

Ward & Lock's Humorous Books. This is the first edition, no date, 187 pp.
See below

1197 JOHN HABBERTON **Other People.** Fcp 8vo. Illustrated. 1/0 sewed 1877 (*Eng Cat*)

Ward & Lock's Humorous Books. This has no date and 173 pp. I think it was issued by Derby Bros., New York, as *Some Folks*, listed in *PW* on Sept. 15, 1877. *Some Folks* was also issued by George Routledge, London, my copy, no date, at 2/0 boards, listed in the *Ath* on Aug. 11, 1877. It is copyright and has 448 pp. It was issued by Carleton, New York, as *Little Guzzy and Other Stories* (*Some Folks*), 1878, with the joint imprint of Sampson Low, London, illustrated, $1.00 paper, $1.50 cloth, advertised in the *New-York Times* on May 19, 1878, as "This week."
See the next item

1198 (JOHN HABBERTON) **The Scripture Club of Valley Rest.** 0/6 sewed 1877 (*Eng Cat*)

This was later *Popular Sixpenny Books* No. 54, circa 1881. It was also issued by

Nimmo, London (1877), and by George Routledge, London (1877), both at 1/0, the latter, my copy, 16.6 cm., anonymous, 159 pp., probably issued in June. The first American edition was issued by G. P. Putnam's Sons, New York, 1877, 18 cm., anonymous, 188 pp., frontispiece, listed in the *Ind* on June 21, and in *PW* on June 9. It was advertised in the *New-York Times* on June 9 at $.50 paper, $1.00 cloth, as postponed to June 12.

1199 ANONYMOUS **Hostess and Guest.** 4to. Illustrated. 1/0 1877 (*Eng Cat*)

Sylvia's Home Help Series No. 3. This is probably the first edition.

1200 SYLVIA **How to Dress Well on a Shilling a Day.** 1/0 sewed 1877 (*Eng Cat*)

This is the second edition. Ward, Lock issued it as *The Lady's Guide to Home Dressmaking and Millinery* (1883), 19 cm., 126 pp., illustrated. See 1876 for the first edition.
Also 1876

1201 ANONYMOUS **Illustrated Guide to the War.** 1/0 1877 (*Eng Cat*)

I cannot trace this.

1202 (JOHN HABBERTON) **The Jericho Road.** Fcp 8vo. 1/0 sewed 1877 (*Eng Cat*)

Ward & Lock's Humorous Books. This is (1877), with 186 pp. It was also issued by George Routledge, London, anonymous, at 1/0 boards, listed in the *Spect* on Feb. 3, 1877. The first edition was issued by Jansen, McClurg & Co., Chicago, 1877, 17.5 cm., anonymous, 222 pp., at $1.00 in black cloth decorated in red and gold. It was listed in *PW* on Dec. 2, 1876, in the *Ind* on Dec. 21, and in the *Nation* on Jan. 11, 1877.

1203 WILLIAM B. JERROLD **Cent per Cent.** Fcp 8vo. 1/0 sewed 1877 (*Eng Cat*)

Ward & Lock's Humorous Books. The first edition was issued by John C. Hotten,

London (1869), 19 cm., 268 pp., with colored illustrations, at 6/0, in green cloth, listed in the *Ath* on Dec. 11, 1869. It had a 24-page catalog at the back. It was reissued by Chatto & Windus, London, 1874, Fcp 8vo, at 2/0 boards, listed in the *Ath* on May 16.

1204 EMANUEL KINK (RICHARD DOWLING) & ARTEMUS WARD (CHARLES F. BROWNE) *On Babies and Ladders. Among the Fenians.* Fcp 8vo. 1/0 sewed 1877 (*Eng Cat*)

Ward & Lock's Humorous Books. This is (1877), in 2 parts. The first edition of the first title was issued by John C. Hotten, London (1873), 16.3 cm., at 1/0, in yellow pictorial wrappers, illustrated by William S. Gilbert et al. It is my copy and was listed in the *Spect* on Sept. 27, and has 167 pp. The first edition of the second title was also issued by Hotten in 1866, my copy, 16.1 cm., 56 pp., 0/6 sewed, listed in the *Spect* on July 7. Hotten reissued it in Apr. 1867, at 0/6 sewed.
Also 1885

1205 SOPHIE MAY (REBECCA S. CLARKE) *Our Helen.* 12mo. 1/0 sewed, 1/6, 2/0 cloth 1877 (*Eng Cat*)

Lily Series No. 61. The first edition was issued by Lee & Shepard, Boston (1874), 18 cm., listed in *PW* on Nov. 28, and in the *Ind* on Dec. 3, 1874. It was also issued with the joint imprint of Lee, Shepard & Dillingham, New York, 1875, 18 cm., 372 pp., illustrated.
Also 1883

1206 DWIGHT L. MOODY *Moody's Talks on Temperance.* 1/0 sewed, 1/6 cloth 1877 (*Eng Cat*)

This has no date, with 128 pp., revised and edited by J. W. Kirton. The first edition was issued by the National Temperance Society & Publishing House, New York, 1877, 19 cm., 248 pp., frontispiece (portrait), edited by James B. Dunn.

1207 DWIGHT L. MOODY *The Faithful Saying.* 1/0 sewed, 1/6 cloth 1877 (*Eng Cat*)

This has no date, a series of addresses, revised. This is the only entry in either the *BM* or the *U Cat.*

1208 MR. BROWN (GEORGE ROSE) *The Goings On of Mrs. Brown at the Tichborne Trial.* Fcp 8vo. 1/0 sewed 1877 (*Eng. Cat*)

Ward & Lock's Humorous Books. This has no date and 162 pp. The first edition was issued by John C. Hotten, London (1872), my copy, 16.2 cm., 162 pp., at 1/0 in pale yellow pictorial wrappers, with a 28-page catalog at the back. It was listed in the *Ath* on May 4. George Routledge, London, issued *Mrs. Brown on the Tichborne Case*, by Arthur Sketchley (George Rose), 1872, a different work, my copy, the first edition, 16.4 cm., 152 pp., at 1/0, in pictorial boards, listed in the *Ath* and in the *Spect* on Jan. 20, 1872.

1209 (AMOS K. FISKE & W. H. DOWNER) *My Mother-in-Law.* 0/6 sewed 1877 (*Eng Cat*)

This was later *Popular Sixpenny Books* No. 52. The present edition has no date and 128 pp. It was also issued by George Routledge, London, with 159 pp., at 1/0 boards, mentioned in editorial matter in the *Ath* on Oct. 20, 1877. The first American edition was issued by Lockwood, Brooks & Co., Boston, 1877, my copy, 17.1 cm., anonymous, 159 pp., $.50, in buff wrappers cut flush, simply printed in black with the title, the front and back identical. There are publisher's ads on pp. (161)–(176) and commercial ads on the inside covers. It was listed in the *Nation* on Sept. 27, and in the *Ind* on Oct. 4, and advertised in the *New-York Times* on Sept. 4, as if ready.

1210 (JOHN HABBERTON) *Other People's Children.* Fcp 8vo. 1/o sewed 1877 (*Eng Cat*)

Ward & Lock's Humorous Books. This has no date and 235 pp., the last chapter written by an English writer and signed H. The first English edition was probably issued by George Routledge, London, 1877, my copy, 17.7 cm., anonymous, 303 pp., at 2/o boards, by special arrangement with the author, the last two chapters being copyrighted in the United Kingdom. It was listed in the *Ath* on June 2. It was also issued by Simpkin, Marshall & Co., London, in 1877, at o/6. The first American edition was issued by G. P. Putnam's Sons, New York, 1877, 18 cm., anonymous, 303 pp., frontispiece, $1.00 paper, $1.25 cloth, listed in *PW* on July 14, and in the *Ind* on July 26. It was advertised in the *New-York Times* on July 14, 20,000 copies, "This noon." In an ad in the *Ath* on June 23, 1877, Routledge stated that another house had issued a noncopyrighted edition in which the last two chapters were omitted. A letter from Habberton appeared in the *Ath* on July 21 complaining about the Ward, Lock issue as being mutilated and an insult to the reader. Ward, Lock answered in the July 28 issue, saying there was no copyright in the main part of the work and that the last two chapters were the only part that could be copyrighted in England and that the proof of this was that Routledge had taken no legal action against them! This did not answer Habberton's criticism that it was a shoddy work!
Also 1891. See below

1211 TITUS A. BRICK, ed. (JOHN C. HOTTEN) *Shaving Them.* Fcp 8vo. 1/o sewed 1877 (*Eng Cat*)

Ward & Lock's Humorous Books. This has no date, a reissue of the first edition, issued and written by John C. Hotten, London. The Ward, Lock catalog of 1877 gave it as 2/6 cloth only. The Hotten edition was (1872), 16.2 cm., 230 pp., 1/o, in pale yellow pictorial wrappers, with a 24-page catalog at the back, and 2/6 in cloth, listed in the *Ath* on Apr. 6. My copies of the Hotten issue are in the pictorial wrappers.

1212 (MAURICE F. EGAN) *That Girl of Mine.* Fcp 8vo. 1/o sewed 1877 (*Eng Cat*)

Ward & Lock's Humorous Books. This has no date and 159 pp., probably the first English edition. The first American edition was issued by T. B. Peterson & Bros., Philadelphia (copyright 1877), 17.5 cm., anonymous, 294 pp.

1213 JOHN TODD *The Student's Manual.* Cr 8vo. 1/o sewed, 1/6, 2/o cloth 1877 (*Eng Cat*)

Friendly Counsel Series No. 11. The first edition was issued by J. H. Butler, Northampton; etc., 1835, 18 cm., 392 pp. The first English edition was issued by L. & G. Seeley, London, 1836, revised by Thomas Dale, 12mo, 6/o, listed in the *Ath* on Sept. 3. The second edition, the same, was listed on June 3, 1837, as *Todd's Student Guide.*

1214 J. G. MONTEFIORE *The History of England in Verse.* 1/o boards 1877 (*Eng Cat*)

The *U Cat* and the *BM* give only (1876), 128 pp., issued by Ward, Lock & Tyler.

1215 CHARLES H. ROSS & AMBROSE CLARKE *The Story of a Honeymoon.* Fcp 8vo. 1/o sewed 1877 (*BM*)

Ward & Lock's Humorous Books. This has no date and 284 pp. The first edition was issued by John C. Hotten, London (1869), with a colored frontispiece, illustrations, at 6/o cloth, with 4 pp. of ads, and a 24-page catalog at the back. It was listed in the *Spect* on Dec. 4, 1869. It was reissued by Chatto & Windus, London, in 1874, Fcp 8vo, illustrated, at 2/o boards, listed in the *Ath* on Mar. 7. The first American edition was issued by G. W. Carleton, New York, 1870, 23.5 cm., 335 pp., illustrated, noticed in the *Ind* on Apr. 21.

1216 FRANCIS BACON *The New Atlantis. The Wisdom of the Ancients. The History of King Henry VII.* A second series of essays. 1/o sewed, 1/6, 2/o cloth   1877 (*BM*)
Books for All Time No. 6. This has no date. For the first series see 1874

1217 ANN & JANE TAYLOR *Hymns for Infant Minds.* 18mo. o/9 sewed, 1/o, 1/6 cloth   1877?
Beeton's Good-Aim Series No. 21. This along with the next item was contained in *The Poetical Works of Ann and Jane Taylor* (1877), p 8vo, illustrated, 3/6 cloth, issued by Ward, Lock. I think the first edition of the present title was issued by T. Conder, etc., London, 1808, anonymous. The second edition was issued, the same, 1810, 24mo, anonymous, 100 pp.; and the fifth edition, the same, 1812, 14 cm., with 100 pp. Eric Quayle in *Early Children's Books* says there were 60 editions before 1890. In the United States it was issued by Munroe, Francis & Parker, Boston, 24mo, 68 pp., illustrated, which the *U Cat* gives as (1809?).

1218 ANN & JANE TAYLOR *Rhymes for the Nursery.* 18mo. o/9 sewed, 1/o, 1/6 cloth 1877?
Beeton's Good-Aim Series No. 22. See the preceding item. The first edition of the present title was issued by Darton & Harvey, London, 1806, 12mo, 95 pp. This contained *Twinkle, Twinkle, Little Star*. Eric Quayle in *Early Children's Books* says the 27th edition appeared in 1835.

1219 ELIZABETH PRENTISS *Little Susy's Six Birthdays.* 18mo. o/9 sewed, 1/o, 1/6 cloth   1877 (*Eng Cat*)
Beeton's Good-Aim Series No. 23. The first English edition of the first series was issued by Sampson Low, London, 1854, by

Her Aunt Susan, 15 cm., 190 pp., 4 colored illustrations. It was issued by Nelson, London, probably both series, in 1875, 12mo, 1/6. Both series were issued 2-vols.-in-1, by A. D. F. Randolph, New York, 1862, illustrated. He issued the first series in 1853, advertised in the *New York Daily Times* on Oct. 17, Sq 16mo, by Aunt Susan, $.50, "Just published." He reissued the first series, 1864, 15 cm., 190 pp., illustrated. This and the following two titles were issued by James Nisbet, London, in 1 vol., second edition, Sq 16mo, 220 pp., at 4/6 cloth, listed by *PC* as published Oct. 31–Nov. 14, 1859.

1220 ELIZABETH PRENTISS *Little Susy's Little Servants.* 18mo. o/9 sewed, 1/o, 1/6 cloth   1877 (*Eng Cat*)
Beeton's Good-Aim Series No. 24. This was issued by A. D. F. Randolph, New York, both series, 2-vols.-in-1 (1856), 15 cm., with a colored frontispiece, which the *U Cat* gives as (1857?). Routledge, London, issued it in 1876, 16mo, at 1/o. See the preceding title.

1221 ELIZABETH PRENTISS *Little Susy's Six Teachers.* 18mo. o/9 sewed, 1/o, 1/6 cloth   1877 (*Eng Cat*)
Beeton's Good-Aim Series No. 25. This was issued by A. D. F. Randolph, New York, 2 vols., both series (1857?); and reissued, 2 vols., 1861 (copyright 1856), 15 cm., illustrated. George Routledge, London, issued it in 1875, 16mo, at 1/o. See the items above.

1222 ÉMILE ERCKMANN & PIERRE CHATRIAN *The Wild Huntsman, and Other Tales.* Small format. 1/o sewed   1877 (*BM*)
This is also given by the *Eng Cat*. It has no date and 184 pp., with a preface by H. F. It contains two stories in addition to the title story.

1223 (MRS. M. A. DENISON) *That Husband of Mine.* Fcp 8vo. 1/o sewed 1877 (*BM*)

Ward & Lock's Humorous Books. This has no date and 183 pp. It was later *Popular Sixpenny Books* No. 53. The first American edition was issued by Lee & Shepard, Boston; etc., 1877, 17.5 cm., anonymous, 227 pp., $.50 paper and $1.00 cloth, advertised in the *New-York Times* on Aug. 11 as "Today." It was listed in the *Nation* and in the *Ind* on Aug. 9. George Routledge, London, issued it, no date, my copy, 16.6 cm., 153 pp., at 1/o boards, listed in the *Ath* on Sept. 15, 1877. Frederick Warne, London, also issued it, with 175 pp., illustrated, at 1/o picture covers, advertised in the *Ath* on Sept. 15, 1877, and listed in the *Acad* on Sept. 15.

1224 FRANCES H. BURNETT *Surly Tim, and Other Stories.* 1/o sewed   Jan. 4, 1878 (*Bks*)

The *Bks* at this time was a monthly so this title was probably issued in Dec. 1877. It has no date and 147 pp. and was received by the *BM* on Dec. 12, 1877. The first edition was issued by Scribner, Armstrong & Co., New York, 1877, 17 cm., 270 pp., $1.25 cloth, listed in the *Nation* on Oct. 18, in *PW* on Oct. 20, and in the *Ind* on Oct. 25. All except one of the stories had appeared in *Scribner's Magazine*. It was advertised in the *New-York Times* on Oct. 16; and the third edition was advertised there, the same, on Oct. 27, as "Now ready." There was an author's note in the review in *Scribner's Monthly* in Dec. 1877, stating that this title and *That Lass o' Lowrie's* were the only two books under her name that had been prepared and corrected for publication in book form under her supervision. It was issued by Chatto & Windus, London, 1878 (1877), with 333 pp., at 2/o boards, by special arrangement with the authoress, and was received by the *BM* on Dec. 5,

1877, and was listed in the *Ath* on Nov. 17, 1877.

Also 1889

1225 ALPHONSE DE LAMARTINE *Genevieve . . . and the Stonemason of Saint Point.* 2/o boards   Jan. 4, 1878 (*Bks*)

Library of Favourite Authors No. 32. The *Bks* was issued monthly at this time so this was probably issued in Dec. 1877. The first edition of the first title was issued in Paris, 1850, 24 cm., 192 pp.; and the first edition of the second title was *Le Tailleur de Pierres de Saint-Point*, Paris, 1851, 319 pp., with a frontispiece. The first English edition of the first title was issued by Henry G. Bohn, London, 1850, with 179 pp., at 1/o; and the first English edition of the second title was the same, 1851, *The Stonemason of Saint-Point*, 18.5 cm., 147 pp., at 1/o; or it was issued by George Routledge, London, *The Stonecutter of Saint Point*, 1851, 17 cm., 188 pp., at 1/o boards, 1/6 cloth, listed in the *Ath* on July 26. The Bohn was listed in the *Ath* on July 19. The first American edition of the first title was either Harper & Bros., New York (1850), 25 cm., with 80 pp., double columns, listed by *Lit World* as published Oct. 19–Nov. 2, translated by A. R. Scoble; or Stringer & Townsend, New York, 1850, 21 cm., 182 pp., advertised in *Lit World* on Oct. 5 as "Just published." The first American edition of the second title was Harper & Bros., New York, 1851, 21 cm., 144 pp., listed by *Lit World* as published July 26–Aug. 17.

1226 (JOHN HABBERTON) *Grown-up Babies and Other People.* Illustrated. 2/o boards   1877?

Household and Railway Books No. 39. This has no date, 17 cm., full-page illustrations, a pictorial yellowback, with a 20-page catalog at the back.

See the preceding two items

1227 GUSTAVE AIMARD (OLIVER GLOUX)
The Pearl of the Andes. 12mo. 1/0 sewed
1877?
This was 18 cm., bound in pink pictorial
wrappers.
Also 1863. See 1880

1228 GUSTAVE AIMARD *Stronghand.*
12mo. 1/0 sewed   1877?
This was 18 cm., bound in pink pictorial
wrappers.
Also 1864. See 1880

1229 GUSTAVE AIMARD *The Rebel Chief.*
12mo. 1/0 sewed   1877?
This was 18 cm., bound in pink pictorial
wrappers. In a joint full-page ad with
Vickers, London, in the *Spect* on Sept. 1,
1877, Vickers offered 18 Aimard titles as
ready at 0/6 sewed each, author's copyright cheap edition, edited by Percy St.
John.

1230 MRS. H. S. MACKARNESS
(M. A. PLANCHÉ, later MACKARNESS)
Only a Penny. 18mo. 0/9 sewed,
1/0, 1/6 cloth   1877?
Beeton's Good-Aim Series No. 26. This is
probably the first edition and was proba-

bly issued late in 1877 or early in 1878, as
the *Eng Cat* gives it as issued in 1878.

1231 (MARY E. BRADDON) *The Lovels of
Arden.* Stereotyped Edition. Small
format. 2/0 boards   1877?
This is my copy, no date, 16.9 cm., 399
pp., with Ward, Lock & Tyler on the title
page, and Ward, Lock & Co. on the front
and back covers. It is in yellow pictorial
boards with plain white endpapers and
has the author's name on the spine only. It
has "Miss Braddon's Novels" from the
Dublin University Magazine on pp. (i)–xii at
the back. The list of Braddon yellowbacks
on the back cover ends with *Weavers and
Weft* (issued in Sept. above).
Also 1872

1232 JOHN HABBERTON *Helen's Babies
and Other People's Children.* Illustrated.
2/0 boards   1877?
Household and Railway Books No. 37. This
contains the two titles previously issued
(see above). It has no date, 16.9 cm., with
separate pagination and a full-page illustrations. It is a pictorial yellowback with
an 18-page catalog.
See above and 1897 for the first title; and
see above and 1891 for the second title

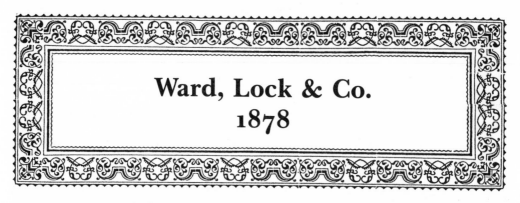

Ward, Lock & Co.
1878

1233 MARY BASKIN *Esther Douglas, and Other Stories.* 12mo. 1/0 sewed, 1/6, 2/0 cloth   Jan. 26 (*Spect*)

Lily Series No. 65. This is the first edition, no date, with 236 pp.

1234 MARY S. NOVELLO *The History of Bluebeard's Wives.* Sq Cr 8vo. Stiff wrappers   Jan.?

This was mentioned in editorial matter in the *Ath* on Feb. 16. I have a copy, no date, with the imprint of Ward, Lock & Tyler, 20.5 × 16 cm., 59 pp., in dark blue stiff wrappers, decorated on the front in gold. It has many new full-page illustrations, in brown, by Novello, plain white endpapers. There is a preface to the second edition (1877) and 3 pp. of publisher's ads at the back. The first edition was issued by Grant & Co., London, 1875, 4to, 43 pp., illustrated, at 5/0, *The History of Bluebeard's Six Wives*, with the illustrations by Cruikshank. It was noticed in the *British Quarterly Review* for Jan. 1876.

1235 HARRIET B. STOWE *Uncle Tom's Cabin.* 12mo. 1/0 sewed   Apr. 3 (*Bks*)

This has 324 pp.
Also 1864, 73

1236 GUSTAVE AIMARD (OLIVER GLOUX) *The Pirates of the Prairies.* 12mo. 1/0 sewed   Apr. 3 (*Bks*)

This has no date, 18 cm., 320 pp., and is probably in pink pictorial wrappers, although I have two titles in the series in white wrappers. There are ads on the endpapers and back cover. It is edited by (Lascelles Wraxall).
Also 1861, 80

1237 GUSTAVE AIMARD *The White Scalper.* 12mo. 1/0 sewed   Apr. 3 (*Bks*)

This has no date, 18 cm., with 352 pp. See the preceding item for a description.
Also 1861, 80

1238 EDWARD P. ROE *A Knight of the Nineteenth Century.* 12mo. 1/0 sewed, 1/6, 2/0 cloth   May 11 (*Spect*)

Lily Series No. 66. This has 404 pp. It was listed in the *Bks* on Mar. 2 at 1/0 sewed, 1/6, and on Apr. 3 at 1/0 sewed. The *Spect* listing was for a 1/6 issue. Ward, Lock issued it in their *Home Treasure Library* (1877), 18 cm., 520 pp., with colored plates, at 3/6 cloth. The first English edition was issued by Ward, Lock in 1877, Cr 8vo, at 10/6, listed in the *Ath* and in the *Spect* on Oct. 13. The first American edition was issued by Dodd, Mead & Co., New York, 1877, 19 cm., 582 pp., $1.50, in green or maroon cloth with cream endpapers. It was advertised in the *New-York Times* on Sept. 29 as "Now ready," and listed in *PW* on Oct. 20, and in the *Nation* and in the *Ind* on Oct. 25.
Also 1882, 86

1239 ANONYMOUS *Dress, Health, and Beauty.* Illustrated. 1/0 sewed   June 1 (*Ath* ad)

Sylvia's Home Help Series No. 5. This was given in editorial matter in the *Ath* on June 22. It is the first edition, no date.

1240 HENRY W. LONGFELLOW

The Poetical Works of Henry W. Longfellow.
1/6 sewed, 2/0 cloth   June 1 (*Ath* ad)

Books for All Time No. 10. This has no date and 586 pp., a reprint of a Moxon issue of 1870, 600 pp., illustrated, edited by W. M. Rossetti. *Ballads and Other Poems* was issued by John Owen, Cambridge, 1842, 132 pp., in yellow boards, in an edition of 350 copies. *Poems* was issued by Carey & Hart, Philadelphia, 1845, 23 cm., 387 pp., illustrated, called the first collected edition, and deposited on Oct. 29. *Poems* was also issued by D. Huntington, Philadelphia, 1845, illustrated, with 19 poems printed for the first time, deposited Oct. 29, and issued about Nov. 24. Harper & Bros., New York, issued *Poems*, 8vo, 117 pp., $.50 paper, listed in the *Knickerbocker* for July 1846. *Ballads, Poems and Drama* was issued by Edward Moxon, London, 1843, printed in the United States, and containing with separate pagination *Ballads—Voices of the Night—The Spanish Student*. He issued the fourth edition at 4/0 boards, listed in the *Spect* on Nov. 18, 1843.
Also 1882

1241 SIR WALTER SCOTT   **The Poetical Works of Sir Walter Scott.** 1/6 sewed, 2/0 cloth   June 1 (*Ath* ad)

Books for All Time No. 11. This has no date and 610 pp., a reissue of the edition issued by Edward Moxon, Son & Co., London, 1870, 18.5 cm., 620 pp., illustrated, edited by W. M. Rossetti. However the Ward, Lock reissue lacked the preface and illustrations. The first collected edition was issued by Constable, Edinburgh; Hurst, London, 12 vols., Fcp 8vo, portrait, 72/0, listed in the *Edinburgh Review* as published July–Oct. 1819.

1242 WILLIAM WORDSWORTH

The Poetical Works of William Wordsworth.
1/6 sewed, 2/0 cloth.   June 1 (*Ath* ad)

Books for All Time No. 12. This has no date and is a reissue without the preface or il-lustrations of an issue of Edward Moxon, Son & Co., London (1871), 22 cm., 568 pp., illustrated, edited by W. M. Rossetti. Ward, Lock took over Moxon in 1870. *Poems* was issued by Longmans, London, 2 vols., in 1807, Fcp 8vo, at 11/0 boards, in various colored boards, some with cloth spines. It was listed in the *Edinburgh Review* as published Apr.–July 1807. *The Poetical Works* was issued by Edward Moxon, London, 6 vols., 1836 (–37), a new edition, in black or green cloth, yellow endpapers. *The Poetical Works* was issued by Cummings, Hilliard & Co., Boston, 4 vols., 1824, 18.5 cm., in drab boards, uncut. It was called the first American collected edition.

1243 JOHN MILTON   **The Poetical Works of John Milton.** 1/6 sewed, 2/0 cloth   June 1 (*Ath* ad)

Books for All Time No. 13. This has no date and 460 pp., a reissue of the Moxon edition of (1871), 18.5 cm., 460 pp., illustrated, edited by Rossetti. This Ward, Lock reissue is without the preface or il-lustrations. *Poems* was issued by Humphrey Moseley, London, 1645, portrait, the first collected edition of the minor poems. It was issued by Thomas Dring, London, 1673, enlarged, 290 pp., portrait.

1244 WILLIAM COWPER   **The Poetical Works of William Cowper.** 1/6 sewed, 2/0 cloth   June 1 (*Ath* ad)

Books for All Time No. 14. This has no date and 600 pp., a reissue of the Moxon edition of 1872, without the preface or illustrations. It was issued by Edward Moxon, Son & Co., London (1872), 18.5 cm., 600 pp., edited by Rossetti. *Poems* was issued by J. Johnson, London, 2 vols., 1782–84, 18 cm. *The Poetical Works* was issued by Benjamin Johnson, Philadelphia, 1806, 15 cm., illustrated. *The Complete Poetical Works* was issued by D. Appleton, New York; etc., 1843, 2 vols., edited by H. Stebbing,

12mo., 416 pp., 445 pp., called the first complete American edition.

1245　JOHN KEATS　*The Poetical Works of John Keats.* 1/6 sewed, 2/o cloth　July 27 (*Spect*)

Books for All Time No. 15. This has no date and 406 pp., a reissue of the Moxon edition of (1872), which was 18.5 cm., 406 pp., illustrated, edited by Rossetti. It was reissued by Moxon (1880), but, of course, Moxon was owned by Ward, Lock, who took over in 1870. *Poems* was issued by C. & J. Ollier, London, 1817, 19 cm., 121 pp. *The Poetical Works* was issued by Galignani, Paris, 1829; and by Wiley & Putnam, New York, 1846, 2-vols.-in-1, 18.5 cm. *The Poetical Works of Coleridge, Shelley and Keats* was issued by Desilver, Thomas & Co., Philadelphia, 1835.

1246　THOMAS HOOD, THE ELDER *The Poetical Works of Thomas Hood.* Series 1. 1/6 sewed, 2/o cloth June 1 (*Ath* ad)

Books for All Time No. 16. *Poems and Verses* was issued by Wiley & Putnam, New York, 2 vols., listed in the *Knickerbocker* for Sept. 1845. *Poems* was issued by Little, Brown, Boston, 2 vols., 1844. In England *Poems* was issued by Edward Moxon, London, 2 vols., 1846, at 12/o, listed in the *Spect.* on Jan. 10, 1846; and *Poems of Wit and Humour* was issued by him, 1847, in 1 vol. The present edition has no date and 400 pp., a reissue of a Moxon edition of the 1870s, the latter illustrated, edited by Rossetti.
See below for the second series

1247　HENRY W. LONGFELLOW *The White Czar; and Other Poems.* 1/o boards　June 1 (*Ath* ad)

This has no date, 17.5 cm., 115 pp., in printed pink boards, with ads on the endpapers. It is a selection from several books of poems. The title poem appeared in the

Atlantic Monthly for Mar. 1878; it first appeared in book form in vol. 20 of *Poems and Places*, 1878, issued in Boston in 31 vols., 1876–79. The title poem was in *Kéramos and Other Poems*, issued by George Routledge, London, 1878, 156 pp., in cloth, deposited Apr. 26, and the same was issued in Boston, 1878, deposited May 1.

1248　EDWARD P. ROE *Near to Nature's Heart.* 12mo. 1/o sewed, 1/6, 2/o cloth June 15 (*Spect*)

Lily Series No. 64. This has no date. Ward, Lock also issued it at 3/6 cloth, 12mo, listed in the *Spect* on July 6, 1878. Ward, Lock & Tyler issued the first English edition, 2 vols., Cr 8vo, at 10/6, listed in the *Ath* on Oct. 7, 1876, and in *PC* on Oct. 17. The first American edition was issued by Dodd, Mead & Co., New York (1876), 19 cm., 556 pp., $1.25, in red, blue, terra cotta, or maroon cloth, pale yellow endpapers. It was advertised in the *New-York Times* on Sept. 30 as "Now ready," and the 15th thousand was advertised on Nov. 30. It was listed in *PW* on Sept. 30, a printing of 12,000 copies; an ad on Sept. 16 stated that the first edition was exhausted, and the second edition was now printing. It was listed in the *Nation* and in the *Ind* on Oct. 12.
Also 1882, 86

1249　MARK TWAIN (SAMUEL CLEMENS) ET AL. *Mark Twain's Nightmare. With Tales, Sketches, and Poetry.* Fcp 8vo. Illustrated. 1/o sewed　June?

Ward & Lock's Humorous Books. This has pieces by F. C. Burnand, H. S. Leigh, et al., and has illustrations by Linley Sambourne, A. B. Frost, et al. It has no date, 167 pp., in wrappers printed in red, blue, and black. There are 24 pp. of ads. Most of the contents are from Beeton's Christmas Annual for 1877 (which see), including *Punch, Brothers, Punch! A Literary*

Nightmare appeared in the *Atlantic Monthly* for Feb. 1876.

1250 CAPTAIN CRAWLEY (GEORGE F. PARDON) *Cricket, Base-Ball and Rounders*. Illustrated. 1/0 sewed   June?

This was in editorial matter in the *Ath* for June 22. There is an entry in the *BM* that may have relevance: *Cricket as Now Played by Frederick de'A. Planché*. *And Base-Ball and Rounders by Captain Crawley*, London and Chilworth (1878). The present title and those below by Crawley were probably all issued together in 1 vol. as *Boy's Book of Outdoor Games*, by Crawley, 12mo, illustrated, 5/0 cloth, listed in the *Spect* on Sept. 2, 1882, issued by Ward, Lock.

1251 DOUGLAS JERROLD *The Brownrigg Papers*. 2/0 boards   1878?

Library of Favourite Authors No. 34. This is edited by W. Blanchard Jerrold, the author's son. The first edition was issued by John C. Hotten, London, 1860, 20.5 cm., 417 pp., at 10/6, in purple cloth, with a colored frontispiece, listed in the *Ath* on June 30. It was issued by Chatto & Windus (Hotten's successors), London, 1874, at 2/0 boards, listed in the *Ath* on May 16.

1252 EDWARD P. ROE *Opening a Chestnut Burr*. 12mo. 2/0 boards   Aug. 3 (*Spect*)

Lily Series double volume. Ward, Lock issued this also at 3/6 cloth, listed in the *Spect* on July 27, 1878. The first edition was issued by Dodd & Mead, New York (1874), 19.5 cm., 561 pp., $1.75 cloth, listed in *PW* on Oct. 3, in the *Ind* on Oct. 8, and advertised in the *New-York Times* on Sept. 28 as "This day." The seventh thousand was advertised in the latter on Oct. 24 as "This day." There were three printings: No. 1 in blue or green cloth; No. 2 in blue cloth; and No. 3 in red cloth, all with yellow endpapers. The first English edition was issued by George Routledge,

London (1874), at 3/6 cloth, listed in the *Ath* and in the *Spect* on Nov. 7.
Also 1886

1253 WILLIAM PALEY *Evidences of Christianity*. 12mo. 1/0, 1/6   Aug. 3 (*Spect*)

Christian Knowledge Series No. 1. This has no date, 18 cm., with 268 pp. The first edition was *A View of the Evidences of Christianity*, issued by R. Faulder, London, 3 vols., 1794, 19 cm. It was also issued by J. Milliken, Dublin, 1794, 21 cm., 664 pp. The first American edition was issued by Thomas Dobson, Philadelphia, 1795, 22 cm., 443 pp. The present edition is edited by F. A. Malleson.

1254 BISHOP JOSEPH BUTLER *The Analogy of Religion*. 12mo. 1/0, 1/6 Aug. 3 (*Spect*)

Christian Knowledge Series No. 2. This has no date and 240 pp., with an introduction and notes by F. A. Malleson. The first edition was issued by J. J. & P. Knapton, London, 1736, 4to, 320 pp. It was issued by George Ewing, Dublin, 1736, with 320 pp. The *U Cat* gives W. C. Allison, New York (1736?), paged 170–539. The second American edition was issued by David West, Boston, 22 cm., with 422 pp., but I don't know the date.
Also 1885

1255 FLAVIUS JOSEPHUS *Antiquities of the Jews*. 1/6 sewed, 2/0 cloth   Aug. 10 (*Spect*)

Books for All Time No. 18. This has no date and 528 pp., translated by W. Whiston. It was written before 100 A.D. It together with the following item were issued in 1 vol. by Ward, Lock, with separate pagination, *The Works of Josephus*, Cr 8vo, at 3/6 cloth, listed in the *Spect* on Aug. 31, 1878. They also issued it in 1 vol., no date, 23 cm., 858 pp., illustrated, probably in 1879. *The Works* was issued in Latin in

1502; and it was issued by Peter Short, London, 1602, 31 cm., with 812 pp.

1256 FLAVIUS JOSEPHUS *Wars of the Jews.* 1/6 sewed, 2/0 cloth   Aug. 10 (*Spect*)

Books for All Time No. 19. This has no date and 284 pp., translated by W. Whiston. See the preceding item. This was written before 100 A.D.

1257 ROSA M. KETTLE (MARY ROSA S. KETTLE) *The Mistress of Langdale Hall.* 2/0 boards   Aug. 31 (*Spect*)

Library of Favourite Authors No. 35. The first edition was issued by Samuel Tinsley, London, 1872, 19.5 cm., 336 pp., with a frontispiece, 4/0 cloth, the first title in a new price experiment. It was listed in the *Ath* on Feb. 17 and by *PC* as published Feb. 16–29, anonymous. The third edition was advertised in the *Spect* on Oct. 5, the same.

1258 GUSTAVE AIMARD (OLIVER GLOUX) *The Prairie Flower.* 12mo. 1/0 sewed Aug. 31 (*Spect*)

This is my copy, no date, 18 cm., 360 pp., in pink pictorial wrappers cut flush. There are ads on the back cover, on the endpapers, and on the verso of the half-title, with a catalog paged (1)–18 at the back.
Also 1861. See 1880

1259 CAPTAIN CRAWLEY (GEORGE F. PARDON) *Rowing, Sculling, and Canoeing.* Illustrated. 1/0 sewed   Aug.?

This has 128 pp. It was mentioned in editorial matter in the *Ath* on Aug. 31. See *Cricket, etc.* above.

1260 CAPTAIN CRAWLEY *Swimming, Skating, Rinking.* Illustrated. 1/0 sewed Aug.?

This was mentioned in editorial matter in the *Ath* on Aug. 11. See *Cricket, etc.* above.

1261 F. C. BURNAND ET AL. *D's Diary.* Illustrated. 1/0 sewed   Nov.

Beeton's Christmas Annual, 19th season. This contains *The Crutch-Handled Stick* by Burnand.

1262 BRET HARTE *The Hoodlum Band, and Other Stories.* Fcp 8vo. 1/0 sewed Dec. 18 (*PC*)

Ward & Lock's Humorous Books. This has no date, 16.5 cm., with 184 pp. The title story first appeared in *Drift from Two Shores*, issued by Houghton, Osgood & Co., Boston, 1878, 15.5 cm., with 266 pp., reviewed in *Scribner's Monthly* for Sept. 1878, and containing also *The Man on the Beach— Jinny—My Friend the Tramp—etc.* The title story appeared in *Temple Bar* (Bentley) for Jan. 1878.

1263 GUSTAVE AIMARD (OLIVER GLOUX) *The Guide of the Desert.* 12mo. 1/0 sewed Dec. (*Bks*)

This is a reissue of the C. H. Clarke edition, with 320 pp. The first edition was *Le Guaranis*, in Paris. The first English edition was issued by C. H. Clarke, London (1867), Fcp 8vo, with 320 pp., at 2/0 boards, listed in the *Ath* on Apr. 13. It was reissued by Clarke at 2/0 boards in 1874, listed in the *Spect* on Oct. 13. George Vickers, London, issued it, 1876, 19 cm., with 120 pp.; reissued by J. & R. Maxwell, London, in 1878 or 1879.
See 1880

1264 RAWDEN CRAWLEY (GEORGE F. PARDON) *Football, Golf, Hockey, and Curling.* Illustrated. 1/0 sewed   Dec. (*Bks*)

This has no date and 96 pp. See *Cricket, etc.* above.

1265 MARY BASKIN *Released.* 12mo. 1/0 sewed, 1/6, 2/0 cloth   Dec. (*Bks*)

Lily Series No. 67. This is the first edition, no date, with 188 pp.

1266 SOPHIE MAY (REBECCA ST. CLARKE) *Quinnebasset Girls.* 12mo. 1/o sewed, 1/6, 2/o cloth   Dec. (*Bks*)

Lily Series No. 68. This is the first English edition. The first edition was issued by Lee & Shepard, Boston (1877), 336 pp., illustrated, $1.50, listed in *PW* on Dec. 15, 1877, and in the *Ind* and the *Nation* on Dec. 20.

1267 ANONYMOUS *Charlie and Rosie.* Illustrated. 2/o boards   Dec. (*Bks*)

This is the first edition, no date, with 168 pp., a book of pictures and stories with musical notes, a book for children.

1268 JOHN W. KIRTON, ed. *The Standard Comic Reciter.* 1/o boards, 1/6 cloth Dec. (*Bks*)

This is the first edition, no date, the contents selected and edited by Kirton. Also 1888

1269 JOHN W. KIRTON, ed. *The Standard Sunday School Reciter.* 1/o boards, 1/6 cloth   1878 (*Eng Cat*)

This is the first edition (1878).

1270 ANONYMOUS *All About the Electric Light.* Illustrated. 1/o   1878 (*Eng Cat*)

This was mentioned in editorial matter in the *Ath* on Jan. 4, 1879. It is the first edition, no date.

1271 ANONYMOUS *All About the Telephone and Telegraph.* 1/o   1878 (*Eng Cat*)

I cannot trace this.

1272 SYDNEY SMITH *Essays, Social and Political.* Second series. 1/o sewed, 2/o cloth   1878 (*Eng Cat*)

Books for All Time No. 7. Ward, Lock issued this also at 3/6 cloth, Cr 8vo, listed in the *Spect* on Oct. 20, 1877.
For the first series see 1874

1273 THOMAS DEQUINCEY *Notes from the Pocket-Book of an Opium-Eater. With Anecdotes.* 1/o sewed, 1/6, 2/o cloth 1878 (*Eng Cat*)

Books for All Time No. 9. No. 8 in this series was not issued. This has no date and is paged 243–435. Pages 1–242 were in No. 3 in the series (see 1874). The title piece appeared serially in the *London Magazine*: Nos. I–III in vol. 8, 1823; No. IV in vol. 9, 1824; and Nos. V and VI in vol. 10, 1824.

1274 ANONYMOUS *The Letter-Writer for Lovers.* Illustrated. o/6   1878 (*Eng Cat*)

The *BM* gives London, Chilworth (1878), illustrated.

1275 H. P. ROCHE *My Adventures at the Seat of War.* o/6   1878 (*Eng Cat*)

I cannot trace this.

1276 CATHERINE SINCLAIR *Modern Accomplishments.* 2/o boards   1878 (*Eng Cat*)

Also 1865, 76

1277 MAX ADELER (CHARLES H. CLARK) *Out of the Hurly-Burly.* 12mo. Illustrated. 2/o boards   1878

This is a reissue in *Household and Railway Books*, my copy, no date, authorized edition, with a copyright preface, 17.8 cm., 398 pp., in white pictorial boards with four small illustrations on the front in red, blue, and black. There is a frontispiece, full-page illustrations, and many textual illustrations. There are ads on the endpapers, back cover, and verso of the title page, and a catalog paged (1)–14 at the back. The series title appears on the spine. Also 1874, 82, 83, 1900

1278 BRET HARTE *Stories, Sketches and Bohemian Papers. Complete . . . with a Memoir.* Wrappers   1878 (*BAL*)

BAL gives this as Ward, Lock & Tyler (1878), in wrappers, with the cover title,

Complete Tales, stated as received at the *BM* on Nov. 18, 1878. If the imprint is as *BAL* gives it and if it was deposited in 1878, then this issue is a reissue of the (1874) issue, using the same title page.
Also 1874

1279 ANONYMOUS *Bicycling.* Illustrated. 1/o sewed   1878
Captain Crawley's Shilling Handbooks. This has no date, 17 cm., 116 pp., by a member of the Dark Blue Bicycle Club.

1280 GUSTAVE AIMARD (OLIVER GLOUX) *The Insurgent Chief.* 12mo. 1/o sewed 1878?
This has no date, 18 cm., in pink pictorial wrappers probably, although I have two titles in white wrappers. This series of reissues is edited by (Lascelles Wraxall). There are ads on the endpapers and back cover. It is a reissue of the C. H. Clarke issue of (1874). The first edition was *Le Montenero*, Paris, 1864, 18 cm. The first English edition was issued by C. H. Clarke, London (1867), 16.5 cm., 344 pp., at 2/o boards, edited by Wraxall, in Apr. It was reissued by Clarke (1874), 2/o, listed in the *Spect* on Oct. 3, with 344 pp. George Vickers, London, issued it, 1876, 118 pp., edited by Percy St. John; reissued by J. & R. Maxwell, London, no date, in white decorated wrappers, in 1878 or 1879.
See 1880

1281 GUSTAVE AIMARD *The Last of the Incas.* 12mo. 1/o sewed   1878?
This is my copy, no date, 18 cm., 317 pp., in white pictorial wrappers in red, green, and black, with ads on the endpapers, back cover, and verso of the half-title. There is a catalog paged (1)–28 at the back. This is a reissue of the 1862 edition.
Also 1862. See 1880

1282 GUSTAVE AIMARD *The Indian Scout.* 12mo. 1/o sewed   1878?
This has no date, a reissue of the 1861 edition, 429 pp. See *The Insurgent Chief* above for binding.
Also 1861. See 1880

1283 GUSTAVE AIMARD *The Border Rifles.* 12mo. 1/o sewed   1878?
Also 1861. See 1880

1284 GUSTAVE AIMARD *The Freebooters.* 12mo. 1/o sewed   1878?
Also 1861. See 1880

1285 GUSTAVE AIMARD *The Red Track.* 12mo. 1/o sewed   1878?
Also 1862. See 1880

1286 GUSTAVE AIMARD *The Queen of the Savannah.* 12mo. 1/o sewed   1878?
Also 1862. See 1880

1287 GUSTAVE AIMARD *The Buccaneer Chief.* 12mo. 1/o sewed   1878?
Also 1864. See 1880

1288 GUSTAVE AIMARD *The Smuggler Chief.* 12mo. 1/o sewed   1878?
Also 1864. See 1880

1289 GUSTAVE AIMARD *The Bee Hunters.* 12mo. 1/o sewed   1878?
Also 1864. See 1880

1290 GUSTAVE AIMARD *Stoneheart.* 12mo. 1/o sewed   1878?
This is my copy, no date, 18 cm., 322 pp., in pink pictorial wrappers in red, green, and black, with ads on the endpapers, back cover, and with a list of titles in this series on the verso of the half-title.
Also 1865. See 1880

1291 LORD BYRON *The Poetical Works of Lord Byron.* 1/6 sewed, 2/o cloth   1878?
Books for All Time No. 17. The number in this series indicates a July date of issue.

This is a reissue of the Moxon edition of 1870, no date, 604 pp., but without the memoir and illustrations. It is edited by W. M. Rossetti. The Moxon issue was 1870, 18.5 cm., 604 pp., illustrated. Ward, Lock issued a new edition, Cr 8vo, at 3/6 cloth, listed in the *Spect* on July 10, 1880. *The Poetical Works* were issued in 8 vols. by James Murray, London, Fcp 8vo, 7/0 each, vols. 1–4 listed in the *Edinburgh Review* as published Mar. 10–June 10, 1815; vol. 5, Sept.–Dec. 1816; vol. 6, Nov. 1817–Mar. 1818; vol. 8, Jan.–Apr. 1820. Murray issued *Poems*, 5 vols., Fcp 8vo, 35/0, in Jan. 1821.

1292 ROBERT BURNS *The Poetical Works of Robert Burns.* 1/6 sewed, 2/0 cloth 1878?

Books for All Time No. 20. This has no date and 512 pp., a reissue of the Moxon edition of (1871), which was 18.5 cm., illustrated, edited with a memoir by W. M. Rossetti. Ward, Lock issued it at 3/6 cloth, listed in the *Spect* on Aug. 5, 1871. I suspect this listing was for the Moxon issue, as Ward, Lock took over Moxon in 1870. The present edition does not have the illustrations or the memoir. *Poems, Chiefly in the Scottish Dialect* was issued by John Wilson, Kilmarnock, 1786, 8vo, 240 pp., at 3/0 sewed, in an edition of 612 copies, published on July 31. *The Poetical Works* was issued by D. Appleton, New York, 1842, 12mo, 575 pp., abridged, edited by James Currie, listed in the *United States Magazine* (monthly) for Dec. 1842.

1293 FELICIA HEMANS *The Poetical Works of Mrs. Felicia Hemans.* 1/6 sewed, 2/0 cloth 1878?

Books for All Time No. 21. This has no date and 595 pp., a reissue of the Moxon issue of (1873), which was edited by W. M. Rossetti with a memoir. The present edition does not have the illustrations or the memoir of the Moxon issue. *Poems* was issued by T. Cadell & W. Davies, London,

1808, 28 cm., 111 pp., illustrated; and by Hilliard, Gray, Little & Wilkins, Boston, 2-vols.-in-1, 1826–27, 25 cm. *The Poetical Works* was issued by Evert Duyckinck, New York, 2 vols., 1828, the fourth American edition. *The Complete Works* was issued by D. Appleton, New York, 1844, reprinted from the last English edition, listed in the *Knickerbocker* for Dec. 1844.

1294 ALEXANDER POPE *The Poetical Works of Alexander Pope.* 1/6 sewed, 2/0 cloth 1878?

Books for All Time No. 22. This has no date and 600 pp., a reissue of the Moxon edition of (1873), which was 18.5 cm., 600 pp., illustrated, 3/6 cloth, edited with a memoir by W. M. Rossetti. The present edition does not have the memoir or the illustrations. *The Works*, vol. 1, was issued by Plintot, London, 1717, 30.5 cm., 468 pp.; and vol. 2 was issued by L. Gilliver, London, 1735, 30 cm., illustrated. *The Works* was issued by B. Lintot, etc., London, 4 parts, 1718, 1716 (parts 2 and 4 were dated 1716). *The Poetical Works* was issued by R. & A. Foulis, Glasgow, 3 vols., 1768, 13 cm., illustrated.

1295 THOMAS CAMPBELL *The Poetical Works of Thomas Campbell.* 1/6 sewed, 2/0 cloth 1878?

Books for All Time No. 23. This is (1878), with 420 pp., a reissue of the Moxon issue of (1871), which was 18.5 cm., 420 pp., illustrated, 3/6 cloth, edited with a memoir by W. M. Rossetti. It was listed in the *Spect* on Jan. 20, 1872, as issued by Ward, Lock, Cr 8vo, 3/6 cloth, edited by Rossetti. I suspect this is the above Moxon issue as Ward, Lock took over Moxon in 1870. The present edition does not have the memoir or the illustrations. *Poems* was issued by Longmans, London, 2-vols.-in-1, 1810, 17 cm. Henry Colburn, London, issued *The Poetical Works*, 2 vols, 1828, 20.5 cm., portrait, 18/0 boards, in June, said to be "Now first collected." *The Poetical Works* was issued by D. W. Farrand & Green, Albany; etc., 2 vols., 1810, 19.5 cm; and by Philip H. Nicklin & Co., Baltimore; Farrand & Green, Albany; etc., 1810, 18 cm., 296 pp.

1296 SAMUEL T. COLERIDGE *The Poetical Works of Samuel T. Coleridge.* 1/6 sewed, 2/0 cloth   1878

Books for All Time No. 24. This is (1878), with 421 pp., a reissue of the Moxon edition of 1871 or 1872, which had 424 pp., illustrations, edited with a memoir by W. M. Rossetti. The present edition does not have the memoir or the illustrations. The Moxon was probably (1872) as such was given by Thomas J. Wise in his bibliography of Coleridge, Cr 8vo, 424 pp., illustrated, edited by Rossetti. *Poems* was issued by J. Cottle & Messrs. Robinson, London, 1797, the second edition, 16.5 cm., 278 pp., 6/0, in dark green boards, advertised in the *Morning Post* as published on Oct. 28. It included poems by Charles Lamb and Charles Lloyd. *Poems* was issued by Longmans, London, 1803, third edition, 18 cm., 202 pp., in drab pink boards. *The Poetical Works* was issued by Pickering, London, 1828, 12mo, 15/0, in Aug.; and by Hooker, Philadelphia, 1842, edited by Herman Hooker, 256 pp.

1297 THOMAS MOORE *The Poetical Works of Thomas Moore.* 1/6 sewed, 2/0 cloth 1878

Books for All Time No. 25. This is (1878), with 595 pp., a reissue of the Moxon edition of (1872), which was illustrated and edited by W. M. Rossetti, with a memoir. The present edition does not have the memoir or the illustrations. *The Poetical Works of the Late Thomas Little* was issued by J. & T. Carpenter, London, 1801, 17 cm., 175 pp., 7/6, in June. *The Poetical Works of Thomas Moore* was issued by E. & J. B. Young & Co., New York, 1800, 18 cm., 670 pp.; and *The Poetical Works of the Late*

Thomas Little was issued by Hugh Maxwell, Philadelphia, 1804, 19 cm., 193 pp.

1298 PERCY B. SHELLEY *The Poetical Works of Percy B. Shelley.* 1/6 sewed, 2/0 cloth   1878?

Books for All Time No. 26. This has no date and 616 pp., a reissue of the Moxon edition of 1870, 616 pp., illustrated, edited and with a memoir by W. M. Rossetti. *The Poetical Works* was issued by William Benbow, London, 1826, vol. 1, part 1; and he issued *Miscellaneous and Posthumous Poems*, 1826. *The Poetical Works* was issued by Edward Moxon, London, 4 vols., 1839, edited by Mrs. Shelley, Cr 8vo, portrait, 5/0 each. Vols. 1–3 were listed in the *Spect* in 1839 on Jan. 26, Mar. 2, and Apr. 6, respectively. *The Poetical Works* was issued by Porter & Coates, Philadelphia, 1839, 24 cm., 391 pp.

1299 THOMAS HOOD, THE ELDER *The Poetical Works of Thomas Hood.* Second series. 1/6 sewed, 2/0 cloth 1878?

Books for All Time No. 27. This is a reissue of a Moxon edition, edited by Rossetti. See the first series above.

1300 JAMES THOMSON *The Poetical Works of James Thomson.* 1/6 sewed, 2/0 cloth   1878

Books for All Time No. 28. This is (1878) with 508 pp., a reissue without the memoir or illustrations of the Moxon edition of (1873). The latter was 18.5 cm., 508 pp., illustrated, edited and with a memoir by W. M. Rossetti. This 1873 edition of Moxon was probably the one listed in the *Spect* on Aug. 2, 1873, Cr 8vo, 3/6 cloth, edited by Rossetti, issued by Ward, Lock. This is possible as Ward, Lock took over Moxon in 1870. *The Poetical Works* was issued by J. E. Shaw, Dublin, 1751, 360 pp., illustrated; and was issued by Benjamin Johnson, Philadelphia, 2 vol., 1804, 14.5

cm., frontispiece (portrait) in vol. 1, and a plate in vol. 2. *Poems* (except *The Seasons*) was issued by Alexander Donaldson, Edinburgh, 1763, 18 cm., 228 pp. Vol. 2 of *The Works* was issued by A. Millar, London, 1736, 4to; he issued 4 vols., 1857, 12mo, illustrated; and he issued 2 vols., 1738.

1301 MARTIN F. TUPPER *Proverbial Philosophy.* 1/6 sewed, 2/o cloth   1878?
Books for All Time No. 29. This is a reissue of a Moxon edition issued by Ward, Lock in 1871, Cr 8vo, 3/6 cloth, listed in the *Spect* on Sept. 16, 1871, edited by W. M. Rossetti, 456 pp., with a portrait, containing both series. Ward, Lock issued a new edition in 1880, Cr 8vo, 3/6 cloth, listed in the *Spect* on July 10. Moxon issued the Bijou edition in 1866, the 200th thousand, listed in *Notes & Queries* on Aug. 4. The first edition of the first series was issued by Joseph Rickerby, London, 1838, 23 cm., 224 pp., 7/o, in blue-black cloth stamped in blind, with 4 pp. of ads at the back. It was listed in the *Ath* on Jan. 27, 1838. He issued the second edition in 1838, revised with additions, p 8vo, 6/o, noticed in the *Spect* on Sept. 29. It was issued in Boston by J. Dowe, reprinted from the London edition, given a short review in *Godey's Lady's Book* for July 1840. The first edition of the second series was issued by J. Hatchard & Son, London, 1842, 20.5 cm., 315 pp., 7/o, listed in the *Spect* on Oct. 15. He advertised the fourth edition in the *Spect* on June 19, 1844, p 8vo, 7/o cloth boards, as "Just published." The second series appeared in *Ainsworth's Magazine* in the second issue, advertised in the *Spect* on Feb. 26, 1842. The first and second series were issued by Herman Hooker, Philadelphia, 1843, an authorized edition, 21 cm., from the fifth London edition, listed in *Godey's Lady's Book* for Dec. 1843. Saxton & Miles, New York, issued an edition for the author, claimed to be the first authorized

American edition, listed in the *Knickerbocker* for Nov. 1845.

1302 ANONYMOUS *Humorous Poems.* 1/6 sewed, 2/o cloth   1878?
Books for All Time No. 30. This has no date and 488 pp., a reissue of the Moxon edition of (1872), which was 18.5 cm., 488 pp., selected and edited by W. M. Rossetti.

1303 ANONYMOUS *American Poems.* 1/6 sewed, 2/o cloth   1878 (*Eng Cat*)
Books for All Time No. 31. This is (1878), 18.5 cm., 512 pp., a reissue of the Moxon edition of about 1872, which had illustrations, was 18.5 cm., 512 pp., with the pieces edited and selected by W. M. Rossetti.

1304 THOMAS DAY *The History of Sandford and Merton.* New and Revised Edition. 12mo. Illustrated. 1/o sewed, 2/o cloth   1878?
Youth's Library of Wonders and Adventures No. 13. This has no date and 286 pp., a reissue of the Ward, Lock & Tyler edition of (1873), which was a new and revised edition with 286 pp., illustrated. The first edition was John Stockdale, London, 3 vols., 1783, 1786, 1789, 16.6 cm., anonymous. In the United States it was issued by W. Young, Philadelphia, 2-vols.-in-1, 1788, the fifth edition corrected. A third vol. was issued by Young, 1791.

1305 BARON MUNCHAUSEN (RUDOLPH E. RASPE) *Baron Munchausen: His Life, Travels, and Adventures.* A New Edition. 12mo. 1/o sewed, 2/o cloth   1878?
Youth's Library of Wonders and Adventures No. 14. This is my copy, no date, 17.1 cm., 163 pp., in white pictorial wrappers, printed in red, blue, and black, with "The Youth's Library" on the front. It has Ward, Lock & Co. on the title page and front cover, commercial ads and Ward, Lock &

Tyler ads on the endpapers, an ad on the back cover, a Ward, Lock & Co. ad on the verso of the half-title, and a Ward, Lock & Co. catalog paged (1)–14 at the back. The first edition was issued by Smith, London, 1786, *Baron Munchausen's Narrative of His Marvellous Travels etc.*, anonymous, a 49-page pamphlet, at 1/0. Smith reissued it, 1786, and then sold the rights to G. Kearsley, London, who had a writer add 15 chapters to Raspe's 5 (chapters 2–6 then and ever since). He issued the fourth edition, 1786, *Gulliver Revived*, 16 cm., 172 pp., illustrated, at 2/0. It was issued in New York, 1787. *Travels and Adventures of Baron Munchausen* was issued by D. Appleton, New York, a new edition, in Nov. 1858, illustrated by Crowquill (Alfred and Charles Forrester), and reissued about Dec. 6, 1859, 8vo, colored plates, $2.50. This Appleton edition was issued in London by Trübner, Cr 8vo, anonymous, illustrated by Crowquill, 7/6, advertised in the *Spect* on Nov. 20, 1858, as "This day." Frederick Warne, London, issued an edition (1878), 32.5 cm., 103 pp., illustrated in color by A. Bichard, 10/6, listed in the *Spect* on Dec. 7, 1878.

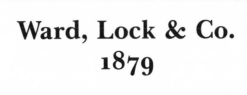

Ward, Lock & Co.
1879

1306 C. J. HAMILTON *Marriage Bonds.*
2/0 boards, 2/6 cloth   Jan. 11 (*Ath*)
Library of Favourite Authors No. 36. This is
probably the first edition. It is given by the
Eng Cat, but otherwise I cannot trace it.
Also 1886

1307 HENRY VIZETELLY *Facts About
Champagne and Other Sparkling Wines.*
Cr 8vo. Illustrated. 1/6, 2/6   Jan. 25 (*Ath*)
This is the first edition, 1879, 19 cm., 235
pp. The 1/6 issue had an ornamental
cover, but whether boards or paper I don't
know. It was advertised by Scribner, Welford, New York, in the *New-York Times* on
May 31, 1879, 12mo, illustrated, $.60
paper.

1308 JAMES MASON, ed. *The Year-Book of
Facts in Science and the Arts. 1878.* Cr 8vo.
2/6 boards, 3/6 cloth   Jan. 25 (*Spect*)
See 1875 for publishing history

1309 JEREMY TAYLOR *The Rule and
Exercises of Holy Living.* 12mo. 1/0,
1/6   1879 (*Eng Cat*)
Christian Knowledge Series No. 3. This is
(1879), edited by F. A. Malleson. The first
edition was issued by Richard Royston,
London, 1650, 14.5 cm., 410 pp., with
Royston on both the printed and engraved title pages. There is also a first edition with Royston on the engraved title
page, but Francis Ash, Worcester, on the
printed title page, 1650. The first American edition was issued by W. W. Woodward, Philadelphia, 1810, 336 pp.

1310 JEREMY TAYLOR *The Rule and
Exercises of Holy Dying.* 12mo. 1/0, 1/6
1879 (*Eng Cat*)
Christian Knowledge Series No. 4. This is
(1879), edited by F. A. Malleson. The first
edition was issued by Richard Royston,
London, 1651, 14.5 cm., 339 pp. A copy
was offered by a dealer, printed in London by Richard Royston and to be sold by
John Courtney Bookseller in Salisbury, 2
vols., 1651. There were variants of the
printed title page, including imprints of
Bristol, Worcester, and Norwich. The first
American edition was issued by W. W.
Woodward, Philadelphia, 1811, 17.5 cm.,
386 pp.

1311 PHILIP DODDRIDGE *Doddridge's
Rise and Progress of Religion.* 12mo. 1/0,
1/6   Feb. 15 (*Spect*)
Christian Knowledge Series No. 5. This is
(1879), edited by F. A. Malleson. The first
edition was issued by J. Waugh, London,
1745, 17 cm., 309 pp. It was issued by D.
Henchman, Boston, 1749, sixth edition,
with 89 and 264 pp.

1312 GUSTAVE AIMARD (OLIVER GLOUX)
The Flying Horseman. 12mo. 1/0 sewed
Mar.?
This is my copy, no date, 18.1 cm., 312
pp., in pink pictorial wrappers, with ads
on the back cover, the endpapers, and on
the verso of the half-title. There is a catalog paged (1)–8 at the back and a list of
the series on the verso of the title page.
The first edition was *Zeno Cabral*, issued at

Paris, 1864, 19 cm., 399 pp. The first English edition was issued by C. H. Clarke, London (1867), at 2/0 boards, 312 pp., in Apr. He reissued it (1874), at 2/0, listed in the *Spect* on Oct. 3, 1874. The present edition is a reissue of the Clarke issue. It was also issued by George Vickers, London, 1876, 19 cm., 120 pp., edited by Percy B. St. John; and reissued by J. & R. Maxwell in 1878 or 1879, 120 pp., in white wrappers.
See 1880

1313 BRET HARTE ET AL. *Bret Harte's Great Deadwood Mystery; With Tales, Sketches and Poetry by F. C. Burnand, J. G. Montefiore, H. S. Leigh, et al.*
Fcp 8vo. Illustrated. 1/0 sewed
Apr. 1 (*PC*)
Ward & Lock's Humorous Books. This is (1879), 16.5 cm., 164 pp., in pictorial wrappers, with ads on the back cover and on the inside covers, and with 28 pp. of ads at the back. It was received at the *BM* on May 22. The title story was in *Beeton's Christmas Annual* for 1878 (which see) on pp. (28)–45, illustrated, and it appeared in *Scribner's Monthly* for Dec. 1878 on pp. 177–188. It was in *The Twins of Table Mountain and Other Stories*, issued by Houghton, Osgood & Co., Boston, 1879, 15.5 cm., 249 pp., listed in *PW* on Nov. 1, in the *Ind* on Nov. 6, and it was deposited Oct. 17, 1879.
Also 1880

1314 ROSA M. KETTLE (MARY ROSA S. KETTLE) *Smugglers and Foresters.* 2/0 boards   Apr. 26 (*Spect*)
Library of Favourite Authors No. 37. This is 1879. The first edition was issued by T. C. Newby, London, 3 vols., 1851, 20 cm., anonymous, 31/6, listed in the *Spect* on Sept. 6. It was issued in *Hodgson's New Series of Novels*, vol. 3, in 1859, 16 cm., 381 pp., at 2/0, listed in the *Spect* on Sept. 10, 1859. It was also issued by Weir, London, 1875, author's edition, Cr 8vo, 406 pp., at

5/0, listed in the *Ath* on Jan. 30, 1875. James Weir & Knight, London, issued the fifth edition, p 8vo, at 5/0, advertised in the *Spect* on Dec. 11, 1875.

1315 EDWARD P. ROE *A Face Illumined.*
2/0 boards   Apr. 26 (*Spect*)
Library of Favourite Authors No. 39. This has no date. The first English edition was issued by Ward, Lock & Co. (1878), Cr 8vo, 10/6, advertised in the *Ath* on Dec. 7, 1878, as "Now ready, by special arrangement with the author," and it was listed on Dec. 14. They issued it at 3/6 cloth, Cr 8vo, listed in the *Spect* on June 21, 1879. The first American edition was issued by Dodd, Mead & Co., New York (1878), 19 cm., 658 pp., advertised in *Lit World* as "Published Nov. 16," and advertised in *PW* on Nov. 16 as "Ready" and listed there on Dec. 21, and listed in the *Nation* on Dec. 12, 1878. It was advertised in the *New-York Times* on Nov. 16, 1878, 12mo, $1.50, as "This day," and a Nov. 23 ad said the second edition was exhausted; the third edition, the 14th thousand, was advertised on Dec. 7 as $1.50.

1316 ROSA M. KETTLE *Hillesden on the Moors.* 12mo. 2/0 boards   May 24 (*Ath*)
Library of Favourite Authors No. 38. This has no date, 17.8 cm., with 331 pp. The first edition was issued by Samuel Tinsley, London, 2 vols., 1873, Cr 8vo, at 21/0, advertised in the *Ath* on May 31 as "Next week," and listed June 21. Weir & Knight issued it as the author's edition, 1877 (1876), at 5/0, listed in the *Spect* on Dec. 23, 1876.

1317 JOHN S. C. ABBOTT *The Life and Achievements of Christopher Columbus.*
12mo. Illustrated. 2/0 boards, 2/6, 3/6 cloth   May (*Bks*)
The Boys' Illustrated Library of Heroes, Patriots, and Pioneers No. 1. This is the first English edition, no date, 18 cm., 345 pp.

The first edition was issued by Dodd & Mead, New York (1875), 19 cm., 345 pp., portrait, listed in the *Ind* on Oct. 7 at $1.50. Dodd & Mead issued this series, called *American Pioneers and Patriots* and issued a new edition in 12 vols., 12mo, at $1.25 each in an ornamental binding, advertised in the *Christian Union* on Dec. 6, 1883. *Christopher Columbus* by Abbott was an article in *Harper's New Monthly Magazine* for May 1869.
Also 1882, 90

1318 JOHN BUNYAN *Pilgrim's Progress.*
12mo. Illustrated. 1/o sewed, 1/6 cloth
May (*Bks*)
Christian Knowledge Series No. 8. This is (1879), with 278 pp. Ward, Lock & Tyler issued this in 1865, a new edition, Fcp 8vo, at 2/6, listed in the *Reader* on May 6; and issued it with a memoir by Dulcken, in 1865, a new edition, Cr 4to, 304 pp., illustrated, 7/6, listed in the *Reader* on Aug. 5. The first edition was issued by Nathaniel Ponder, London, part 1, 1678, 15 cm., 232 pp.; part 2, 1684, 224 (i.e., 210) pp., illustrated. Thomas Fleet, Boston, issued the 17th edition, 1744, with 166 (176) pp.; and John M'Culloch, Philadelphia, issued three parts in 1 vol., 1789, part 3 being spurious.
Also 1882

1319 ALEXANDER KEITH *The Evidence of Prophecy.* Cheap Edition. 12mo. 1/o, 1/6
May?
Christian Knowledge Series No. 7. This is (1879), slightly abridged. It was issued by the Religious Tract Society, London (1830?), 162 pp., with a frontispiece, taken from a Waugh & Innes, Edinburgh, issue, 1828, 12mo, 346 pp., *Evidence of the Truth of the Christian Religion*. This latter edition was reissued by J. & J. Harper, New York, 1832, 18 cm., 284 pp. Waugh & Innes issued *Sketch of the Evidence from Prophecy*, 1823, with 214 pp. *The Evidence of Prophecy* was issued by the American

Tract Society, New York (1833), 15 cm., 144 pp., illustrated.

1320 MAX ADELER (CHARLES H. CLARK)
Random Shots. Copyright. 12mo.
Illustrated. 2/o boards   June 14 (*Ath*)
Household and Railway Books No. 40. This is the first English edition, my copy, no date, 18.1 cm., 326 pp., with both full-page and textual illustrations by Arthur B. Frost. It is in yellow boards, pictorially printed on the front in red, blue, and black, with the series title on the spine, and No. 40 on the front cover. There are ads on the back cover, the endpapers, and the verso of the half-title, and a leaf of ads and a 24-page catalog at the back. The first American edition was issued by J. M. Stoddart, Philadelphia, 1879, 18.5 cm., 326 pp., illustrated, listed in the *Ind* and in the *Nation* on June 26, and in *PW* on June 28. It was advertised in the *New-York Times* on June 14, illustrated, $.75 paper, $1.00 cloth, as "Ready."
Also 1883, 89, 1900

1321 WILLIAM PALEY *Horae Paulinae.*
12mo. 1/o sewed, 1/6 cloth   June 21
(*Spect*)
Christian Knowledge Series No. 9. This is (1879), edited and an introduction and notes by F. A. Malleson. The first edition was issued by R. Faulder, London, 1790, 21.5 cm., 426 pp.

1322 ROSA M. KETTLE (MARY ROSA S. KETTLE *Under the Grand Old Hills.*
2/o boards   June 28 (*Spect*)
Library of Favourite Authors No. 40. This has no date. The first edition was issued by James Weir & Knight, London, 1875, author's edition, Cr 8vo, at 5/o, advertised and listed in the *Ath* on June 19. The second edition, the same, was advertised in the *Spect* by Weir & Knight on Dec. 11, 1875.

1323 JOHN S. C. ABBOTT
Benjamin Franklin. 12mo.
Illustrated. 2/o boards, 2/6,
3/6 cloth   June?

Heroes, Patriots, and Pioneers No. 2. This
has no date, 17.5 cm., 373 pp. The first
edition was issued by Dodd, Mead & Co.,
New York (1876), 18.5 cm., 373 pp., illustrated, No. 12, the last volume in their series. It was listed in the *Nation* on June 1
and in the *Ind* on June 8 and advertised in
the *New-York Times* on May 27, at $1.50.
Also 1890

1324 STEPHEN W. FULLOM *The Man of
the World.* 2/o boards   July 5 (*Spect*)
Household and Railway Books No. 41. This
has no date.
Also 1858.

1325 WILLIAM PALEY *Natural Theology.*
12mo. 1/o, 1/6   July 5 (*Spect*)
Christian Knowledge Series No. 6. This is
(1879), 19 cm., 269 pp., edited by Francis
Young. The first edition was issued by R.
Faulder, London, 1802, 22.5 cm., 586 pp.
It was issued in the United States by John
Morgan, Philadelphia, 1802, 21.5 cm.,
402 pp.; and by D. & S. Whiting, Albany,
1803, 18 cm., 368 pp.

1326 ANONYMOUS *Fun for Everybody.*
Illustrated. 1/o sewed   July (*Bks*)
Comic Holiday Books No. 4. This is the first
edition, 1879, illustrated by J. Leech,
Theodore Hook, et al. It is a collection of
new humorous stories.

1327 MARIA EDGEWORTH *Helen.* 12mo.
1/o sewed, 1/6, 2/o cloth   July (*Bks*)
Lily Series No. 69. This has no date and
probably had 402 pp. The first edition
was issued by Bentley, London, 3 vols.,
1834, 19.5 cm., at 31/6, listed in the *Ath* on
Mar. 1 and published Feb. 22, according
to the Bentley private catalog. Bentley issued it as *Standard Novels* No. 71, 1838,

with 455 pp. It was issued by Bentley in
1875, advertised in the *Spect* on July 4 as
"Just published." It was issued in the
United States by Carey, Lea & Blanchard,
Philadelphia; etc., 2 vols., 1834, 21.5 cm.,
advertised in the *National Gazette and Literary Record* on Apr. 15, and reviewed in
the *Knickerbocker* for May. The cost book
of Carey & Lea states that 1,500 copies
were finished on Apr. 4, 1834, and it states
that Harper printed it on them ten days
after their issue came out but that they
sold all they printed. With no copyright it
was dog eat dog!

1328 JOHN S. C. ABBOTT
George Washington. 12mo.
Illustrated. 2/o boards, 2/6,
3/6 cloth   July?

Heroes, Patriots, and Pioneers No. 3. This is
(1879), with 360 pp. The cloth edition had
11 leaves of ads and was bound in red pictorial cloth. It was mentioned in editorial
matter in the *Ath* on Aug. 9. The first edition was issued by Dodd & Mead, New
York (copyright 1875), 18.5 cm., 360 pp.,
illustrated, $1.50, No. 11 of their series,
listed in the *Nation* on Jan. 6, 1876, and
advertised in the *New-York Times* on Dec.
11, 1875.
Also 1890

1329 JOHN S. C. ABBOTT *The Puritan
Captain.* 12 mo. Illustrated. 2/o boards,
2/6, 3/6 cloth   Aug. 16 (*Spect*)
Heroes, Patriots, and Pioneers No. 4. This
has no date and 512 pp. The first edition
was *Miles Standish, the Puritan Captain*, issued by Dodd & Mead, New York, 1872,
18.5 cm., 372 pp., illustrated, $1.50 cloth,
listed in the *Ind* and in the *Nation* on Jan.
9, 1873.
Also 1890

1330 JOHN S. C. ABBOTT *Boone, the
Backwoodsman.* 12mo. Illustrated. 2/o
boards, 2/6, 3/6 cloth   Aug. 30 (*Spect*)
Heroes, Patriots, and Pioneers No. 5. This
has no date, 17.5 cm., with 331 pp. The

first edition was *Daniel Boone, the Pioneer of Kentucky,* issued by Dodd & Mead, New York, 1872, 18.5 cm., 331 pp., illustrated, $1.50 cloth, No. 1 of the series, listed in *Godey's Lady's Book* for Feb. 1873, and thus probably issued in Nov. or Dec. 1872. It was advertised in the *New-York Times* on Nov. 28, 1872, as "This day."
Also 1890

1331 ANONYMOUS *Pictorial Guide to London.* [New edition]. Illustrated.
1/o   Sept. 6 (*Spect*)
This has no date, 17 cm., probably with 222 pp., 62 pp. It was reissued passim, always with no date.
Also 1889, 97

1332 ANONYMOUS *Babies, and How to Take Care of Them.* Illustrated. 1/o sewed, 1/6 cloth   Oct. 25 (*Spect*)
Sylvia's Home Help Series No. 4. This is the first edition with 114 pp. and with a preface signed J. C.

1333 ANONYMOUS *The House and Furniture.* Illustrated. 1/o sewed, 1/6 cloth   Oct. (*Bks*)
Sylvia's Home Help Series No. 6. This is the first edition, no date, with 202 pp.

1334 MARK TWAIN (SAMUEL L. CLEMENS) *The Innocents Abroad.* 2/o boards   Oct. (*Bks*)
Also 1874, 84. See 1873, 75

1335 JOHN S. C. ABBOTT *The Terror of the Indians.* 12mo. Illustrated. 2/o boards, 2/6, 3/6 cloth   Oct.?
Heroes, Patriots, and Pioneers No. 6. This is the first English edition, the life of David Crockett (1879), 17.5 cm., 350 pp. The first edition was *David Crockett,* issued by Dodd & Mead, New York, 1874, 18.5 cm., 350 pp., illustrated, listed in the *Nation* on July 2, and advertised in the *New-York Times* on Sept. 19, as No. 6, already pub-

lished. The present edition was mentioned in editorial matter in the *Ath* on Nov. 8.

1336 JOHN S. C. ABBOTT *The Hero of the Prairies.* 12mo. Illustrated. 2/o boards, 2/6, 3/6 cloth   Nov. 15 (*Spect*)
Heroes, Patriots, and Pioneers No. 7. This is the first English edition, the life of Kit Carson (1879), with 348 pp. The first edition was issued by Dodd & Mead, New York, as *Kit Carson,* 1873, 18.5 cm., 348 pp., illustrated, $1.50 cloth, listed in the *Nation* on Dec. 4, 1873, and in the *Ind* on Dec. 18. It was advertised in the *New-York Times* on Nov. 22, 1873, as No. 5, "This day."

1337 ANONYMOUS *Sylvia's Home Journal Christmas Number.* 1/o   Nov. 25 (*Ath*)
This was the second year of issue.

1338 DANIEL DEFOE *Robinson Crusoe.* 12mo. Illustrated. 1/o sewed, 2/o cloth Nov. (*Bks*)
Youth's Library of Wonders and Adventures No. 15.
Also 1863, 64, 68, 85

1339 MARY M. SHERWOOD (M. M. BUTT, later SHERWOOD) *The History of the Fairchild Family.* 12mo. 1/o sewed, 1/6, 2/o cloth   Nov. (*Bks*)
Lily Series No. 70.
Also 1875

1340 MAX ADELER ET AL. *Seven Poor Tradesmen.* 8vo. Illustrated. 1/o sewed Nov. (*Bks*)
This is Beeton's Christmas Annual, the 20th season, my copy, 21.2 cm., 128 pp., many textual illustrations, double columns, with contributions from Adeler, Henry Frith, J. G. Montefiore, et al. It has white wrappers, decorated in red, blue, and black on the front with many small illustrations. There are ads on the inside

covers and on the back cover. It proceeds as follows: Beeton's Christmas Annual Advertiser, 8 pp.; 6 pp. of ads, the last 2 on blue paper; 128 pp. of text; a yellow slip insert; Beeton's Christmas Annual Advertiser, 2 pp.; text (131)–135; the advertiser again, 17 pp.

1341　MRS. A. G. F. ELIOT JAMES　*A Guide to Indian Household Management.* 1/o sewed, 1/6 cloth　Nov.?

Sylvia's Home Help Series No. 7. It is mentioned in editorial matter in the *Ath* on Nov. 22. It is the first edition (1879), with 90 pp.

1342　JOHN W. KIRTON　*Intoxicating Drinks.* 12mo. 1/o boards　Dec. 20 (*Spect*)

This is the first edition, my copy, no date, 18 cm., 144 pp., with commercial ads on the endpapers and on the back cover. It is bound in gray boards, printed and with a small illustration on the front cover in red and black. It has a preface (Dec. 1, 1879). The *Spect* listing is for 1/6, so possibly it was also issued in cloth at 1/6.

1343　JOHN S. C. ABBOTT　*The Spanish Cavalier.* 12mo. Illustrated. 2/o boards, 2/6, 3/6 cloth　Dec. (*Bks*)

Heroes, Patriots, and Pioneers No. 8. This has no date and 351 pp., the first English edition, the life of De Soto. The first edition was *Ferdinand De Soto. The Discoverer of the Mississippi,* issued by Dodd & Mead, New York, 1873, 18.5 cm., 351 pp., illustrated, $1.50 cloth, listed in the *Nation* and in the *Ind* on May 8.

1344　ÉMILE ERCKMANN & PIERRE CHATRIAN　*Daniel Rock.* 12mo. 1/o sewed　Dec. (*Bks*)

This has no date, with 170 pp. The first edition was *Maître Daniel Rock,* issued in Paris, 1861, with 334 pp. The first English edition was issued by John C. Hotten,

London, as *Peace,* translated by H. L. Williams, no date, 12mo, 1/o sewed, about Dec. 7, 1872.

1345　JOSEPH COOK (FLAVIUS J. COOK) *Boston Monday Lectures. Life and Soul. . . . Biology and Transcendentalism.* 1/o sewed, 1/6 cloth　1879 (*Eng Cat*)

This has no date and 182 pp. Vol. I, issued by Ward, Lock, Cr 8vo, 5/o, was listed in the *Spect* on Sept. 9, 1882. *Transcendentalism* was also issued by David Bryce & Son, Glasgow, 1878, 245 pp.; and R. D. Dickinson, London, issued all six lectures, 1879, a new edition, revised, in 6 vols., 1879, the student's edition, at 1/6 cloth each, advertised in the *Times Weekly Edition* (London) on Nov. 14, 1879. Vol. I of the Boston Monday Lectures was *Biology,* issued by James R. Osgood & Co., Boston, 1877, 19.5 cm., 325 pp., with three colored plates, advertised in the *New-York Times* on Sept. 30 at $1.50 as "This day." The fourth edition was advertised, the same, on Oct. 6; and the tenth edition was advertised, the same, on Nov. 28. Vol. II was *Transcendentalism,* issued by Osgood (copyright 1877), with some copies dated 1878, 19.5 cm., 305 pp., advertised in the *New-York Times* on Nov. 28, 1877, $1.50, "This day." Vol. III was *Orthodoxy,* issued by Osgood in 1878, 343 pp., at $1.50, advertised in the *New-York Times* on Jan. 27, 1878, as "This day." This was apparently not issued by Ward, Lock.
For vol. IV see 1881

1346　RAWDON CRAWLEY (GEORGE F. PARDON)　*Lawn Tennis, Croquet, Badminton, etc.* 1/o sewed　1879 (*Eng Cat*)

This is probably the first edition. *Beeton's Book of Games: Badminton,* by Crawley, was listed in the *Reader* on Apr. 21, 1866, 18mo, o/6 sewed, issued by Beeton, London.

1347 ANONYMOUS *The Contented Home.* 18mo. Illustrated. 1/o cloth 1879 (*Eng Cat*)

Good-Aim Books No. 27. This is (1879), 174 pp., illustrated, the first edition.

1348 MARIE VON ROSKOWSKA *Help One Another.* 18mo. 1/o cloth   1879 (*Eng Cat*)

Good-Aim Books No. 28. This is a translation by J. Frederick Smith of *In Mitten der Nordsee*, which was issued by the Amerikanische Tratatgesellschaft, New York, no date, 16mo, 128 pp. It was issued by the Lutheran Board of Publication, Philadelphia, as *Die Halligen*, 1869, 16 mo.

1349 ANONYMOUS *Buried in the Snow.* 18mo. Illustrated. 1/o cloth   1879 (*BM*)

Good-Aim Books No. 29. This is (1879), 161 pp., translated from the German. It was issued by the Lutheran Board of Publication, Philadelphia, 1870, 17 cm., 161 pp., illustrated.

1350 ANONYMOUS *The Lost Child.* 18mo. Illustrated. 1/o cloth   1879 (*Eng Cat*)

Good-Aim Books No. 30. The Beeton name has been dropped from this series, and it is now issued only in cloth. This is the first English edition of this title, no date, 200 pp., translated from the German.

1351 MARY A. PAULL, later RIPLEY *Summer House Stories.* 18mo. 1/o cloth   1879 (*Eng Cat*)

Good-Aim Books. This is the first edition, with 145 pp. The *Eng Cat* gives it as published in 1879, and the *BM* gives it as (1880).

1352 JOHN W. KIRTON, ed. *The Standard Popular Reciter.* 1/o boards, 1/6 cloth 1879 (*Eng Cat*)

This is the first edition, no date. Also 1888

1353 JULES VERNE *Around the World in Eighty Days.* 12mo. Illustrated. 1/o sewed, 2/o cloth.   1879 (*Eng Cat*)

Youth's Library of Wonders and Adventures No. 16. This has no date and 141 pp., a different translation from the Osgood and Low editions. *Le Tour de Monde en Quatre-Vingt Jours* appeared in *Le Temps*, Paris, Nov. 6–Dec. 22, 1872; and the first book edition was issued by Hetzel, Paris (1873), 18 cm., 312 pp. The first edition in English was issued by James R. Osgood & Co., Boston, 1873, *The Tour of the World in Eighty Days*, translated by G. M. Towle. It was listed in the *Nation* on July 3 and in *PW* on July 5. It was reissued, 1874, *Around the World in Eighty Days*, about Dec. 18, 1873, 20 cm., 315 pp., illustrated, in the Towle translation. It was issued by Porter & Coates, Philadelphia, from the Osgood plates, 1873, *Around the World in Eighty Days*. The first English edition was issued by Sampson Low, London, 1874 (1873), 18.5 cm., 315 pp., illustrated, 7/6, with a 32-page catalog (Oct. 1872), in the Towle translation. It was advertised in the *Ath* on Nov. 8 as "Ready," and listed on Nov. 15, 1873. Low issued the author's edition, 1876, my copy, 18.5 cm., 192 pp., frontispiece and six full-page illustrations, 1/o stiff wrappers, 2/o cloth, listed in the *Ath* on May 6, 1876. My copy is in the stiff wrappers. Low reissued it in 1879, a new edition, Cr 8vo, 3/6 cloth, listed in the *Spect* on Oct. 4. George Routledge, London, issued it as *Round the World in Eighty Days*, 1879 (1878), translated by Henry Frith.

Ward, Lock & Co.
1880

1354 JOHN MASON, ed. *The Year-Book of Facts in Science and the Arts. For 1879.* Cr 8vo. 2/6 boards, 3/6 cloth   Jan. 10 (*Spect*)
See 1875 for publishing details

1355 JOHN S. C. ABBOTT *The Buccaneer Chiefs.* 12mo. Illustrated. 2/o boards, 2/6, 3/6 cloth   Jan. 10 (*Spect*)
Heroes, Patriots, and Pioneers No. 11. This is the first English edition (1880), with 373 pp. The first edition was issued by Dodd & Mead, New York, as *Captain William Kidd and the Early Buccaneers*, 1874, 18.5 cm., 373 pp., illustrated, $1.50 cloth, advertised in the *Ind* and in the *Nation* on Sept. 24 as "Now ready," and listed in the latter on Oct. 22.
Also 1882

1356 JAMES MASON, ed. *How to Excel in Study.* 1/o sewed, 1/6, 2/o cloth   Jan. 31 (*Spect*)
Friendly Counsel Series No. 12. This is the first edition (1880), 196 pp., with the series title on the cover.

1357 HENRY VIZETELLY *Facts About Port and Madeira.* 12mo. 1/6 ornamental cover, 2/6 cloth   Feb. 28 (*Spect*)
This is the first edition with the imprint Ward, Lock & Co., London; Scribner & Welford, New York, 1880. It is 18 cm., with 211 pp. The Scribner & Welford was advertised in the *New-York Times* on Mar. 27, 1880, 12mo, illustrated, $.60 picture boards, as "This day." It was listed in *PW* on May 8, 1880.

1358 ANONYMOUS *The Sixpenny Economical Cookery Book.* o/6 sewed   Feb. (*Bks*)
This has no date, a new edition, 124 pp., illustrated.
Also 1861, 75

1359 (CAPTAIN CRAWLEY) GEORGE F. PARDON *Popular Gymnastics, Athletics, Pedestrianism, etc.* Illustrated. 1/o sewed   Feb. (*Bks*)
This is the first edition, no date, 16 cm., 160 pp., with the preface signed by Rawden Crawley.

1360 BRET HARTE, MARK TWAIN, ET AL. *Bret Harte's Deadwood Mystery and Mark Twain's Nightmare. Tales, Sketches and Poetry.* 2/o boards   Mar. 1 (*PC*)
Household and Railway Books No. 42. This had pieces by F. C. Burnand, H. S. Leigh, et al. also.
See 1879 for the first title and 1878 and 1885 for the second

1361 JOHN W. KIRTON *The Standard Speaker and Elocutionist.* 12mo. 1/o boards, 1/6 cloth   Apr. 10 (*Spect*)
This is the first edition, no date, with 248 pp.
Also 1888

1362 ROSA M. KETTLE (MARY ROSA S. KETTLE) *The Wreckers.* 12mo. 2/o boards   Apr. 10 (*Spect*)
Library of Favourite Authors No. 42. This has no date and 402 pp. The first edition

was issued by T. C. Newby, London, 3 vols., 1857, p 8vo, anonymous, 31/6, listed in the *Spect* on May 9. The second edition was issued by James Weir & Knight, London, 1876 (1875), p 8vo, 5/o cloth, listed in the *Spect* on Dec. 18, 1875.

1363 ANONYMOUS *British Ferns and Mosses.* 12mo. Illustrated. 1/o boards Apr. (*Bks*)

Useful Handbooks. This is my copy, no date, 17.3 cm., 136 pp., with many textual illustrations. There are ads on the endpapers and the back cover, and there is an 18-page catalog at the back. It is in white boards, decorated with ferns on the front in red, green, and black, with the series title on the front.

Also 1861, 69

1364 ANONYMOUS *Wild Flowers.* 12mo. Illustrated. 1/o boards Apr. (*Bks*)

Useful Handbooks. This has no date and 140 pp.

Also 1861, 69

1365 ANONYMOUS *Marine Botany and Sea-Side Objects.* 12mo. Illustrated. 1/o boards Apr. (*Bks*)

Useful Handbooks. This has no date.

Also 1861, 69

1366 WILLIAM SHAKESPEARE *The Complete Works of Shakespeare.* 2/6 boards Apr. (*Bks*)

This probably has no date, and it has 974 pp., with a biography by W. M. Rossetti.

Also 1887

1367 ROSA M. KETTLE (MARY ROSA S. KETTLE) *Fabian's Tower.* 12mo. 2/o boards May 8 (*Ath*)

Library of Favourite Authors No. 41. This is my copy, no date, 17.6 cm., 340 pp., in pictorial yellow boards, printed in red, blue, and black, with the series title on the spine. There are ads on the endpapers,

the back cover, and on the versos of the halftitle and title page, and there are 6 pp. of ads at the back. The first edition was issued by T. C. Newby, London, 3 vols., 1852, p 8vo, anonymous, 31/6, listed in the *Spect* on May 29. James Weir & Knight, London, issued the author's edition, 1875, Cr 8vo, 5/o cloth, listed in the *Spect* on Apr. 17, 1875. The third edition was issued by them, p 8vo, 5/o cloth, listed in the *Spect* on Dec. 11, 1875. Hodgson, London, issued it as *Hodgson's New Series of Novels* No. 7, 1860, anonymous, 336 pp., at 2/o, listed in the *Spect* on May 26.

1368 RICHARD COBBOLD *Freston Tower.* 12mo. 1/o sewed, 1/6, 2/o cloth May 8 (*Spect*)

Lily Series No. 71. This has no date and 303 pp.

Also 1865, 70, 75

1369 F. C. ARMSTRONG *The Sunny South.* 12mo. 2/o boards May 22 (*Spect*)

Library of Favourite Authors No. 46. This has no date and is a reissue of the 1866 edition. Sadleir had a copy, after 1884, a yellowback issued by Ward, Lock in the *Select Library of Fiction*.

Also 1866, 90

1370 ALBANY FONBLANQUE, JR. *A Lease for Lives.* 12mo. 2/o boards May 22 (*Spect*)

Household and Railway Books No. 44. This is a reissue of *Hector Mainwaring*, with no date and 259 pp.

Also 1861 as *Hector Mainwaring*

1371 STEPHEN W. FULLOM *The King and the Countess.* 12mo. 2/o boards May 29 (*Spect*)

Household and Railway Books No. 43.

Also 1857, 58

1372 ANONYMOUS *A Boy's Life Aboard Ship.* 12mo. Illustrated. 1/o sewed, 2/o cloth 1880 (*Eng Cat*)

Youth's Library of Wonders and Adventures No. 17. The first edition was issued by Ward & Lock, Fcp 8vo, 3/6 cloth, in 1860.

1373 SAILOR CHARLEY *Life in a Whaler.*
12mo. 1/o sewed, 2/o cloth   May (*Bks*)
Youth's Library of Wonders and Adventures
No. 18. The first edition was issued by
Ward & Lock in 1860, Fcp 8vo, at 3/6
cloth. The *U Cat* gives also (1860), 18 cm.,
pp. (201)–424, illustrated. I conjecture
that this and the previous title were issued
in 1 vol. at some time, with continuous
pagination.

1374 JOHN S. C. ABBOTT *Through Prairie
and Forest; or, The Adventures of de La
Salle.* 12mo. Illustrated. 1/o boards, 2/6,
3/6 cloth   May?
Heroes, Patriots, and Pioneers No. 9. This
was mentioned in editorial matter in the
Ath on July 17. It has no date and 384 pp.
The first edition was issued by Dodd &
Mead, New York, as *The Adventures of
Chevalier de la Salle*, illustrated, listed in
the *Nation* on June 10, 1875, and listed in
Godey's Lady's Book for July 1875. It was advertised in the *Ind* on Apr. 29, 1875, as *La
Salle, Pioneer of the Northwest*; and advertised thus in the *New-York Times* on May 8,
1875, 12mo, illustrated, $1.50 cloth, vol. 8
in the series. I cannot explain this strange
publishing record.

1375 ROSA M. KETTLE (MARY ROSA S.
KETTLE) *The Sea and the Moor.*
12mo. 2/o boards   June 5 (*Spect*)
Library of Favourite Authors No. 44. This
has no date and 310 pp. The first edition
was issued by James Weir & Knight, London, 1877, author's edition, 18.5 cm., 310
pp., 5/o cloth, advertised and listed in the
Ath on Apr. 14.

1376 (WILLIAM H. THOMPSON)
Life in a Debtor's Prison. 12mo.
2/o boards   June 5 (*Spect*)
Household and Railway Books No. 45. This is
probably the first edition, 1880, with 283
pp.
Also 1885

1377 UNCLE JOHN *The Wonders of the
World.* 12mo. Illustrated. 1/o sewed,
2/o cloth   June (*Bks*)
Youth's Library of Wonders and Adventures
No. 21. This is the first edition, no date,
with 313 pp.

1378 ANONYMOUS *Artistic Homes.*
12mo. Illustrated. 1/o sewed   July 3
(*Spect*)
Sylvia's Home Help Series No. 10. This is the
first edition, no date, 18 cm., 121 pp.

1379 WILLIAM JONES *How to Make Home
Happy.* 12mo. 1/o sewed   1880 (*BM*)
Sylvia's Home Help Series No. 11. This is a
reissue, no date, with 309 pp.
Also 1860

1380 ANONYMOUS *Hints and Helps for
Everyday Emergencies.* 12mo. 1/o sewed
July (*Bks*)
Sylvia's Home Help Series No. 12. This has
no date, 18 cm., with 112 pp.
Also 1860

1381 JAMES MASON, ed. *The Holiday
Companion and Traveller's Guide.*
1/o boards   July (*Bks*)
This is the first edition, no date, with 156
pp.
See an anonymous entry for 1882

1382 CATHERINE J. HAMILTON
The Flynns of Flynnville. 2/o boards
July?
Library of Favourite Authors No. 47. This is
the first edition, no date, with 277 pp.

1383 (EDWIN T. FREEDLY) *Money; How
to Get, How to Keep, etc.* [New and revised
edition]. 1/o sewed, 1/6, 2/o cloth   Aug. 7
(*Spect*)
The first edition was *A Practical Treatise on
Business*, issued by Lippincott, Grambo,
Philadelphia, 1852, 20 cm., 312 pp. It was

issued with the same title by T. Bosworth, London, 1853, 20 cm., 282 pp., the second English edition from the fifth American edition. Partridge, London, issued *Money: How to Get It*, 1853, 17 cm., 259 pp. It was issued by George Routledge, London, as *How to Make Money*, 1853, 228 pp., at 1/0 boards, listed in *PC* as published Mar. 14–30. He reissued it in May 1859. Also 1883

1384 ANONYMOUS *The Skin in Health and Disease.* 12mo. 1/0   Aug. 14 (*Spect*)

1385 ANONYMOUS *The Marvels of Nature, in Earth, in Sky, and Sea.* 12mo. Illustrated. 1/0 sewed, 2/0 cloth
Aug. (*Bks*)

Youth's Library of Wonders and Adventures No. 20. This is probably the first edition. It was also issued in the *Family Gift Series* at 2/6 cloth (1880), and in the *People's Standard Library* at 2/0 cloth (1880), with 338 pp., illustrated.

1386 ANONYMOUS *Penny Popular Proverbs.* 0/1 sewed   Aug. (*Bks*)

Penny Educational and Useful Books No. 12. This series eventually had 36 titles.

1387 ANONYMOUS *Penny All About Things.* 0/1 sewed   Aug. (*Bks*)

Penny Educational and Useful Books No. 13.

1388 ANONYMOUS *Penny Natural Philosophy.* 0/1 sewed   Aug. (*Bks*)

Penny Educational and Useful Books No. 14.

1389 (FRANCES NOTLEY) *Forgotten Lives.* 2/0 boards   Aug.?

This is a reissue in *Library of Favourite Authors.*
Also 1876

1390 EDWARD EGGLESTON & LILLIE E. SEELYE *The Shawnee Prophet; or, The Story of Tecumseh.* 12mo. Illustrated. 2/0 boards, 2/6, 3/6 cloth   Aug.?

Heroes, Patriots, and Pioneers No. 10. This was mentioned in editorial matter in the

Ath on Sept. 11. It is the first English edition (1880), 18 cm., 327 pp. It begins a series of five titles issued in the United States by Dodd, Mead & Co., New York, *Eggleston's Series of Famous American Indians.* The series of five vols. was reviewed in *Scribner's Monthly* for Mar. 1881; and the five vols. were reissued in 1883, 12mo, $1.25 each, about Dec. 6, 1883. The present title was issued by Dodd, Meade & Co., 1878, as *Tecumseh and the Shawnee Prophet*, 18.5 cm., 332 pp., listed by *Lit World* as published in Oct. The third thousand was advertised in the *Ind* on Oct. 17.

GUSTAVE AIMARD (OLIVER GLOUX)
Boy's Own Story Books of Daring and Adventure.   13 vols. Illustrated.
2/0 boards, 2/6 cloth each
Sept. 4 (*Ath* ad)

Aimard's tales are combined two to the vol.

1391 **No. 1. *The Foster Brothers (The Indian Chief and Red Track).*** For the first title see 1861, 76, and below. For the second title see also 1862, 78

1392 **No. 2. *The Kings of the Desert (The Insurgent Chief and The Flying Horseman).*** For the first title see also 1878, and for the second see also 1879

1393 **No. 3. *The Forest Chieftain (The Guide of the Desert and The Bee Hunters).*** For the first title see also 1878, and for the second see also 1865, 78

1394 **No. 4. *The White Buffalo (The Prairie Flower and The Indian Scout).*** For the first title see also 1861, 78, and for the second see also 1861, 78

1395 **No. 5. *The Chief of the Dark Hearts (The Adventurers and The Pearl of the Andes).*** For the first title see also 1863, 76, and for the second see also 1863, 77

1396 **No. 6. *The Prairie Rovers (Last of the Incas and The Rebel Chief).*** For the first title see also 1862, 78, and for the second see also 1864, 77

1397 **No. 7. *The Robbers of the Forest (The Border Rifles and The Freebooters).***

For the first title see also 1861, 78, and
for the second see also 1861, 78

1398 **No. 8.** *Red Cedar (The Pirates of the*
Prairies and The Trapper's Daughter).
For the first title see also 1861, 78, and
for the second see also 1861 and below

1399 **No. 9.** *The Texan Rangers (The Buc-*
caneer Chief and The Trail Hunter). For
the first title see also 1864, 78, and for
the second see also 1861

1400 **No. 10.** *Pale Face and Red Skin*
(Stoneheart and The Smuggler Chief). For
the first title see also 1865, 78, and for
the second see also 1864, 78

1401 **No. 11.** *Loyal Heart (The White*
Scalper and The Trappers of the Arkan-
sas). For the first title see also 1861, 78,
and below. For the second see also 1864,
76

1402 **No. 12.** *The Mexican's Revenge*
(Stronghand and The Queen of the Savan-
nah). For the first title see also 1864, 77,
and for the second see also 1862, 78

1403 **No. 13.** *Eagle Head (The Tiger*
Slayer and The Gold-Seekers). For the
first title see also 1860, 76, and below.
For the second title see also 1860

1404 ANONYMOUS *The Economical*
Housewife. 12mo. Illustrated. 1/0 sewed
Sept. 4 (*Ath*)
Sylvia's Home Help Series No. 13. This is the
first edition (1880), with 118 pp.

1405 ANONYMOUS *The Cow. A Guide to*
Dairy-Management and Cattle-Raising.
12mo. Illustrated. 1/0 boards   Sept. (*Bks*)
Country Life Books No. 1. This is the first
edition (1880), 17.5 cm., 136 pp.

1406 ANONYMOUS *Poultry: How to*
Manage, etc. 12mo. Illustrated.
1/0 boards   Sept. (*Bks*)
Country Life Books No. 2. This is the first
edition (1880), with 130 pp.

1407 ANONYMOUS *Fun for All.*
Illustrated. 1/0 sewed   Sept. (*Bks*)
Comic Holiday Books No. 5. This is the first
edition (1880), with 120 pp., a collection
of jokes and jests.

1408 JAMES RUSSELL LOWELL
The Poetical Works of James Russell Lowell.
2/0 sewed, 3/6 cloth   Sept. (*Bks*)
The 3/6 edition was listed in the *Spect* on
July 10 and again as a new edition, Cr 8vo,
on Oct. 16. One of these was *Moxon's Popu-*
lar Poets with 623 pp., and the other one
had 400 pp. *Poems* was issued by John Ow-
ens, Cambridge, 1844, 18.5 cm., 279 pp.;
and by C. E. Mudie, London, 1844, 18
cm., 279 pp. A second series was issued by
G. Nichols, Cambridge; etc., 1848 (1847),
19 cm., 184 pp., in boards. Thomas Delf,
American Literary Agency, London, imported *Poems* and advertised it in the *Ath*
on Oct. 4, 1851, 2 vols., 12mo, at 12/0.
These Ward, Lock issues had an introduction by W. M. Rossetti.

1409 ANONYMOUS *Ward and Lock's*
Universal Instructor. Part 1. Illustrated.
0/1 sewed, 0/6 sewed   Oct. 23 (*Spect* ad)
This was issued in 0/1 weekly Nos. and 0/6
monthly parts. The *Spect* ad said part 1
"On Oct. 25." It was issued in book form
in 3 vols. (1880–84), Roy 8vo, 7/6 each.
There was a reissue, probably in serial
form, in 1890, 1891. I think it was issued
in the United States by W. H. Stelle & Co.,
New York, as the *U Cat* gives their imprint
jointly with Ward, Lock.

1410 ANONYMOUS *Ward and Lock's*
Home Book. Part 1. Illustrated.
0/6 sewed   Oct. 23 (*Spect* ad)
This has plain and colored illustrations.
The *Spect* ad said part 1 "On Oct. 25." It
was issued in monthly parts and was issued in 1 vol. in 1881, p 8vo, 1,056 pp., at
7/6.

1411 ANONYMOUS *Ward and Lock's Book of Farm Management and Country Life. Part 1.* Illustrated. o/6 sewed   Oct. 23 (*Spect* ad)

This was issued in monthly parts and in 1 vol. in 1881, 19.5 cm., 1,370 pp., with a colored frontispiece and partly colored plates, at 7/6.

1412 FRANCES CASHEL HOEY *No Sign, and Other Tales.* 2/o boards   Oct.?

Library of Favourite Authors No. 48.
Also 1876

1413 FRANCES CASHEL HOEY *The Blossoming of an Aloe.* 2/o boards   Oct.?

Library of Favourite Authors No. 49.
Also 1876, 86

1414 ELIZABETH LYNN LINTON *The Mad Willoughbys, and Other Tales.* 2/o boards Oct.?

Library of Favourite Authors No. 50.
Also 1875

1415 SIR WILLIAM MATHEWS *Oratory and Orators.* 1/o sewed, 1/6, 2/o   Nov. 27 (*Spect*)

Friendly Counsel Series No. 14. This was also given as No. 15 in the publisher's lists, and since there is no other No. 15, it seems likely that a number was skipped. This is revised and edited by J. W. Kirton (1880), with 226 pp. The first edition was issued by S. C. Griggs, Chicago (copyright 1878), possibly issued in 1879, 19.5 cm., 456 pp. The first English edition was issued by Hamilton, Adams, London, 1879, p 8vo, 5/o, fron the seventh American edition. Also 1882

1416 MAX ADELER (CHARLES H. CLARK) ET AL. *The Fortunate Island.* Illustrated. 1/o sewed   Nov. 27 (*Ath*)

This is Beeton's Christmas Annual, the 21st season. In addition to the title story by Adeler, there are stories by Henry Frith, J. G. Montefiore, and Marion Couthouy for a total of 135 pp. This is an example of the complexity of the Ward, Lock operation. The title story was one of the stories in *An Old Fogey, and Other Stories,* with the title, *Professor Baffin's Adventures* (see 1881). The main ingredients of this annual were used in *A Desperate Adventure, and Other Stories* (see 1886), a combination of stories also used in *Transformations* (see 1883) and *The Drolleries of a Happy Island* (see 1883). *The Fortunate Island and Other Stories* was issued by Lee & Shepard, Boston; etc., 1882, 333 pp., illustrated, with all the stories save one the same as in *An Old Fogey and Other Stories.* It was listed in the *Nation* and in the *Ind* on Dec. 15, 1881, and in *PW* on Dec. 17.

1417 ANONYMOUS *Sylvia's Home Journal Christmas Number.* 1/o sewed   Nov.
Also 1881

1418 JAMES MASON, ed. *The Year-Book of Facts in Science and the Arts. For 1880.* 2/6 boards, 3/6 cloth   Dec. 25 (*Spect*)
See 1875 for publishing details.

1419 LILY SPENDER (MRS. J. K. SPENDER) *Godwyn's Ordeal.* 12mo. 1/o sewed, 1/6, 2/o cloth   Dec. (*Bks*)

Lily Series No. 72. This is (1880), with 345 pp. The first edition was issued by Hurst & Blackett, London, 3 vols., 1879, 19.5 cm., 31/6, listed in the *Ath* on Sept. 13. The dedication reads "To my five elder girls and boys, to whom the first volume was read as it was written on the seashore during a happy summer holiday."

1420 (EMMA JANVIER) *Madeleine.* 12mo. 1/o sewed, 1/6, 2/o cloth   Dec. (*Bks*)

Lily Series No. 73. This has no date and 143 pp. I think this is by Janvier, and if so, it was first published by the Presbyterian Board of Publication, Philadelphia (1861), 100 pp., and 1 plate. If this is the work by Julia Kavanagh, it was first issued by Bentley at 10/6 in 1848; and it was issued by Ward, Lock in 1884 (which see) and 1886 (which see).

1421 ANONYMOUS *Sylvia's Book of Home Needlework.* 12mo. Illustrated. 1/o sewed, 1/6 cloth   Dec. (*Bks*)

Sylvia's Home Help Series No. 15. This is the first edition (1880), with 76 pp., and diagrams.
Also 1885

1422 WILLIAM COBBETT *A Grammar of the English Language.* New Edition. 1/o sewed, 2/o cloth   1880 (*Eng Cat*)

This is (1880), 163 pp., carefully annotated and with a preface signed J. M. The first edition was probably Clayton & Kingsland, New York, 1818, 17.5 cm., 184 pp. It was issued by Thomas Dolby, London, 1819, 18 cm., 186 pp.

1423 BRET HARTE *Poems and Prose of Bret Harte.* 1/o   1880 (*Eng Cat*)

This is a reissue of the 1872 edition. Chatto & Windus, London, issued the *Complete Works of Bret Harte* in 4 vols., the first two about Aug. 1880, and vols. 3 and 4 about Oct. 1880, corrected and revised by the author. The present edition obviously could not then be complete!
Also 1872

1424 SIR WALTER SCOTT *Waverley.* Demy 8vo. o/6 sewed   1880 (*BM*)

Sixpenny Standard Novels No. 1. This has no date and 141 pp. This series was later identified as *Popular Sixpenny Books*. The first edition was issued by Archibald Constable, Edinburgh; etc., 3 vols., 1814, 18.9 cm., anonymous. The second edition in 3 vols., anonymous, 21/o, was listed in the *Edinburgh Review* as published May–Aug. 1814; and the third edition, the same, was listed as published Aug.–Nov. 1814. In the United States it was issued by Van

Winkle & Wiley, New York, 2 vols., 1815, 17.5 cm., anonymous; and by Wells & Lilly, etc., Boston, 2-vols.-in-1, 1815, 17.5 cm., anonymous.
Also 1882, 92

1425 SIR WALTER SCOTT *Kenilworth.* Demy 8vo. o/6 sewed   1880 (*BM*)

Sixpenny Standard Novels No. 2. This has no date and 147 pp. This series was later identified as *Popular Sixpenny Books*. The first edition was issued by A. Constable & Co., etc., Edinburgh; etc. 3 vols., 1821, 19.5 cm., anonymous, listed by the *Quarterly Review* as published Oct.–Dec. 1820, 3 vols., at 31/6. In the United States it was issued by M. Carey, Philadelphia, 2 vols., 1821, 18 cm., anonymous; and by J. Seymour, New York, 2 vols., 1821, 18 cm., anonymous; and by S. G. Goodrich, Hartford, 1821, 24 cm., anonymous, 300 pp.
Also 1883

1426 SIR WALTER SCOTT *Ivanhoe.* Demy 8vo. o/6 sewed   1880 (*BM*)

Sixpenny Standard Novels No. 3. This has no date and 145 pp. The series was later identified as *Popular Sixpenny Books*. The first edition was issued by A. Constable & Co., Edinburgh; etc., 3 vols., 1820, 19.5 cm., with a preface signed Laurence Templeton. It was issued in Dec. 1819 and listed by the *Edinburgh Review* as published Oct. 1819–Jan. 1820, 3 vols., at 30/o. The first American edition was issued by M. Carey & Son, Philadelphia, 2 vols., 1820.
Also 1882

1427 SIR WALTER SCOTT *The Antiquary.* Demy 8vo. o/6 sewed   1880 (*BM*)

Sixpenny Standard Novels No. 4. This has no date and 131 pp. The series was later identified as *Popular Sixpenny Books*. The first edition was issued by A. Constable & Co., etc., Edinburgh; etc., 3 vols., 1816, 19.5 cm., anonymous, at 24/o, listed in the

Edinburgh Review as published Mar.–June 1816. The first American edition was issued by Van Winkle & Wiley, New York, 2 vols., 1816.
Also 1883

1428 ANONYMOUS ***The Child's Own Book of Poetry.*** 18mo. Illustrated. 1/o cloth 1880 (*Eng Cat*)
Good-Aim Books No. 32. This is the first edition (1880), with 168 pp.

1429 ANONYMOUS ***Cottage Cookery Book.*** o/6 1880 (*Eng Cat*)
This is the first edition (1880), with 106 pp. A new edition, revised and enlarged, was noticed in the *Spect* on Nov. 5, 1881.
Also 1886, 90

1430 GUSTAVE AIMARD (OLIVER GLOUX) ***The Trapper's Daughter.*** 12mo. 1/o sewed 1880?
This is my copy, no date, 17.9 cm., 381 pp., in pale yellow wrappers, printed in red, blue, and black. It has ads on the back cover, on the endpapers, a list of the series on the verso of the title page, a 16-page catalog at the back, and a 4-page insert at the back for the *Select Library of Fiction*. It was issued by John Maxwell; George Vickers, London (1879), 12mo, 128 pp., at o/6 sewed. It was also issued by C. H. Clarke (1875?), 381 pp., at 2/o boards.
Also 1861 and above

1431 GUSTAVE AIMARD ***The White Scalper.*** 12mo. 1/o sewed 1880?
This is in pictorial wrappers, 17.9 cm., with ads on the back cover and on the endpapers. C. H. Clarke, London, issued it (1874), 17.5 cm., 352 pp.; and George Vickers, London, issued it, 1876, 19 cm., 126 pp., at o/6 sewed, advertised in the *Ath* on Nov. 4; and Beadle & Adams, New York, issued it in 1881, 33 cm., 28 pp., about Sept. 28, as *Beadle's Dime Novel* No. 153.
Also 1861, 78, and above

1432 GUSTAVE AIMARD ***The Tiger Slayer.*** 12mo. 1/o sewed 1880?
This is my copy, no date, 17.9 cm., 339 pp., in pink pictorial wrappers, printed in red, green, and black, with ads on the endpapers and back cover, and with an ad on the verso of the half-title. There are publisher's ads paged (1)–6 at the back. This was issued by J. & R. Maxwell; George Vickers, London (1879), with 127 pp., at o/6 sewed; and by Beadle & Co., New York (1869), 20 cm., 98 pp., about Dec. 28, 1869, as *American Tales* No. 60.
Also 1860, 76, and above

1433 GUSTAVE AIMARD ***The Indian Chief.*** 12mo. 1/o sewed 1880?
This is my copy, no date, 17.9 cm., 324 pp., in pink pictorial wrappers in red, green, and black, with ads on the endpapers and back cover. There is a list of the series on the verso of the title page and a 22-page catalog at the back. This was issued by J. & R. Maxwell; George Vickers, London (1879), 12mo, 127 pp., at o/6 sewed; and by C. H. Clarke, London (1875), 324 pp., at 2/o boards.
Also 1861, 76, and above

1434 EDGAR ALLAN POE ***Tales of Mystery, Imagination, and Humour.*** Cr 8vo. Illustrated. 2/o boards. 1880?
This is my copy, a reissue in *Library of Favourite Authors*, no date, 18.3 cm., 395 pp., in yellow pictorial boards, with the series title on the spine. There are ads on the endpapers and back cover, and there is a 14-page catalog at the back. Ward, Lock issued it as *Minerva Library* No. 10, Cr 8vo, with portrait and illustrations, 2/o cloth, advertised in the *Times Weekly Edition* (London) on Jan. 31, 1890.
Also 1873. See 1864

Ward, Lock & Co.
1881

1435 JOSEPH COOK *Boston Monday Lectures. God and the Conscience. Love and Marriage.* Second series. 1/o sewed, 1/6 cloth Jan. 29 (*Spect*)

This has no date and 159 pp., selected from *Conscience* and from *Marriage*. The first title was first issued by Houghton, Osgood & Co., Boston, 1879, 19.5 cm., 279 pp., given a short review in *Harper's New Monthly Magazine* for Feb. 1879, a 12mo vol., consisting of 10 Monday evening lectures given in the fall of 1877. It was reviewed in *Scribner's Monthly* for Apr. 1879. It was issued in London by Richard D. Dickinson, 1879, 143 pp. (see 1879). *Marriage* was first issued by Houghton, Osgood & Co., Boston, 1879, 19.5 cm., 270 pp., noticed in *Harper's New Monthly Magazine* for Aug. 1879, and thus probably issued in June or July. It was issued in London by Dickinson, 1879, 120 pp.
See 1879 for the first series

1436 ANONYMOUS *Sylvia's Book of the Toilet.* 12mo. Illustrated. 1/o sewed, 1/6 cloth Jan.?

Sylvia's Home Help Series No. 14. This has 106 pp. and the *BM* gives it as (1881). It was advertised in the *Ath* on Sept. 4, 1880, as "Just ready," which is unreliable. It was mentioned in editorial matter there on May 18, 1881! But this does not preclude an 1880 issue date.

1437 ANONYMOUS *Children and What to Do with Them.* 12mo. 1/o sewed, 1/6 cloth Feb. (*Bks*)

Sylvia's Home Help Series No. 16. This is (1881), with 117 pp.

1438 ANONYMOUS *How to Choose and Manage a Farm Profitably.* 12mo. Illustrated. 1/o boards Mar. (*Bks*)

Country Life Books No. 3. This is (1881), with 144 pp., probably the first edition.

1439 THOMAS B. MACAULAY *Reviews and Essays.* Third series. 1/o sewed, 2/o cloth Mar. (*Bks*)

Books for All Time No. 12. This is (1881), with 244 pp., a duplicate of pp. 1–240 of *Reviews and Essays*, issued by Ward, Lock (1881), with 384 pp. It has a new title page and 4 pp. of index added.
For the first and second series see 1874, 75, respectively

1440 FREDERICK MARRYAT *Mr. Midshipman Easy.* Demy 8vo. o/6 picture wrapper Mar. (*Bks*)

Sixpenny Standard Novels No. 9. This was later identified as *Sixpenny Books* No. 9. It is (1881), with 112 pp. The first edition was issued by Saunders & Otley, London, 1836, 3 vols., 19 cm., anonymous, 31/6, listed in the *Ath* on Sept. 3, and reviewed on Sept. 10. The first American edition was issued by Carey & Hart, Philadelphia, 1836, 21 cm., anonymous, 274 pp. Bentley issued it as *Standard Novels* No. 66, 1838, anonymous, 387 pp. The present edition was reissued, probably in 1892.
Also 1883

1441 FREDERICK MARRYAT *Peter Simple.* Demy 8vo. o/6 picture wrapper Mar. (*Bks*)

Sixpenny Standard Novels No. 12. This was later identified as *Sixpenny Books* No. 12.

The first English edition was issued by Saunders & Otley, London, 3 vols., 1834, 19 cm., anonymous, 31/6, advertised in the *Ath* on Nov. 9 as "Just published," and listed on Nov. 16, 1833. The third edition, revised, was advertised in the *Spect* on May 9, 1835, as "Just ready." The first American edition was issued by E. L. Carey and A. Hart, Philadelphia; etc., 1833, 1834, 3 vols. Vol. 1 was issued, 1833, with no volume number, 19 cm., anonymous, 216 pp., and contained a publisher's ad stating that it was issued alone, as there was no probability of its early completion. It was reviewed in the *Knickerbocker* for Dec. 1833. There were 18 pp. of ads (Sept. 1833). It ran intermittently in the *Metropolitan Magazine*, June 1832–Dec. 1833. Vol. 2 was dated 1833, and vol. 3 was dated 1834, both being numbered vols. It was also issued by Merklein, Chambersburg, 1834, 2-vols.-in-1, 14 cm., 487 pp. Bentley issued it as *Standard Novels* No. 62, 1838, with 462 pp. The present edition is (1881), with 128 pp.
Also 1883

1442 ANONYMOUS *Sheep, Pigs, and Other Live Stock.* 12mo. Illustrated. 1/0 boards Mar.?
Country Life Books No. 4. This is (1881), with 118 pp., mentioned in editorial matter in the *Ath* on May 7. It is probably a first edition.

1443 WILLIAM CARLETON *Traits and Stories of the Irish Peasantry.* 10 vols. Demy 8vo. 0/6 colored wrappers each Apr. (*Bks*)
These were later identified as *Sixpenny Books* Nos. 76–85. Ward, Lock issued this in 2 vols. (1881), illustrated, with the author's last corrections; and the present issue is a reissue of it without the introduction or the illustrations. Ward, Lock also issued it in 1 vol., a new edition, at 7/6, listed in the *Spect* on Aug. 13. The first edition of the first series was issued by William Curry, Jr., & Co., Dublin, 2 vols.,

1830, 17.5 cm., anonymous, illustrated, 14/0, listed in *Fraser's Magazine* (monthly) for June 1830. The first edition of the second series was issued by W. F. Wakeman, Dublin; etc., 3 vols., 1833, 19 cm., anonymous, illustrated, 31/6 boards. It was advertised in the *Ath* on Dec. 15, 1832, as "This day." Carey & Hart, Philadelphia, issued the tales in three series of 2 vols. each, 20 cm., 1833, 1833, 1834, respectively. It was reviewed in the *Knickerbocker* in Nov. and Sept. 1833 and in June 1834, respectively. The review of the second series gave the imprint as Carey & Hart, Philadelphia; etc., and stated that it omitted many of the tales.

1444 ANONYMOUS *Corn, Roots, and Other Crops of the Farm.* 12mo. Illustrated. 1/0 boards Apr. (*Bks*)
Country Life Books No. 5. This is the first edition (1881), with 134 pp.

1445 SYLVIA *Sylvia's Book of Bazaars and Fancy Fairs.* Cr 8vo. Illustrated. 1/0 boards Apr. (*Bks*)
The Lady's Bazaar and Fancy Fair Books No. 1. This is the first edition (1881), with 96 pp.

1446 ANONYMOUS *Penny Biographical Series.* 8 vols. 0/1 each Apr. (*Bks* ad)
This series continued until 1892 and reached 53 vols. The first eight vols. were Gladstone, Beaconsfield, Nelson, Wellington, Luther, Chatham, Chaucer and Humboldt.

1447 ANONYMOUS *Benjamin Disraeli, Earl of Beaconsfield.* Cr 8vo. Portrait. 1/0 sewed Apr. (*Bks*)
This is the first edition (1881), 19 cm., 117 pp.

1448 FRANCES E. M. NOTLEY *In the House of a Friend.* 2/0 boards May 28 (*Spect*)
Library of Favourite Authors No. 51. This is the first edition (1881), with 527 pp. Sad-

leir had a yellowback issued by Ward, Lock, with no date, in the *Select Library of Fiction*. This would have been after 1881 when Ward, Lock took over most of the titles in this series from Chapman & Hall. They issued titles of their own in the series also, and in the case of the present title the number given was 632 in the series.

1449 ANONYMOUS *Gardening*. 12mo. Illustrated. 1/o boards   May (*Bks*)
Country Life Books No. 7. This is (1881), with 150 pp.
See 1861, 90, 92

1450 ANONYMOUS *Fun for the Million*. Illustrated. 1/o sewed   May (*Bks*)
Comic Holiday Books No. 6. This is (1881), with pieces by Dickens, Jerrold, C. H. Ross, Tom Hood, Theodore Hook, Mark Twain, et al. It is illustrated by Cruikshank, W. S. Gilbert, et al. The first English edition was issued by John C. Hotten, London (1873), Fcp 4to, illustrated, 1/o sewed, about Sept. 1. It was issued in the United States by D. Appleton & Co., New York, 1868, advertised in the *New-York Times* on Oct. 10, 1868, Sq 12mo, at $.50 paper, "This day." It was listed in *ALG&PC* (fortnightly) on Oct. 15.

1451 ANONYMOUS *The Horse and How to Manage Him*. 12mo. Illustrated. 1/o boards   May?
Country Life Books No. 6. This may be the first edition (1881), with 122 pp.
See 1862

1452 GEORGE C. EGGLESTON *Red Eagle*. 12mo. Illustrated. 2/o boards, 2/6, 3/6 cloth   June 11 (*Ath*)
Heroes, Patriots, and Pioneers No. 12. This was listed in the *Spect* at 2/6 on both June 11 and Aug. 20. It is the first English edition (1881), 346 pp., a duplicate of the Dodd, Mead & Co., New York, issue with a new title page and a slight variation in the

prefatory matter. It was reviewed in the *Ath* on Oct. 29. The first edition was the Dodd, Mead issue, *Red Eagle and the Wars with the Crick Indians of Alabama* (copyright 1878), 19 cm., 346 pp., frontispiece, $1.25, as *Famous American Indians Series* No. 2. It was advertised in the *New-York Times* on Dec. 14, 1878, and listed in *Lit World* (fortnightly) on Jan. 4, 1879.

1453 EDWARD EGGLESTON & ELIZABETH E. SEELYE *The Rival Warriors*. 12mo. Illustrated. 2/o boards, 2/6, 3/6 cloth June 11 (*Ath*)
Heroes, Patriots, and Pioneers No. 13. This was listed in the *Spect* at 2/6 on June 11 and Aug. 20. It is the first English edition (1881), with 370 pp. The first edition was issued by Dodd, Mead & Co., New York, 1879, *Brant and Red Jacket*, 19 cm., 370 pp., illustrated, listed in the *Ind* on Dec. 18, 1879. The English edition was reviewed in the *Ath* on Oct. 29, 1881.

1454 ANONYMOUS *The Book of Fancy Needlework*. 12mo. Illustrated. 1/o sewed, 1/6 cloth   June (*Bks*)
Sylvia's Home Help Series No. 18. This is the first edition, no date, 78 pp., and it has the wrapper title *Sylvia's Fancy Needlework Instruction Book*. *Ladies' Handbook of Fancy Needlework* was listed in the *Spect* on June 24, 1882, Cr 8vo, 5/o; and the *Handbook of Plain and Fancy Needlework* was listed in the *Spect* on Nov. 4, 1882, Cr 8vo, 2/6.

1455 SYLVIA *Sylvia's Book of New Designs in Knitting, Netting and Crochet*. Cr 8vo. Illustrated. 1/o boards   June (*Bks*)
Bazaar and Fancy Fair Book No. 2. This is (1881), mentioned in editorial matter in the *Ath* on Oct. 1. It is pp. 97–192 of *The Lady's Bazaar and Fancy Fair Book*, with a special title page and index.

1456 SYLVIA **Sylvia's Illustrated Embroidery Book.** Cr 8vo. Illustrated. 1/0 boards June (*Bks*)

Bazaar and Fancy Fair Books No. 3. This was mentioned in editorial matter in the *Ath* on Oct. 1. It is pp. 193–288 of *The Lady's Bazaar and Fancy Fair Book*, with a special title page and index.

1457 HENRY W. DULCKEN, ed. **The Boy's Handy Book of Natural History.** 12mo. Illustrated. 1/0 sewed, 1/6, 2/0 cloth June (*Bks*)

Youth's Library of Wonders and Adventures No. 26. The first edition was issued by Ward, Lock & Tyler in 1869, no date, Cr 8vo, 384 pp., illustrated, at 5/0 cloth, listed in the *Spect* on Oct. 30.

1458 MAX ADELER (CHARLES H. CLARK) **An Old Fogey and Other Stories.** 12mo. Illustrated. 2/0 boards July 9 (*Ath*)

Household and Railway Books No. 42. This is my copy, no date, 17.5 cm., 372 pp., with a frontispiece and full-page and textual illustrations by Arthur Frost et al. It is in white pictorial boards, printed in red, blue, and black, with the series title on the spine. There are ads on the endpapers, back cover, and 4 pp. at the back. There is a known copy in this series, no date, in pink boards, with the frontispiece and 4 pp. of ads, but also with a 24-page and a 48-page catalog. For a discussion of the publishing history of this title see *The Fortunate Island*, 1880 above. This title was later *Select Library of Fiction* No. 432.
Also 1883, 89, 1901, 05

1459 EDWARD EGGLESTON & ELIZABETH E. SEELYE **The Indian Princess.** 12mo. Illustrated. 2/0 boards, 2/6, 3/6 cloth July 9 (*Spect*)

Heroes, Patriots, and Pioneers No. 14. This is the first English edition (1881), with 310 pp. It was listed in the *Spect* at 2/6 on both July 9 and Aug. 20. The first edition was

Pochahontas, issued by Dodd, Mead & Co., New York (1879), 19 cm., 310 pp., illustrated, as *Famous American Indians Series* No. 3. It was listed in *PW* on Nov. 1.

1460 EDWARD EGGLESTON & ELIZABETH E. SEELYE **The Mexican Prince.** 12mo. Illustrated. 2/0 boards, 2/6, 3/6 cloth July 9 (*Spect*)

Heroes, Patriots, and Pioneers No. 15. This was listed by the *Spect* at 2/6 on July 9 and Aug. 20. It is the first English edition (1881), with 385 pp., reviewed in the *Ath* on Oct. 29, 1881. The first edition was *Montezuma and the Conquest of Mexico*, issued by Dodd, Mead & Co., New York, 1880, 19 cm., 385 pp., with a frontispiece and two portraits, bound in black and tan pictorial cloth. It was listed in *PW* on Oct. 9 and in the *Nation* on Oct. 21.

1461 SYLVIA **Sylvia's Book of Artistic Knickknacks.** Cr 8vo. Illustrated. 1/0 boards July (*Bks*)

Bazaar and Fancy Fair Books No. 4. This has no date and has pp. 289–384 from *The Lady's Bazaar and Fancy Fair Book*, with a special title page and an index. The latter title was issued by Ward, Lock in 1881, Cr 8vo, at 5/0 cloth, listed in the *Spect* on Sept. 24.

1462 FANNY BURNEY (FRANCES BURNEY, later MADAME D'ARBLAY) **Evelina.** 12mo. 2/0 boards Aug. 20 (*Spect*)

Library of Favourite Authors No. 15. This is a reissue of No. 15 in this series, first issued in 1874. It has 379 pp. It was later *Select Library of Fiction* No. 437.
Also 1874

1463 HENRY J. BYRON **Paid in Full.** 12mo. 2/0 boards Aug. 20 (*Spect*)

Library of Favourite Authors No. 52. This is (1881), with 460 pp., a reissue of the 1868 issue.
Also 1868, 84

1464 THE BROTHERS GRIMM, W. HAUFF, ET AL. ***Grimm's Fairy Tales and Other Popular Stories.*** 12mo. Illustrated. 1/0 sewed, 1/6, 2/0 cloth   Aug. 20 (*Spect*)

Youth's Library of Wonders and Adventures No. 19. This was also issued in the *Family Gift Series* (1881), Cr 8vo, 312 pp., illustrated, at 2/6 cloth. *Household Tales and Popular Stories* was issued in a new edition in 1872, 12mo, 316 pp., at 3/6 cloth, listed in the *PC* as published Jan. 16–31, 1872. The first edition of the Grimm was *Kinder- und Haus-Märchen*, issued by G. Reimer, Berlin, 3 vols., 18 cm., vol. 1, 1812; vol. 2, 1815; vol. 3, 1818. He issued a 2-vol. edition, 1819, specially designed for young people, illustrated, which became known throughout the English-speaking world as *Grimm's Fairy Tales*. The first English edition of the Grimm was *German Popular Stories*, issued by C. Baldwyn, London, 1823, 12mo, illustrated by Cruikshank, 7/0, in pictorially printed paper-covered boards. It was listed in the *Quarterly Review* as published July–Sept. 1822, translated by Edgar Taylor. There was a second vol., issued by James Robins & Co., London; etc., 1826; and Robins also reprinted the first vol., 1825, 18 cm., 240 pp. Vol. 2 was listed by the *Quarterly Review* as published Jan.–Mar. 1826. In the United States it was issued as *The Fairy Ring* by E. Kearny, New York, 1849, 18 cm., 376 pp., illustrated.

1465 GASTON TISSANDIER ***Popular Scientific Recreations, Part 1.*** Illustrated. 0/7 sewed   Oct. 1 (*Spect*)

This was to be completed in 12 monthly parts. It is translated and enlarged from the French of Tissandier, issued at Paris, 1881, as *Recreations Scientifiques*, 341 pp., illustrated. A third edition, entirely revised, was issued at Paris (1883), 329 pp., illustrated. Ward, Lock issued it (1882), 24 cm., 781 pp., illustrated, listed in the *Spect* on Oct. 14, at 7/6 and 9/0. A reissue in 12 monthly 0/6 parts, illustrated, began in

Nov. 1884. They advertised it in the *Spect* on Dec. 18, 1886, Roy 8vo, 7/6. A reissue in 0/6 monthly parts, a new and enlarged edition, illustrated, began in Oct. 1889. They issued it in 1889, Roy 8vo, 800 pp., illustrated, 7/6 cloth, advertised in the *Spect* on Nov. 2, 1889. In the United States it was issued by W. H. Stelle & Co., New York (copyright 1883), 25 cm., 781 pp.

1466 ANONYMOUS ***The Thrift Book. Part 1.*** Illustrated. 0/6 sewed Oct. 1 (*Spect*)

This was issued in ten monthly parts and in 1 vol. (1882), 652 pp., at 6/0 cloth.

1467 ANONYMOUS ***The Illustrated History of the World. Part 1.*** 0/7 sewed   Oct. 29 (*Spect*)

This was issued in 28 monthly parts and when completed was issued in 2 vols., Roy 8vo, 7/6 cloth, 12/0 half-calf each. Ward, Lock, Bowden & Co. reissued it in 28 monthly 0/6 parts, advertised in the *Times Weekly Edition* (London), on Oct. 21, 1892, as "On Oct. 25."

1468 F. L. M (F. L. MORSE) ***Onward to the Heights of Life.*** 12mo. 1/0 sewed, 1/6, 2/0 cloth   Oct. 29 (*Spect*)

Lily Series No. 74. This is the first English edition (1881), with 376 pp. The first edition was issued by D. Lothrop & Co., Boston (copyright 1880), 18 cm., 376 pp., with a frontispiece.

1469 ANONYMOUS ***Funny People.*** Demy 8vo. Illustrated. 1/0 sewed   Oct. (*Bks*)

Comic Holiday Books No. 7. This is the first edition (1881), in prose and verse.

1470 CHARLES DICKENS ***The Posthumous Papers of the Pickwick Club.*** Illustrated. 2/0 boards   Oct. (*Bks*)

This is (1881), with 535 pp., illustrated by Arthur Frost. It was later *Select Library of Fiction* No. 424, and then later renum-

bered as 203. The first edition was in 20 monthly parts at 1/0 each, 23 cm., illustrated, part 1 being advertised in the *Ath* on Mar. 26, 1836, as "On Mar. 31"; part 2 advertised on May 21 as "Just published." The 1-vol. issue was from Chapman & Hall, London, 1837, 8vo, 609 pp., illustrated, 21/0, advertised in the *Ath* on Oct. 21 as "On Nov. 14," and listed Nov. 11. The illustrations were by "Phiz" and Seymour. In the United States it was issued in 5 vols., 1836–37, 20 cm., by Carey, Lea & Blanchard, Philadelphia. Vol. 1 was noticed in the *Southern Literary Messenger* for Nov. 1836. However, vol. 2 was reviewed in the *Knickerbocker* for Mar. 1837, as from Carey, Lea & Blanchard, Philadelphia; Wiley & Putnam, New York, and the completed work was reviewed there in Mar. 1838 as from Wiley & Putnam! It was also issued by James Turney, Jr., New York, in 26 parts, 25.5 cm., illustrated, in picture wrappers in varying shades of blue-green and apple-green. He issued it in 1 vol., bound up from the parts, 1838, 23 cm., 609 pp., illustrated by Seymour, "Phiz," and Crowquill. The parts were issued in 1836–38. It was also issued by W. H. Colyer, New York, 1838, 2 vols., 12mo, illustrated, with the same illustrators as for the Turney issue.
Also 1883

1471 ANONYMOUS ***Our Leisure Hours.*** 12mo. Illustrated. 1/0 sewed, 1/6 cloth Oct. (*Bks*)
Sylvia's Home Help Series No. 17. I cannot trace this.

1472 EDWARD BULWER LYTTON ***The Last Days of Pompeii.*** Demy 8vo. 0/6 picture wrapper Oct. (*Bks*)
Sixpenny Standard Novels No. 6. This is (1881), with 128 pp. It was later identified as *Popular Sixpenny Books* No. 6. The first edition was issued by Bentley, London, 3 vols., 1834, 20.5 cm., anonymous, 31/6, advertised in the *Ath* on Sept. 6 as "At

once," and listed on Sept. 27. He issued it as *Standard Novels* No. 72, 1839, with 419 pp.; and Chapman & Hall, London, issued it in 1 vol., 1850, with 304 pp. The first American edition was issued by Harper & Bros., New York, 2 vols., 1834, 19.5 cm., anonymous, pink muslin with labels, and with 28 pp. of ads, numbered, and 8 pp. unnumbered at the back of vol. 2. It was reviewed in the *Knickerbocker* for Nov. 1834 and noticed in the *Southern Literary Messenger* for Jan. 1835.
Also 1883

1473 FREDERICK MARRYAT ***Jacob Faithful.*** Demy 8vo. 0/6 picture wrapper Oct. (*Bks*)
Sixpenny Standard Novels No. 11. It was later identified as *Popular Sixpenny Books* No. 11. The present edition is (1881), with 128 pp. The first edition was issued by Carey & Hart, Philadelphia; etc., 3 vols., 1834, 19 cm., anonymous, vols. 2 and 3 each having two 12-page catalogs at the back (Mar. 1834 and Oct. 1833). It ran in the *Metropolitan Magazine* from Sept. 1833 to Dec. 1834. The first English edition was issued by Saunders & Otley, London, 3 vols., 1834, 22 cm., anonymous, 31/6, listed in the *Ath* on Sept. 30. The second edition, revised, was advertised in the *Spect* on May 9, 1835, as "Just ready." Bentley issued it as *Standard Novels* No. 63, 1838, with 407 pp.
Also 1883, 1902

1474 ANONYMOUS ***Sylvia's Home Journal Christmas Number.*** 1/0 sewed Nov. 19 (*Ath* ad)
The Christmas number for 1891 was advertised in the *Times Weekly Edition* (London) on Nov. 20, 1891, 96 pp., 2 colored plates, 1/0.
Also 1879, 80

1475 MISS E. MARLITT (EUGENIE JOHN)
The Second Wife. 12mo. 2/o boards,
2/6 cloth   Nov. 19 (*Ath*)

Library of Select Authors. This is (1881), with
318 pp., a different translation from the
German than for the Bentley edition.
This was later *Select Library of Fiction* No.
433 and is the first title I've found in this
new Ward, Lock series, the *Library of Select
Authors.* The first edition was issued in
Leipzig, 2 vols., 1874, as *Die Zweite Frau.*
The first English edition was issued by
Bentley, London, 3 vols., 1875, Cr 8vo,
31/6, translated by Annie Wood. It was advertised in the *Ath* on Oct. 16 as "Ready"
and reviewed on Oct. 30. The first edition
in English was issued by J. B. Lippincott,
Philadelphia, 1874, 18 cm., 302 pp.,
translated by Mrs. Wister, and listed in
PW on July 4, in the *Ind* on July 9, and in
the *Nation* on July 16.

1476 ANTHONY TROLLOPE **Dr. Wortle's
School.** 12mo. 2/o boards, 2/6 cloth
Nov. (*Bks*)

Library of Select Authors. This has no date,
17.9 cm., 397 pp., pictorial yellow boards.
There are ads on the endpapers and back
cover and on 12 pp. at the back. It is the
first yellowback edition with the series title
on the spine. It ran in *Blackwood's Magazine,* May to Dec. 1880. The first English
edition was issued by Chapman & Hall,
London, 2 vols., 1881, 12/o, with a 28-
page catalog (Nov. 1880) in vol. 2. It was
advertised in the *Ath* on Dec. 25, 1880, as
"On Jan. 1"; advertised in the *Spect* on Jan.
8 as "This day"; and listed in both on Jan.
22, 1881. In the United States it was issued by Harper & Bros., New York, 1880,
my copy, as *Franklin Square Library* No.
155, 28.2 cm., 36 pp., $.15 paper, with a
caption title and text beginning immediately below on p. (1). It is dated Dec. 31,
1880, and p. 36 of text is completed with
ads, and the fourth page of ads is the back
of the issue. The list of the series in the ads
ends with No. 155. It was received at the

Library of Congress on Jan. 3, 1881, listed
in *PW* on Jan. 8, in the *Ind* on Jan. 13, and
advertised in the *New-York Times* on Dec.
31, 1880, as "This day." It was also issued
by George Munro, New York, 1881, as
Seaside Library No. 910, 4to, 35 pp., $.10
paper, received at the Library of Congress
on Jan. 6, 1881, listed in *PW* on Jan. 15,
and advertised in the *New-York Times* on
Jan. 3, 1881, as "Out today." There is a
picture of the present yellowback in *Victorian Publisher's Book-Bindings in Paper* by
Ruari McLean, 1983, on p. 99, showing it
in white pictorial boards, printed in dark
and light blue and red, ads on the back
(1889), with *Library of Select Novels* at the
foot of the spine and "The Works of Anthony Trollope" at the head.
Also 1882

1477 PANSY & FAYE HUNTINGTON
(ISABELLA M. ALDEN & THEODOSIA
FOSTER) **Perry Harrison's Mistake.** 12mo.
1/o sewed, 1/6, 2/o cloth   Nov. (*Bks*)

Lily Series No. 75. This is the first edition
(1881), with 375 pp.

1478 GEORGE MEREDITH **The Tragic
Comedians.** 12mo. 2/o boards   Nov. (*Bks*)

Library of Select Authors. This is my copy, no
date, 18 cm., 309 pp., pink pictorial
boards, with the series title on the spine.
There are ads on the endpapers and back
cover (one with a date 1881), and there
are 6 pp. of ads at the back. This was later
Select Library of Fiction No. 422. Ward,
Lock, Bowden & Co. issued it, 1892, as
Warwick House Library No. 3, 258 pp., portraits, 6/o cloth, revised and corrected by
the author. It was listed in *Review of Reviews* (New York) for Feb. 1892. It was
reissued in June. It was issued at 3/6 cloth
in July 1892, reissued in Dec. The first
edition was issued by Chapman & Hall,
London, 2 vols., 1880, 18.5 cm., 12/o, enlarged from the *Fortnightly Review,* where
it ran from Oct. 1880 until Feb. 1881. It
was listed in the *Ath* on Dec. 18, 1880, and

in the *Spect* on Dec. 25, but was advertised in the *Ath* on Jan. 1, 1881, as "On Jan. 1." The first American edition was issued by George Munro, New York, 1881, as *Seaside Library* No. 939, 32 cm., 30 pp., at $.10 paper, dated Feb. 18. It was listed in *PW* on Mar. 5 and advertised in the *New-York Times* on Feb. 25 as "Out Today." Roberts Bros., Boston, issued it, 16mo, $1.50 cloth, and 12mo, $2.00 cloth, with an introduction by Clement Shorter, advertised in the *New-York Times* on Jan. 22, 1892.

1479 HAWLEY SMART *Social Sinners.* 12mo. 2/o boards Nov. (*Bks*)

Library of Select Authors. This is (1881), with 352 pp. It was later *Select Library of Fiction* No. 423. The first edition was issued by Chapman & Hall, London, 3 vols., 1880, 19 cm., 31/6, listed in the *Spect* on Oct. 30. Also 1901

1480 WILLIAM H. AINSWORTH *Hilary St. Ives.* 2/o boards, 2/6 cloth Nov.?

Library of Select Authors. This has no date, 18 cm., 380 pp., in pink pictorial boards, with a printer's date of Nov. 1881. The first edition was issued by Chapman & Hall, London, 3 vols., 1870, 19 cm., 31/6, listed in the *Ath* on June 18. They issued it at 2/o boards as *Select Library of Fiction* No. 374, about Apr. 6, 1878. George Routledge, London, issued it in 1881, Cr 8vo, 3/6 cloth, listed in the *Spect* on Jan. 22, 1881. A Chapman & Hall ad in the *Bks* for July 4, 1881, advertised for sale all the proprietor's interests in the *Select Library of Fiction*, including plates, illustrations, and wrapper blocks, and it stated that tenders were to be made to W. H. Smith & Son (who of course were the proprietors). In ads of July 16 and Aug. 4, Ward, Lock & Co. announced the purchase from Smith of the copyrights, plant, and stock of many titles in the series by Trollope, Melville, Lever, Smart, Mrs. Oliphant, Ainsworth, Henry Kingsley, Charles C. Clarke,

Mrs. Linton, G. P. R. James, and James Grant. They announced that they would be issued in the *Library of Select Authors.* Not all titles were so issued, however, as many of them were still reissued under the *Select Library of Fiction* umbrella, first with the old Chapman & Hall numbers and then with new ones. Chatto & Windus purchased copyrights, stock, and cases of many others by James Payn, Percy Fitzgerald, Hamilton Aïdé, Lady Duffus Hardy, et al. Frederick Warne, Diprose & Bateman, Macmillan and others purchased titles also, and some titles probably were not disposed of.

1481 GEORGE R. EMERSON *William Ewart Gladstone.* 8vo. Frontispiece. 1/o boards Nov.?

This is (1881), 23 cm., 427 pp., mentioned in editorial matter in the *Ath* on Dec. 3. The first edition was issued by Ward, Lock & Co., in 1881, Demy 8vo, 6/o cloth, advertised in *Notes & Queries* on Oct. 29, 1881, as "Just ready." Also 1882, 86

1482 MISS E. MARLITT (EUGENIE JOHN) *The Little Moorland Princess.* 12mo. 2/o boards, 2/6 cloth Dec. 3 (*Ath*)

Library of Select Authors. This has no date, 18 cm., 387 pp., pale blue pictorial boards, with a printer's date (Nov. 1881), and with the series title on the spine. My copy is of a later issue with ads on the endpapers (one with a date Mar. 26, 1891), the back cover, and 8 pp. of ads at the back. It has the 1881 covers and title page. This title was later *Select Library of Fiction* No. 434. The first edition was issued in Leipzig, 2 vols., 1872, as *Das Haideprinzesschen.* The first English edition was issued by Sampson Low, London, who issued it jointly with Tauchnitz of Leipzig, 2 vols., 1872, 18 mo, 1/6 sewed, 2/o flexible cloth each, *The Princess of the Moor.* It was listed in the *Ath* on Oct. 19. The first American edition was issued by J. B. Lippincott, Philadelphia, 1872, with the present title, and 408 pp. It was listed in the *Ind* on Feb. 2 and in *PW* on Feb. 8, translated by Mrs. A. L. Wister. *See color photo section*

1483 FREDERICK A. MALLESON
Jesus Christ, His Life and Work. 12mo. 1/o sewed, 1/6 cloth   Dec. 24 (*Spect*)
Christian Knowledge Series No. 12. The first edition was issued by Ward, Lock & Co. in 1880, 375 pp., and 1 plate.

1484 ANONYMOUS ***Trees, and How to Grow Them.*** 12mo. Illustrated. 1/o boards Dec. (*Bks*)
Country Life Books No. 10. This is the first edition (1881), with 112 pp.

1485 H. G. O. VERE ***Three Wonderful Travellers.*** Illustrated. 1/o sewed Dec. (*Bks*)
Comic Holiday Books No. 8. This is the first edition (1881), 110 pp., illustrated by E. Griset.

1486 ANONYMOUS ***Fifty Celebrated Men.*** 12mo. Illustrated. 1/o sewed, 1/6, 2/o cloth   Dec. (*Bks*)
Youth's Library of Wonders and Adventures No. 23. This is (1881), with 311 pp. It was issued in the *Family Gift Series* also in 1881, Cr 8vo, with portraits, 2/6 cloth, listed in the *Spect* on Sept. 17. The first edition was issued by Ward & Lock (1862), Sq 12mo, 311 pp., illustrated, 3/6 cloth.

1487 ELISHA NOYCE ***The Boy's Own Book of the Manufactures and Industries of the World.*** 12mo. Illustrated. 1/o sewed, 1/6, 2/o cloth   1881 (*Eng Cat*)
Youth's Library of Wonders and Adventures No. 22. It was issued in the *Family Gift Series*, Cr 8vo, 334 pp., at 2/6 cloth, listed in the *Spect* on Sept. 24, 1881. It is a reissue of *Boy's Book of Industrial Information*, issued by Ward & Lock, 1858, 304 pp., at 5/o, reduced to 3/6 in 1862.

1488 ANONYMOUS ***Great Inventors.*** Illustrated. 12mo. 1/o sewed, 1/6, 2/o cloth   1881?
Youth's Library of Wonders and Adventures No. 24. This was also issued in the *Family Gift Series*, Cr 8vo, illustrated, 2/6 cloth, probably in 1881. The first edition was issued by Ward & Lock (1864), 18 cm., 308 pp., illustrated, 3/6 cloth, listed in the *Reader* on Oct. 29.

1489 ANONYMOUS ***The Boy's Handy Book of Sports, Pastimes, Games and Amusements.*** 12mo. Illustrated. 1/o sewed, 1/6, 2/o cloth   1881 (*Eng Cat*)
Youth's Library of Wonders and Adventures No. 25. This is (1881), with 374 pp. It was also issued in the *Family Gift Series*, Cr 8vo, illustrated, 2/6 cloth, probably in 1881 also. The first edition was issued by Ward & Lock (1863), 374 pp., illustrated.

1490 ANONYMOUS ***The Etiquette of Modern Society.*** 12mo. Illustrated. 1/o sewed, 1/6 cloth   1881 (*Eng Cat*)
Sylvia's Home Help Series No. 19. This is the first edition (1881), with 103 pp. It was mentioned in editorial matter in the *Ath* on Jan. 21, 1882.

1491 FRANZ HOFFMANN ***Trust in God.*** 1/o   1881 (*Eng Cat*)
This is probably the first English edition (1881), 176 pp., translated from the German. It was issued as *René* by the Lutheran Board of Publication, Philadelphia, 1870, 17.5 cm., 176 pp., illustrated.

1492 SYLVESTER JUDD ***Margaret.*** 2/o boards   1881 (*Eng Cat*)
This was later *Select Library of Fiction* No. 478.
Also 1874

1493 KARL G. NIERITZ ***Help in Need.*** 18mo. 0/9 sewed, 1/o cloth   1881 (*Eng Cat*)
Beeton's Good-Aim Series. This is the first English edition, translated from the German (1881), with 120 pp.

1494 (SARAH WHITEHEAD) *Rose Douglas.*
2/o boards   1881 (*Eng Cat*)

The first edition was issued by Smith, Elder & Co., London, 2 vols., 1851, p 8vo,
21/o, by S. R. W., about Feb. 24. They issued it at 1/o sewed, 18 cm., anonymous,
320 pp., about Dec. 21, 1861. Chapman &
Hall, London, issued it as *Select Library of
Fiction* No. 146 (1869), third edition, 19
cm., still anonymous, 320 pp., a 2/o yellowback, probably in July. The first American edition was issued by D. Appleton &
Co., New York, 1851, 19.5 cm., 372 pp., by
S. R. W., listed by *Lit World* as published
Apr. 5–19, and listed by the *Ind* on Apr.
24.
Also 1882

1495 GEORGE J. WHYTE MELVILLE
M. or N. New Edition. p 8vo. 2/o boards
1881

Library of Select Authors. This was Sadleir's
copy, which he gave as (1881), 18.2 cm.,
348 pp., in pink pictorial boards with the
series title at the foot of the spine. It was
Select Library of Fiction No. 393 and was issued with this series title on the cover, and
when the series was renumbered it became No. 121. The first edition was issued
by Chapman & Hall, London, 2 vols.,
1869, 20 cm., 21/o, listed in the *Ath* on
Oct. 16. They reissued it as a 2/o yellowback, 1872, 18.6 cm., listed in the *Ath* on
Nov. 18, 1871. They reissued it as *Select Library of Fiction* No. 393, 2/o boards, in the
fall of 1879. The first American edition
was issued by Leypoldt, Holt & Williams,
New York, 1871, 8vo, 159 pp., paper
bound, listed in *ALG&PC* on Apr. 15, and
in the *Nation* on Apr. 13.
Also 1902

1496 GEORGE J. WHYTE MELVILLE
Black but Comely. New Edition.
p 8vo. 2/o boards   1881   *See color photo section*

Library of Select Authors. This is my copy, no
date, with the Chapman & Hall imprint
on the title page, and with Ward, Lock &
Co. on the front cover. It is 18.2 cm., 336
pp., pink pictorial boards, printed in red,
blue, and black, with the No. 402 on the
front cover, and the series title at the foot
of the spine. It has a printer's date of May
1881 and "The Works of Whyte Melville"
at the head of the spine. There are ads on
the endpapers and back cover, the one on
the back with a date of 1881. The 8 pp. of
ads at the back are for W. H. Smith & Son
and Chapman & Hall. The first edition
was issued by Chapman & Hall, London, 3
vols., 1879, Cr 8vo, 31/6, listed in the *Ath*
on Jan. 4, 1879. They reissued it as *Select
Library of Fiction* No. 402, a 2/o yellowback,
listed in the *Ath* on Sept. 27, 1879. They
also issued a second edition in 3 vols., advertised in the *Spect* on Feb. 1, 1879, as
"This day"; and issued it at 6/o, Cr 8vo,
listed in the *Spect* on Apr. 15, 1879. Ward,
Lock issued this as *Select Library of Fiction*
No. 402, and when the series was renumbered it became No. 130.
Also 1901

1497 ANTHONY TROLLOPE *The Prime
Minister.* [New edition]. 12mo. 2/o
boards   1881

This is my copy, 1881, 17.8 cm., 547 pp.,
pale pink pictorial boards, printed in red,
blue, and black with "Select Library" at
the foot of the spine, and a printer's date
(July 11, 1881). The title page bears the
imprint of Ward, Lock & Co., and the
endpapers have their ads, but it is bound
in a Chapman & Hall *Select Library of Fiction* case with a Chapman & Hall ad on the
back cover and the No. 362 on the front
cover. The first English edition was in 8
parts by Chapman & Hall, London, 1875,
1876, at 5/o sewed each. Part 1 was listed
in the *Spect* on Dec. 4, 1875, and part 8 was
listed July 1, 1876. It was issued in 4 vols.,
1876, at 42/o, listed in the *Spect* and in the
Academy on July 1, and reviewed in the *Ath*
on July 1. They issued it in 1 vol., 1877,
547 pp., at 6/o cloth, about Nov. 4, 1876.

Belford Bros., Toronto, used these sheets for their issue, 1876, 19 cm. The first yellowback edition was issued by Chapman & Hall, 1877, a new edition, 17.8 cm., 547 pp., at 2/6 boards, 3/6 cloth, as *Select Library of Fiction* No. 362, with printer's date (June 14, 1877). It was issued about July 28, and reissued as the fourth edition in 1878 with printer's date (July 10, 1878). The No. 362 was on the cover of the yellowback. The first edition was issued by Harper & Bros., New York; and by Porter & Coates, Philadelphia, issued simultaneously about May 17, 1876. They were both listed in *PW* on May 20 and both reviewed in the *New York Daily Tribune* on June 9. The Harper was also listed in the *Ind* on May 25. Old records in the Morgan Library, of Harper's, contain the agreement between Harper and Porter & Coates, and the latter company advertised their issue as from advance sheets by arrangement with Harper. This Porter & Coates edition was (1876), 17.5 cm., 690 pp., $.75 in gray wrappers, and $1.25 and $1.50 in cloth.

1498 ANTHONY TROLLOPE
Is He Popenjoy? New Edition.
2/o boards, 2/6 cloth   1881

This is my copy in smooth green cloth blocked in black and gold with "Select Library of Fiction" on the front cover, figured endpapers. It has the imprint of Chapman & Hall on the title page, no date, 18.4 cm., 421 pp., with printer's date (June 3, 1881), and with Ward, Lock & Co. on the spine, and their 20-page catalog at the back. I suspect this is the cloth counterpart of a yellowback edition issued in the *Library of Select Novels*, as it certainly was issued in the latter form with no date. The boards issue was *Select Library of Fiction* No. 384, and under the renumbering it became No. 17. The first edition was issued by Chapman & Hall, London, 3 vols., 1878, 31/6, with a 24-page catalog of Sampson Low (Nov. 1877) at the back of

vol. 3. It was issued about Apr. 6, was listed in the *Acad* on Apr. 27, and advertised in the *Spect* on Apr. 6 as "This day." It ran in *All the Year Round* in a Bowdlerized form from Oct. 13, 1887, until July 13, 1878. Chapman & Hall issued a new edition, 1878, Cr 8vo, 421 pp., at 6/o cloth, listed in the *Spect* on Oct. 5; and they reissued it at 6/o about Nov. 30, 1879. They issued the first yellowback edition, 1879, third edition, 18.2 cm., 421 pp., my copy, *Select Library of Fiction* No. 384, yellow pictorial boards printed in red, blue, and black, with the wrong No., 386, on the front, and the series title on the spine. It was 2/o boards, 3/o cloth, and was reissued as the fourth edition, 1880. The first American edition was issued by Harper & Bros., New York (1878), *Franklin Square Library* No. 1, 29.5 cm., 105 pp., triple columns, $.15 paper. This is my copy and has a wrapper called a title leaf of the same stock as the text; the inside of the front and both sides of the back have publisher's ads, and the series was always dated very accurately but unfortunately the title leaf is frequently missing in the rare copies still in existence, as it is in my two copies. This series was started by Harpers to compete with George Munro's *Seaside Library*, and in the same format, quarto paper. Harper advertised them as having the advantage of being thrown away after reading, and most of them were so treated! According to J. Henry Harper, they paid £20 for this. The list of the *Library of Select Novels* at the back ends with No. 611. This No. 1 was advertised in the *Ind* on May 30, listed in *PW* on May 25, and advertised in *Harper's Weekly* on June 1.

1499 CHARLES LEVER *Charles O'Malley, the Irish Dragoon.* New Edition. 12mo.
2/6 boards   1881

Library of Select Authors. This is my copy, no date, 17.8 cm., 604 pp., pale pink boards, printed in red, blue, and black, with the series title at the foot of the spine, and "The Works of Charles Lever" at the head of the spine. It has a preface (1872) and a printer's date (Nov. 1881). There are ads on the endpapers and back cover and a 22-page catalog at the back. This was *Select Library of Fiction* No. 18 at 2/6 and changed to No. 59 later. Ward, Lock issued it at 7/6 cloth, Roy 8vo, listed in the *Spect* on Oct. 25, 1879. It ran in the *Dublin University Magazine* from Apr. 1840 until Dec. 1841. It was issued in 22-parts-in-21, illustrated by "Phiz," 1/0: part 1 being advertised in the *Ath* on Feb. 1, 1840, as "On Mar. 30"; and part 2 advertised on May 2, issued by William Curry, Jr., Dublin; etc. The parts were issued from Mar. 30 until Nov. 30, 1841. It was issued by Curry in 2 vols., 1841, 23 cm., illustrated by "Phiz," 24/0: vol. 1 listed in the *Ath* on Mar. 18, 8vo, 12/0; and vol. 2 listed on Dec. 18, 8vo, 12/0. Vol. 2 was advertised in the *Ath* on Nov. 6, 1841, as "On Nov. 30." Chapman & Hall, London, issued it in 2 vols., 8vo, reduced to 7/0 each, listed by *PC* as published July 14–29, 1850. They reissued it in 2 vols., 1857, Cr 8vo, 8 illustrations in each vol., 4/0 each, advertised in *Notes & Queries* on Feb. 5, 1859, as a reissue in 2 vols. at 4/0 each. They issued it in 2 vols. as *Select Library of Fiction* Nos. 18 and 19, 1862, 2/0 boards each: vol. 1 listed in the *Ath* on Apr. 19; and vol. 2 on May 10, reissued 1865, 1866. They issued it in 2 vols., p 8vo, illustrated, 12/0, listed in the *Reader* on June 10, 1865. They issued the 12th edition at 3/0 boards in Mar. 1867. Routledge, London, issued it in his *Octavo Novels*, illustrated, 6/0, listed in the *Spect* on Feb. 11, 1871. In the United States parts 1–17 ran in the supplement to the *Museum of Foreign Literature*, E. Littell & Co., Philadelphia, Jan. 1838–May 1839. Carey & Hart, Philadelphia issued it in parts, illustrated by "Phiz"; parts 1 and 2 noticed in *Godey's Lady's Book* for Nov. 1840; and parts 9–12 reviewed there in Dec. 1840. They issued it in 2 vols., 1840, 1841, 25

cm., illustrated by "Phiz." The first editions both English and American were anonymous, edited by Harry Lorrequer. Also 1883, 85

1500 CHARLES READE *It Is Never Too Late to Mend.* A New Edition. 12mo. 2/6 boards   1881

This is my copy, no date, 18 cm., 462 pp., in yellow pictorial boards, printed on the front with 4 illustrations in red, green, and black. There is an inscribed date (Oct. 28, 1881) and ads on the endpapers, back cover, and a 16-page catalog at the back. Also 1872

1499 EDWARD BULWER LYTTON *Paul Clifford.* Demy 8vo. 0/6 picture wrappers   1881

Sixpenny Standard Novels No. 5. This was later identified as *Popular Sixpenny Books* No. 5. It is (1881), with 113 pp. The first edition was issued by Henry Colburn & Richard Bentley, London, 3 vols., 1830, 20 cm., 31/6, with the dedication signed E. L. B., published on May 4 according to the Bentley private catalog. They issued the second edition with a new preface, some additions, and a few deletions, reviewed in the *Spect* on Sept. 25, 1830. It was issued as *Bentley Standard Novels* No. 47, 1835, with 469 pp. Chapman & Hall issued it in 1½ d weekly numbers and 0/7 monthly parts: the first monthly part advertised in the *Spect* as "On Mar. 31," 1848; and part 4 was advertised on July 1. They issued it in 1 vol., 1848, 20 cm., 308 pp., frontispiece by "Phiz," 3/6 cloth, with a new preface. Another author's story occupied pp. (289)–308. It was listed in the *Spect* on Aug. 19, 1848. George Routledge, London, purchased from Lytton the limited right of issuing a cheap series of 19 works for a period of 10 years, for which he paid £20,000, and the contract was renewed. In Apr. 1873, Routledge purchased all the copyrights of Lytton's works. He issued the present title at 1/6 boards, 2/0 cloth, in his *Railway Library* about Feb. 1, 1854. The first American edition was issued by J. & J. Harper, New York, 2 vols., 1830, anonymous, in boards, with a pink muslin spine and yellow labels.

1502 EDWARD BULWER LYTTON *Pelham.*
Demy 8vo. 0/6 picture wrappers   1881
Sixpenny Standard Novels No. 7. This was later identified as *Popular Sixpenny Books* No. 7. It has no date, 22.5 cm., 124 pp., double columns. The first edition was issued by Henry Colburn, London, 3 vols., 1828, 19.5 cm., anonymous, 31/6, in May. He issued the second edition in 3 vols., 1828, 8vo, anonymous, 31/6, listed in the *Ath* on Oct. 29. It was issued as *Colburn's Modern Novelists* in 2 vols., 5/0 each: vol. 1 advertised in the *Spect* on Jan. 17, 1835; and vol. 2 on Feb. 14, a revised edition with a new introduction and a portrait, published by Bentley for Colburn. Chapman & Hall, London, issued it in 5 parts, 0/7 sewed each, part 5 advertised in the *Spect* on Dec. 2, 1848; and they then issued it in 1 vol., 1849, 19.5 cm., 304 pp., frontispiece, 3/6 cloth, advertised in the *Spect* on Dec. 16, 1848, as "This day."
Also 1883

1503 EDWARD BULWER LYTTON
Eugene Aram. Demy 8vo. 0/6 picture wrappers   1881
Sixpenny Standard Novels No. 8. The first edition was issued by Colburn & Bentley, London, 3 vols., 1832, 20 cm., anonymous, 24/0, published Jan. 1, 1832, according to the Bentley private catalog, listed and reviewed in the *Spect* on Jan. 6. It was issued as *Bentley's Standard Novels* No. 34, 1833, anonymous, 453 pp. Chapman & Hall, London, issued it in 1849, a new edition with a new preface, thoroughly revised, Cr 8vo, with a frontispiece by "Phiz," 3/6 cloth, listed in the *Spect* on May 17. The first American edition was issued by J. & J. Harper, New York, 2 vols., 1832, 18.5 cm., anonymous, as *Library of*

Select Novels Nos. 19 and 20. It was listed in the *New-England Magazine* (Boston) in Mar. as "Recent."
Also 1883

1504 FREDERICK MARRYAT *Japhet in Search of a Father.* Demy 8vo. 0/6 picture wrappers   1881
Sixpenny Standard Novels No. 10. This is (1881), with 114 pp. The first English edition was issued by Saunders & Otley, London, 3 vols., 1836, p 8vo, anonymous, 31/6, advertised in the *Ath* on Nov. 28, 1835, as "Just ready," and listed on Dec. 19. It ran in the *Metropolitan Magazine* from Oct. 1834 to Jan. 1836. Bentley issued it as *Standard Novels* No. 64, 1838, anonymous, 401 pp. In the United States it was issued by Wallis & Newell, New York, 4 parts, in 1835, 1836, anonymous; by Carey & Hart, Philadelphia, 2 vols., 1835, 19 cm., anonymous; and by H.C. Boswell, Trenton, 1835, 22 cm., 167 pp., by Marryat. See the discussion in Sadleir I, p. 233 for these American editions, parts of which preceded the first English book edition.
Also 1883

1505 ANNIE THOMAS (MRS. PENDER CUDLIP) "*'He Cometh Not,' She Said.*"
New Edition. 2/0 boards   1881 (*U Cat*)
This was probably in the *Library of Select Authors*. The *U Cat* gives 1881, 18 cm., 374 pp. The first edition was issued by Chapman & Hall, London, 3 vols., 1873, 19 cm., 31/6, listed in the *Ath* on Apr. 12. They issued it as *Select Library of Fiction* No. 268, at 2/0 boards, listed in the *Spect* on Feb. 27, 1875. The first American edition was issued by Harper & Bros., New York, 1873, as *Library of Select Novels* No. 396, 8vo, 125 pp., $.50 paper, listed in the *Ind* on June 26 and in *PW* on June 28.
Also 1883

1506 ANONYMOUS **Beeton's Riddle Book.**
p 8vo. Illustrated. 1/o boards   1881?

This is my copy, no date, 18.2 cm., 152 pp., in white pictorial boards, printed in red, green, and black. There are textual and full-page illustrations, with ads on the endpapers, back cover, versos of the half-title and title page, and with a 16-page catalog at the back.

Also 1868

Ward, Lock & Co.
1882

Ward, Lock & Co. opened a branch at 10 Bond Street, New York, in June 1882.

1507 EDWARD P. ROE *Without a Name.*
2/0 Jan. 28 (*Spect*)

This has no date and 478 pp. It was also listed by the *Spect* on Apr. 29 at 2/6, and was issued as *Lily Series* No. 77 about this time, 1/0 sewed, 1/6, 2/0 cloth. The first English edition was issued by Ward, Lock & Co., 2 vols. (1881), Cr 8vo, at 10/6, listed in the *Ath* on Dec. 17, 1881. Frederick Warne, London, issued it at 1/0 sewed, 1/6 cloth, no date, 387 pp., listed in the *Spect* on Dec. 24, 1881, and by the *Bks* as published in Jan. 1882. Ward, Lock issued it as *Select Library of Fiction* No. 453, at 2/0 boards, 2/6 cloth, listed in the *Spect* on Sept. 9, 1882. The No. was later changed to 375. The first American edition was issued by Dodd, Mead & Co., New York (copyright 1881), 19 cm., 560 pp., in green, maroon, or purple-brown cloth, with yellow endpapers. It has 6 pp. of ads. The first edition was 20,000 copies, to sell at $1.50. It was advertised in *Lit World* on Oct. 8 as "On Oct. 10," listed in *PW* on Oct. 22, and advertised in the *New-York Times* on Oct. 15 as "Next week," and as "Now published," on Oct. 21. They reissued it in May 1885, in quarto paper; issued a second edition, the 23rd thousand, advertised in the *New-York Times* on Dec. 3, 1881, as "Next week"; and issued the third edition, the 26th thousand, advertised on Dec. 17.
Also 1886

1508 JOHN LANG *Captain Macdonald.*
1/0 sewed Jan. (*Bks*)
Shilling Novels No. 1.
Also 1856, 58, 60, 70, 85

1509 SIR WILLIAM MATHEWS *Beeton's British Orators and Oratory.* 8vo. 1/0 sewed, 1/6, 2/0 cloth Jan.?
Friendly Counsel Series No. 15. This is a reissue in this series, no date, 20 cm., 161 pp. It was mentioned in editorial matter in the *Ath* on Feb. 25.
Also 1880

1510 ANONYMOUS *Beeton's Art of Public Speaking.* 8vo. 1/0 sewed, 1/6, 2/0 cloth Jan.?
Friendly Counsel Series No. 16. This is (1882), with 128 pp. The *U Cat* says that it has "Ward & Lock's Shilling Library" on the front, a fact that I cannot explain, there being no such series! This was mentioned in editorial matter in the *Ath* on Feb. 25 and could very well have been issued in 1881. *Beeton's Public Speaker*, Cr 8vo, 3/6 cloth, was listed in the *Spect* on June 5, 1875. The *BM* gives *Beeton's Complete Orator, Including the Art of Public Speaking and British Orators and Oratory*, 2 parts (1881).
Also 1885

1511 WILLIAM H. AINSWORTH *The Constable de Bourbon.* 2/0 boards, 2/6 cloth Jan.?
Select Library of Fiction No. 370, later No. 77. It has no date, 387 pp., blue pictorial

boards with printer's date (Jan. 1882), and a 20-page catalog at the back. The first edition was issued by Chapman & Hall, London, 3 vols., 1866, p 8vo, 31/6, listed in the *Ath* on June 23. They issued it as *Select Library of Fiction* No. 370, 1878, 17.7 cm., 387 pp., 2/o boards, my copy, with printer's date (Jan. 14, 1878), listed in the *Ath* on Feb. 16. George Routledge, London, issued it, Cr 8vo, illustrated, 3/6, listed in the *Spect* on Oct. 9, 1880.

1512 WILLIAM M. THACKERAY
The Yellowplush Correspondence and Other Tales. 1/o   Feb. 4 (*Spect*)

This is (1882), with 127 pp. The first edition of *The Yellowplush Correspondence* was issued by Carey & Hart, Philadelphia, 1838, 12mo, anonymous, 238 pp., the first collected edition of any of Thackeray's writings to appear in England or America. It was collected from *Fraser's Magazine*, where it ran from Nov. 1837 until July 1838. The first American reprint in full was issued by D. Appleton & Co., New York, 1852, *The Yellowplush Papers*. The first English edition was *Memoirs of Mr. Charles James Yellowplush*, which appeared in vol. 1 of *Comic Tales and Sketches*, issued by Hugh Cunningham, London, 2 vols., 1841, edited and illustrated by Mr. M. A. Titmarsh, Cr 8vo, 21/o, containing also *Major Gahagan—The Bedford Row Conspiracy—The Fatal Boots*, all from periodicals, listed in the *Ath* on Apr. 24. It has additions and deletions from and to the Carey & Hart edition.
See 1883

1513 ANONYMOUS **Children's Fancy Work.** 12mo. 1/o boards   Feb. (*Bks*)

Sylvia's New Needlework Books No. 1. This is the first edition (1882), with 96 pp. It has the title, "The Child's Fancy Work and Doll Book" on the cover.

1514 JOHN S. C. ABBOTT **The Buccaneer Chiefs.** 2/o boards   Feb.?

This is a reissue of the 1880 edition.
Also 1880

1515 CHARLES LEVER **Nuts and Nutcrackers.** New Edition. 12mo. Illustrated. 2/o boards   Feb.?

Library of Select Authors. This is my copy, no date, 17.9 cm., 232 pp., with textual illustrations by "Phiz." It is in white pictorial boards printed in red, green, and black, with the series title at the foot of the spine and with "The Works of Charles Lever" at the head. It has ads on the endpapers and back cover and a 16-page catalog at the back. This was *Select Library of Fiction* No. 372 and later No. 56. It ran in the *Dublin University Magazine*, Jan. 1842–May 1843, off and on. The first edition was issued by W. S. Orr, London, 1845, Fcp 8vo, anonymous, 232 pp., with illustrations by "Phiz." They issued the second edition, the same, 1845. Chapman & Hall, London, issued the third edition, 1857, my copy, 16.7 cm., 232 pp., illustrations by "Phiz." It is anonymous at 1/o boards, issued in Aug., in yellow boards, decorated and printed in black. The first Orr edition was advertised in the *Spect* on Dec. 21, 1844, at 5/o fancy cloth boards. Chapman & Hall issued it as *Select Library of Fiction* No. 251, in 1875, in 1/o stiff wrappers; and reissued it about Jan. 12, 1878, a new edition, at 2/o boards, as *Select Library of Fiction* No. 372, with the No. on the front cover, and a 32-page catalog at the back.

1516 MAX ADELER (CHARLES H. CLARK) **Out of the Hurly-Burly.** Medium 4to. Illustrated. o/6 sewed   Mar. 6 (*Ath*)

People's Edition No. 1. This is (1882), with 64 pp.
Also 1874, 78, 83, 1900

1517 THOMAS HOOD, THE ELDER
Hood's Own. First series. Medium
4to. Illustrated. o/6 sewed
Mar. 6 (*Ath*)

People's Edition No. 2. This is (1882). Ward,
Lock also issued it at 2/0, the fourth edition, listed in the *Spect* on Apr. 29, 1882. It
was later *Popular Sixpenny Books* No. 37. It
was issued in monthly 1/0, Demy 8vo, illustrated parts by A. H. Baily & Co., London. No. 1 was advertised in the *Spect* on
Jan. 6, 1838, as "On Jan. 25"; No. 2 advertised on Mar. 3; and No. 12 advertised as
"On Mar. 1, 1839." He issued it in 1 vol.,
1839, 23 cm., 568 pp., illustrated. Edward
Moxon, London, issued it, 1846, 23 cm.,
568 pp., illustrated, 10/6, listed in the *Spect*
on Oct. 10. In the United States it was issued in parts by G. Dearborn & Co., New
York, illustrated. No. 1 was noticed in the
New York Review (quarterly) for July 1838
and listed in the *American Monthly Magazine* as published Mar. 15–May 26, 1838.

1518 ANONYMOUS **Arabian Nights'
Entertainments.** Medium 4to. Illustrated.
o/6 sewed   Mar. (*Bks*)

People's Edition No. 3. This is (1882), with
64 pp. F. J. Harvey Darton, in *Children's
Books in England*, states that the first English translation was from Galland, 1704–
17. This was *Popular Sixpenny Books* No. 38,
later. It was issued as *Youth's Library of Wonders and Adventures* No. 30, in 1882, illustrated, 1/0 sewed, 1/6 cloth. It was issued
as *Dalziel's Illustrated Arabian Nights' Entertainments*, circa 1878, edited by H. W.
Dulcken, 26.5 cm., 822 pp.
Also 1863, 86, 89

1519 ANNA H. DRURY **Misrepresentation.**
[New edition]. 12mo. 2/0 boards
Apr. 29 (*Spect*)

Sadleir had a copy in the *Select Library of
Fiction*, issued by Ward, Lock after 1881, a
new edition. It probably had the No. 345,
which was later changed to No. 655. The

first edition was issued by J. W. Parker &
Son, London, 2 vols., 1859, p 8vo, 18/0,
advertised in the *Ath* on Nov. 12 as "This
day," and listed on Nov. 12 also. They issued the second edition, listed in the *Spect*
on Sept. 7, 1861. Chapman & Hall, London, issued the third edition in 1861, 19.5
cm., 476 pp., 5/0 cloth; and they reissued
it as *Select Library of Fiction* No. 79, the fifth
edition, at 2/0 boards, listed in the *Spect* on
Apr. 14, 1866; and again in late 1876 or
early 1877 as *Select Library of Fiction* No.
345, at 2/0 boards. The first American
edition was issued by Harper & Bros.,
New York, 1860, 23 cm., 211 pp., $.50 pa-
per, in their *Library of Select Novels*, listed in
APC&LG (weekly) on Jan. 7, 1860.

1520 JOHN BUNYAN **The Pilgrim's
Progress.** Medium 4to. Illustrated.
o/7 sewed   Apr. (*Bks*)

People's Edition No. 4. This is (1882), 64
pp., with the same illustrations as for the
1879 edition. This was later *Popular Sixpenny Books* No. 39. It was also issued as
Youth's Library of Wonders and Adventures
No. 27, at 1/0 sewed, 1/6 cloth, probably in
1882.
Also 1879

1521 ANONYMOUS **Dogs and Cats:
How to Manage and Keep Them.**
Illustrated. 1/0 boards   Apr. (*Bks*)

County Life Books No. 11. This is the first
edition (1882), with 118 pp. It was mentioned in editorial matter in the *Spect* on
July 1.

1522 HENRY W. LONGFELLOW
Longfellow's Poems. Medium 4to.
Illustrated. o/6 sewed   Apr. (*Bks*)

People's Edition No. 5. This is (1882), 64
pp., illustrated by Major Seccombe. It was
later *Popular Sixpenny Books* No. 40.
Also 1878

1523 THOMAS HOOD, THE ELDER
Hood's Own. Second series.
Medium 4to. Illustrated.
0/6 sewed   Apr. (*Bks*)
People's Edition No. 8. I've not been able to locate the first edition of this, but it was probably issued before the author's death in 1845. Edward Moxon, London, issued it, 1861, 22 cm., 564 pp., illustrated, at 10/6, with a preface by the author's son, Tom Hood. It was advertised in *Notes & Queries* on Feb. 9 as "Just published" and listed in the *Spect* on Jan. 26. It was later *Popular Sixpenny Books* No. 43.

1524 ANONYMOUS **Bees, Rabbits, and Pigeons.** 12mo. Illustrated. 1/o boards Apr.?
Country Life Books No. 8. This is the first edition (1882), 18 cm., 106 pp. It was mentioned in editorial matter in the *Spect* on July 1.

1525 ANONYMOUS **Country Sports.** 12mo. Illustrated. 1/o boards   Apr.?
Country Life Books No. 9. This is the first edition (1882), 18 cm., 112 pp. It was mentioned in editorial matter in the *Spect* on July 1.

1526 HAWLEY SMART **The Great Tontine.** 12mo. 2/o boards, 2/6 cloth   May 6
(*Spect*) *See color photo section*
Library of Select Authors. This is my copy, no date, 18 cm., 408 pp., white pictorial boards, printed in red, blue, and black, with the series title, "Select Authors," at the foot of the spine. There are ads on the endpapers (one with the date Aug. 1881), the back cover, and 8 pp. at the back. This was *Select Library of Fiction* No. 542, later changed to No. 176. The first edition was issued by Chapman & Hall, London, 3 vols., 1881, 20 cm., 31/6, listed in the *Ath* on Oct. 22. I have another copy of the present edition at 2/o boards, identical to the above described copy except that it is

in pale blue pictorial boards. My copies do not have a printer's date, but a known copy, the same as described for my copies, did have such (Aug. 1882). The first American edition was issued by George Munro, New York, 1883, 32.5 cm., 57 pp., in paper, *Seaside Library* No. 1679, listed in *PW* on Aug. 4, 1883.
Also 1901

1527 ANNIE THOMAS (MRS. PENDER CUDLIP) **Best for Her.** 12mo. 2/o boards, 2/6 cloth   May 20 (*Ath*)
This is (1882), 372 pp., probably in the *Library of Select Authors.* It was *Select Library of Fiction* No. 543 and later changed to No. 353. The first edition was issued by Tinsley Bros., London, 3 vols., 1882, listed in the *Ath* on Jan. 28. The first American edition was issued by George Munro, New York (1883), in quarto paper, as *Seaside Library* No. 1608, listed in *PW* on Apr. 28.

1528 MAX ADELER (CHARLES H. CLARK) **Elbow-Room.** Medium 4to. Illustrated.
0/6 sewed   May (*Bks*)
People's Edition No. 9. This is (1882), with 64 pp.
Also 1876, 83, 1902

1529 ANNA H. DRURY **The Brothers.** New Edition. 2/o boards, 2/6 cloth May?
Select Library of Fiction No. 185, later changed to No. 656. This is (1882), 349 pp., probably with Chapman & Hall on the title page. The first edition was issued by Chapman & Hall, London, 2 vols., 1865, 21/o, listed in the *Ath* on Sept. 30. They issued it in 1 vol., 1868, Cr 8vo, frontispiece, 5/o, listed in the *Spect* on Dec. 21, 1867. They reissued it as *Select Library of Fiction* No. 185, at 2/o boards, in Aug. 1871.

1530 EMILY EDEN **The Semi-Attached Couple.** 2/o boards, 2/6 cloth   May?
Select Library of Fiction No. 204, later changed to No. 662. The first edition was

issued by Bentley, London, 2 vols., 1860, 21 cm., 21/0, by E. E., edited by Lady Theresa Lewis; Lady Lewis's name did not appear. It was issued on Aug. 28 according to the Bentley private catalog. He issued it in the third series of *Standard Novels* in 1860 or 1861 at 2/6 white cloth, 3/0 claret cloth, with 351 pp.; and reissued it, 1865, new edition, by E. E., at 2/0 boards, on Sept. 27. Chapman & Hall, London, issued it as *Select Library of Fiction* No. 204, anonymous, 2/0 boards, probably in Oct. 1872. The first American edition was issued by T. O. H. P. Burnham, Boston, 1861, 18.5 cm., anonymous, 360 pp., listed in *APC&LG* (weekly) on Apr. 20.

1531 HOLME LEE (HARRIET PARR)
Gilbert Massenger. 2/0 boards, 2/6 cloth   May?

Select Library of Fiction No. 240, later changed to No. 674. The first edition was issued by Smith, Elder & Co., London, 1855, at 6/0, listed in the *Ath* on Oct. 27. They issued a new edition, 1862, 17 cm., 250 pp., at 1/0 sewed, about Dec. 21, 1861. Chapman & Hall, London, issued it as *Select Library of Fiction* No. 240, a new edition, at 2/0 boards, listed in the *Ath* on May 23, my copy, 17.8 cm., 250 pp., in yellow pictorial boards in red, blue, and black, with a printer's date (Jan. 30, 1874).

1532 HOLME LEE (HARRIET PARR)
Hawksview. 2/0 boards, 2/6 cloth   May?

Select Library of Fiction No. 239, later changed to No. 673. The first edition was issued by James Blackwood, London, 1859, at 7/6, listed in the *Ath* on June 25. The third thousand was issued at 2/0 boards, about Oct. 1, 1859. Smith, Elder & Co., London, issued a new edition, 1862, 247 pp., 1/0 sewed, about May 24. Chapman & Hall, London, issued it as *Select Library of Fiction* No. 239 at 2/0 boards, listed in the *Ath* on May 23, 1874. The first American edition was issued by W. A. Townsend & Co., New York, 1860, 19.5

cm., 330 pp., $1.00, listed in *APC&LG* (weekly) on June 9.

1533 HOLME LEE (HARRIET PARR)
Thorney Hall. 2/0 boards, 2/6 cloth May?

Select Library of Fiction No. 241, later changed to No. 675. The first edition was issued by Smith, Elder & Co., London, 1855, 19.5 cm., 338 pp., 6/0, listed in the *Ath* on Mar. 10. A new edition was issued, 1862, 1/0 sewed, about Dec. 21, 1861. Chapman & Hall, London, issued it at 1/0 sewed, a new edition (1869); and they issued it as *Select Library of Fiction* No. 241, at 2/0 boards, about May 23, 1874.

1534 ELIZA METEYARD **Mainstone's Housekeeper.** 2/0 boards, 2/6 cloth May?

Select Library of Fiction No. 347, later changed to No. 781. The first edition was issued by Hurst & Blackett, London, 3 vols., 1860, 18.5 cm., 31/6, listed in the *Ath* on May 26. Chapman & Hall, London, issued it as *Select Library of Fiction* No. 57, 1865, 437 pp., at 2/0 boards, listed in the *Ath* on Mar. 25; and reissued it as No. 347 in late 1876 or early 1877. The first American edition was issued by A. K. Loring, Boston, 1864, 18 cm., 523 pp., $1.75, advertised in the *New-York Times* on Mar. 18 as "This morning," and listed in *APC&LG* (fortnightly) on Apr. 1. A second edition was advertised in the *New-York Times* on Mar. 28 as "Tomorrow"; and a fourth edition was advertised at $1.25 on Apr. 12.

1535 JEAN MIDDLEMASS **Wild Georgie.**
New Edition. 2/0 boards, 2/6 cloth   May?
Select Library of Fiction No. 284, later changed to No. 625. This has no date and 380 pp. The first edition was issued by Hurst & Blackett, London, 3 vols., 1873, Cr 8vo, 31/6, listed in the *Ath* on Apr. 5. Chapman & Hall, London, issued it in 1875, 380 pp., 2/0 boards, as *Select Library*

of Fiction No. 284, listed in the *Ath* on July 24.

1536 ANONYMOUS ***The Holiday Companion and Tourist Guide.***
1/o boards   June 3 (*Ath* ad)

I cannot trace this. It is probably the issue with this title, edited by James Mason (see 1880).

1537 ANONYMOUS ***Holiday Trips Around London.*** Illustrated. 1/o boards   June 3 (*Ath* ad)

I cannot trace this.

1538 SYLVIA ***Sylvia's Book of Ornamental Needlework.*** Illustrated. 1/o boards   June (*Bks*)

Sylvia's New Needlework Books No. 3. This is (1882), with pp. 193–288 of *The Lady's Handbook of Fancy Needlework*, which was issued by Ward, Lock in 1882, 19 cm., 383 pp., illustrated, 5/o.

1539 SYLVIA ***Sylvia's Book of Macramé Lace.*** Illustrated. 1/o boards   June (*Bks*)

Sylvia's New Needlework Books No. 4. This is (1882), pp. 289–383 of the title given in the preceding item.

Also 1883, 85

1540 JOHN HABBERTON ***Mrs. Mayburn's Twins.*** 1/o sewed   June (*Bks*)

Ward & Lock's Humorous Books. This is (1882), with 134 pp. The first English edition was *Just One Day*, issued by George Routledge, London (1879), author's copyright edition, anonymous, 150 pp., 1/o boards, listed by *PC* as published May 16–31. The first American edition was issued by George R. Lockwood, New York, 1879, with the Routledge title, 17.5 cm., anonymous, 172 pp., listed in the *Ind* on May 29 and in the *Nation* on June 5. It was issued with the present title by T. B. Peterson & Bros., Philadelphia (1882), 188 pp., listed in the *Nation* on Mar. 30.

1541 MIGUEL CERVANTES ***Don Quixote. Part 1.*** Medium 4to. Illustrated. 0/6 sewed   June (*Bks*)

People's Edition No. 6. This was later *Popular Sixpenny Books* No. 41. This is a new edition, with some chapters omitted, of the revision of Jarvis's translation, previously issued by S. O. Beeton, London, in 10 parts (1864, 1865), 640 pp., illustrated, incomplete. This latter work was reissued by Frederick Warne, London, 1866, 766 pp., illustrated; and by Ward, Lock in 1870 and 1879, 766 pp., illustrated. The first edition was in 2 parts, in Madrid, 1605, 1615. It was issued in England in 2 vols.: vol. 1 by Edward Blount & W. Barret, London, 1612; and vol. 2 by Blount, 1620. It was issued in the United States by Conrad, Philadelphia; etc., 4 vols., 1803.

For part 2 see 1883

1542 ANTHONY TROLLOPE ***Lotta Schmidt and Other Stories.*** [New edition]. 2/o boards, 2/6 cloth   June (*Bks*)

Select Library of Fiction No. 188, later changed to No. 10. The 2/o edition was in a handsome binding of illuminated decorative boards in red, blue, and green, 18 cm., 369 pp., with the series title on the front cover and spine, and the words, "The Works of Anthony Trollope" on the spine. The 2/6, my copy, is in green smooth cloth blocked in black, with figured endpapers, and the series title on the front. It has a printer's date (May 1882) and 10 pp. of ads at the back. Ward, Lock reissued it, a new edition, with a printer's date (Nov. 12, 1883). The first edition was issued by Alexander Strahan, London, 1867, my copy, 20 cm., 403 pp., at 10/6, in maroon cloth, listed in the *Spect* on Sept. 14. Strahan issued it, 1870, Cr 8vo, 425 pp., at 5/o cloth, about May 21. Chapman & Hall issued it, 1870, 425 pp., in bright green cloth with ads on the endpapers. They issued the first yellowback edition (1871), a new edition, 369 pp., 2/o boards listed in the *Ath* on Sept. 16, and 2/6 cloth issued in Nov. It was advertised in the *Spect* by Chapman & Hall on July 6, 1872, at 3/o cloth. They issued the fourth edition, 1876, 17 cm., with printer's date (Apr. 10, 1876). George Routledge, New York, issued it in the United States at $2.50 cloth, advertised in the *Nation* on Oct. 17, 1867. The first yellowback edition from Chapman & Hall was as *Select Library of Fiction* No. 188.

1543 MATILDA BETHAM-EDWARDS
The White House by the Sea. 12mo.
2/o boards, 2/6 cloth   June?

Select Library of Fiction No. 289, later changed to No. 551. The first edition was issued by Smith, Elder & Co., London, 2 vols., 1857, 19 cm., 21/o, advertised in the *Ath* on Nov. 28 as "Now ready." It was reissued at 1/o sewed, 1/6 cloth, a new edition, 1864, about May 1. Chapman & Hall, London, issued it as *Select Library of Fiction* No. 289, at 2/o boards, listed in the *Ath* on Oct. 16, 1875.

1544 ANNE MANNING ***The Ladies of Bever Hollow.*** 12mo. 2/o boards,
2/6 cloth   June?

Select Library of Fiction No. 214, later changed to No. 772. The first edition was issued by Bentley, London, 2 vols., 1858, 17.5 cm., anonymous, 12/o, listed in the *Ath* on June 12. He issued it in 1 vol., 1858, a new edition, anonymous, 357 pp.; and reissued it in the third series, his *Standard Novels* at 2/6 white cloth, 3/o claret cloth, in May 1860. Chapman & Hall, London, issued it as *Select Library of Fiction* No. 214, anonymous, 2/o boards, listed in the *Ath* on Aug. 30, 1873.

1545 MISS E. MARLITT (EUGENIE JOHN)
The Old Maid's Secret. 12mo. 2/o boards,
2/6 cloth   June?

Select Library of Fiction No. 235, later changed to No. 387. The first edition was *Das Geheimnis der Alten Mamsell*, Leipzig, 2

vols., 1868. The first edition in English was issued by J. B. Lippincott & Co., Philadelphia, 1868, as *The Old Mam'selle's Secret*, translated by Mrs. Wister, advertised in the *New-York Times* on Apr. 11, 12mo, 297 pp., $1.75 cloth, as ready. It was advertised there on June 23, 1887, a cheap edition, $.25 paper. The first British edition was probably a Dublin house issued jointly with Strahan, London, 1871. *The Old Maid's Secret*, translated by H. J. G., 10/6, advertised by Strahan in the *Spect* on Nov. 11, and again advertised there on June 22, 1872, a new edition, Cr 8vo, 6/o. Chapman & Hall, London, issued it with the Strahan title, *Select Library of Fiction* No. 235, at 2/o boards, about Jan. 10, 1874.

1546 ANNE MARSH, later MARSH-CALDWELL ***Father Darcy.*** 12mo.
2/o boards, 2/6 cloth   June?

Select Library of Fiction No. 102, later changed to No. 451. Chapman & Hall, London, issued it with the No. 102, a new edition, 2/o boards, in 1867, and issued it in late 1876 or early 1877 as No. 350. Also 1864

1547 GEORGE J. WHYTE MELVILLE
Songs and Verses. 12mo. 2/o boards,
2/6 cloth   July 15 (*Ath* ad)

Library of Select Authors. This was later *Select Library of Fiction* No. 600, and still later, No. 132, although, of course it was not fiction! It has no date and 238 pp., with the series title on the spine, and "The Works of Whyte Melville" on the spine for the 2/o issue. The first edition was issued by Chapman & Hall, London, 1869, 20 cm., 136 pp., 5/o cloth, listed in the *Ath* on July 24. It was revised and enlarged on several occasions as new editions came out, Chapman & Hall issuing at least eight editions. They issued a second edition in 1871, p 8vo, 190 pp., at 2/o, advertised in the *Ath* on Nov. 11. I have copies in boards at 2/o, no dates, 18.3 cm., pictorial boards in red, blue, and black, with plain white endpapers, and a publisher's ad on the back cover. The first is a fourth edition, 188 pp., yellow boards; and the second is a fifth edition, in white boards, 232 pp., with 12 more poems than in the fourth edition. This and the following title were issued in 1 vol. in 1879, a new edition at 6/o cloth, listed in the *Spect* on Nov. 22. Also 1883. See 1903

1548 GEORGE J. WHYTE MELVILLE
The True Cross. 12mo. New Edition.
2/o boards, 2/6 cloth   July 15
(*Ath* ad)
Library of Select Authors. This is my copy, no date, 17.6 cm., 241 pp., pale pink decorated boards, with a printer's date (Nov. 1881). It has the series title at the bottom of the spine and "The Works of Whyte Melville" at the top. There are ads on the endpapers, back cover, and 12 pp. at the back. It was given as *Select Library of Fiction* No. 601 and called uniform with it, although it is in verse. The No. was later changed to 133. The first edition was issued by Chapman & Hall, London, 1873, 12mo, 241 pp., 8/o, listed in the *Ath* on Feb. 22. It was reissued at 2/o boards, listed in the *Ath* on Mar. 21, 1874, 241 pp. It and the preceding title were issued in 1 vol. (see above).
See 1903

1549 EDWARD P. ROE *A Knight of the Nineteenth Century.* 2/o boards, 2/6 cloth July 15 (*Ath* ad)
Select Library of Fiction No. 523, later changed to No. 376.
Also 1878, 86

1550 EDWARD P. ROE *Near to Nature's Heart.* 2/o boards, 2/6 cloth   July 15 (*Ath* ad)
Select Library of Fiction No. 524, later changed to No. 377.
Also 1878, 86

1551 CHARLES LEVER *Paul Gosslett's Confessions.* New Edition. 2/o boards, 2/6 cloth   July 15 (*Ath* ad)
Select Library of Fiction No. 532, later changed to No. 58. It has 152 pp. It ran in *St. Paul's Magazine*, passim, Feb. 1868–July 1868. The first book edition was issued by Virtue & Co., London, 1868, Cr 8vo, anonymous, 152 pp., frontispiece, 2/6 cloth, listed in the *Ath* on Oct. 31. George Routledge, London, issued it at 1/o sewed, about May 14, 1870; and Chapman & Hall, London, issued it as *Select Library of Fiction* No. 264 in 1875, at 1/o sewed; and also in 1879, listed in *Spect* on Sept. 6, 1879, 12mo, 1/o.

1552 GEORGE R. EMERSON *William Ewart Gladstone.* Frontispiece (portrait). 1/o boards   July (*Bks*)
This is 1882, 22 cm., 322 pp. It was reissued, 1893, 22 cm., 400 pp., illustrated, with a continuation by D. Williamson.
Also 1881, 86

1553 CHARLES CLARKE *The Beauclercs Father and Son.* 2/o boards, 2/6 cloth July?
Select Library of Fiction No. 168, later changed to No. 337. It ran in *Fraser's Magazine* from Nov. 1865 to Sept. 1866. The first edition was issued by Harper & Bros., New York, 1866, as *Library of Select Novels* No. 286, 25 cm., 90 pp., double columns, $.50 paper, advertised in the *New York Times* on Dec. 1, 1866, as "This day," and listed in *ALG&PC* (fortnightly) on Dec. 15. The first book edition in England was issued by Chapman & Hall, London, 3 vols., 1867, 20.5 cm., 31/6, listed in the *Spect* on Feb. 16. It was reissued as *Select Library of Fiction* No. 168 (1870), a new edition, 396 pp., 2/o boards, about July 16.

1554 CHARLES CLARKE *A Box for the Season.* New Edition. 1/o boards, 2/6 cloth   July?
Select Library of Fiction No. 207, later changed to No. 338. It has no date, 18.3

cm., 247 pp., with the series title on the cover. The first edition was issued by Chapman & Hall, London, 2 vols., 1864, p 8vo, 21/0, listed in the *Ath* on Jan. 16. It was reissued as a new edition, 1873, as *Select Library of Fiction* No. 207, my copy, 17.9 cm., 247 pp., 2/0, yellow pictorial boards in red, blue, and black, with a printer's date (Oct. 21, 1872). It was listed in the *Ath* on Mar. 22.

1555 ELEANOR EDEN *Dumbleton Common.* 2/0 boards, 2/6 cloth July?

Select Library of Fiction No. 127, later changed to No. 661. The first edition was issued by Bentley, London, 2 vols., 1867, 20 cm., 21/0, listed in the *Ath* on Feb. 23. Chapman & Hall, London, issued it as *Select Library of Fiction* No. 127, a new edition, 1868, at 2/0 boards, with purple ads on the endpapers, listed in the *Ath* on May 23.

1556 GERALDINE E. JEWSBURY *Constance Herbert.* [New edition]. 1/0 boards, 2/6 cloth   July?

Select Library of Fiction No. 59, later changed to No. 571. The first edition was issued by Hurst & Blackett, London, 3 vols., 1855, p 8vo, 31/6, listed in the *Ath* on Mar. 17. Chapman & Hall, London, issued it as *Select Library of Fiction* No. 59, 1865, 2/0 boards, listed in the *Ath* on Apr. 29. The first American edition was issued by Harper & Bros., New York, 1855, 23 cm., 123 pp., $.37½ paper, as *Library of Select Novels* No. 198, advertised in the *New-York Times* on June 20 as "On June 21."

1557 ANNE MARSH, later MARSH-CALDWELL *Mount Sorel.* New Edition. 2/0 boards, 2/6 cloth   July?

Select Library of Fiction No. 349, later changed to No. 454. The first English edition was issued by Chapman & Hall, London, in 4 parts, 3/0 sewed each, in p 8vo

monthly vols., the beginning of a new *Monthly Series* as No. 1. Part 1 was listed in the *Ath* on Dec. 28, 1844; part 2 on Feb. 1, 1845, as was also vol. I at 7/0; part 3 on Mar. 1; Vol. II, p 8vo, 7/0, listed Mar. 29. Sadleir apparently had this title and *The Whiteboy* interchanged! Thomas Hodgson, London, issued it as *Parlour Library* No. 134 (1856), 365 pp.; and it was reissued in that series by C. H. Clarke, London, at 1/6 boards, in 1860, and again at 2/0 boards about Jan. 11, 1862. Chapman & Hall, London, issued *Select Library of Fiction* No. 97, at 2/0 boards, listed in the *Bks* as published in Feb. 1867. They reissued it as No. 349 in late 1876 or early 1877. The first American edition was issued by Harper & Bros., New York, 1845, 156 pp., listed in *Godey's Lady's Book*, anonymous, for June 1845.

1558 JOHN MILLS *The Belle of the Village.* 2/0 boards, 2/6 cloth   July?

Select Library of Fiction No. 40, later changed to No. 582. The first edition was issued by Henry Colburn, London, 3 vols., 1852, 21 cm., anonymous, 31/6, listed in the *Ath* on July 31. Chapman & Hall, London, issued the second edition, 1864, as *Select Library of Fiction* No. 40, 369 pp., 2/0 boards, listed in the *Ath* on Jan. 2, 1864.

1559 ROSA M. KETTLE (MARY ROSA S. KETTLE) *My Home in the Shires.* 12mo. 2/0 boards, 2/6 cloth   July?

Select Library of Fiction No. 462, later changed to No. 612. This is my copy, no date, 18 cm., 346 pp., yellow pictorial boards, printed in red, blue, and black, with the series title, "Select Library," on the spine. It has a printer's date (June 1882), and there are ads on the endpapers, the back cover, and 20 pp. at the back. There is a cut-down page at the back advertising the author's novels at 5/0, to be had from the author at her home address! The first edition was issued by Weir, London, 1876, author's edition, at 5/0.

1560 PHINEAS T. BARNUM Struggles and Triumphs. 12mo. 2/0 boards   Aug. 5 (*Spect*)

This is (1882), 367 pp., brought up to the year 1882. The first American edition was issued by J. B. Burr & Co., Hartford, 1869, 22 cm., 780 pp., illustrated, listed in the *Ind* on Oct. 21 and in *ALG&PC* (fortnightly) on Nov. 1. The first English edition was issued by Sampson Low, London, 1869, 780 pp., illustrated, 10/6. He issued it at 2/6 boards, illustrated, about Sept. 3, 1870. There was a steady stream of updates issued by Courier, Buffalo, from 1871 to 1889, always adding a few pages.
Also 1889

1561 EDWARD P. ROE A Day of Fate. 2/0 boards, 2/6 cloth   Aug. (*Bks*)

Select Library of Fiction No. 452, later changed to No. 374. This has no date and 367 pp. The first English edition was issued by Ward, Lock & Co. (1880), 2 vols., 5/0 cloth each. Vol. 1 was listed in the *Ath* on Aug. 14 and by *PC* as published Oct. 1–14; vol. 2 was listed in the *Ath* on Oct. 23 and by *PC* on Nov. 1. The first American edition was issued by Dodd, Mead & Co., New York (copyright 1880), 19 cm., 450 pp., $1.50, in an edition of 20,000 copies, advertised in the *New-York Times* on Oct. 2 as "Ready." It has 6 pp. of ads and is bound in purple-brown or tan cloth with yellow endpapers, or blue cloth with figured endpapers in brown, or in green cloth with yellow endpapers. It was listed in the *Ind* on Oct. 14 and listed in *PW* and *Lit World* on Oct. 9, but listed in the *Nation* on Sept. 30. There was a second edition advertised in the *New-York Times* on Nov. 16 as "Now ready."
Also 1886

1562 ADELINE D. T. WHITNEY Odd or Even? 2/0 boards, 2/6 cloth Aug. (*Bks*)

Select Library of Fiction No. 525, later changed to No. 710. The first English edition was issued by Ward, Lock & Co., 2 vols. (1880), Cr 8vo. Vol. 1 was listed in the *Spect* on May 1, 5/0; and 2 vols. were listed June 5 at 10/6. They issued it in the *Family Gift Series* (1881), Cr 8vo, 583 pp., at 2/6 cloth. The first American edition was issued by Houghton, Osgood & Co., Boston, 1880, 19 cm., 505 pp., listed in the *Ind* on Apr. 19, *PW* on May 1, and *Lit World* on May 8.
Also 1886

1563 GEORGIANA M. CRAIK Riverston. 2/0 boards, 2/6 cloth   Aug.?

Select Library of Fiction No. 154, later changed to No. 494. The first edition was issued by Smith, Elder & Co., London, 3 vols., 1857, 21 cm., advertised in the *Ath* on Oct. 17 as "Now ready." Chapman & Hall issued it as *Select Library of Fiction* No. 154 (1869), a new edition, 407 pp., at 2/0 boards, listed in the *Spect* on July 24. They reissued it in the series with the No. 346 in late 1876 or early 1877.

1564 GERALDINE JEWSBURY The Sorrows of Gentility. 2/0 boards, 2/6 cloth   Aug.?

Select Library of Fiction No. 44, later changed to No. 569. This ran in the *Ladies' Companion*. It was in the Sept. 7, 1850, issue, and chapter 10 was in the Oct. 26 issue. The first book edition was issued by Hurst & Blackett, London, 2 vols., 1856, p 8vo, 21/0, listed in the *Ath* on May 17. Chapman & Hall, London, issued it as *Select Library of Fiction* No. 44, the second edition, 1864, 17.5 cm., 346 pp., listed in the *Ath* on Mar. 12.

1565 ANNE MARSH, later MARSH-
CALDWELL *Emilia Wyndham.*
New Edition. 2/0 boards,
2/6 cloth   Aug.?

Select Library of Fiction No. 110, later
changed to No. 453. Chapman & Hall,
London, issued it in this series as No. 110,
12mo, 352 pp., at 2/0 boards, listed by the
Bks as published in July 1867. They reissued it, 1872, my copy, 18 cm., 352 pp., a
new edition, 2/0 boards, in yellow pictorial
boards, printed in red and blue.
Also 1864

1566 LADY HARRIET ANNE SCOTT
The Only Child. 2/0 boards,
2/6 cloth   Aug.?

Select Library of Fiction No. 56, later
changed to No. 763. The first edition was
issued by Hurst & Blackett, London, 2
vols., 1858, 21 cm., 21/0, listed in the *Ath*
on Mar. 6. The present issue is my copy,
no date, 18 cm., 321 pp., yellow pictorial
boards, with 3 illustrations on the front in
red, blue, and black. It has a printer's date
(June 1882) and has the series title, "Select Library," on the spine. There are ads
on the endpapers, back cover, and 26 pp.
at the back. Chapman & Hall, London, issued it in this series, 1865, at 2/0 boards,
listed in the *Ath* on Mar. 4; and issued the
third edition in 1870, at 1/0 sewed.

1567 EMILIE CARLÉN (EMILIE FLYGARE,
later CARLÉN) *Twelve Months of
Matrimony.* 2/0 boards, 2/6 cloth
Sept. 9 (*Spect*)

Select Library of Fiction No. 496, later
changed to No. 711.
See *The Events of One Year*, 1855

ANONYMOUS Penny Biographical Series.
3 vols.   Sept.?

These were mentioned in editorial matter
in the *Spect* on Oct. 28.
1568 **No. 45.** *John Bright*
1569 **No. 47.** *Victor Hugo*
1570 **No. 48.** *William Pitt*

1571 CHARLES LEVER *Tales of the Trains.*
[New edition]. 2/0 boards, 2/6 cloth
Oct.?

Select Library of Fiction No. 531, later
changed to No. 57. The first edition was
issued by William S. Orr, London; etc.,
1845, 16 cm., by Tilbury Tramp, 156 pp.,
illustrated, the illustrations being by
"Phiz," 2/6, bound in red cloth. It ran in
the *Dublin University Magazine* from Jan. to
May 1845, and Orr issued it in 5 parts in
buff wrappers. Part 1 was listed in the *Ath*
on June 7, 1845. Chapman & Hall issued
it, 1857, by Tilbury Tramp, 127 pp., at 1/6
boards, listed in the *Ath* on Aug. 15; and
they issued it, 1875, as *Select Library of Fiction* No. 262, a new edition, 175 pp., 1/0
sewed, by Lever, about Apr. 10. I have a
copy, 1875, in stiff pale blue wrappers, a
new edition, with a pictorial cover and the
series title on the spine. It has a printer's
date (May 19, 1876).

1572 ANONYMOUS *A Curious Company.*
Illustrated. 1/0 sewed   Nov. 18 (*Ath* ad)
Beeton's Christmas Annual, the 23rd
season.

1573 BRET HARTE *Two Men of Sandy Bar
(a Drama) and New Poems.* 1/0 sewed
Nov. (*Bks*)
Also 1877

1574 JOHN TODD *The Sunday School
Teacher.* 1/0 sewed, 1/6, 2/0 cloth
1882 (*Eng Cat*)

Friendly Counsel Series No. 17. The first edition was issued by Butler, Northampton,
Mass.; etc., 1837, 19 cm., 432 pp., as *The
Sabbath School Teacher.* The sixth edition
was issued in London, 1838, 12mo, with a
preface by H. Althans, with the present
title.

1575 JOHN TODD *Lectures to Children
and Young Men.* Series 1 and 2. 1/0 sewed,
1/6, 2/0 cloth   Nov. (*Bks*)

Friendly Counsel Series No. 18. Ward, Lock
issued Todd's complete works, 6 parts

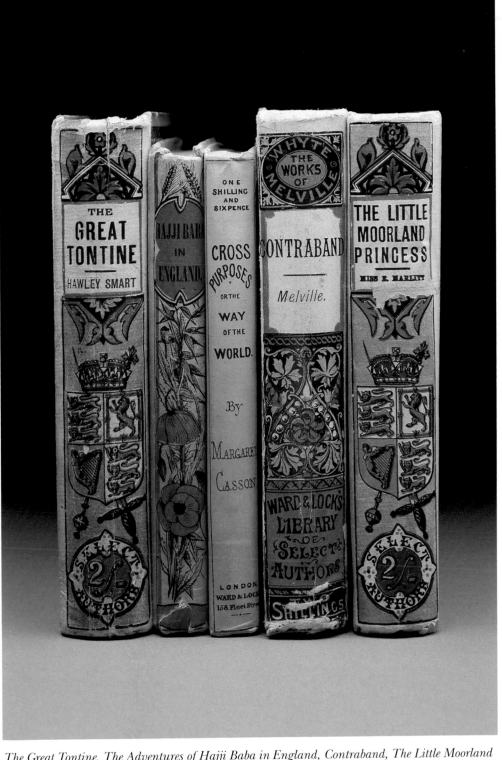

*The Great Tontine, The Adventures of Hajji Baba in England, Contraband, The Little Moorland
Princess*

Love's Provocations. See page 7

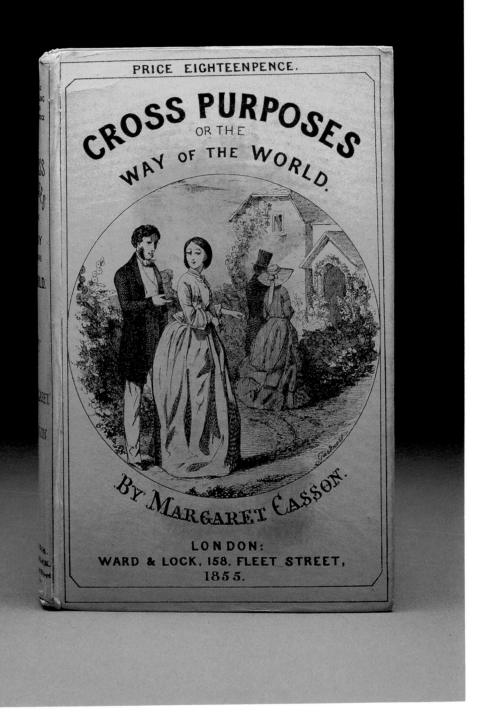

Cross Purposes in the Way of the World. See page 7

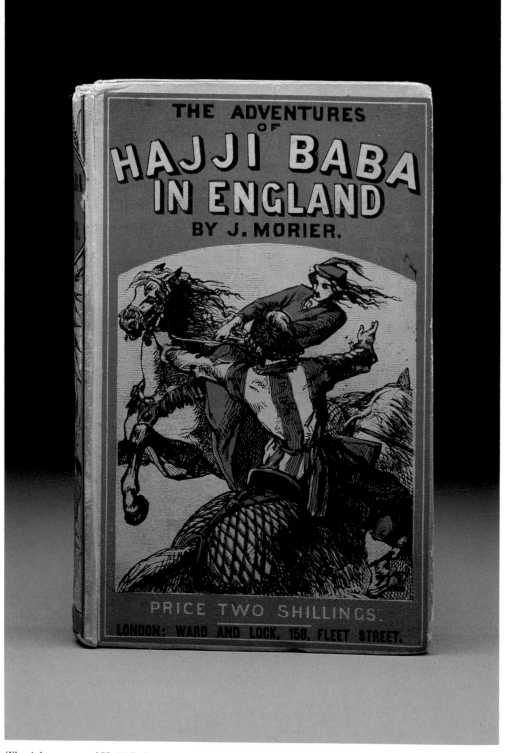

The Adventures of Hajji Baba in England. See page 9

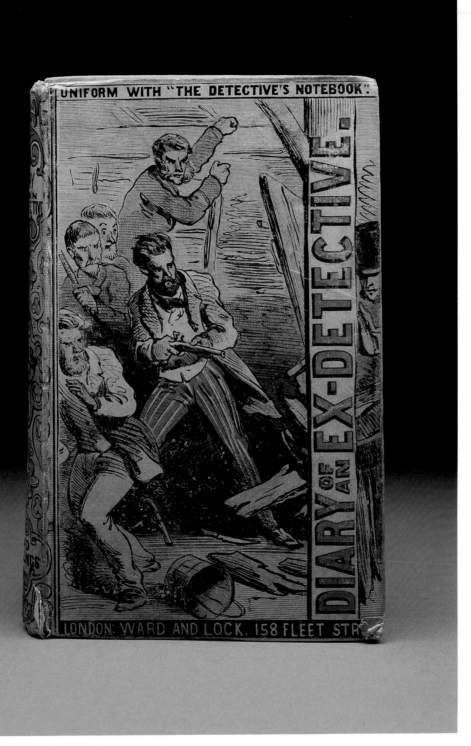

Diary of an Ex- Detective. See page 36

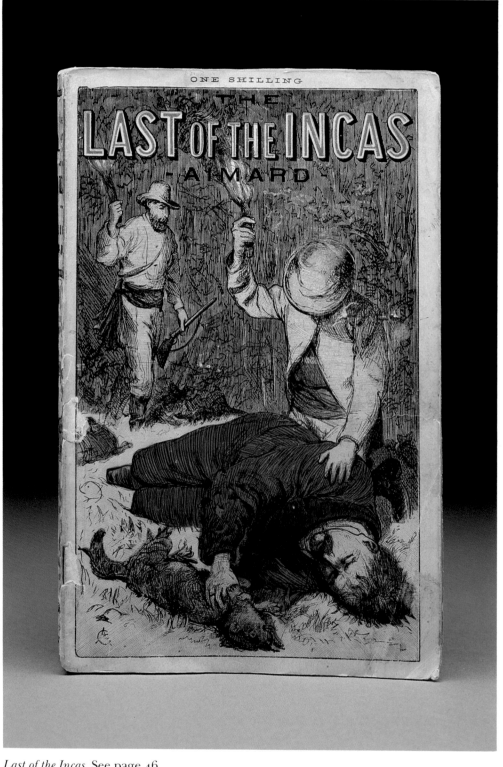

Last of the Incas. See page 46

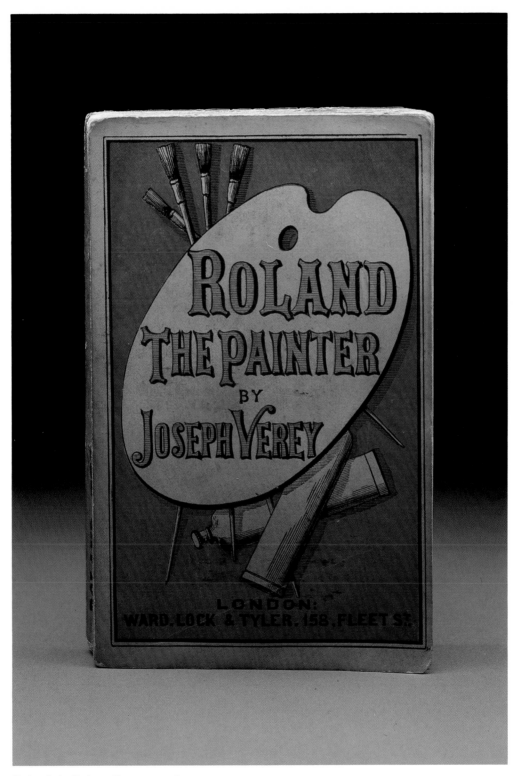

Roland the Painter. See page 48

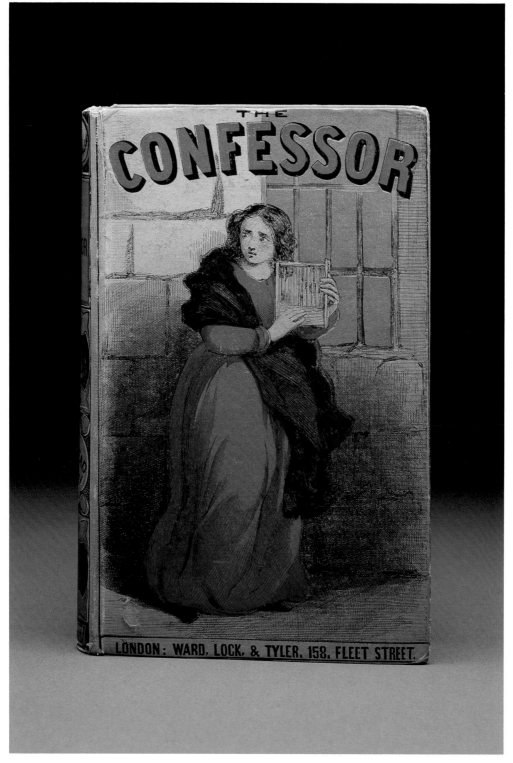

The Confessor. See page 66

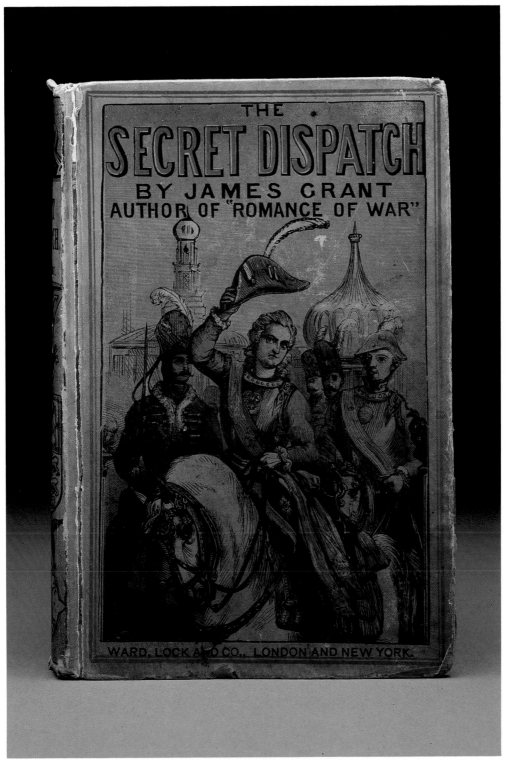

The Secret Dispatch. See page 340

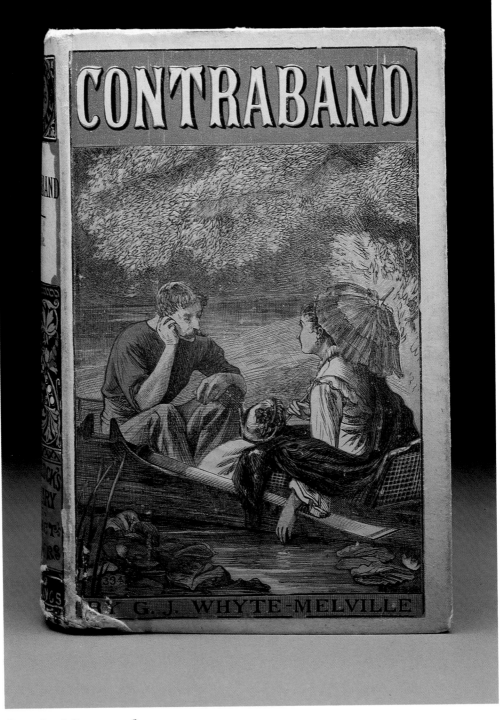

Contraband. See page 360

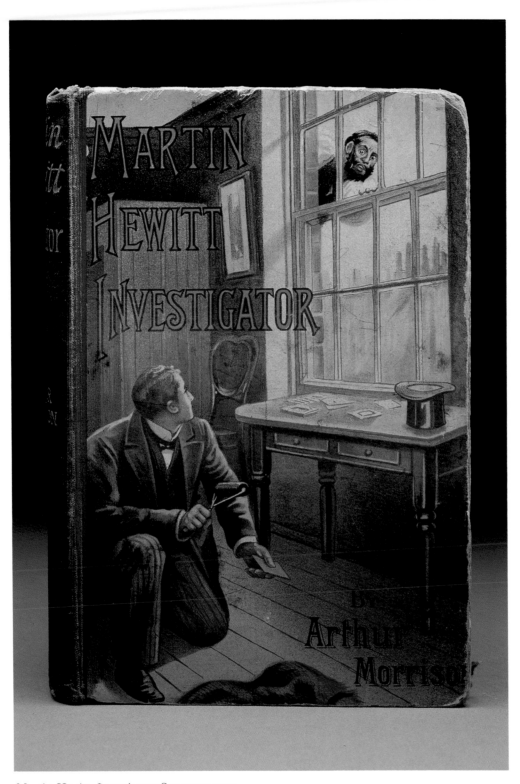

Martin Hewitt, Investigator. See page 370

Pharos the Egyptian. See page 380

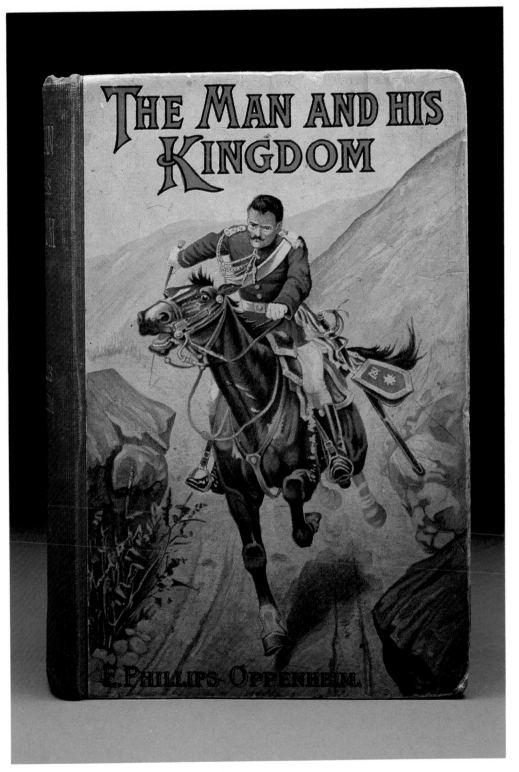

The Man and His Kingdom. See page 381

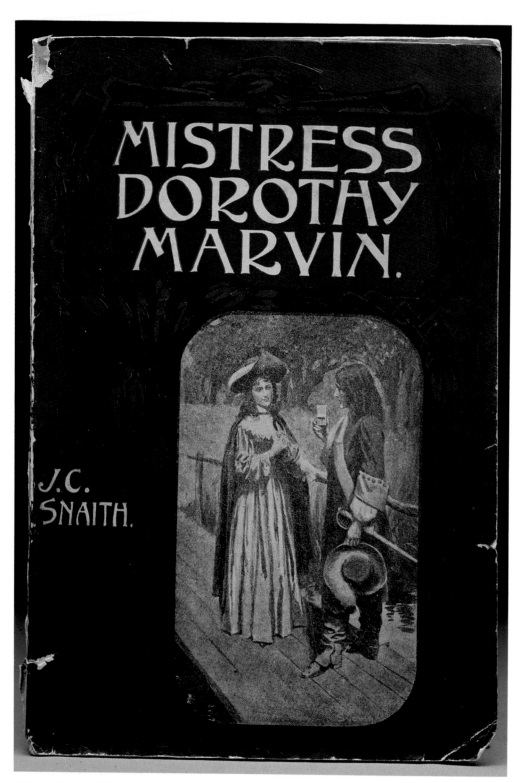

Mistress Dorothy Marvin. See page 382

Rosine and Sister Louise. See page 383

The Temptress. See page 391

(1882). The first series of *Lectures to Children* was issued by J. H. Butler, Northampton, Mass., 1834, 16 cm., 218 pp., illustrated; and the 12th edition was issued in 1841. The same was issued by the Religious Tract Society, London, 1835, revised, 16 cm., 138 pp.; and *Familiar Lectures to Children* was issued by J. W. Parker, London, 1835, abridged, anonymous, 160 pp., edited by Hobart Caunter. The second series was issued by Hopkins, Bridgman, Northampton, 1858, 275 pp., illustrated; and was issued in London (1859).

1576 JOHN TODD **Simple Sketches.**
1/o sewed, 1/6, 2/o cloth   Nov. (*Bks*)
Friendly Counsel Series No. 19. The first edition was issued by J. H. Butler, Northampton, Mass.; etc., 1838, edited by J. Brace, 16 cm., 304 pp.; and a second vol. was issued by E. P. Little, Pittsfield, Mass., 1845, edited by Brace, 16 cm., 288 pp. It was issued by T. Nelson, Edinburgh, 1848, 260 pp., illustrated.

1577 JOHN S. C. ABBOTT **The Life and Achievements of Christopher Columbus.**
12mo. 2/o boards   Nov. (*Bks*)
Also 1879

1578 S. R. W. (SARAH WHITEHEAD) **Rose Douglas.** 2/o boards, 2/6 cloth Nov.?
Select Library of Fiction No. 146, later changed to No. 769. This is probably dated 1882, a new edition, with the imprint of Chapman & Hall, London.
Also 1881

1579 WILLIAM H. MAXWELL **The Fortunes of Hector O'Halloran and His Man Mark Anthony O'Toole.** Illustrated. 2/o boards, 2/6 cloth Nov.?
Select Library of Fiction No. 515, later changed to No. 516. This has no date and 412 pp. Bentley, London, issued it in 13 monthly parts, in 1842, 1843, illustrated by Leech, in 1/o tan wrappers. Part 1 was advertised by Bentley, London; etc., in the *Ath* on Mar. 5, 1842, for the end of Mar.; part 2 was advertised on Apr. 30; and part 5 on Sept. 3. Bentley issued it in 1 vol. (1843), 23 cm., 412 pp., illustrated by Leech, 14/o, issued on May 16 according to the Bentley private catalog. Thomas Tegg, London, issued it in 1845, 8vo, 412 pp., illustrated, 9/o, listed in the *Ath* on July 26. The *U Cat* gives the Tegg issue as 1850, and the *BM* gives it as 1853. Bentley issued it as *Standard Novels* No. 121, 1851, with 432 pp. The *Standard Novels* copyrights were sold at an auction on Feb. 26 and 27, 1856; and George Routledge issued it at 2/o boards, listed in the *Ath* on Apr. 24, 1858. D. Appleton & Co., New York, issued it in parts, and the Sept. 1842 issue of the *United States Magazine* (monthly) stated that 3 parts had already appeared, and the parts were still appearing in June 1843. It was issued in book form by D. Appleton & Co., New York; George S. Appleton, Philadelphia, 1843, 22 cm., 412 pp., 23 illustrations by Leech, listed in the *United States Magazine* for July 1843.

1580 CHARLES DICKENS, ed. **The Pic-Nic Papers.** 2/o boards, 2/6 cloth   Nov.?
Select Library of Fiction No. 517, later changed to No. 229.
Also 1859, 62, 65, 70

1581 MISS F. LEVIEN **Almost a Quixote.**
2/o boards, 2/6 cloth   Dec. 23 (*Ath*)
Select Library of Fiction No. 528, later changed to No. 795. This is probably the first edition, no date, with 268 pp.

1582 LOUISA M. ALCOTT **Good Wives.**
2/o   1882 (*Eng Cat*)
Also 1871

1583 (HENRY B. ADAMS) *Democracy, An American Novel.* 12mo. o/6 sewed 1882 (*Eng Cat*)

Popular Sixpenny Books No. 57. This is my copy, no date, 18 cm., 186 pp., yellow pictorial wrappers in red, blue, and black. It has a printer's date (Sept. 1882) and has ads on the endpapers, the back cover, and 6 pp. at the back. The first edition was issued by Henry Holt, New York, 1880, 17.5 cm., anonymous, 374 pp., as *Leisure Hour Series* No. 112, in cloth, listed in the *PW* on Apr. 10 and the *Ind* on Apr. 15. This is my copy. Holt issued it at $.25 paper, probably in the *Leisure Moment Series*, a new edition, 16mo, anonymous, advertised in the *New-York Times* on Oct. 14, 1882, as "Ready," and advertised again on Apr. 7, 1883, *Leisure Moment Series*, $.30 paper, "Ready today." The first English edition was issued by Macmillan & Co., London, 1882, 19 cm., anonymous, 280 pp., 4/6, advertised in the *Ath* on May 27 as "Just ready." They issued it at 1/0 sewed about Mar. 10, 1883.

1584 JOSEPH H. INGRAHAM *The Throne of David.* 2/0 1882 (*Eng Cat*)
Also 1874

1585 WILLIAM JAY *Prayers for the Use of Families.* 12mo. 1/0 sewed, 1/6 cloth 1882 (*Eng Cat*)

Christian Knowledge Series No. 11. The first edition was issued by Gye, Bath; etc., 1820, 9/0, in May, as *The Domestic Minister's Assistant*. Hamilton, Adams, London, issued the 13th edition, 1831, 439 pp. The first American edition was issued by H. Whipple, Salem, Mass., 1821, 18 cm., 284 pp., from the second English edition.

1586 SYLVIA *Sylvia's Lady's Illustrated Lace Book.* 1/0 boards 1882 (*Eng Cat*)

Sylvia's New Needlework Books No. 2. I cannot trace this.

1587 VICTOR HUGO *Cosette and Marius.* 2/0 boards 1882

Sadleir gives this as (1882) and says it is in the style of the *Library of Select Authors*. It was *Select Library of Fiction* No. 426, later changed to No. 196.
Also 1876. See 1887

1588 VICTOR HUGO *Jean Valjean.* 2/0 boards 1882 (*Eng Cat*)

Sadleir gives this as (1882) and says it is in the *Favourite Authors* style. It was *Select Library of Fiction* No. 425, later changed to No. 197.
Also 1876, 87

1589 ANONYMOUS *The Penny Historical Series. The Elizabethan Age—The Mutinies at Spithead—Guy Fawkes, etc.* 1882 (*Eng Cat*)

There were eventually 48 titles in this series of *Penny Books for the People*. The *BM* gives only 11 parts (1882–86). Actually *The Elizabethan Age* was the 15th title in the series.
See 1883

1590 CHARLES LEVER *One of Them.* New Edition. 12mo. 2/0 boards 1882

Library of Select Authors. This is my copy, no date, 18 cm., 420 pp., white pictorial boards, printed in red, green, and black, with a printer's date (Mar. 1882). It has a dedication dated Dec. 20, 1860, and has the series title at the foot of the spine, with the words "The Works of Charles Lever" at the head. There are ads on the endpapers, back cover, and 18 pp. at the back. This was also *Select Library of Fiction* No. 35, later changed to No. 43. In England Chapman & Hall, London, issued it 15 parts in 14, 1/0 each, in pink printed wrappers, illustrated by "Phiz" (Dec. 1858–Jan. 1861). They issued it in 1 vol., 1861, 22.5 cm., 471 pp., illustrated by "Phiz," 16/0, listed in the *Ath* on Jan. 5, 1861, and advertised also as "This day."

They issued it as *Select Library of Fiction* No. 35, at 2/0 boards, listed in the *Ath* on June 13, 1863. They issued it in 1865, a new edition, p 8vo, 420 pp., illustrated, 6/0 cloth, listed in the *Reader* on July 8. I have a copy, issued by them, the 10th edition, no date, 420 pp., 2/0 boards, with a printer's date (Aug. 23, 1869). They reissued it at 2/0 boards, 1873, a new edition. In the United States it was issued in parts by Harper & Bros., New York, part 1 advertised in the *New-York Times* on Dec. 3, 1859, 8vo, $.05 paper. They issued it in 1 vol. in 1861, 24 cm., 187 pp., $.50 paper, illustrated by "Phiz," advertised in the *New-York Times* on Jan. 26 as "This day," and listed in the *Ind* on Jan. 31.

1591 GEORGE J. WHYTE MELVILLE **Tilbury Nogo.** New Edition. 12mo. 2/0 boards 1882

Library of Select Authors. This is my copy, no date, 18.2 cm., 363 pp., with a preface (Apr. 1, 1858), white pictorial boards, printed in red, tan, and black. There is a printer's date (Nov. 1881), and the series title is at the foot of the spine and "The Works of Whyte Melville" is at the head. There are ads on the endpapers, back cover, an inserted leaf at the front, and 16 pp. at the back. This was *Select Library of Fiction* No. 387, later changed to No. 115. The first edition was issued by Chapman & Hall, London, 2 vols., 1854, 20 cm., anonymous, 21/0, listed in the *Ath* on June 17. They issued it in 1 vol. in 1861, anonymous, listed in the *Spect* on June 15. They issued the fourth edition in May 1866, 18.2 cm., 363 pp., 2/0 boards, as *Select Library of Fiction* No. 80, another tale occupying pp. (325)–363. I have a copy, new edition, 1874, 18.2 cm., 363 pp., *Select Library of Fiction* No. 80 on the front cover, 2/0 boards. They issued the 10th edition, 1876, at 2/0, possibly in cloth; and in the fall of 1879 issued a new edition at 2/0 boards, as No. 387 in the series. I have a copy, 1880, new edition, 18.2 cm., 363

pp., 2/0 boards in the series, with the No. 80 on the front.

1592 ANTHONY TROLLOPE **Ralph the Heir.** New Edition. 12mo. 2/0 boards, 2/6 cloth 1882

Select Library of Fiction No. 203, later changed to No. 12. I have copies both in boards and in cloth, both with no date, 17.9 cm., 470 pp., both with the printer's date (June 1882), and both with the same 8 pp. of publisher's ads at the back. The 2/6 is in smooth green cloth, blocked in black with figured endpapers, with the series title on the front and spine, and Ward, Lock & Co., on the title page and at the base of the spine. The 2/0 is in white pictorial boards, printed in red, blue, and black, with the No. 203 on the front, and with a Chapman & Hall ad on the back cover, but with Ward, Lock & Co. on the title page. It has the series title on the spine. The first edition was issued by Hurst & Blackett, London, 3 vols., 1871, Cr 8vo, 31/6, my copy, listed in the *Spect* on Apr. 8. The complete copyright was sold by Trollope to Virtue & Co. for £2,520, and before it was published Virtue sold it to Strahan. Strahan issued it in 19, 0/6 monthly parts (Jan. 1870–July 1871), and issued it also as a supplement to *Saint Paul's Magazine*. He issued an illustrated edition, 1871, 22.5 cm., 434 pp., at 10/6, in green cloth, my copy. Chapman & Hall issued a new edition in 1872, 470 pp., 2/6 boards, 3/6 cloth, as *Select Library of Fiction* No. 203, in July; reissued as new editions, 1876 and 1878. George Routledge, London, issued it as an *Octavo Novel*, 1872, a new edition, 22.6 cm., 434 pp., with 18 illustrations, at 6/0 cloth, my copy, in dark green cloth, listed in the *Spect* on Jan. 27. Routledge, New York, issued it at $3.00 in Oct. 1873. Ward, Lock issued a new edition, 470 pp., with printer's date (Apr. 15, 1884). D. Appleton & Co., New York, paid $1,500 to Virtue & Co. for advance sheets and issued it as a supplement to *Appleton's*

Journal (Jan. 22, 1870–May 27, 1871). They thought better of issuing it in book form and sold the rights to Harper & Bros., New York, who issued the first American book issue, 1871, 23.9 cm., 282 pp., illustrated, double columns, $1.75 cloth and $1.25 paper, my copy in olive cloth. It was listed in the *Nation* on June 8 and advertised in the *New-York Times* on June 2 as "This day."

1593 ANTHONY TROLLOPE *Dr. Wortle's School.* 12mo. 2/0 boards   1882
Library of Select Authors. Select Library of Fiction No. 421. These are my copies, both having no date and 397 pp., with printer's date (June 1882), both with the same 12-page catalog at the back, and both 18 cm. The copy in the *Select Library of Fiction* is in the attractive illuminated decorative boards, the same on the front and back, with plain pale yellow endpapers, the series title on the front, back, and spine, and "The Works of Anthony Trollope" at the head of the spine. The *Library of Select Authors* copy has the series title at the foot of the spine and "The Works of Anthony Trollope" at the head, bound in yellow pictorial boards, with ads on the endpapers and back cover.
Also 1881

1594 EDWARD BULWER LYTTON *Paul Clifford.* 12mo. 2/0 boards   1882
Select Library of Fiction No. 507, later changed to No. 264. The *BM* gives (1882), 312 pp.
Also 1881

1595 CHARLES LEVER *Tony Butler.* New Edition. 12mo. 2/0 boards   1882
Library of Select Authors. This is my copy, no date, 18 cm., 420 pp., pale pink pictorial boards, printed in red, blue, and black, with the No. 225 on the front. It has the series title at the foot of the spine and "The Works of Charles Lever" at the

head, printer's date (June 1882), with ads on the endpapers and back cover, and with a 22-page catalog at the back. This was *Select Library of Fiction* No. 225, later changed to No. 52. It ran in *Blackwood's Magazine* (Oct. 1863–Jan. 1865). The first book edition was issued by William Blackwood & Sons, Edinburgh and London, 3 vols., 1865, p 8vo, anonymous, 31/6, listed in the *Ath* on Jan. 21. Chapman & Hall, London, issued it in 3 vols., 1872, a new edition, by Lever, with Blackwood sheets and new prelims, and with Chapman & Hall on the spine, having no appearance of a remainder! They issued it in 1873 as *Select Library of Fiction* No. 225, at 2/6 boards, 3/6 cloth, listed in the *Ath* on May 3. They issued a new edition, 1878, 18 cm., 420 pp. George Routledge, London, issued it in 1878, Cr 8vo, 3/6 cloth, listed in the *Spect* on May 11. The first American edition was issued by Harper & Bros., New York, 1865, 23 cm., anonymous, 257 pp., at $1.00 paper, $1.50 cloth, advertised in the *New-York Times* on Mar. 11 as "This day," and listed in *ALG&PC* (fortnightly) on Mar. 15. It was reprinted from *Blackwood's Magazine.*

1596 CHARLES LEVER *A Rent in a Cloud. St. Patrick's Eve.* New Edition. 2/0 boards   1882
This is probably in the *Library of Select Authors*, but the copy I examined was re-bound, no date, with a printer's date (Feb. 1882). It was *Select Library of Fiction* No. 193, later changed to No. 49. It has 370 pp., with the second title occupying pp. (243)–370. Chapman & Hall, London, issued it (1871), a new edition, 18 cm., 370 pp., 2/0 boards, as *Select Library of Fiction* No. 193; and reissued it (1875), a new edition, the same. The first edition of the first title was issued by William Blackwood & Sons, Edinburgh and London, 1865. There are no copies in the *U Cat* or in the *BM*! Chapman & Hall issued it in 1869, 242 pp., at 1/0 sewed and 5/0 cloth; and is-

sued it in 1870, a new edition, 17.5 cm., 242 pp., with a printer's date (May 31, 1870). The first American edition of the first title was issued by T. B. Peterson & Bros., Philadelphia, 1870, 24 cm., 111 pp., double columns, $.50, advertised in the *New-York Times* on Nov. 21, and listed in *Christian Union* on Dec. 10. The first edition of the second title was issued by Chapman & Hall, 1845, 17 cm., 203 pp., illustrated by "Phiz," 5/o cloth, and listed in the *Ath* on Mar. 29. They issued it in 1866, illustrated, 1/o sewed, in Nov. or Dec. (*Bks*); and reissued it, 1867, illustrated, 1/o, probably in stiff wrappers, as *Select Library of Fiction* No. 115, in Nov. or Dec. (*Bks*). The first American edition of the second title was issued by Harper & Bros., New York, 1845, 24 cm., 38 pp., noticed in *Southern Literary Messenger* for June.

1597 MARK LEMON *Leyton Hall and Other Tales.* New Edition. 12mo.
2/o boards   1882

Select Library of Fiction No. 325. This is my copy, no date, 18 cm., 376 pp., white pictorial boards, printed in red, green, and black, with the series title on the spine. It has a printer's date (May 1882) and has ads on the endpapers, the back cover, and a 22-page catalog at the back. Under renumbering this became No. 725. The first edition was issued by Hurst & Blackett, London, 3 vols., 1867 (1866), p 8vo, 31/6, listed in the *Ath* on Dec. 8, 1866. Chapman & Hall, London, issued it in 1876, as *Select Library of Fiction* No. 325, at 2/o boards, listed in the *Ath* on May 20. In the United States it was issued by T. B. Peterson & Bros., Philadelphia, in 1867, 8vo, 176 pp., listed in *Godey's Lady's Book* for Jan. 1868.

1598 SCRUTATOR (KNIGHTLEY W. HORLOCK) *The Country Gentleman.* New Edition. 12mo. 2/o boards   1882

Select Library of Fiction No. 72, later changed to No. 596. This is my copy, no

date, 17.8 cm., 358 pp., white pictorial boards, printed in red, blue, and black, with the No. 72 on the front, and the series title on the spine. It has a printer's date (June 1882). The first edition was issued by Hurst and Blackett, London, 3 vols., 1862, 20 cm., 31/6, listed in the *Ath* on Mar. 1. Chapman & Hall issued a new edition, 1863, my copy, 19.4 cm., 358 pp., with a frontispiece and a vignette title page, 5/o white cloth, listed in the *Reader* on Oct. 3. They issued the third edition in 1865, 2/o boards, as *Select Library of Fiction* No. 72, listed in the *Reader* on Nov. 4. They continued to reissue it, passim, and I have a new edition, 1873, a 2/o yellowback, with ads of 1876.

1599 WILLIAM H. AINSWORTH
Cardinal Pole. New Edition. 12mo.
2/o boards   1882

Select Library of Fiction No. 335, later changed to No. 73. This is my copy, no date, 18 cm., 416 pp., yellow pictorial boards, printed in red, blue, and black, with ads on the endpaper and back cover, and an 18-page catalog at the back. It has a replaced spine and a printer's date (Jan. 1882). The first edition was issued by Chapman & Hall, London, 3 vols., 1863, p 8vo, 31/6, listed in the *Ath* on Aug. 1. They issued the second edition, Cr 8vo, 400 pp., at 5/o cloth, listed in the *Reader* on Aug. 6, 1864. They issued it as *Select Library of Fiction* No. 60, at 2/o boards, my copy, 17.5 cm., 400 pp., dated 1865, listed in the *Ath* on May 27. They reissued it in the same series as No. 335, at 2/o boards, in 1876.
Also 1894

1600 JANE AUSTEN *Northanger Abbey. Persuasion.* New Edition. p 8vo. 2/o boards   1882

Select Library of Fiction No. 166, later changed to No. 190. This is my copy, 1882, 18.2 cm., 212 pp. (213)–440 pp., in light green pictorial boards, printed in red, blue, and black, with the series title on the spine. It has separate title pages for the two stories, the second with no date. The imprint is Ward, Lock & Co., and it is in a *Select Library of Fiction* case, Chapman & Hall ads on the endpapers, the back cover, and 8 pp. at the back, and with Ward, Lock on the front cover. The first edition was issued by John Murray, London, 4 vols., 1818, anonymous, 24/0 in boards, with a biographical notice of the author, listed by the *Quarterly Review* as published July–Sept. 1817. Bentley, London, issued both titles in 1 vol. as *Standard Novels* No. 28, 1833, 440 pp. Chapman & Hall, London, issued it as *Select Library of Fiction* No. 166, 440 pp., at 2/0 boards, about Apr. 16, 1870. Carey & Lea, Philadelphia, issued the first title, 2 vols., 1833, 18.5 cm.; and the second title, 2 vols., 1832. The first title was 19.5 cm., issued in an edition of 1,250 copies, finished on Jan. 20, 1833, and advertised in the *National Gazette and Literary Register* on Jan. 24. The second title was 19.5 cm., in an edition of 1,250 copies, to sell for $.84 wholesale. It was finished on Nov. 6, 1832, and advertised in the *National Gazette and Literary Register* on Nov. 8 as "This day." I cannot explain the *Quarterly Review* listing, as the 4 Murray vols. were advertised in the *Morning Chronicle* on Dec. 19, 1817, as "Tomorrow," and on Dec. 20 as "This day," and were advertised in the *Courier* on Dec. 17, 1817, as "On Dec. 20."

1601 W. M. L. JAY (JULIA L. M. WOODRUFF) *Shiloh.* 12mo. 2/0 boards   1882

Select Library of Fiction No. 519, later changed to No. 602. This is my copy, no date, 17.9 cm., 519 pp., white pictorial boards, printed in red, blue, and black, with the series title on the spine. It has an inscribed date (1882) and a printer's date (Aug. 1882). There are ads on the endpapers, back cover, and in a 28-page catalog at the back.
Also 1874

1602 CHARLES LEVER *Harry Lorrequer.* New Edition with Autobiographical Introduction. 12mo. 2/0 boards   1882

Library of Select Authors. This is my copy, no date, 18 cm., 379 pp., with an introduction (1872), in cream pictorial boards, printed in red, green, and black with "Harry Lorrequer's Confessions" on the front, the series title at the foot of the spine, and "The Works of Charles Lever" at the head. It has a printer's date (May 1882), No. 22 on the front cover, and ads on the endpapers, back cover, and in a 24-page catalog at the back. This was *Select Library of Fiction* No. 22, later changed to No. 40. The first appearance was in 11, 1/0 parts in pink wrappers, William Curry, Jr., & Co., Dublin, illustrated by "Phiz," part 1 listed in the *Spect* on Mar. 9, 1839, and part 10 on Dec. 21. He issued it in 1 vol., *The Confessions of Harry Lorrequer*, 1839, 22 cm., illustrated by "Phiz," 12/0, listed in the *Ath* on Jan. 25, 1840. It was issued by Chapman & Hall, London, 1857 (1856), 22 cm., 344 pp., illustrated; and reissued, 1859, Cr 8vo, 8 illustrations by "Phiz," 4/0, advertised in *Notes & Queries* on Feb. 5. They issued it in 1862, as *Select Library of Fiction* No. 22, with a frontispiece, 2/0 boards, listed in the *Ath* on June 28. They issued a new edition in 1865, p 8vo, 379 pp., at 6/0, listed in the *Reader* on Jan. 28. I have a copy, 1879, new edition, with an autobiographical introduction, at 2/0 boards, with a printer's date (Sept. 14, 1878) and an introduction (1872). The first American edition was issued by Carey & Hart, Philadelphia, 1840, 23.5 cm., anonymous, 402 pp., noticed in the *Knickerbocker* for Nov.
Also 1884

1603 SIR WALTER SCOTT *Waverley.* 2/0 boards   1882 (*BM*)

Select Library of Fiction No. 503, later changed to No. 230. The *BM* gives this as (1882), with 418 pp.
Also 1880

1604 SIR WALTER SCOTT *Ivanhoe.*
2/0 boards   1882 (*BM*)

Select Library of Fiction No. 505, later changed to No. 232. The *BM* gives this as (1882), with 397 pp.
Also 1880

1605 FRANCES E. TROLLOPE
Aunt Margaret's Trouble. New Edition.
12mo. 2/0 boards   1882

Select Library of Fiction No. 212, later changed to No. 459. This is my copy, 1882, 18.1 cm., 292 pp., pale green pictorial boards, printed in orange, tan, and black, in the Chapman & Hall *Select Library of Fiction* clothing. It has the No. 212 on the front, the series title on the spine, and there is a printer's date (Apr. 16, 1880). There are ads for the series on the endpapers, the back cover, and on 8 pp. at the back. It was issued by Chapman & Hall, London, 1880, a new edition, 292 pp., as No. 212 in the series, and the present issue apparently used the sheets of that issue. The first edition was issued by Chapman & Hall, London, 1866, 19 cm., anonymous, 292 pp., 8/0, listed in the *Ath* on Aug. 11. They issued the second edition in 1866, anonymous, 292 pp., 8/0, advertised in the *Spect* on Oct. 20 as "This day"; reissued the second edition about Dec. 1, 1866. They issued the fourth edition in 1870, at 1/0 sewed, listed by the *Bks* as published in Apr. They issued a 2/0 yellowback as *Select Library of Fiction* No. 212, about Apr. 12, 1873. The first American edition was issued by T. B. Peterson & Bros., Philadelphia, 1870, by Miss Dickens! It was listed in *Godey's Lady's Book* for Nov. and thus probably issued in Aug. or Sept. It was listed in *Lippincott's Magazine* for Mar. 1870, 8vo, 57 pp., by Miss Dickens, and thus probably issued in Jan. or Feb.
Also 1884

1606 G. P. R. JAMES *Bernard Marsh.*
12mo. 2/0 boards   1882?

Library of Select Authors. This has no date, 18 cm., 380 pp., my copy, white pictorial boards with the front cover in red, blue, and black, and with the series title at the foot of the spine. There are ads on the endpapers, the back cover, and 8 pp. at the back, and I date it from the ads. The first edition was issued by Bentley, London, 2 vols., 1864, 19 cm., at 21/0, advertised in the *Ath* on Apr. 23 as "On Apr. 25," and listed on Apr. 30. Ward & Lock gave it the No. 230 in the *Select Library of Fiction*, later changed to No. 435. Chapman & Hall, London, issued it, 1873, as *Select Library of Fiction* No. 230, 17.9 cm., 380 pp., at 2/0 boards, my copy, with a printer's date (Apr. 22, 1873), listed in the *Ath* on May 31.

1607 ELIZABETH WETHERELL (ANNA WARNER) *Carl Krinken.* 12mo. 1/0 sewed, 1/6, 2/0 cloth   1882?

Lily Series No. 76. The first edition was issued by George P. Putnam, New York, 1854, with a preface signed Amy Lothrop (Anna Warner). It was vol. 1 of *Ellen Montgomery's Bookshelf*, mentioned in editorial matter in the *Ind* on Jan. 5, 1854. In England it was issued by James Nisbet & Co., etc., London, 1854, 16 cm., anonymous, 255 pp., illustrated, with the cover title, *The Christmas Stocking*, and a preface signed Amy Lothrop, and dated Dec. 13, 1853. It was also issued by Clarke, Beeton, London, 1855 (1854), *The Christmas Stocking*, 155 pp., at 1/0; by Piper, Stephenson, & Spence, London, 1855 (1854), with a different title page; and by Frederick Warne, London, in 1865.

Shilling Novels. 12 vols. 1/0 sewed each
1882?

These were probably issued in 1882, although the later titles could have been issued in 1883.

1608 **No. 2.** JOHN LANG *Clever Criminals.* Also 1870, 71

1609 **No. 3.** CHARLES ROSS *The Eldest Miss Simpson.* Also 1866

1610 **No. 4.** JOHN MILLS *The Flyers of the Hunt.* Illustrated. Also 1865, 73

1611 **No. 5.** JOHN LANG *The Forger's Wife.* Also 1855, 58, 70

1612 **No. 6.** JOHN MILLS *The Life of a Racehorse.* Illustrated. Also 1854, 56, 65, 73, 85

1613 **No. 8.** JOHN LANG *My Friend's Wife.* Also 1859, 70

1614 **No. 9.** JOHN LANG *The Secret Police.* Also 1859, 70, 83

1615 **No. 10.** JOHN MILLS *Stable Secrets.* Illustrated. Also 1865, 73, 85

1616 **No. 11.** ANGUS REACH & C. W. SHIRLEY BROOKS *A Story with a Vengeance.* Illustrated. Also 1868

1617 **No. 13.** JOHN LANG *Too Clever by Half.* Illustrated. Also 1870

1618 **No. 14.** JOHN LANG *Too Much Alike.* Also 1854, 58, 70

1619 **No. 16.** *Yankee Humour and Uncle Sam's Fun.* Introduction by W. Jerdan. Illustrated. Also 1860, 65

1620 ANNA BARBAULD & DR. JOHN AIKEN *Evenings at Home.* Illustrated. 1/o sewed, 1/6 cloth   1882?

Youth's Library of Wonders and Adventures No. 28. It was also issued in the *Family Gift Series*, Cr 8vo, illustrated, 2/6 cloth; and in *The Good Worth Library* illustrated, 3/6 cloth. The first edition was issued by J. Johnson, London, 6 vols., 1792–96. In the United States, *The Works of Mrs. Barbauld* was issued by David Reed, Boston, 3 vols., 1826; and by G. & C. Carvill, New York, 2 vols., 1826.

1621 (JOSEPH JOHNSON) *Famous Boys and How They Became Great Men.* Illustrated. 1/o sewed, 1/6 cloth   1882?

Youth's Library of Wonders and Adventures No. 29. This was also issued in the *Family Gift Series*, Cr 8vo, 2/6 cloth; and in the *Good Worth Library*, illustrated, 3/6 cloth. The first edition was issued by Darton & Co., London, 1860, 18 cm., anonymous,

293 pp., illustrated. The first American edition was issued by W. A. Townsend & Co., New York, 1861, 300 pp., illustrated. Ward, Lock issued it with no date and 302 pp., which the *BM* gives as (1879).

1622 WILLIAM H. AINSWORTH *Old Court.* Cr 8vo. 2/o boards   1882?

Select Library of Fiction No. 371, later changed to No. 78. This has no date, 18.2 cm., 380 pp., with ads on the endpapers and a 10-page catalog at the back. The first edition was issued by Chapman & Hall, London, 3 vols., 1867, p 8vo, 31/6, listed in the *Ath* on June 1. They issued it as *Select Library of Fiction* No. 371, 2/o boards, listed in the *Ath* on Jan. 26, 1878.

1623 HENRY KINGSLEY *Reginald Hetherege.* 12mo. 2/o boards   1882?

Select Library of Fiction No. 201, later changed to No. 109. This has no date, 18.1 cm., 355 pp., with a printer's date (Oct. 1882), and a 20-page catalog at the back. This was not in the Chapman & Hall series, and the No. 201 was created by Ward, Lock when putting this title in the *Select Library of Fiction* from its *Favourite Author's* issue in 1875.
Also 1875

1624 AMELIA B. EDWARDS *Monsieur Maurice and Other Tales.* New Edition. 2/o boards   after 1881

Select Library of Fiction No. 307, later changed to No. 401. This was Sadleir's copy, and he gave it as after 1881. The first edition was issued by Hurst & Blackett, London, 3 vols., 1873, p 8vo, 31/6, listed in the *Ath* on Aug. 30. It contains seven stories. Chapman & Hall, London, issued it as No. 307 in the series, listed in the *Ath* on Feb. 12, 1876.

1625 IVAN TURGENIEFF *Virgin Soil.*
2/0 boards, 2/6 cloth   Jan. 6 (*Spect*)
Select Library of Fiction No. 483 in the new numbering. During 1883 Ward, Lock began a new numbering system for this series. If only a new No. is given, this implies that it was not issued with an old No. The present edition is (1883), 315 pp., a duplicate of the Henry Holt, New York, issue, with a new title page. The first edition in English was issued by Henry Holt, New York, 1877, *Leisure Hour Series* No. 88, 17 cm., 315 pp., in cream cloth printed in black, with endpaper ads (June 13, 1877). It was translated from the French edition by T. S. Perry, listed in the *Ind* on June 14, and in *PW* on June 23. The second edition was issued in Paris (1877), *Terres Vierges*. The first English edition was issued by Macmillan & Co., London, 1878, Cr 8vo, 346 pp., 10/6, in green cloth, translated by A. W. Dilke. It was listed in the *Spect* on June 22.

1626 HARRIET L. CHILDE-PEMBERTON
Original Readings and Recitations.
"Prince" . . . and Other Poems. 1/0 sewed
Jan. (*Bks*)
This is the first edition (1883), with 79 pp.
Also 1886

1627 WILLIAM M. THACKERAY
The Yellowplush Correspondence and the Fitzboodle Papers.
0/6 sewed   Jan. (*Bks*)
Popular Sixpenny Books No. 64. This should be compared with the 1882 title where it

was given as with 127 pp. I'm giving the present title, 19 cm., 441 pp., as from a *U Cat* entry which gives (1883?), with "Yellowplush Papers" on the spine, with the present title, containing *Cox's Diary* and *The Fatal Boots* also. It may not be the present title.
See 1882

1628 PHINEAS T. BARNUM *The Art of Money-Getting.* 0/6 sewed   Feb. (*Bks*)
Popular Sixpenny Books No. 59. This is probably the first English edition (1883), with 60 pp. It was issued in the United States by J. S. Ogilvie, New York (copyright 1882), 18.5 cm., 59 pp.

1629 MIGUEL CERVANTES *Don Quixote.*
Part 2. Medium 4to. Illustrated. 0/6 sewed   Feb. (*Bks*)
People's Edition No. 7. This was later *Popular Sixpenny Books* No. 43. The *Eng Cat* gives it as issued in 1882.
For part 1 see 1882

1630 ELIZABETH S. PHELPS, later WARD
That Dreadful Boy, Trotty. 8vo. 0/6 sewed.
Mar. (*Bks*)
Popular Sixpenny Books No. 56.
Also 1877. See 1872

1631 (METTA FULLER, later VICTOR)
A Bad Boy's Diary. 8vo. 1/0 sewed
Mar. (*Bks*)
Popular Sixpenny Books No. 60. This is (1883), with 96 pp. The first edition was

issued by J.S. Ogilvie & Co., New York
(copyright 1881), 17 cm., 276 pp., containing *A Bad Boy's Diary* and *More Leaves
from a Bad Boy's Diary*. They previously issued the first title as part 1, listed in *PW* on
Mar. 27, 1880; and the complete work in 1
vol. was listed there on Dec. 18, 1880. In
England it was issued by Alfred Hays,
London (1882), anonymous, 276 pp., at
1/0, containing both parts, advertised in
the *Times Weekly Edition* (London) on Jan.
26, 1883, as "Just published." It was also
issued as *A Bad Boy's Diary*, unabridged, by
Simpkin, Marshall, London, both parts,
4to, anonymous, 31 pp., which the *BM*
gives as (1883), and which the *Eng Cat*
gives as issued in 1882. It was also issued
by George Routledge, London, in 1883,
both parts, as *A Bad Boy's Diary and More
Leaves from a Bad Boy's Diary*, Demy 8vo,
160 pp., at 0/6 sewed, listed by the *Bks* as
published in Feb., and advertised by Routledge in the *Ath* on Mar. 3. It was also issued by Frederick Warne, London (1883),
both parts, unabridged edition, as *A Bad
Boy's Diary*, my copy, anonymous, 126 pp.,
at 0/6 sewed, listed in the *Bks* as issued in
Jan. 1883, and advertised in the *Ath* on
Feb. 3 that the first and second editions of
10,000 each had sold out, and that the
third edition of 10,000 was "Now ready."

1632 (METTA FULLER, later VICTOR)
The Blunders of a Bashful Man. 8vo.
o/6 sewed   Mar. (*Bks* ad)

Popular Sixpenny Books No. 61. This is
(1883), with 84 pp. The first edition was
issued by J.S. Ogilvie & Co., New York
(1881), 17 cm., 168 pp., illustrated, listed
in *PW* on Oct. 29. In England it was issued
by Frederick Warne, London (1883),
anonymous, 125 pp., illustrated, at 0/6
sewed, listed by the *Bks* as issued in Feb. It
was also issued by George Routledge,
London (1883), Demy 8vo, anonymous,
93 pp., at 0/6 sewed, listed by the *Bks* as
published in Feb., and advertised by Routledge in the *Ath* on Mar. 3. I cannot explain a *New-York Times* ad by Ogilvie on

June 23, 1881, for this title, at $.10 paper,
People's Library No. 41, as "Just issued"!

1633 (METTA FULLER, later VICTOR)
Catching a Husband. 8vo. o/6 sewed
Mar. (*Bks*)

Popular Sixpenny Books No. 62. This is
(1883), with 95 pp., containing *Miss Slimmens' Window* and *Miss Slimmens' Boarding
House*. The first appearance of the first title was in *Godey's Lady's Book*, Jan.–June
1859, and the first book edition was issued
by Derby & Jackson, New York, 1859, *Miss
Slimmens' Window and Other Papers*, 18.5
cm., anonymous, 312 pp., $1.00, by Mrs.
Mark Peabody. It contained three other
stories in addition to the title story and
was listed in the *Ind* on Sept. 15 and in
APC&LG on Sept. 17. They issued the second edition at $1.00, advertised in the
New-York Times on Sept. 30, 1859. J.S.
Ogilvie & Co., New York, issued *Miss Slimmens' Window*, anonymous, 149 pp., illustrated, $.10, advertised in the *New York
Times* on May 10, 1881, as "This morning." The first appearance of the second
title was in *Godey's Lady's Book*, Jan.–Sept.
1860. The first book edition was issued by
J.S. Ogilvie & Co. (1882), 17.5 cm., anonymous, 188 pp., listed in *PW* on June 19.
George Munro, New York, issued both titles in the *New York Monthly Fashion Bazaar*
in Oct. 1884, anonymous, entitled *In Quest
of a Husband*. It was also issued in England
by George Routledge, London (1883), my
copy, anonymous, 191 pp., at 0/6 sewed,
advertised in the *Ath* on Mar. 3, and listed
by the *Bks* as published in Mar., with the title *Miss Slimmens' Boarding House and Miss
Slimmens' Window*. It was also issued by
Frederick Warne, London (1883), as *Miss
Slimmens in Search of a Husband*, containing
both stories, anonymous, 128 pp., o/6
sewed, listed by the *Bks* as issued in Mar.

1634 JOEL C. HARRIS ***Uncle Remus and
His Sayings.*** Illustrated. o/6 sewed   Mar.
(*Bks*)

Popular Sixpenny Books No. 63. This is
(1883). This first appeared in the *Consti-*

tution (Atlanta), in 1880; and the first book edition was issued by D. Appleton & Co., New York, 1881 (1880), *Uncle Remus. His Songs and Sayings*, 19.5 cm., 231 pp., listed in the *Ind* on Dec. 2, 1880, and in *PW* on Dec. 4. It was advertised in the *New-York Times* on Nov. 20, 1880, 12mo, illustrated, $1.50 cloth, "This day." The fourth edition was advertised as "Just ready," $1.50, in a Dec. 21 ad; and a new edition, illustrated, $.50 paper, was advertised on June 13, 1885. The first English edition of part of the work was issued by David Bogue, London, 1881, as *Uncle Remus and His Legends of the Old Plantation*, 19 cm., 192 pp., illustrated by F. Church and J. Moser, 5/o, in pictorial gray-green cloth, with a 32-page catalog (June 1880). It was listed in the *Ath* on Mar. 5. They issued it at 2/6, listed in the *Spect* on Sept. 9, 1882. It was also issued by George Routledge, London, 190 pp., at 1/o sewed, dated 1881, and advertised in the *Ath* on Apr. 30, and listed by *PC* as published May 1–15. It was also issued by Trübner, London, probably the Appleton edition imported, with the Appleton title "On our table" in the *Ath* on Aug. 20, 1881, and hence probably issued about June.

1635 MARION HARLAND (MARY V. HAWES, later TERHUNE) *Her Wedding Day*. 12mo. 1/o sewed, 1/6, 2/o cloth   Mar. (*Bks*)

Lily Series No. 78. This is (1883), with 224 pp. This was possibly *Colonel Floyd's Wards*, issued by Sheldon, New York, 1863, with *Husks*. It was also probably *Helen Gardner's Wedding Day*, issued by Carleton, New York; etc., 1870, 17.5 cm., 382 pp.

1636 MAX ADELER (CHARLES H. CLARK) *An Old Fogey and Other Stories*. Medium 4to. Illustrated. o/6 sewed   Mar. (*Bks*)

People's Edition. This was also *Popular Sixpenny Books* No. 44. The *Bks* also listed it as published in May.

Also 1881, 89, 1901, 05

1637 MAX ADELER (CHARLES H. CLARK) *Random Shots*. Medium 4to. Illustrated. o/6 sewed   Mar. (*Bks*)

People's Edition. This was also listed in the *Bks* as issued in May. It was also issued as *Select Library of Fiction* No. 431, later changed to No. 324, 2/o boards, 2/6 cloth, advertised in the *Ath* on July 14.

Also 1879, 89, 1900

1638 WILLIAM H. AINSWORTH *Myddleton Pomfret*. 1/o boards, 2/6 cloth   Mar.?

Select Library of Fiction No. 373, later changed to No. 79. This has no date and 383 pp., with a printer's date (Mar. 1883). The first edition was issued by Chapman & Hall, London, 3 vols., 1868, 20 cm., 31/6, listed in the *Ath* on Mar. 28. They issued it, 1878, as No. 373 in the series, 383 pp., 2/o boards, listed in the *Ath* on Mar. 16 as a new edition. George Routledge, London, issued it in 1880, Cr. 8vo, 3/6 cloth, listed in the *Spect* on Dec. 18.

1639 STANLEY HUNTLEY *Mr. and Mrs. Spoopendyke*. o/6 sewed   Apr. (*Bks*)

Popular Sixpenny Books No. 65. This has no date and 93 pp. The first edition was issued by W. B. Smith & Co., New York (copyright 1881), 17.5 cm., 145 pp., as *Satchel Series* No. 35, listed in *Literary News* for Aug. It was also issued in London by T. H. Roberts (1883), an unabridged edition, anonymous, 31 pp.

1640 (H. M. JOHNSON) *The Adventures of an Amateur Tramp*. 12mo. Illustrated. 1/o sewed   Apr. (*Bks*)

Ward & Lock's Humorous Books No. 78. This is the first edition (1883), 18 cm., 179 pp., illustrated by Matt Stretch.

1641 KATHERINE KING *The Queen of the Regiment*. 2/o boards, 2/6 cloth   Apr. (*Bks*)

Select Library of Fiction No. 678, new numbering. The first edition was issued by Hurst & Blackett, London, 3 vols., 1872,

Cr 8vo, 31/6, listed in the *Ath* on Mar. 9. Chapman & Hall, London, issued a new edition, 1875, my copy, 18 cm., 387 pp., 2/o boards, as *Select Library of Fiction* No. 283, listed in the *Ath* on Aug. 28. The first American edition was issued by James R. Osgood, Boston, 1874, 8vo, listed by *Lit World* as published in May and noticed on June 1.

1642 ANNIE THOMAS (MRS. PENDER CUDLIP) *"'He Cometh Not.' She Said."* [Fourth edition]. 12mo. 2/o boards, 2/6 cloth   Apr. (*Bks*)

Select Library of Fiction No. 268, later changed to No. 347. This has 374 pp. I think this has no date, 4 pp. of ads, with ads on the endpapers and back cover, bound in pale blue boards, as there is such a known copy with the No. 268 on the front.

Also 1881

1643 ANNIE THOMAS *A Laggard in Love.* 12mo. 2/o boards, 2/6 cloth   Apr. (*Bks*)

Select Library of Fiction No. 376, later changed to No. 351. The first edition was issued by Chapman & Hall, London, 3 vols., 1877, Cr 8vo, 31/6, listed in the *Spect* on Nov. 17. It was issued by them in this series as No. 376, at 2/o boards, listed in the *Ath* on June 15, 1878.

1644 ANONYMOUS *Penny Books for the People.* Historical series. 16 vols. o/1 sewed each   May (*Bks*)

See 1882

1645 MAX ADELER (CHARLES H. CLARK) *Transformations.* Illustrated. 1/o boards May (*Bks*)

Ward & Lock's Humorous Books No. 79. This has no date, a first edition, 122 pp., illustrated by Matt Stretch. It contains *Mrs. Shelmire's Djinn* and *A Desperate Adventure,* by Adeler.

See *A Desperate Adventure, and Other Stories,* 1886

1646 IVAN TURGENIEFF *Dimitri Roudine.* 2/o boards, 2/6 cloth   May (*Bks*)

Select Library of Fiction No. 486, new numbering. This is (1883), a duplicate of the New York edition with a new title page. The first edition in English was issued by Holt & Williams, New York, 1873, 271 pp., at $1.25, *Leisure Hour Series* No. 21. It is 17 cm., translated from the French and German versions. It was listed in *Old and New,* a monthly (Boston), for Sept., reprinted from *Every Saturday.* There was a second issue, issued by Henry Holt & Co., 1873, in decorated mustard cloth. It was issued in Paris (1862), with 341 pp.

1647 CHARLES DICKENS *The Pickwick Papers.* 8vo. Illustrated. o/6 sewed, 1/o cloth   May (*Bks*)

Popular Sixpenny Books No. 13. The illustrations are by A. B. Frost.

Also 1881

1648 IVAN TURGENIEFF *Smoke.* p 8vo. 2/o boards, 1/6 cloth   May (*Bks*)

Select Library of Fiction No. 484, new numbering. This is (1883), 18.5 cm., 291 pp., a duplicate of the New York edition with a new title page. The first edition was *Duim,* Moscow (1867), reviewed in the *Spect* on Mar. 28, 1868. It was issued in Paris as *Fumée,* 1867, 25 cm., 176 pp., by Hetzel. The first edition in English was issued by Bentley, London, 2 vols., 1868, 20 cm., translated by Rowland Crawley from the French version, listed in the *Spect* on Nov. 21, at 21/o. The first American edition was issued by Holt & Williams, New York, 1872, 17 cm., 291 pp., *Leisure Hour Series* No. 2. It is in decorated cloth with ads on the front endpapers having a date (July 6, 1872), listed in *Old and New,* a Boston monthly, for Aug. 1872. It was translated by William F. West from the French version and was reviewed in the *Atlantic Monthly* for Aug. and in *Scribner's Monthly* for Nov. 1872. *See color photo section*

1649 KATHERINE KING *Lost for Gold.*
12mo. 2/o boards, 2/6 cloth   May (*Bks*)

Select Library of Fiction No. 677, new numbering. The first edition was issued by Hurst & Blackett, London, 3 vols., 1873, Cr 8vo, 31/6, listed in the *Ath* on May 3. Chapman & Hall, London, issued it in this series as No. 273, 1875, at 2/o boards, listed in the *Ath* on July 3. It was issued by Ellis, Melbourne (1875), 19 cm., 379 pp., illustrated.

1650 CHARLES LEVER *Charles O'Malley.*
1/o sewed   May (*Bks*)

Shilling Novels No. 17. This was also issued as *Popular Sixpenny Books* No. 17, illustrated, o/6 sewed, 1/o cloth, listed in the *Bks* as issued in Oct. 1883.
Also 1881, 85

1651 CHARLES DICKENS *The Life and Adventures of Nicholas Nickleby.* 8vo.
Illustrated. o/6 sewed   May (*Bks*)

Popular Sixpenny Books No. 14. This is (1883), with 259 pp., and the original illustrations by "Phiz." Ward, Lock also issued it as *Select Library of Fiction* No. 521, later changed to No. 204, no date, 18.2 cm., 548 pp., in pictorial yellow boards, with a 16-page catalog at the back. It was first issued by Chapman & Hall, London, in 20 parts in 19, 1/o monthly parts in green wrappers, illustrated by "Phiz." No. 1 was issued on Mar. 31, 1838; and the double part, Nos. 19 and 20, was listed in the *Spect* on Oct. 5, 1839. They issued it in 1 vol., 1839, 22 cm., 628 pp., illustrated by "Phiz," at 21/o, listed in the *Ath* on Oct. 26. When Chapman & Hall issued a new serial edition of Dickens's works, this was No. 9 through No. 17, in the o/7 monthly parts. No. 17 was advertised in the *Spect* on May 27, 1848. It was then issued in 1 vol. in 1848, Cr 8vo, 499 pp., frontispiece, 15/o, listed in the *Spect* on June 3. In the United States it was issued by Carey, Lea & Blanchard, Philadelphia, in 20 monthly parts, in yellow wrappers with a design by "Phiz," illustrated. A notice in the *Knickerbocker* for July 1838 said "Now publishing." It was issued by Lea & Blanchard, 1839, 24 cm., 404 pp., with 2 illustrations by "Phiz," in boards with a maroon cloth spine. It was also issued by William H. Colyer, New York, 2 vols., 1839, 19 cm., with an engraved title page and 4 plates by "Phiz." It was also issued by James Turney, Jr., New York, in 1838, 1839, in parts, in green paper covers, with the same design as for the English part issue, illustrated. He issued it in 1 vol., 1839, 8vo, 624 pp., illustrated.

1652 JOHN DANGERFIELD (OSWALD CRAWFURD) *Grace Tolmar.* 12mo. 2/o boards, 2/6 cloth   June 16 (*Spect*)

Select Library of Fiction No. 564, new numbering.
Also 1876

1653 ANTHONY TROLLOPE *Harry Heathcote of Gangoil.* Third Edition.
12mo. Illustrated. 2/o boards   June (*Bks*)

Library of Select Authors. This is my copy, no date, 17.9 cm., 313 pp., white pictorial boards, printed in red, blue, and black, with the series title at the foot of the spine, and "The Works of Anthony Trollope" at the head. There is a printer's date (May 1883), a 20-page catalog at the back, and ads on the endpapers and back cover. The third edition, 2/6 cloth, was listed by the *Bks* as issued in Oct. 1883. This was *Select Library of Fiction* No. 21 in the new numbering system. I also have a copy, no date, fourth edition, 18.5 cm., 313 pp., illustrated, smooth green cloth, blocked in black, with the "Select Library of Fiction" on the front cover and spine. It has figured endpapers and a printer's date (Nov. 1883). It has the same 20-page catalog at the back as the third edition above. The first edition was issued by Harper & Bros., New York, 1874, as *Library of Select Novels* No. 407, 23.1 cm., 61 pp., double col-

umns, illustrated, $.25 paper, with the list
of the series in the ads ending with No.
406. It was listed in *PW* on Jan. 31 and in
the *Ind* on Feb. 5. It ran in *Littell's Living
Age* from Jan. 24 to Mar. 7, 1874. In England it was the Christmas No. of *The
Graphic* for 1873, with 6 illustrations by
different artists. It was issued in 1 vol. by
Sampson Low, London, 1874, 19 cm., 313
pp., 10/6, my copy, with a 48-page catalog
(Oct. 1873) at the back. I have a copy of
the second edition issued by Low, 1874,
using the original sheets, 10/6, in scarlet
cloth, advertised in the *Spect* on Nov. 28 as
"Now ready." Low issued it with the 6 illustrations used in the *Graphic*, 1874, at 5/0,
in green, red, blue, or violet cloth, listed in
the *Spect* on Feb. 5, 1875.

1654 ANONYMOUS *Esther's Sacrifice.*
12mo. 2/0 boards, 2/6 cloth   June (*Bks*)
Select Library of Fiction No. 771, new numbering. This is the first edition (1883),
with 327 pp., a story for girls.

1655   GEORGE A. BRINE *The King of the
Beggars. The Life and Adventures of
George Atkins Brine.* p 8vo. 1/0 boards
June (*Bks*)
This is the first edition (1883), 19 cm., 185
pp. It was *Shilling Novels* No. 21, probably
in 1884.
Also 1886

1656   (EMILY JOLLY) *Caste.* 12mo.
2/0 boards, 2/6 cloth   June (*Bks*)
Select Library of Fiction No. 293, later
changed to No. 693. The first edition was
issued by Hurst & Blackett, London, 3
vols., 1857, 20 cm., anonymous, 31/6, advertised in the *Ath* on Nov. 14 as "Next
week," and listed on Nov. 21. Chapman &
Hall, London, issued it as *Select Library of
Fiction* No. 293, at 2/0 boards, listed in the
Ath on Aug. 28, 1875. The first American
edition was issued by Harper & Bros.,
New York (1867), 8vo, 23 cm., anony-

mous, 136 pp., double columns, $.50 pa-
per, advertised in the *New-York Times* on
Sept. 9, "This day," and listed in *Godey's
Lady's Book* for Dec., and thus probably issued in Sept. or Oct.

1657   ELSE JUNCKER (ELSE SCHMIEDEN)
Margaret's Ordeal. 12mo. 2/0 boards,
2/6 cloth   June (*Bks*)
Select Library of Fiction No. 797, new numbering. This is probably the first English
edition (1883), with 224 pp. It is translated from the German by Mrs. A. L. Wister. The first edition in English was issued
by J. B. Lippincott & Co., Philadelphia,
1878, as *Margarethe*, 19 cm., 336 pp.,
translated by Mrs. Wister.

1658   BEATRICE REYNOLDS *My First
Season.* 12mo. 2/0 boards, 2/6 cloth
June (*Bks*)
Select Library of Fiction No. 534, later
changed to No. 590. The first edition was
issued by Smith, Elder & Co., London,
1855, p 8vo, 10/6, edited by Elizabeth S.
Sheppard, listed in the *Ath* on Sept. 15.
They issued a new edition, 1864, 17 cm.,
256 pp., at 1/0 sewed, 1/6 cloth, about May
1. Chapman & Hall, London, issued *Select
Library of Fiction* No. 250, 1/0 stiff wrappers, early in 1875, I think. The first
American edition was issued by W. P. Fetridge, New York; etc., 1856, 19 cm., 284
pp., $.75, listed by *APC&LG* as published
Jan. 5–12, 1856, and advertised in the
New York Daily Times on Feb. 22 as "Just
published."

1659   JULIA S. H. PARDOE *The Jealous
Wife.* 12mo. 2/0 boards, 2/6 cloth   June
(*Bks*)
Select Library of Fiction No. 644, new numbering. The first edition was issued by
Hurst & Blackett, London, 3 vols., 1855,
p 8vo, 31/6, listed in the *Ath* on June 23. It
was issued by C. H. Clarke, London, *Parlour Library* No. 244, at 2/0 boards, a sec-

ond edition, listed in the *Ath* on Oct. 2, 1858, and also in 1861. David Bryce, London, issued it at 2/0 boards, advertised in the *Ath* on Sept. 26, 1857. Chapman & Hall, London, issued it as *Select Library of Fiction* No. 61, 381 pp., 2/0 boards, advertised in the *Sat Rev* on May 27, 1865. The first American edition was issued by W. P. Fetridge & Co., New York; etc., 1855, advertised in the *New York Daily Times* on Aug. 11, 8vo, $.50 paper, from advanced sheets, "On Aug. 15." It was listed in the *Knickerbocker* for Oct. and in *Harper's New Monthly Magazine* for Sept.

1660 EDWARD P. ROE *From Jest to Earnest.* 2/0 boards, 2/6 cloth   July 14 (*Ath* ad)

Select Library of Fiction No. 526, later changed to No. 378.
Also 1876, 86, 92

1661 MAX ADELER (CHARLES H. CLARK) *Out of the Hurly-Burly.* Illustrated. 2/0 boards, 2/6 cloth   July 14 (*Ath* ad)

Select Library of Fiction No. 429, later changed to No. 322.
Also 1874, 78, 82, 1900

1662 ARTHUR S. HARDY *But Yet a Woman.* 8vo. 0/6 sewed, 1/0 cloth July 17 (*PC*)

Popular Sixpenny Books No. 58. This is (1883), with 183 pp. The first edition was issued by Houghton, Mifflin & Co., Boston, 1883, 18.5 cm., 348 pp., $1.25, listed in the *Ind* on Apr. 26, in *PW* on Apr. 28, and in the *Nation* on May 3. An ad in the *Christian Union* on Apr. 19 stated that the first edition had sold out before publication and that a second edition was forthcoming immediately, and it was listed on Apr. 26. The first English edition was issued by Macmillan & Co., London, 1883, Cr 8vo, 275 pp., 4/6 cloth, 1/0 sewed, listed in the *Ath* on June 23, and advertised in the *Times Weekly Edition* (London)

on June 15. It was also issued by Frederick Warne, London (1883), 248 pp., at 0/6 sewed, 1/0 cloth, listed in *PC* on July 17.

1663 EARL OF DESART (WILLIAM CUFFE) *Kelverdale.* 12mo. 2/0 boards, 2/6 cloth July (*Bks*)

Select Library of Fiction No. 386, later changed to No. 785. The first edition was issued by Hurst & Blackett, London, 3 vols., 1879 (1878), Cr 8vo, 31/6, listed in the *Spect* on Dec. 28, 1878. Chapman & Hall, London, issued it in the series as No. 386, at 2/0 boards, listed in the *Ath* on July 26, 1879. The first American edition was issued by Harper & Bros., New York (1879), *Franklin Square Library* No. 40, 29 cm., 60 pp., $.15 paper, with a caption title, advertised in the *New-York Times* on Feb. 7 as "This day," and listed in *PW* on Feb. 15. It ran in *Vanity Fair* (weekly) in 1877, 1878.

1664 THOMAS A. TROLLOPE *Marietta.* [New edition]. 12mo. 2/0 boards, 2/6 cloth   July (*Bks*)

Select Library of Fiction No. 500, new numbering. This is (1883), with 419 pp. The first edition was issued by Chapman & Hall, London, 1862, 2 vols., p 8vo, 21/0, listed in the *Ath* on June 7. They issued the second edition in 1 vol., 19 cm., 419 pp., dated 1862, advertised in the *Spect* on Sept. 27. They issued the third edition in 1863, 419 pp., 5/0 cloth, listed in the *Reader* on Aug. 1. They issued the fourth edition as No. 74 in the series, at 2/0 boards, listed in *PC* in Mar. 1866; and reissued it, my copy, a new edition, 1874, 419 pp., at 2/0 boards, with a printer's date (Sept. 7, 1874). The first American edition was issued by T. B. Peterson & Bros., Philadelphia (1868), 19 cm., 420 pp., $1.50 paper and $1.75 cloth, advertised in the *New-York Times* on June 20 as "This day," listed in *ALG&PC* (fortnightly) on July 1.

1665 IVAN TURGENIEFF *Fathers and Sons.*
2/o boards, 2/6 cloth   July (*Bks*)
Select Library of Fiction No. 485, new numbering. This is the first English edition (1883), 19 cm., 248 pp., a duplicate of the New York edition with a new title page. The first edition in English was issued by Leypoldt & Holt, New York, 1867, *Leisure Hour Series* No. 3, 17 cm., 248 pp., $1.50, translated from the Russian by Eugene Schuyler, with the author's approval. It was advertised in the *New-York Times* on June 8 as "Immediately," and as if ready on June 10; and advertised in the *Nation* on June 6 as "Early in June." It was issued by George Munro, New York, as *Seaside Library* No. 1624, in 1883, 4to, $.20 paper, advertised in the *New-York Times* on Apr. 28 as recent. Henry Holt, New York, issued a second edition in the *Leisure Hour Series*, 1872, 248 pp., in decorated mustard cloth.

1666 HENRY COCKTON *Valentine Vox.*
Illustrated. o/6 sewed   Aug. 18 (*Ath* ad)
Popular Sixpenny Books No. 16. This was first issued in 20 illustrated parts by Robert Tyas, London, part 1 listed in the *Spect* on Apr. 6, 1839, and parts 19 and 20 listed on Oct. 10, 1840. Tyas issued it in 1 vol., 1840, 22 cm., 620 pp., 21/o, listed in the *Ath* on Oct. 17. George Routledge, London, issued it very early as he advertised it in the *Illustrated London News* on Nov. 16, 1844, 8vo, 60 plates, reduced to 10/6. I think he reissued it, 1846, 8vo, 620 pp., illustrated, 10/6. It was issued by Henry Lea, London, in 1859 at 2/o boards; and Routledge issued it in 1853, a new and carefully revised edition, at 2/o boards, 2/6 cloth, listed in the *Ath* on May 28; and he issued it at least 11 more times! The first American edition was issued by Carey & Hart, Philadelphia, 1841, 24 cm., 395 pp., illustrated, reviewed in the *Southern Literary Messenger* for Oct.

(FRANCIS C. YOUNG) *Every Man His Own Mechanic Series*   3 vols. Illustrated. 1/o boards each   Aug. 18 (*Ath* ad)
1667 No. 1. Household Carpentry and Joinery
1668 No. 2. *Ornamental and Constructional Carpentry*
1669 No. 3. *Household Building Art and Practice*
These were issued in 1 vol. as *Every Man His Own Mechanic*, with a preface signed F.Y., 21 cm., 816 pp., illustrated, 7/6, probably in 1881; and the eighth edition was issued, 1890, 924 pp., illustrated.

1670 ANONYMOUS *Etiquette for Ladies.*
1/o cloth boards   Aug. (*Bks*)
Shilling Useful Books.
Also See 1875

1671 OLIVER W. HOLMES *The Autocrat of the Breakfast Table.* 2/o boards, 2/6 cloth   Sept. 15 (*Ath*)
Select Library of Fiction No. 441, new numbering. This is (1883), with 279 pp.
Also 1865, 70

1672 HAWLEY SMART *At Fault.* 12mo. 2/o boards, 2/6 cloth   Sept. 15 (*Ath*)
Library of Select Authors. This is my copy, no date, 17.9 cm., 410 pp., white pictorial boards, printed in red, green, and black, with the series title on the spine. It has a printer's date (Sept. 1883), an inscribed date (Nov. 6, 1883), and ads on the endpapers, back cover, and 6 pp. at the back. This was *Select Library of Fiction* No. 177 in the new numbering system. The third edition at 2/o boards was advertised in the *Sat Rev* for Nov. 3, 1883. The first edition was issued by Chapman & Hall, London, 3 vols., 1883, advertised in the *Ath* on Mar. 17 as "This day," and reviewed on Mar. 31. The first American edition was issued by George Munro, New York, 1883, *Seaside Library* No. 1582, 32.5 cm., 58 pp., $.20 paper, advertised in the *New-York Times* on

Mar. 16 as "Out today," and listed in *PW* on Apr. 14, but not received.
Also 1897, 1901, 02

1673 THORPE TALBOT **Philiberta.** 12mo. 2/o boards, 2/6 cloth   Sept. 15 (*Ath*)
Select Library of Fiction No. 798, new numbering. This is the first English edition (1883), 18 cm., 366 pp., with 16 pp. of ads at the back, and ads on the endpapers and back cover. It is the *Melbourne Leader* £100-prize tale.

1674 SOPHIE MAY (REBECCA S. CLARKE) **Our Helen.** 2/o boards, 2/6 cloth   Sept. 15 (*Spect*)
Select Library of Fiction No. 799, new numbering.
Also 1877

1675 (HENRY FRITH) **Speeches and Toasts.** Cr 8vo. 1/o boards   Oct. (*Bks*)
Shilling Useful Books. This is the first edition (1883), with 136 pp. A new edition with added toasts was issued (1883), 19 cm., 142 pp., listed in the *Bks* as published in Nov. A new edition was issued, entirely rewritten and enlarged, 1903, 155 pp., with portraits; and it was still being issued as late as 1953!

1676 ANONYMOUS **Stepping Stones to Thrift.** 8vo. 1/o sewed, 1/6, 2/o cloth   Oct. (*Bks*)
Friendly Counsel Series No. 20. This is the first edition (1883), with 248 pp.

1677 SYLVIA **Sylvia's Book of Macramé Lace.** 1/o boards   Oct. (*Bks*)
Shilling Useful Books.
Also 1882, 85

1678 FREDERICK MARRYAT **Japhet in Search of a Father.** 2/o boards, 2/6 cloth   Oct. (*Bks*)
Select Library of Fiction No. 512, later changed to No. 299. It is (1883), with 295

pp. This first appeared in the *Metropolitan Magazine* from Oct. 1834 to Jan. 1836. The first book edition was issued by Saunders & Otley, London, 3 vols., 1836 (1835), 21 cm., anonymous, 31/6, advertised in the *Ath* on Nov. 28, 1835, as "Just ready," and listed on Dec. 19. Bentley issued it as *Standard Novels* No. 64, 1838, anonymous, 401 pp. In the United States it was issued by Wallis & Newell, New York, 1835, anonymous, 223 pp., after being issued in 4 parts from Apr. 1835 to Feb. 1836. It was also issued by Carey & Hart, Philadelphia; etc., 1835, 19 cm., anonymous, 196 pp., with a 24-page catalog (Jan. 1835), but containing only part of the story. It was also issued by H.C. Boswell, Trenton, 1835, 23 cm., 167 pp., by Marryat. The American issues are so complicated it is best to refer to Sadleir I, page 233.
Also 1881

1679 (CHARLES BARNARD ET AL.) **Beeton's Christmas Annual.** Illustrated. 1/o sewed. Nov. (*Bks*)
This was the 24th season for this annual (1883), 21.7 cm., 135 pp., yellow pictorial wrappers, printed in red, blue, and black. One of the stories was *A Dead Town* by Barnard.
See 1885

1680 ANNA K. GREEN, later ROHLFS **X, Y, Z.** o/6 sewed   Nov. (*Bks*)
Popular Sixpenny Books No. 86. This is the first English edition (1883), with 95 pp., Sadleir's copy, in yellow stiff wrappers cut flush, decorated in yellowback style, and lettered in red and black on the front. It has ads on the back cover, endpapers, inside wrappers, and 16 pp. at the back. The first edition was issued by G. P. Putnam's Sons, New York, 1883, 17 cm., 97 pp., listed in *PW* on June 30 and in both the *Nation* and the *Ind* on July 5.

1681 ANONYMOUS ***Beeton's Domestic Recipe Book.*** 1/0   Dec.?
This is the first edition (1883), with 144 pp.

1682 JOHN LANG ***The Secret Police.***
0/6 sewed   1883 (*Eng Cat*)
Popular Sixpenny Books No. 87.
Also 1859, 70, 82

1683 EDWIN T. GREEDLY ***Money.***
1/6   1883 (*Eng Cat*)
Also 1880

1684 (GEORGE A. LAWRENCE) ***Hagarene.***
Sixth Edition. 2/0 boards   1883 (*Sadleir*)
Select Library of Fiction No. 270, later changed to No. 774. This is Sadleir's copy (1883), with 396 pp. The first edition was issued by Chapman & Hall, London, 3 vols., 1874, 20 cm., anonymous, 31/6, listed in the *Ath* on Oct. 24. They issued it in the series as No. 270, a new edition, 17.8 cm., anonymous, 396 pp., my copy, in pink pictorial boards, listed in the *Ath* on Apr. 17, 1875; and reissued it at 2/0 boards, the fifth edition, 1876, anonymous, 396 pp. I have a reissue of 1879, 2/0 boards, with a printer's date (Jan. 1879), but the title page is missing. The first American edition was issued by Harper & Bros., New York, 1875, *Library of Select Novels* No. 429, 24 cm., anonymous, 148 pp., $.75 paper, listed in *PW* on Jan. 30 and in the *Ind* on Feb. 4.

1685 GEORGE J. WHYTE MELVILLE ***Roy's Wife.*** Seventh Edition. 2/0 boards   1883 (*Sadleir*)
Library of Select Authors. This is Sadleir's copy (1883), with 334 pp., in yellow pictorial boards, with the series title at the foot of the spine, and "The Works of Whyte Melville" at the head. It was *Select Library of Fiction* No. 401, later changed to No. 129. This first appeared in the *Gentleman's Mag-*

azine, where it ran Jan.–Aug. 1878. The first edition was issued by Chapman & Hall, London, 2 vols., 1878, 20 cm., 21/0, listed in the *Ath* on July 13. They issued it as No. 401 in the series at 2/0 boards, listed in the *Ath* on Sept. 6, 1879; and issued it in 1878, Cr 8vo, 6/0, listed in the *Spect* on Nov. 9; and again listed, the same, on Jan. 18, 1879.
See 1901

1686 FREDERICK MARRYAT ***Mr. Midshipman Easy.***
2/0 boards, 2/6 cloth   1883
Select Library of Fiction No. 511, later changed to No. 298. It is (1883), with 283 pp. It was reissued as No. 298 in the early 1890s.
Also 1881

1687 FREDERICK MARRYAT ***Jacob Faithful.*** 2/0 boards, 2/6 cloth   1883
Select Library of Fiction No. 513, later changed to No. 300. It is (1883), with 302 pp. It was reissued as No. 300 in the early 1890s.
Also 1881, 1902

1688 FREDERICK MARRYAT ***Peter Simple.***
2/0 boards, 2/6 cloth   1883
Select Library of Fiction No. 514, later changed to No. 301.
Also 1881

1689 ANTHONY TROLLOPE ***La Vendée.***
New Edition. 12mo. 2/0 cloth   1883
Library of Select Authors. This is my copy, no date, 17.8 cm., 397 pp., yellow pictorial boards, printed in red, blue, and black, with the series title at the foot of the spine, and "The Works of Anthony Trollope" at the head. It has a printer's date (Sept. 1883), with ads on the endpapers, back cover, and 14 pp. at the back, the latter giving the new numbering for the *Select*

Library of Fiction. I also have an earlier is-sue, probably 1881, in the *Select Library of Fiction*, in smooth green cloth blocked in black, with figured endpapers, and series title on the front and spine. It is 18.6 cm., 397 pp., with a 14-page catalog at the back, different from the one above. The first edition was issued by Henry Colburn, London, 3 vols., 1850, p 8vo, 31/6, 500 copies, listed in *PC* as published May 29–June 14, and advertised in the *Spect* on May 18, as "Ready." My copy is in dark green cloth, but it was also issued in boards. Colburn issued unsold sheets, bound up in 1 vol., 1850, in red cloth; and there was a second issue in 3 vols. later in 1850. It was remaindered to T. C. Newby, London, who issued it in 3 vols. in dark blue cloth. Chapman and Hall, London, issued it as *Select Library of Fiction* No. 242, 1874, new edition, 397 pp., at 2/o boards, 3/o cloth, listed in the *Spect* on June 27. It has a printer's date (June 13, 1874). It was reissued as a third edition, 1874, with a printer's date (Aug. 1, 1874); as a fourth edition, with a printer's date (Jan. 19, 1875); and in a new edition, 1878 and (1879). The 3/o cloth issue in the series was in russet cloth with greenish-black endpapers and has a frontispiece. Ward, Lock gave it the No. 242 in the series, later changed to No. 13.

1690 GEORGE J. WHYTE MELVILLE
Songs and Verses. Tenth Edition, with Numerous Additions.
12mo. 2/o boards   1883
Library of Select Authors. This is my copy, no date, 17.9 cm., 238 pp., pale blue pictorial boards, printed in red and black, with the series title at the foot of the spine, and "The Works of Whyte Melville" at the head. There is a printer's date (Sept. 1883) and ads on the endpapers, back cover, and 10 pp. at the back, the latter

giving the new numbering system for the *Select Library of Fiction*.
Also 1882. See 1903

1691 HENRY KINGSLEY *Austin Elliot.*
New Edition. 2/o boards   1883
This was probably in the *Library of Select Authors*, but the copy I examined was re-bound. It has a printer's date (Jan. 1883). This was *Select Library of Fiction* No. 200, later No. 108. The first edition was issued by Macmillan & Co., London and Cam-bridge, 2 vols., 1863, 19.5 cm., at 21/o, listed in the *Ath* on May 23. They issued a second edition in 2 vols., 1863, at 21/o, ad-vertised in the *Spect* on June 20 as "This day." They issued the third edition, adver-tised in the *Reader* on July 4, 1863, as "This day," and also listed in the *Reader* on Jan. 6, 1866, p 8vo, 409 pp., at 6/o. A new edition was advertised in the *Spect* on Mar. 3, 1866, Cr 8vo, 6/o, issued by Macmillan. Chapman & Hall issued it as *Select Library of Fiction* No. 200, the fourth edition, 1872, 409 pp., at 2/o boards, 3/o cloth, listed by *PC* as published July 16–Aug. 1. They reissued it, 1875, a new edition, at 2/o boards. The first American edition was issued by Ticknor & Fields, Boston, 1863, 20 cm., 352 pp., at $1.25, advertised in the *New-York Times* on July 30 as "This day," and listed in *APC&LG* (fortnightly) on Aug. 15.

1692 MAX ADELER (CHARLES H. CLARK)
ET AL. **The Drolleries of a Happy Island
. . . with Other Tales and Sketches.**
Illustrated. 1/o sewed   1883
Ward & Lock's Humorous Books. The title story was first issued in Beeton's Christ-mas annual for 1880. *The Fortunate Island and Other Stories* was issued by Lee & Shep-ard, Boston, listed in the *Atlantic Monthly* for Feb. 1882.
See 1880 and *A Desperate Adventure and Other Stories*, 1886

1693 JANE AUSTEN **Sense and Sensibility.**
New Edition. 12mo. 2/o boards   1883
Select Library of Fiction No. 163, later
changed to No. 187. This is my copy, no
date, 18 cm., 331 pp., white pictorial
boards, printed in red, blue, and black,
with the series title on the spine, and the
No. 163 on the front. It has an inscribed
date (Oct. 1884), a printer's date (Nov.
1883), and a memoir of the author (Oct. 5,
1832). There are ads on the endpapers,
back cover, and 4 pp. at the back. The first
edition was issued by T. Egerton, London,
3 vols., 1811, by "A Lady," 12mo, anonymous, 15/o, listed by the *Edinburgh Review*
as published Aug.–Nov. 1811. It was also
listed there, the same, as published July–
Nov. 1812. Bentley, London, issued it as
Standard Novels No. 23, 1833, 331 pp., with
a memoir of the author. Chapman & Hall,
London, issued it as *Select Library of Fiction*
No. 163, 1870, a new edition, 331 pp., at
2/o boards, 2/6 Roxburghe, in Apr., from
the Bentley plates. They reissued it, a new
edition, in 1872, at 2/o boards. The first
American edition was issued by Carey &
Lea, Philadelphia, 2 vols., 1833, 19 cm.

1694 MAX ADELER (CHARLES H. CLARK)
Elbow-Room. Authorized Edition. 12mo.
Illustrated. 2/o boards   1883
Library of Select Authors. This is my copy, no
date, 17.8 cm., 384 pp., white pictorial
boards, printed in red, blue, and black,
with the series title on the spine. There is
a printer's date (Nov. 1883) and a preface
to the English edition (Nov. 6, 1876). It
has a frontispiece and many textual illustrations by Arthur B. Frost, with ads on
the endpapers, back cover, and a catalog
paged 15–30 at the back, the latter being
of a later date, probably 1887–89. This
was advertised in the *Ath* on July 14, 1883,
as *Select Library of Fiction* No. 430, at 2/o
boards, 2/6 cloth. Under the renumbering
it became No. 323. I have never seen the
Library of Select Authors mentioned in any
Ward, Lock ad or catalog! This is amazing

considering the large number of titles issued with that name on the spine.
Also 1876, 82, 1902

1695 EDWARD BULWER LYTTON **The Last
Days of Pompeii.** 2/o boards   1883
Select Library of Fiction No. 508, later
changed to No. 265. This is (1883), with
326 pp.
Also 1881

1696 EDWARD BULWER LYTTON **Pelham.**
2/o boards   1883
Select Library of Fiction No. 509, later
changed to No. 267.
Also 1881

1697 EDWARD BULWER LYTTON
Eugen Aram. 2/o boards   1883
Select Library of Fiction No. 510, later
changed to No. 266. The *BM* gives this as
(1883), with 329 pp.
Also 1881

1698 JOHN W. KIRTON, ed. **Standard
Temperance Dialogues.** 1/o boards, 1/6
1883 (*BM*)
This is the first edition, no date, with 192
pp.
See 1888

1699 MICHAEL SCOTT **The Cruise of the
Midge.** o/6 sewed   1883?
Popular Sixpenny Books No. 15. This ran in
Blackwood's Magazine in 1834–35, concluding in June 1835. The first English edition
was issued by William Blackwood & Sons,
Edinburgh; etc., 2 vols., 1836, Fcp 8vo,
anonymous, at 12/o, listed in the *Ath* on
Feb. 6. The first edition was issued in 4
vols: Allen & Ticknor, Boston, vol. 1,
1834, 19 cm.; vol. 2, Carey & Hart, Philadelphia; etc., 1834; vols. 3 and 4, Carey &
Hart, the same, 1835, all anonymous.
Wallis & Newell, New York, issued it,
1835, 18.5 cm., with 318 pp.

1700 HANS C. ANDERSEN *Andersen's Popular Tales.* Illustrated. 1/0 sewed, 1/6 cloth 1883?

Youth's Library of Wonder and Adventure No. 31. This was also issued in the *Family Gift Series*, Cr 8vo, illustrated, 2/6 cloth, and in the *Good Worth Library*, illustrated, 3/6 cloth. Ward, Lock issued *Fairy Tales* in 1875, no date, 21.5 cm., 525 pp., an illustrated edition with 14 colored plates and others, with the prelims (Oct. 1875), listed in the *Spect* on Oct. 23, at 7/6. They issued *Popular Tales for Children*, no date, 503 pp., illustrated, 3/6 cloth, listed in the *Spect* on Dec. 25, 1875, at 3/6, and on Jan. 8, 1876, at 5/0. The first editions were *Eventyr*, Copenhagen: the first collection (4 tales), 1835; the second collection (3 tales), 1835; the third collection (2 tales), 1837. In England Chapman & Hall, London, issued *Wonderful Stories for Children*, 1846, 16.6 cm., 127 pp., 4 colored plates, consisting of 10 tales, translated by Mary Howitt, who learned Danish in order to do it. William Pickering, London, issued *Danish Fairy Legends and Tales*, 1846, 16 cm., 197 pp., at 6/0, translated by Caroline Peachey. It contains 14 stories and was listed in the *Ath* on May 16. Joseph Cundall, London, issued the *Danish Story Book and the Nightingale and Other Stories*, 2 vols., 1846, translated by Charles Boner, the first series being in Sq 16mo, listed in the *Ath* on May 9, at 3/6 cloth. H. G. Bohn, London, issued *A Poet's Bazaar*, 1846, translated by Beckwith, containing 3 tales. In the United States, *Wonderful Stories for Children* was issued by Wiley & Putnam, New York, 1846, Sq 16mo, 142 pp.; and they issued a second series also, 1843, illustrated. H. G. Bohn, London, issued *Danish Fairy Legends and Tales in Bohn's Illustrated Library*, containing 12 additional stories from *Historier* of 1852, 1853. It claimed to be the most complete edition of the fairy tales and was listed in books received in *Notes & Queries* for Mar. 23, 1861. *Tales for the Young* was issued by James Burns, London, 1847, 230 pp., partly colored illustrations.

1701 HANS C. ANDERSEN *Andersen's Popular Stories.* Illustrated. 1/0 sewed, 1/6 cloth 1883?

Youth's Library of Wonder and Adventure No. 32. This was also issued in the *Family Gift Series*, Cr 8vo, illustrated, 2/6 cloth, and in the *Good Worth Library*, illustrated, at 3/6 cloth. Ward, Lock & Tyler issued *Stories for the Young*, no date, 439 pp., illustrated, 3/6 cloth, listed in the *Spect* on Jan. 8, 1876.

1702 FRANCIS R. GOULDING *The Young Marooners.* Illustrated. 1/0 sewed, 1/6 cloth 1883?

Youth's Library of Wonder and Adventure No. 33. The *U Cat* gives an edition by Ward, Lock & Tyler in the 1860s, 17 cm., 306 pp., illustrated; and Ward, Lock issued *The Adventures of the Young Marooners* (1882), 17.5 cm., 306 pp. It was also issued in the *Family Gift Series*, Cr 8vo, illustrated, 2/6 cloth, and in the *Good Worth Library*, illustrated, at 3/6 cloth. The first edition was issued by S. Martien, Philadelphia, 1852, 422 pp., illustrated, received by the Library of Congress on Jan. 11, 1853, and listed by *Lit World* as published Feb. 5–Mar. 5, 1853. The first English edition was *The Young Marooners on the Florida Coast*, issued by James Nisbet, etc., London, 1853, 17 cm., 263 pp., illustrated, 2/6 cloth, listed in the *Ath* on Apr. 16. It was also issued by Thomas Nelson & Sons, London and Edinburgh, 1853, Fcp 8vo, 256 pp., 2/0 cloth, listed in the *Ath* on Nov. 26, as *Robert and Harold*. George Routledge, London, issued it as *Robert and Harold*, 1855, 12mo, illustrated, edited and revised, in decorated cloth.

1703 JOHN G. EDGAR *The Crusades and the Crusaders.* Illustrated. 1/0 sewed, 1/6 cloth 1883?

Youth's Library of Wonder and Adventure No. 34. Ward, Lock also issued it in the *Family*

Gift Series, illustrated, at 2/6 cloth, and in the *Good Worth Library*, illustrated, at 3/6 cloth. The *BM* gives London, 1869 (1859), and the *Eng Cat* gives a new edition issued by Kent & Co., London, in 1860, Fcp 8vo, 3/6 cloth. Cassell & Co., London, issued *The Boy Crusaders* in 1865, Fcp 8vo, 283 pp., illustrated, 3/6 cloth, listed in the *Reader* on June 24. Ward, Lock & Tyler issued it with no date in 1866, 16 cm., 408 pp., illustrated, 3/6 cloth, listed in the *Reader* on Feb. 3. In the United States it was issued by Ticknor & Fields, Boston, 1860, author's edition, 17.5 cm., 380 pp., illustrated.

Ward, Lock & Co.
London and New York
1884

The New York office was moved from 10 Bond Street to 31 Bond Street; the new address was given in a PW *ad of Nov.*

1704 IVAN TURGENIEFF **Liza, or a Noble Nest.** 12mo. 2/0 boards, 2/6 cloth Jan. 12 (*Spect*)

Select Library of Fiction No. 487, new numbering. This is (1884), 17.5 cm., 318 pp., translated by W. R. S. Ralston. The first edition was in Moscow, 1859, 19 cm., 320 pp. The first edition in English was issued by Chapman & Hall, London, 2 vols., 1869, translated by Ralston, listed in the *Spect* on July 17, at 12/0. The first American edition was issued by Holt & Williams, New York, 1872, translated by Ralston, $1.25 in the *Leisure Hour Series*, advertised in the *New-York Times* on Nov. 16 as "Just ready," and listed by *Lit World* as published in Nov.

1705 (JULIA C. DE WINTON, later STRETTON) **Woman's Devotion.** 2/0 boards, 2/6 cloth Mar. 15 (*Ath*)

Select Library of Fiction No. 206, later changed to No. 530. The first edition was issued by Hurst & Blackett, 3 vols., 1855, 21 cm., anonymous, listed in the *Ath* on Aug. 11. Chapman & Hall, London, issued it in the series as No. 206, in 1872, 2/0 boards, listed in the *Spect* on Oct. 19.

1706 (MATILDA C. HOUSTOUN) **Lilian's Penance.** 2/0 boards, 2/6 cloth Mar. 29 (*Ath*)

Select Library of Fiction No. 777, new numbering. The first edition was issued by

Hurst & Blackett, London, 3 vols., 1873, Cr 8vo, anonymous, 31/6, listed in the *Ath* on July 5. Chapman & Hall, London, issued it in the series as No. 290, a new edition, anonymous, 404 pp., at 2/0 boards, listed in the *Ath* on Sept. 18, 1875.

1707 (EMILY JOLLY) **Bruna's Revenge, and Other Tales.** 2/0 boards, 2/6 cloth Mar. 29 (*Ath*)

Select Library of Fiction No. 691, new numbering. The first edition was issued by Hurst & Blackett, London, 3 vols., 1872, Cr 8vo, anonymous, 31/6, listed in the *Ath* on Jan. 27. Chapman & Hall, London, issued it in the series as No. 282, a new edition, 400 pp., at 2/0 boards, listed in the *Ath* on Aug. 7, 1875.

1708 MARIE BLAZE DE BURY **All for Greed.** [New edition]. 2/0 boards, 2/6 cloth Mar. 29 (*Ath*)

Select Library of Fiction No. 379, later changed to No. 783. This edition has no date. It ran in *St. Paul's Magazine* from Oct. 1867 to May 1868, and was issued in 2 vols. by Virtue & Co., London, 1868, 20 cm., frontispiece, 21/0, with a dedication signed A. A. A. It was listed in the *Ath* on Apr. 4. Chapman & Hall, London, issued it in the series as No. 379, 1878, a new edition, 346 pp., at 2/0 boards, listed in the *Ath* on Sept. 28. In America it was issued by Littell & Gay, Boston, in *Tales of the Living Age,* 93 pp., at $.38, listed in *Godey's Lady's Book* for Sept. 1868, and hence probably issued in June or July.

1709 THOMAS A. TROLLOPE
Giulio Malatesta. New Edition.
2/o boards, 2/6 cloth   Mar.?

Select Library of Fiction No. 90, later changed to No. 503. This has no date and 427 pp. The first edition was issued by Chapman & Hall, London, 3 vols., 1863, 21 cm., 31/6, listed in the *Ath* on May 30. They issued it at 5/o in 1864; and issued the third edition, 1866, as No. 90 in the series, 427 pp., at 2/o boards, listed in the *Reader* on Nov. 24. I have a reissue, 1874, a new edition, 2/o boards, with a printer's date (Aug. 28, 1874), and with endpaper ads of 1879.

1710 WILLIAM M. THAYER *From Log-Cabin to White House.* Illustrated.
o/6 sewed   Apr. 5 (*Ath* ad)

Popular Sixpenny Books No. 88. This has no date and 327 pp. The first edition was issued by James H. Earle, Boston, which the *U Cat* gives both as (copyright 1880), 19 cm., 478 pp., illustrated, and as 1881, 19 cm., 416 pp., frontispiece. It was listed in the *Ind* on Feb. 24, 1881. It is a life of President Garfield. Ward, Lock issued it at 2/o boards, 2/6, 3/6 cloth, illustrated, in 1884, *Heroes, Patriots, and Pioneers* No. 17. The first English edition was issued by Hodder & Stoughton, London, 1881, 20 cm., 344 pp., portrait, advertised in the *Ath* on Sept. 24 at 5/o as "Now ready." They issued the third edition at 5/o, with a portrait and an added chapter, advertised in the *Times Weekly Edition* (London) on Oct. 14, 1881, as "This day." They advertised the fifth edition, the same, on Nov. 25, 1881. It was advertised there on Feb. 1, 1884, at 1/o, 1/6, 3/6, with a portrait, as "Now ready." They issued the 40th edition, 1893, 348 pp., illustrated. Frederick Warne, London, issued it at o/6 sewed, 1/o

cloth, advertised in the *Ath* on Apr. 5, 1884.

1711 G. R. EMERSON ***General Gordon.***
Illustrated. o/6 sewed, 1/o cloth   Apr. 5 (*Ath* ad)

Popular Sixpenny Books No. 89. This is probably the first edition and, I think, has no date and 152 pp.
Also 1885

1712 (JULIA C. DE WINTON, later **STRETTON)** ***Lords and Ladies.*** 2/o boards, 2/6 cloth   Apr. 12 (*Ath*)

Select Library of Fiction No. 529, new numbering. The first edition was issued by Hurst & Blackett, London, 3 vols., 1866, 20 cm., anonymous, 31/6, listed in the *Ath* on Aug. 11. Chapman & Hall, London, issued it in the series as No. 314, at 2/o boards, listed in the *Ath* on Feb. 12, 1876. The first American edition was issued by A. K. Loring, Boston, 1866, 23 cm., anonymous, 150 pp., listed in *ALG&PC* (fortnightly) on Dec. 14, 1866.

1713 BILL NYE (EDGAR W. NYE)
Boomerang Shots. 8vo. Illustrated.
o/6 sewed   Late Apr.

Popular Sixpenny Books No. 90. This is the first English edition (1884), 21 cm., 124 pp. The first edition was as *Bill Nye and Boomerang,* issued by Bedford, Clark, Chicago, 1881, 19 cm., 286 pp., illustrated.
See *Comic Stories,* 1888

1714 (JULIE C. DE WINTON, later **STRETTON)** ***The Ladies of Lovel-Leigh.***
2/o boards, 2/6 cloth   Apr.?

Select Library of Fiction No. 295, later changed to No. 526. The first edition was issued by Hurst & Blackett, London, 3 vols., 1862, Cr 8vo, anonymous, 31/6, listed in the *Ath* on June 28. Chapman & Hall, London, issued it as No. 295 in the series, at 2/o boards, listed in the *Ath* on Aug. 28, 1875.

1715 ANNA C. STEELE *Broken Toys.*
2/o boards, 2/6 cloth   Apr.?

Select Library of Fiction No. 383, later changed to No. 707. The first edition was issued by Chapman & Hall, London, 3 vols., 1872, Cr 8vo, 31/6, listed in the *Ath* on Jan. 27. It was put in the series as No. 383, 1879, at 2/o boards, listed in the *Ath* on May 17. An edition in 3 vols. by Chapman & Hall was listed in *PC* as published May 1–15, 1872, p 8vo, 31/6, possibly a second edition. The first American edition was issued by James R. Osgood & Co., Boston, 1872, 163 pp., listed in *PW* on May 30, and by *Lit World* as published in June.

1716 ANNIE THOMAS (MRS. PENDER CUDLIP) *A Narrow Escape.* 2/o boards, 2/6 cloth   Apr.?

Select Library of Fiction No. 349, new numbering. The first edition was issued by Chapman & Hall, London, 3 vols., 1875, 20 cm., 31/6, listed in the *Ath* on Aug. 14. They issued it in the series as No. 322, at 2/o boards, listed in the *Ath* on Apr. 15, 1876. The first American edition was issued by William F. Gill & Co., Boston (copyright 1876), 22.5 cm., 215 pp., double columns, listed in *PW* on May 27, 1876, and in the *Ind* on June 15.

1717 LADY HARRIET THYNNE *Off the Line.* 2/o boards, 2/6 cloth   Apr.?

Select Library of Fiction No. 294, later changed to No. 778. The first edition was issued by Hurst & Blackett, London, 2 vols., 1867, p 8vo, 21/o, listed in the *Ath* on Mar. 9. Chapman & Hall, London, issued it in the series as No. 294, at 2/o boards, listed in the *Ath* on Aug. 28, 1875.

1718 (JULIA C. STRETTON) *Three Wives.* 2/o boards, 2/6 cloth   Apr.?

Select Library of Fiction No. 525, new numbering. The first edition was issued by Hurst & Blackett, London, 3 vols., 1868,

18.5 cm., anonymous, 31/6, listed in the *Ath* on Aug. 8. Chapman & Hall, London, issued it in the series as No. 302, at 2/o boards, listed in the *Ath* on Nov. 20, 1875.

1719 TOBE HODGE (CHARLES MCILVAINE) *A Legend of Polecat Hollow.* Illustrated. o/6 sewed.   Apr.?

Popular Sixpenny Books No. 92. The *BM* and the *U Cat* give only the second edition (1884). It has 69 pp. It was issued in New York in *The Continent* for June 1884, 28.5 cm., illustrated by A. B. Frost.

1720 BILL NYE (EDGAR W. NYE) *Hits and Skits.* Illustrated. o/6 sewed   Early May

Popular Sixpenny Books No. 91. This is probably the first edition (1884), with 124 pp.

See *Comic Stories*, 1888

1721 HAWLEY SMART *Hard Lines.*
New Edition. p 8vo. 2/o boards, 2/6 cloth   May 31 (*Ath*)

Library of Select Authors. This is my copy, no date, 18.2 cm., 362 pp., yellow pictorial boards, printed in red, green, and black, with the series title at the front of the spine, and the No. 178 on the front cover. There are ads on the endpapers, back cover, and on 16 pp. at the back. There is a printer's date (Apr. 12, 1884), and an inscribed date of June 11, 1884. This was *Select Library of Fiction* No. 178 in the new numbering. The first edition was issued by Chapman & Hall, London, 3 vols., 1883, 19 cm., 31/6, listed in the *Ath* on Sept. 15. They issued a new edition at 6/o cloth, advertised in the *Spect* on Jan. 12, 1884.

Also 1901

1722 ANTHONY TROLLOPE
South Australia, Western Australia, and New Zealand. 12mo. 2/o boards, 3/6 cloth   Late May

This is my copy, no date, 17.9 cm., pages (1)–146; (1)–166, in yellow pictorial boards, printed in red, green, and black. It has an uncolored folding map at the front, another one preceding p. (85), and a third map preceding p. (1) of New Zealand. There are ads on the endpapers, back cover, and 18 pp. at the back, with a printer's date (Apr. 6, 1884). This and the following item were listed in Ward, Lock catalogs as uniform with the *Select Library of Fiction*. The first edition was issued by Chapman & Hall, London, 2 vols., 1873, *Australia and New Zealand*, 36/0, listed in the *Ath* and in the *Spect* on Feb. 15. Each vol. had four maps in color, one at the front and three in a pocket at the back, my copy. They issued it at 7/6 in 2 vols., listed in the *Spect* on Nov. 20, 1875. The first Australian book issue was issued by George Robertson, Melbourne, 1873, "Authorized Australian Edition," 23 cm., 691 pp., at 18/0, issued in June. It was previously issued in 7 wrappered parts, No. 1 about Mar. 10, 1873; and it ran in *The Australasian* from Feb. 22, 1873, to June 20, 1874. Chapman & Hall issued it in 4 vols., 1874, at 3/0 cloth each, with uncolored maps: *New Zealand*, 166 pp., about Apr. 18; *Victoria and Tasmania*, 195 pp., about June 6; *New South Wales and Queensland*, 209 pp., about June 27; and *South Australia and Western Australia*, 146 pp., about July 25. They issued it in 4 vols., 1875, with folding colored maps, at 2/0 boards, 2/0 stiff wrappers each, uniform with the *Select Library of Fiction*, listed in the *Spect* on May 22.

See below

1723 ANTHONY TROLLOPE *New South Wales, Queensland, Victoria, and Tasmania.* 12mo. 2/0 boards, 3/6 cloth Late May

This has no date and 3 uncolored maps. See the preceding item.

Also below

1724 KATHERINE KING *Off the Roll.* 2/0 boards, 2/6 cloth   May?

Select Library of Fiction No. 354, later changed to No. 679. The first edition was issued by Hurst & Blackett, London, 3 vols., 1875, p 8vo, 31/6, listed in the *Ath* on Sept. 4. Chapman & Hall, London, issued it in the series as No. 354, at 2/0 boards, listed in the *Ath* on June 2, 1877. The first American edition was issued by Harper & Bros., New York, 1875, my copy, 22.5 cm., 197 pp., $.75 paper, listed in the *Ind* on Dec. 9, 1875.

1725 KATHERINE KING *Our Detachment.* 2/0 boards, 2/6 cloth   May?

Select Library of Fiction No. 680, new numbering. The first edition was issued by Hurst & Blackett, London, 3 vols., 1875, p 8vo, 31/6, listed in the *Ath* on Jan. 2. Chapman & Hall, London, issued it in the series as No. 355, at 2/0 boards, listed in the *Ath* on May 19, 1877. The first American edition was issued by Harper & Bros., New York, 1875, 24 cm., 147 pp., $.50 paper, listed by *Lit World* as published in May.

1726 ANNA C. STEELE *Gardenhurst.* 2/0 boards, 2/6 cloth   May?

Select Library of Fiction No. 363, later changed to No. 706. The first edition was issued by Chapman & Hall, London, 3 vols., 1867, 20 cm., 31/6, listed in the *Ath* on Nov. 7. A second edition in 3 vols. was advertised in the *Spect* on Mar. 21, 1868. It was issued in the series as No. 363, at 2/0 boards, listed in the *Ath* on Aug. 18, 1877.

1727, 1728, 1729, 1730 ANTHONY TROLLOPE *New South Wales and Queensland. New Zealand. South Australia and Western Australia. Victoria and Tasmania.* 4 vols. 1/0 boards each June 5 (*Bks* ad)

These are reprints of the 4 vols. of the Chapman & Hall issue of 1874, each with an uncolored folding map. They have a pictorial front cover and a pink back cover with ads. The second title has 22 pp. of ads at the back; and the third title has 2 pp. of ads at the front and 10 pp. at the back; and all four have ads on the endpapers. I have a rebound copy of *New Zealand*, no date, 166 pp., an uncolored folding map at the back, no ads, and a printer's date (Apr. 6, 1884). The 4 vols. were listed by the *Bks* as published in Sept. 1884 at 1/0 sewed each, as *Shilling Useful Books* Nos. 52–55, in pale yellow wrappers with different scenes on the front covers from the Chapman & Hall 1875 edition. Also above

1731   EDWARD P. ROE   *His Sombre Rivals.*
2/0 boards, 2/6 cloth   June?
Select Library of Fiction No. 379, new numbering. This was also *Lily Series* No. 79, later in 1884, with 282 pp. The first American edition was issued by Dodd, Mead & Co., New York (copyright 1883), 19 cm., 487 pp., $1.25, in an edition of 25,000 copies, bound in terra-cotta, green, or maroon cloth, with yellow endpapers. It was advertised in the *New-York Times* on Sept. 29 as "This day," listed in the *Nation* on Oct. 11, and deposited on Sept. 19. The first English edition was issued by Frederick Warne, London (1883), Fcp 8vo, 282 pp., at 1/0 sewed, 1/6 cloth, advertised in the *Ath* on Sept. 22, and listed in *PC* on Oct. 25.
Also 1886

1732   WAT BRADWOOD (WALTER BRADFORD WOODGATE)   *The O.V.H.*
New Edition. 12mo. 2/0 boards, 2/6 cloth   June?
Select Library of Fiction No. 770, new numbering. This is my copy, no date, 17.8 cm., 418 pp., yellow pictorial boards, printed in red, green, and black, with the series title on the spine, and a printer's date (Feb. 14, 1884). There are ads on the endpapers, back cover, and a 24-page catalog at the back. The first edition was issued by

Chapman & Hall, London, 3 vols., 1869, 20 cm., 31/6, listed in the *Ath* on June 26. They issued it in the series as No. 173, a new edition, my copy, no date, 418 pp., at 2/0 boards, listed in the *Spect* on Sept. 3, 1870. They reissued it as the third edition in 1871; and as the fourth edition, 1877, at 2/0 boards, a known copy.

1733   HENRY J. BYRON   *Paid in Full.*
12mo. 2/0 boards, 2/6 cloth   June?
Select Library of Fiction No. 750, new numbering. This is my copy, no date, 17.9 cm., 460 pp., yellow pictorial boards, printed in red, green, and black, with a printer's date (Apr. 15, 1884). It has the series title on the spine and ads on the endpapers, back cover, and 14 pp. at the back.
Also 1868, 81

1734   ANTHONY TROLLOPE   *Ayala's Angel.*
2/0 boards, 2/6 cloth   July 12 (*Ath*)
Select Library of Fiction No. 30, new numbering. This is the first yellowback edition (1884), with 459 pp. The first edition was issued by Chapman & Hall, London, 3 vols., 1881, listed in the *Ath* on May 21, my copy. They issued it at 6/0, 1882, with 459 pp., about May 20. The *Cincinnati Commercial* paid £50 for early sheets and it ran from Nov. 6, 1880, to July 23, 1881. Harper & Bros., New York, issued it, 1881, *Franklin Square Library* No. 197, 28.1 cm., 109 pp., $.20 paper, dated July 22, 1881. The list of the series in the ads ends with No. 196. It was listed in *PW* on July 30 and in the *Nation* on Aug. 4. It was also issued by George Munro, New York, 1881, as *Seaside Library* No. 1047, 31.5 cm., 96 pp., $.20 paper. It is dated Aug. 4, was deposited Aug. 13, and was listed in *PW* on Aug. 13.

1735   BERTHA LEITH ADAMS, later CAFFAN
Aunt Hepsy's Foundling. New Edition.
2/0 boards, 2/6 cloth   July 26 (*Spect*)
Select Library of Fiction No. 900, new numbering. This is (1884), with 315 pp. The

first English edition was issued by Chapman & Hall, London, 3 vols., 1881, at 31/6, listed in the *Ath* on Jan. 22. The second edition was advertised in the *Spect* on Apr. 30, 3 vols., as "Next week." A new edition was advertised in the *Times Weekly Edition* (London) on Mar. 10, 1882, Cr 8vo, 6/o, as "Now ready." The first American edition was issued by George Munro, New York (1880), as *Seaside Library* No. 906, 32 cm., 60 pp., $.20 paper, advertised in the *New-York Times* on Jan. 3, 1881, as "Out today," and it was listed in *PW* on Jan. 8.

1736 MARK TWAIN (SAMUEL L. CLEMENS) **The Innocents Abroad.** o/6 sewed   July?

Popular Sixpenny Books No. 93. This was also issued by Ward, Lock & Bowden, Ltd., in the wrappers of G. M. Rose & Sons, Toronto, a later Canadian edition. It was in printed green wrappers decorated in blue, 299 pp., and 14 pp. of Ward, Lock ads.

Also 1873, 74, 75, 79

1737 BRET HARTE **The Heathen Chinee with East and West Poems and Parodies.** o/6 sewed   July?

Popular Sixpenny Books No. 94. This is a reissue of the 1873 edition, 150 pp., in illustrated wrappers, with "Beeton's Humorous Books" on the cover.

Also 1873

1738 ANNA M. HALL (MRS. S. C. HALL) **The Whiteboy.** New Edition. 2/o boards, 2/6 cloth   Aug. 2 (*Spect*)

Select Library of Fiction No. 756, new numbering. This is (1884), with 316 pp. The first edition was in 4 parts and then 2 vols., from Chapman & Hall, London, at 3/o each. Part 1 was advertised in the *Ath* on Apr. 26, 1845, as "This day"; part 2 was issued June 1; vol. 1 was advertised in the *Ath* on May 31, at 7/o, as "This day." Part 3 was advertised there on June 28 as "This

day"; and 2 vols. were listed in the *Ath* on Aug. 2, 1845, p 8vo, at 14/o. Sadleir gives an incorrect sequence, having confused this title with *Mount Sorel* by Anne Marsh. Chapman & Hall issued it in the series as No. 4, 1855, 2/o boards, with a preface (Jan. 1855), about Feb. 3. They reissued it (1880), in cream pictorial boards (Sadleir's copy). The first American edition was issued by Harper & Bros., New York, 1845, reviewed in the *Harbinger* (weekly) on Dec. 20, 1845.

1739 HAWLEY SMART **Salvage.** 2/o boards, 2/6 cloth   Aug. 2 (*Spect*)

Library of Select Authors. This is (1884), with 440 pp., a collection of stories. It was *Select Library of Fiction* No. 179 in the new numbering. The first edition was issued by Chapman & Hall, London, 1884, at 10/6, listed in the *Spect* on Mar. 1.

Also 1894

1740 JULIA KAVANAGH **Madeleine.** New Edition. 2/o boards, 2/6 cloth Aug. 2 (*Spect*)

Select Library of Fiction No. 773, new numbering. This is (1884), with 256 pp., a known copy with 28 pp. of ads, and ads on the endpapers and back cover. The first edition was issued by Bentley, London, 1848, 19 cm., 352 pp., 10/6, listed in the *Ath* on Oct. 21, and published then according to the Bentley private catalog. He issued the second edition, 1851, 17 cm., 256 pp., with a new preface, listed in the *Spect* on July 5. He issued a new edition, Fcp 8vo, illustrated, at 3/6, about Jan. 31, 1857; and issued it at 2/6 in canvas in the fall of 1860. Chapman & Hall, London, issued it in the series as No. 215, at 2/o boards, listed in the *Ath* on June 28, 1873. The first American edition was probably issued by D. Appleton & Co., New York, 1852, 19 cm., 300 pp., listed by *Lit World* as published Mar. 20–Apr. 10. It was also issued by Kilner, Philadelphia, probably in the 1850s, 18 cm., 300 pp.

Also 1886

1741 THOMAS A. TROLLOPE *Lindisfarn Chase.* New Edition. 2/o boards, 2/6 cloth Aug. 2 (*Spect*)

Select Library of Fiction No. 87, later changed to No. 502. It is (1884), with 522 pp. It ran in Ward, Lock's *Victoria Magazine* from June 1863 to Aug. 1864. The first English edition was issued by Chapman & Hall, London, 3 vols., 1864, 20 cm., at 31/6, listed in the *Ath* on Oct. 22. They issued a new edition, p 8vo, 522 pp., at 5/o, listed in the *Reader* on Oct. 7, 1865; and issued it in the series as No. 87, the third edition, at 2/o boards, listed in the *Spect* on Aug. 18, 1866. The first edition was issued by Harper & Bros., New York, 1864, 24 cm., 274 pp., $1.50 paper, $2.00 cloth, as *Library of Select Novels*, advertised in the *New-York Times* on Oct. 5 as "This day," and listed in *ALG&PC* (fortnightly) on Oct. 15.

1742 ANNIE THOMAS (MRS. PENDER CUDLIP) *Denis Donne.* New Edition. 2/o boards, 2/6 cloth Aug. 9 (*Ath*)

Select Library of Fiction No. 344, new numbering. This is (1884), with 410 pp. The first edition was issued by Tinsley Bros., London, 3 vols., 1864, listed in the *Ath* on July 30. They issued the second edition, revised, in 3 vols., advertised in the *Spect* on Sept. 17, 1864; and issued a new edition, 414 pp., 6/o, advertised in the *Spect* on June 17, 1865, as "This day." Chapman & Hall, London, issued the third edition in 1868 as No. 118 in the series, at 2/o boards, listed in the *Spect* on Jan. 18; and they issued the fourth edition (1869), at 2/o boards. The first American edition was issued by Harper & Bros., New York, 1865, 25 cm., 147 pp., $.50 paper, as *Library of Select Novels* No. 256. It was advertised in the *New-York Times* on July 12 as "This day," and listed in *ALG&PC* (fortnightly) on Aug. 1.

1743 ELIZABETH C. GREY (MRS. COLONEL GREY) *The Daughters.* 2/o boards, 2/6 cloth Aug. 16 (*Spect*)

Select Library of Fiction No. 577, new numbering. This is (1884), with 381 pp. Also 1865

1744 ÉMILE ERCKMANN & PIERRE CHATRIAN *Waterloo.* 2/o boards, 2/6 cloth Aug. 16 (*Ath* ad)

Select Library of Fiction No. 878, new numbering. This was also issued by Ward, Lock, Bowden & Co., 1892, 19 cm., 307 pp.
Also 1872. See 1875

1745 ROSA M. KETTLE *La Belle Marie.* 12mo. 2/o boards, 2/6 cloth Aug. 23 (*Ath*)

Select Library of Fiction No. 614, new numbering. This is (1884), with 341 pp. The first edition was issued by L. Booth, London, 2 vols., 1862, 19 cm., anonymous, at 21/o, advertised in the *Spect* on May 10. James Weir & Knight, London, issued it, 1880, Cr 8vo, 341 pp., at 5/o, listed in the *Ath* on June 12.

1746 JULIA PARDOE *The Rival Beauties.* 2/o boards, 2/6 cloth Aug. 23 (*Spect*)

Select Library of Fiction No. 645, new numbering. The first edition was issued by Bentley, London, 3 vols., 1848, 20 cm., 31/6, listed in the *Ath* on Apr. 1 C. H. Clarke, London, issued it as *Parlour Library* No. 254, listed in the *Ath* on Nov. 30, 1861. Chapman & Hall, London, issued it as No. 62 in the series, at 2/o boards, listed in the *Reader* on June 10, 1865; and reissued it in the series, 1867. In the United States it was advertised by Stringer & Townsend, New York, in the *New York Daily Times* on June 14, 1854, anonymous, as "Recent," a sequel to *The Royal Favorite*, the latter advertised by Stringer & Townsend in the same, anonymous, illustrated, $.50, as "This morning," on May 12, 1854.

It was issued by W. P. Fetridge, New York, advertised in the *New York Daily Times* on Dec. 19, 1855, as "This day," and listed in *APC&LG* (weekly) on Dec. 22. It was also issued by T. B. Peterson & Bros., Philadelphia, no date, 23 cm., 194 pp.

1747 (JULIA DE WINTON, later STRETTON) *Mr. and Mrs. Asheton.* New Edition. 2/o boards, 2/6 cloth   Aug.?

Select Library of Fiction No. 47, later changed to No. 524. This is (1884), with 365 pp. The first edition was issued by Hurst & Blackett, London, 3 vols., 1860 (1859), 20 cm., anonymous, at 31/6, listed in the *Ath* on Nov. 5, 1859. Chapman & Hall, London, issued it in the series as No. 47, anonymous, 365 pp., at 2/o boards, listed in the *Ath* on July 30, 1864.

1748 KATHERINE S. MACQUOID *Forgotten by the World.* New Edition. 12mo. 2/o boards, 2/6 cloth   Sept.?

Select Library of Fiction No. 737, new numbering. This is (1884), with 594 pp. It ran in the *Sunday Magazine* (Strahan) from Oct. 1868, concluding in 1869. The first English edition was issued by Hurst & Blackett, London, 3 vols., 1870 (1869), Cr 8vo, anonymous, 31/6, listed in the *Ath* on Dec. 11, 1869. Strahan, London, issued it, Cr 8vo, a new edition, at 6/o, listed in the *Spect* on Aug. 16, 1873. Chapman & Hall, London, issued it in the series as No. 319, at 2/o boards, listed in the *Ath* on Apr. 1, 1876. In the United States it was issued by George Routledge, New York, 12mo, anonymous, 594 pp., at $1.50 paper, printed in London, listed in *Putnam's Monthly* (New York) for Nov. 1869 as issued since the Aug. issue.

1749 FRANCES E. TROLLOPE *Aunt Margaret's Trouble.* Sixth Edition. 12mo. 2/o boards, 2/6 cloth   Sept.?

Select Library of Fiction No. 459, new numbering. This is (1884), 17.5 cm., with 292 pp.
Also 1882

1750 (EMILY JOLLY) *Mr. Arle.* New Edition. 12mo. 2/o boards, 2/6 cloth   Sept.?

Library of Select Authors. This is (1884), 17.8 cm., 330 pp., white pictorial boards, printed in red, blue, and black, with the series title at the foot of the spine. There are ads on the endpapers, back cover, and ads at the back consisting of 1 leaf, then pp. 1–11, and then 5 unnumbered pp. My copy is as described but has a date of July 12, 1889, in an ad on the endpapers. This was given the *Select Library of Fiction* No. 690 in the new numbering. The first edition was issued by Hurst & Blackett, London, 2 vols., 1856, p 8vo, anonymous, at 21/o, listed in the *Ath* on Nov. 1, 1856. Chapman & Hall, London, issued it as No. 301 in the series, 1876, a new edition, anonymous, 330 pp., at 2/o boards, listed in the *Ath* on Nov. 20, 1875.

1751 ANNA K. GREEN, later ROHLFS *Hand and Ring.* [Second edition]. o/6 sewed   Oct. 4 (*Ath*)

Popular Sixpenny Books No. 99. It is (1884), with 168 pp. The first edition was issued by G. P. Putnam's Sons, New York, 1883, 20 cm., 608 pp., illustrated, $1.50 cloth, advertised in the *New-York Times* on Oct. 27 as "Next week," listed in the *Ind* on Nov. 8, and in the *Nation* on Nov. 15. An ad in the *New-York Times* on Nov. 24 said that there had been three large editions in three weeks. A new edition was advertised there on Aug. 26, 1884, 16mo, $.50 paper, *Knickerbocker Novels* No. 18, "Today"; and a new edition, 4to, $.20 paper, was advertised there on Feb. 20, 1886, as "Now ready." The first English edition was issued by G. P. Putnam's Sons, New York and London, Cr 8vo, at 6/o, listed in the *Ath* on May 17, 1884.
Also 1904

1752 KATHERINE MACQUOID *A Bad Beginning.* New Edition. 12mo. 2/o boards, 2/6 cloth   Oct. 11 (*Ath*)

Select Library of Fiction No. 735, new numbering. This is (1884), with 280 pp. The first edition was issued by Smith, Elder & Co., London, 2 vols., 1862, anonymous, at 21/0, listed in the *Ath* on Oct. 11. They reissued it, 1866, 17.5 cm., 280 pp., at 1/0 sewed, listed in the *Reader* on Sept. 1. Chapman & Hall, London, issued it in the series as No. 202, a new edition, at 2/0 boards, listed in the *Ath* on June 1, 1872.

1753 ANNA K. GREEN, later ROHLFS
The Sword of Damocles. Cr 8vo. o/6 sewed   Oct.?

Popular Sixpenny Books No. 97. This is my copy, the first English edition (1884), 19.6 cm., 174 pp., double columns, yellow pictorial wrappers, printed in red, green, and black, with the cover picture by Corbould. It has ads on the verso of the half-title, on the back cover, and has ads at the back consisting of 1 leaf, then pp. 1–8, and then 8 unnumbered pp. The first edition was issued by G. P. Putnam's Sons, New York, 1881, 19 cm., 540 pp., $1.50 cloth, listed in *PW* on Apr. 30, and in the *Ind* on May 5.
Also 1904

1754 JOHN HABBERTON **The Bowsham Puzzle and My Friend Moses.** o/6 sewed 1884 (*Eng Cat*)

Popular Sixpenny Books No. 95. This is 1884, with 188 pp., the first English edition. The first edition was issued by Funk & Wagnalls, New York, my copy, 1884, 19.5 cm., 222 pp., $.25 paper, the *Standard Library* No. 110. It was listed in the *Ind* on Mar. 20, in *PW* on Mar. 22, and in the *Nation* on Mar. 27.

1755 ARTEMUS WARD (CHARLES F. BROWNE) **Letters to "Punch," Among the Witches and Other Humorous Papers.** o/6 sewed   1884 (*Eng Cat*)

Popular Sixpenny Books No. 96. This has no date, clothed in pictorial wrappers, with the cover title, "Artemus Ward's Letters to Punch."
See *Artemus Ward in London*, 1874

1756 ANNA K. GREEN, later ROHLFS
A Strange Disappearance. o/6 sewed Oct.?

Popular Sixpenny Books No. 98. This is (1884), with 153 pp. Either this or the Routledge edition was the first English edition. George Routledge, London, issued it (1884), 128 pp., o/6 sewed, listed in *PC* as published Sept. 15–Oct. 1. The first edition was issued by G. P. Putnam's Sons, New York, 1880, 17 cm., 280 pp., $.50 paper, $1.00 cloth, advertised in the *New-York Times* on Nov. 29, *Knickerbocker Novels* No. 5, "Next week," and advertised as "Now ready" on Dec. 11, 1879. It was advertised there on June 13, 1885, at $.20 paper. The first edition was listed in *PW* on Dec. 20, 1879.
Also 1904

1757 MARK TWAIN (SAMUEL L. CLEMENS)
The Jumping Frog and Other Stories and Sketches. o/6 sewed   1884 (*Eng Cat*)
Popular Sixpenny Books No. 100.
Also 1874, 76. See *American Drolleries*, 1875

1758 ANNA K. GREEN, later ROHLFS
The Leavenworth Case. o/6 sewed   Oct.?

Popular Sixpenny Books No. 101. This is (1884), with 284 pp. This was issued in England by Strahan, London, Cr 8vo, 475 pp., 3/6, listed in the *Spect* on Apr. 19, 1884. It was also issued by George Routledge, London, 159 pp., at o/6 sewed, probably in Sept. 1884. The first edition was issued by G. P. Putnam's Sons, New York, 1878, 20 cm., 475 pp., illustrated, $.75 paper, $1.50 cloth, listed in the *Nation* on Nov. 21, in the *Ind* on Nov. 28, and in *PW* on Dec. 7. A new edition was advertised in the *New-York Times* on Aug. 19, 1879, the same; and a new edition was also advertised there on Dec. 11, 1879, 16mo, $.60 paper, $1.25 cloth, as "Now ready."
Also 1902

1759 ELIZABETH C. GREY (MRS. COLONEL GREY) *Mary Seaham.* 1/0 boards, 2/6 cloth   Oct.?

Select Library of Fiction No. 575, new numbering. The first edition was issued by Henry Colburn, London, 3 vols., 1852, 20 cm., 31/6, listed in the *Ath* on May 22. The second edition was issued by Chapman & Hall, London, as No. 38 in the series, 415 pp., at 2/0 boards, listed in the *Ath* on Oct. 31, 1863. In the United States it was issued by T. B. Peterson, Philadelphia, in 1852, 23 cm., 211 pp., listed in *Godey's Lady's Book* for Nov., and hence probably issued in Aug. or Sept.

1760 SAMUEL LOVER *Handy Andy.* Illustrated. 0/6 sewed   Oct.?

Popular Sixpenny Books No. 18. This is (1884), with 157 pp. The first issue was in 12 monthly 1/0 parts (Jan. 1, 1842–Dec. 1, 1842), by Frederick Lover & Richard Groombridge, London. They issued it in 1 vol., 1842, 21.5 cm., 380 pp., illustrated, at 13/0 cloth, listed in the *Ath* on Dec. 10. It is based on 2 short stories from *Tales from Bentley's Miscellaney.* It was issued by Henry G. Bohn, London, 1845, 23 cm., 380 pp., illustrated, at 7/6; and by David Bryce, London, at 2/0 boards, the latter advertised in *Notes & Queries* on July 15, 1854, as "On July 29." The entire stock of Bryce (over 100,000 vols.) was sold at a Hodgson auction, June 2–5, 1858, and the copyright was sold at a Hodgson auction on June 8, 1858, the property of Bryce, for £390. In the United States it was issued in parts by D. Appleton & Co., New York; etc.; a listing in the *United States Magazine* (monthly) for Sept. 1842 stated that 7 parts, illustrated, had already been issued. A notice in the *Knickerbocker* for Jan. 1843 stated that the part issue was now over and that it was now issued in two forms, 1843, illustrated.

1761 EDWIN LANKESTER, ed. *Haydn's Domestic Medicine. Part 1.* Illustrated. 0/6 sewed   Nov. 1 (*Spect* ad)

This was originally by Joseph T. Haydn. It is a serial issued in 12 monthly parts. Moxon, London, published this Lankester edition, 1874, *Haydn's Dictionary of Popular Medicine and Hygiene,* 646 pp., at 7/6. Ward and Lock issued it in serial form (1878, 1879), a new edition, with 685 pp. In the United States it was apparently issued by True & Co., Augusta, Maine (1882), 24 cm., 1,008 pp., with plates and frontispiece.

1762 ANONYMOUS *Beeton's Christmas Annual.* 1/0 sewed   Nov.

This contains *Uncle Oldenthorpe's Legacy.* See 1885

1763 CHARLES LEVER *Jack Hinton.* 1/0 sewed   Nov.?

Shilling Novels No. 24. This was originally issued as vol. 1 of *Our Mess,* vols. 2 and 3 containing *Tom Burke of "Ours." Jack Hinton* ran in the *Dublin University Magazine* (Mar.–Dec. 1842). *Our Mess* was issued, 35-parts-in-34, illustrated by "Phiz," 1/0, part 1 advertised in the *Ath* on Oct. 30, 1841, as "On Jan. 1." Vol. 1 was issued by William Curry, Jr. & Co., Dublin; etc., as were the monthly parts. The book issue dated 1843, edited by Lever, 23 cm., illustrated by "Phiz," 14/0, listed in the *Ath* on Dec. 31, 1842. This vol. 1 was reissued by Curry, 1845, 396 pp., illustrated. Chapman & Hall issued it, 8vo, reduced to 7/0, listed by *PC* as reduced July 14–29, 1850. They issued it Cr 8vo, with 8 illustrations by "Phiz," at 4/0, advertised in *Notes & Queries* on Feb. 5, 1859. They issued it as *Select Library of Fiction* No. 17, at 2/0 boards, listed in the *Ath* on Apr. 5, 1862. This began a resurrection of this series by W. H. Smith, who issued the series for his railway book stalls, under cover of Chapman & Hall. It was reissued at 2/0 boards, a yellowback in the series, with a new introduction and with a printer's date (Oct. 17, 1878). They issued a new edition in 1865, p 8vo, 404 pp., illustrated, 6/0, listed in the *Reader* on Apr. 1. The first American edition was issued by Carey & Hart, Philadelphia, 1843, 24 cm., 400 pp., illustrated by "Phiz."

1764 BAYLE ST. JOHN *Maretimo.*
2/0 boards, 2/6 cloth   Nov.?

Select Library of Fiction No. 761, new numbering. This is (1884). I have not been able to trace the first edition. Chapman & Hall, London, issued it (1856), small format, 311 pp., at 2/0 boards, as No. 13 in the series, listed in the *Ath* on Aug. 9. They reissued it in 1862 at 1/0 boards. The 1856 issue is Sadleir's copy, a yellowback.

1765 AUGUSTUS MAYHEW ET AL.
Paved with Gold. 2/0 boards, 2/6 cloth
Dec. 6 (*Ath*)

Select Library of Fiction No. 724A, new numbering. This is (1884), with 408 pp. Chapman & Hall, London; etc., issued it in 13 monthly 1/0 parts in white wrappers, illustrated by "Phiz," part 1 listed in the *Spect* on Mar. 7, 1857, and part 13 advertised there on Feb. 27, 1858, as "On Mar. 1." Parts 1–5 and 13 were by the Brothers Mayhew, and the rest was by Augustus. Chapman & Hall issued it in 1 vol., 1858, 22.5 cm., 408 pp., illustrated by "Phiz," 14/0, advertised in the *Spect* on Mar. 6. They issued the third edition, no date, in cloth, but with a blocking differing from the first edition. George Routledge, London, issued the fourth edition, 1872, 23 cm., 408 pp., illustrated by "Phiz," 6/0 cloth, listed by *PC* as published May 1–15.

1766 SAMUEL WARREN *Passages from the Diary of a Late Physician.* 1/0 sewed
Dec.?

Shilling Novels No. 22. This is (1884), with 284 pp. It ran in *Blackwood's Magazine*, 1830–37. The first edition was issued by J. & J. Harper, New York, 2 vols., 1831, 16 cm., anonymous; and they issued it in 3 vols., 1838. The first English edition was issued by William Blackwood, Edinburgh; etc., 2 vols., 1832, Fcp 8vo, anonymous, 12/0, listed in the *Ath* on Mar. 17. They issued the fourth edition in 2 vols., 1835, 17 cm., anonymous, illustrated, 12/0, still advertised in the *Spect* on Jan. 14, 1837. They issued the third vol., 1838, 17 cm., by Warren, illustrated, 6/0, listed in the *Ath* on Dec. 9, 1837. Wolff has a presentation copy of the second edition in 2 vols., 1833, inscribed May 9, 1833, and with a notice to the reader (Feb. 3, 1832). The seventh edition, 2 vols. at 12/0, was advertised in the *Spect* on June 1, 1844, as "This day." George Routledge, London, issued it (1884), 503 pp., 2/0 boards, listed by *PC* as published Aug. 1–15; and Frederick Warne, London, issued it in 2 vols., at 0/6 sewed each, or in 1 vol. at 1/0 sewed, probably in Dec. 1884.
Also 1885

1767 SAMUEL WARREN *Ten Thousand a Year.* 1/0 sewed   Dec.?

Shilling Novels No. 23. This is (1884), with 429 pp. George Routledge, London, also issued it (1884), 704 pp., 2/0 boards, listed by *PC* as published July 16–31; and Frederick Warne, London, also issued it in 1884, probably in Sept., in 2 vols., 0/6 sewed each, or in 1 vol., 1/0 sewed. It ran in *Blackwood's Magazine* (Oct. 1839–Aug. 1841). The first edition was issued by Carey & Hart, Philadelphia, 6 vols., 1840, 1841, the last 2 vols. in 1841, 19.5 cm., anonymous, in boards, cloth backs, and paper labels, listed as 5 vols., unfinished, in the *New York Review* (quarterly) for Jan. 1841, and vol. 5 was listed in the *U.S. Magazine* (monthly) for July 1841. The first English edition was issued by William Blackwood & Sons, Edinburgh and London, 3 vols., 1841, 19.5 cm., anonymous, 31/6, listed by the *Edinburgh Review* as

published Oct. 1841–Jan. 1842, and Wolff's presentation copy in gray-purple cloth was inscribed Nov. 15, 1841. They issued a revised edition, p 8vo, 31/6 for 3 vols., listed in the *Ath* on Nov. 13, 1841. They issued a second edition, completely revised, 3 vols., illustrated, 18/0, the three vols. listed in the *Spect* on Mar. 1, Apr. 12, and May 10, 1845, respectively.
Also 1886

1768 CHARLES LEVER *Harry Lorrequer.*
0/6 sewed   Dec.?
Popular Sixpenny Books No. 19.
Also 1882

1769 LAWRENCE L. LYNCH (EMMA MURDOCH, later VAN DEVENTER)
Shadowed by Three. 0/6 sewed   Dec.?
Popular Sixpenny Books No. 103. This is the first edition in England (1884), with 165 pp. The first edition was issued by Donnelley, Gassett, & Loyd, Chicago (1879), 17.5 cm., 738 pp., illustrated, listed in *PW* on Dec. 6, 1879.

1770 THOMAS L. PEACOCK *Melincourt.*
2/0 boards, 2/6 cloth   Dec.?
Select Library of Fiction No. 759, new numbering. The first edition was issued by T. Hookham, Jr. & Co., London; etc., 3 vols., 1817, 17.5 cm., anonymous, 18/0, listed by the *Edinburgh Review* as published Dec. 1816–Mar. 1817. It was issued by Chapman & Hall, London, 1856, as No. 14 in the series, 18 cm., 315 pp., 2/0 boards, with a new preface, listed in the *Ath* on Apr. 12. It was issued in the United States by Moses T. J. Maxwell, Philadelphia, 2-vols.-in-1, 1817, 14.5 cm., anonymous.

1771 JAMES GREENWOOD *The Little Ragamuffins.* Illustrated. 1/0 sewed
1884 (*Eng Cat*)
Shilling Novels No. 18. This is (1884), with 359 pp. This was also issued as *Youth's Library of Wonder and Adventure* No. 41, illus-

trated, 1/0 sewed, 1/6 cloth. The first American edition was *The True History of a Little Ragamuffin*, issued by Harper & Bros., New York, 1866, 8vo, anonymous, $.50 paper, listed in the *Nation* on May 1, and advertised in the *New-York Times* on May 1 as "This day." The first English edition was issued by S. O. Beeton, London, 1866, anonymous, 359 pp., listed in the *Spect* on Feb. 24. Ward, Lock & Tyler, London, issued it (1867), a new edition, 359 pp., frontispiece and added illustrated title page and 12 full-page illustrations by "Phiz" and J. G. Thomson, 10/6. The author's name appears only on the title page, and there is a 16-page catalog at the back. Wolff had two copies of this, one in powder blue and the other in red-brown, both with dark cream endpapers. Wolff thought the date was (1866), and the Osborne Collection gave it as (1870), both probably incorrect as the above item shows.

1772 JOHN LATOUCHE (OSWALD J. F. CRAWFURD) *Travels in Portugal.*
Third Edition. p 8vo. Map, Frontispiece.
2/0 boards   1884 (*Eng Cat*)
Library of Favourite Authors. This is my copy, no date, 18.4 cm., 336 pp., with a map in red and black, pink pictorial boards in red, blue, and black, with gray endpapers with ads. There is a preface to the second edition (Sept. 20, 1875), a preface to the third edition (Sept. 1878), and 4 pp. of Moxon ads at the back. It first appeared in *New Quarterly Magazine* No. 1, Oct. 1, 1873, and concluded in issue No. 5, Oct. 1, 1874. The first edition was issued by Ward, Lock & Tyler (1875), 22 cm., 354 pp., illustrated, 10/6, listed in the *Spect* on June 26. They issued the second edition in 1875, Demy 8vo, illustrated, 10/6, advertised in the *Spect* on Sept. 25 as "On Oct. 1." Ward, Lock & Co. issued the third edition (1878), 336 pp., frontispiece and map, at 6/0, advertised in the *Spect* on Nov. 23 as "Now ready." The first Ameri-

can edition was issued by G. P. Putnam's Sons, New York, 1875, 22 cm., 354 pp., illustrated, listed in *PW* on Oct. 9.

1773 (EMILY JOLLY) *Entanglements.*
New Edition. 2/0 boards   1884 (*Eng Cat*)
Select Library of Fiction No. 291, later changed to No. 689. This is (1884), with 260 pp. The first edition was issued by Smith, Elder & Co., London, 2 vols., 1862, 29 cm., anonymous, 21/0, listed in the *Ath* on Dec. 13. They issued it, 1865, anonymous, at 1/0 sewed, about Dec. 30, 1865. Chapman & Hall, London, issued it at 1/0 sewed, probably in 1869; and issued it as *Select Library of Fiction* No. 291, anonymous, at 2/0 boards, listed in the *Ath* on Sept. 18, 1875; and reissued it, my copy, at 2/0 boards, in Oct. 1876.

1774 FRANCES E. TROLLOPE
The Sacristan's Household. 2/0 boards
1884 (*Eng Cat*)
Select Library of Fiction No. 462, new numbering. This is (1884), with 425 pp. The first edition was issued by Virtue & Co., London, 2 vols., 1869, 20 cm., anonymous, illustrated, 21/0, listed in the *Ath* on Apr. 10. Virtue sold it to Strahan, London. Virtue advertised it on Apr. 3, 1869; and Strahan advertised it on May 8, 1869. It ran in *St. Paul's Magazine* (July 1868–June 1869). Chapman & Hall, London, issued it in the series as No. 308, at 2/0 boards, listed in the *Ath* on Feb. 26, 1876. The first American edition was issued by Harper & Bros., New York, 1869, 24 cm., anonymous, 158 pp., illustrated, noticed in the *Ind* on June 24, and advertised in *Harper's Weekly* on June 26.

1775 FRANCES E. TROLLOPE *A Charming Fellow.* New Edition. 12mo. 2/0 boards
1884
Select Library of Fiction No. 460, new numbering. This is my copy, no date, 17.7 cm., 367 pp., yellow pictorial boards, printed in red, green, and black, with the series title on the spine, and the No. 460 on the front cover. There are ads on the endpapers and back cover, a printer's date (Mar. 12, 1884), and a leaf of ads plus ads on pp. 1–8, plus 2 more pp. of ads at the back. The first edition was issued by Chapman & Hall, London, 3 vols., 1876 (1875), 19 cm., 31/6, listed in the *Ath* on Dec. 18, 1875. They issued it in the series as No. 326, at 2/0 boards, listed in the *Ath* on June 24, 1876.

1776 GEORGE J. WHYTE MELVILLE
"Bones and I." New Edition. 12mo.
2/0 boards   1884?
Library of Select Authors. This is my copy, no date, 17.8 cm., 287 pp., yellow pictorial boards, printed in red, blue, and black, with the series title at the foot of the spine, and "The Works of Whyte Melville" at the head. It has ads on the endpapers, back cover, and ads at the back consisting of 1 leaf, then pp. 1–9, and then 15 pp. This was *Select Library of Fiction* No. 392, later changed to No. 120. The first edition was issued by Chapman & Hall, London, 1868, 19.5 cm., 287 pp., at 9/0, listed in the *Ath* on June 20. They issued it, Cr 8vo, at 5/0, listed in the *Spect* on June 12, 1869; and they issued the third edition, 1871, 19 cm., 287 pp., at 2/0 boards, listed in the *Ath* on Aug. 12. It was reissued and put in the series as No. 392, at 2/0 boards, in the fall of 1879. There are known copies of the present edition in pale pink boards, no date, with ads on the endpapers, back cover, and 14 pp. at the back; and also the same except for 26 pp. of ads at the back. Ward, Lock & Bowden reissued it as a new edition with 287 pp. in the 1890s.
Also 1903

1777 ÉMILE ERCKMANN & PIERRE CHATRIAN *The States General.*
12mo. 2/0 boards   1884?
Select Library of Fiction No. 881, new numbering. This is my copy, no date, 17.7 cm.,

274 pp., yellow pictorial boards, printed in red, blue, and black, with the series title on the spine, and ads on the endpapers, back cover, and 18 pp. at the back. There is a known copy (circa 1893) in the series, in blue pictorial boards, with an initial ad leaf, ads on the endpapers, back cover, and 18 pp., at the back, the front cover illustrated by J. T. Schuler.
Also 1871, 75

1778   CÉCILE J. B. GÉRARD   **Lion Hunting and Sporting Life in Algeria.** 1/o sewed, 1/6 cloth   1884?
Youth's Library of Wonder and Adventure No. 36. This is illustrated. The *Eng Cat* gives an edition from Ward, Lock & Tyler in 1874, p 8vo, illustrated by Doré, 5/o. Ward, Lock also issued it in the *Family Gift Series*, Cr 8vo, illustrated by Doré, 2/6 cloth. The first edition was *La Chasse au Lion*, Paris, 1850, 250 pp. The first English edition was issued by Addey & Co., London, 1856, 18 cm., 224 pp., illustrated, 2/6.

1779   FREDERICK C. L. WRAXALL   **The Backwoodsman.** 1/o sewed, 1/6 cloth   1884?
Youth's Library of Wonder and Adventure No. 37. Ward, Lock & Tyler issued this in 1871, at 5/o, listed in the *Spect* on July 15; and they also issued it in the *Family Gift Series*, Cr 8vo, 2/6 cloth. The first edition was issued by John Maxwell & Co., London, 1864, 19.5 cm., 428 pp., illustrated, 6/o, edited by Wraxall, listed in the *Ath* on Oct.

1. The first American edition was issued by T. O. H. P. Burnham, Boston; etc., 1865, 302 pp., illustrated, listed in the *Nation* on Sept. 28, and in *ALG&PC* (fortnightly) on Oct. 2.
Also 1886

1780   ANONYMOUS   **Hunting Adventures in Forest and Field.** 1/o sewed, 1/6 cloth   1884?
Youth's Library of Wonder and Adventure No. 38. I cannot trace this. It was also issued in the *Family Gift Series*, Cr 8vo, illustrated, 2/6 cloth.

1781   THOMAS A. TROLLOPE   **La Beata. A Tuscan Romeo and Juliet.** New Edition. 12mo. 2/o boards   1884?
Select Library of Fiction No. 504, new numbering. This has no date, 18 cm., 329 pp. Both Sadleir and the *U Cat* think it was circa 1884. The first edition was issued by Chapman & Hall, London, 2 vols., 1861, p 8vo, 16/o, listed in the *Ath* on May 11, *La Beata*. The second edition, the same, was advertised in the *Spect* on June 22, 1861, as "This day." They issued the third edition, 1862, at 5/o, with *A Tuscan Romeo and Juliet*, now first printed, listed in the *Spect* on May 3. They issued it in the series as No. 73, listed in the *Reader* on Dec. 30, 1865; and reissued it in the series as No. 344, a new edition, 1877, my copy, 329 pp., at 2/o boards, with a printer's date (Oct. 28, 1876), the No. 344 on the front, and with the ads for the series ending with No. 404, which was issued in Feb. 1879.

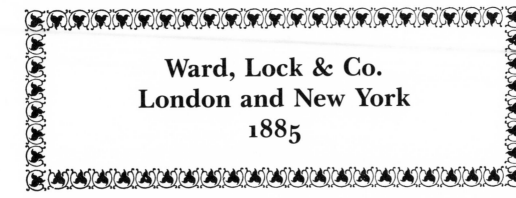

Ward, Lock & Co.
London and New York
1885

1782 OSWALD J. F. CRAWFURD **The World We Live In.** New Edition. 2/o boards, 2/6 cloth   Jan. 24 (*Ath*)

Select Library of Fiction No. 952, new numbering. This is (1885). The first edition was issued by Chapman & Hall, London, 2 vols., 1884, advertised in the *Times Weekly Edition* (London) on July 4, 1884, 2 vols., 12/o, and listed in the *Spect* on June 28. A new edition was advertised in the *Times Weekly Edition* on Aug. 29, Cr 8vo, 5/o, "This day." The first American edition was issued by G. P. Putnam's Sons, New York and London, 1884, 16 cm., 351 pp. $.50 paper, $1.00 cloth, listed in *PW* on Aug. 30, and advertised in the *New-York Times* on Aug. 26, *Transatlantic Series* No. 19, "This day."

1783 GEORGE PAYNE **Oonah.** 1/o sewed Jan.?

Shilling Novels No. 25. This is the first edition (1885), with 138 pp.

1784 EMMANUEL KINK (RICHARD DOWLING) & ARTEMUS WARD (CHARLES BROWNE) **Babies and Ladders; Artemus Ward Among the Fenians.** o/6 sewed 1885 (*Eng Cat*)

Popular Sixpenny Books No. 103.
Also 1877

1785 BRET HARTE **Sensation Novels Condensed.** o/6 sewed   Feb.?

Popular Sixpenny Books No. 107.
Also 1875

1786 BRET HARTE **The Pagan Child and Other Sketches.** o/6 sewed   Mar.?

Popular Sixpenny Books No. 104. This was also issued by Ward, Lock, Bowden & Co. in the 1890s, 18.5 cm., with 185 pp.
Also 1876, 78

1787 MARK TWAIN (SAMUEL L. CLEMENS) **Eye Openers.** o/6 sewed   1885 (*Eng Cat*)

Popular Sixpenny Books No. 106.
Also 1875. See *Funny Stories and Humorous Poems*, 1875

1788 ANNIE THOMAS (MRS. PENDER CUDLIP) **False Colours.** 2/o boards, 2/6 cloth   Apr. 18 (*Spect*)

Select Library of Fiction No. 354, new numbering. This was also listed in the *Ath* on June 20, at 2/o boards. The first edition was issued by Tinsley Bros., London, 1869, 3 vols., p 8vo, 31/6, listed in the *Ath* on May 8. George Routledge, London, issued it, 1871, at 2/o boards, listed in the *Spect* on Apr. 29. He ran it in *The Broadway* (New York), starting in Oct. 1868, illustrated, continuing into 1869. Annie Thomas married the minister, Pender Cudlip, and Charlotte Yonge, in a letter (Dec. 22, 1869), wondered how he could permit her to write such an immoral book! The first American edition was issued by Harper & Bros., New York, 1869, 8vo, 152 pp., $.50 paper, in the *Library of Select Novels*, listed in the *Nation* on Sept. 2, and advertised in the *New-York Times* on Sept. 4 as "This day."

1789 OCTAVE FEUILLET **The Journal of a Woman.** 0/6 sewed   Apr.?

Popular Sixpenny Books No. 110. This is (1885), with 136 pp. The first edition was *Le Journal d'une Femme*, Paris, 1878, 19 cm., 343 pp. The present edition is probably the first English edition. *A Woman's Diary and The Little Countess* was issued by Vizetelly, London, in 1881, 18 cm., 220 pp., 1/0 sewed, 1/6 cloth, advertised in the *Ath* on Feb. 26. In the United States it was issued by George Munro, New York (1878), 32 cm., 18 pp., as *A Woman's Journal, Seaside Library* No. 428, advertised in the *New-York Times* on Nov. 30 at $.10 as "Out today." It was also issued by D. Appleton & Co., New York, *The Diary of a Woman*, 1879, advertised in the *New-York Times* on Dec. 12, 1878, 16mo, $.50 paper, $.75 cloth, as "This day."

1790 AGLEN A. DOWTY **Connubial Bliss.** 0/6 sewed   1885 (*Eng Cat*)

Popular Sixpenny Books No. 111.
Also 1872

1791 HENRY KINGSLEY **The Harveys.** New Edition. 12mo. 2/0 boards, 2/6 cloth Apr.?

Library of Select Authors. Select Library of Fiction No. 110 in the new numbering. It is my copy, no date, 17.7 cm., 353 pp., yellow pictorial boards, printed in red, blue, and black, with the series title on the spine, and the No. 110 on the front. There are ads on the endpapers and back cover, and there is a 22-page catalog at the back. The first edition was issued by Tinsley Bros., London, 2 vols., 1872, advertised in the *Ath* on Dec. 9, 1871, as "This day" and reviewed on Dec. 16. It has a 16-page catalog (Dec. 1871) at the back of vol. 2. They issued it, 1872, 6/0, in blue cloth, with a 16-page catalog (Feb. 1872) at the back; and issued it at 2/0 boards, 2/6 cloth,

listed in the *Ath* on Feb. 22, 1873. George Routledge announced in the *Ath* on May 29, 1875, that he had purchased the copyright and stock of this title and, in fact, issued it promptly at 2/0 boards. The first American edition was issued by J. B. Lippincott, Philadelphia, 1872, 18 cm., 353 pp., a copyright edition, listed in *PW* on Oct. 3 and in the *Ind* on Oct. 10, probably with A. Asher, Berlin, also in the imprint.

1792 HENRY KINGSLEY **Stretton.** 2/0 boards, 2/6 cloth   Apr.?

This was probably in the *Library of Select Authors*. It was given the *Select Library of Fiction* No. 111, in the new numbering. It has no date and 394 pp. The first edition was issued by Tinsley Bros., London, 3 vols., 1869, 18.5 cm., at 31/6, listed in the *Ath* on May 29. He issued it at 6/0 in 1870, listed in the *Spect* on Mar. 5. George Routledge, London, issued it at 2/0 boards, with 394 pp., listed in the *Ath* on June 15, 1872; and reissued it at 2/0 boards in Aug. 1879. He ran it in *The Broadway* (New York), beginning with the first issue of his new periodical in Sept. 1868, with chapters 1–8 and 1 illustration. Chapters 12–16 were in the Dec. issue. In the United States it was issued by Lepoldt & Holt, New York, 1869, 23.5 cm., 250 pp., with 4 illustrations, at $1.00 paper and $1.50 cloth, an authorized edition, listed in the *Nation* on June 17, and advertised in the *New-York Times* on June 12. They issued it at $.50 paper, $1.50 cloth, advertised there on June 26. It was also issued by Harper & Bros., New York, 1869, 22 cm., 144 pp., illustrated, $.40 paper, listed in the *Nation* on July 1, and advertised in the *New-York Times* on June 19 as "This day."

1793 (WILLIAM H. THOMPSON) **Life in a Debtor's Prison.** 2/0 boards, 2/6 cloth May?

Select Library of Fiction No. 803, new numbering. This used the 1880 edition title page. It has the series title on spine.
Also 1880

1794 WAT BRADWOOD (WALTER
BRADFORD WOODGATE) *Ensemble.*
New Edition. 12mo. 2/0 boards,
2/6 cloth   May?

Select Library of Fiction No. 770A, new
numbering. This is my copy, no date, 17.7
cm., 384 pp., yellow pictorial boards,
printed in red, green, and black, with the
series title on the spine. There are ads on
the endpapers, back cover, and on pp. 9–
11, 14, 15, 34–36 at the back. There is a
known copy in the series, in blue boards, a
new edition, with ads on the endpapers,
back cover, and on pp. 9–16 and 33–40 at
the back. The first edition was issued by
Chapman & Hall, London, 3 vols., 1870,
20 cm., 31/6, listed in the *Ath* on Apr. 30.
They issued it in the series as No. 236,
1874, a new edition, my copy, 17.9 cm.,
387 pp., yellow pictorial boards, with
printer's date (Nov. 18, 1873), listed in the
Ath on Jan. 10.

1795 (HENRY F. KEENAN) *The Money-
Makers.* 1/0 sewed   May?

Shilling Novels No. 26. This is the first English edition, no date, with 319 pp. The
first American edition was issued by D.
Appleton & Co., New York, 1885, 18.5
cm., anonymous, 337 pp., listed in the *Ind*
on Feb. 5.

1796 RICHARD RUSSELL *India's Danger
and England's Duty.* Illustrated. Maps.
1/0 sewed   May?

Shilling Useful Books. This is (1885), with
127 pp., the first English edition. It was issued by W. Bryce, Toronto (1885?), 18
cm., 127 pp., folding maps and
illustrations.

1797 WILLIAM G. CRAVEN
The Margravine. 12mo. 2/0 boards,
2/6 cloth   June 6 (*Ath*)

Select Library of Fiction No. 809, new numbering. This is my copy, no date, 17.6 cm.,
292 pp., white pictorial boards, printed in
red, blue, green, and brown with black let-

tering, with the series title on the spine.
There are ads on the endpapers and back
cover, with a 22-page catalog at the back.
The first edition was Chapman & Hall,
London, 2 vols., 1870, illustrated.

1798 WANDERER (ELIM H. D'AVIGDOR)
Hunt-Room Stories and Yachting Yarns.
Illustrated. 2/0 boards, 2/6 cloth
June 6 (*Ath*)

Select Library of Fiction No. 808, new numbering. This is 1885, with 287 pp. The
first edition was issued by Chapman &
Hall, London, 1884, 22.5 cm., anonymous, 287 pp., illustrated, 12/6, advertised in the *Times Weekly Edition* (London)
on May 30, as "This day." It is reprinted
from the *Court Circular* and *The Country
Gentleman*, illustrated by E. Giberne.

1799 HENRY KINGSLEY *Hornby Mills;
and Other Stories.* 2/0 boards, 2/6 cloth
June 6 (*Ath*)

This is probably in the *Library of Select Authors* but was given the *Select Library of Fiction* No. 114, in the new numbering. It is
(1885), with 412 pp. The first edition was
issued by Tinsley Bros., London, 2 vols.,
1872, 19.5 cm., 21/0, containing nine
stories, listed in the *Ath* on Apr. 27. They
issued it at 2/0 boards, 2/6 cloth, 1872,
listed in the *Ath* on Jan. 18, 1873. Wolff
had a copy of the 2/0 Tinsley yellowback.
George Routledge, London, in an ad in
the *Ath* on May 29, 1875, announced that
they had purchased the copyright and
stock of this title, which they promptly issued at 2/0 boards.

1800 ANNIE THOMAS (MRS. PENDER
CUDLIP) *Sir Victor's Choice.* 2/0 boards,
2/6 cloth   June 6 (*Ath*)

Select Library of Fiction No. 355, new numbering. This is (1885), with 409 pp. The
first edition was issued by John Maxwell &
Co., London, 3 vols., 1864, p 8vo, 31/6,
listed in the *Ath* on Mar. 5. It was reissued,
1865, a new edition, Cr 8vo, 409 pp., at

6/o, listed in the *Reader* on Apr. 22, 1865. George Routledge, London, issued it, 1867, at 2/o boards, listed in the *Ath* on Sept. 28.

1801   WILLIAM ADAMSON   *The Abbot of Aberbrothock.* 12mo. 2/o boards, 2/6 cloth June 13 (*Ath*)   See color photo section

Select Library of Fiction No. 802, new numbering. This is my copy, the first edition (1885), 17.6 cm., 383 pp., white pictorial boards, printed in red, blue, and black, with the series title on the spine, and the No. 802 on the front cover. There are ads on the endpapers and back cover, with a 30-page catalog at the back with a mishmash of non-sequential numbering and non-numbering.
Also 1886

1802   JAMES GREENWOOD   *Martyrs by Proxy, and Other Stories.* o/6 sewed June?

Popular Sixpenny Books No. 108. This is the first edition (1885), with 121 pp.

1803   JAMES GREENWOOD
A Queer Showman, and Other Stories.
o/6 sewed   June?

Popular Sixpenny Books No. 109. This is the first edition (1885), with 128 pp.

1804   W. S. HAYWARD   *The Diamond Cross.*
2/o boards, 2/6 cloth   June?

Select Library of Fiction No. 651, new numbering. This has no date.
Also 1875

1805   JOHN LANG   *Captain Macdonald.*
o/6 sewed   June?

Popular Sixpenny Books No. 112.
Also 1856, 58, 60, 70, 82

1806   HENRY KINGSLEY   *Old Margaret.*
New Edition. 2/o boards, 2/6 cloth
June?

This is probably in the *Library of Select Authors* but was given the *Select Library of Fic-*

tion No. 112, new numbering. It has no date and 378 pp. The first edition was issued by Tinsley Bros., London, 2 vols., 1871, p 8vo, 21/o, listed in the *Ath* on July 1. They issued it in 1 vol., 1872, a new edition, at 6/o, listed in the *Spect* on Feb. 3. Routledge, London, bought the copyright and stock about May 29, 1875, and issued it at 2/o boards. Tinsley Bros. issued it at 2/o boards, 2/6 cloth, listed in the *Spect* on Sept. 7, 1872. The first American edition was issued by J. B. Lippincott, Philadelphia, 1872, listed in the *Nation* on July 18 and in *PW* on July 25.

1807   HENRY KINGSLEY   *Valentin.*
Revised and Corrected. 2/o boards, 2/6 cloth   June?

This is probably in the *Library of Select Authors* but was given the *Select Library of Fiction* No. 113, new numbering. It is (1885), with 310 pp. The first edition was issued by Tinsley Bros., London, 2 vols., 1872, 19.5 cm., at 21/o, with a 16-page catalog (Feb. 1872), listed in the *PC* as published Sept. 17–30. It appeared in *Routledge's Every Boy's Annual for 1873*, issued the latter part of 1872, a copy of which was in the Sadleir collection; he described it as having a dust jacket of dark yellow paper, printed in black. Routledge issued the revised and corrected edition (1874), 18 cm., 310 pp., illustrated, in cloth with a 32-page catalog.

1808   (MAURICE F. EGAN)   *That Girl of Mine.* o/6 sewed   1885 (*Eng Cat*)
Popular Sixpenny Books No. 113.
Also 1877

1809   CHARLES G. LELAND   *Hans Breitmann's Barty and Other Ballads.*
o/6 sewed   1885 (*Eng Cat*)
Popular Sixpenny Books No. 115.
Also 1877

1810 THOMAS HOOD, THE ELDER
Poems of Wit and Humour.
[Twenty-first edition]. o/6 sewed
1885 (*Eng Cat*)
Popular Sixpenny Books No. 116.
Also 1873

1811 THOMAS HOOD, THE ELDER
Whims in Prose and Verse. Illustrated.
o/6 sewed   1885 (*Eng Cat*)
Popular Sixpenny Books No. 117. Ward, Lock, Bowden & Co. issued Hood's *Whimsicalities in Prose and Verse*, no date, 464 pp., illustrated, in the early 1890s, containing, I think, the present title and the following one.
Also 1873

1812 THOMAS HOOD, THE ELDER
Oddities in Prose and Verse. Illustrated.
o/6 sewed   1885 (*Eng Cat*)
Popular Sixpenny Books No. 118.
Also 1873

1813 ARTEMUS WARD (CHARLES F. BROWNE) *Artemus Ward: His Book.*
o/6 sewed   1885 (*Eng Cat*)
Popular Sixpenny Books No. 119.
Also 1865, 67, 72

1814 CHARLES LEVER *Charles O'Malley.*
2/o boards, 2/6 cloth   June?
Select Library of Fiction No. 59, new numbering.
Also 1881, 83

1815 OSWALD J. F. CRAWFURD *Horses and Riders and Other Essays.* 2/o boards
July 4 (*Ath*)
Library of Favourite Authors. Select Library of Fiction No. 1120, new numbering. This is the first edition (1885), with 235 pp. There is a known copy, no date, 17.8 cm., a yellowback, with a catalog at the back dated 1876! I cannot explain this. The only entry in the *BM* and in the *U Cat* is (1885). The series of *Favourite Authors*

here given is not the original series of this name but a new series in which the present title is No. 29. The original series terminated in 1881.

1816 ELIZABETH C. GREY *The Opera-Singer's Wife.* 2/o boards, 2/o cloth
July 25 (*Ath*)
Select Library of Fiction No. 578, new numbering. This is (1885), with 352 pp.
Also 1870

1817 WATERS (WILLIAM RUSSELL)
Romance of the Seas. 2/o boards, 2/6 cloth
July?
Select Library of Fiction No. 748, new numbering. This is given by the *Eng* but not by the *BM* or the *U Cat's* in any edition whatsoever. The first edition was probably issued by C. H. Clarke, London, *Parlour Library* No. 266, Sadleir's copy, no date, a 2/o yellowback in small format, issued about Mar. 17, 1862. Sadleir could not trace it.

1818 ALEXANDER WHAMOND
James Tacket. [Fourth edition].
2/o boards, 2/6 cloth   July?
Select Library of Fiction No. 811, new numbering. This is (1885), with 235 pp. The *BM* gives a second edition as Edinburgh, 1877.

1819 HAMILTON AÏDÉ *Introduced to Society.* 2/o boards, 2/6 cloth   Aug. 8
(*Spect*)
Select Library of Fiction No. 920, new numbering. This is (1885), with 406 pp. The first edition was issued by Chapman & Hall, London, 2 vols., 1884, 18 cm., at 12/o, listed in the *Ath* on Mar. 8. They issued it at 5/o in 1 vol., Cr 8vo, listed in the *Spect* on June 7, 1884. The first American edition was issued by George Munro, New York (1885), as *Seaside Library Pocket Edition* No. 383, listed in *PW* on Mar. 7, 1885.

1820 HARRIETTE SMYTHIES
Guilty; or, Not Guilty. 1/o sewed
Aug.?
Shilling Novels No. 28.
Also 1866

1821 CHARLES BARNARD *A Dead Town.*
1/o sewed   Aug.?
Shilling Novels No. 29. This was also issued
as *Popular Sixpenny Books* No. 143, o/6
sewed, probably in Nov. 1885.
See 1883

1822 (JOHN T. TROWBRIDGE) *The Three
Scouts.* o/6 sewed   Aug.?
Popular Sixpenny Books No. 131. This is
(1885), 20 cm., 174 pp.
Also 1868

1823 WILLIAM H. THOMES *Life at
the Gold Mines of Ballarat.* o/6 sewed
1885 (*Eng Cat*)
Popular Sixpenny Books No. 120. This is
probably the first edition (1885), with 122
pp.

1824 CHARLES D. CLARK *Warncliffe,
the Wanderer.* o/6 sewed   Sept.?
Popular Sixpenny Books No. 121. This is a
reissue (1885), of the first edition issued
by J. S. Marr, Glasgow (1866), where it was
issued as *Fireside Series* No. 5. The Marr
edition was issued jointly with Simpkin,
Marshall, London, at o/6.

1825 WILLIAM H. THOMES
A Gold-Hunter's Adventures.
o/6 sewed   1885 (*Eng Cat*)
Popular Sixpenny Books No. 122. This is
(1885), with 125 pp. The first edition was
The Gold Hunters' Adventures, issued by Lee
& Shepard, Boston; etc., 1864, 20 cm.,
564 pp., illustrated.
Also 1890

1826 GEORGE L. AIKEN *The Household
Skeleton.* o/6 sewed   Sept.?
Popular Sixpenny Books No. 123. This is a
reissue (1885), 122 pp., of the first British

edition, issued jointly by J. S. Marr, Glasgow, and Simpkin, Marshall, London, at
o/6 in 1866, 122 pp. The *BM* gives the
American News Co., New York (1865), 80
pp., *Fireside Series* No. 8.

1827 BRET HARTE *Sandy Bar: With
Other Stories, Sketches, Legends and Tales.*
o/6 sewed   Sept.?
Popular Sixpenny Books No. 129.
Also 1873

1828 JOHN MILLS *Stable Secrets and
The Life of a Racehorse.* Illustrated.
2/o boards, 2/6 cloth   Oct. 17 (*Ath*)
Select Library of Fiction No. 584, new
numbering.
Also 1865, 73, 82 for the first title. Also
1854, 56, 65, 73, 82 for the second title

1829 HAWLEY SMART *A Race for a Wife.*
1/o sewed   1885 (*Eng Cat*)
Shilling Novels No. 27. This ran serially in
the *Temple Bar Magazine,* starting in the
Jan. 1870 issue. The first book edition was
issued by Bentley, London, 1870, 19 cm.,
308 pp., at 10/6, listed in the *Spect* on Apr.
2, 1870. Chapman & Hall, London, issued
it as a new edition, at 2/o boards, listed in
the *Ath* on Aug. 17, 1872. They reissued it
as *Select Library of Fiction* No. 263, at 1/o
sewed, in 1875; and reissued it as No. 367,
at 2/o boards, in 1877. The first American
edition was issued by D. Appleton & Co.,
New York, 1870, 23 cm., 100 pp., double
columns, $.50 paper, in their *Library of
Choice Novels.* It was advertised in the *New-
York Times* on Apr. 20 as "This day," and
listed in the *Nation* on Apr. 21.
Also 1902

1830 E. WERNER (ELIZABETH
BÜRSTENBINDER) *Riven Bonds.*
1/o sewed   Oct.?
Shilling Novels No. 30. This is (1885), 292
pp., in the same translation as the first English edition. The first English edition was

issued by Eden Remington, London, 2 vols., 1877, p 8vo, at 21/o , listed in the *Ath* on Dec. 15. It was translated by Bertha Ness from the German. There was a German edition, *Gesprengte Fesseln*, issued at Leipzig in 2 vols., 1875, 18 cm. The first edition in English was *Broken Chains* issued by James R. Osgood & Co., Boston, 1875, 23.5 cm., 133 pp., listed in the *Ind* on Dec. 17, 1874.

1831 E. WERNER (ELIZABETH BÜRSTENBINDER) *Sacred Vows.*
1/o sewed   Oct.?

Shilling Novels No. 31. This is (1885), 307 pp., translated by Bertha Hess from the German. The first English edition was issued by Remington, London, 3 vols., 1878, listed in the *Ath* on May 18. It was also issued as *At the Altar* by Sampson Low, London, 2 vols., 1878, at 21/o, translated by Mrs. Parker, listed in the *Contemporary Review* for Feb. 1879. There was a German edition, 2-vols.-in-1, at Leipzig, 1873, *Am Altar*. The first edition in English was issued by J. B. Lippincott, Philadelphia, 1872, 18.5 cm., 343 pp.

1832 T. S. ARTHUR *Ten Nights in a Bar-Room.* Memorial Edition.
o/6 sewed   1885 (*Eng Cat*)

Popular Sixpenny Books No. 135. This is (1885), 191 pp., revised by J. W. Kirton. The first edition was issued by J. W. Bradley, Philadelphia, 1854, 19 cm., 240 pp., frontispiece, listed in the *Ind* on Sept. 21, but noticed in *Godey's Lady's Book* for Aug. 1854. However, it was listed with varying imprints, all 1854, including Lippincott, Grambo, Philadelphia; J. W. Bradley; and also L. P. Crown & Co., Boston . . . ; J. W. Bradley. The first British edition was issued by the Scottish Temperance League, Glasgow, 1855, 156 pp., which was listed by *PC* at 1/6 cloth, as published by Houlston, London, Aug. 30–Sept. 14, 1855. James Blackwood, London, issued the 11th thousand at o/6, 1/o, in 1870, 180 pp.

1833 OSWALD J. F. CRAWFURD *A Woman's Reputation.* New Edition. 2/o boards, 2/6 cloth   Oct.?

Select Library of Fiction No. 953, new numbering. This is (1885), with 391 pp. The first edition was issued by Chapman & Hall, London, 2 vols., 1885, Cr 8vo, 12/o, listed in the *Ath* on June 13. A second edition was advertised in the *Times Weekly Edition* on July 24, 1885.
Also 1886

1834 FRANCES H. BURNETT *Theo.*
o/6 sewed   Oct.?

Popular Sixpenny Books No. 137. The first American edition was issued by T. B. Peterson & Bros., Philadelphia (copyright 1877), 17.5 cm., 232 pp., $.50 paper and $1.00 cloth, listed in *PW* on Sept. 22, 1877. The *Eng Cat* and the *BM* both give it as issued by Ward, Lock and by Frederick Warne, London (1877), with 177 pp. The Warne was Fcp 8vo, at 1/o sewed, and a Warne edition was "On our table" in the *Ath* for Dec. 8, 1877 (thus issued some months earlier). The first Canadian edition was issued by J. R. Robertson, Toronto, 1877, 21.5 cm., 41 pp., double columns. Charles Scribner's Sons, New York, issued an authorized edition, 16mo, 183 pp., $.30 paper, advertised in the *New-York Times* on May 17, 1879, as "This day."
Also 1889

1835 HENRY KINGSLEY *Hetty and Other Stories.* 12mo. 2/o boards, 2/6 cloth   Oct.?

Select Library of Fiction No. 102, new numbering. This may have been in the *Library of Select Authors*. It is (1885), with 344 pp. The first edition was issued by Harper & Bros., New York, 1869, *Library of Select Novels* No. 325, 23.5 cm., 69 pp., $.25 paper, in pinkish-buff wrappers. It was advertised in the *New-York Times* on July 30, as "This day," entitled *Hetty*, and listed in the *ALG&PC* (fortnightly) on Aug. 16.

The first English edition was issued by Bradbury, Evans & Co., London, 1871, either as *Hetty*, 18 cm., 381 pp., with a frontispiece, or as *Hetty and Other Stories*, 19 cm., 344 pp., frontispiece, containing four stories. Sadleir gives the nod to *Hetty*.

1836 HENRY KINGSLEY *Mademoiselle Mathilde.* 12mo. 2/o boards, 2/6 cloth Oct.?

Select Library of Fiction No. 101, new numbering. This is (1885), with 399 pp. It ran in the *Gentleman's Magazine* (Bradbury, Evans), beginning in the Apr. 1867 issue. The first book edition was issued by Bradbury, Evans & Co., London, 3 vols., 1868, 18.5 cm., reviewed in the *Contemporary Review* for Dec. 1868. They issued it in 1 vol., 1870, 12mo, 399 pp., 2/6 cloth, listed in the *Spect* on Nov. 5.

1837 HAWLEY SMART *From Post to Finish.* 12mo. 2/o boards, 2/6 cloth   Oct. 31 (*Spect*)

Library of Select Authors. Select Library of Fiction No. 180, new numbering. This is my copy, no date, 17.7 cm., 364 pp., blue pictorial boards, printed in red, blue, green, and black, with the front cover signed "Corbould," and with the No. 180. The series title is on the spine, and there are ads on the endpapers and back cover, with a catalog paged 1–14 at the back. The first edition was issued by Chapman & Hall, London, 3 vols., 1884, 20 cm., 31/6, advertised in the *Times Weekly Edition* (London) on Dec. 19, 1884, and in the *Spect* on Dec. 6 as "On Dec. 6." They issued it in 1 vol. in 1885, at 6/o, listed in the *Spect* on May 2. The first American edition was issued by Harper & Bros., New York (1884), *Franklin Square Library* No. 436, 29.5 cm., 82 pp., $.25 paper, advertised in the *New-York Times* on Dec. 27, 1884, as "This day," and listed in *PW* on Jan. 3, 1885. It was also issued by George Munro, New York (1885), as *Seaside Library* No. 1942, in quarto paper, listed in *PW* on

Mar 14. He also issued it as *Seaside Library Pocket Edition* No. 348, 18 cm., 224 pp., listed in *PW* on Mar. 21, 1885.
Also 1891, 99, 1904

1838 EDWARD P. ROE *An Original Belle.* 1/o sewed   Nov. 1 (*PC*)

Shilling Novels No. 32. This is probably the first edition or a reprint thereof (1885), with 384 pp. *BAL* says it was listed in *PC* on Nov. 1, but actually it was advertised in the *Spect* on Sept. 26, 1885, as the second edition, at 1/o, "Now ready," the first edition being exhausted on the day of publication, according to the ad. It was also issued as *Lily Series* No. 91, in 1885, at 1/o sewed, 1/6, 2/o cloth, and it was advertised in the *Ath* on Nov. 14, 1885, at 2/6. The first American edition was issued by Dodd, Mead & Co., New York (1885), 19.5 cm., 533 pp., blue cloth with yellow endpapers, with or without 8 pp. of ads. It was listed in the *Nation* and in the *Ind* on Oct. 1, and advertised in the *New-York Times* on Sept. 23, 25,000 copies, $1.50 cloth, "This day." It was advertised in *PW* on Sept 12 as "On Sept. 20."

1839 HANNAH LYNCH *Defeated.* Illustrated. 1/o sewed   Nov.

This is Beeton's Christmas Annual, 1885, with 188 pp.
Also 1886

1840 MARK TWAIN ET AL. *Mark Twain's Nightmare. With Tales, Sketches, and Poetry.* By Mark Twain, F. C. Burnand, H. S. Leigh, et al. Illustrated. o/6 sewed 1885 (*Eng Cat*)

Popular Sixpenny Books No. 132.
Also 1878. See 1880

1841 SAMUEL WARREN *Passages from the Diary of a Late Physician.* 2 vols. o/6 sewed each   1885?

Popular Sixpenny Books Nos. 133, 134.
Also 1884

1842, 1843, 1844 ALBERT SMITH
The Gent. The Flirt. Evening Parties.
3 vols. o/6 sewed, 1/o half red cloth each
1885?
Popular Sixpenny Books Nos. 139, 140, 141.
For the first title see also 1856, 72, 75. For
the second title see also 1856, 72, 75. For
the third title, the same

1845 ANONYMOUS *Uncle Oldenthorpe's
Legacy.* o/6 sewed   Nov.?
Popular Sixpenny Books No. 144.
See Beeton's Christmas Annual, 1884

1846 BRET HARTE & JOAQUIN MILLER
**Thompson's Prodigal and Other Stories.
By Bret Harte. With a Story of Wild
Western Life. By Joaquin Miller.**
o/6 sewed   Dec. 7 (*PC*)
Popular Sixpenny Books No. 136. This is
probably the first book edition (1885). It
was advertised in the *Ath* on Sept. 26.

1847 ANNIE WEBB, later WEBB-PEPLOE
Julamerk. 1/o sewed, 1/6, 2/o cloth
1885 (*Eng Cat*)
Lily Series No. 81. Ward, Lock issued this
in 1882, 12mo, anonymous, 489 pp., illustrated, 3/6, listed in the *Spect* on Feb. 11.
The first edition was in 3 vols., 1849,
12mo, 31/6, listed in the *Spect* on Feb. 10 as
issued by Simpkin, Marshall. It probably
had a second imprint also as it was reviewed in the *Spect* on Oct. 6, 1849, as issued by Yorke, Clarke & Co. A second edition was issued by Simpkin, Marshall,
London; J. M. Burton, Ipswitch, with a
frontispiece and an illustrated title page,
at 5/6, and is the edition, I think, listed in
the *Spect* on Nov. 29, 1851, which gave no
information. It was issued as *Run and Read
Library* No. 9, by Clarke, Beeton, London;
J. M. Burton, Ipswitch, 1854, 17.3 cm.,
with 489 pp., with frontispiece and illustrated title page, listed in the *Ath* on Dec.
2, 1854. The *Run and Read* edition was
also listed in the *Spect* on Feb. 17, 1855. All

in all this title has a messy publishing
history!

1848 ANNIE WEBB, later WEBB-PEPLOE
The Martyrs of Carthage. 1/o sewed, 1/6,
2/o cloth   1885 (*Eng Cat*)
Lily Series No. 82. The first edition was issued by Bentley, London, 2 vols., 1850, 18
cm., 12/o, listed in the *Spect* on Feb. 2. He
issued a new edition (1857), the third, Cr
8vo, illustrated, 5/o, listed in the *Spect* on
May 23; and reissued it in 1860, Fcp 8vo,
443 pp., at 2/6 canvas, about Sept. 29. He
issued a new edition, 1868, 16.5 cm., 443
pp., with a frontispiece.

1849 MARY SHERWOOD (M. M. BUTT)
The Nun. 1/o sewed, 1/6, 2/o cloth   1885
Lily Series No. 83.
Also 1864, 69, 76

1850 JOHANN C. VON SCHMID **The Basket
of Flowers.** 1/o sewed, 1/6, 2/o cloth
1885 (*Eng Cat*)
Lily Series No. 84.
Also 1872

1851 ANNIE-WEBB, later WEBB-PEPLOE
The Five-Pound Note: An Autobiography.
1/o sewed, 1/6, 2/o cloth   1885
Lily Series No. 85.
Also 1865, 75

1852 ANNIE WEBB, later WEBB-PEPLOE
The Pilgrims of New England. 1/o sewed,
1/6, 2/o cloth   1885
Lily Series No. 86.
Also 1875

1853 ANONYMOUS **Beeton's Art of Public
Speaking.** 1/o sewed, 1/6 cloth   1885
(*Eng Cat*)
The *BM* gives *Beeton's Complete Orator, In-
cluding the Art of Public Speaking and British
Orations and Orators*, Ward, Lock & Co.
(1886), with 306 pp.
See 1882

1854 BISHOP JOSEPH BUTLER
The Analogy of Religion. 1/o sewed,
1/6 cloth   1885 (*Eng Cat*)
This is edited by F. A. Malleson.
Also 1878

1855 ANONYMOUS *Dictionary of Every-Day Difficulties in Reading, Writing and Speaking.* 1/o boards   1885 (*Eng Cat*)
Shilling Useful Books. This is probably the first edition. It has no date and 364 pp.

1856 JOHN FOSTER *Decision of Character and Other Essays.* 1/o sewed, 1/6 cloth
1885 (*Eng Cat*)
Also 1876, 86

1857 GEORGE R. EMERSON *General Gordon.* Illustrated. 1/o sewed, 1/6 cloth
1885 (*Eng Cat*)
Youth's Library of Wonder and Adventure No. 42. This was listed in the *Spect* as issued by Ward, Lock at 2/6, Cr 8vo, in *England's Heroes, etc.*, on May 23, 1885. The *BM* gives the sixth edition (1885), 162 pp., and the *U Cat* gives the eighth edition, revised, 19 cm., 162 pp., portrait, folding map, illustrations (1885).
Also 1884

1858 JAMES GREENWOOD *Wild Sports of the World.* Illustrated. 1/o sewed, 1/6
1885 (*Eng Cat*)
Youth's Library of Wonder and Adventure No. 43. This has 426 pp. This was first issued by S. O. Beeton, London, in eight monthly parts, 23 cm., portraits, folding maps, colored plates, starting in May 1861, in the *Boy's Own Library.* A title page was included in part 8. Ward, Lock issued it in *Beeton's Boy's Own Library,* Demy 8vo, with colored plates, 5/o cloth, in 1870. Beeton, himself, offered the 50th thousand in 1864. Ward, Lock issued a new edition, 8vo, at 7/6, listed in the *Spect* on Oct. 16, 1880. The first American edition was issued by Harper & Bros., New York, 1870,

21.5 cm., 474 pp., illustrated, $2.50 cloth, advertised in the *New-York Times* on Nov. 27, 1869, as "This day," and noticed in the *Ind* on Dec. 16. The first English book edition was issued by S. O. Beeton, London, 1862, 426 pp., colored plates, portraits, folding maps. There is a known copy, London, 1864, the second impression, in the original red cloth.

1859 ANONYMOUS *Brave British Soldiers and the Victoria Cross.* Illustrated. 1/o sewed, 1/6 cloth   1885?
Youth's Library of Wonder and Adventure No. 44. I put this in here because of the No. in the series, but the *Eng Cat* gives it as issued in 1886. The first edition was issued by S. O. Beeton, London, in 1866, in his *Boy's Own Library.* Ward, Lock & Tyler took over his titles and the use of his name in 1866, and they issued it as *Beeton's Boy's Own Library,* Demy 8vo, illustrated, 5/o cloth. The *BM* gives *Our Soldiers and the Victorian Cross,* issued by Ward, Lock & Tyler (1867), with an added title page with the imprint of S. O. Beeton, 383 pp. The present edition is a reissue, no date, 383 pp., of the *Boy's Own Library,* edited by S. O. Beeton.

1860 JAMES GREENWOOD *Silas Horner's Adventures.* Illustrated. 1/o sewed, 1/6 cloth   1885 (*Eng Cat*)
Youth's Library of Wonder and Adventure No. 45. This has no date, 346 pp., with the running title *Silas the Conjuror.* The first edition was issued by S. O. Beeton, London (1866), *Silas the Conjuror,* 22 cm., 346 pp., illustrated, 5/o cloth, listed in the *Spect* on Apr. 21. Ward, Lock & Tyler reissued it with the Beeton title as *Beeton's Boy's Own Library,* 1874, Demy 8vo, 347 pp., illustrated, 5/o cloth, listed in the *Spect* on Nov. 21, 1874.

1861 JOSEPH M. GRANVILLE *Doubts, Difficulties, and Doctrines.* 1/o sewed 1885 (*Eng Cat*)
Shilling Useful Books. The first edition was issued by Ward, Lock, 1883, 247 pp., at 2/6.

1862 CHRISTOPH VON HUFELAND *The Art of Prolonging Life.* 1/o sewed, 1/6 cloth 1885 (*Eng Cat*)
Also 1876

1863, 1864, 1865 ELIZABETH PRENTISS *Only a Dandelion and Other Stories. "Follow Me," and Other Stories. Nidworth, and His Three Magic Wands.* 3 vols. 1/o sewed, 1/6, 2/o cloth each 1885 (*Eng Cat*)
Lily Series Nos. 87, 88, 89.
Also 1875 for all three titles and also 1888 for the first title

1866 (JANE E. HORNBLOWER) *Nellie of Truro.* 1/o sewed, 1/6, 2/o cloth 1885 (*Eng Cat*)
Lily Series No. 90.
Also 1864, 76

1867 ANONYMOUS *Professions and Occupations.* 1/o 1885 (*Eng Cat*)
Shilling Useful Books. I cannot trace this.

1868 SYLVIA *Sylvia's Book of Macramé Lace.* Illustrated. 1/o boards 1885 (*Eng Cat*)
Shilling Useful Books. This is (1885) and has pp. 289–384 of *The Lady's Book of Ornamental Needlework.* Ward, Lock also issued a new and enlarged edition with no date, with pp. 289–416 of the above book, illustrated.
Also 1882, 83

1869 ANONYMOUS *Sylvia's Book of Home Needlework.* p. 8vo. Illustrated. 1/o boards 1885
This is my copy, no date, 18.5 cm., 76 pp., green decorated boards, with ads on the endpapers, back cover (one with a date 1885), and at the back consisting of 4 pp. plus pp. 5–20.
Also 1880

1870 GEORGE J. WHYTE MELVILLE *Riding Recollections.* 12mo. 2/o boards 1885?
Library of Select Authors. Select Library of Fiction No. 410, later changed to No. 131. It is my copy (1885), 17.8 cm., 251 pp., yellow pictorial boards, printed in red, green, and black, with the series title at the foot of the spine, the words "The Works of Whyte Melville" at the head, and with the No. 410 on the front cover. There are ads on the endpapers and back cover and a catalog paged 81–96 at the back. The first edition was issued by Chapman & Hall, London, 1878, 21 cm., 251 pp., illustrated, at 12/o, listed in the *Ath* on Mar. 23. They reissued it many times, the ninth edition, my copy, being 1880, 251 pp., 2/o boards, 2/6 cloth, with the series No. 410, probably issued in May. I also have a copy of the eighth edition, 1880, 18.1 cm., 251 pp., not in the *Select Library of Fiction*, with a printer's date (Jan. 13, 1880), listed in the *Ath* on Feb. 21. The second through the fifth editions were issued at 12/o, from Apr. 1878 to June 1879. Another edition was issued in 1879, Cr 8vo, 6/o, listed in the *Spect* on Aug. 9. In New York, Scribner & Welford issued the fourth edition, Cr 8vo, illustrated, at $3.00 cloth, advertised in the *New-York Times* on Aug. 12, 1878, and listed in *PW* on Aug. 17.
Also 1901

1871 CATHERINE SINCLAIR *Holiday House.* 12mo. 2/o boards 1885?
Select Library of Fiction No. 852, new numbering. This is my copy, no date, 17.5 cm., 346 pp., plus a 1-page postscript, bound in blue pictorial boards, printed with three smaller illustrations on the front in red, blue, and black. It has the series title on the spine, ads on the endpapers and

back cover, and a 24-page catalog at the back.
Also 1865, 72

1872 MARY W. PORTER Poor Papa.
Illustrated. o/6 sewed   1885?
Popular Sixpenny Books No. 114. The first English edition was Hodder & Stoughton, London, 1879, anonymous, 218 pp.; reissued, 1885, 218 pp., illustrated, at 1/o. The first American edition was issued by D. Lothrop & Co., Boston (copyright 1879), 17.5 cm., 218 pp., illustrated.

**1873 OLIVER OPTIC (WILLIAM T. ADAMS)
Adventures of a Midshipman.** o/6 sewed 1885?
Popular Sixpenny Books No. 124. This has no date and 128 pp.; I think the first edition was issued by J. S. Marr & Sons, Glasgow, 1866, 128 pp.

**1874 OLIVER OPTIC (WILLIAM T. ADAMS)
The Brave Old Salt.** o/6 sewed   1885?
Popular Sixpenny Books No. 125. This has no date and 115 pp. The first edition was issued by Lee & Shepard, Boston, 1865, 18 cm., 330 pp., *Army and Navy Series* No. 6; and reissued, 1866, the same, but with a plate. Simpkin, Marshall, London, issued it in 1867, 12mo, at o/6.

1875 HENRY HAZELTON The Light Dragoon. o/6 sewed   1885?
Popular Sixpenny Books No. 126. This was issued by Simpkin, Marshall, London, in 1867, 12mo, at o/6.

1876 HENRY HAZELTON The Gambler's Last Pledge. o/6 sewed   1885?
Popular Sixpenny Books No. 127. This is (1885), with 128 pp. It was issued by Simpkin, Marshall, London, in 1867, 12mo, at o/6.

1877 ANONYMOUS The Bad Boy's Start in Life. o/6 sewed   1885?
Popular Sixpenny Books No. 128. I cannot trace this.

1878 JOHN T. TROWBRIDGE Cudjo's Cave.
o/6 sewed   1885?
Popular Sixpenny Books No. 130.
Also 1868

**1879 ALEXANDRE DUMAS, THE YOUNGER
The Count of Monte Cristo.** 2 vols. o/6 sewed each   1885?
Popular Sixpenny Books Nos. 142, 142a. This is an unabridged edition.
Also 1858, 88

1880 DANIEL DEFOE Robinson Crusoe.
Demy 8vo. Illustrated. 1/o sewed, 1/6 cloth   1885?
Youth's Library of Wonder and Adventure No. 46.
Also 1863, 64, 68, 79

1881 ANONYMOUS The Noble Wife.
Illustrated. 1/o sewed, 1/6 cloth   1885 ?
Youth's Library of Wonder and Adventure No. 47. I cannot trace this.

1882 ANONYMOUS The Triumph of Truth.
1/o sewed, 1/6 cloth   1885?
Youth's Library of Wonder and Adventure No. 48. I cannot trace this.

1883 ANONYMOUS The Faithful Servant.
1/o sewed, 1/6 cloth   1885?
Youth's Library of Wonder and Adventure No. 49. I cannot trace this. These titles sound as if they belong in a Sunday School library, issued by a religious publishing company. I wonder how much wonder or adventure they contain!

1884 FRANZ HOFFMANN The Widow's Son. Illustrated. 1/o sewed, 1/6 cloth 1885?
Youth's Library of Wonder and Adventure No. 50. The *BM* gives this as issued by Ward, Lock (1881), 246 pp., illustrated, in the *Sunday School Library*. It is translated from the German.

1885 FRANZ HOFFMANN *The Greek Slave.* Illustrated. 1/o sewed, 1/6 cloth 1885?

Youth's Library of Wonder and Adventure No. 51. The first edition was issued by the Lutheran Board of Publication, Philadelphia, 1870, 17 cm., 239 pp., illustrated, translated from the German by J.C. Brodführer. The *BM* gives an issue by Ward, Lock (1881), illustrated, in the *Sunday School Library*.

1886 ANONYMOUS *The Hero Martyr.* Illustrated. 1/o sewed, 1/6 cloth 1885?

Youth's Library of Wonder and Adventure No. 52. I cannot trace this.

1887 ANONYMOUS *The Pilgrim King.* Illustrated. 1/o sewed, 1/6 cloth 1885?

Youth's Library of Wonder and Adventure No. 53. I cannot trace this.

1888 MARGARET OLIPHANT *At His Gates.* New Edition. 12mo. 2/o boards 1885 (*BM*)

Select Library of Fiction No. 159, new numbering. This has no date, 446 pp., greenish-white pictorial boards, Sadleir's copy. The first edition was issued by Tinsley Bros., London, 3 vols., 1872, 18 cm., 31/6, listed in the *Spect* on Oct. 12. Sadleir's presentation copy is inscribed with the date Oct. 1872. They issued it at 2/o boards, 2/6 cloth, listed in the *Ath* on July 19, 1873. The first American edition was issued by Scribner, Armstrong & Co., New York, 1873, 8vo, 231 pp., illustrated, $1.00 paper, $1.50 cloth, advertised in the *New-York Times* on Dec. 7, 1872, as *Library of Choice Novels* No. 1, "This day."

1889 MARGARET OLIPHANT *Lucy Crofton.* 12mo. New Edition. 2/o boards 1885?

Select Library of Fiction No. 377, later changed to No. 158. This has no date, 19 cm., 307 pp. Sadleir's copy was in pale lilac pictorial boards, and he thought it was issued after 1889. The *U Cat* gives (1885?).

The first edition was issued by Hurst & Blackett, London, 1860 (1859), 18 cm., anonymous, 317 pp., at 10/6, listed in the *Ath* on Dec. 24, 1859. Chapman & Hall, London, issued it as No. 377 in the series, 1878, a new edition, my copy, 18.1 cm., 307 pp., 2/o boards, listed in the *Ath* on July 27. The first American edition was issued by Harper & Bros., New York, 1860, 17 cm., anonymous, 222 pp., at $.75, listed in the *Ind* on Feb. 16 and in *APC&LG* on Feb. 18.

1890 MARGARET OLIPHANT *Madonna Mary.* New Edition. 2/o boards 1885?

Select Library of Fiction No. 296, later changed to No. 151. It has no date and 415 pp. Sadleir's copy was in pale green pictorial boards, and he thought it was issued after 1882. I don't know when it was issued. It ran serially in *Good Words* (Strahan) from Jan.–Dec. 1866. The first book edition was issued by Hurst & Blackett, London, 3 vols., 1867 (1866), 18.5 cm., 31/6, listed in the *Ath* on Nov. 3, 1866. Chapman & Hall, issued it as No. 296 in the series, at 2/o boards, listed in the *Ath* on Sept. 11, 1875; and issued a new edition, 1880, with 415 pp. In the United States it ran serially in *Littell's Living Age* and was issued by Littell, Son & Co., Boston, 22.5 cm., 225 pp., which the *U Cat* gives as (1867). The first American edition, I think, was issued by Harper & Bros., New York, 1866, *Library of Select Novels* No. 282, 23 cm., 182 pp., double columns, $.50 paper, advertised in the *New-York Times* on Dec. 5, 1866, as "This day," and advertised in *Harper's Weekly* on Dec. 15 as "Just published."

1891 MARGARET OLIPHANT *The Days of My Life.* New Edition. 2/o boards 1885?

Select Library of Fiction No. 316, later changed to No. 152. This had no date and 364 pp. Sadleir's copy was in greenish-white pictorial boards, and he thought it was issued after 1889, but it doesn't fit there. I don't know when it was issued as the numbering in the series is of no help as the Ward, Lock new numbers were assigned strictly by authors, with no relation to order of issue. The first edition was issued by Hurst & Blackett, London, 3 vols., 1857, 19 cm., anonymous, 31/6, listed in the *Ath* on Feb. 14. Chapman & Hall issued it as No. 316 in the series, a new edition, 17.5 cm., 364 pp., listed in the *Ath* on Apr. 1, 1876. The first American edition was issued by Harper & Bros., New York, 1857, 19.5 cm., anonymous, 428 pp., $.75 muslin, advertised in the *New-York Times* on Apr. 9 as "This day."

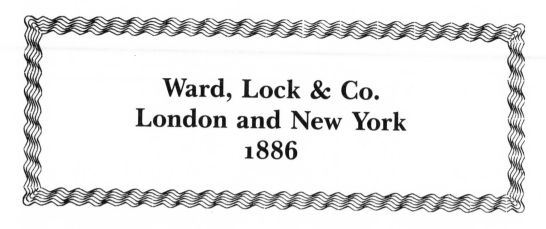

Ward, Lock & Co.
London and New York
1886

1892 MAX ADELER (CHARLES H. CLARK)
ET AL. *A Desperate Adventure and Other Stories.* Illustrated. 2/0 boards, 2/6 cloth
Feb.?

Select Library of Fiction No. 326, new numbering. This is (1886), with 255 pp. It contains a combination of stories from *Transformations* (see 1883) and *The Drolleries of a Happy Island* (see 1883). *Mrs. Shelmire's Djinn* and the title story from the former are by Adeler.

1893 WILLIAM M. THACKERAY
The Fitz-Boodle Papers, etc. 0/6 sewed
Feb.?

Popular Sixpenny Books No. 148. This is (1886), paged 129–244. The title piece ran in *Fraser's Magazine,* Jan. 1842–Apr. 1843. The first book edition of the title piece, and the only complete edition, was published by D. Appleton & Co., 1852, 276 pp., *The Confessions of Fitz-Boodle; and Some Passages in the Life of Major Gahagan.* The first English edition of the title piece was issued by Bradbury & Evans, London, 1857, 219 pp., in yellow wrappers, *The Fitz-Boodle Papers; and Men's Wives.* They issued the title piece in vol. 4 of *Miscellanies,* 1857; both of these English issues omitted some material. Both of the stories in the former appeared in *Fraser's Magazine,* *Men's Wives* running Mar.–Nov. 1843.

1894 FREDERICK C. L. WRAXALL
The Backwoodsman. 2/0 boards,
2/6 cloth Feb.?

Select Library of Fiction No. 794, new numbering.
Also 1884

1895 RALPH W. EMERSON *Representative Men and English Traits.* 8vo. 0/3 sewed, 0/6 cloth Mar. 15 (*Ath*)

Popular Library of Literary Treasures No. 1. This new series was edited by George T. Bettany. The first three titles were in double columns, but this was then abandoned. This has no date, with 128 pp. The first edition of the first title was probably issued by John Chapman, London, 1850, 20 cm., 215 pp., at 5/0, in his *Catholic Series,* advertised in both the *Ath* and *Spect* as "On Jan. 1, 1850," and listed in both on Jan. 5. There are publisher's ads (Sept. 1849). It was issued with the sanction of the author and, in fact, from a manuscript sent by Emerson. Henry G. Bohn, London, issued it, 1850, in their *Shilling Series,* 18 cm., 143 pp., containing an ad signed by Bohn and dated Feb. 1, 1850, stating that he had made arrangements with the American publisher for early sheets and that he had received them but found that he had been forestalled. In a letter from Emerson to Chapman, Emerson stated that the American publisher's promise to Bohn was wholly unauthorized by him. It was also issued by George Routledge, London, 1850, 17.5 cm., 182 pp., at 1/o boards, 1/6 cloth, with "Popular Library" on the cover, advertised in the *Spect* on Feb. 2, 1850, as "Just ready." He issued the 12th thousand, 1855. The first American edition was issued by Phillips, Sampson & Co., Boston; etc., 1850, 19 cm., 285 pp., deposited Dec. 28, 1849. There are presentation copies known, dated Dec. 1849. The first edition of the second title was issued by Phillips, Sampson & Co., Boston, 1856, 18.5 cm., 312 pp., at $1.00, listed in *APC&LG* (weekly) on Aug. 2, and in the *Ind* on Sept. 4. I cannot explain an ad in the *New York Daily Times* on Nov. 15, 1855, saying "On Dec. 10"! The first English edition was issued by George Routledge, London, 1856, small format, 176 pp., 1/o, green boards printed with the title in blue on the front, with 4 pp. of ads (Sept. 1856), "Printed by arrangement with the author." It has a yellow slip inserted advertising Lytton's works. It was also in blue cloth. It was listed in the *Ath* on Sept. 6. He reissued it with 176 pp., new editions, 1857 and 1882. It was also issued by Sampson Low, London, Cr 8vo, 312 pp., at 6/o, listed by *PC* as published Oct. 30–Nov. 14, 1856. It was also issued by Knight & Son, London, 12mo, 176 pp., at 1/o boards, listed by *PC* as for the Low edition.

1896 THOMAS B. MACAULAY *Lord Clive, Warren Hastings, History of the Popes, and Lord Holland.* 8vo. o/3 sewed, o/6 cloth Mar. 22 (*Ath*)

Popular Library of Literary Treasures No. 2. This is 1886, with 123 pp. This series was started in imitation of Cassell & Co.'s *Cassell's National Library* issued at o/3 sewed, o/6 cloth, 18mo, No. 1 of which, *Warren Hastings*, was issued in Dec. 1885. The first separate book editions of the first three essays were in 1/o sewed volumes, issued by Longmans in 1851, listed in the *Ath* on May 3, May 10, and Sept. 27, respectively.

They were all from *Critical and Historical Essays*, which itself was a collection of essays from the *Edinburgh Review*. The second essay was in that periodical for Oct. 1841. *Critical and Miscellaneous Essays* was issued in 2 vols. by Weeks, Jordan & Co., Boston, 1840, the first printing in book form of some of the essays. Carey & Hart, Philadelphia, pirated these 2 vols. and added a third vol. and issued 3 vols., 1841; they issued vol. 4, 1843; and vol. 5, 1844, these containing mostly essays in first book form. *Critical and Historical Essays* was issued by Longmans, London, 3 vols., 1843, the first English edition in book form of some of the essays, 8vo, 36/o, listed in the *Spect* on Mar. 28.
See 1874

1897 ANONYMOUS *The Irish Problem and England's Difficulty.* 1/o sewed   Mar. 27 (*Ath* ad)

Shilling Useful Books. This is the first edition (1886), with 274 pp.
Also 1887

1898 PLUTARCH *The Lives of Alexander the Great, Julius Ceasar and Pompey.* 8vo. o/2 sewed, o/6 cloth   Mar. 29 (*Ath*)

Popular Library of Literary Treasures No. 3. This is 1886, 123 pp., translated by J. & W. Langhorne.

1899 MARY E. KENNARD *The Right Sort.* Illustrated. 2/o boards, 2/6 cloth   Apr. 3 (*Ath*)

Select Library of Fiction No. 818, new numbering. This is (1886), 18 cm., 446 pp., frontispiece and plates by Edgar Giberne, with 26 pp. of ads and an inserted ad slip, in pale pink pictorial boards. There are ads on the endpapers and back cover. The first edition was issued by Remington & Co., London, 3 vols., 1883, Cr 8vo, 31/6, listed in the *Ath* on Oct. 27. Chapman & Hall, London, issued a new edition in

1884, Cr 8vo, illustrated, 6/o, listed in the *Spect* on May 3.
Also 1900, 02

1900 JOHN LOCKE ***Some Thoughts Concerning Education.*** 8vo. o/3 sewed, o/6 cloth   Apr. 5 (*Ath*)

Popular Library of Literary Treasures No. 4. This is 1886, 160 pp., with an introduction by J. S. Blackie. The first edition was issued by A. & J. Churchill, London, 1693, 18 cm., anonymous, 262 pp. Gray & Bower, Boston, issued it, 1830, 18.5 cm., 371 pp., including *A Treatise on Education* by Milton. Ward, Lock issued *Locke's Essays* in the *World Library*, 700 pp., at 3/6 cloth. They abstracted the present title for *Books for All Time*, 19 cm., paged 404–556, at 1/o cloth, issued in the early 1890s.

1901 THOMAS DEQUINCEY ***Confessions of an Opium Eater and Letters to a Young Man.*** 8vo. o/3 sewed, o/6 cloth   Apr. 12 (*Ath*)

Popular Library of Literary Treasures No. 5. This is 1886, with 127 pp. It is a reissue of parts of the collection in *Books for All Time* (1874), and has a preface by G. T. Bettany. See 1874

1902 HENRY W. LONGFELLOW ***Voices of the Night, Tales of a Wayside Inn, and Miscellaneous Poems.*** 8vo. o/3 sewed, o/6 cloth   Apr. 19 (*Ath*)

Popular Library of Literary Treasures No. 6. This is (1886), with 120 pp. The first edition of the first title was issued by John Owen, Cambridge, 1839, 18.5 cm., 144 pp., about Dec. 15, 1839. He issued the second edition, 1840, 12mo, 184 pp., which had a short review in the *New York Review* for July 1840. I am puzzled by the English editions. The *BM* and the *U Cat* give no English editions for 1840 or 1841, but an edition is listed in the *Ath* in 1840 and in the *Spect* for Feb. 22, 1840, no publisher given in either case. *Voices of the*

Night and Other Poems was issued by H. G. Clarke & Co., London, 1843, unauthorized, in paper wrappers, listed in *PC* on Dec. 1, 1843, and in the *Spect* on Dec. 9. *Voices of the Night* was also issued by Edward Moxon, London, 1843, listed in *PC* on Jan. 1, 1844. I suspect his edition was imported. He issued an edition at 4/o boards, listed in the *Spect* on Nov. 18, 1843. An imported edition was listed in the *Spect* on June 4, 1842, sixth edition, with no publisher given. *BAL* is not of much help here. The first edition of the second title was issued by George Routledge, London, 1864, 244 pp., in cloth with a frontispiece, listed in the *Ath* on Nov. 7, 1863. He also issued it, 1864, 17 cm., 140 pp., at 1/o sewed, listed in the *Reader* on Nov. 28, 1863. The first American edition was issued by Ticknor & Fields, Boston, 1863, 16mo, 225 pp., at $1.25, probably issued on Nov. 25, 1863, listed in *APC&LG* (fortnightly) on Dec. 15. The 20th thousand was advertised in the *New-York Times* on Feb. 27, 1864, 16mo, $1.25, as "Lately issued." Eight of the poems appeared in the *Atlantic Monthly* from 1859–63.

1903 HAWLEY SMART ***Tie and Trick.*** p 8vo. 2/o boards, 2/6 cloth May 15 (*Ath*)

Library of Select Authors. Select Library of Fiction No. 181, new numbering. This is my copy, no date, 18.3 cm., 402 pp., yellow pictorial boards, printed in red, green, and black, with the series title on the spine. There are ads on the endpapers, back cover, and on 6 pp. at the back. The first English edition was issued by Chapman & Hall, London, 3 vols., 1885, Cr 8vo, 31/6, listed in the *Spect* on Feb. 28, and advertised in the *Times Weekly Edition* on Mar. 6 as "This day." They issued it in 1 vol., 1885, 402 pp. The first American edition was issued by Harper & Bros., New York, 1885, *Franklin Square Library* No. 442, 29.5 cm., 66 pp., $.20 paper, listed in *PW* on Jan. 31, in the *Nation* on Jan. 22, and advertised in the *New-York Times* on Jan. 17 as "This day." It was also issued by George Munro, New York (1885), in the *Seaside Library Pocket Edition* No. 367, listed in *PW* on Mar. 14, 1885. Also 1902

1904 MARK TWAIN (SAMUEL L. CLEMENS) *The New Pilgrim's Progress.* o/6 sewed 1886 (*Eng Cat*)
Popular Sixpenny Books No. 149.
Also 1873, 74, 75

1905 JULES VERNE *Twenty Thousand Leagues Under the Sea.* 2 vols. o/6 sewed each   1886?
Popular Sixpenny Books Nos. 150, 151.
Also 1876

1906 ANONYMOUS *Original Readings and Recitations. Prince . . . and Other Poems.* o/6 sewed   1886?
Popular Sixpenny Books No. 152. I think this has no date and 145 pp.
Also 1883

1907 SAMUEL WARREN *Ten Thousand a Year.* 2 vols. o/6 sewed each   1886?
Popular Sixpenny Books Nos. 154, 155.
Also 1884

1908 MARK TWAIN (SAMUEL L. CLEMENS) *The Mississippi Pilot.* o/6 sewed   1886?
Popular Sixpenny Books No. 156.
Also 1877

1909 JULES VERNE *On the Track.* o/6 sewed   1886?
Popular Sixpenny Books No. 157.
Also 1876

1910 JULES VERNE *The Ice Desert.* o/6 sewed   1886?
Popular Sixpenny Books No. 158.
Also 1875. See 1876

1911 MARK TWAIN ET AL. *Practical Jokes with Artemus Ward, Including the Story of the Man Who Fought Cats.* o/6 sewed June 1 (*PC*)
Popular Sixpenny Books No. 159. This has no date and 176 pp. It is a reprint of Twain items except for eight sketches, and it has five sketches of doubtful origin, credited to Twain, 37 pieces total. The first edition was issued by John C. Hotten, London (1872), 17.5 cm., 176 pp., at 1/o sewed, 2/6 cloth, listed in *PC* on Sept. 2. The wrappers edition was in pictorial yellow wrappers printed in blue. I think this is the same as *Beeton's Humorous Books* No. 34, issued by Ward, Lock & Tyler in 1875.

1912 CATHERINE L. PIRKIS *Wanted, an Heir.* 2/o boards, 2/6 cloth   June 12 (*Ath*)
Select Library of Fiction No. 825, new numbering. This is (1886), with 401 pp. The first edition was issued by Hurst & Blackett, London, 3 vols., 1881, 20 cm., 31/6, listed in the *Ath* on July 30.

1913 (ROBERT H. NEWELL) *The Orpheus C. Kerr Papers.* o/6 sewed   1886?
Popular Sixpenny Books No. 160.
Also 1865, 73

1914 GEORGE A. BRINE *The King of the Beggars.* o/6 sewed   June?
Popular Sixpenny Books No. 161.
Also 1883

1915 ANTONIO GELLENGA *Jenny Jennett.* 12mo. 2/o boards, 2/6 cloth   July 10 (*Ath*)
Select Library of Fiction No. 826, new numbering. This is my copy, no date, 18 cm., 296 pp., yellow pictorial boards, printed in red, blue, and black, with the series title on the spine. There are no endpapers, and ads on the front and back pastedowns and on the back cover. The first edition was issued by Chapman & Hall,

London, 2 vols., 1886, Cr 8vo, 21/0, listed in the *Ath* on Jan. 23.

1916 VICTOR HUGO *Under Sentence of Death . . . Together with Told Under Canvas (Bug-Jargal) and Claude Gueux.*
2/0 boards, 2/6 cloth   July 10 (*Ath*)

Select Library of Fiction No. 200, new numbering. This has 331 pp. and was translated by Sir George Campbell. The first edition of the first title was issued in Paris, 1829, *Le Dernier Jour d'un Condamné*, 19 cm., anonymous, 259 pp., in tan wrappers. The first English edition of the first title was issued by Smith, Elder & Co., London, as *The Last Days of a Condemned*, 1840, 19 cm., 192 pp., at 7/6, with a 40-page preface by the translator, Sir P. H. Fleetwood, and a 40-page postscript by Hugo, strongly attacking capital punishment. This postscript occupies pp. (155)–192. It was listed in the *Spect* on May 23. The first edition of the second title was issued in Paris, 1826, 16 cm., anonymous, 386 pp., with a frontispiece, in tan wrappers. The first English edition was *The Slave King*, issued by Smith, Elder & Co., London, 1833, 319 pp., at 6/0, *Library of Romance* No. 6, listed in the *Ath* on June 1. The first American edition was issued by Carey, Lea & Blanchard, Philadelphia, 1833, 18 cm., 259 pp., *Library of Romance* No. 6. The cost book of Carey & Lea states that they printed 1,250 copies, finished on July 30, 1833. The *BM* gives *Capital Punishment . . . Claude Gueux*, issued by R. Hardwick, London, 1865, 32 pp., and the *U Cat* gives *Capital Punishment, Claude Gueux, The Last Days of a Condemned*, issued by Carleton, New York, 1869, 16mo, 275 pp. Ward, Lock issued the present title in the *Royal Library*, 2/0 cloth (1886).

1917 MARK HOPE (EUSTACE MURRAY) *An Amateur Lunatic.* 1/0 sewed   July?

Shilling Novels No. 33. The first edition was issued by Chapman & Hall, London, as *Dark and Light Stories*, 1879, at 6/0, about

Oct. 25. They issued it, 1880, as *Select Library of Fiction* No. 409, 322 pp., 2/0 boards, listed in the *Ath* on Apr. 17.

1918 OLIVER W. HOLMES *Elsie Venner.* 1/0 sewed   July?

Shilling Novels No. 34. This ran in the *Atlantic Monthly* as *The Professor's Story*, from Jan. 1860 to Apr. 1861. The first book edition was issued by Ticknor & Fields, Boston, 2 vols., 1861, 18 cm., at $1.75, in brown cloth. There were four printings. It was advertised in the *New-York Times* on Feb. 16 as "This day," and the fifth thousand was advertised there on Mar. 25 as "This day"; Fields, Osgood & Co., Boston, advertised it there on May 5, 1869, a cheap and popular edition, 16mo, $2.00. It was advertised in the *Ind* on Feb. 21 as "This day," and listed in *APC&LG* (weekly) on Feb. 23. The first English edition was issued by Macmillan & Co., London, 1861, the author's English edition, Fcp 8vo, at 6/0, listed in the *Ath* on Mar. 2 and advertised there on Feb. 23 as "Next week." George Routledge, London, issued it, 428 pp., at 2/0 boards, 2/6 cloth, listed in the *Ath* on Mar. 16, 1861. The 2/6 issue was in orange cloth, 17 cm. It was also issued by C. H. Clarke, London (1861), as *Parlour Library* No. 247, 376 pp., 2/0 boards, listed in the *Ath* on Sept. 28.

1919 CHARLES E. CRADDOCK (MARY N. MURFREE) *Down the Ravine.* 1/0 sewed   Aug.?

Shilling Novels No. 36. This is (1886). The first edition was issued by Houghton, Mifflin & Co., Boston and New York, 1885, 18.5 cm., 196 pp., illustrated, $1.00 cloth, listed in the *Ind* on June 4, and in *Lit World* on May 30.

1920 THOMAS MILLER *Royston Gower.* 2/0 boards, 2/6 cloth   Aug.?

Select Library of Fiction No. 754, new numbering.
Also 1874

1921 WATERS (WILLIAM RUSSELL)
The Privateer Captain. 2/0 boards,
2/6 cloth   Aug.?
Select Library of Fiction No. 748A, new
numbering.
Also 1874

1922 BYRON WEBBER **Pigskin and
Willow, with Other Sporting Stories.**
2/0 boards, 2/6 cloth   Aug. 28 (*Ath*)
Select Library of Fiction No. 834, new numbering. This is (1886), with 363 pp. The
first edition was issued by Tinsley Bros.,
London, 3 vols., 1879, 20 cm., 31/6, advertised in the *Ath* on Feb. 1 as "Next
week" and on Feb. 22 as "Ready." Hogg,
London, issued it in 1883, Cr 8vo, at 3/6,
listed in the *Spect* on Mar. 12. Two of the
stories first appeared in *Bailey's Magazine*.

1923 SAMUEL LAING, THE YOUNGER
A Sporting Quixote. 2/0 boards,
2/6 cloth   Sept. 4 (*Ath*)
Select Library of Fiction No. 828, new numbering. This is (1886), with 435 pp. The
first edition was issued by Chapman &
Hall, London, 2 vols., 1886, 20 cm., 21/0,
listed in the *Ath* on Mar. 20.

1924 EDWARD P. ROE **He Fell in Love with
His Wife.** 1/0 sewed, 1/6, 2/0 cloth, 2/0
boards, 2/6, 3/6 cloth   Sept. 18 (*Ath*)
Lily Series No. 97. *Select Library of Fiction*
No. 381, new numbering. *Shilling Novels*
No. 43. This is (1886), with 333 pp. The
1/0, 1/6 cloth issue was advertised in the
Ath on Sept. 18 as "Now ready," and the
2/6 issue was listed on Oct. 9. *BAL* states
that there was a listing in *PC* on both Oct.
1 and Oct. 15 and in the *Bks* for Nov. but
gives no details. The first American edition was issued by Dodd, Mead & Co.,
New York (1886), 19.5 cm., 333 pp.,
$1.50, blue cloth with yellow endpapers,
in an edition of 25,000. It was advertised
in the *New-York Times* on Sept. 15 as "This
day"; advertised in *PW* on Sept. 4 as "On

Sept. 15" and listed on Oct. 9; and advertised in the *Ind* on Sept. 23 as "Just published" and listed on Oct. 6. *BAL* gives an
inscribed copy (Sept. 20).

1925 OLIVER W. HOLMES
Wit and Humour: Poems. 0/6 sewed
1886 (*Eng Cat*)
Popular Sixpenny Books No. 162.
Also 1875. See Mark Twain and Holmes,
1875

1926 EDMOND F. V. ABOUT **The Soldier
Lover.** 0/6 sewed   Sept.?
Popular Sixpenny Books No. 163. This is
(1886), with 190 pp., translated from the
French by Elton Locke. The first edition
was *Trente et Quarante Sans Dot. Les Parents
de Bernard*, Paris, 1859, 18 cm., 343 pp.
The present edition is probably the first
edition in English.

1927 JOHN PHOENIX (GEORGE H. DERBY)
Squibbs and Drolleries. 0/6 sewed   1886
(*Eng Cat*)
Popular Sixpenny Books No. 164. I think the
first edition was *Phoenixiana*, issued by D.
Appleton & Co., New York, 1856, 19.5
cm., 274 pp., illustrated. They issued the
11th edition, 1856, also. The editor's preface is signed J. J. A. (John J. Ames). S. O.
Beeton, London, issued it with the same
title (1865), 17 cm., 255 pp., the preface
signed as above. Carleton, New York, issued *The Squibb Papers*, 1865, 19 cm., 247
pp., illustrated.

1928 LEIGH HUNT (JAMES H. L. HUNT)
One Hundred Romances of Real Life.
0/6 sewed   Sept.?
Popular Sixpenny Books No. 165. This is
(1886). The first edition was issued by
Whittaker & Co., London, 1843, 24.5 cm.,
with 132 pp. uncut, 3/6 cloth, annotated
and selected by Hunt. It originally appeared in the *London Journal*. Whittaker
issued the second edition in 1846, all the

same except for the date. It was issued by Hamilton, Adams & Co., London; etc., a new edition, 1888, 21 cm., 320 pp., 3/6, in green cloth.

1929 ANONYMOUS *Ward and Lock's Illustrated History of England. Part 1.*
o/6 sewed   Oct. 8

This is an entirely new work, issued in 14 monthly o/6 parts. Part 1 was advertised in the *Times Weekly Edition* on Oct. 8, 1886, as "Ready."

1930 CHARLES DICKENS *The Mudfog Society, and Other Sketches and Stories.*
2/o boards, 2/6 cloth   Oct. 9 (*Ath*)

Select Library of Fiction No. 228, new numbering. This is (1886), 382 pp., and contains (in addition to the *Mudfog Papers*) *A Christmas Carol*, *Sketches of Young Couples*, and *Sunday Under Three Heads*. Dickens wrote three Mudfog papers for *Bentley's Miscellany*, and they appeared in Jan. and Oct. 1837, and in Sept. 1838. The first one was *The Public Life of Mr. Tulrumble, Once Mayor of Mudfog*, which was issued by Carey, Lea & Blanchard, Philadelphia, 1837. The full title also included "With Other Tales and Sketches from *Bentley's Miscellany*, and the *Library of Fiction*." It was 18.5 cm., 208 pp. Bentley, London, issued it, 1880, 18 cm., 198 pp., 2/6, in red cloth, with 6 pp. of ads, *The Mudfog Papers, etc.*, containing pieces collected from *Bentley's Miscellany*, called "now first collected," and listed in the *Spect* on Aug. 21. He issued the second edition, Cr 8vo, 2/6 cloth, listed in the *Spect* on Oct. 9, 1880. In the United States it was issued by Henry Holt & Co., New York, 1880, 16mo, 249 pp., an authorized edition, as *Leisure Hour Series* No. 114. It was advertised in the *New-York Times* on Sept. 1 as "Just published." It was also issued by Harper & Bros., New York, 1880, by courtesy of Henry Holt, 29 cm., 16 pp., triple columns, paper with a caption title, advertised in the *New-York Times* on Sept. 2. It was also issued by George

Munro, New York, *Seaside Library* No. 827, 4to paper, $.10, advertised in the *New-York Times* on Sept. 4, 1880, as "Out today." *The Mudfog Society, etc.* was also issued by Ward, Lock as *Popular Sixpenny Books* No. 33, illustrated, o/6 sewed, in Nov. 1886, I think.

1931 FRANCIS M. CRAWFORD *An American Politician.* 12mo.
2/o boards, 2/6 cloth   Oct. 9 (*Ath*)

Select Library of Fiction No. 965, new numbering. This is (1886), with 364 pp. It was reissued in the *Warwick House Library* at 3/6 cloth in the 1890s. The first American edition was issued by Houghton, Mifflin & Co., Boston, 1885 (1884), 18.5 cm., 356 pp., at $1.25 cloth, listed in *PW* on Nov. 15, and in the *Nation* on Nov. 20. The first English edition was issued by Chapman & Hall, London, 2 vols., 1884, 18 cm., 12/o, advertised in the *Times Weekly Edition* on Nov. 14, 1884, as "This day," and listed in the *Spect* on Nov. 15.

1932 FRANCIS M. CRAWFORD *To Leeward.*
2/o boards, 2/6 cloth   Oct. 23 (*Ath* ad)

Select Library of Fiction No. 966, new numbering. This is my copy, no date, 18 cm., 307 pp., white pictorial boards, printed in red, green, blue, and black, with the series title on the spine, and a cover by Corbould. It has ads on the endpapers, back cover, and 6 pp. at the back. The first American edition was issued by Houghton, Mifflin & Co., Boston, 1884, 18.5 cm., 411 pp., at $1.25, advertised in the *New-York Times* on Dec. 9, 1883, as "This week" and as if ready on Dec. 15; listed in the *Nation* and the *Ind* on Dec. 20 and in *PW* on Dec. 22. The first English edition was issued by Chapman & Hall, London, 2 vols., 1884, 18 cm., 12/o, advertised in the *Times Weekly Edition* on Dec. 7, 1883, and listed in the *Spect* on Nov. 24. They issued the second edition in 2 vols., advertised in the *Times Weekly Edition* on Dec. 21, 1883, as "This day"; and a new edition at 5/o was listed in the *Spect* on Feb. 2, 1884. It was issued by Macmillan & Co., New York, 404 pp., at $1.00, listed in the *Review of Reviews* (New York) for May 1893.

1933 JOHN MILLS **The Wheels of Life.** 1/o sewed   Oct.?

Shilling Novels No. 37.

Also 1854 and see *The Briefless Barrister*, 1857

1934 EDWARD P. ROE **Opening a Chestnut Burr.** 1/o sewed, 1/6, 2/o   1886 (*Eng Cat*)

Lily Series No. 93. I think this was issued about the same time as *Shilling Novels* No. 39.

Also 1878

1935 EDWARD P. ROE **A Day of Fate.** 1/o sewed, 1/6, 2/o cloth   1886 (*Eng Cat*)

Lily Series No. 95. *Shilling Novels* No. 41, about the same time, I think.

Also 1882

1936 EDWARD P. ROE **A Face Illumined.** 1/o sewed, 1/6, 2/o cloth   1886 (*Eng Cat*)

Lily Series No. 96. *Shilling Novels* No. 42, probably about the same time.

Also 1879

1937 EDWARD P. ROE **Driven Back to Eden.** 1/o sewed, 1/6, 2/o, 2/6, 3/6 Nov. 13 (*Spect*)

Lily Series No. 98. *Shilling Novels* No. 44. This ran serially in the *St. Nicholas Magazine*, Feb.–June 1885. The present edition is the first English edition (1886), 276 pp., with a preface dated 1885. The 2/o was listed in the *Spect* on Nov. 13. The first edition was issued by Dodd, Mead & Co., New York, 1885, 19 cm., 291 pp., illustrated, $1.50 cloth, with 8 pp. of ads, in green-blue or blue cloth with yellow endpapers. It was listed in the *Ind* and in the *Nation* on Oct. 1, and advertised in *PW* on Sept. 12 as "On Sept. 20." A second edition was advertised in *PW* on Oct. 10 as "On Oct. 10."

1938 JEANNIE G. BETTANY, later KERNAHAN **Two Legacies.** 1/o sewed Nov. 27 (*Ath* ad)

Shilling Novels No. 59. This is the first edition (1886), with 162 pp.

1939 BENJAMIN L. FARJEON **The Nine of Hearts.** 1/o sewed   Nov. 27 (*Ath* ad)

Shilling Novels No. 66. This is the first edition (1886), with 220 pp. Ward, Lock issued it in New York (1886), at $.30 paper, listed in *PW* on Dec. 11, 1886. It was also issued in the United States by Harper & Bros., New York, 1886, *Handy Series* No. 107, 19 cm., 216 pp., at $.25, with a cover title. It was listed in the *Nation* and the *Ind* on Dec. 23, 1886, and in *PW* on Jan. 15, 1887. There were at least two other piracies in New York later in 1887.

Also 1891

1940 VICTOR HUGO **"Ninety-Three."** 2/o boards, 2/6 cloth   Nov. 27 (*Ath* ad)

Select Library of Fiction No. 202, new numbering. This is (1886), 327 pp., translated by Sir G. Campbell. The first edition was *Quatrevingt Treize*, Paris; etc., 3 vols., 1874, 23 cm., reviewed in the *Ath* on Feb. 28, 1874. The first book edition in English was issued by Harper & Bros., New York, 1874, *Library of Select Novels* No. 414, 23.5 cm., 143 pp., frontispiece (portrait), $1.75 cloth, translated by F. R. Benedict and J. H. Friswell. There is an additional frontispiece, and the list of the series in the ads ends with No. 413. It was advertised in the *New-York Times* on Mar. 25 as "This day" and listed in *PW* on Mar. 28. It was advertised there also on Apr. 24, 8vo, $.75 paper, as "This day." This issue was 1874, 19.5 cm., 356 pp. It was issued in French in the United States by the Librairie du Courier des Etats Unis, New York, 1874, reviewed in *Scribner's Monthly* for June 1874. It was also issued by the *Evening Telegraph*, Philadelphia, 1874, 23.5 cm., 163 pp., translated by E. B. d'E. Picot. The

first English edition was issued by Sampson Low, London, 3 vols., 1874, 20 cm.,
31/6, translated by Benedict and Friswell,
advertised in the *Ath* on July 4 as "On July
14." Low had advertised on Jan. 3, 1874,
that the publication was delayed for a few
months so that it could be issued serially in
The Graphic. It was also issued by Low, Cr
8vo, illustrated, at 6/o, listed in the *Ath* and
the *Spect* on Feb. 27, 1875. George Routledge, London, issued it (1885), 383 pp.,
2/o boards, listed in the *Ath* on Aug. 22,
with the Low translation.
Also 1887

1941 ANONYMOUS *Sylvia's Art of Church
Embroidery.* Illustrated. 1/o boards
Nov. 27 (*Ath* ad)
Sylvia's Needlework Books No. 5. I cannot
trace this.

1942 ANNIE ASHMORE (MRS. J. M.
SIMPSON) *Worth His Weight in Gold.*
1/o sewed   Nov.
This is Beeton's Christmas Annual for
1886, the first edition of this story.
Also 1887

1943 SIR GILBERT CAMPBELL ET AL.
On a Winter's Night, etc. o/6 sewed
Nov.
This was a Sixpenny Christmas Annual,
no date, with 102 pp. There were three
other pieces in addition to the title story,
one of which was a play by Campbell.
Also 1887

1944 EDWARD P. ROE *Barriers Burned
Away.* 1/o sewed   Nov.?
Shilling Novels No. 38. It was also issued as
Lily Series No. 92 about this time. It had
been issued in the *Lily Series* as a double
vol. in 1878. Ward, Lock issued it in 1877,
Cr 8vo, 3/6 cloth, listed in the *Spect* on
Sept. 29. This appeared in *The Evangelist*.
The first edition was issued by Dodd,
Mead & Co., New York, 1872, 18.5 cm.,

488 pp., illustrated, in orange or green
cloth with yellow endpapers. It was listed
in the *PW* on Nov. 28, the *Ind* on Dec. 5,
and the *Nation* on Jan. 16, 1873. They issued it in 1882, 4to, 76 pp., $.20 paper,
advertised in the *New-York Times* on May
19 as "This day," having sold 100,000 copies. The first English edition was issued by
George Routledge, London (1874), 3/6
cloth, listed in the *Ath* on Oct. 17 and in
PC on Nov. 1. He advertised it in the *Ath*
on Feb. 3, 1877, Fcp 8vo, at 1/o sewed, 1/6,
2/o cloth.

1945 VICTOR HUGO *The Workers of the
Sea.* 2/o boards, 2/6 cloth   Dec. 4 (*Ath*)
Select Library of Fiction No. 201, new numbering. This is (1886), 343 pp., translated
by Sir Gilbert Campbell. The first French
edition was *Les Travailleurs de la Mer*, Paris,
3 vols., 1866, published at the same time
as the first English edition of Sampson
Low. It was also issued at Bruxelles, 3
vols., 1866, 23 cm., which was reviewed in
the *Ath* on Mar. 24 and in the *Spect* on Mar.
31. The first Low edition was in 3 vols.,
1866, 20 cm., 24/o, the authorized English
translation by W. Moy Thomas. It had ads
at the back of vol. 3 (Mar. 30, 1866) and a
16-page catalog (Feb. 1, 1866). It was advertised in the *Ath* on Mar. 24 as "Ready"
and listed March. 31. Low issued it in 3
vols., the second edition, at 24/o, advertised in the *Spect* on May 12, 1866, as "Now
ready." He issued it, 1867, 2 illustrations
by Dore, 6/o, listed in *Notes & Queries* on
Jan. 12; and issued it, 1869, Sq Demy 8vo,
illustrated, 10/6, listed in the *Spect* on Oct.
9. He issued it at 2/o boards, listed in the
Spect on Aug. 13, 1870. The Low titles
were always *Toilers of the Sea*. In the United
States it ran in the *Semi-Weekly Tribune*,
New York, beginning on May 5, 1866, and
running for about 8 weeks. The original
edition in French was issued for America
by F. W. Christern, New York, 8vo, at
$2.00, listed in the *Nation* on Mar. 29,
1866. The review in the *Nation* on Mar. 29

gave the imprint as Bruxelles; Christern. The first American edition in English was issued by Harper & Bros., New York, 1866, 24 cm., 155 pp., frontispiece (portrait), $.75 paper, advertised in the *New-York Times* on Apr. 10, 1866, as "This day," and listed in *ALG&PC* (fortnightly) on Apr. 16. George Routledge, London, issued it, 1886, my copy, 18.5 cm., 370 pp., translated by Thomas, the authorized English edition.
Also 1887

1946 (CHARLES E. CRADDOCK (MARY N. MURFREE) *In the Clouds.* 12 mo. 2/o boards, 2/6 cloth   Dec. 4 (*Ath*)
Select Library of Fiction No. 971, new numbering. This is the first English edition, listed also in the *Spect* on Dec. 4. It ran in the *Atlantic Monthly*, Jan.–Dec. 1886. The book edition was issued by Houghton, Mifflin, Boston and New York, 1887 (1886), 18.5 cm., 452 pp., $1.25, advertised in the *New York-Times* on Nov. 28, 1886, and listed in the *Nation* and the *Ind* on Dec. 2, and in *PW* on Dec. 11.

1947 EDWARD P. ROE *What Can She Do?* 1/o sewed, 1/6, 2/o cloth   Dec.?
Lily Series No. 94. *Shilling Novels* No. 40.
Also 1876

1948 ANONYMOUS *Sinbad the Sailor, Aladdin, and Other Stories from the Arabian Nights' Entertainments.*
o/3 sewed, o/6 cloth   1886 (*Eng Cat*)
Popular Library of Literary Treasures No. 7.
This is (1886), with 159 pp.
See 1863, 82, 89

1949 FRANCIS BACON *Essays, Civil and Moral.* o/3 sewed, o/6 cloth 1886 (*Eng Cat*)
Popular Library of Literary Treasures No. 8.
See 1874, 77

1950 OLIVER GOLDSMITH *The Vicar of Wakefield.* o/3 sewed, o/6 cloth   1886 (*Eng Cat*)
Popular Library of Literary Treasures No. 9.
Also 1855, 64

1951 ANONYMOUS *Captain Cook's First Voyage Round the World.* o/3 sewed, o/6 cloth   1886 (*Eng Cat*)
Popular Library of Literary Treasures No. 10. This is an abridgment (1886). The *BM* gives this as in 2 parts, but I have found no evidence for this. The first edition was *An Account of the Voyages Undertaken by the Order of His Present Majesty* ... by John Hawkesworth, issued by A. Leathley, etc., Dublin, 3 vols., 1773, 21 cm. It was also issued by W. Strahan & T. Cadell, London, 3 vols., 1773, 20.5 cm., with plates and maps.
Also 1891

1952 JOHN FOSTER *Decision of Character.* o/3 sewed, o/6 cloth 1886 (*Eng Cat*)
Popular Library of Literary Treasures No. 11.
Also 1876, 85

1953 JOHN MILTON *Miscellaneous Poems, Sonnets, etc.* o/3 sewed, o/6 cloth   1886 (*Eng Cat*)
Popular Library of Literary Treasures No. 12. This is edited by Bettany. I cannot trace this.

1954 PLUTARCH *Famous Greeks.* o/3 sewed, o/6 cloth   1886 (*Eng Cat*)
Popular Library of Literary Treasures No. 13. This is 1886, 126 pp., translated by J. & W. Langhorne. It contains Aristides, Themistocles, Pericles, et al.

1955 WILLIAM COBBETT *Advice to Young Men.* o/3 sewed, o/6 cloth 1886 (*Eng Cat*)
Popular Library of Literary Treasures No. 14. This is 1886, 127 pp., with notes and a life

of the author. It contains sections 1–181 only of the complete edition.

See 1875

1956 RICHARD H. BARHAM *The Witches' Frolic, the Black Mousquetaire, and Other Ingoldsby Legends.* o/3 sewed, o/6 cloth 1886 (*Eng Cat*)

Popular Library of Literary Treasures No. 15. This is 1886, with 114 pp. The first edition of the *Ingoldsby Legends* by Thomas Ingoldsby was in three series, issued by Bentley, London, 1840, 1842, 1847, respectively, 8vo, 10/6 each. Bentley reissued them many times and in many forms, including an issue in 1857, Cr 8vo, at 5/0; a 4to issue in 1881; a selection at o/6 sewed, with 64 pp., illustrated by Cruikshank, Leech, Tenniel; and an illustrated edition, Demy 8vo, at 1/0, issued about Jan. 16, 1886. Carey & Hart, Philadelphia, issued selections from series 1 and 2, 1844, 19.5 cm., 192 pp., illustrated, listed in the *Knickerbocker* for Nov. 1844. The third series was issued in Philadelphia, 1847; and D. Appleton & Co., New York, issued the first series, 1852, 320 pp.

1957 SAMUEL T. COLERIDGE *The Ancient Mariner, Christabel, and Miscellaneous Poems.* o/3 sewed, o/6 cloth 1886 (*Eng Cat*)

Popular Library of Literary Treasures No. 16. This is (1886), with 124 pp. The first appearance in book form of the first title was in *Lyrical Ballads with a Few Other Pieces*, by William Wordsworth, printed for T. N. Longman & O. Rees, London, 1798. A first printing of 500 copies had a first imprint as above, but the major portion were sold to J. & A. Arch, London, who put its imprint on them, 1798, 12mo, anonymous, 68, 69–210 pp. The first appearance in book form of the second title was in *Christabel; Kubla Khan; The Pains of Sleep*, issued by John Murray, London, 1816, 22 cm., 64 pp., at 4/6, listed by the *Edinburgh Review* as published Mar.–June 1816. It

was issued by Wells & Lilly, Boston, 1816, 16 cm., 63 pp.

1958 ANONYMOUS *The Little Hunchback, The Barber, The Sleeper Awakened, and The Forty Thieves.* o/3 sewed, o/6 cloth 1886 (*Eng Cat*)

Popular Library of Literary Treasures No. 17. These are from the *Arabian Nights' Entertainments* (1886), with 144 pp.

See 1863, 82, 89

1959 THOMAS B. MACAULAY *Lays of Ancient Rome and Other Poems.* o/3 sewed, o/6 cloth 1886 (*Eng Cat*)

Popular Library of Literary Treasures No. 18. This is (1886), with 100 pp. The first edition was issued by Longmans, 1842, 20.5 cm., 191 pp., listed as "In press," July–Sept. 1842, in the *Edinburgh Review*. A second edition, Sq Cr 8vo, 192 pp., 10/6 cloth, was listed there as published Oct.–Dec. 1842. It was issued by Carey & Hart, Philadelphia, 1843, 19 cm., 122 pp., both of these editions entitled *Lays of Ancient Rome*.

1960 RALPH W. EMERSON *Essays: Love, Friendship and Character.* o/3 sewed, o/6 cloth 1886 (*Eng Cat*)

Popular Library of Literary Treasures No. 19. I cannot trace this. The first series of Essays (Love, Friendship, etc.), 12 in number, was issued by James Monroe & Co., Boston, 1841, 12mo, 303 pp., listed in the *New York Review* (monthly) for Apr. 1841. In England it was issued by James Fraser, London, 1841, Fcp 8vo, 10/0, with a preface by Thomas Carlyle, listed in the *Spect* on Aug. 21. James Monroe & Co. also issued the second series, probably in 1844. It was issued in England by John Chapman, London, 1845, p 8vo, 3/0 sewed, 3/6 cloth, listed in the *Spect* on Nov. 16, 1844.

1961 THOMAS À KEMPIS (THOMAS HÄMMERLEIN) *The Imitation of Christ.* o/3 sewed, o/6 cloth 1886 (*Eng Cat*)

Popular Library of Literary Treasures No. 20. This has 149 pp. *De Imitatione Christi* was first issued at Augsburg (1473). The first English translation, by William Atkinson and Margaret, Duchess of Beaufort, was issued in 1503.

1962 RICHARD H. BARHAM
The Smuggler's Leap, Bloudie Jacke of Shrewsberrie . . . and Other Ingoldsby Legends. o/3 sewed, o/6 cloth   1886 (*Eng Cat*)

Popular Library of Literary Treasures No. 21. This is (1886), with 118 pp. *The Smuggler's Leap* was in the Sept. 1841 issue of *Bentley's Miscellany*.
See No. 15 above

1963 JOHANN W. VON GOETHE
Faust. Part 1. o/3 sewed, o/6 cloth 1886 (*Eng Cat*)

Popular Library of Literary Treasures No. 22. This has 152 pp., translated in the original meters by Bayard Taylor. Part 1 was issued in Germany in 1808, and there was an English translation, 8vo, at 12/0 boards, listed in the *Edinburgh Review* as published Jan.–July 1833. Part 2 was issued in Germany in 1832, and both parts were issued at Heidelberg, 1832, 18 cm., 223 pp. A combined text was issued at Suttgart & Tübingen, 1834. An English translation by J. L. Bernays, with other poems, of part 2, 8vo, 10/6, was listed by the *Edinburgh Review* as published Oct. 1839–Jan. 1840; and a different translation at 9/0 was listed the same. Both parts were issued by A. Taylor, London, 2 vols., 1838, 19.5 cm. The first English edition of the Taylor translation was issued by A. Strahan, London, 2 vols., 1871, 19 cm., at 28/0; and it was issued in the United States by Fields, Osgood & Co., Boston, 2 vols., 1871, 25.5 cm.

1964 RALPH W. EMERSON ***The Conduct of Life, Social Aims, and Other Essays.***
o/3 sewed, o/6 cloth   Dec.?

Popular Library of Literary Treasures No. 23. This has 123 pp. The first edition of the

first title, containing nine essays, was issued by Ticknor & Fields, Boston, 1860, 18 cm., 288 pp., issued at $1.00 in brown muslin, advertised in the *Ind* on Dec. 6, 1860, as "This day," and listed in *APC&LG* (weekly) on Dec. 15. The first English edition of the first title was issued by Smith, Elder & Co., London, 1860, author's edition, 21. cm., 287 pp., simultaneously at 6/0 and 1/0 cloth, claimed to be the only editions published in conjunction with the author. They were listed in the *Ath* on Dec. 8, 1860, and both advertised in *Notes & Queries* on Jan. 26, 1861. I think the 1/0 cloth issue was 17.5 cm., with 203 pp. George Routledge, London, issued it, 189 pp., at 1/0 boards, about Jan. 5, 1861.

1965 ANONYMOUS ***Beeton's Cottage Cookery Book.*** o/3 sewed, o/6 cloth 1886 (*Eng Cat*)
Also 1880, 90

1966 ANONYMOUS ***Fifty Famous Women.*** Portraits. 1/0 sewed, 1/6 cloth   1886 (*Eng Cat*)

Youth's Library of Wonder and Adventure No. 65. The first edition was probably from Ward & Lock (1864), Fcp 8vo, 312 pp., illustrated, 3/6 cloth, listed in the *Reader* on Oct. 29. They issued it in the *Family Gift Series*, probably in 1879, with the portraits, at 2/6 cloth; and, I think, they issued it in the 1890s with 312 pp. and the portraits.

1967 JULIA KAVANAGH ***Madeleine.*** 1/0 sewed   1886 (*Eng Cat*)

Shilling Novels No. 58. The *Eng Cat* entry is 2/0 boards, which must be an error.
Also 1884

1968 ADELINE D. T. WHITNEY
Odd or Even? 1/0 sewed, 1/6, 2/0 cloth 1886 (*Eng Cat*)

Lily Series No. 80.
Also 1882

1969 ANONYMOUS *Mrs. Beeton's Sixpenny Cookery Book.* o/6 sewed 1886 (*Eng Cat*)
Shilling Useful Books. This is probably the first edition. Ward, Lock issued it, 1910, 152 pp., illustrated; and also 1923, with 256 pp.
Also 1890

1970 HAWLEY SMART *Broken Bonds.*
New Edition. 12mo. 2/o boards 1886?
Library of Select Authors. Select Library of Fiction No. 321, later changed to No. 165. This is my copy, no date, 17.6 cm., 379 pp., white pictorial boards, printed in red, blue, and black, with the series title on the spine. There are ads on the endpapers, back cover, and 16 pp. at the back. The first edition was issued by Hurst & Blackett, London, 3 vols., 1874, 19 cm., 31/6, listed in the *Spect* on Jan. 24. Chapman & Hall, London, issued it in the series as No. 321, 379 pp., at 2/o boards, listed in the *Ath* on Apr. 15, 1876; and reissued it, my copy, 1877, third edition, 17.7 cm., 379 pp., at 2/o boards
Also 1900, 02

1971 HAWLEY SMART *Play or Pay.* 12mo. 2/o boards 1886?
Library of Select Authors. Select Library of Fiction No. 375, later changed to No. 172. This is my copy, no date, 17.7 cm., 242 pp., yellow pictorial boards, printed in red, green, and black, with the series title on the spine and the No. 375 on the front. It has ads on the endpapers, back cover, and 8 pp. at the back. The front cover is by Corbould. The first edition was issued by Chapman & Hall, London, 1878, p 8vo, 10/6, listed in the *Ath* on Dec. 22, 1877. They issued it as No. 375 in the series, my copy, 1878, 18 cm., 242 pp., at 2/o boards, listed in the *Ath* on Apr. 13. They reissued it in 1880, a new edition, at 2/o boards.
Also 1889, 1903

1972 HENRY KINGSLEY *Silcote of Silcotes.*
New Edition. 12mo. 2/o boards 1886?
Library of Select Authors. Select Library of Fiction No. 198, later changed to No. 106. This is my copy, no date, 17.8 cm., 439 pp., yellow pictorial boards printed in red, blue, and black, with the series title on the spine and the No. 198 on the front. It has ads on the endpapers, back cover, and 14 pp. at the back. Ward, Lock & Bowden, Ltd., issued it, 1895, a new edition, 20 cm., 365 pp., with a frontispiece, 3/6 cloth. This ran serially in *Macmillan's Magazine*, July 1866–Sept. 1867. The first English edition was issued by Macmillan & Co., London, 3 vols., 1867, 18.5 cm., at 31/6, listed in the *Ath* on Oct. 19. They issued the second edition, 1869, 439 pp., at 6/o cloth, listed in the *Spect* on Dec. 25, 1869. Chapman & Hall, London, issued it, 1872, the third edition, as No. 198 in the series, 19 cm., 439 pp., 2/o boards, listed in the *Ath* on Apr. 27. They issued the fifth edition, 12mo, at 3/o cloth in the series, listed by *PC* as published Nov. 1–15, 1872. The first American edition was issued by Ticknor & Fields, Boston, 1867, author's edition, 23.5 cm., 138 pp., double columns, $.75 paper, advertised in the *New-York Times* on Sept. 25 as "This day," and listed in *ALG&PC* (fortnightly) on Oct. 1.

1973 EDWARD P. ROE *From Jest to Earnest.* 1/o sewed 1886?
Shilling Novels No. 53.
Also 1876, 83, 92

1974 EDWARD P. ROE *Near to Nature's Heart.* 1/o sewed 1886?
Shilling Novels No. 54.
Also 1878, 82

1975 EDWARD P. ROE *Without a Home.* 1/o sewed 1886?
Shilling Novels No. 55.
Also 1882

1976 EDWARD P. ROE *A Knight of the Nineteenth Century.* 1/o sewed   1886?
Shilling Novels No. 56.
Also 1878, 82

1977 EDWARD P. ROE *His Sombre Rivals.*
1/o sewed   1886?
Shilling Novels No. 57.
Also 1884

1978 ANONYMOUS *The Child's Life of Jesus Christ.* 1/o sewed, 1/6 cloth   1886?
Youth's Library of Wonder and Adventure No. 54. This is illustrated. Cassell, London, issued a book with this title (1882), 4to, illustrated, 21/o; and *The Child's Life of Jesus* was issued by Sheldon & Co., New York, 1867, 22 cm., with colored illustrations. Whether either one is appropriate, I don't know.

1979 ANONYMOUS *The Good Sailor Boy.*
1/o sewed, 1/6 cloth   1886?
Youth's Library of Wonder and Adventure No. 55. I cannot trace this.

1980 FRANZ HOFFMANN *The Christian Prince.* Illustrated. 1/o sewed, 1/6 cloth   1886?
Youth's Library of Wonder and Adventure No. 56. The *BM* gives Ward, Lock (1882), 316 pp., illustrated, in the *Sunday School Library.* The first American edition was *Prince Wolfgang,* 1871, 316 pp., illustrated, issued by the Lutheran Board of Publication, Philadelphia. It was translated by J. F. Smith.

1981 ANONYMOUS *The Faithful Missionary.* Illustrated. 1/o sewed, 1/6 cloth   1886?
Youth's Library of Wonder and Adventure No. 57. I cannot trace this.

1982 ANONYMOUS *The Boy Pilot.*
Illustrated. 1/o sewed, 1/6 cloth   1886?
Youth's Library of Wonder and Adventure No. 58. I cannot trace this.

1983 FRANZ HOFFMANN *Fidelity Rewarded.* Illustrated. 1/o sewed, 1/6 cloth   1886?
Youth's Library of Wonder and Adventure No. 59. The first edition was *Geier Wälty,* issued by the Lutheran Board of Publication, Philadelphia, 1870, 17 cm., 196 pp., illustrated, at $1.00, translated by M. A. Manderson. Ward, Lock issued it with the same title (1882), 172 pp., illustrated, in the same translation.

1984 FRANZ HOFFMANN *Virtue Triumphant.* Illustrated. 1/o sewed, 1/6 cloth   1886?
Youth's Library of Wonder and Adventure No. 60. The first American edition was *Anton the Fisherman,* issued by the Lutheran Board of Publication, Philadelphia, 1870, 17.5 cm., 172 pp., illustrated. Ward, Lock issued it (1882), 172 pp., illustrated, in the same translation as for the American edition, by M. A. Manderson. It was in the *Sunday School Library.*

1985 ANONYMOUS *Famous Friendships of Men and Women Eminent in Politics, Literature, etc.* Illustrated. 1/o sewed, 1/6 cloth   1886?
Youth's Library of Wonder and Adventure No. 61. This was issued by Ward, Lock (1883), with 176 pp.

1986 ANONYMOUS *Romantic Tales of Royal Palaces.* Illustrated. 1/o sewed, 1/6 cloth   1886?
Youth's Library of Wonder and Adventure No. 62. This was issued by Ward, Lock (1883), with 161 pp.

1987 ANONYMOUS *Notable Women of Our Own Times.* Portraits. 1/o sewed, 1/6 cloth 1886?
Youth's Library of Wonder and Adventure No. 63. This was issued by Ward, Lock (1883), with 164 pp.

1988 GEORGE R. EMERSON *William Ewart Gladstone.* 1/0 sewed, 1/6 cloth 1886?
Youth's Library of Wonder and Adventure No. 64.
Also 1881, 82

1989 HANNAH LYNCH *Defeated.* 0/6 sewed 1886?
Popular Sixpenny Books No. 166.
Also 1885

1990 OSWALD J. F. CRAWFURD *A Woman's Reputation.* 1/0 sewed 1886?
Shilling Novels No. 60.
Also 1885

1991 FRANCES HOEY (MRS. CASHEL HOEY) *The Blossoming of an Aloe.* 1/0 sewed 1886?
Shilling Novels No. 61.
Also 1876, 80

1992 WILLIAM ADAMSON *The Abbot of Aberbrothock.* 1/0 sewed 1886?
Shilling Novels No. 62.
Also 1885

1993 GEORGIANA CRAIK, later MAY *Lost and Won.* 1/0 sewed 1886?
Shilling Novels No. 63. The first edition was issued by Smith, Elder & Co., London, 1859, 20.5 cm., 296 pp., 10/6, listed in the *Ath* on Jan. 29. They issued a second edition, 1859, with 305 pp.; and issued it, 1862, a new edition, 252 pp., at 1/0 sewed, listed in the *Ath* on May 24.

1994 C.J. HAMILTON *Marriage Bonds.* 1/0 sewed 1886?
Shilling Novels No. 64.
Also 1879

1995 FRANCES E. TROLLOPE *Veronica.* 1/0 sewed 1886?
Shilling Novels No. 65. The first edition was issued by Tinsley Bros., London, 3 vols., 1870, Cr 8vo, anonymous, 31/6, reprinted from *All the Year Round*, and listed in the *Ath* on Apr. 2. Chapman & Hall, London, issued it as *Select Library of Fiction* No. 179 (1871), a new edition, 2/0 boards, listed in the *Spect* on Mar. 18; and reissued it as No. 337 in the series (third edition), 2/0 boards, listed in the *Ath* on Nov. 11, 1876. The first American edition was issued by Harper & Bros., New York, 1870, 24 cm., anonymous, 175 pp., $.50 paper, advertised in the *New-York Times* on Sept. 1 as "This day," and listed in the *Nation* on Sept. 8.

Ward, Lock & Co.
London and New York
1887

I think Ward, Lock opened a Melbourne office in 1884 or 1885, but Melbourne was not used in the imprint until 1887 or later.

1996 VICTOR HUGO **The Workers of the Sea.** o/6 sewed   Apr.?
Popular Sixpenny Books No. 168.
Also 1886

1997 JULES VERNE **Round the Moon.** o/6 sewed   1887?
Popular Sixpenny Books No. 169.
Also 1877

1998 JULES VERNE **A Journey into the Interior of the Earth.** o/6 sewed   1887?
Popular Sixpenny Books No. 170.
Also 1875, 77

1999 JULES VERNE **Five Weeks in a Balloon.** o/6 sewed   1887?
Popular Sixpenny Books No. 171.
Also 1875, 77

2000 LAWRENCE L. LYNCH (EMMA MURDOCH, later VAN DEVENTER)
The Diamond Coterie. o/6 sewed Apr.?
Popular Sixpenny Books No. 173. This is (1887), with 160 pp. Glover and Greene give the first edition as issued by H. A. Sumner & Co., Chicago, 1884, 557 pp., brown pictorial cloth. It was listed in *PW* on Dec. 20, 1884, but not received. The *U Cat* gives R. R. Donnelley & Sons, Chicago, 1884, 19 cm., 557 pp., illustrated. This

Donnelley issue was in red, decorated cloth. The present edition is the first English edition. George Routledge, London, issued it, 1887, 154 pp., at o/6 sewed, probably in July.

2001 EMMA MURDOCH, later VAN DEVENTER **The Detective's Daughter.** o/6 sewed   May?
Popular Sixpenny Books No. 176. This is (1887), 188 pp., probably the first English edition. The first edition was entitled *Madeline Payne*, issued by A. T. Loyd, Chicago, 1884, 19.5 cm., 457 pp., illustrated, by L. L. Lynch.
Also 1904

2002 LAWRENCE L. LYNCH (EMMA MURDOCH), later VAN DEVENTER)
Out of a Labyrinth. o/6 sewed May?
Popular Sixpenny Books No. 177. This is the first English edition (1887), with 137 pp. The first edition was issued by A. T. Loyd, Chicago, 1885, 19.5 cm., 471 pp., illustrated, by L. L. Lynch.

2003 CHARLES DICKENS **The Life and Adventures of Martin Chuzzlewit.** o/6 sewed   June (*Bks* ad)
Popular Sixpenny Books No. 22. The first appearance was as 20 parts in 19, issued

by Chapman & Hall, London, from Jan. 1843 to July 1884. They were 22.5 cm., illustrated by "Phiz," and edited by "Boz." They issued it in 1 vol., 1844, 22 cm., 624 pp., illustrated, at 21/0, by Dickens, with a preface (June 25, 1844). It was listed in the *Ath* on July 13. In the United States it was issued in 7 parts, $.06½ each, in blue wrappers, illustrated by "Phiz," and edited by "Boz." Part 1 was noticed in the *Southern Literary Messenger* for May 1843, and part 3 noticed in the issue for Nov. 1843. A listing in the *Knickerbocker* for Mar. 1843 said that the first two chapters had appeared, and a listing for May 1843 stated that up to the last part had appeared. Harpers issued it in 1 vol., 1844, 312 pp., illustrated. Lea & Blanchard, Philadelphia, also issued it, without the author's permission, having been refused advance sheets. It is dated 1844, 8vo, 320 pp., illustrated by "Phiz," partly colored, by Dickens, noticed in the *Southern Literary Messenger* for Sept. 1844. It was also issued by the New World Press, J. Winchester, New York, with no date, 29 cm., 150 pp., probably in 1843 and 1844, as an extra number of the *New World*. It was reviewed in the *Knickerbocker* for Sept. 1844. A listing for May 1843 in this magazine stated that the New World office was also issuing it.

2004 EMMA MURDOCH, later VAN DEVENTER **The Rival Detectives.**
o/6 sewed June (*Bks* ad)
Popular Sixpenny Books No. 172. This is the first English edition (1887). The first edition was in Chicago, 1885, the *BM* giving H. A. Sumner & Co., with the title *Dangerous Ground*, 462 pp., illustrated; and the *U Cat* giving the same title, issued by A. T. Loyd & Co., 19.5 cm., 462 pp., illustrated.

2005 RICHARD COBBOLD **The History of Margaret Catchpole.** o/6 sewed June (*Bks* ad)
Popular Sixpenny Books No. 174.
Also 1864, 67, 73, 77

2006 VICTOR HUGO **Ninety-Three.**
o/6 sewed June (*Bks* ad)
Popular Sixpenny Books No. 175. This is (1887), with 187 pp.
Also 1886

2007 JAMES F. COOPER **The Spy.**
o/6 sewed June (*Bks* ad)
Popular Sixpenny Books No. 183. This is (1887), with 150 pp. The first edition was issued by Wiley & Halsted, New York, 2 vols., 1821, 18.5 cm., anonymous, published on Dec. 22, 1821, and listed in the *North American Review* for Jan. 1822. Charles Wiley, New York, issued the fourth edition, 1824, in 2 vols. The first English edition was issued by W. B. Whittaker, London, 3 vols., 1822, 18 cm., anonymous, 21/0, in Mar., listed by the *Edinburgh Review* as published Feb.–June 1822. Colburn & Bentley, London, issued it as *Standard Novels* No. 3, 1831, revised, corrected, and with a new introduction, 410 pp.

2008 JAMES F. COOPER **The Last of the Mohicans.** o/6 sewed June (*Bks* ad)
Popular Sixpenny Books No. 186. This is (1887), with 150 pp. The first edition was issued by Carey & Lea, Philadelphia, 2 vols, 1826, 19 cm., anonymous. Editorial matter in the *New York Mirror* on Feb. 18, 1826, stated that it had been published the previous week. They issued the second edition, 2 vols., 1826, 20 cm. The first English edition was issued by John Miller, London, 3 vols., 1826, 18 cm., anonymous, listed in the *Literary Gazette* on Mar. 18, and listed by the *Quarterly Review* as published Apr.–June 1826. Colburn & Bentley, London, issued it as *Standard Novels* No. 6, 1831, revised, corrected, and with a new introduction, 401 pp., in July.

2009 JAMES F. COOPER **The Pathfinder.**
o/6 sewed June (*Bks* ad)
Popular Sixpenny Books No. 189. The first edition was issued by Bentley, London, 3

vols., 1840, 20.5 cm., anonymous, 31/6, on Feb. 25, listed in the *Ath* on Mar. 7, and advertised in the *Spect* on Feb. 22 as "On Feb. 26." The first American edition was issued by Lea & Blanchard, Philadelphia; etc., 2 vols., 18 cm., anonymous, on Mar. 14, reviewed in the *Knickerbocker* for Apr. Bentley issued it as *Standard Novels* No. 90, 1843, 472 pp.

2010 JAMES F. COOPER *Eve Effingham.*
0/6 sewed   June (*Bks* ad)
Popular Sixpenny Books No. 190. This has no date and 160 pp. The first edition was *Home as Found*, issued by Lea & Blanchard, Philadelphia, 2 vols., 1838, 19 cm., anonymous, deposited on Nov. 9, 1838, and reviewed in the *Knickerbocker* for Dec. 1838. The first English edition was issued by Bentley, as *Eve Effingham*, 3 vols., 1838, 20.5 cm., anonymous, advertised in the *Ath* on Dec. 1 as "Just published," and listed there and in the *Spect* on Dec. 8.

2011 VICTOR HUGO *Les Misérables.*
2 vols. 0/6 sewed each   June (*Bks* ad)
Popular Sixpenny Books Nos. 198, 199. It was also issued as *Shilling Novels* No. 67, at 1/0 sewed, complete, in 1887.
Also 1876, 82

2012 SARAH S. HAMER *Christine's Crook.*
1/0 sewed, 1/6, 2/0 cloth   Aug.
Lily Series No. 100. This is (1887), with 297 pp. It was advertised in the *Ath* on Aug. 13 as "Just issued." The *BM* gives another edition from Ward, Lock (1887), 297 pp. Ward, Lock issued the first edition.

2013 JOHN W. KIRTON *Victoria: True Royalty.* 1/0 sewed, 1/6 cloth   Aug.
Youth's Library of Wonder and Adventure No. 73. This is (1887), with 408 pp. It was advertised in the *Ath* on Aug. 13 at 1/0 sewed, 1/6 without illustrations, and at 2/6, 3/6, 5/0, all with illustrations and all cloth. It was listed in the *Spect* on June 18,

1887, Cr 8vo, 2/6 cloth. The first edition was probably issued by Ward, Lock.

2014 THEODORE F. MUNGER *On the Threshold.* 1/0 sewed, 1/6 cloth   Sept.?
Friendly Counsel Series. This contains essays for young men. The first edition was issued by Houghton, Mifflin & Co., Boston, 1881 (1880), 18.5 cm., 228 pp., $1.00, listed in *PW* on Dec. 25, 1880, and in the *Ind* on Dec. 30. The 14th thousand was advertised in the *New-York Times* on Dec. 14, 1884, at $1.00. The first English edition was issued by Ward, Lock (1883), Cr 8vo, 228 pp., at 3/6 cloth, listed in the *Spect* on Oct. 6. They issued it in 1891 at 2/0 cloth.

2015 SOPHIE MAY (REBECCA S. CLARKE)
Drones' Honey. 1/0 sewed, 1/6, 2/0 cloth
Oct. 8 (*Ath*)
Lily Series No. 106. This is (1887), 217 pp., and is the first English edition. The first American edition was issued by Lee & Shepard, Boston, 1887, 8vo, 281 pp., listed in the *Nation* on June 16, and the *Ind* on June 23.

2016 WILLIAM SHAKESPEARE
Complete Works. 0/6 sewed, 1/0 cloth
Oct. 22 (*Ath* ad)
Popular Sixpenny Books No. 44. This has 800 pp., but it is still unbelievable that it contained the complete works! It was advertised in the *Times Weekly Edition* on Sept. 30, 1887, complete, in double columns.
Also 1880

2017 ARTHUR CONAN DOYLE *A Study in Scarlet.* 8vo. 1/0 sewed   Nov.
This is Beeton's Christmas Annual, 28th season. It has no date, 21.5 cm., 138 pp., the title story occupying pp. 1–95, followed by two plays, one by R. André and the other by C. J. Hamilton. It is in white wrappers with many ads in front and ads

on pp. 139–168. The imprint on the front cover is Ward, Lock & Co., London, New York & Melbourne, and on the title page it is just the same without the Melbourne. This is the first appearance of the first Sherlock Holmes story and is one of the scarcest books known to collectors! Ward, Lock paid Doyle £25 for the complete copyright, and he received nothing further! He never published with them again. Three firms refused it before its acceptance by Ward, Lock in 1886, who in a letter to Doyle of Oct. 31, stated that it would be issued in 1887 as the market was flooded with cheap fiction in 1886. The first American edition was issued by J. B. Lippincott & Co., Philadelphia, 1890, 18.1 cm., 214 pp., and 2 pp. of ads, in their *Series of Select Novels* No. 107. It is in tan wrappers, printed in dark brown, and dated Mar. 1, 1890. It was listed in *PW* and in *Public Opinion* on Mar. 29 and in the *Ind* on Mar. 27, at $.50. It was also issued in light blue cloth with brown rosebud endpapers, at $.75, in Sept. 1890. Also 1888, 99, 1902 *See color photo section*

2018 JOHN FORSTER **The Life and Times of Oliver Goldsmith. Part 1.** Illustrated. o/6 sewed Nov. 25

This was advertised in the *Times Weekly Edition* (London) on Dec. 18, 1887, 12 monthly o/6 parts, illustrated, with part 1 to be issued "On Nov. 25." Ward, Lock issued it in 2 vols. (1888), 22 cm., illustrated, with a preface (1871). They issued it in their *Minerva Library*, 1890, 18.5 cm., 472 pp., illustrated, 2/o cloth, listed in the *Spect* on Apr. 5. The first edition was issued by Bradbury & Evans, London, 1848, 21 cm., 704 pp., illustrated; and they issued the second edition in 2 vols., 1854, 22.5 cm.; and reissued it in 1 vol., a new edition, 1855, illustrated. Chapman & Hall, London, issued it, 1863, the fourth edition, 20 cm., 472 pp., illustrated.

2019 WILLIAM HONE **Hone's Every-Day Book. Part 1.** Illustrated. o/6 sewed Nov. 25

This was advertised in the *Times Weekly Edition* (London) on Dec. 8, 1887, 27 monthly o/6 parts, with Part 1 "On Nov. 25." Ward, Lock issued it in 2 vols., 1888–89, 23.5 cm., illustrated by Cruikshank et al. *The Every-Day Book* was originally published weekly from Jan. 1825 to Dec. 1826, 105 numbers in 2 vols. Hone published it in 2 vols., 1825, illustrated; and Hunt & Clarke, London, published it for him, 2 vols., 1826, illustrated. *The Table-Book* was originally issued in weekly numbers from Jan. 1827 to Jan. 1828, in 55 numbers in 2 vols. They were both issued by W. Tegg & Co., London, 4-vols.-in-3, with a preface (1827), 22 cm., illustrated. They were issued in London in 3 vols., in 1831, *The Table-Book* forming vol. 3; and reissued in London, 3 vols., 1838.

2020 GEORGE R. EMERSON & RICHARD RUSSELL **The Irish Problem.** o/6 sewed 1887 (*Eng Cat*)

Sixpenny Useful Books. This is (1887), 18.5 cm., with 274 pp. See 1886

2021 SUSAN COOLIDGE (SARAH C. WOOLSEY) **What Katy Did Next.** Illustrated. 1/o sewed, 1/6, 2/o cloth 1887 (*Eng Cat*)

Lily Series No. 99. This is (1887), with 288 pp. The first American edition was issued by Robert Bros., Boston, 1886, 17.5 cm., 323 pp., illustrated, $1.50 cloth, listed in the *Ind* and the *Nation* on Oct. 28 and in *PW* on Oct. 30. The first English edition was issued by Frederick Warne, London, Cr 8vo, illustrated, 3/6 cloth, advertised in the *Ath* on Oct. 23, 1886. Warne issued it, 16mo, at 1/o sewed, 1/6 cloth, about Oct. 1, 1887.

2022 LEW WALLACE (LEWIS WALLACE)
Ben-Hur. 1/0 sewed, 1/6, 2/0 cloth
1887 (*Eng Cat*)

Lily Series No. 101. This has no date, 18
cm., 422 pp., with 28 pp. of ads at the
back. The cloth issue is in olive cloth, decorated in gray and black. There was a
Ward, Lock edition (1887), 17.7 cm., 422
pp., with 26 pp. of ads, in red, decorated
cloth. I have a Ward, Lock issue in wrappers, probably about 1911. The first edition was issued by Harper & Bros., New
York, 1880, 17.5 cm., 552 pp., $1.50 cloth,
advertised in the *New-York Times* on Nov.
12 as "This day." It was listed in the *Ind* on
Nov. 18 and listed in *PW* on Dec. 11. *BAL*
stated that it was in powder blue cloth with
gray endpapers, in an edition of 2,500
copies, published Nov. 12 according to the
publisher's records and deposited Oct. 22.
A known copy is cited (Nov. 16, 1880).
Harpers agreed on Nov. 9, 1880, to fur-
nish plates for the English edition. Harpers reissued it many times, always at
$1.50 and with 552 pp. The *New York Times
Book Review* on Jan. 13, 1900, stated that
Ben-Hur was now in its 92nd edition and
that 680,000 copies had been sold. The
first English edition was issued by Sampson Low, London, 1881, 17.5 cm., 552
pp., at 6/0 cloth, with 32 pp. of ads at the
back, listed in the *Ath* on Feb. 26. They issued a new edition, at 6/0, advertised in
the *Spect* on Mar. 12, 1881. Frederick
Warne, London, issued it (1884), 16mo,
458 pp., 1/0 sewed, 2/0 cloth; and reissued
it at 2/0 cloth in 1887.

2023 RICHARD RUSSELL **India's Danger
and England's Duty.** 0/6 sewed 1887
(*Eng Cat*)

Sixpenny Useful Books.
Also 1885

2024 ANONYMOUS **Ward and Lock's
Pictorial and Historical Guide to
Killarney.** Small format. Illustrated.
1/0 boards 1887?

This is my copy, no date, 16.2 cm., 118
pp., green glazed boards, printed in

black, with green endpapers with ads.
There is an ad on the back cover, ads in
front, and on pp. 1–85 plus 3 pp. at the
back. It has 2 folding maps and colored
plates. Ward, Lock issued many of these
guides covering the British Isles. I base
the date on the ads. The first edition was
probably in 1883.

2025 ANNIE ASHMORE (MRS. J. M.
SIMPSON) **Worth His Weight in Gold.**
0/6 sewed 1887

Popular Sixpenny Books No. 178.
Also 1886

2026 SIR GILBERT CAMPBELL ET AL.
On a Winter's Night. 0/6 sewed 1887

Popular Sixpenny Books No. 179.
Also 1886

2027 JAMES F. COOPER **The Pilot.**
0/6 sewed 1887

Popular Sixpenny Books No. 184. This has
no date. The first edition was issued by
Charles Wiley, New York, 2 vols., 1823, 20
cm., anonymous. The first English edition
was issued by John Miller, London, 3 vols.,
1824, 20 cm., anonymous, 21/0, listed in
the *Literary Gazette* on Jan. 31, 1824. Colburn & Bentley, London, issued it as *Standard Novels* No. 1, 1831, 420 pp., 6/0, listed
in the *Spect* on Mar. 19.

2028 JAMES F. COOPER **Lionel Lincoln.**
0/6 sewed 1887

Popular Sixpenny Books No. 185. This has
no date, with 156 pp. The first edition was
issued by Charles Wiley, New York, 2 vols.,
1825, 1824, the second vol. being dated
1824, published Feb. 5, 1825, and deposited on Dec. 7, 1824, reviewed in the
United States Literary Gazette on Feb. 26,
1825. The first English edition was issued
by John Miller, London, 3 vols., 1825, 19
cm., anonymous, 21/0, listed in the *Literary Gazette* on Feb. 26 and in the *Edinburgh
Review* as published Jan.–Apr. 1825.
Bentley, London, issued it as *Standard Nov-*

els No. 20, 1832, 408 pp., revised, corrected, and with a new preface.

2029 JAMES F. COOPER *The Prairie.* o/6 sewed 1887

Popular Sixpenny Books No. 187. This has no date. The first printing was by Hector Bossange, Paris, 3 vols., 1827, anonymous, in wrappers. According to a contract between Cooper and Colburn, advance sheets from the Paris printing were to be sent to Colburn, and he had the right to publish it one to three days before the Paris edition. He issued the first English edition, 3 vols., 1827, 18 cm., anonymous, 24/0, listed in the *Literary Gazette* on Apr. 28. The first American edition was issued by Carey, Lea & Carey, Philadelphia, 2 vols., 19 cm., anonymous, about May 17, listed in the *United States Literary Gazette* for June. The cost book of Carey & Lea states that they printed 5,000 copies and that they paid Cooper $5,000. Colburn & Bentley, London, issued it as *Standard Novels* No. 17, 1832, 443 pp., revised, corrected, and with a new preface.

2030 JAMES F. COOPER *The Water Witch.* o/6 sewed 1887

Popular Sixpenny Books No. 188. This has no date and 159 pp. The first edition was issued by Walther, Dresden, 3 vols., 1830, anonymous, which *BAL* states was issued before Sept. 18. The first English edition was issued by Colburn & Bentley, London, 3 vols., 1830, 18.5 cm., anonymous, 31/6, listed in the *Ath* on Oct. 16. The first American edition was issued by Carey & Lea, Philadelphia, 2 vols., 1831, 21 cm., anonymous. The cost book for Carey & Lea states that it was published Dec. 11, 1830, and it was reviewed in the *North American Review* for Apr. 1831. It was issued as Bentley's *Standard Novels* No. 36, 1834, 429 pp., revised, corrected, and with a new preface.

2031 ANONYMOUS *Lives and Adventures of Remarkable Imposters.* o/6 sewed 1887

Popular Sixpenny Books No. 195. The *Eng Cat* gives this as issued in 1887.
See 1876

2032 ANONYMOUS *Lives and Adventures of Celebrated Claimants.* o/6 sewed 1887 (*Eng Cat*)

Popular Sixpenny Books No. 196.
See 1876

2033 ÉMILE ERCKMANN & PIERRE CHATRIAN *The Alsatian Schoolmaster.* o/6 sewed 1887

Popular Sixpenny Books No. 197.
Also 1872, 75

2034 B. ELIOT G. WARBURTON *The Crescent and the Cross.* o/6 sewed 1887 (*Eng Cat*)

Popular Sixpenny Books No. 201. This is from the first edition of 1845 and has 229 pp. The first edition was issued by Henry Colburn, London, 2 vols., 1845, 20 cm., illustrated, 25/0, listed in the *Ath* on Nov. 16, 1844. He issued the second through fourth editions in 2 vols., revised and corrected, from Apr. 1845 to Feb. 1846. He issued the fifth edition, 550 pp., illustrated, 10/6, with a new preface, listed by *PC* as published Nov. 30–Dec. 14, 1850. At a sale of Colburn copyrights by Southgate and Barrett on May 26, 1857, Hurst & Blackett paid 420 g for the copyright and 58/10/0 for the stock, according to editorial matter in *Notes & Queries* for June 6. This seems peculiar inasmuch as Hurst & Blackett were successors to Henry Colburn and that they had been issuing this title for at least two years before the sale. They issued the 11th edition, 1855, 20 cm., 380 pp., illustrated, 6/0; and issued the 12th edition at 6/0 in Nov. 1856; and issued the 15th edition at 5/0 in Mar. 1859. The first American edition was issued by Wiley & Putnam, New York, 2 vols., 1845, 18 cm., in their *Library of Choice Reading*. It was listed in *Godey's Lady's Book* for July 1845 and noticed in the *Knickerbocker* for July.

2035 ANONYMOUS *Amusing Anecdotes, etc.* o/6 sewed   1887
Popular Sixpenny Books No. 202.
See 1875

2036 ÉMILE GABORIAU *Monsieur Lecoq.* 1/o sewed   1887 (*Eng Cat*)
Shilling Novels No. 68. The first edition was issued in Paris, 2 vols., 1869. The first edition in English was issued by George Munro, New York, 1879, 2 parts, my copy, *Seaside Library* No. 465, 4to paper, $.20 each, dated Mar. 28. The first part was advertised in the *New-York Times* on Feb. 6, and the second part on Mar. 22 as "On Mar. 28" and on Mar. 28 as "Out today." The second part was also advertised in the *Ind* on Apr. 3 as "Out today." Estes & Lauriat, Boston, issued it, 1880, listed in *PW* on May 8, the *Ind* on May 20, and the *Nation* on June 10. The first English edition was issued by Vizetelly, London, 2 vols., 1881, 17.2 cm., 1/o each in scarlet wrappers, *Lecoq the Detective*. I have a set of the second edition, 2 vols., 1884, the same. He issued the 45th thousand in 2 vols., 1887; and issued it in 1 vol., 2/6 scarlet cloth, about Apr. 4, 1885. I think Glover and Greene must be in error in stating that the first English translation was issued by Estes & Lauriat in 1880, as the above discussion makes clear.
Also 1888

2037 JOHN W. KIRTON *Standard Irish Reciter.* o/6 sewed, 1/o, 1/6 cloth   1887 (*Eng Cat*)
I cannot trace this.

2038 ANONYMOUS *Sylvia's Monograms and Initials for Embroidery.* 1/o boards 1887 (*Eng Cat*)
Sylvia's Needlework Books No. 6. I cannot trace this.

2039 J. TILLOTSON *Uncle John's Chats with Young Folks.* 1/o cloth 1887 (*Eng Cat*)
Good Aim Series. I cannot trace this.

2040 MRS. WILLIAM H. HUNT *Children at Jerusalem.* 1/o sewed, 1/6 cloth   1887?
Youth's Library of Wonder and Adventure No. 66. The first edition was issued by Ward, Lock, no date, 189 pp., with a frontispiece, 3/6 cloth, issued in late 1880 or early 1881.

2041 JOHN W. KIRTON, ed. *Bible Heroes.* 1/o sewed, 1/6 cloth   1887?
Youth's Library of Wonder and Adventure No. 67. *Sacred Heroes and Martyrs* was first issued by E. B. Treat & Co., New York; etc., 1870, 23.5 cm., 623 pp., illustrated, by Joel F. Headley. Ward, Lock issued it with the same title (1876), in the *Christian Life Series*, revised and edited by Kirton.

2042 JOHN W. KIRTON, ed. *First Heroes of the Cross.* 1/o sewed, 1/6 cloth   1887?
Youth's Library of Wonder and Adventure No. 68. This is probably the second part of the work mentioned in the preceding entry.

2043 JAMES MASON? *Thrilling Adventures in the Arctic Regions.* Illustrated. 1/o sewed, 1/6 cloth   1887?
Youth's Library of Wonder and Adventure No. 69. This and the following entry may be from an earlier issue by Ward, Lock, of *Ice World Adventures; or, Voyages and Travels in the Arctic Regions* by James Mason, issued after 1875, Cr 8vo, illustrated, 5/o cloth.

2044 JAMES MASON? *In Search of Franklin.* Illustrated. 1/o sewed, 1/6 cloth 1887?
Youth's Library of Wonder and Adventure No. 70. See the preceding item.

2045 F. C. ARMSTRONG *The Sailor Hero.*
1/0 sewed, 1/6 cloth   1887?

Youth's Library of Wonder and Adventure
No. 71.
Also 1863, 73

2046 FRANCIS PALGRAVE (FRANCIS
COHEN, later PALGRAVE) *A History of
the Anglo-Saxons.* Illustrated. 1/0 sewed,
1/6 cloth   1887?

Youth's Library of Wonder and Adventure No.
72. The first edition was *The History of En-*
gland. Vol. 1. *Anglo-Saxon Period*, issued by
John Murray, London, 1831, 391 pp.,
with maps and illustrations. No more
were issued. William Tegg, London, reissued it, 1867, 332 pp., with the maps and
illustrations, as *History of the Anglo-Saxons*.
Ward, Lock reissued this Tegg edition
(1887), 20 cm., 332 pp., illustrated, 3/6
cloth, in their *World Library*.

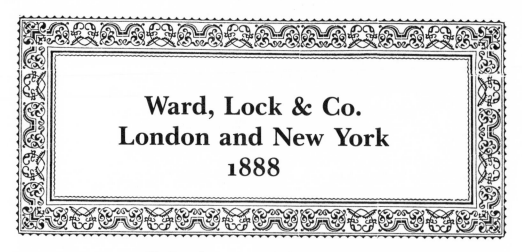

Ward, Lock & Co.
London and New York
1888

2047 THOMAS CARLYLE **The French Revolution.** Cr 8vo. 1/0 sewed, 2/0 cloth Mar. 10 (*Spect*)

Famous Books for All Time. This has no date and 624 pp. It was reissued in the *Minerva Library*, 1891, illustrated, in cloth. It was issued as *Popular Sixpenny Books* Nos. 45–47, at 0/6 sewed each, advertised in the *Ath* on Mar. 10, 1888. The 0/6 issue of the present edition was in pale blue wrappers, printed in dark blue, with ads on the back cover and on the inside covers. The first edition was issued by James Fraser, London, 3 vols., 19.5 cm., 31/6, advertised in the *Ath* on May 27, 1837, as "Just published." He issued the second edition in 3 vols., at 25/0, advertised in the *Spect* on Nov. 30, 1839, as if ready. Chapman & Hall, London, issued the third edition, 3 vols., p 8vo, 31/6, in cloth, advertised in the *Spect* on Mar. 4, 1848. The first American edition was issued by C. C. Little & J. Brown, Boston, 2 vols., 1838 (1837), 20.5 cm., about Dec. 25, 1837, listed in the *New York Review* (quarterly) for Apr. 1838 as published Jan. 1–Mar. 15, 1838.

2048 THOMAS CARLYLE *Sartor Resartus, Heroes and Hero-Worship, Past and Present.* Cr 8vo. 1/0 sewed, 2/0 cloth Mar. 10 (*Ath* ad)

Famous Books for All Time. This is (1888), 19 cm., with 192, 176, and 203 pp. It was reissued in the *Minerva Library* (1891),

18.5 cm., illustrated, 2/0 cloth, listed in the *Spect* for Feb. 14, 1891. Ward, Lock issued the three titles in 3 vols., 0/6 sewed each, as *Popular Sixpenny Books* Nos. 48–50, all (1888), with 192, 176, and 203 pp., respectively. They were advertised in the *Ath* on Mar. 10, 1888. The first title ran in *Fraser's Magazine*, Nov. 1833–Aug. 1834. The first book issue was from James Fraser, London, 1834, 22 cm., anonymous, in 3 books, 50 copies being printed for friends. Saunders & Otley, London, issued it, 1838, 20 cm., 310 pp., by D. Teufelsdröckh, noticed in the *Spect* on Aug. 11. Fraser issued a second edition, 1841, Demy 8vo, 352 pp., at 10/6 cloth, with the author's name on the binding only, advertised in the *Spect* on Feb. 20. Chapman & Hall, London, issued the third edition, 21 cm., 324 pp., 10/6 cloth, advertised in the *Spect* on Dec. 16, 1848, as "This day." The first American edition of the first title was issued by James Monroe, Boston, 1836, anonymous, 299 pp., in three books, with a preface by (Ralph W. Emerson). There was another American edition of 1,000 copies sold before the first English edition came out. This must mean before the Saunders & Otley edition. The first edition of the second title was *On Heroes, Hero-Worship, and the Heroic in History*, issued by Chapman & Hall, London, 1840. They issued the second edition, Cr 8vo, 382 pp., 9/0, listed in the *Ath* on May 7,

1842; and issued the third edition at 9/0 before Dec. 22, 1849. James Fraser, London, issued it, 1841, 19 cm., 393 pp., at 10/6, 6 lectures, reprinted with corrections and additions, advertised in the *Spect* on Feb. 20. In the United States it was issued by D. Appleton & Co., New York, 1841, 18.5 cm., 283 pp., with pp. (281)–283 being ads; and by Scribners, New York, 1841, 255 pp., both listed in the *United States Magazine* (monthly) for July. The first edition of the third title was issued by Chapman & Hall, 1843, at 10/6, listed in the *Ath* on Apr. 29. It was 20 cm., with 399 pp. They issued a second edition before Dec. 22, 1849. The first American edition was issued by Charles C. Little & James Brown, Boston, 1843, 20 cm., 296 pp. There was a very long review in *The New Englander* (New Haven) for Jan. 1844, attributing it to Harper & Bros., New York, 1843.

2049 ELIZABETH S. PHELPS, later WARD
The Gates Between. 1/0 sewed, 1/6,
2/0 cloth   Mar. 10 (*Ath*)

Lily Series No. 112. The first English edition was issued by Ward, Lock (1887), copyright, 19 cm., 185 pp., 2/0, gray cloth with pale yellow endpapers. It has 2 pp. of ads at the front and 16 pp. at the back. It was deposited at the Bodleian on Nov. 27 and listed in the *Ath* and the *Spect* on Sept. 17. They issued a second edition at 2/0 cloth, advertised in the *Spect* on Nov. 19, 1887, as "Now ready." The first American edition was issued by Houghton, Mifflin & Co., Boston and New York; etc., 1887, 18 cm., 222 pp., $1.25, with 12 pp. of ads. It was in tan, blue, or green cloth with yellow endpapers or in a different stamping with brown endpapers. From Sept. 14, 1887, to Feb. 12, 1895, 10,250 copies were printed and bound. It was deposited on Sept. 19, advertised in the *New-York Times* on Sept. 18, and listed in the *Ind* on Sept. 22.

2050 EDWARD P. ROE **The Earth
Trembled.** 1/0 sewed, 1/6, 2/0 cloth
Mar. 10 (*Ath*)

Lily Series No. 111. *Shilling Novels* No. 69. The first English edition was issued by Ward, Lock (1887), copyright, 18.5 cm., 395 pp., 2/0, gray cloth with endpapers printed in gray with an overall leafy pattern. It was listed in the *Spect* and the *Ath* on Sept. 17. They issued a second edition at 2/0 cloth, advertised in the *Spect* on Nov. 19, 1887, as "Now ready." The first American edition was issued by Dodd, Mead & Co., New York, 1887, 19 cm., 452 pp., at $1.50 cloth, advertised in the *New-York Times* on Sept. 28 as "Ready," and listed in *Public Opinion* on Oct. 1, and in the *Nation* and *Ind* on Oct. 6. There was a second edition of 5,000 copies, the same, advertised in the *New-York Times* on Nov. 30 as "On Dec. 1," noting that 25,000 copies of the first edition had been sold. The third edition, the 31st thousand, the same, was advertised on Jan. 24, 1888, as "Now ready."

2051 GEORGE BLACK **First Aid: A Book of
Ready Reference in Times of Emergency.
A Manual of Instruction for Ambulance
Students, etc.** p 8vo. Illustrated.
2/0 boards   Mar. 10 (*Ath* ad)

This is (1888), with 215 pp. The first edition was issued by Ward, Lock (1887), Cr 8vo, 215 pp., illustrated, 2/6 cloth, listed in the *Spect* on Nov. 19.

GASTON TISSANDIER *Scientific Recreation
Series.* 8 vols. Illustrated. 1/0 sewed,
1/6 cloth   Apr. 7 (*Ath* ad)

Youth's Library of Wonder and Adventure Nos. 74–77 and 87–90. The ad in the *Ath* gave these as in the *Scientific Recreation Series* and an Oct. 1888, Ward, Lock catalog gave them as in the *Youth's Library* as above. I think they were all translated from *Les Recreations Scientifiques*, by Tissandier, Paris, 1881, 341 pp., illustrated, which was issued in a third edition, entirely revised (1883), with 329 pp. It was translated by Henry Frith and issued by Ward, Lock in the early 1880s, enlarged, as *Popular Scientific Recreations in Natural Philosophy, Astronomy, etc.*, 24 cm., 781 pp., illustrated, at 7/6 and 9/0. It was issued in the United States by W. H. Stelle & Co., New York (copyright 1883), 25 cm., 781 pp., illustrated. I think when the eight titles of the present entry were issued they had *Scientific Recreation Series* on their covers as I've verified for Nos. 76 and 90. The eight vols. were as follows:

2052 **No. 74.** *Marvels of the Elements.* 182 pp.

2053 **No. 75.** *Marvels of Heat, Light, and Sound.*

2054 **No. 76.** *Marvels of Invention and Scientific Puzzles.* 113 pp.

2055 **No. 77.** *Marvels of Earth, Air, and Water.* 129 pp. See 1881

2056 **No. 87.** *Marvels of Geology and Physical Geography.* 183 pp.

2057 **No. 88.** *Marvels of Animal and Plant Life.* 134 pp.

2058 **No. 89.** *Marvels of Electricity and Magneticism.* 152 pp.

2059 **No. 90.** *Marvels of Astronomy.*

2060 EDWARD P. ROE *Found Yet Lost.*
1/0 sewed, 1/6, 2/0 cloth　Apr. 16 (*PC*)

Lily Series No. 113. *Shilling Novels* No. 70. This is the first English edition (1888), with 180 pp. The first American edition was issued by Dodd, Mead & Co., New York (1888), 19 cm., 222 pp., $.25, blue wrappers, printed on the front with "This limited edition is published for Dodd, Mead & Co. exclusively for Butler Bros., New York and Chicago." It was deposited on Mar. 29 and advertised in the *New-York Times* on Mar. 27 as a first edition of 50,000 copies. It was listed in *PW* on Apr. 14 and 28, and in the *Ind* and the *Nation* on Apr. 26.

2061 EARL OF BEACONSFIELD (BENJAMIN DISRAELI) *Vivian Grey.* 0/6 sewed　Apr.?

Popular Sixpenny Books No. 209. This is (1888), 22 cm., 247 pp. The first edition was issued by Henry Colburn, London, 5 vols.: vols. 1 and 2, 1826, and vols. 3–5, 1827, anonymous. Colburn paid £500 for it. Vols. 1 and 2 were issued at 18/0 about Apr. 22, and vols. 3–5 were issued at 31/6 about Feb. 17, 1827. David Bryce, London, issued it, 1853, a new edition, small format, 416 pp., 2/0 boards, by Disraeli, in Dec. 1853. In the United States it was issued by Collins & Hannay, E. Duyckinck, etc., New York, 1826, 19.5 cm., anonymous, 224 pp.; and by Carey, Lea & Carey, Philadelphia, 2 vols., 1827, 21 cm. The cost book of Carey and Lea states that 500 copies of part 1 were finished on Apr. 25, 1827, and the same for 500 copies of part 2. The second American edition, 750 copies of 2 vols. each, was finished July 20, 1827.

2062 EARL OF BEACONSFIELD *Coningsby.* 0/6 sewed　Apr.?

Popular Sixpenny Books No. 210. This is (1888), with 191 pp. The first edition was issued by Henry Colburn, London, 3 vols., 1844, 19.5 cm., 31/6, listed in the *Ath* on May 11. He issued the second edition, the same, advertised in the *Spect* on July 27, 1844, as "Now ready." It was issued with *The Wondrous Tale of Alroy* in 3 vols., with a portrait, advertised in the *Illustrated London News* on Jan. 3, 1846. He issued the fifth edition of *Coningsby*, 1849, Fcp 8vo, 471 pp., 6/0, with a new preface (May 1849) and a frontispiece (portrait), in May. David Bryce, London, issued it, 1853, small format, at 1/6 boards, in Aug. In the United States it was issued by Carey & Hart, Philadelphia, 1844, 22.5 cm., 159 pp., noticed in the *Southern Quarterly Review* for Oct. 1845. It was also issued by W. H. Colyer, New York, 1844, 24 cm., 136 pp., the cover dated 1845.

2063 EARL OF BEACONSFIELD (BENJAMIN DISRAELI) *Henrietta Temple.*

o/6 sewed   Apr.?

Popular Sixpenny Books No. 211. This is (1888), 22 cm., 169 pp. The first edition was issued by Henry Colburn, London, 3 vols., 19 cm., anonymous, 31/6, listed in the *Ath* on Dec. 3, 1836. David Bryce, London, issued it, 1853, small format, 331 pp., 1/6 boards, in Apr.; Disraeli censored and cut all reprints according to Wolff. The first American edition was issued by Carey & Hart, Philadelphia; etc., 2 vols., 1837, anonymous, noticed in the *Knickerbocker* for Mar. and in the *Southern Literary Messenger* for May.

2064 EARL OF BEACONSFIELD *Venetia.*

o/6 sewed   Apr.?

Popular Sixpenny Books No. 212. This is (1888), 22 cm., 193 pp. The first edition was issued by Henry Colburn, London, 3 vols., 1837, 19.5 cm., anonymous, at 31/6, the dedication signed Δ. It was listed in the *Ath* on May 20. David Bryce, London, issued it, 1853, a new edition, small format, 336 pp., 1/6 boards, in Mar. The first American edition was issued by Carey & Hart, Philadelphia, 2 vols., 1837, anonymous.

2065 EARL OF BEACONSFIELD *Sybil.*

o/6 sewed   Apr.?

Popular Sixpenny Books No. 213. This is (1888), 22 cm., 195 pp. The first edition was issued by Henry Colburn, London, 3 vols., 1845, 19.5 cm., 31/6, listed in the *Ath* on May 10. A second edition in 3 vols. was advertised in the *Spect* on June 28, 1845, as "Now ready." David Bryce, London, issued it, 1853, a new edition, small format, 336 pp., 1/6 boards, in May. The first American edition was issued by Carey & Hart, Philadelphia, 1845, 24 cm., 125 pp., 3-vols.-in-1, $.25, buff printed wrappers, listed in *Godey's Lady's Book* for July 1845.

2066 EARL OF BEACONSFIELD *Contarini Fleming.* o/6 sewed   Apr.?

Popular Sixpenny Books No. 214. This is (1888), 22 cm., 130 pp. The first edition was issued by John Murray, London, 4 vols., 1832, 18 cm., anonymous, 24/0 in boards, listed in the *Ath* on May 19. Edward Moxon, London, issued a second edition, 4 vols., 1834. David Bryce, London, issued it, 1853, a new edition, small format, 277 pp., 1/6 boards, in June. This and *The Wondrous Tale of Alroy* were issued by Colburn in 3 vols., advertised in the *Spect* on Dec. 20, 1845, with a portrait. The first American edition was issued by J. & J. Harper, New York, 2 vols., 1832, 18.5 cm., anonymous.

2067 EARL OF BEACONSFIELD *The Wondrous Tale of Alroy.*

o/6 sewed   Apr.?

Popular Sixpenny Books No. 215. This is (1888), 22 cm., 104 pp. The first edition was in *The Wondrous Tale of Alroy. The Rise of Iskander,* issued by Saunders & Otley, London, 3 vols., 1833, 20 cm., anonymous, at 31/6, listed in the *Ath* on Mar. 9. It has ads in vol. 2 (Feb. 1833). The first title was issued with the preceding title in 3 vols., by Colburn (see the preceding item). David Bryce, London, issued it, 1853, at 1/6 boards, in July. The first American edition, with the English title, was issued by Carey, Lea & Blanchard, Philadelphia, 2 vols., 1833, 20.5 cm., anonymous, listed in the *Knickerbocker* for July as lately published or in press.

2068 EARL OF BEACONSFIELD *The Young Duke.* o/6 sewed   Apr.?

Popular Sixpenny Books No. 216. This is (1888), 22 cm., 146 pp. The first edition was issued by Colburn & Bentley, London, 3 vols., 1831, 19 cm., anonymous, 31/6, listed in the *Spect* on Apr. 23 and published on Apr. 21, according to the Bentley private catalog. They paid £500 for it.

David Bryce, London, issued it, 1853, a new edition, small format, 304 pp., 1/6 boards, in Oct. The first American edition was issued by J. & J. Harper, New York, 2 vols., 1831, 16.5 cm., anonymous.

2069 HENRY W. DULCKEN, ed. *The Life of William the First, Emperor of Germany.* 1/0 sewed   Apr.?

This is the first edition, 1888, 18 cm., 112 pp., with illustrations and portraits. It was mentioned in editorial matter in the *Ath* for May 19.

2070 ARCHIBALD C. GUNTER *Mr. Barnes of New York.* 0/6 sewed   May?

Popular Sixpenny Books No. 207. The first American edition was probably Deshler, Welch & Co., New York, 1887, my copy, 20 cm., 250 pp., listed in the *Nation* on Apr. 14, and in *PW* on Apr. 30 (not received). It was listed in the *Atlantic Monthly* for July 1887, and thus probably issued in Apr. It was also issued with the Home Publishing Co., New York, imprint, 1887, 21 cm., 250 pp., in green cloth. This company was founded and operated by Gunter. In England it was issued by Henry Vizetelly & Co., London, 1887, 250 pp.; and by George Routledge, London, 1887, 192 pp., 1/0 sewed, 1/6, the 1/6 published in Sept. Both of these English editions were "On our table" in the *Ath* on Oct. 19, 1887, thus probably issued a few months earlier. It was advertised in the *New-York Times* on June 26, 1887, with no publisher given.
Also 1903

2071 HAWLEY SMART *A False Start.* 2/0 boards, 2/6 cloth   June 2 (*Ath*)

Select Library of Fiction No. 182, new numbering. This was probably in the *Library of Select Authors* with the series title at the base of the spine. It ran serially in *London Society*, chapters 10–14 being in the May 1887 issue. The first edition was issued by Chapman & Hall, London, 3 vols., 1887,

Cr 8vo, 31/6, listed in the *Ath* on May 28. There was a new edition, Cr 8vo, advertised by Chapman & Hall in the *Spect* on Dec. 24, 1887. In the United States it was issued by D. Appleton & Co., New York, 1888, 12mo, 462 pp., $.50 paper, advertised in the *New-York Times* on Apr. 12 as "This day," and listed in *PW* on Apr. 21. It was also issued by Rand McNally, New York, 1888, listed in *PW* on Mar. 24, and in *Lit World* (fortnightly) on Mar. 31. It was also issued by John W. Lovell, New York (1888), *Lovell's Library* No. 1141, 12mo, paper, listed in *PW* on Apr. 7, and in *Public Opinion* on Apr. 21.
Also 1891, 1902

2072 ARTHUR CONAN DOYLE *A Study in Scarlet.* Illustrated. 1/0 sewed   June?

Shilling Novels No. 76. This is the first separate edition, 1888, 18 cm., 169 pp., with the *Select Library of Fiction* list in the ads ending with No. 889. It was also issued as *Warwick House Library* No. 1, 1891, a new edition, illustrated, in cloth with buff sides and a red back, the second separate English edition, with imprint Ward, Lock, Bowden & Co., London, New York, and Melbourne. It was 19.3 cm., 224 pp., 3/6, in three-quarter beige cloth, with a red cloth spine, and with green flower and leaf endpapers. There are ads on pp. (225)–(248). It was published in Dec. 1891 and advertised in the *Spect* on Feb. 27, 1892, a new edition, Cr 8vo, with 40 illustrations by Hutchinson, 3/6, as "Just ready." It was issued in New York in Feb. 1892, illustrated, $1.50, with plain white endpapers. The present edition is Ward, Lock & Co., London and New York, in white wrappers blocked in pink and lettered in red, with ads on the back cover and on the inside wrappers. There are ads on pp. (171)–(184), and all edges are cut. It has 6 illustrations by Doyle's father and was published July 2–16, 1888. There was a second impression in Mar. 1889 at 1/0. The third English edition was issued by

Ward, Lock & Bowden, Ltd., London, New York, and Melbourne, 1895, 24.2 cm., 64 pp., illustrated, issued as a supplement to the *Windsor Magazine*, Christmas 1895. It is in white wrappers blocked in red and black, with ads on the back cover and on the inside wrappers. It was published in Nov. 1895.

Also 1887, 99, 1902

2073 G. A. COLMACHE *An Undiscovered Crime.* o/6 sewed   June?

Popular Sixpenny Books No. 217. This is (1888), 192 pp., probably the first edition. The *BM* gives only the third edition (1888), with 192 pp.

2074 LAWRENCE L. LYNCH (EMMA MURDOCH, later VAN DEVENTER) *A Mountain Mystery.* o/6 sewed   June?

Popular Sixpenny Books No. 218. This has no date, 202 pp., with ads on pp. (203)–(224). It is clothed in white pictorial wrappers, lettered and decorated in red, blue, and black. It is probably the first English edition. The first edition was issued by A. Sumner & Co., Chicago, listed in *PW* on Sept. 4, 1886, but not received. It was also issued by A. T. Loyd, Chicago, 1887, 600 pp., illustrated.

Also 1904

2075 ALEXANDRE DUMAS, THE ELDER *The Count of Monte Cristo.* 2 vols., o/6 sewed each   July?

Popular Sixpenny Books Nos. 142, 142A. It was also issued at the same time as *Shilling Novels* No. 72 (1888), 252 pp., 1/0 sewed, 2/0 cloth, an unabridged edition.

Also 1858, 85

2076 THOMAS CARLYLE *Cromwell's Letters and Speeches.* 3 vols., o/6 sewed each   Aug. 18 (*Ath* ad)

Popular Sixpenny Books Nos. 35–37. The Aug. 18 ad said "Just out." Ward, Lock

also issued it in 1 vol. (1888), 819 pp., 1/0 sewed, 2/0 cloth, as *Famous Books of All Time*, being the three sixpenny vols. in one. It was reprinted from the second revised edition. Ward, Lock, Bowden & Co. issued it, 1892, 3-vols.-in-1, 18 cm., 819 pp., illustrated, 2/0 cloth, in the *Minerva Library*, listed in the *Spect* on July 2. The first edition was issued by Chapman & Hall, London, 2 vols., 1845, 23.5 cm., portrait, listed in the *Ath* on Nov. 22 and reviewed on Dec. 6, 13, and 20. They issued a supplement, 1846, 23.5 cm., 224 pp. They issued the third edition, 4 vols., p 8vo, portrait, 42/0, advertised in *Notes & Queries* for Dec. 22, 1849, but probably issued before this date. George Routledge, London, issued it, 1888, 3 vols., and in 1 vol., 1/0 sewed, 2/0 cloth. The first American edition was issued by Wiley & Putnam, New York, 2 vols., in 4 parts, in the *Library of Choice Reading*, 22 cm., portrait, briefly reviewed in the *Knickerbocker* for Jan. 1846.

2077 HENRY W. DULCKEN *Self Instruction in German.* 1/0 sewed, 2/0 cloth   Aug. 18 (*Ath* ad)

Shilling Useful Books. This is the first edition (1888), with 282 pp. The ad said 1/0, "Just ready."

2078 JULES A. L. KUNZ *Lessons on French Grammar.* 1/0 sewed, 2/0 cloth Aug. 18 (*Ath* ad)

Shilling Useful Books. The ad said "Just ready." The *BM* gives (1886), 315 pp., and the *Eng Cat* gives Cr 8vo, 2/0, 1886–88.

2079 PANSY (ISABELLA M. ALDEN) *Three People.* 1/0 sewed, 1/6, 2/0 cloth Sept. 29 (*Ath* ad)

Lily Series No. 114. This is (1888), with 288 pp. It was later *Pansy Series* No. 9, 1/0 decorated cloth. The first edition was probably D. Lothrop & Co., Boston (1872), 18 cm., 412 pp., illustrated. The *BM* gives London (1878).

2080 PANSY (ISABELLA M. ALDEN) *Esther Reid.* 1/0 sewed, 1/6, 2/0 cloth   Sept. 29 (*Ath* ad)

Lily Series No. 115. This is (1888), with 248 pp. It was later *Pansy Series* No. 10, 1/0 decorated cloth. It was issued by T. Nelson & Sons, London, 1887, 238 pp.; and by George Routledge, London, 1887, Cr 8vo, 319 pp., 2/0, listed in the *Spect* on Aug. 27.

2081 PANSY *Esther Reid Yet Speaking.* 1/0 sewed, 1/6, 2/0 cloth   Sept. 29 (*Ath* ad)

Lily Series No. 116. This is (1888), with 275 pp. It was later *Pansy Series* No. 11. The first edition was issued by D. Lothrop & Co., Boston (copyright 1882), 17 cm., 447 pp., illustrated, $1.50 cloth, advertised in the *New-York Times* on Dec. 11, 1883. George Routledge, London, issued it, 1887, 376 pp.

2082 PANSY *Julia Reid.* 1/0 sewed, 1/6, 2/0 cloth   Sept. 29 (*Ath* ad)

Lily Series No. 117. This is (1888), with 264 pp. It was later *Pansy Series* No. 12, 1/0 decorated cloth. The first edition was probably issued by D. Lothrop & Co., Boston (copyright 1872), 12mo, 372 pp., with a frontispiece. It was also issued by the Western Tract & Book Society, Cincinnati, 1872, the same. The first English edition was probably issued by George Routledge, London, 1887, 375 pp.

2083 PANSY *Four Girls at Chautauqua.* 1/0 sewed, 1/6, 2/0 cloth   1888 (*Eng Cat*)

Lily Series No. 102. This is (1888), with 291 pp. It was later *Pansy Series* No. 1, 19.4 cm., 1/0 decorated cloth. The first edition was issued by D. Lothrop & Co., Boston (1876), 474 pp., illustrated, listed in the *Ind* on Aug. 3. The first English edition was issued by George Routledge, London, 1887, Cr 8vo, 382 pp., at 2/0 cloth, listed in the *Spect* on Apr. 30.

2084 PANSY *The Chautauqua Girls at Home.* 1/0 sewed, 1/6, 2/0 cloth 1888 (*Eng Cat*)

Lily Series No. 103. This is (1888), with 287 pp. It was later *Pansy Series* No. 2, 19.4 cm., 1/0 decorated cloth. The first edition was issued by D. Lothrop & Co., Boston (1877). Routledge, London, issued it, 1887, 380 pp., at 1/0, 1/6, 2/0, all in cloth.

2085 PANSY *Christie's Christmas.* 1/0 sewed, 1/6, 2/0 cloth   1888 (*Eng Cat*)

Lily Series No. 104. This is (1888), with 236 pp. It was later *Pansy Series* No. 3, 19.4 cm., 1/0 decorated cloth. The first edition was issued by D. Lothrop & Co., Boston (copyright 1884), 443 pp., illustrated, advertised in the *Christian Union* on May 14, 1885, 12mo, illustrated, $1.50 cloth. George Routledge, London, probably issued it in 1887, Cr 8vo, at 2/0 cloth, listed in the *Spect* on May 27.

2086 PANSY *An Endless Chain.* 1/0 sewed, 1/6, 2/0 cloth   1888 (*Eng Cat*)

Lily Series No. 107. This is (1888), with 283 pp. The first edition was issued by D. Lothrop & Co., Boston (1884), 18.5 cm., 497 pp., with a frontispiece. The first English edition was issued by George Routledge, London, 1887, 380 pp., 2/0 cloth. The Lothrop edition was listed in the *Ind* on Apr. 3, 1884.

2087 PANSY *Ruth Erskine's Crosses.* 1/0 sewed, 1/6, 2/0 cloth   1888 (*Eng Cat*)

Lily Series No. 108. This is (1888). The first edition was issued by D. Lothrop & Co., Boston (copyright 1879), 19 cm., 434 pp., illustrated. The first English edition was issued by George Routledge, London (1887), 383 pp., 2/0 cloth, listed in the *Ath* on July 30.

2088 PANSY *Links in Rebecca's Life.* 1/0 sewed, 1/6, 2/0 cloth   1888 (*Eng Cat*)

Lily Series No. 109. This is (1888), with 258 pp. The first edition was issued by D.

Lothrop & Co., Boston (copyright 1878), 12mo, 422 pp., with a frontispiece. The first English edition was issued by Hodder & Stoughton, London, 1882, 422 pp., listed in the *British Quarterly Review* for Jan. 1883, and thus probably issued Sept.–Nov. 1882.

2089 PANSY ***Mrs. Solomon Smith Looking On.*** 1/o sewed, 1/6, 2/o cloth 1888 (*Eng Cat*)

Lily Series No. 110. This is (1888), with 265 pp. It is probably the first English edition. The first edition was issued by D. Lothrop & Co., Boston (1882), 19 cm., 456 pp., with a frontispiece, listed in the *Ind* on Sept. 7.

2090 JANE AUSTEN ***Sense and Sensibility.*** 1/o sewed, 1/6, 2/o cloth Sept. 29 (*Ath* ad)

Lily Series No. 119.
Also 1883

2091 JANE AUSTEN ***Pride and Prejudice.*** 1/o sewed, 1/6, 2/o cloth Sept. 29 (*Ath* ad)

Lily Series No. 120. Ward, Lock issued this as a new edition as *Select Library of Fiction* No. 167, later changed to No. 191, 1881, 17 cm., with 6 pp. of ads. The first edition was issued by T. Egerton, London, 3 vols., 1813, 19 cm., anonymous, at 18/o, listed in the *Edinburgh Review* as published Nov. 1812–Feb. 1813. The first American edition was issued by Carey & Lea, Philadelphia, 2 vols., 1832, 20 cm., anonymous, from the third London edition.

2092 JANE AUSTEN ***Emma.*** 1/o sewed, 1/6, 2/o cloth Sept. 29 (*Ath* ad)

Lily Series No. 121. Ward, Lock also issued this as *Select Library of Fiction* No. 164, later changed to No. 188, 1881, a new edition, 17.5 cm., 435 pp. The first edition was issued by John Murray, London, 3 vols., 1816, 18.5 cm., anonymous, 21/o, listed in the *Quarterly Review* as published Oct.–Dec. 1815, advertised in the *Morning Chronicle* on Dec. 23, 1815, as "This day." It was in various colors of paper boards with contrasting spines and paper labels. The first American edition was issued by M. Carey, Philadelphia, 2 vols., 1816, actually 3-vols.-in-2, anonymous, at $2.00 or $2.50, probably in the late spring or early summer. It was issued by Carey, Lea & Blanchard, Philadelphia, 2 vols., 1832. Bentley issued it as *Standard Novels* No. 25, 1833, 435 pp.

2093 JULIA MAGRUDER ***Honoured in the Breach.*** 1/o sewed, 1/6, 2/o cloth Sept. 29 (*Ath* ad)

Lily Series No. 124. This is the first English edition (1888), with 239 pp. It appeared in *Lippincott's Magazine*, 1888, vol. 41, on pp. (287)–389.

2094 EDWARD P. ROE ***An Unexpected Result and Other Stories.*** 1/o sewed, 1/6, 2/o cloth Sept. 29 (*Ath* ad)

Lily Series No. 125. This has no date, with 116 pp. This was also *Shilling Novels* No. 80. The first edition was issued by Dodd, Mead & Co., New York (copyright 1883), 18 cm., 134 pp., with 2 pp. of ads. It was deposited on Apr. 26, 1883, listed in *PW* on May 5, and listed in the *Ind* on May 10. It was bound in maroon, mustard, or grass-green cloth with brown endpapers and contained three stories. The first English edition was issued by George Routledge, London, 1883, 128 pp., possibly just the title story. It was listed in *PC* on June 1.

2095 ÉMILE GABORIAU ***Monsieur Lecoq.*** 2 vols. o/6 sewed each 1888 (*BM*)

Popular Sixpenny Books Nos. 203, 204. The first vol. was "The Detective's Dilemma," and vol. 2 was "The Detective's Triumph." Also 1887

2096 VICTOR HUGO *The History of a Crime.* o/6 sewed   1888 (*Eng Cat*)

Popular Sixpenny Books No. 205. This is (1888), translated by Sir Gilbert Campbell. The first edition was *Histoire d'un Crime*, Paris, 2 vols., 1877, 25 cm., vol. 1 reviewed in the *Ath* on Oct. 13, and vol. 2 reviewed on Mar. 23, 1878. The first English edition was issued by Sampson Low, London, 4 vols.: vols. 1 and 2, 1877; vols. 3 and 4, 1878. It was translated by T. H. Joyce and Arthur Locker, 20 cm., each 2 vols. at 21/0. The first two were listed in the *Ath* on Dec. 15, 1877, and the last two were listed in the *Spect* on June 22, 1878. Low issued it, Cr 8vo, 6/0, listed in the *Spect* on May 31, 1879; and reissued it, the same, advertised in the *Times Weekly Edition* on June 5, 1885. In the United States it was issued by George Munro, New York, as *Seaside Library* No. 179, 4to, 23 pp., in paper, at the end of 1877 or in early 1878. It was also issued by Harper & Bros., New York, 2 vols. (1878), *Franklin Square Library* Nos. 2 and 3, 4to, illustrated, $.25 paper, advertised in the *New-York Times* on Feb. 8, 1878, as "This day." No. 3, also at $.25, was advertised there on Apr. 25, 1878, as "This day." It was advertised as No. 2, complete, 4to, 69 pp., $.10 paper, there on May 25, 1878, my copy. Harpers also issued it, 1878, 23.5 cm., 103 pp., illustrated.

2097 ÉMILE GABORIAU *In Deadly Peril.* o/6 sewed, 2/o boards, 2/6 cloth   1888

Popular Sixpenny Books No. 206. *Select Library of Fiction* No. 1031, new numbering. The o/6 edition was (1888), 201 pp. The 2/o edition is given by the *Eng Cat*. The translation is by Sir Gilbert Campbell. The first edition was *La Corde au Cou*, Paris, 1873, 489 pp. The first American edition was probably issued by James R. Osgood & Co., Boston, 1874, my copy, 23 cm., 212 pp., as *Within an Inch of His Life*, listed in *PW* on Aug. 1, and in *APC&LG* on Aug. 6. The *American Catalog* and Glover and Greene give Estes & Lauriat, Boston, 1874. The first English edition was issued by Vizetelly & Co., London, 1881, 17.2 cm., 255 pp., in 1/o scarlet wrappers, with blue endpapers with ads. It was entitled *In Peril of His Life*. He issued the second edition, the same, about Sept. 23, 1882; and the third edition, my copy, the same, 1884; and the 40th thousand, 1886. He issued it with *Intrigues of a Poisoner*, 1885, at 2/6 in scarlet cloth.

Also 1904

2098 BENJAMIN BROADAXE *The Bad Boy and His Sister.* Illustrated. o/6 sewed   1888 (*Eng Cat*)

Popular Sixpenny Books No. 208. This is the first edition (1888), with 102 pp.

2099 JOYCE E. MUDDOCK, later PRESTON-MUDDOCK *Stormlight.* o/6 sewed   Sept. 29 (*Ath* ad)

Popular Sixpenny Books No. 220. This is the first edition, 1888, 171 pp. It was also issued as *Warwick House Library* No. 2, 1892, a new edition, Cr 8vo, 457 pp., at 3/6 cloth, listed in the *Spect* on Jan. 23.

Also 1893, 1903

2100 G. NORWAY *The Brand of Cain.* 8vo. o/6 sewed   Sept. 29 (*Ath* ad)

Popular Sixpenny Books No. 221. This is the first edition (1888), 96 pp.

2101 G. A. COLMACHE *Under Spell of the Dark Powers.* o/6 sewed   Sept. 29 (*Ath* ad)

Popular Sixpenny Books No. 222. This is the first edition (1888), 107 pp.

2102 ALFRED H. POULTNEY *"B" Confidential.* o/6 sewed   Sept. 29 (*Ath* ad)

Popular Sixpenny Books No. 223. This is the first edition, 1888, 122 pp. It was reissued circa 1891, 122 pp.

2103 DOUGLAS HARRISON
How Mr. Skelton's Sin Found Him Out.
8vo. o/6 sewed   Sept. 29 (*Ath* ad)
Popular Sixpenny Books No. 224. This is the first edition (1888), 148 pp.

2104 PETER ANTON *Masters in History. Gibbon, Macaulay, Grote, Motley.*
Illustrated. 1/o sewed, 1/6 cloth
Sept. 29 (*Ath* ad)
Youth's Library of Wonder and Adventure No. 91. This was first issued by Macniven & Wallace, Edinburgh; etc., 1880, 18 cm., 252 pp., 2/6, 3/o cloth, advertised in the *Spect* on Nov. 6. It was issued by Frederick Warne, London, Cr 8vo, at 1/6 in 1884; and by Ward, Lock about 1885, at 1/o cloth. At about this time the title of the series was shortened to *Youth's Library*, no doubt reflecting the lack of adventure in the new titles!

2105 JAMES C. WATT *Great Novelists. Scott, Thackeray, Dickens, Lytton.*
Illustrated. 1/o sewed, 1/6 cloth
Sept. 29 (*Ath* ad)
Youth's Library No. 92. Ward, Lock issued this at 1/o cloth, probably in 1885 or 1886. The first edition was issued by Macniven & Wallace, Edinburgh; etc., 1880, 18 cm., 260 pp., at 2/6. Frederick Warne, London, issued it in 1884, Cr 8vo, 260 pp., at 1/6. See *England's Essayists* below.

2106 HENRY J. NICOLL *Thomas Carlyle.*
Illustrated. 1/o sewed, 1/6 cloth
Sept. 29 (*Ath* ad)
Youth's Library No. 93. Ward, Lock issued it, probably in 1885, 255 pp., 1/o cloth. The first edition was issued by Macniven & Wallace, Edinburgh; etc., 1881, 18 cm., 248 pp., with a frontispiece (portrait). They issued a revised edition in 1881, with 255 pp. Frederick Warne, London, issued it in 1884, 255 pp., at 1/6.

2107 PETER ANTON *England's Essayists. Addison, Bacon, DeQuincey, Lamb.*
Cr 8vo. Illustrated. 1/o sewed, 1/6 cloth
Sept. 29 (*Ath* ad)
Youth's Library No. 94. The first edition was issued by Macniven & Wallace, Edinburgh; etc., 1883, 18 cm., 252 pp., at 2/6. Frederick Warne, London, issued it at 1/6 in 1884. This and *Great Novelists* above were issued about this time in 1 vol., at 3/6 cloth.

2108 HENRY J. NICOLL *Brilliant Speakers.* Cr 8vo. Illustrated. 1/o sewed, 1/6 cloth   Sept. 29 (*Ath* ad)
Youth's Library No. 95. This was combined with the next item and issued in the *Good Worth Library*, 1 vol., at 3/6, in Sept. 1888. The first edition of the present title was issued by Macniven & Wallace, Edinburgh; etc., 1880, 18 cm., 254 pp., at 2/6 and 3/o cloth, with the title, *Great Orators. Burke, Fox, Sheridan, Pitt*, advertised in the *Spect* on Nov. 6 as "Just published." It was reissued by Frederick Warne, London, with the latter title, in 1884, at 1/6.

2109 HENRY J. NICOLL *Great Scholars. Buchanan, Bentley, Porson, Parr and Others.* Illustrated. 1/o sewed, 1/6
Sept. 29 (*Ath* ad)
Youth's Library No. 96. This was also issued in Sept. combined with the previous title, 1 vol., 3/6, in the *Good Worth Library*. The first edition was issued by Macniven & Wallace, Edinburgh; etc., 1880, 18 cm., 251 pp., 2/6, 3/o cloth, advertised in the *Spect* on Nov. 6. Frederick Warne, London, issued it in 1884, 18 cm., 251 pp., 1/6.

2110 CHARLES & MARY LAMB *Tales from Shakespeare.* Illustrated. 1/o sewed, 1/6 cloth   Sept. 29 (*Ath* ad)
Youth's Library No. 97. The first edition was issued by T. Hodgkins, London, 2 vols., 1807, 17.5 cm., illustrated. Charles Lamb

said that he wrote 6 of the 20 pieces. The first six editions did not have Mary Lamb's name on the title page. According to Percy Muir, 8 of the 20 tales were issued as single numbers by Godwin, London, previous to the above first edition. A second edition was issued by Godwin, 2 vols., 1809, 12mo, according to the *Eng. Cat.* The first American edition was issued by Bradford & Inskeep, Philadelphia; etc., 2 vols., 1813, 20 cm.

2111 ROBERT C. ADAMS *On Board the "Rocket."* Illustrated. 1/o sewed, 1/6 Sept. 29 (*Ath* ad)

Youth's Library No. 98. This is the first English edition. It was issued by D. Lothrop & Co., Boston (copyright 1879), 18.5 cm., 335 pp., illustrated, and included sailor's songs with music.

2112 JAMES GREENWOOD *Strange Tales.* 1/o sewed   Sept.?

Shilling Novels No. 72. This was given by the *Eng. Cat*, but otherwise I cannot trace it.

2113 BILL NYE *Comic Stories.* 1/o sewed 1888?

Shilling Novels No. 74. This is possibly a 1-vol. issue of *Boomerang Shots* and *Hits and Skits* of 1884.
See 1884

2114 WILLIAM A. CLOUSTON, ed. *Choice Anecdotes and Good Sayings of the Witty and Wise.* 1/o sewed   1888 (*Eng Cat*)

Shilling Novels No. 75. It may be noted that these last three items are not "Novels" despite the series designation. The *BM* gives Ward, Lock (1883), 272 pp., in prose and verse, probably at 2/o cloth. It was listed in the *Spect* on Nov. 17, 1888, at 2/o, probably in the *People's Standard Library*, Cr 8vo, in cloth.

2115 FRANCES P. COBBE *False Beasts and True.* 1/o sewed   1888 (*Eng Cat*)

Shilling Novels No. 78.
Also 1875

2116 WILLIAM F. WILLIAMS *England's Battles by Sea and Land. Part 1.* Illustrated. o/6 sewed   Oct. 26

This was issued in 20 monthly parts, in collaboration with W. C. Stafford. Part 1 was advertised in the *Times Weekly Edition* (London) on Oct. 12, as "On Oct. 26." It is a new edition, issued in 2 vols., in Nov. 1890. The *BM* gives 6 vols. (1854–59).

2117 HERMANN J. KLEIN & DR. THOMÉ *God's Glorious Creation. Part 1.* Illustrated. o/6 sewed   Oct. 26

This is a reissue in 18 monthly parts. Part 1 was advertised in the *Times Weekly Edition* (London) on Oct. 12 as "On Oct. 26." The first edition was *Die Erde und Ihr Organisches Lebens*, Stuttgart, 2 vols. (1880, 1881), plates and illustrations, with vol. 1 by Klein and vol. 2 by Thomé. The first English edition was issued by Ward, Lock (1881, 1882), 25.5 cm., 832 pp., with plates, maps, illustrations, and diagrams, translated and with a signed preface by Janet Minshull. It is entitled *Land, Sea and Sky*. It was issued in the United States by W. H. Stelle & Co., New York (copyright 1883), 25.5 cm., 832 pp., with illustrations, maps, and diagrams. Ward, Lock reissued it (1884), entitled *God's Glorious Creation*, 25 cm., 376 pp., with illustrations and plates, a duplicate of the first English edition, with new title pages on the two parts, new prefatory matter, but with the running title *Land, Sea and Sky*.

2118 ANONYMOUS *The Land and the Bible. Part 1.* Illustrations. Maps. o/6 sewed   Oct. 26

This was issued in monthly parts. Part 1 was advertised in the *Times Weekly Edition* (London) on Oct. 12 as "On Oct. 26." I cannot trace this!

2119 HANNAH C. O'NEILL & EDITH A. BARNETT *Our Nurses and the Work They Have to Do.* Cr 8vo. 1/0 sewed, 2/0 cloth Oct. 27 (*Spect* ad)

Shilling Useful Books. This is the first edition (1888), with 197 pp. It was advertised in the *Ath* on Sept. 29 as "At once."

2120 VICTOR HUGO *Han of Iceland.* 8vo, 0/6 sewed; 12mo, 2/0 boards, 2/6 cloth Nov. 10 (*Spect*) *See color photo section*

Popular Sixpenny Books No. 219. *Select Library of Fiction* No. 202B, new numbering. The sixpenny issue is my copy, no date, 21.5 cm., 138 pp., double columns, white pictorial wrappers cut flush and printed in red, blue, and black. It has ads on the back cover, the inside covers, 1 p. at the front, and pp. 139–160 at the back. The translation is by K. Aungle. The first edition was *Han D'Island*, Paris, 4 vols., 1823, 17 cm., anonymous. The first English edition was issued by Robins & Co., London, 1825, 20 cm., anonymous, 225 pp., at 7/6, *Hans of Iceland*. It was illustrated by Cruikshank and was listed by the *Quarterly Review* as published Apr.–June 1825. In the United States it was issued by J. Winchester, New York (1844?), 22.5 cm., 141 pp., *Hans of Iceland*, translated by J. T. Hudson. It was listed in *Godey's Lady's Book* for Apr. 1844 and was probably issued in Mar. 1844.

2121 MRS. A BLITZ *Romance of Australian Squatting, Mining, and Social Life. Digger Dick's Darling, and Other Tales.* 1/0 sewed Nov.?

Shilling Novels No. 79. This is the first edition, 1888, 256 pp.

2122 HAWLEY SMART *Saddle and Sabre.* 12mo. 2/0 boards, 2/6 cloth Nov.?

Library of Select Authors. Select Library of Fiction No. 183, new numbering. It is my copy, no date, 17.7 cm., 399 pp., yellow pictorial boards, printed in red, green, and black, with the series title at the foot of the spine. There are ads on the endpapers, back cover, and 8 pp. at the back. The first English edition was issued by Chapman & Hall, London, 3 vols., 1888 (1887), 19.5 cm., at 31/6, listed in the *Ath* on Dec. 10, 1887. In the United States it was issued by Frank F. Lovell, New York, *Household Library* No. 96, 19 cm., 352 pp., with a wrapper date of Dec. 22, 1887, and probably issued at the end of 1887. It was also issued by John W. Lovell, New York (1888), *Lovell's Library* No. 1103, 19 cm., 352 pp., with wrapper date (Nov. 23, 1887), and listed in *PW* on Jan. 21, 1888. It was also issued by M. J. Ivers, New York (1888), listed in *PW* on Jan. 21, 1888.

2123 SIR GILBERT CAMPBELL ET AL. *The Mystery of Mandeville Square, etc.* Illustrated. 1/0 sewed Dec. 7

This is Beeton's Christmas Annual, the 29th season, advertised in the *Times Weekly Edition* (London) on Dec. 7, 1888, as "Just ready." It is (1888), 192 pp. It contains first editions, including *The Mystery of a Handsome Cap* by R. André. The title story at least was put in *Shilling Novels* as No. 84 and in *Popular Sixpenny Books* as No. 240, probably in 1889.

2124 ANONYMOUS *The Magic Lantern.* 12mo. Illustrated. 1/0 sewed 1888 (*Eng Cat*)

Shilling Useful Books. This was by A Practiced Hand, the first edition, 1888, 18 cm., 151 pp.

2125 JOHN W. KIRTON, ed. *Standard Popular Reciters and Dialogues.* 9 vols. 0/6 sewed each 1888 (*Eng Cat*)

Also from 1877 to 1887

2126 CHARLES E. CRADDOCK (MARY N. MURFREE) *The Story of Keedon Bluffs.* (Copyright). 2/0 boards 1888 (*BM*)

Select Library of Fiction No. 972, new numbering. This is my copy, no date, 18.2 cm.,

257 pp., pale blue pictorial boards, printed in red and black, with the series title on the spine. It has ads on the endpapers, back cover, and 26 pp. at the back. The first English edition was issued by Ward, Lock (1887), 2/o cloth, listed in the *Ath* on Dec. 10, 1887, and in the *Spect* on Dec. 3. The present copy has endpaper ads for after 1904 but with title page and catalog at the back consistent with a date of 1888. The first American edition was issued by Houghton, Mifflin & Co., Boston and New York, 1888, 18.5 cm., 257 pp., $1.00, advertised in the *New-York Times* on Dec. 4, 1887, advertised in the *Nation* on Dec. 1 as "On Dec. 3" and listed Dec. 8, and listed in *PW* on Dec. 17.

2127 ELIZABETH PRENTISS *Only a Dandelion and Other Stories.* 1/o sewed, 1/6 cloth   1888 (*Eng Cat*)
Also 1875, 85

2128 ANNIE N. PRICE *True to the Best.* 1/o sewed, 1/6, 2/o cloth   1888 (*Eng Cat*)
Lily Series No. 105. The *BM* gives this as (1888), with 278 pp. The *Eng Cat* gives Ward, Lock, 1887, 8vo, 2/6.

Ward, Lock & Co.
London and New York
1889

Ward, Lock moved their New York office from 31 Bond Street to 35 Bond Street by Aug. 1889.

2129 W. H. PARKINS *How I Escaped.*
2/0 boards   Jan. 12 (*Ath*)

Select Library of Fiction No. 837, new numbering. It is the first edition, 1889, 19 cm., 180 pp., a duplicate of the American edition with a new title page, edited by Archibald C. Gunter. The first American edition was issued by the Home Publishing Co., New York, 1889 (copyright 1888), 19 cm., 180 pp., first listed in *PW* on Feb. 23, 1889, but not received, and later listed on June 8. It was listed in *Public Opinion* on June 22. Ward, Lock advertised this in the *Ath* on Aug. 17, 1889, as 2/0 cloth! This seems unlikely and not a Ward, Lock practice.

2130 THOMAS N. PAGE *In Ole Virginia.*
2/0 boards   Feb. 9 (*Spect*)

Select Library of Fiction No. 836, new numbering. It is (1889), with 230 pp. It was advertised in the *Ath* on Aug. 17, 1889, at 2/0 cloth as was the previous item, and it certainly is unusual for Ward, Lock. They issued it as *Warwick House Library* No. 8, a new edition, 1893, 230 pp., 3/6. The present edition is the first English edition. The first edition was issued by Charles Scribner's Sons, New York, 1887, 19 cm., 230 pp., $1.25 cloth, containing six tales, listed in the *Ind* on June 2. It was reissued in 1896, 8vo, $1.50 cloth, listed in the *New York Times Book Review* on Oct. 24.
Also 1893

2131 PIERRE C. DE MARIVAUX *The Hand of Destiny.* 0/6 sewed   Feb.?

Popular Sixpenny Books No. 228. This is (1889), with 160 pp., translated by Sir Gilbert Campbell. The first edition was *La Vie de Marianne*, Paris, in 11 or 12 parts, 1735– . The *BM* gives 11 parts, 1735–41, parts 1 and 2 being of the second edition, 1736. *The Life of Marianne* was issued by Charles Davis & Paul Vaillant, London, 3 vols., 1736–42, 17 cm. *The Virtuous Orphan* was issued by Jacob Robinson, London, 4 vols., 1743, a second edition, 17 cm.

2132 ANONYMOUS *A Mysterious Revenge.* 0/6 sewed   Feb.?

Popular Sixpenny Books No. 230. This is the first edition (1889), with 177 pp.

2133 ARTHUR LOUIS (ARTHUR L. KEYSER) *Dollars or Sense?* 12mo. 2/0 boards, 2/6 cloth   Mar. 23 (*Ath*)

Select Library of Fiction No. 835, new numbering. This is my copy, no date, 18 cm., 376 pp., white pictorial boards, printed in red, blue, and black, with the series title on the spine, and with a cover by Prowse. There are ads on the endpapers, back cover, and 6 pp. at the back. One of the endpaper ads is dated July 12, 1889. It is the first English edition. The first edition was issued by Brentano Bros., New York,

1886, 19.5 cm., 376 pp., listed in *PW* on Oct. 16, and in *Lit World* (fortnightly) on Oct. 16.

2134 MARGARET W. DELAND *John Ward, Preacher.* o/6 sewed   Mar.?

Popular Sixpenny Books No. 238. Later issued in the *Pansy Series* at 1/0 cloth. This is 1889, 288 pp. The first edition was issued by Houghton, Mifflin & Co., Boston and New York, 1888, 20 cm., 473 pp., $1.50, listed in *PW* and in *Lit World* (fortnightly) on Apr. 28, and in the *Ind* on May 3. The third edition was advertised in the *Atlantic Monthly* for July 1888, at $1.50; and the sixth edition was advertised in the *New-York Times* on Sept. 23, 1888, at $1.50; and the *Riverside Paper Series* No. 1, at $.50 paper, was advertised there on June 2, 1889. I am in doubt as to the first English edition. It could have been issued by Frederick Warne, London, in 1888, as *Popular Library* No. 1, at 1/0 sewed, 1/6 cloth, with 288 pp. It was advertised as such in a display ad in the *Ath* on Feb. 23, 1889. *Popular Library* Nos. 1 and 2 were advertised in the *Ath* on June 16, 1888, No. 2 as "Just published." This leads one to think that No. 1 was issued before June 16, 1888. It was also issued by Longmans, London, 1888, a reissue of the American edition, Cr 8vo, at 6/0, advertised as "Now ready," and listed in the *Ath* on June 23. They claimed in their ads that they paid royalties to the authoress and that their edition was the only authorized edition in England. They issued the third edition, Cr 8vo, 473 pp., at 6/0, advertised in the *Spect* on Oct. 6, 1888; and reissued it at 2/0 boards, 2/6 cloth, listed in the *Ath* on Mar. 2, 1889.

2135 ANNIE WEBB, later WEBB-PEPLOE *Naomi.* 12mo. 1/0 sewed, 1/6, 2/0 cloth Mar.?

Lily Series No. 126. This was also *Shilling Novels* No. 82 and was issued later in the *Pansy Series* at 1/0 cloth. The present edition is (1889), with 351 pp. It was issued after May 1, 1893, 19 cm., 351 pp., with a frontispiece. The first edition was issued by Harvey & Darton, London, 1841, Fcp 8vo, at 7/6, listed in the *Spect* on Dec. 26, 1840. It was advertised there, the same, on Sept. 11, 1841, and Mar. 12, 1842. The second edition was listed in the *Spect* on May 28, 1842. The first American edition was issued by Herman Hooker, Philadelphia, 1851, 422 pp., from the ninth London edition, noticed in the *Ind* on Jan. 9, 1851, and listed by *Lit World* as published Jan. 25–Feb. 8.

2136 ÉMILE GABORIAU *The Slaves of Paris.* 2 vols. o/6 sewed each   Apr.?

Popular Sixpenny Books Nos. 225, 226. These have the subtitles, *Caught in the Net* and *The Champdoce Mystery*. They were translated by Sir Gilbert Campbell and have no date. The first edition was *Les Esclaves de Paris*, Paris, 2 vols., 1868, as *Le Chantage* and *Le Secret des Champdoce*. The first edition in English was issued by George Munro, New York, 1879, 2 parts, *Seaside Library* No. 476, 32 cm., paper, with a caption title and with wrapper date (Mar. 1879). It was advertised in the *Ind* on Apr. 3 as "Out today." It was also issued by Estes & Lauriat, Boston, in 1882, 24 cm., 270 pp., in paper, listed in the *Ind* on Aug. 31 and in *PW* on Sept. 2. The first English edition was issued by Vizetelly & Co., London, 2 vols., in Mar. 1884, 227 and 211 pp., in 1/0 scarlet wrappers. My copy is the second edition, the same, 1884; and it was reissued, 1886, the 30th thousand, the same; and it was issued in 1 vol., 1885, in scarlet cloth at 2/6, about Apr. 4.
Also 1904

2137 ANONYMOUS *Ward and Lock's Pictorial Guide to London.* Illustrated. Maps. 1/0 boards, 1/6 cloth   May 18 (*Spect* ad)

This has no date, 16.5 cm., probably with 284 pp.
Also 1879, 97

2138 ANONYMOUS ***Ward and Lock's Pictorial Guide to Paris.*** Illustrated. Map. 1/0 boards, 1/6 cloth   May 18 (*Spect* ad)

This is the first edition, no date. It was advertised in the *Times Weekly Edition* (London) as *Ward and Lock's Guide to Paris and the Exhibition* on July 26, 1889, with maps, plans, colored plates, 1/0, 1/6 cloth. It was issued by Ward, Lock & Co., Ltd., 1900; and the fifth edition, revised, was issued, probably around 1903, 16.5 cm., 224 pp., illustrated, and with a map. A new edition of the guide to Paris was advertised in the *Ath* on May 12, 1894, at 1/0 cloth.

2139 GEORGE BLACK, ed. ***The Doctor.*** 0/6   May?

Sixpenny Manuals. This is probably *The Household Doctor*, edited by Black, the second, revised edition of which was issued by Ward, Lock, 1889, 264 pp., advertised in the *Spect* on May 18, 1889, as "Just ready." The present edition has no date and 113 pp.

2140 ELIZABETH BENJAMIN ***Jim the Parson.*** 1/0 sewed, 1/6 cloth   May?

Lily Series No. 130. This is probably the first English edition. Ward, Lock issued it as *Temperance Gift Book Series* No. 1, at 1/6, on Oct. 19, 1889. The first American edition was issued by John W. Lovell, New York (1887), as *Lovell's Library* No. 1077, 19 cm., 244 pp., in wrappers, listed in *PW* on Dec. 24, 1887.

2141 CHARLES MATTHEW ***Bazi Bazoum.*** 0/6 sewed   July?

Popular Sixpenny Books No. 239. This is the first edition, 1889, with 182 pp. It was issued in the United States by Street & Smith, New York, as *Mabel Seymour*, 1891, 19.5 cm., 203 pp.

2142 AUGUSTA J. EVANS, later WILSON ***Vashti.*** 1/0 sewed, 2/6 cloth   Aug.?

Shilling Novels No. 90. *Lily Series* No. 133. This is (1889), with 365 pp. The first edi-

tion was issued by G. W. Carleton, New York; Sampson Low, London, 1869, 18.5 cm., 473 pp., at $2.00, listed in *ALG&PC* (fortnightly) on Dec. 1, 1869, and advertised in the *New-York Times* on Nov. 13 as "This morning." The latter ad should be taken with a grain of salt as Carleton ads were very unreliable. This title, for example, was advertised from Nov. 1 on as "Ready." I presume this was to be issued in London by Sampson Low, but I have found no evidence of this. Ward, Lock put it in the *Pansy Series* later at 1/6 cloth.

2143 ALESSANDRO MANZONI ***The Betrothed Lovers.*** 2/0 boards, 2/6 cloth   Oct. 5 (*Spect*)

Select Library of Fiction No. 915, new numbering. This was also issued in the *Minerva Library*, 1889, 19 cm., 456 pp., 2/0 cloth, with a frontispiece (portrait), listed in the *Spect* on Oct. 5, 1889, at the same time as the present edition. The first edition was *I Promessi Sposi*, Milano, 3 vols., 1825, 1826 (i.e., 1827), issued in June 1827. It was issued at Pisa, as *The Betrothed Lovers*, 3 vols., 1828, Cr 8vo, anonymous, at 21/0, translated by Charles Swan, and listed by the *Quarterly Review* as published Apr.–June 1828. It was issued in London by Rivington, 3 vols., Cr 8vo, 21/0, in June 1828. It was issued as *Bentley's Standard Novels* No. 43, as *The Betrothed*, 1834, 452 pp. In the United States it was issued as *Lucia, the Betrothed*, by G. Dearborn, New York, 2 vols., 1834, 19 cm.; and by D. Green, Washington, 1834, 22 cm., 249 pp., as *I Promessi Sposi*, in English.

2144 JOHN W. KIRTON ***Rays of Sunshine for Every Home.*** Cr 8vo. 1/0 sewed, 1/6, 2/0 cloth   Oct. 19 (*Spect*)

Friendly Counsel Series. This is the first edition (1889), with 155 pp.

2145 G. T. BETTANY *The World's Religions. Part 1.* Illustrated. o/6 sewed Oct. 25

This was issued in 14 monthly parts, part 1 advertised in the *Spect* on Oct. 26 as "On Oct. 25." It was reissued in 14 monthly parts at o/6 sewed each, illustrated, part 1 advertised in the *Times Weekly Edition* (London) on Feb. 19, 1892, as "On Feb. 25." The present part issue was issued in 1 vol., Royal 8vo, illustrated, 7/6, advertised in the *Spect* on Dec. 13, 1890. There were separate issues of some of the religions as *Great Indian Religions* by Bettany, Cr 8vo, 2/6, was listed in the *Spect* on Nov. 5, 1892; and *Hinduism* by Bettany, at 3/6, was listed there on Nov. 5, 1892, also.

2146 SIR GILBERT CAMPBELL ET AL. *A Wave of Brain Power by Sir G. Campbell . . . Minette's Birthday by R. André, etc.* Demy 8vo. 1/o sewed   Oct. 26 (*Ath* ad)

This is Beeton's Christmas Annual, the 30th season, the first edition, 1889, with 194 pp. A second edition was issued in Nov., advertised in the *Ath* on Nov. 30 as "Now ready."

2147 JEANNIE G. BETTANY, later KERNAHAN *The House of Rimmon.* 12mo. 2/o boards, 2/6 cloth   Nov. 13 (*Ath*)

Select Library of Fiction No. 910, new numbering. This is 1889, with 379 pp. The first edition was issued by Remington, London, 3 vols., 1885, 19 cm., 31/6, listed in the *Ath* on July 18.

2148 PHINEAS T. BARNUM *Struggles and Triumphs.* 12mo. Illustrated. 1/o sewed Nov. 22

Shilling Novels No. 100. This was advertised in the *Times Weekly Edition* (London) on Nov. 22. It is my copy, 1889, 17.7 cm., 398 pp., with a frontispiece, and 32 full-page illustrations. It is brought down to 1889 and is in yellow wrappers cut flush, printed and with a portrait in black. It is

the first title in my collection with the Ward, Lock imprint including Melbourne in the address. It has ads on the endpapers, back cover, and 10 pp. at the back. The preface (Sept. 1889) states that the work was originally written in 1869. Also 1882. See 1855

2149 FRANCES H. BURNETT *That Lass o' Lowrie's.* 1/o sewed   Dec.? *Shilling Novels* No. 97. Also 1877

2150 FRANCES H. BURNETT *Theo.* 1/o sewed   Dec.? *Shilling Novels* No. 98. Also 1885

2151 FRANCES H. BURNETT *Surly Tim's Troubles.* 1/o sewed   Dec. 14 (*Ath*) *Shilling Novels* No. 99. Also 1877

2152 CHARLOTTE BRONTË *Jane Eyre, an Autobiography.* 2/o boards, 2/6 cloth Dec. 21 (*Spect*)

Select Library of Fiction No. 1081, new numbering. This has no date, with 271 pp. The first edition was issued by Smith, Elder & Co., London, 3 vols., 1847, edited by Currer Bell, p 8vo, 31/6, advertised in the *Ath* on Oct. 16 as "On Oct. 23," and noticed then also. The second edition, the same, was advertised in the *Spect* on Jan. 22, 1848, as "Just published." The third edition, the same, was advertised in the *Illustrated London News* on Apr. 15, 1848; and the fourth edition 19 cm., 457 pp., 6/o, dated 1850, was listed by *PC* as published May 14–29, 1850. In the United States it was issued by Wilkins, Carter & Co., Boston, 1848, 19 cm., 483 pp.; and by Harper & Bros., New York, 1848, *Library of Select Novels* No. 109, 24 cm., 174 pp., reviewed in the *Harbinger* (weekly) on Jan. 22, 1848. The *U Cat* gives also Porter, Philadelphia, 1847, 495 pp.

2153 AUGUSTA J. EVANS, later WILSON
Beulah. 1/0 sewed, 1/6 cloth   1889?

Lily Series No. 127. *Shilling Novels* No. 81.
This is (1889), with 384 pp. The first edition was issued by Derby & Jackson, New
York, 1859, 19 cm., 510 pp., $1.25, listed
in the *Ind* on Sept. 29, and advertised in
the *New-York Times* on Sept. 22 as "On
Sept. 24." The third edition was advertised there on Sept. 30, at $1.25; and the
seventh thousand was advertised there on
Oct. 1, at $1.25, as "Now ready." The *Eng
Cat* gives Knight, London, 12mo, 2/0, issued in 1860; and the *BM* gives London
(1861). Ward, Lock issued it in the *Pansy
Series* later, at 1/0 cloth.

2154 AUGUSTA J. EVANS, later WILSON
Infelice. 1/0 sewed, 1/6 cloth   1889
(*Eng Cat*)

Lily Series No. 128. *Shilling Novels* No. 83.
This is (1889), with 424 pp. Ward, Lock
later put it in the *Pansy Series* at 1/0 cloth.
The first edition was issued by G. W.
Carleton, New York; Sampson Low, London, 1876, 19 cm., 572 pp., listed in the
Ind on Dec. 9, 1875. Nicholson, London,
issued it in 1883. Presumably it was issued
by Sampson Low in England, but I've
found no evidence of this.

2155 EDWARD P. ROE **"Miss Lou."**
1/0 sewed, 1/6 cloth   1889 (*Eng Cat*)

Lily Series No. 129. *Shilling Novels* No. 85.
The first English edition was issued by
Ward, Lock (1888), 368 pp., 2/0 cloth, 2/6,
3/6, advertised in the *Ath* on Sept. 8 as
"Now ready" and listed on Sept. 15, and
listed in *PC* on Sept. 15. The first Ameri-
can appearance was as a serial in *Cosmopol-
itan Magazine*, where it began in the Mar.
1888 issue. The first book edition in the
United States was issued by Dodd, Mead
& Co., New York, 1888, 19 cm., 368 pp.,
$1.50 cloth, deposited on Sept. 7, listed in
Lit World (fortnightly) on Oct. 13, and in
PW on Oct. 20. It was advertised in the

New-York Times on Sept. 22, as "Just published." It is in blue-green cloth with yellow endpapers, 3 pp. of ads; and there is
another printing, the same, but with a
slightly different collation.

2156 AUGUSTA J. EVANS, later WILSON
St. Elmo. 1/0 sewed, 1/6, 2/6 cloth
1889 (*Eng Cat*)

Lily Series No. 131. *Shilling Novels* No. 88.
This is (1889), with 376 pp. It was later issued in the *Pansy Series*, no date, 19.5 cm.,
439 pp., at 1/0 cloth. The first edition was
issued by G. W. Carleton, New York;
Sampson Low, London, 1867, 18.4 cm.,
571 pp., $2.00, listed in the *Ind* on Dec. 27,
1866, and advertised in the *New-York Times*
on Dec. 19, 1866, as "This morning."
Sampson Low issued it in England in
1883.

2157 AUGUSTA J. EVANS, later WILSON
At the Mercy of Tiberius. 1/0 sewed,
1/6 cloth   1889?

Lily Series No. 132. *Shilling Novels* No. 89.
This has no date and 397 pp. It was issued
in the *Pansy Series* at 1/0 cloth in Aug.
1891. The first edition was issued by G. W.
Carleton, New York; Sampson Low, Lon-
don, 1887, 19 cm., 616 pp., listed in the
Nation on Oct. 27, and in *PW* on Oct. 29.
Presumably it was issued by Sampson
Low, but I have found no evidence of this.

2158 AUGUSTA J. EVANS, later WILSON
Macaria. 1/0 sewed, 1/6 cloth   1889
(*Eng Cat*)

Lily Series No. 134. *Shilling Novels* No. 91.
This has no date and 380 pp. About 1891
it was issued in the *Pansy Series* at 1/0 cloth.
The first American edition was issued by
West & Johnston, Richmond, 1864, 22
cm., anonymous, 183 pp. It was also is-
sued by John Bradburn, New York, 1864,
19 cm., 469 pp., $1.50, advertised in the
New-York Times on June 25 as "This day."
The first English edition was issued by

Saunders, Otley & Co., London, 3 vols., 1864, 31/6, listed in the *Spect* on Nov. 12.

2159 AUGUSTA J. EVANS, later WILSON
Inez. 1/o sewed, 1/6 cloth   1889 (*Eng Cat*)
Lily Series No. 135. *Shilling Novels* No. 92. This has no date and 251 pp. It was issued somewhat later in the *Pansy Series* at 1/o cloth. The first edition was issued by Harper & Bros., New York, 1855, 19 cm., anonymous, 298 pp., $.75 in muslin, advertised in the *New York Daily Times* on Feb. 23, 1855, as "This day," and noticed in *Harper's New Monthly Magazine* for Mar. 1855. The first English edition was issued by Sampson Low, London, Cr 8vo, anonymous, 6/6, in 1855.

2160 JOSEPH HOCKING **Elrad, the Hic.**
Cr 8vo. 1/o sewed, 1/6 cloth   Nov. 22
Lily Series No. 136. *Shilling Novels* No. 96. This is the first edition (1889), 221 pp., advertised in the *Times Weekly Edition* (London) on Nov. 22, 1889, as "Just ready."

2161 MAX ADELER (CHARLES H. CLARK)
Random Shots. Illustrated. 1/o sewed 1889 (*Eng Cat*)
Ward & Lock's Humorous Books No. 82. Also 1879, 83, 1900

2162 MAX ADELER (CHARLES H. CLARK)
An Old Fogey and Other Stories.
Illustrated. 1/o sewed   1889 (*Eng Cat*)
Ward & Lock's Humorous Books No. 83. Also 1881, 83, 1901, 05

2163 JOHN W. KIRTON **True Nobility.**
1/o sewed, 1/6 cloth   1889 (*Eng Cat*)
Youth's Library No. 99. This is the life of the seventh Earl of Shaftesbury. The first edition was issued by Ward, Lock (1886), 18.5 cm., 425 pp., illustrated, 2/6 cloth, in the *Family Gift Series*, listed in the *Spect* on Nov. 13.

2164 FRANCIS WATT **The Life and Opinions of the Right Hon. John Bright.**
Cr 8vo. Illustrated. 1/o sewed, 1/6 cloth 1889 (*Eng Cat*)
Youth's Library No. 100. This is (1889), 19 cm., 312 pp. The first edition was issued by J. Sangster & Co., London (1887), 312 pp., illustrated.

2165 JOHN W. KIRTON, ed. **The Way to Victory.** 1/o sewed, 1/6 cloth   1889 (*Eng Cat*)
Youth's Library No. 102. This is the first edition, no date, 404 pp.

2166 ANONYMOUS **The Enquirer's Oracle.**
1/o cloth   1889 (*Eng Cat*)
Shilling Useful Books. The first edition was issued by Ward, Lock (1884), 437 pp., at 2/o boards, 2/6 cloth.

2167 ANONYMOUS **Sylvia's Illustrated Crochet Book.** 1/o boards   1889 (*Eng Cat*)
Sylvia's Needlework Books No. 7. This is probably the first edition.

2168 GEORGE J. WHYTE MELVILLE
Sister Louise. New Edition. 12mo. 2/o boards   1889
Library of Select Authors. Select Library of Fiction No. 127, new numbering. This is my copy, no date, 18 cm., 268 pp., with a dedication (Oct. 1875). The imprint contains Melbourne in the address. It is in white pictorial boards, printed in red, blue, and black, with the series title at the foot of the spine and "The Works of Whyte Melville" at the head. There are ads on the endpapers, back cover, and 10 pp. at the back. The first edition was issued by Chapman & Hall, London, 1876, 18 cm., 268 pp., illustrated, 16/o, listed in the *Ath* on Dec. 25, 1875. It has a 32-page catalog (Dec. 1875) at the back. They issued it at 2/o boards, 2/6 cloth, listed in the *Ath* on May 5, 1877; and they issued it as No. 399 in the series, at 2/o boards, in the fall of

1879. The first American edition was issued by George Munro, New York, 1882, as *Seaside Library* No. 1350, 32.5 cm., 37 pp., $.20 paper, advertised in the *New-York Times* on Aug. 17, as a late issue, and listed in *PW* on Aug. 12.

Also 1901

2169 F. C. ARMSTRONG **The Medora.** 12mo. 2/o boards 1889?

Select Library of Fiction No. 642, new numbering. This is my copy, no date, 17.7 cm., 382 pp., without Melbourne in the imprint. It is in white pictorial boards, printed in red, blue, and black, with the series title on the spine, and the No. 642 on the front cover. There are ads on the endpapers and back cover. There is a date (July 12, 1889) on an endpaper ad. The first edition was issued by T. C. Newby, London, 3 vols., 1857, 19.5 cm., anonymous. It was issued by Henry Lea, London (1859), 382 pp., 2/o boards; and reissued at 2/o boards about July 9, 1864. C. H. Clarke, London, issued it (1863), a new edition, Fcp 8vo, 382 pp., 2/o boards, listed in the *Ath* on Apr. 18, 1863.

2170 HANS C. ANDERSEN **The Improvisatore.** A New and Carefully Corrected Edition. 12mo. 2/o boards 1889?

Select Library of Fiction No. 734, new numbering. This is my copy, no date, 17.8 cm., 340 pp. This is in the clothing of the *Library of Select Authors*, which series title appears on the spine. Melbourne appears in the imprint. It is in white pictorial boards, printed in red, blue, and black, with ads on the endpapers, back cover, and 6 pp. at the back. An endpaper ad has a date, 1889. It was translated by Mary Howitt and has a life of Andersen on pp. (vii)–xxxvii.

Also 1857, 63, 73

2171 HAWLEY SMART **Play or Pay.** New Edition. 12mo. 2/o boards 1889?

Library of Select Authors. Select Library of Fiction No. 172, new numbering. This is my copy, no date, 17.7 cm., 242 pp., with Melbourne in the imprint. It is in white pictorial boards, printed in red, green, blue, and black, with the series title at the foot of the spine, and with the No. 375 on the front cover. The cover picture is by Corbould, and there are ads on the endpapers, back cover, and 8 pp. at the back. An endpaper ad has a date, 1889.

Also 1886, 1903

2172 GEORGE J. WHYTE MELVILLE **Katerfelto.** New Edition. 12mo. 2/o boards 1889?

Library of Select Authors. Select Library of Fiction No. 126, new numbering. This is my copy, no date, 18 cm., 341 pp., with Melbourne in the imprint. It is in pale green pictorial boards, printed in orange, blue, and black, with the series title at the foot of the spine, and "The Works of Whyte Melville" at the head. It has ads on the endpapers, back cover, and 4 pp. at the back. One of the endpaper ads has a date, 1889. The first edition was issued by Chapman & Hall, London, 1875 (1874), 291 pp., illustrated, 16/o, listed in the *Ath* on Dec. 19, 1874. It has a 32-page catalog (Nov. 1874). The third edition was issued in 1875, Demy 8vo, illustrated, 16/o, listed in the *Spect* on Feb. 27. It was issued in 1875, 8vo, at 8/o, listed in the *Spect* on Oct. 30. It was reissued many times including the 15th thousand at 2/o boards, listed in the *Ath* on June 24, 1876; the 17th thousand, my copy, in 1878; and as No. 398 in the series in the fall of 1879. In the United States it was issued by Scribner, Welford, and Armstrong, New York, 1875, 8vo, with 12 illustrations, $1.50, listed in the *Nation* on Feb. 11. It was also issued by Porter & Coates, Philadelphia, 1875,

listed in *PW* on Mar. 20, and in the *Ind* on
Mar. 25.
Also 1900. See 1901

2173 SIR GILBERT CAMPBELL
Prince Goldenblade. 1/o sewed,
1/6 cloth   1889?
Youth's Library No. 105. The first edition
was issued by Ward, Lock, 1889, illustrated, 2/o, listed in the *Spect* on Dec. 18,
1889. It has 159 pp.

2174 ANONYMOUS *Arabian Nights'*
Entertainments. 1/o sewed   1889?
Shilling Novels No. 86.
Also 1863, 82. See 1886

2175 SIR GILBERT CAMPBELL *Wild and*
Weird. 1/o sewed   1889?
Shilling Novels No. 93. The first edition was
issued by Ward, Lock, 1889, 18.5 cm.,
with 162, 143, and 175 pp., at 5/o, containing Russian, English, and Italian tales.
The present edition contains the Russian
tales, 162 pp.

2176 SIR GILBERT CAMPBELL
Dark Stories from the Sunny South.
1/o sewed   1889 (*BM*)
Shilling Novels No. 94. This is 1889, with
175 pp., containing the Italian tales (see
the preceding items).

2177 SIR GILBERT CAMPBELL *Mysteries of*
the Unseen. 1/o sewed   1889 (*BM*)
Shilling Novels No. 95. This is 1889, with
143 pp., containing the English tales (see
the preceding items).

2178 F.C. ARMSTRONG *The Young*
Commander. 2/o boards   1889?
Select Library of Fiction No. 636, new numbering. This was Sadleir's copy, no date,
12mo. The *BM* gives an edition (1885)
from Ward, Lock. The first edition was issued by T.C. Newby, London, 3 vols.,
1856, 21 cm., anonymous. It was issued by
C. H. Clarke, London (1863), 12mo, at 2/o
boards in their *Standard Novels Library*, a
new edition, 371 pp., and issued about
Mar. 28. It was issued by George Routledge, London, 1873, in his *Railway Li-*
brary, at 2/o boards, about Sept. 29.

In an ad in the Spect *on Nov. 1, 1890, the address in the imprint was London, New York, and Melbourne.*

2179 (ADRIEN PAUL) *Willis the Pilot.*
Illustrated. 1/o sewed, 1/6 cloth   Jan.?
Youth's Library No. 101. This is (1890), 295 pp., translated by Henry Frith. The first edition was *Le Pilote Willis*, Tours, 2 vols., 1855, 18 cm., illustrated. The first English edition was issued by C. H. Clarke, London (1857), anonymous, 342 pp., illustrated, 3/6 cloth. They reissued it illustrated, at 2/o cloth, about Nov. 27, 1869; and illustrated, at 2/6 cloth, in 1882. The first American edition was issued by Mayhew & Baker, Boston, 1858 (1857), 17.8 cm., anonymous, 350 pp., illustrated, listed in *APC&LG* (weekly) on Dec. 4, 1857, and listed in the *Ind* on Dec. 24.

2180 EDWARD BELLAMY *Looking Backward, 2000–1887.* o/6 sewed, 1/6 cloth   Feb. 15 (*PC*)
Popular Sixpenny Books No. 244. This has no date, with 248 pp. The *BM* gives a third edition, issued by Ward, Lock, no date, 19 cm., 236 pp., but I've found no evidence of this. The first edition was issued by Ticknor & Co., Boston, 1888, 19 cm., 470 pp., at $1.50, listed in the *Ind* on Jan. 26, and in *PW* on Jan. 28. Houghton, Mifflin & Co., Boston, advertised it in the *New-York Times* on Sept. 22, 1889, the 12th thousand, from new plates, at $.50 paper

and $1.00 cloth. The first English edition was issued by William Reeves, London (1889), 256 pp., in light blue printed wrappers, listed in *PC* on Apr. 1. It was also issued by George Routledge, London, at 1/o sewed, 1/6 cloth, listed in *PC* on Feb. 1, 1890. He also issued it, 156 pp., at o/6 sewed, in Feb. 1890. Frederick Warne, London, also issued it (1890), 192 pp., at o/6 sewed, listed in *PC* on Feb. 15, 1890.

2181 EDWARD BELLAMY *Dr. Heidenhoff's Process.* o/6 sewed, 1/o cloth   Feb.?
Popular Sixpenny Books No. 245. The first edition was issued by D. Appleton & Co., New York, 1880, my copy 16.5 cm., 140 pp., $.25 paper, as *New Handy-Volume Series* No. 54, listed in the *Nation* on June 17, and in *PW* on June 19. The first British edition was issued by David Douglas, Edinburgh; etc., 1884, 19 cm., 234 pp., at 6/o, listed in the *Ath* on Feb. 16, and in *PC* on Feb. 15. It was also issued by George Routledge, London (1890), 96 pp., o/6 sewed, listed in *PC* on Feb. 15. Frederick Warne, London, also issued it (1890), 126 pp., o/6 sewed, listed in the *Bks* for Feb. It was also issued by William Reeves, London (1890), 139 pp., and a portrait, listed in *PC* on Feb. 15.

2182 ANONYMOUS *Kitchen and Flower Gardening for Pleasure and Profit.* Cr 8vo. Illustrated. 1/o boards   Mar. 29 (*Ath* ad)

This has 160 pp. and was advertised in the *Times Weekly Edition* (London) on Mar. 28, 1890.

Also 1892. See 1861, 81

2183 ANONYMOUS *Mrs. Beeton's Sixpenny Cookery Book for the People.* o/6 limp cover   Mar. 29 (*Ath* ad)

Also 1886

2184 ANONYMOUS *Beeton's Penny Cookery Book.* o/1 sewed   Mar. 29 (*Ath* ad)

The *U Cat* gives Ward, Lock & Tyler, no date (fifth edition), 14 cm., 64 pp., which would have been issued in the period 1865–77. A new edition was issued, 1908, 90 pp.

2185 EDWARD BELLAMY *Miss Ludington's Sister.* o/6 sewed, 1/o cloth   Mar.?

Popular Sixpenny Books No. 247. This has no date, 19 cm., 125 pp. The first edition was issued by James R. Osgood & Co., Boston, 1884, 17.5 cm., 260 pp., at $1.25, listed in *PW* on July 5, and in the *Ind* on July 3. The first British edition was issued by David Douglas, Edinburgh; etc., 1884, Cr 8vo, at 6/o, another copy of the American edition, with a different title page, listed in the *Ath* on Sept. 27. It was also issued by William Reeves, London, listed in *PC* on Mar. 15, 1890; and by Frederick Warne, London (1890), 123 pp., at o/6 sewed, listed in *PC* on Mar. 15.

2186 EDWARD BELLAMY *Six to One.* o/6 sewed, 1/o cloth   May?

Popular Sixpenny Books No. 251. This is 1890, 19 cm., 119 pp. The first edition was issued by G. P. Putnam's Sons, New York, 1878, 16mo, anonymous, 176 pp., $.40 paper, $.75 cloth, listed in the *Ind* on Aug. 1, and listed by *Lit World* as published in

July. Putnam issued a new edition, revised, 1890, 16mo, $.35 paper, listed in *PW* on Feb. 1, and advertised in the *New-York Times* on Feb. 11. The first English edition was issued by Sampson Low, London, 1878, anonymous, 126 pp., at 1/o sewed, 2/6 cloth, advertised in the *New-York Times* on Nov. 29, and in the *Spect* on Nov. 9 as "Now ready." They reissued it in 1879, at 1/o, listed by the *Bks* as published in July.

2187 MARION HARLAND (MARY V. HAWES, later TERHUNE) *Jessamine.* 1/o sewed, 1/6, 2/o cloth   May?

This is probably a reissue in the *Lily Series*. Also 1876

2188 RONALD M. SMITH *Stanley in Tropical Africa.* Illustrated. 1/o sewed, 1/6 cloth   May?

Youth's Library No. 106. This is the first edition, 1890, 18 cm., 196 pp. Ward, Lock issued the second edition and the third edition, 1890, 196 pp., illustrated.

2189 W. S. HAYWARD *Eulalie.* 1/o sewed June?

Shilling Novels No. 103. Also 1874

2190 JOHN W. KIRTON *Standard Humorous Dialogues.* o/6 sewed, 1/o, 1/6 cloth July (*Eng Cat*)

This is probably the first edition. It was in the spring 1906 Ward, Lock catalog at o/6 sewed, 1/o cloth, *Kirton's Standard Reciters* No. 10.

2191 WILLIAM M. THACKERAY *Vanity Fair.* 1/o   July?

Select Library of Fiction No. 926, new numbering, and the *Minerva Library* each contained this, the former at 2/o boards and the latter at 2/o cloth. It was also issued about this time as *Shilling Novels* No. 108, possibly the present edition. The first two at least had 565 pp. It was first issued by the *Punch* office, London, 20 parts in 19, printed by Bradbury & Evans, London. They ran from Jan. 1847 to July 1848, illustrated, at 1/0, in yellow wrappers. Parts 19 and 20 were advertised in the *Spect* on July 1, 1848, as "This day." Bradbury & Evans issued the first book edition, 1848, 22.5 cm., 624 pp., illustrated, advertised in the *Ath* on July 1 as "This day," and listed on July 22. They reissued it, 1853, 589 pp., at 6/0, advertised in the *Spect* on Jan. 28, 1854, as "This day." They reissued it in 1856, a new edition, p 8vo, 584 pp., at 6/0, listed by *PC* as published Aug. 15–30. The first American edition was issued by Harper & Bros., New York, 1848, 24 cm., 332 pp., illustrated, double columns, in purple cloth, having been previously issued in 2 parts. Part 2 and the complete edition were listed by *Lit World* as published Aug. 19–26, and it was reviewed in the *Knickerbocker* for Sept.

2192   MRS. K. F. HILL   *A Mysterious Case.*
o/6 sewed   Aug.?

Popular Sixpenny Books No. 253. This is the first English edition (1890), with 126 pp. The first edition was issued by Street & Smith, New York, 1889, 19.5 cm., 226 pp., frontispiece, *Secret Service Series* No. 23. Also 1903

2193   E. M. C. (ELVINA M. CORBOULD)
The Knitter's Note Book. 24mo.
Illustrated. 1/0 boards   Aug.?

Sylvia's Needlework Books No. 9. This is the first edition (1890), with 62 pp.

2194   FLAVIUS JOSEPHUS   *The Works of Flavius Josephus. Part 1.* o/6 sewed
Sept. 25

This was issued in 13 monthly o/6 parts, translated by Whiston, a reissue, part 1 advertised in the *Times Weekly Edition* (London) as "On Sept. 25." Ward, Lock issued it in 1878–79, 23 cm., 858 pp., illustrated, and it was listed in the *Spect* on Feb. 17, 1883, Cr 8vo, 3/6, as issued by Ward, Lock. The first edition of the Whiston translation was issued by J. Cundell, London, 2 vols., 1806, a new edition. Bell & Sons, London, issued the Whiston translation in 2 vols., 1889, 12mo, at 3/6 each; and Nelson, London, issued the same, 1881, 8vo, with 36 illustrations, at 4/0.

2195   EDWARD GIBBON   *The History of the Decline and Fall of the Roman Empire. Part 1.* o/6 sewed   Sept. 25

This was issued in monthly parts, part 1 advertised as in the previous item, unabridged and carefully revised.
Also 1882

2196   EDWIN DAVIES, ed.   *Great Thoughts on Great Truths. Part 1.* o/6 sewed
Sept. 25

This is a reissue in 12 monthly o/6 parts, part 1 advertised as in the previous two items. Ward, Lock first issued this in 1882–83, in parts, with 727 pp.

2197   ANONYMOUS   *Housewife's Treasury of Domestic Information. Part 1.*
Illustrated. o/6 sewed   Sept. 25

This is a reissue in 13 monthly o/6 parts. Part 1 was advertised as in the preceding items. Ward, Lock first issued it in 1883, p 8vo, 1,056 pp., at 7/6.

2198   LAWRENCE L. LYNCH (EMMA MURDOCH, later VAN DEVENTER)
The Lost Witness. o/6 sewed
Sept. (*Eng Cat*)

Popular Sixpenny Books No. 260. This is the first English edition (1890), 192 pp., in pictorial wrappers, printed in red, blue, and black, with an ad on the back cover. The first edition was issued by Laird & Lee, Chicago, 1890, 19.5 cm., 557 pp., *Library of Choice Fiction* No. 1, listed in *PW* on June 28.

2199 (MARIETTA E. HOLLEY)
Sweet Cicely. p 8vo. Illustrated.
2/o boards, 2/6 cloth   Oct. 25 (*Ath*)

Select Library of Fiction No. 896, new numbering. This is my copy, no date, with Melbourne in the imprint, 18.7 cm., 381 pp., with a frontispiece (portrait) and many illustrations. It is in yellow pictorial boards, printed in red, green, and black, with the No. 896 on the front cover. The author is given as "Josiah Allen's Wife," and it has a pictorial spine with no series title, which I suspect was used for all the forthcoming Holley titles. There are ads on the back cover, on the endpapers, and in a 24-page catalog at the back. It was reviewed in the *Ath* on Jan. 10, 1891, and the *BM* gives Ward, Lock, 1891, 381 pp. The first edition was issued by Funk & Wagnalls, New York, etc., 1885, 20 cm., anonymous, 381 pp., illustrated, $2.00, listed in the *Nation* on Dec. 3, and in *Lit World* and in *PW* on Dec. 12.

2200 ANONYMOUS ***Our National Cathedrals. Part 1.*** Illustrated. 1/o sewed
Oct. 31

This was a reissue in 27 monthly parts, part 1 being advertised in the *Times Weekly Edition* (London) on Oct. 31 as "Now ready." The first edition was issued by Ward, Lock, in 3 vols., 1887–89, 24.5 cm., with colored plates and frontispieces, having first been issued serially. Part 1 was advertised in the *Spect* on Oct. 23, 1886, as "On Oct. 26," and vol. 1 was advertised on Nov. 5, 1887, at 10/6, as "Just ready." Three vols. were advertised at 31/6 on Oct. 27, 1888.

2201 ANONYMOUS ***Ward & Lock's Technical Dictionary. Part 1.*** Illustrated. 0/3 sewed   Oct. 31

This is probably the first issue, in 10 monthly 0/3 parts. Part 1 was advertised in the *Times Weekly Edition* (London) on Oct. 31 as "Now ready." I cannot trace it.

2202 HENRY W. DULCKEN, ed. ***Worthies of the World. Part 1.*** Portraits. 0/6 sewed
Oct. 31

This was issued in about 14 monthly 0/6 parts. Part 1 was advertised in the *Times Weekly Edition* (London) on Oct. 31 as "Now ready." It was first issued by Ward, Lock, first in serial form and then in 1 vol. Part 1 at 0/6 sewed was advertised in the *Spect* on Oct. 23, 1880, as "On Oct. 25"; and it was advertised in 1 vol., on Oct. 1, 1881, Roy 8vo, portraits, 7/6, for the fall 1881 issue.

2203 GEORGE BLACK, ed. ***Household Medicine. Part 1.*** Illustrated. 0/6 sewed
Nov. 28

This is a reissue in 15 monthly 0/6 parts. Part 1 was advertised in the *Times Weekly Edition* (London) on Nov. 28 as "Now ready." It was issued in 1 vol., advertised in the *Spect* on Dec. 13, 1890, Roy 8vo, illustrated, 10/6. The first edition was issued serially by Ward, Lock in 1881, 1882, and in 1 vol. in 1882, Roy 8vo, 828 pp., at 7/6, listed in the *Spect* on Oct. 14. It was reissued, 1897.

2204 SIR GILBERT CAMPBELL
The Vanishing Diamond. 0/6 sewed
Dec.?

Popular Sixpenny Books No. 261. I suspect that this was probably issued in Nov. as Beeton's Christmas Annual at 1/o sewed. The *BM* gives only (1891), with 141 pp.

2205 FRANCES E. & ALICE M. CALLOW
Home Theatricals Made Easy. Illustrated. 0/6 sewed   Dec.?

Popular Sixpenny Books No. 262. The first edition was issued by T. H. Roberts & Co., London, 1881, 4to, 84 pp. The present issue is a reissue with no date. The *BM* gives the present edition as 4to, but I suspect that it is Demy 8vo, as are all the books in this series.

2206 DOUGLAS W. JERROLD *Mrs. Caudle's Curtain Lectures.* o/6 sewed 1890?

Popular Sixpenny Books No. 252. The first edition was issued by the *Punch* office, London, 1846, 17.5 cm., 142 pp., illustrated by Leech, 2/6 sewed, edited (or rather written) by Jerrold. It was reprinted from *Punch* and was listed in the *Ath* on Dec. 20, 1845. A new edition was issued with the same imprint, with 1 illustration by Leech, 2/6, advertised in the *Spect* on May 23, 1846, as "Just ready." Bradbury & Evans, London, issued a new edition, 12mo, 93 pp., 1/0 sewed, listed by *PC* as published Sept. 30–Oct. 14, 1856. In the United States it was issued by J. Winchester, New York, 1845, 22 cm., anonymous, 26 pp., probably containing the first 10 lectures. He also issued it, 1845, 22 cm., 48 pp., probably containing all 15 lectures. It was also issued by W. Taylor, New York, 1845, 8vo, anonymous, 26 pp.; and by Carey & Hart, Philadelphia, 1845, 18.5 cm., anonymous, 42 pp., illustrated, containing the first 10 lectures only, and listed in the *Knickerbocker* for July 1845.

2207 ANONYMOUS *Leah, the Jewish Maiden.* 12mo. 2/0 boards 1890?

Select Library of Fiction No. 788, new numbering. This is my copy, no date, without Melbourne in the imprint, 17.9 cm., 316 pp., in white pictorial boards, printed in red, blue, and black, with the series title on the spine. There are ads on the endpapers, back cover, and in a 16-page catalog at the back.
Also 1864, 70, 73

2208 W. M. L. JAY (JULIA L. M. WOODRUFF) *Holden with the Cords.* 1/0 sewed, 1/6 cloth 1890

Lily Series No. 137. This was also issued in the *Good Tone Library* at 2/6 cloth, which the *BM* gives as (1883).
Also 1877

2209 PANSY (ISABELLA M. ALDEN) *Wise and Otherwise.* 1/0 sewed, 1/6 cloth 1890 (*BM*)

Lily Series No. 138. This is (1890), with 275 pp. The first edition was issued by the Western Tract Society, Cincinnati, 1873, 19 cm., 388 pp., illustrated. D. Lothrop & Co., Boston, issued it, 1874, the same. In England it was issued by George Routledge, London; and by Partridge & Co., London, from 1887–89, the former with 414 pp., and the latter with 320 pp. Ward, Lock also issued it in the *Pansy Series*, Cr 8vo, at 1/0 cloth.

2210 PANSY *The King's Daughter.* 1/0 sewed, 1/6 cloth 1890 (*BM*)

Lily Series No. 139. This has no date and 247 pp. It was also issued in the *Pansy Series* by Ward, Lock, about the same time, Cr 8vo, at 1/0 cloth. The first edition was issued by D. Lothrop & Co., Boston, 1873, 19 cm., 305 pp., with a frontispiece. Partridge, London, issued it with 319 pp., probably in 1888; and George Routledge, London, issued it with 310 pp., probably in 1889 or 1890. The first British edition was issued by J. Gemmell, Edinburgh, in 1883 or 1884, at 1/6, probably with Simpkin, Marshall, London.

2211 PANSY *A New Graft on the Family Tree.* 1/0 sewed, 1/6 cloth 1890 (*BM*)

Lily Series No. 141. This was also issued in the *Pansy Series*, probably about 1890, Cr 8vo, 1/0 cloth. The first edition was issued by D. Lothrop & Co., Boston, unknown date, 19 cm., 476 pp., illustrated. The first English edition was issued by T. Nelson & Sons, London, 1887 (1886), 275 pp., 2/0. George Routledge, London, issued it, 1889, 331 pp.

2212 SUSAN WARNER *Hope and Rest.* 1/0 sewed, 1/6 cloth 1890 (*BM*)

Lily Series No. 142. This is (1890), 437 pp., deposited at the *BM* on Sept. 5, 1890. The first American edition was *The Hills of the Shatemuc*, issued by D. Appleton & Co., New York, 1856, 19.5 cm., anonymous, 516 pp., and 8 pp. of ads. It was issued in various colors of cloth and with various colors of endpapers. The Boston Athenaeum copy was received on Sept. 28, 1856, and it was advertised in the *New York Daily Times* on Sept. 19, at $1.25 cloth and, with illustrations, $1.50 cloth, as "Tomorrow." A new edition was advertised there on Oct. 8 as "Now ready." The first English edition was issued by Sampson Low, London; Thomas Constable & Co., Edinburgh, 1856, anonymous, 514 pp., in 12mo at 2/6 boards, and p 8vo at 6/0, an authorized edition, listed in the *Ath* on Aug. 23. Low editions at 1/6 boards, 2/6 boards, 3/0 cloth, and 6/0 cloth were listed by *PC* as published Sept. 15–30, 1856. Low advertised in the *Ath* on Nov. 22, 1856, a 1/6 boards issue, Fcp 8vo, with a frontispiece; a 2/6 boards edition, illustrated; a 3/0 cloth edition, illustrated; and a 6/0 cloth edition, p 8vo, illustrated. These all had the American title. It was also issued by George Routledge, London, at 1/6 boards, listed in the *Spect* on Oct. 4, 1856, and by *PC* as published Sept. 15–30. He issued it in 1874, about June 13, at 1/0 sewed, 1/6, 2/0 cloth. Both of these had the American title. He issued it in 1877, at 1/0 sewed, 1/6 cloth, about Sept. 1, as *Hope's Little Hand*. It was issued by C. H. Clarke, London, at 1/0 boards, advertised and listed in the *Ath* on Sept. 20, 1856, and listed by *PC* as published Sept. 15–30. It had the American title. It was also issued in the *Run and Read Library* by Simpkin, Marshall, London; Burton, Ipswitch, in 1857, 17.5 cm., 514 pp., at 1/6 boards, in green paper boards, with the series title on the spine and front. It was entitled *Rufus and Winthrop*, deposited on June 17, and listed by *PC* on June 1. It has a frontispiece, a vignette title page, and illustrations. It was reissued as *The Hills of*

the *Shatemuc*, 420 pp., 1/0 boards, listed in *PC* on Nov. 1, 1857.

2213 EDWARD P. ROE *A Young Girl's Wooing.* 1/0 sewed, 1/6 cloth 1890 (*BM*)
Lily Series No. 143. *Shilling Novels* No. 101. This is (1890), with 320 pp. The first American edition was issued by Dodd, Mead & Co., New York (copyright 1884), 19 cm., 482 pp., $1.50 cloth, bound in terra-cotta, green, or gray cloth, with yellow endpapers. It has 2 pp. of ads and was advertised in the *New-York Times* on Oct. 11, 1884, 25,000 copies, "This day"; and advertised in *PW* on Oct. 11 as "On Oct. 11," and listed on Oct. 18. The first English edition was issued by Frederick Warne, London (1884), Cr 8vo, 408 pp., 6/0, advertised as "Now ready," and listed in the *Ath* on Oct. 25. They reissued it at 1/0 sewed, 1/6 cloth, listed by the *Bks* as published in Jan. 1886.

2214 EDWARD P. ROE *Taken Alive, and Other Stories.* 1/0 sewed, 1/6 cloth 1890 (*BM*)
Lily Series No. 144. This was also issued as or designated as *Shilling Novels* No. 102. It is 1890, with 191 pp. The first American edition was issued by Dodd, Mead & Co., New York (1889), 20 cm., 375 pp., with a portrait, $1.50 cloth. It contains *Found Yet Lost, The Queen of Spades, An Unexpected Result,* and an autobiography. It was listed in *PW* on Nov. 2 and advertised on Oct. 26 as "Just issued." *BAL* had not seen and had not located a copy! The first edition was issued by Frederick Warne, London, 1886, at 0/6 sewed, with the American title, listed in *PC* on Feb. 15. *The Queen of Spades and Other Stories,* with the autobiography, was issued by Warne at 1/0 sewed, 1/6 cloth, listed in the *Spect* on Sept. 22, 1888, and in *PC* on Oct. 15. For *Found Yet Lost* see Ward, Lock (1888), and for *An Unexpected Result* see Ward, Lock (1888). This latter title was also issued by George Routledge, London, about June 1, 1883, with 128 pp.

The Queen of Spades with the autobiography was in *Lippincott's Magazine* in 1888.

2215 G. T. BETTANY **The Red, Brown, and Black Men of America and Australia.** p 8vo. Illustrated. Maps. 1/o sewed, 1/6 cloth 1890 (*BM*)

Youth's Library No. 108. This was book No. 4 of *The World's Inhabitants*, 1890, 18.5 cm., 289 pp., with the series title on the cover. The first edition of the latter title was issued by Ward, Lock, 1889, 25 cm., 949 pp., illustrated, 7/6, advertised in the *Spect* on Oct. 27, 1888. It was issued in parts, o/6 monthly, for 12 months, illustrated, with part 1 advertised in the *Times Weekly Edition* (London) on Oct. 28, 1887, as "Now ready." The present title was issued by Ward, Lock & Co., New York, at $1.00 cloth, listed in *Literary Digest* for Nov. 22, 1890.

2216 G. T. BETTANY **The Dark Peoples of the Land of Sunshine.** p 8vo. Illustrated. 1/o sewed, 1/6 cloth 1890 (*BM*)

Youth's Library No. 109. This was book No. 3 of *The World's Inhabitants* (see the preceding title). It is 1890, with 221 pp. It was issued by Ward, Lock & Co., New York, 12mo, illustrated, $1.00 cloth, listed in the *Literary Digest* on Nov. 22, 1890.

J. S. C. ABBOTT *Youth's Library.* 5 vols. Illustrated. 1/o sewed, 1/6 cloth each 1890?

These are reissues of *Heroes, Patriots, and Pioneers* of 1879.

2217 **No. 103. The Life and Achievements of Christopher Columbus.** Also 1879, 82

2218 **No. 104. The Puritan Captain.** Also 1879

2219 **No. 107. George Washington.** Also 1879

2220 **No. 115. Benjamin Franklin.** Also 1879

2221 **No. 116. Prince of Pioneers.** (Daniel Boone). See *Boone, the Backwoodsman,* 1879.

2222 F. C. ARMSTRONG **The Two Midshipmen.** 1/o sewed 1890?

Shilling Novels No. 104. The first edition was issued by T. C. Newby, London, in 1854. Routledge, London, issued it in his *Railway Library* at 2/o boards, about Nov. 2, 1867; and reissued it at 2/o boards in Apr. 1877.

2223 F. C. ARMSTRONG **The Cruise of the Daring.** 1/o sewed 1890?

Shilling Novels No. 105.

Also 1863, 73

2224 F. C. ARMSTRONG **The Sunny South.** 1/o sewed 1890?

Shilling Novels No. 106.

Also 1866, 80

2225 F. C. ARMSTRONG **The Queen of the Seas.** 1/o sewed 1890?

Shilling Novels No. 107. The first edition was issued by T. C. Newby, London, 3 vols., 1864, 20.5 cm., at 31/6, listed in the *Reader* on Oct. 1. It was issued by Chapman & Hall, London, 1866, *Select Library of Fiction* No. 81, at 2/o boards, about May 26; and reissued, the third edition, 1867, 373 pp., at 2/o boards. It was issued in the United States by the American News Co., New York, listed in *ALG&PC* (fortnightly) on Jan. 15, 1867.

2226 W. H. THOMAS **A Gold-Hunter's Adventures.** 1/o sewed 1890?

Shilling Novels No. 109.

Also 1885

Ward, Lock, Bowden & Co.
London, New York, and Melbourne
1891

By Sept. 1891, an office was opened in Sydney, Australia. George Locke, one of the founders of the firm, died in 1891, reported in the Ath on Aug. 15. The style of the firm was changed to Ward, Lock, Bowden & Co. on July 27, 1891. James Bowden came to work for the company in 1869 and began to share in the profits in 1879, eventually becoming a managing partner. The new copyright law, preventing piracies in England and the United States, took effect in 1891. The first book in the United States to be entered under the new law was The Faith Doctor *by Edward Eggleston, issued by Appleton & Co., New York, 12mo, at $1.50, listed in the* Christian Union *on Oct. 17, 1891.*

2227 MARIETTA E. HOLLEY *My Opinions and Betsy Bobbet's.* Illustrated. 2/o boards, 2/6 cloth   Jan. 17 (*PC*)

Select Library of Fiction No. 898, new numbering. This is (1891), with 482 pp. The first edition was issued by the American Publishing Co., Hartford; etc., 1873, 20.5 cm., 432 pp., illustrated, by Josiah Allen's Wife. The first English edition was issued by George Routledge, London (1873), 250 pp., 1/o sewed, containing also *A Lady's Life Among the Mormons* by Mrs. Stenhouse. It was listed in the *Ath* on Aug. 16.

2228 GASTON TISSANDIER *Half Hours of Scientific Amusement; or Practical Physics and Chemistry Without Apparatus.* Illustrated. 1/o sewed, 1/6 cloth   Feb. 7 (*PC*)

Youth's Library No. 105? This is from *Les Récréations Scientifiques*, Paris, 1881, with 341 pp., 222 pp., translated by Henry Frith. Ward, Lock issued it, 1890, 19 cm., 141 pp., with *Scientific Recreation Series* on the cover.

2229 (MARIETTA E. HOLLEY) *Samantha Among the Brethren.* Illustrated. 2/o boards, 2/6 cloth   Feb. 14 (*Ath*)

Select Library of Fiction No. 895, new numbering. The first edition was issued by Funk & Wagnalls, New York, etc., 1890, 20 cm., 437 pp., illustrated, by Josiah Allen's Wife. It is in red cloth and has a publisher's appendix on pp. (389)–437, listed in *Public Opinion* on Nov. 15, in *PW* on Dec. 6, and in *Lit World* (fortnightly) on Dec. 20. The first English edition was issued by Ward, Lock in 1890, 387 pp., at 5/o cloth, by Josiah Allen's Wife, listed in The *Spect* on Nov. 15.

2230 HAY FORBES *A Detective in Italy.* o/6 sewed   Feb. 21 (*PC*)

Popular Sixpenny Books No. 263. This has 144 pp. and probably has no date. An ad in the *Ath* on May 16, 1891, said "Just ready."

2231 LAWRENCE L. LYNCH (EMMA MURDOCH, later VAN DEVENTER) *Moina.* [Third edition]. 2/o boards   Mar. 14 (*Ath*)

Select Library of Fiction No. 848, new numbering. This is 1891, 459 pp., with a 12-

page catalog. The first edition was issued by Ward, Lock, 1891, Cr 8vo, 459 pp., 2/6 cloth, listed in the *Ath* on Feb. 21, and in *PC* on Jan. 10 and Feb. 28. The first American edition was issued by Laird & Lee, Chicago, 1891, 20 cm., 520 pp., illustrated, *Library of Choice Fiction* No. 20. It was listed in the *Nation* on July 2 and in *PW* on July 4.
Also 1892, 1903

2232 MARIETTA E. HOLLEY *Josiah Allen's Wife.* Illustrated. 2/0 boards, 2/6 cloth
Mar. 21 (*Ath*)
Select Library of Fiction No. 897, new numbering. This is 1891, 578 pp., probably the first English edition. The first edition was issued by the American Publishing Co., Hartford, 1877, 20.5 cm., anonymous, 580 pp., illustrated. It was listed in *PW* on Feb. 2, 1878, thus causing a question as to the 1877 date on the title page (given by both Wright and by the *U Cat*). The *BM* gives 1878.

2233 JOHN W. KIRTON, ed. *The Standard Little Folks' Reciter.* 0/6 sewed, 1/0, 1/6 cloth Mar.?
This is the first edition (1891), with 244 pp. It was in the spring 1906, Ward, Lock catalog as *Kirton's Standard Reciters* No. 11, Cr 8vo, 0/6 sewed, 1/0 cloth.

2234 B. L. FARJEON *The Nine of Hearts.*
0/6 sewed Apr. 14 (*PC*)
Popular Sixpenny Books No. 264.
Also 1886

2235 MARIETTA E. HOLLEY *My Wayward Partner.* Illustrated. 2/0 boards, 2/6 cloth
Apr. 25 (*Ath*)
Select Library of Fiction No. 899, new numbering. This is the first English edition (1891), with 490 pp. The first edition was issued by the American Publishing Co., Hartford, 1880, 20.5 cm., 490 pp., by Josiah Allen's Wife. It was advertised in the

Ind on Jan. 6, 1881. The first Canadian edition was issued by Rose-Belford, Toronto, 1881, 294 pp., in cloth.

2236 GEORGE P. MERRICK *Work Among the Fallen.* Cr 8vo. 1/0 leatherette
May 2 (*PC*)
This is the first edition (1891), 19 cm., 62 pp., and an introduction by F. W. Farrar.

2237 CHAUNCEY THOMAS *The Crystal Button.* 0/6 sewed May 16 (*PC*)
Popular Sixpenny Books No. 267. This is (1891), with 147 pp. The first edition was issued by Houghton, Mifflin & Co., Boston and New York, 1891, 18 cm., 302 pp., $1.25, edited by George Houghton. It was listed in the *Ind* on Feb. 5 and in *PW* on Feb. 7. It was advertised in the *New-York Times* on Jan. 25. The first English edition was issued by George Routledge, London, 1891, 160 pp., 0/6 sewed, listed in *PC* on Apr. 4.

2238 MARION HARLAND (MARY HAWES, later TERHUNE) *Mark Hale, Shoemaker.*
1/0 sewed, 1/6 cloth May 16 (*Ath*)
Lily Series No. 157. I cannot trace this.

2239 ADELINE D. T. WHITNEY *Ascutney Street.* 1/0 sewed, 1/6 cloth May 23 (*PC*)
Lily Series No. 156. The first edition was issued by Houghton, Mifflin & Co., Boston, 1890, 19 cm., 259 pp., $1.50, listed in *Public Opinion* on Oct. 4 and in *PW* on Oct. 11. The first English edition was issued by Ward, Lock, 1890, 259 pp., 5/0, printed in Cambridge, Mass., and listed in the *Ath* on Nov. 8.

2240 PANSY (ISABELLA M. ALDEN) *The Hall in the Grove.* 1/0 sewed, 1/6 cloth June 13 (*PC*)
Lily Series No. 140. This has no date and 429 pp. It was later put in the *Pansy Series*, Cr 8vo, at 1/0 cloth. The first edition was issued by D. Lothrop & Co., Boston

(1882), 431 pp., illustrated, listed in the *Literary News* (monthly) for Mar. 1882.

2241 PANSY (ISABELLA M. ALDEN)
Interrupted. 1/0 sewed, 1/6 cloth
June 20 (*PC*)

Lily Series No. 145. This is (1891), with 443 pp. It was later placed in the *Pansy Series*, Cr 8vo, at 1/0 cloth. The first edition was issued by D. Lothrop & Co., Boston (1885), 19 cm., 443 pp., with a frontispiece, $1.50 cloth. It was listed in the *Ind* on Mar. 5. The first English edition was issued by Hodder & Stoughton, London, 1886, p 8vo, 443 pp., at 5/0 cloth.

2242 SIR GILBERT CAMPBELL ***The Great Grub Street Conspiracy.*** [Third edition]. 8vo. 0/6 sewed   June 27 (*PC*)

Popular Sixpenny Books No. 265. This is given by the *Eng Cat*, but otherwise I cannot trace it.

2243 EDMUND BOISGILBERT (IGNATIUS DONNELLY) ***Caesar's Column.*** 0/6 sewed
June 27 (*PC*)

Popular Sixpenny Books No. 270. This is (1891), with 242 pp. The first edition was issued by F. J. Schulte & Co., Chicago (1890), 20.5 cm., 367 pp., listed in *PW* on Apr. 12, and in the *Ind* on Apr. 17. The present edition is the first English edition. It was also issued by Sampson Low, London, 1891, authorized edition, by Donnelly, 367 pp., 3/6 cloth, listed in the *Spect* on July 4, and in the *Ath* on July 11. It was also issued by Frederick Warne, London, 1891, 19 cm., 216 pp., at 0/6 sewed, listed in *PC* on July 4.

2244 HENRY KINGSLEY ***The Recollections of Geoffrey Hamlyn.*** 1/0   July 11 (*PC*)

I think this was probably a *Shilling Novel* at 1/0 sewed. I have not discovered that numbers were assigned to the very few remaining titles in this series. The first edition was issued by Macmillan & Co., Cambridge and London, 3 vols., 1859, 19.5 cm., at 31/6, with a 24-page catalog (Apr. 15, 1859). It was advertised in the *Ath* on Apr. 16 as "Next week" and listed Apr. 23. They issued the second edition at 6/0, advertised in the *Spect* on June 16, 1860. Chapman & Hall issued it as *Select Library of Fiction* No. 195, the third edition, at 2/0 boards, with a printer's date (Feb. 3, 1872), listed in the *Ath* on Mar. 9, 1872. They issued it at 3/0 cloth in Nov. 1872. The first American edition was issued by Ticknor & Fields, Boston, 1859, 19 cm., 525 pp., at $1.25, listed in the *Ind* on June 2 and in *APC&LG* on June 4.
Also 1900

2245 HAWLEY SMART ***From Post to Finish.***
1/0   July 11 (*PC*)

This is probably in the *Shilling Novels Series*.
Also 1885, 99, 1904

2246 HAWLEY SMART ***Saddle and Sabre.***
1/0   July 11 (*PC*)

This is probably in the *Shilling Novels Series*.
Also 1888, 1901

2247 HAWLEY SMART ***A False Start.***
1/0   July 11 (*PC*)

This is probably in the *Shilling Novels Series*.
Also 1888, 1902

2248 THOMAS COBB ***The House by the Common.*** 0/6 sewed   July 18 (*PC*)

Popular Sixpenny Books No. 266. This is probably the first edition. The *BM* gives only Ward, Lock, 1891, 98 pp., illustrated.

2249 E. CURTIS ***Dr. Malchi.*** 0/6 sewed
Aug. 1 (*PC*)

Popular Sixpenny Books No. 269. This is the first edition (1891), 20 cm., 148 pp.

2250 ISABELLA M. BEETON *Mrs. Beeton's Household Management. Part 1.*
Illustrated. o/6 sewed   Sept. 25

This is a reissue in 13 monthly o/6 parts, revised, with colored plates, advertised in the *Times Weekly Edition* on Sept. 25, part 1, "Now ready." This was first issued in 24 parts in tan printed wrappers, by S. O. Beeton, London, 18.5 cm., 1,112 total pp., with partly colored illustrations. The parts were issued during 1859–61; and it was issued in 1 vol., 1861. He reissued it, the same, 1863. Ward, Lock & Tyler issued it in 1868 or 1869, a new edition, revised and corrected, 19 cm., 1,139 pp., partly colored illustrations. They reissued it in 1879–80 in parts; and in 1 vol. in 1880, 1,296 pp., 7/6. They reissued it in 1888, Cr 8vo, 1,644 pp., 7/6, colored plates. The present parts issue led to a 1 vol. issue in 1892, with a total of 1,644 pp. They issued a large paper edition, Roy 8vo, at 21/0, in Jan. 1893. They continued to reissue it up through 1950 at least.

2251 ANONYMOUS *The Child's Instructor. Part 1.* Illustrated. o/6 sewed   Sept. 25

This is a reissue in 13 monthly o/6 parts. Part 1 was advertised in the *Times Weekly Edition* on Sept. 25 as "Now ready." It was first issued in parts in 1882, 1883, with a total of 622 pp., illustrated. The first book edition was then issued (1883), 25 cm., with tables, maps, music, and portraits, at 7/6. This edition was also issued by Ward, Lock in New York, no date, probably around 1884.

2252 PANSY (ISABELLA M. ALDEN) *One Commonplace Day.* 1/0 sewed, 1/6 cloth   Sept.?

Lily Series No. 158. This was also placed in the *Pansy Series*, Cr 8vo, at 1/0 cloth. The first edition was issued by D. Lothrop & Co., Boston (1885), 18.5 cm., 513 pp., listed in the *Ind* on Sept. 17. The first English edition was issued by Hodder & Stoughton, London, 1886, as *The Master Hand*, p 8vo, 513 pp., at 5/0.

2253 SIR GILBERT CAMPBELL *New Detective Stories.* o/6 sewed   Oct. 3 (*PC*)

Popular Sixpenny Books No. 271. This is the first edition (1891), with 116 pp.

2254 ANONYMOUS *Joe Miller's Jest Book.* o/6 sewed   Oct.?

Popular Sixpenny Books No. 272.
Also 1856, 72

2255 JOHN HABBERTON *Other People's Children.* o/6 sewed   Oct.?

Popular Sixpenny Books No. 273.
Also 1877

2256 THOMAS P. O'CONNOR *Charles Stewart Parnell.* 12mo.
Frontispiece (portrait).
1/0 sewed, 2/0 cloth   Oct. 24 (*Spect*)

This is the first edition (1891), 223 pp., advertised in the *Times Weekly Edition* on Oct. 23 as ready.

2257 PANSY (ISABELLA M. ALDEN) *Chrissy's Endeavor.* 1/0 sewed, 1/6 cloth   Oct. 31 (*PC*)

Lily Series No. 160. This was also issued in the *Pansy Series*, Cr 8vo, at 1/0 cloth. The first edition was issued by D. Lothrop & Co., Boston (1889), 19 cm., 374 pp., with a frontispiece, advertised in the *Ind* on July 11 as "New books," and listed in *Literary News* (monthly) for Sept. The first British edition was issued by Oliphant, Anderson & Ferrier, Edinburgh and London (1890), Cr 8vo, 374 pp., at 1/0, 2/0, listed in the *Ath* on Mar. 8.

2258 CHARLOTTE BRONTË *Shirley.* o/6 sewed   Nov. 28 (*PC*)

Popular Sixpenny Books No. 276. This was also issued in the *Minerva Library*, 1891, 557 pp., illustrated, 2/0 cloth, listed in the

Spect on Nov. 7. It was also issued as *Select Library of Fiction* No. 1082, new numbering, at 2/0 boards, 2/6 cloth, probably about this time. The first edition was issued by Smith, Elder & Co., London, 3 vols., 1849, 21 cm., at 31/6, by Currer Bell. It has a catalog (Oct. 1849) at the back of vol. 1 and was advertised in the *Ath* on Oct. 20 as "On Oct. 31," and listed on Nov. 3. It was advertised in the *Spect* on Oct. 27 as "Now ready." They issued a new edition, Cr 8vo, at 6/0, listed in the *Spect* on Nov. 27, 1852; and issued a new edition, 1853, with 580 pp. There were many reissues, all with 534 pp. The first American edition was issued by Harper & Bros., New York, 1850, 206 pp., in buff printed wrappers, as *Library of Select Novels* No. 132, advertised in *Lit World* on Nov. 24, 1849, as "Just published."

2259 SIR GILBERT CAMPBELL
The Romance of the Ruby, etc.
Illustrated. 1/0 sewed   Dec. 19 (*PC*)
This is Beeton's Christmas Annual. It was also issued as *Popular Sixpenny Books* No. 286, probably in 1892. *A Ruby Beyond Price* was issued by the Minerva Publishing Co., New York (copyright 1891), 18.5 cm., 219 pp.

2260 MARY C. LEE **In the Cheering-Up Business.** Illustrated. 1/0 sewed, 1/6 cloth Dec.?
Lily Series No. 162. This is the first English edition, 1891, 322 pp. The first edition was issued by Houghton, Mifflin, Boston and New York, 1891, 18 cm., 322 pp., at $1.25, listed in *PW* on Feb. 21, and in the *Nation* and the *Ind* on Feb. 26.

2261 CECIL M. NORRIS **"Never Say Die!"**
Illustrated. 1/0 sewed, 1/6 cloth   Jan. 2, 1892 (*PC*)
Youth's Library No. 111. This is the first edition, 1891, with 153 pp.

2262 AMELIA B. EDWARDS **In the Days of My Youth.** 12mo. 2/0 boards   1891?
Library of Select Authors. Select Library of Fiction No. 398, new numbering. This is my copy, with the Ward, Lock, Bowden & Co. imprint, no date, 17.9 cm., 392 pp., in pale green pictorial boards, printed in red, green, and black, with the series title at the foot of the spine. There are ads on the back cover, the endpapers, and 2 pp. at the back. One of the endpapers has a date in an ad (Mar. 26, 1891). The first edition was issued by Hurst & Blackett, London, 3 vols., 1873, 31/6, listed in the *Ath* on Jan. 4, 1873. It was advertised in *Notes & Queries* on Dec. 21, 1872, as "Just ready." Chapman & Hall, London, issued it in the series as No. 272, at 2/0 boards, listed in the *Ath* on June 12, 1875. The first American edition was issued by Porter & Coates, Philadelphia, 1874, 19 cm., 454 pp., in the *International Series*, listed in the *Nation* and the *Ind* on Jan. 22, 1874.

2263 JAMES GRANT **The Secret Dispatch.**
12mo. 2/0 boards   1891? *See color photo section*
Library of Select Authors. Select Library of Fiction No. 428, new numbering. This is my copy, with the Ward, Lock & Co. imprint, no date, 18 cm., 250 pp., clothed in yellow pictorial boards, printed in red, blue, and black, with the series title at the foot of the spine. There are ads on the back cover and the endpapers, an ad in one of the latter having a date (Mar. 26, 1891). The first edition was issued by Virtue, London, 1869, p 8vo, at 10/6, advertised in the *Ath* on June 23 as "This day." Chapman & Hall, London, issued it in the series as No. 159, a new edition, 250 pp., 2/0 boards, listed in the *Spect* on Sept. 4, 1869; and they reissued it in 1872 and in 1874.

2264 PANSY (ISABELLA M. ALDEN)
The Man of the House. 1/0 sewed, 1/6 cloth   1891 (*BM*)
Lily Series No. 146. This is (1891), with 310 pp. It was also issued in the *Pansy Series*, Cr

8vo, at 1/o cloth. The first edition was is-
sued by D. Lothrop & Co., Boston (1883),
18 cm., 514 pp., illustrated, listed in the
Christian Union on Mar. 8, 1883. The first
English edition was issued by George
Routledge, London, 1887, 310 pp.

2265 PANSY (ISABELLA M. ALDEN)
The Pocket Measure. 1/o sewed,
1/6 cloth   1891 (*BM*)

Lily Series No. 147. This is (1891), with 376
pp. It was also issued in the *Pansy Series*, Cr
8vo, at 1/o cloth. The first edition was issued by D. Lothrop & Co., Boston (copyright 1881), 17.5 cm., 515 pp., with a frontispiece. The first English edition was
issued by George Routledge, London,
1887, 376 pp.

2266 PANSY ***Household Puzzles.***
1/o sewed, 1/6 cloth   1891?

Lily Series No. 148. This was also issued in
the *Pansy Series*, Cr 8vo, at 1/o cloth. This
has no date and 319 pp. The first edition
was issued by D. Lothrop & Co., Boston
(1874), 18 cm., 370 pp., with a frontispiece. The first English edition was issued
by George Routledge, London, 1889, 319
pp., at 1/o.

2267 PANSY ***Tip Lewis and His Lamp.***
1/o sewed, 1/6 cloth   1891?

Lily Series No. 150. This has no date and
256 pp. It was also issued in the *Pansy Series*, Cr 8vo, at 1/o cloth. The first edition
was issued by Hoyt, Boston (1867), 17 cm.,
360 pp., illustrated. It was reissued by D.
Lothrop, Boston, listed in the *Christian
Union* on May 8, 1884. The first English
edition was issued by George Routledge,
London (1890), 256 pp., at 2/o, 2/6, in
Apr.

2268 PANSY ***Sidney Martin's Christmas.***
1/o sewed, 1/6 cloth   1891?

Lily Series No. 151. This was also issued in
the *Pansy Series*, Cr 8vo, at 1/o cloth. This

contains other stories in addition to the title story. The first edition was issued by D.
Lothrop & Co., Boston (1879), 18 cm.,
610 pp., illustrated. The first English edition was issued by George Routledge,
London, 314 pp., at 1/o, 2/6, in Apr. 1890.

2269 PANSY ***Little Fishers and Their Nets.***
1/o sewed, 1/6 cloth   1891?

Lily Series No. 152. This was also issued in
the *Pansy Series*, Cr 8vo, at 1/o cloth. The
first edition was issued by D. Lothrop &
Co., Boston (1878), 12mo, illustrated.
The first English edition was issued by
George Routledge, London, 1887, Cr
8vo, anonymous, 375 pp., 2/o, listed in the
Spect on Apr. 30.

2270 PANSY ***Spun from Fact.*** 1/o sewed,
1/6 cloth   1891?

Lily Series No. 153. This was also issued in
the *Pansy Series*, Cr 8vo, at 1/o cloth. The
first edition was issued by D. Lothrop &
Co., Boston (1886), 338 pp., $1.50, listed
in the *Christian Union* on July 1 and noticed on Aug. 5. The first English edition
was issued by George Routledge, London,
1887, 380 pp., 2/o.

2271 PANSY ***The Randolphs.*** 1/o sewed,
1/6 cloth   1891?

Lily Series No. 154. This has no date and
317 pp. It was also issued in the *Pansy Series*, Cr 8vo, at 1/o cloth. The first edition
was issued by D. Lothrop & Co., Boston;
etc. (copyright 1876), 19 cm., 440 pp., illustrated. The first English edition was issued by George Routledge, London,
1889, 317 pp., 1/o.

2272 FAYE HUNTINGTON (MRS.
THEODOSIA FOSTER) ***Echoing and
Re-Echoing.*** 1/o sewed, 1/6 cloth   1891?

Lily Series No. 155. This was issued uniform with the *Pansy Series*, Cr 8vo, at 1/o
cloth, probably in 1891 also. The first edition was issued by D. Lothrop & Co., Bos-

ton (copyright 1878), 12mo, 309 pp., with a frontispiece. The first English edition was issued by George Routledge, London, 1887, Cr 8vo, at 2/0, listed in the *Spect* on Apr. 23.

2273 RETLAW SPRING **Hedged with Thorns.** 1/0 sewed, 1/6 cloth   1891?
Lily Series No. 159.
Also 1875

2274 PANSY **A Sevenfold Trouble.**
1/0 sewed, 1/6 cloth   1891?
Lily Series No. 161. This was also issued in the *Pansy Series*, Cr 8vo, at 1/0 cloth. The first edition was issued by D. Lothrop & Co., Boston (1889), 19 cm., 431 pp., illustrated. The first British edition was issued by Oliphant, Anderson & Ferrier, Edinburgh and London (1890), 431 pp.

2275 JAMES COOK **Captain Cook's First Voyage Round the World.** 1/0 sewed, 1/6 cloth   1891?
Youth's Library No. 110. Ward, Lock issued *The Three Famous Voyages of Captain James Cook Round the World* in parts in 1888, 1889. Part 1 was advertised in the *Times Weekly Edition* on Dec. 18, 1887, 0/6 sewed, "On Nov. 25." It was issued in 15 monthly parts and resulted in a 1 vol. issue in 1889, 25.5 cm., 1,152 pp., illustrated. They issued the *Voyages of Discovery of Captain James Cook* (1892), 2 vols., 14.5 cm., illustrated, 10/0, edited by Hawkesworth.
Also 1886

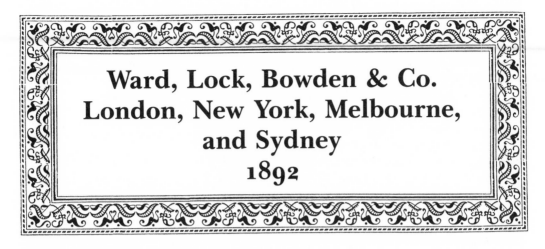

Ward, Lock, Bowden & Co.
London, New York, Melbourne, and Sydney
1892

By Sept. 24, 1892, the New York branch was moved to East 12 Street.

2276 GEORGE HASTINGS *Philip Henson, M.D.* o/6 sewed   Jan. 9 (*PC*)

Popular Sixpenny Books No. 277. This is the first English edition, 1892, 239 pp. The first edition was issued by E. Brandus & Co., New York, 1891, 19.5 cm., 349 pp., *Vanity Fair Series* No. 1.

2277 JOHN W. KIRTON *Cheerful Homes.* 1/o sewed, 1/6 cloth   Mar. 12 (*PC*)

Friendly Counsel Series. The first edition was issued by Ward, Lock, Cr 8vo, 3/6 cloth, listed in the *Spect* on Jan. 6, 1883.

2278 LAWRENCE L. LYNCH (EMMA MURDOCH, later VAN DEVENTER) *Moina.* 2 vols. o/6 sewed each Mar. 12 (*PC*)

Popular Sixpenny Books Nos. 279, 280. These have the titles, *A Detective Mystery* and *A Mystery Solved.*
Also 1891, 1903

2279 GODFREY H. PIKE *Charles Haddon Spurgeon.* o/6 sewed   Mar. 26 (*PC*)

This was issued by Hodder & Stoughton, London, 1886, 312 pp.; and also by the Religious Tract Society, Edinburgh, 1886, 312 pp. It was issued, probably in condensed form, by Cassell & Co., London, 1892, 128 pp., at 1/o, listed in the *Times Weekly Edition* on Apr. 15. In the United States it was issued by Funk & Wagnalls, New York; etc., 1892, 19.5 cm., 307 pp., with portraits, an introduction by William C. Wilkinson, and a final chapter by James C. Fernald.

2280 ANONYMOUS *Kitchen and Flower Gardening.* Illustrated. 1/o boards Mar. 26 (*PC* ad)

See 1861, 81, 90

2281 BENJAMIN L. FARJEON *Self-Doomed.* o/6 sewed   Apr. 21 (*PC*)

Popular Sixpenny Books No. 281. The first English edition was issued by Griffith, Farran & Co., London (1885), 123 pp., noticed in the *British Quarterly Review* for Oct. 1885, and thus probably issued July–Sept. 1885. In the United States it was issued by Harper & Bros., New York, 1885, 17.5 cm., 140 pp., $.25 paper, *Handy Series* No. 27, listed in *PW* on Oct. 17, and advertised in the *New-York Times* on Oct. 12, as "This day." It was also issued by George Munro, New York (1885), 12mo paper, *Seaside Library Pocket Edition* No. 607, probably in Oct.

2282 FRANK E. SMEDLEY **Frank Fairlegh.**
0/6 sewed   May 7 (*PC*)

Popular Sixpenny Books No. 278. The first
edition was issued by Arthur Hall, Virtue
& Co., London, 1850, 11 cm., anonymous, 496 pp., illustrated by Cruikshank,
16/0. This ran in *Sharpe's London Magazine*
(weekly), published by T. B. Sharpe, London, concluding temporarily in the June
1846 issue, resuming in the Jan. 1847 issue, and concluding in the May 1848 issue, after an irregular appearance. It was
issued in 15 monthly parts, 22 cm., illustrated, in pale green wrappers, printed in
black, running Jan. 1849–Mar. 1850. Arthur Hall & Co., London, advertised part
1, with 2 illustrations, at 1/0, in the *Spect*,
as "On Jan. 1, 1849." They advertised it at
2/6 boards, 3/6 cloth, in the *Spect* on Oct.
28, 1854, as "This day." They reissued it,
the same, advertised in the *Spect* on June
20, 1857. George Routledge, London, issued it at 2/6 boards, 3/6 cloth, advertised
in the *Ath* on Aug. 6, 1870; and reissued it
in their *Octavo Novels*, a new edition, illustrated by Cruikshank, at 6/0, listed in the
Ath on May 20, 1871. An early American
edition was issued by H. Long & Brother,
New York (1851), anonymous, 188 pp.,
probably with the illustrations, advertised
in *Lit World* on Mar. 22, and reviewed in
the *Southern Quarterly Review* for Apr.
1851. It was also issued by T. B. Peterson,
Philadelphia, anonymous, listed in *Godey's
Lady's Book* for Nov. 1850.

2283 HENRY W. DULCKEN **Pictures of
London.** 1/0 sewed   June 4 (*PC*)

This is the first edition (1892), containing
pictures in color, with short descriptions
by Dulcken. It was printed in Holland.

2284 SIR GEORGE BADEN-POWELL ET AL.
**Our Boys and Girls, and What to Do with
Them.** Cr 8vo. 1/0 sewed, 2/0 cloth
June 4 (*PC*)

Shilling Useful Books. This was listed in the
Times Weekly Edition on May 27; it was is-

sued by Ward, Lock, Bowden & Co., New
York, $.45 cloth, listed in the *Literary Digest*
on Oct. 18, 1892.

2285 LAWRENCE L. LYNCH
(EMMA MURDOCH, later VAN DEVENTER)
A Slender Clue. 2/0 boards
June 25 (*Ath*)

Select Library of Fiction No. 849, new numbering. This is 1892, 348 pp., in yellow
pictorial boards. The first English edition
was issued by Ward, Lock, Bowden & Co.,
1891, 19 cm., 348 pp., at 2/6 cloth, listed
in the *Ath* on Dec. 5, 1891. The first American edition was issued by Laird & Lee,
Chicago, 1891, 20 cm., 650 pp., illustrated, *Library of Choice Fiction* No. 35.
Also 1893, 1904

2286 ANONYMOUS **With the Wits.**
Roy 8vo. Illustrated. 0/6 sewed
July 16 (*PC*)

Popular Sixpenny Books No. 274. This is the
first English edition (1892), 96 pp., a collection of jokes, anecdotes, poems, etc., by
leading American humorists. The first
edition was issued by J. B. Lippincott &
Co., Philadelphia, 1891, 24 cm., 96 pp.,
illustrated.

2287 M. W. WATKINS-PITCHFORD
Brothers in Arms. p 8vo. 0/6 sewed
July 23 (*PC*)

Popular Sixpenny Books No. 282. The first
edition was issued by the Church Sunday
School Union, London, 1883, anonymous, 141 pp.

2288 JULIEN GORDON (JULIE G. CRUGER)
Vampires. Mademoiselle Réséda.
2/0 boards, 2/6 cloth   Aug. 13 (*PC*)

Select Library of Fiction No. 959, new numbering. The first English edition was issued by Ward, Lock, 1891, 299 pp., 6/0,

Warwick House Library No. 10. The first American edition was issued by J. B. Lippincott & Co., Philadelphia, 1891, 18.5 cm., 299 pp. It ran in *Lippincott's Magazine* for May 1891, pp. 539–573.

2289 WILLIAM T. LEQUEUX *Strange Tales of a Nihilist.* o/6 sewed   Sept. 24 *(PC)*

Popular Sixpenny Books No. 284. This is 1892, with 149 pp. It was listed in the *Times Weekly Edition* on Oct. 7, 1892, at 1/o. It was issued in the colonial edition, 1896, as *A Secret Service*, Cr 8vo, 3/6, listed in the *Spect* on Aug. 29, 1896, and in the *Times Weekly Edition* on Sept. 11. The present edition is the first English edition. The first American edition was issued by the Cassell Publishing Co., New York (copyright 1892), with the present title, 18.5 cm., 314 pp., $.50 paper, *Sunshine Series* No. 130. It was listed in *Public Opinion* and *PW* on Oct. 1 and in the *Ind* on Oct. 6. Ward, Lock & Bowden, New York, issued it, 302 pp., $1.00 cloth, listed in *PW* on Oct. 10, 1896, but not received. The latter was entitled *A Secret Service*.

Also 1899, 1903

2290 CHARLES KINGSLEY *Alton Locke.* o/6 sewed, 2/o boards   Oct. 1 *(PC)*

Popular Sixpenny Books. Select Library of Fiction No. 1052, new numbering. I have not been able to assign numbers to the *Popular Sixpenny Books* from this point on, whether because they were no longer employed or because they were never given in the publisher's ads or lists. Ward, Lock also issued it in their *Warwick House Library*, 1892, and in the *Minerva Library* at 2/o cloth. The former has 311 pp. and an introduction by C. Kernahan. The first edition was issued by Chapman & Hall, London, 2 vols., 1850, 21 cm., anonymous, at 18/o, listed by *PC* as published Aug. 14–29. Wolff's copy had a 32-page catalog (Nov. 1849) at the back of vol. 2. The second edition, the same, was advertised in the *Spect* on Jan.

11, 1851, as "On Jan. 15." The third edition, 1853, Cr 8vo, anonymous, at 7/o, was advertised in the *Spect* on Sept. 18, 1852, "On Sept. 25." It was issued at 2/o boards, 1856 (1855), Sadleir's copy, 17 cm., in yellow pictorial boards with a specially drawn spine, listed in the *Ath* on Dec. 15, 1855. Macmillan & Co., Cambridge, issued it, 1862, a new edition, 20 cm., 309 pp., with a new preface, listed in the *Spect* on Apr. 26. The first American edition was issued by Harper & Bros., New York, 1850, 19.5 cm., anonymous, 371 pp., noticed in the *Southern Quarterly Review* for Jan. 1851, and listed by *Lit World* a published Nov. 17–30, 1850.

2291 (FRANCIS C. YOUNG) *Every Man His Own Mechanic. Part 1.* Illustrated. o/6 sewed   Oct. 25

This was advertised in the *Times Weekly Edition* on Oct. 21 as "On Oct. 25," a reissue in 13 monthly parts. Ward, Lock first issued it (1880, 1881), 816 pp., illustrated, with a preface signed F.Y. (Francis C. Young); and it was issued in 1 vol. in 1881, 8vo, illustrated, at 7/6. They issued it (1883), in parts at 1/o each, and then in 2 vols. It was reissued in o/6 monthly parts, a new edition, revised and enlarged, illustrated, part 1 advertised in the *Spect* on Oct. 26, 1889, as "On Oct. 25," and then issued in 1 vol. at 7/6, advertised in the *Spect* on Dec. 13, 1890.

2292 F. L. MCDERMOTT *Julius Vernon.* o/6 sewed   Dec. 3 *(PC)*

Popular Sixpenny Books. This is also given by the *Eng Cat*, but otherwise I cannot trace it.

2293 LETTICE GALBRAITH ET AL. *The Spine of the Coin.* Illustrated. 1/o sewed   Dec. 10 *(PC)*

This is Beeton's Christmas Annual, containing also *Stranger Than Fiction* by C.

Kernahan; *The Man with the Fatal Finger* by William Le Queux; and *The Head of the Family* by R. Andre. It was issued in *Popular Sixpenny Books* in 1893, with 164 pp.

2294 WILLIAM M. THACKERAY
The History of Pendennis. Illustrated.
2/0 Dec.?

This is probably the *Minerva Library* issue, 1892, 783 pp., at 2/0 cloth, with an introduction by H. W. Dulcken. It was also issued in *Popular Sixpenny Books*, 2 vols., and as *Select Library of Fiction* No. 927, new numbering. It was first issued in 24 in 23 monthly parts by Bradbury & Evans, London, from Nov. 1848 to Dec. 1850, with a 3 month hiatus due to Thackeray's illness. They issued it in 2 vols., 1849, 1850, 22.5 cm., illustrated, 26/0. Vol. 1 was listed in the *Ath* on Jan. 12, 1850, and vol. 2 was listed Dec. 7, 1850. They issued it in 1 vol., 1856 (1885), Cr 8vo, 652 pp., at 7/0, listed by *PC* as published Oct. 1–13, 1855. It was reissued, the same, 1858. Smith, Elder & Co., London, issued it in 2 vols., 1868–70, 21 cm., illustrated; and reissued it in 2 vols. several times. They issued it in 1 vol., 1871, Cr 8vo, 5/0, listed in the *Spect* on Oct. 28. The first American edition was issued by Harper & Bros., New York, 2 vols., 1850, 24 cm., illustrated, containing paragraphs omitted in the English edition. It was listed in the *United States Magazine* (monthly) for Apr. 1851 and reviewed in the *Southern Quarterly Review* for Apr. 1851. They had previously issued it in 8 parts, part 4 about Mar. 9, 1850; part 7 on Dec. 13; and part 8 in Feb. or Mar. 1851, $.25 each.

2295 THOMAS COBB *Wedderburn's Will.*
0/6 sewed 1892 (*BM*)
Popular Sixpenny Books. This is the first edition, 1892, 153 pp.

ANONYMOUS *New Needlework Series.*
8 vols. Illustrated. 0/1 sewed each.
1892 (*BM*)
The *BM* gives *Sylvia's Needlework Books*, 17 parts, 1892.
2296 **No. 1. *Crochet Edgings***
2297 **No. 2. *Cross-Stitch***
2298 **No. 3. *Knitting***
2299 **No. 4. *Bazaar Articles***
2300 **No. 5. *Knitted and Crochet Comforts***
2301 **No. 6. *Fancy Needlework***
2302 **No. 7. *Crochet, second series***
2303 **No. 8. *Canvas Embroidery***

2304 EDWARD P. ROE *From Jest to Earnest.* 12mo. 1/0 sewed 1892?

This is probably a reissue of the *Shilling Novels* issue of 1886. It is my copy, and the front cover has only London and New York in the imprint. It has no date, with both Melbourne and Sydney in the title page imprint, 17.5 cm., 288 pp. It is in very fragile white wrappers, printed in black, and cut flush.
Also 1876, 83, 86

2305 HENRY KINGSLEY *Ravenshoe.*
12mo. New Edition. 2/0 boards 1892?
Library of Select Authors. Select Library of Fiction No. 104, new numbering. This is my copy, with Melbourne and Sydney in the imprint, 18.1 cm., 430 pp., in white pictorial boards, printed in red, blue, and black, with the series title at the foot of the spine. There are ads on the back cover, the endpapers, and 6 pp. at the back. One of the endpaper ads has a date (Mar. 26, 1891), and there is an inscribed date (Oct. 25, 1894). The Sydney office was opened by Sept. 1891, and closed in Nov. 1894. The first appearance was in *Macmillan's Magazine*, where it ran from Jan. 1861 to July 1862, Macmillan & Co., Cambridge, issued it in 3 vols., 1862, 19.5 cm., at 31/6, advertised in the *Ath* on May 24 as "On

May 28," and listed May 31. They issued the second edition, the same, advertised in the *Spect* on Aug. 23, 1862, as "Next week." They issued a new edition, 1864, Cr 8vo, 430 pp., at 6/0, listed in the *Reader* on Aug. 6. Chapman & Hall, London, issued the fifth edition, no date, 2/0 boards, *Select Library of Fiction* No. 196, with a printer's date (Dec. 22, 1871), listed in the *Ath* on Mar. 2, 1872. The third edition [sic!] was issued by Chapman & Hall in 1872, 12mo, 3/0 cloth, in the series, listed by *PC* as published Nov. 1–15. They issued a new edition at 2/0 boards, 1876. Ward, Lock issued it in 1894 or 1895, a new edition, Cr 8vo, 449 pp., with a frontispiece, at 3/6 cloth. The first American edition was issued by Ticknor & Fields, Boston, 1862, 19 cm., 430 pp, at $1.25, advertised in the *New-York Times* on June 11, as "Just ready," issued at the same time as the English edition. It was listed in *APC&LG* (monthly) on June 1. The fourth edition was advertised in the *New-York Times* on July 8, 1862, at $1.25.

Also 1903

2306 JOHN M. WILSON *The Trials of Margaret Lyndsay and Lights and Shadows of Scottish Life.* 12mo. 2/0 boards 1892?

Select Library of Fiction No.? This is my copy, without Sydney in the imprint. The front cover and ads have the imprint Ward, Lock & Co., London, New York, and Melbourne. It is an unusual issue in the series as the text is in very fine print in double columns, and I have never discovered it to be in any list of the series put out by the publisher nor have I found it anywhere else so listed. It is 18 cm., with 111 pp., and pp. (5)–133. It is in white pictorial boards, printed in red, blue, and black, with the series title on the spine. There is a page of ads at the front, 6 pp. at the back, ads on the endpapers, and on the back cover. The first edition of the first title was issued by William Blackwood,

Edinburgh; etc., 1823, 20.5 cm., anonymous, 403 pp., 10/6, issued in Mar. They issued a new edition, Fcp 8vo, anonymous, 6/0 cloth, listed in the *Spect* on Nov. 16, 1839; and issued it Fcp 8vo, anonymous, at 2/6, advertised in the *Spect* on Feb. 15, 1845, as "This day." In the United States it was issued by Wells & Lilly, Boston, 1823, 18 cm., anonymous, 267 pp.; and by E. Bliss & E. White, etc., New York, 1823, 20.3 cm., anonymous, 283 pp. The first edition of the second title was issued by William Blackwood, Edinburgh; etc., 1822, 19.5 cm., anonymous, 430 pp., in May. A new edition, Fcp 8vo, anonymous, 6/0, was listed in the *Spect* on Jan. 26, 1839; and the same was advertised in the *Spect* on Nov. 2, 1839, as "Just published." A new edition, Fcp 8vo, anonymous, at 2/6, 3/6, 6/6, was listed in the *Spect* on Dec. 14, 1844; and a new edition, Fcp 8vo, anonymous, at 3/0 cloth, was advertised in the *Spect* on Dec. 20, 1845, as "Lately published." It was issued in the United States by C. Ewer, etc., Boston, 1822, anonymous; and by E. Bliss & E. White, New York, 1822, 12mo, 311 pp.

2307 SIR WALTER SCOTT *Waverley.* 12mo. 2/0 boards 1892?

Select Library of Fiction No. 230, new numbering. This is my copy, with Sydney in the imprint on the title page but with Ward, Lock & Co., London, New York, and Melbourne on the front cover and in the ads. It has no date, 18 cm., 407 pp., with notes on pp. (408)–418. It is in yellow pictorial boards, printed in red, blue, and black, with the series title on the spine, and with a 26-page catalog at the back. There are ads on the endpapers and the back cover. In front there is an ad on 2 pp.; a General Preface on pp. (3)–17 (Jan. 1, 1829); an appendix to the General Preface No. I on pp. (18)–30; No. II on pp. 30–43; No. III on pp. 43–46; an introduction to Waverley on pp. (47)–50;

and finally the preface for the third edition on pp. (51)–54.
Also 1880, 82

2308 THEODORE HOOK *Jack Brag.*
2/o boards 1892?
Library of Select Authors. Select Library of Fiction No. 536, new numbering. This is Sadleir's copy, which he gives as after 1891. Chapman & Hall issued it in the series as No. 99 in 1867.
Also 1865

2309 CHARLES DICKENS
David Copperfield. o/6 sewed 1892?
Popular Sixpenny Books. This was also issued in the *Royal Library*, 1892, Cr 8vo, 2/o cloth. The first appearance in England was as 20-parts-in-19, issued by Bradbury & Evans, London, in green wrappers with a design by "Phiz." They ran from May 1, 1849, to Nov. 1, 1850. They issued it in 1 vol., 1850, 23 cm., 624 pp., illustrated by "Phiz," 21/o, listed in the *Ath* on Nov. 16, 1850. In the United States it was issued 20-parts-in-19, illustrated by "Phiz," at $.12½ each, in buff wrappers. The first 11 parts were issued by John Wiley, New York, No. 1 reviewed in the *Ind* on June 21, 1849; No. 2 on July 19. These were called authorized. The next 7 parts were issued by G. P. Putnam, New York, 1850; and the last double part was issued by Wiley, 1850. The complete edition was issued by Wiley, 2 vols., 1850, illustrated by "Phiz," listed by *Lit World* as published Nov. 17–30. It was also issued in 2 parts by G. P. Putnam, 1850, bound from the parts, with a frontispiece, engraved title page, and illustrations by "Phiz." The engraved title page has the imprint of John Wiley, New York, 1850, and the printed title pages could be cancels. Part 1 was listed by *Lit World* as published Apr. 27–May 11, 1850, and part 2, Nov. 30–Dec. 14, 1850. It was also issued 20-parts-in-19 by Lea & Blanchard, Philadelphia, 1849, 1850, Roy

8vo, illustrated by "Phiz," double columns, in printed yellow wrappers at $.05 each, 1 illustration in each of 8 parts. No. 4 was listed in *Godey's Lady's Book* for Nov. 1849. They also issued it in 2 parts, part 1 listed by *Lit World* as published Mar. 16–23, 1850. Part 2, the double No. 19 and 20, and the complete issue in 1 vol., were advertised in *Lit World* on Nov. 23, 1850, as "This day." The 1 vol. issue, 1851, complete, 23 cm., 327 pp., illustrated by "Phiz," double columns, was listed in *Lit World* as published Nov. 17–30. It was listed in the *United States Magazine* (monthly) for Jan. 1851, with 5 illustrations, $.37½. It was also issued by W. F. Burgess, New York (1850), 24 cm., 264 pp., frontispiece and illustrations by J. W. Orr, a portrait on the title page, double columns. It was listed by *Lit World* as published Nov. 17–30, 1850. It was also issued by T. B. Peterson, Philadelphia, listed in *Godey's Lady's Book* for May 1850. Bradbury & Evans and Chapman & Hall jointly advertised it in the *Spect* in 2 vols., 6/o each; vol. 1 as "On Feb. 28" and vol. 2 as "On Mar. 31," 1859, with vignette title pages.
Also 1900

2310 ANONYMOUS *The Missing Brother.*
o/6 sewed 1892?
Popular Sixpenny Books No. 283. I cannot trace this.

2311 WILLIAM OWEN *The Good Soldier.*
1/o sewed, 1/6 cloth 1892?
Youth's Library No. 112. The first edition was issued jointly by Simpkin, Marshall, London; and J. M. Burton, Ipswitch (1858), Fcp 8vo, at 1/6 boards, 2/6 cloth, listed in the *Spect* on Mar. 20, 1858; and reissued as *Run and Read Library* No. 62, 12mo, at 1/6 boards, about July 7, 1860. It is the life of General Havelock.

2312 WILLIAM OWEN *The Martyrs of the Indian Rebellion.* Illustrated. 1/0 sewed, 1/6 cloth   1892?

Youth's Library No. 113. This has no date and 144 pp. The first edition was *Memorials of Christian Martyrs . . . in the Indian Rebellion*, issued by Simpkin, Marshall, London; J. M. Burton, Ipswitch, 1859, Cr 8vo, 236 pp., with a frontispiece, 3/6. It was advertised in the *Ath* on Apr. 9. It was reissued as *Run and Read Library* No. 53, 1/6 boards, about Sept. 24, 1859.

2313 ANONYMOUS *Famous Heroes in Field and Forum.* Illustrated. 1/0 sewed, 1/6 cloth   1892?

Youth's Library No. 114. I cannot trace this.

On May 1, 1893, the style became Ward, Lock & Bowden, Ltd.

2314 HENRY HERMAN *His Angel.* [Third edition]. 2/o boards   Mar. 4 (*Ath*)

Select Library of Fiction No. 970, new numbering. The first edition was issued by Ward, Lock, Bowden & Co., 1891, 19.5 cm., 240 pp., illustrated, 6/o, listed in the *Spect* on Dec. 5, 1891. It was also issued as *Warwick House Library* No. 7, Cr 8vo, 240 pp., illustrated, 3/6 cloth, dated 1891. It was also issued, Cr 8vo, at 3/6 cloth, listed in the *Spect* on Oct. 29, 1892. The first American edition was issued by M. J. Ivers, New York, listed in the *Nation* on Mar. 8, 1894. However, Ward, Lock, Bowden & Co., New York, issued it at $.50 paper, listed in the *Literary Digest* for Feb. 6, 1892.

2315 JOYCE E. MUDDOCK, later PRESTON-MUDDOCK *Stormlight.* [Eighth edition]. 2/o boards   Mar. 4 (*Ath*)

Select Library of Fiction No. 968, new numbering. It was listed in *PW*, but not received, on Feb. 27, 1892, issued by Ward, Lock, Bowden & Co., New York, a new edition, at $1.50 cloth. It was listed in *Literary Digest* on June 18, 1892, issued by the same, illustrated, $1.00 cloth.

2316 ÉMILE HERISSÉ *The Art of Pastry-Making, etc.* Cr 8vo. Illustrated. 2/o linen boards   Mar. 11 (*Spect* ad)

The first edition was issued by Ward, Lock, Bowden & Co., 1893, p 8vo, 151 pp., at 2/6, issued in Jan. They issued a second edition, 1895, 20 cm., 151 pp., illustrated; and they issued new editions, revised, 1912, 1923, and (1929). It is translated from the French.

2317 ADELINE D. T. WHITNEY *A Golden Gossip.* 1/o sewed, 1/6 cloth   Mar. 25 (*PC*)

Lily Series No. 164. The first edition was issued by Houghton, Mifflin & Co., Boston and New York, 1892, 19.5 cm., 348 pp., $1.50, *Neighborhood Story* No. 2. It was listed in the *Ind* on Mar. 10 and in *PW* on Mar. 12. The first English edition was issued by Ward, Lock, Bowden & Co., 1892, Cr 8vo, 348 pp., 2/6 cloth, listed in the *Ath* on Nov. 19, 1892.

2318 MARY E. WILKINS, later FREEMAN *The Pot of Gold, and Other Stories.* 1/o sewed, 1/6 cloth   Mar. 25 (*PC*)

Lily Series No. 163. The first edition was issued by D. Lothrop & Co., Boston (copyright 1892), 18.5 cm., 324 pp., $1.50 in blue cloth. It was listed in the *Nation* on Mar. 10 and in *PW* on Mar. 12, 1892. It is the first edition for 3 of the children's stories, and the other 13 appeared in one or the other of four different books. The first English edition was issued by Ward, Lock, Bowden & Co., 1892, 290 pp., 2/6 cloth, listed in the *Ath* on Nov. 19.

2319 THOMAS N. PAGE *In Ole Virginia.* 2/0 boards　Mar.?

This is probably a reissue of *Select Library of Fiction* No. 836.
Also 1889

2320 JOHN W. KIRTON, ed. *The Young Abstainers' Reciter.* o/6 sewed, 1/0 cloth Apr. 8 (*PC*)

Standard Reciters No. 12. This is the first edition, 1893, 255 pp.

2321 LAWRENCE L. LYNCH (EMMA MURDOCH, later VAN DEVENTER) *A Slender Clue.* 2 parts.
o/6 sewed each　May 20 (*PC*)

Popular Sixpenny Books. Part 1 was *Forging the Chain,* and part 2 was *Joining the Links.* Also 1892, 1904

2322 WILTON WOLRIGE *Witness from the Dead, and Other Stories.* o/6 sewed June 24 (*PC*)

Popular Sixpenny Books. This is probably the first edition. It is also given by the *Eng Cat,* but otherwise I cannot trace it.

2323 WILTON WOLRIGE ET AL. *A Ghostly Witness, and Other Stories.* o/6 sewed Aug. 5 (*PC*)

Popular Sixpenny Books. This is the first edition, 1893, 101 pp. The title story is by Wolrige.

2324 MARY E. WILKINS, later FREEMAN *A Humble Romance, and Other Stories.* o/6 sewed, 1/0 sewed, 1/6 cloth Aug. 12 (*PC*)

Popular Sixpenny Books. Lily Series No. 165. The *PC* listing is for the o/6 edition. The first edition was issued by Harper & Bros., New York, 1887, 17.5 cm., 436 pp., $1.25, containing 28 stories. It was listed in the *Ind* on June 16 and in *PW* on June 18. The title story was in *Harper's New Monthly Magazine* for June 1884. The first British edition was issued by David Douglas, Edinburgh, 1890, 13 cm., 309 pp., received by the *BM* on Mar. 11, and listed in *PC* on Mar. 15. It was listed in *Review of Reviews* (London), for Aug. 1891, at 1/0, in the *American Authors Series* of David Douglas. Also 1894

2325 IGNATIUS DONNELLY *The Golden Bottle.* o/6 sewed　Oct. 14 (*PC*)

Popular Sixpenny Books. This is 1893, with 246 pp. A second edition was advertised in *PC* on Oct. 7, the ad stating that the first edition was exhausted on the day of publication. The first edition was issued by D. D. Merrill Co., New York and St. Paul, 1892, 19 cm., 313 pp., $.50 paper and $1.25 cloth, listed in the *Ind* on Oct. 20, and in *PW* on Oct. 22. In England it was issued by Sampson Low, London, 1892, a duplicate of the Merrill edition, printed in the United States, with a different title page. It was listed by the *Times Weekly Edition* on Jan. 20, 1893, $.50 paper, and listed in the *Bks* for Feb. 1893. The *U Cat* gives W. Bryce, Toronto (1892?), 246 pp.

2326 THOMAS P. O'CONNOR *Sketches in the House.* 12mo. 1/0 sewed　Oct. 14 (*PC*)

This is the first edition, 1893, 18 cm., 288 pp., reprinted from the *Weekly Sun,* where it appeared as *At the Bar of the House.* Ward, Lock issued a second edition, 1893.

2327 HENRY HERMAN *The Crime of a Christmas Toy.* Illustrated. 1/0 sewed Nov. 11 (*PC*)

This is Beeton's Christmas Annual. It is the first edition, 168 pp.
Also 1900

2328 LETTICE GALBRAITH *New Ghost Stories.* 0/6 sewed   Dec. 2 (*PC*)

Popular Sixpenny Books. This is the first edition, 1893, 138 pp.

2329 F. L. MCDERMOTT *The Last King of Yewle.* 0/6 sewed   1893 (*BM*)

Popular Sixpenny Books. This is the first English edition, 1893, 115 pp. Ward, Lock issued a second edition, also 1893. The first American edition was issued by the Cassell Publishing Co., New York (copyright 1893), 18 cm., 162 pp., as *Unknown Library* No. 21, the series title and No. appearing on the cover.

2330 WILLIAM CARLETON *The Squanders of Castle Squander.* 12mo. 2/0 boards 1893?

Select Library of Fiction No. 715, new numbering. This is my copy, no date, with Ward, Lock & Co., London and New York, on the title page, and Ward, Lock & Bowden, Ltd., London, New York, and Melbourne on the front cover. It is 17.7 cm., 414 pp., in white pictorial boards, printed in red, blue, and black, with the series title on the spine. There are ads on the endpapers and back cover.

Also 1876

Ward, Lock & Bowden, Ltd.
London, New York, Melbourne, and Sydney
1894

By Sept. 22, 1894, the Melbourne office was moved to Mackillop Street. The Sydney office was closed after Nov. 24, 1894.

2331 MARY E. WILKINS, later FREEMAN
A Humble Romance, and Other Stories.
2/o boards   Jan.?
Select Library of Fiction No. 963, new numbering.
Also 1893

2332 LAWRENCE L. LYNCH
(EMMA MURDOCH, later VAN DEVENTER)
A Dead Man's Step. [Second edition].
2/o boards   May 12 (*Ath*)
Select Library of Fiction No. 849A, new numbering. This has 424 pp. The first edition was issued by Ward, Lock & Bowden, Ltd., 1893, 19 cm., 424 pp., listed in the *Ath* on July 1, at 2/6 cloth. The first American edition was issued by Rand, McNally, Chicago and New York, 1893 (1894), 20.5 cm., 583 pp., as *Rialto Series* No. 6, the series name appearing on the cover. It was listed in *Public Opinion* and the *Nation* on Mar. 22, 1894; in *PW* on Mar. 24 as 1893 (1894); and in the *Ind* on Mar. 29, 1894.
Also 1895

2333 EDGAR FAWCETT   ***A New Nero.***
0/6 sewed   May 19 (*PC*)
Popular Sixpenny Books. This is the first English edition, 1894, 247 pp. The first edi-

tion was issued by P. F. Collier, New York, 1893, 18 cm., 288 pp., *The New Nero*, deposited Apr. 26.

2334 HAWLEY SMART   ***False Cards.***
2/o boards   May 26 (*PC*)
Select Library of Fiction No. 167, new numbering. This probably had *Library of Select Authors* on the spine. The first edition was issued by Hurst & Blackett, London, 3 vols., 1873 (1872), 19.5 cm., at 31/6, listed in the *Ath* on Nov. 23, 1872. Chapman & Hall, London, issued it as No. 328 in the series, 398 pp., 2/o boards, listed in the *Ath* on May 20, 1876. They reissued it, a new edition, no date, my copy, 18.1 cm., 398 pp., 2/o boards; and reissued it, a new edition, 1880, probably at 2/o boards.
Also 1902

2335 HOUGHTON TOWNLEY   ***His Own Accuser.*** 0/6 sewed   Aug. 18 (*PC*)
Popular Sixpenny Books. This is the first edition, with 156 pp.

2336 MRS. A. BLITZ   ***An Australian Millionaire.*** 2/o boards   Sept. 8 (*Ath*)
Select Library of Fiction No. 990, new numbering. The first edition was issued by

Ward, Lock & Bowden, Ltd., 3 vols., 1893, at 31/6, listed in the *Ath* on May 20. They also issued it in the *Warwick House Library*, Cr 8vo, 498 pp., with a frontispiece, dated 1894, 3/6 cloth, listed in the *Times Weekly Edition* on June 22, 1894.

2337 THOMAS COBB *The Disappearance of Mr. Derwent.* o/6 sewed Sept. 15 (*PC*)
Popular Sixpenny Books. This is probably the first edition, 1894, 178 pp. The first American edition was issued by F. Tennyson Neely, Chicago and New York (1894), 263 pp., listed in the *Outlook*, New York (weekly) on Aug. 4, and listed in the *Ind* on Aug. 9.

2338 A. DONNISON *Winning a Wife in Australia.* 2/o boards Nov. 3 (*PC*)
Select Library of Fiction No. 995, new numbering. The first edition was issued by Ward, Lock & Bowden, Ltd. (1894), Cr 8vo, 360 pp., with a frontispiece, 3/6 cloth. This was the *Warwick House Library* edition, listed in the *Ath* on July 14, 1894.

2339 W. FERRARS-AUBURN *Boot-and-Saddle Stories.* p 8vo. 1/o sewed Nov. 10 (*PC*)
Shilling Novels. This is the first edition, 1894, 195 pp. A second edition was issued, also 1894.

2340 E. P. OPPENHEIM *A Monk of Cruta, etc.* Illustrated. 1/o sewed Dec. 1 (*PC*)
This is Beeton's Christmas Annual, 1894, the 35th year. It is a first English edition, Demy 8vo, 158 pp., illustrated, 1/o sewed, advertised in the *Times Weekly Edition* on Nov. 23. The first American edition was issued by F. Tennyson Neely, Chicago and New York, 1894, 20 cm., 340 pp., listed in *PW* on Dec. 15.
Also 1901

2341 GEORGE J. WHYTE MELVILLE *Market Harborough. Inside the Bar.*
12mo. 1/o boards 1894
Library of Select Authors. Select Library of Fiction No. 123, new numbering. This is my copy, with the imprint on the title page being Ward, Lock & Bowden, Ltd., London, New York, and Melbourne; the imprint on the front cover being Ward, Lock & Co., London and New York; and the imprint of the catalog at the back being Ward, Lock & Bowden, Ltd., London. It has no date, 18.2 cm., with 213 pp., (217)–393 pp., in blue pictorial boards, printed in red, green, brown, and black. It has "The Works of Whyte Melville" at the head of the spine and the series title at the foot. There are ads on the endpapers, back cover, and in a catalog paged (1)–16 at the back. There is a reliable date of 1894 on one of the endpaper ads and 1893 on another. I conclude that this was issued between June 1882 and 1887, a new edition, 393 pp., with the *Select Library of Fiction* on the cover. The first edition of the first title was issued by Chapman & Hall, London, 1861, 20 cm., anonymous, 312 pp., at 9/o, listed in the *Ath* on Mar. 16. The first edition of the second title was with the fourth edition of the first title, 1862, 19 cm., 393 pp., at 5/o, listed in the *Spect* on May 3. The second edition of the first title was issued at 9/o, advertised in the *Spect* on Apr. 27, 1861, as "This day"; and the third edition, the same, was advertised on July 13, 1861. Chapman & Hall issued it (both titles in 1 vol.) as No. 105 in the series, 1867, at 2/o boards, listed in the *Spect* on June 8, the sixth edition, my copy. They reissued it as No. 395 in the series in the fall of 1879; and issued the 15th edition, no date, at 2/o boards. All the Ward, Lock yellowbacks have both titles on the title page but, as in my copy, only the first title on the front cover. I have a copy of the fourth edition of the

first title, which contains the first edition of the second title; it has continuous pagination, with a half-title for the second story, bound in buff linen, with the date 1862 on the front, spine, and title page. Also 1901, 03

2342 WILLIAM H. AINSWORTH *Cardinal Pole.* New Edition. p 8vo. 2/o boards 1894

Select Library of Fiction No. 73, new numbering. This is my copy, with the imprint on the title page being Ward, Lock & Bowden, Ltd., London, New York, and Melbourne; on the front cover as Ward, Lock & Co., London and New York; and on the catalog at the back as Ward, Lock & Bowden, Ltd. It has no date, 18.2 cm., 416 pp., in pale blue pictorial boards, printed in red and black, with the series title on the spine. There are ads on the endpapers and back cover and in a 28-page catalog at the back, the latter of date about Dec. 1, 1894. There is a very reliable date of 1894 in one of the endpaper ads and a date of Nov. 4, 1893, in another. Also 1882

2343 HAWLEY SMART *Salvage.* 2/o boards   1894

Library of Select Authors. Select Library of Fiction No. 179, new numbering. This is my copy, with the various imprints as in the preceding item. It has no date, 18.1 cm., 440 pp., containing 11 stories. It is bound in pale blue pictorial boards, printed in red and black, with the series title on the spine. It has ads on the endpapers, back cover, and 2 pp. at the back. One endpaper ad has a reliable date of 1894 and another has a date of Nov. 4, 1893. Also 1884

2344 EDWARD SCOTT *How to Dance.* o/6 sewed, 1/o cloth   1894?

Sixpenny Manuals No. 11. This may have been issued in early 1895, as the *BM* gives

a new edition, revised and partly rewritten, 1895, 102 pp. However, I cannot trace the first edition. Also 1897

2345 GEORGE J. WHYTE MELVILLE *The Brookes of Bridlemere.* p 8vo. 2/o boards   1894?

Library of Select Authors. Select Library of Fiction No. 119, new numbering. This is my copy, no date, with Ward, Lock & Bowden, Ltd., London, New York, and Melbourne on the title page and Ward, Lock & Co., Ltd., London, New York, and Melbourne, on the front cover, 18.2 cm., 419 pp. It is clothed in pale blue pictorial boards, printed in red and black, with "The Works of Whyte Melville" at the head of the spine and the series title at the foot. It has ads on the endpapers and back cover and a 22-page catalog of date about Oct. 1892 at the back. The endpaper ads have dates of Nov. 4, 1893, and also 1894. This was probably issued earlier at 2/o boards, with the No. 391 on the front cover, the 13th edition. This is a good example of why it is difficult to date Ward, Lock yellowbacks. The imprint on the front cover is in a style that began in Oct. 1896; and the catalog at the back has the imprint of Ward, Lock, Bowden & Co., London, New York, Melbourne, and Sydney, which was adopted in mid-1891, and the Sydney office was closed after Nov. 24, 1894; and the title page imprint is of a style begun on May 1, 1893. The first edition was issued by Chapman & Hall, London, 3 vols., 1864, 20 cm., 31/6, listed in the *Ath* on Nov. 5. They issued the second edition, the same, advertised in the *Spect* on Jan. 21, 1865, as "Now ready"; and the third edition, the same, was advertised on Feb. 18, 1865, as "This day"; and the fourth edition, p 8vo, 419 pp., with a frontispiece, 6/o, was advertised on Nov. 18, 1865, as "This day." They issued it at 2/o boards in 1868; and again, 1871, the sixth edition at 2/o boards listed in the *Ath* on May 20. It was issued in the fall of 1879 as No. 391 in the series, the 11th edition, but not in the series clothing. The first American edition was probably issued by D. Appleton & Co., New York, 1872, 19 cm., 419 pp., noticed in *Lit World* (monthly) on Oct. 1.

Also 1903. See 1901

Ward, Lock & Bowden, Ltd.
London, New York, and Melbourne
1895

The Melbourne office was moved to Little Collins Street by May 1895.

2346 LAWRENCE L. LYNCH
(EMMA MURDOCH, later VAN DEVENTER)
Against Odds. 2/o boards
Feb. 16 (*Ath*)

Select Library of Fiction No. 851, new numbering. This probably has 312 pp. The first English edition was issued by Ward, Lock & Bowden, Ltd., 1894, 19 cm., 312 pp., at 2/6 cloth, listed in the *Spect* on June 9, and in the *Ath* on June 23. The first American edition was issued by Rand, McNally, Chicago and New York, 1894, 19.5 cm., 272 pp., *Globe Library* No. 183, the series title appearing on the cover. It was listed in *Public Opinion* and the *Ind* on June 14, *PW* on June 23, and the *Nation* on June 28.
Also 1903

2347 COULSON KERNAHAN (JOHN COULSON KERNAHAN) *God and the Ant.*
Oblong 8vo. 1/o sewed   Apr. 20 (*PC*)

This is the first edition (1895), 19 cm., 60 pp. It was advertised at times as 1/o sewed and at times as 1/o leatherette. The 28th thousand at 1/o sewed was advertised in the *Ath* on Nov. 23, 1895. It was issued in the United States by Ward, Lock & Bowden, Ltd., New York (1895), 18 cm., 48 pp., $.25 paper, advertised in the *Ind* on Apr. 11 and June 20 and listed Apr. 18, and listed in *PW* on Aug. 3.
Also 1896, 99

2348 E. P. OPPENHEIM *The Peer and the Women.* 0/6 sewed   May 18 (*PC*)

Popular Sixpenny Books. The *BM* gives 1895, with 226 pp.; and the *U Cat* gives 1895, with 256 pp. It was reissued, 1910, 1912, and 1913, 20 cm., 320 pp., with a frontispiece. The first edition was issued by J. A. Taylor & Co., New York (1892), 19 cm., 259 pp., with "Mayflower Library No. 4" on the front cover. It was listed in *Public Opinion* and in *PW* on Mar. 19 and in *Lit World* (fortnightly) on Apr. 9.

2349 LAWRENCE L. LYNCH
(EMMA MURDOCH, later VAN DEVENTER)
A Dead Man's Step. 1/o sewed
May 25 (*PC*)
Also 1894

2350 W. FERRARS-AUBURN *With Lance and Pennon.* 1/o sewed   July 6 (*PC*)
Shilling Novels. This is the first edition, 1895, 185 pp.

2351 JOSEPH HOCKING *The Weapons of Mystery.* 1/o sewed   Oct. 12 (*PC*)
Shilling Novels. This is 1895, with 192 pp. It was reissued in 1899, Cr 8vo, at 3/6 cloth, listed in the *Spect* on Jan. 21. The first edition was issued by George Routledge, London, 1890, 192 pp., 1/o sewed, in Sept.

2352 EDGAR FAWCETT *The Ghost of Guy Thyrle.* p 8vo. 2/o boards   Oct. 12 (*Ath*)
Library of Select Authors. Select Library of Fiction No. 978, new numbering. This is my copy, the first English edition, 1895, 18.2 cm., 284 pp., yellow pictorial boards, printed in red and black, with the series title at the foot of the spine. There are ads on the endpapers, back cover, and 4 pp. at the back. The first edition was issued by Peter F. Collier, New York (1895), 18 cm., 282 pp., in nonpictorial wrappers printed in black on white. It is dated Mar. 21, 1895, on the front cover, and it was deposited Apr. 1.

2353 BICKNELL DUDLEY *A Gentleman from Gascony.* p 8vo. 2/o boards   Oct. 12 (*Ath*)
Select Library of Fiction No. 964, new numbering. This is the first English edition, my copy, no date, 18.3 cm., 300 pp., yellow pictorial boards, printed in red, blue, and black. It has a decorative spine not on any other yellowback in my collection. There are ads on the endpapers, back cover, and 20 pp. at the back. The first American edition was issued by Street & Smith, New York, 1895, 19.5 cm., 300 pp., with "Criterion Series No. 11" on the front cover.

2354 HENRY BACON *Etretat.* 2/o sewed   Oct. 19 (*PC*)
This is the first English edition. The *BM* gives Paris (1895); and the *U Cat* gives Brentano, Paris (189–?), 17 cm., 132 pp., illustrated.

2355 DOUGLAS SLADEN *The Japs at Home.* Fifth Edition. 2/6 boards, 3/6 cloth   Oct. 26 (*PC*)
This is 20.5 cm., 354 pp., and at least one of the editions is illustrated. It was advertised in the *Spect* on Nov. 9, 1895, as "Just ready," "The Japs at Home, to Which Is Added for the First Time, 'Bits of China.'" The first edition was issued by Hutchinson & Co., London, 1892, 21.5 cm., 339 pp., illustrated, 15/o, listed in the *Spect* on Oct. 15, and in the *Times Weekly Edition* on Oct. 14. The second edition was advertised in the *Spect* on Nov. 5, 1892, the same, as "Now ready." In the United States it was issued by J. B. Lippincott & Co., Philadelphia, illustrated, at $3.50, listed in the *Literary Digest* on Nov. 19, 1892.

2356 FREDERICK G. WEBB *The Dash for the Colours, and Other Ballads and Sketches.* 1/o cloth   Oct.?
This is the first edition, 1895, 151 pp.

2357 HENRY HERMAN *Lady Turpin.* Illustrated. 1/o sewed   Dec. 12 (*PC*)
This is Beeton's Christmas Annual, 1895. It is the first edition of this story, with 170 pp.
Also 1899, 1903, 05

2358 R. W. ATKINSON *Popular Guide to the Professions.* 1/o sewed, 1/6 cloth   Dec. 21 (*PC*)
Shilling Useful Books. This is the first edition, 1895, 131 pp.

Ward, Lock & Co., Ltd.
London, New York, and Melbourne
1896

The style of the firm was changed to Ward, Lock & Co., Ltd., between Aug. 8 and 29, 1896, as James Bowden retired from the firm in June 1896 and ceased to take any part in the management on June 30. He started his own publishing company at 10 Henrietta Street, mentioned in editorial matter in the Ath *on Aug. 1, 1896. It is baffling to note the changes of address of the Melbourne office. I think they were at Mackillop Street on Sept. 8, 1894, having moved from St. James's Street. They were at Little Collins Street on Apr. 27, 1895; back on Mackillop on Apr. 11, 1896; back to Little Collins on Jan. 2, 1897; and back to Mackillop on May 15, 1897. I much doubt this perpetual motion and think it possible that the head office in London was confused and when placing their ads in the periodicals were careless.*

2359 EDGAR FAWCETT **Her Fair Fame; and The Story of a Statue.** 2/0 boards
July 11 (*Ath*)

Select Library of Fiction No. 979, new numbering. This probably has 263 pp. The first English edition was issued by Ward, Lock & Bowden, Ltd., 1894, 20 cm., 263 pp., with a frontispiece, 3/6 cloth. It was in the *Warwick House Library* and was listed in the *Ath* on July 14 and in *PC* on July 21. The first American edition was *Her Fair Fame*, issued by Merrill & Baker, New York, 1894, 18.5 cm., 220 pp., $1.00 listed in *Public Opinion* on Aug. 9, and in *PW* on Aug. 11.

2360 TIGHE HOPKINS **Kilmainham Memories.** Cr 8vo. Illustrated. 1/0 sewed
Sept. 19 (*PC*)

This is the first edition, 1896, 19 cm., 96 pp. There was a second edition, 1896, 96 pp.

2361 WILLIAM PETT RIDGE **An Important Man and Others.** Illustrated. 1/0 sewed
Sept. 19 (*PC*)

Shilling Novels. This is the first edition, 1896, 192 pp., containing stories and sketches.
Also 1900

2362 LAWRENCE L. LYNCH
(EMMA MURDOCH, later VAN DEVENTER)
No Proof. 2/0 boards   Oct. 3 (*PC*)

Select Library of Fiction No. 852, new numbering. The first English edition was issued by Ward, Lock & Bowden, Ltd. (1895), 18.5 cm., 354 pp., 2/6 cloth, listed in the *Ath* on Oct. 5. The first American edition was issued by Rand, McNally, Chicago and New York (copyright 1895), 19.5 cm., 354 pp., with "Globe Library No. 221" on the cover. It was listed in the *Nation* on Sept. 26, in *Public Opinion* and the *Ind* on Oct. 3, and in *PW* on Oct. 12, 1895.

2363 CAMPBELL RAE-BROWN *The Race with Death; and Other Ballads and Readings.* 1/o   Oct. 24 (*PC*)

This is the first edition, 1896, 98 pp., a book of recitations. A *PC* ad said 1/o sewed, "On Nov. 7," and *Bks* gives it as 1/o sewed, published in Oct., but an 1898 catalog gives it as 1/o cloth, and a 1906 catalog gives it as o/6 sewed, 1/o cloth.

2364 COULSON KERNAHAN *God and the Ant.* [40th thousand]. Oblong 8vo. 1/o sewed   Nov. 28 (*PC*)

This was also listed in *PC* on Feb. 27, 1897, a new edition, long 12mo, 60 pp., at 2/o.
Also 1895, 99

2365 ANDREW ACWORTH *A New Eden.* o/6 sewed   Dec. (*Bks*)

Popular Sixpenny Books. This is the first edition (1896), 134 pp.
Also 1897

2366 ELIZABETH P. TRAIN *A Social Highwayman.* Illustrated. 1/o sewed Dec. (*Bks*)

This is Beeton's Christmas Annual, 1896, the 37th year. It is the first English edition of this story. It was also issued with *A Professional Beauty* in 1 vol. (1898), Cr 8vo, 352 pp., illustrated, 3/6 cloth, listed in the *Ath* on Sept. 10, 1898. It ran in *Lippincott's Magazine* in 1895, and the first American edition was issued by J. B. Lippincott & Co., Philadelphia, 1896 (1895), 16.5 cm., 196 pp., illustrated, $.75, in the *Lotus Library*, which words appear on the cover. It was listed in *Public Opinion* and in the *Ind* on Nov. 21, 1895, and in *Lit World* on Nov. 30.
Also 1899, 1903, 05

2367 E. P. OPPENHEIM *False Evidence.* [Second edition]. 1/o sewed   Dec. (*Bks*)
Shilling Novels. I cannot locate the first edition, as both the *BM* and the *Eng Cat* give

only the second edition (1896), Cr 8vo, 189 pp. It was issued by Ward, Lock & Co., Ltd., New York, listed in *PW* on Jan. 16, 1897, $.40 paper; listed the same in the *Ind* on July 8, 1897, $.25 paper; and listed the same in *Lit World* (fortnightly) on July 10. The first edition was probably in 1896, as the *U Cat* gives Ward, Lock & Bowden (1896?), 20 cm., 189 pp., which would have been before Oct.
Also 1897, 1902

2368 GEORGE J. WHYTE MELVILLE *Contraband.* 2/o boards   1896

Library of Select Authors. Select Library of Fiction No. 122, new numbering. This is my copy, no date, 18.1 cm., 353 pp., pale blue pictorial boards, printed in red, green, and black, with "The Works of Whyte Melville" at the top of the spine, and the series title at the foot. It has the No. 394 on the front and has ads on the endpapers, back cover, and in a 26-page catalog at the back. The imprint is Ward, Lock & Co., Ltd., London, New York and Melbourne. The first edition was issued by Chapman & Hall, London, 2 vols., 1871 (1870), 20 cm., at 21/o, listed in the *Ath* on Dec. 10, 1870. It was reissued at 2/o boards, listed in the *Ath* on Nov. 18, 1871. It was again reissued, 1878, my copy, a new edition, 18.9 cm., 316 pp., 2/o, in yellow pictorial boards. It was reissued, 1874, a new edition, 316 pp., 2/6 cloth, probably in the cloth edition of the series; and again reissued in the fall of 1879 as No. 394 in the series, at 2/o boards. It was issued in New York by George Munro as *Seaside Library* No. 1343, 4to, $.20 paper, advertised in the *New-York Times* on Aug. 3, 1882, as "Out today."
Also 1902   *See color photo section*

The New York office was closed temporarily on Nov. 1, 1897.

2369 SHAN F. BULLOCK *Ring o' Rushes.*
16mo. 1/6 limp leatherette, 2/o cloth
Feb. 27 (*Spect*)
Seven Seas Series No. 1. The first English edition was issued by Ward, Lock & Co., Ltd., 1896, 195 pp., and 2 plates. The first American edition was issued by Stone & Kimball, New York, 1896, 17.5 cm., 230 pp., $1.25, containing 11 tales. It was listed in the *Outlook*, New York (weekly) on Nov. 28, 1896, and listed in the *New York Times Book Review* on Nov. 28.

2370 GEORGE KNIGHT *The Circle of the Earth.* 1/6 limp leatherette, 2/o cloth
Mar. 20 (*PC*)
Seven Seas Series No. 2. This is the first edition, 1897, 217 pp. It was listed in *PC* also on May 15, 1897, the same.

COULSON KERNAHAN *Strange Sin Series.*
3 vols. o/6 leatherette, 1/o cloth each
A Book of Strange Sins containing all three plus a fourth title issued in 1898, was issued in 1 vol., 1893, 19 cm., 195 pp., 3/6 cloth, listed in the *Spect* on Nov. 11, and advertised in the *Times Weekly Edition* on Nov. 3 as "At once"; a second edition, the same, was advertised in the latter on Dec. 18, 1893. They issued it in New York, 1894 (1893), 19.5 cm., 195 pp., $.50 paper, listed in *Public Opinion* and in the *Ind* on Nov. 23, 1893, and in *PW* on Dec. 9.

L. C. Page & Co., Boston issued all four in 4 vols., 1901, 19.5 cm., $.35 each, in the *Day's Work Series*, all listed in *PW* on Oct. 26, 1901.

2371 No. 1. *A Literary Gent.* May 8 (*PC*)
This is (1897), 19 cm., 61 pp., and a portrait. The Page issue was the same.

2372 No. 2. *The Lonely God.* Aug. 28 (*PC*)
This is (1897), 52 pp., and a frontispiece, and contains also "A Suicide" and "A Lost Soul." It was listed in the *Times Weekly Edition* on July 23, 1897, at 1/o. The Page issue was the same.

2373 No. 3. *The Apples of Sin.* Dec. (*Bks*)
This is (1897), 47 pp., and a frontispiece, including "The Garden of God" on pp. (37)–47. The Page edition was the same.

2374 LUCY H. YATES *A Handbook of Fish Cookery.* 18mo. 1/o May 15 (*PC*)
This is the first edition, 1897, 15.5 cm., 87 pp.

2375 W. FERRARS-AUBURN *In Camp and Barrack.* Cr 8vo. 1/o sewed May 22 (*PC*)
Shilling Novels. This is the first edition, 1897, 182 pp.

2376 DAVID WILLIAMSON
Queen Victoria. o/6 sewed, 1/o limp
May, June (*PC*)
This is the first edition, 1897, 64 pp. It was listed at 1/o in the *Times Weekly Edition* on

May 14, 1897, and in *PC* at 1/0 on May 15, 4to, and the 0/6 issue was listed in *PC*, Roy 8vo, on June 26. It was also issued by W. Bryce, Toronto, 1897, 27 cm., 64 pp., illustrated.

2377 ROWLAND GREY (LILIAN K. ROWLAND-BROWN) *The Craftsman.* 16mo. 1/6 limp leatherette, 2/0 cloth June 12 (*Spect*)
Seven Seas Series No. 3. This is the first edition (1897), 198 pp.

2378 ANONYMOUS *A Popular and Pictorial Guide to London.* Small format. Maps, plans. 1/0 limp   June 26 (*PC*)
The *PC* listing is for the 14th edition. The *U Cat* gives it as 1897, 16th edition, and also, 1898, 16th edition, 16.5 cm., 352 pp. The 26th edition was listed in the *Times Literary Supplement* (London) on Apr. 21, 1905, *A Pictorial and Descriptive Guide to London and Its Environs*, entirely rewritten and reillustrated, 17.2 cm., 336 pp., at 1/0. *A New Guide to London* was announced in the *Spect* on July 28, 1894, 360 pp., illustrated, maps, plans, at 1/0.
Also 1879, 89

2379 RICHARD MARSH *The Mystery of Philip Bennion's Death.* Cr 8vo. 1/0 sewed July 3 (*PC*)
Shilling Novels. This is the first edition (1897), 172 pp. It was issued by Ward, Lock in New York, 1899, 20 cm., 240 pp., with a frontispiece. It was issued in England in 1899, Cr 8vo, illustrated, 3/6, advertised in the *Ath* on June 17 as "Just ready."
Also 1900, 04

2380 E. P. OPPENHEIM *False Evidence.* 1/0 sewed   Aug. 7 (*Acad*)
This was probably a reissue of the *Shilling Novels* edition of 1896. It was issued in New York by Ward, Lock, 12mo, in paper,

listed in the *New York Times Book Review* on July 17, 1897.
Also 1896, 1902

2381 LAWRENCE L. LYNCH (EMMA MURDOCH, later VAN DEVENTER) *The Last Stroke.* Cr 8vo. 2/0 cloth Aug. 21 (*Spect*)
This is the first English edition (1897), 19 cm., 319 pp., 2/0, green pictorial cloth blocked in colors, and listed in the *Ath* on Aug. 14 and in *PC* on Aug. 28. It was also issued at 2/0 boards as *Select Library of Fiction* No. 853, new numbering, at a date unknown to me. The first edition was issued by Laird & Lee, Chicago (copyright 1896), 19.5 cm., 290 pp., $.25 paper, *Pinkerton Detective Series* No. 29, which words were on the cover. It was listed in *PW* and in the *New York Times Book Review* on Dec. 5, 1896.
Also 1901, 02

2382 ANDREW ACWORTH *A New Eden.* 0/6 sewed   Aug.?
Popular Sixpenny Books, a reissue of the edition of 1896.
Also 1896

2383 MRS. H. F. WICKEN *Australian Table Dainties and Appetizing Dishes.* Cr 8vo. 1/0 sewed   Sept. 18 (*PC*)
This is the first edition, 1897, 154 pp.

2384 HARRIET L. CHILDE-PEMBERTON *Dead Letters, and Other Narrative and Dramatic Pieces.* Cr 8vo. 1/0   Sept. 18 (*PC*)
The first edition was issued by Ward, Lock, 1896, Cr 8vo, 125 pp., in Dec. at 1/0.
Also 1900

2385 ELIZABETH P. TRAIN ET AL. *A Professional Beauty, etc.* Illustrated. 1/0 sewed   Nov. 20 (*PC*)
This is Beeton's Christmas Annual, 1897. It is the first English edition of the title

story. It contains also stories by Ada Cambridge, A. R. Thomson, and Ethel Turner. Ward, Lock issued this story by Train along with *A Social Highwayman* in 1 vol. (1898), 316 pp., 352 pp., in Sept. The first American edition of the present Train story was *The Autobiography of a Professional Beauty*, issued by J. B. Lippincott & Co., Philadelphia, 1896, 17 cm., 233 pp., illustrated, $.75, in their *Lotus Library*. It was listed in the *Ind* on Mar. 26 and ran in *Lippincott's Magazine* in 1894, pp. (569)–668.

2386 GUY BOOTHBY ET AL.
The Christmas Number of the Windsor
Magazine. Illustrated. 1/o sewed
Nov. 27 (*Spect* ad)

This contains 12 stories by Boothby, Meade, Westall, Zangwill, et al., plus articles, and also contains the beginning of *Kronstadt* by Max Pemberton.

2387 EDWARD SCOTT *How to Dance and Guide to the Ballroom.* Entirely New Edition. 12mo. o/6 sewed, 1/o cloth Dec. 18 (*PC*)

This is a reissue in *Sixpenny Manuals* (1897), 122 pp. The o/6 issue was listed in *PC* as I've given it, and the 1/o issue was listed on Dec. 24.
Also 1894

2388 BERNARD LAZARE *A Judicial Error.*
o/6 sewed   Dec.?

This is the first English edition (1897), 111 pp., translated from the French, *Une Erreur Judiciaire*, issued at Bruxelles,

1896, 20.5 cm., 24 pp., cover title. A second edition was issued at Paris, 1897, 19 cm., 94 pp. The book concerns the Dreyfus case.

2389 HAWLEY SMART *At Fault.*
1/o sewed   1897?
Also 1883, 1901, 02

2390 (JOHN HABBERTON) *Helen's Babies.*
Cr 8vo. Wrappers   1897?

This is my copy, no date, with the imprint of Ward, Lock & Co., Ltd., London, New York, and Melbourne, 19.6 cm., 160 pp., white pictorial wrappers, printed in black, with ads on the inside covers. The authors' name is on the front cover only.
Also 1877

2391 ANONYMOUS *Elementary Carpentry and Joinery.* Cr 8vo. Illustrated. 1/o boards   1897?

Shilling Useful Books. This is my copy, with the same imprint as in the preceding item, no date, 19.2 cm., 222 pp., white pictorial boards, printed in red, blue, and black. There are ads on the endpapers and back cover, and the series title does not appear. The ad on the front endpapers is for the *Pansy Series* at 1/o cloth each, Cr 8vo, those by Pansy being numbered 1–28, those by other authors numbered 38–74, and those by Charles Sheldon are numbered 91–97. The missing numbers apparently leave room for future additions.
Also 1883

Ward, Lock & Co., Ltd.
London, New York, and Melbourne
1898

2392 GEORGE GIFFEN **With Bat and Ball.**
Portraits. 2/6 boards, 3/6 cloth   Feb. 26
(*Spect*)
This is the first edition, 1898, small 8vo,
240 pp. The third edition at 2/o cloth was
issued in June 1899.

2393 COULSON KERNAHAN **A Strange Sin.**
Cr 8vo. Frontispiece. o/6 leatherette, 1/o
cloth   Mar. (*Bks*)
Strange Sin Series No. 4. For details on this
series see 1897. The present title was issued by L. C. Page & Co., Boston, 1901, in
the *Day's Work Series*, listed in *PW* on Oct.
26.

2394 B. D. DE TASSINARI **An Italian
Fortune-Hunter.** 1/o sewed   Mar. (*Bks*)
This is the first edition (1898), 182 pp.

2395 ERNEST E. WILLIAMS
Marching Backward. Long 8vo.
1/o sewed   May 7 (*Acad*)
This is the first English edition (1898),
160 pp., reprinted from the *Daily Mail* of
Nov. 5–16, 1897. The first American edi-
tion was issued by the Home Market Club,
Boston, 1898, 22.5 cm., 32 pp.

2396 ORME AGNUS (JOHN C.
HIGGINBOTHAM) **Countess Petrovski.**
1/o sewed   May 21 (*Acad*)
This is the first edition (1898), 184 pp.
Also 1900

2397 ANONYMOUS *Penny Handbooks*
16 vols. o/1 sewed each   July (Bks)
These had 96 pp. each. No. 1 was *Gardening*; No. 2 was *Cookery*; No. 3 was *The Toilet*,
etc. The spring 1906, Ward, Lock catalog
listed Nos. 1–26 (some missing) with *Golf*
given as No. 22. Golf was listed in the *Acad*
on May 13, 1899.

2398 M. BIRD **The Seeker.** 12mo.
1/o sewed   Aug. (Bks)
This is the first edition (1898), 17.5 cm.,
181 pp.

2399 COULSON KERNAHAN **The Apples of
Sin.** o/6 leatherette, 1/o cloth   Oct. (*Ath*)
This is a reissue of the 1897 edition.
Also 1897

2400 CHARLES M. SHELDON **In His Steps.**
o/6 sewed, 1/o cloth, 1/6 cloth   Dec. 10
(*Acad*)
Sheldon Library No. 1. This is (1898), with
307 pp. The o/6 issue is Cr 8vo, with a
frontispiece, in a tinted wrapper; the 1/o
issue is Cr 8vo, with the frontispiece, in
cloth; and the 1/6 issue is large Cr 8vo, illustrated, in cloth. Ward, Lock issued it
about the same time in the new *Lily Series*,
large Cr 8vo, illustrated, 1/6 cloth; and in
the *Pansy Series*, Cr 8vo, 1/o cloth. There
were many English editions in 1898, including H. R. Allenson, London, 1898, an
authorized edition, 282 pp.; the Sunday
School Union (1898), 265 pp.; S. W. Par-

tridge & Co., London, 1898, 319 pp., as *Our Exemplar*; and George Routledge, 19.5 cm., 288 pp., at 1/0 cloth, in Nov. 1898. The American editions were also confusing. Wright gives the first edition as issued by Fleming Revell Co., New York, Chicago, and Toronto, 1897, 20 cm., 282 pp. It was also issued by the Advance Publishing Co., Chicago, 1897, 20 cm., 282 pp., listed in the *Ind* on June 24, 1897, and listed by the *Outlook*, New York (weekly) on June 18, 1897, at $1.00. The Advance edition was listed in *Review of Reviews*, New York, for June 1898, 282 pp., $.75;

listed in the *Nation* on Mar. 3, 1898; and in *Public Opinion* on Mar. 10, 1898. The *PW* for Sept. 2, 1899, listed at least five different American houses, in addition to the above two, as issuing it then or shortly thereafter.

2401 CHARLES J. WILLS & GODFREY BURCHETT *The Dean's Apron, etc.* 8vo. Illustrated. 1/0 sewed   Dec. 10 (*Acad*)

This is Beeton's Christmas Annual, 1898. It is the first edition, with 232 pp. It was issued at 3/6 cloth, listed in the *Times Weekly Edition* on Aug. 10, 1900.

Ward, Lock & Co., Ltd.
London, New York, and Melbourne
1899

2402 CHARLES M. SHELDON
The Crucifixion of Phillip Strong.
Illustrated. o/6 sewed, 1/o cloth,
1/6 cloth   Jan. (*Bks*)

Sheldon Library No. 2. This is (1899), with
309 pp. Ward, Lock also issued it about
the same time in the new *Lily Series*, large
Cr 8vo, illustrated, 1/6 cloth, and in the
Pansy Series, Cr 8vo, 1/o cloth. The first
edition was issued by A. C. McClurg &
Co., Chicago, 1894, 18.5 cm., 267 pp.,
$1.00, listed in the *Nation* on Nov. 22, and
in the *New-York Times* on Nov. 1. The first
English edition was either issued by the
Sunday School Union, London, or by
S. W. Partridge & Co., London. The former is (1898), 267 pp., issued in Dec.
1898; and the latter is 1899, 288 pp., issued in Dec. 1898. There were at least
seven other houses in England who issued
it in 1899, including George Routledge,
London (1899), 255 pp., with a frontispiece, at o/6 sewed, 1/o cloth, in Feb.;
Simpkin, Marshall, London (1899), 79
pp., at o/3 sewed, in Apr.

2403 CHARLES M. SHELDON *His Brother's
Keeper.* Illustrated. o/6 sewed, 1/o cloth,
1/6 cloth   Feb. 18 (*Acad* ad)

Sheldon Library No. 3. This is (1899), with
320 pp. See the preceding item for other
Ward, Lock issues. The first edition was is-
sued by the Congregational Sunday-
School and Publishing Society, Boston
and Chicago (copyright 1896), 19.5 cm.,
381 pp., illustrated, $1.50, listed in *Lit
World* on Oct. 3, the *Ind* on Oct. 8, and *PW*
on Oct. 10, 1896. The first English edition
was issued by either the Sunday School
Union, London, or by S. W. Partridge,
London. The former is (1899), 281 pp., in
Jan.; and the latter is 1899, 318 pp., in
Jan. It was also issued by H. R. Allenson,
London, 1899, 318 pp.; and by George
Routledge, London (1899), the latter with
318 pp., with a frontispiece, at o/6 sewed,
1/o cloth, in Mar.

2404 CHARLES M. SHELDON
Richard Bruce. Illustrated. o/6 sewed,
1/o cloth, 1/6 cloth   Mar. 11 (*Acad*)

Sheldon Library No. 4. This is (1899), with
313 pp. For other Ward, Lock issues see
Jan. above. The first edition was issued by
the Congregational Sunday-School and
Publishing Society, Boston and Chicago
(1892), 19.5 cm., 355 pp., illustrated,
$1.50, listed in the *Christian Union* on Nov.
26, 1892, and in *PW* on Dec. 3 (no lists on
Nov. 19 or 26 in the latter). The first English edition was probably issued by H. R.
Allenson, London (1899), 313 pp., in Jan.
1899. At least four other houses in England issued it in 1899, including the Sunday School Union, London (1899), 355
pp.; George Routledge, London (1899),
326 pp., frontispiece, o/6 sewed, 1/o cloth,
in Apr.; and Frederick Warne, London,
1899, 19 cm., 288 pp., illustrated, 1/6
sewed, 2/o cloth, probably in Mar.

2405 BERTRAM MITFORD *The Curse of Clement Waynflete.* Fourth Edition. Illustrated. 2/0 boards   Mar. (*Bks*)

2/0 Copyright Novels No. 1. This begins this long series of cheap issues of copyright novels. They have a front cover in colorful, pictorial, lithographed boards and a red or blue cloth spine. The present title is my copy, no date, 18.6 cm., 312 pp., with a frontispiece and 2 full-page illustrations, a blue cloth spine and plain white endpapers, and an ad on the back cover. The first edition was issued by Ward, Lock & Bowden, Ltd., 1894, 19 cm., with 4 full-page illustrations, 3/6 cloth, listed in the *Ath* on Oct. 13. The second edition was also 1894, and the third edition was 1896, these being the same as the first edition. It was issued by the New York branch at $1.00 cloth, listed in *PW* on Dec. 15, 1894, but not received.

2406 CHARLES M. SHELDON *Malcolm Kirk.* 0/6 sewed, 1/0 cloth, 1/6 cloth   Mar.?

Sheldon Library No. 6. This is (1899), with 240 pp. For other Ward, Lock issues see Jan. above. The first edition was issued by the Church Press, Chicago (1898), 17 cm., 264 pp., illustrated, listed in the *Nation* on Apr. 7 and the *Ind* on Apr. 14. The first English edition was probably H. R. Allenson, London, 1899, 255 pp., in Feb.; or the Sunday School Union, London (1899), 255 pp., in Feb. It was also issued by S. W. Partridge, London, 1899, 224 pp., also a possible first English edition. It was also issued by George Routledge, London (1899), 192 pp., with a frontispiece, 0/6 sewed, 1/0 cloth, in Mar.; and by Frederick Warne, London, Cr 8vo, 1/6 sewed, 2/0 cloth, probably in Mar. 1899.

2407 CHARLES M. SHELDON *The Twentieth Door.* Illustrated. 0/6 sewed, 1/0 cloth, 1/6 cloth Apr. 1 (*Acad*)

Sheldon Library No. 5. This is (1899), 19.5 cm., 320 pp. For other Ward, Lock issues

see Jan. above. The first edition was issued by the Congregational Sunday-School and Publishing Society, Boston and Chicago (1893), 19.5 cm., 357 pp., illustrated, $1.50, listed in the *Ind* and *Public Opinion* on Oct. 5, and in *PW* on Oct. 14. The first English edition was probably issued by H. R. Allenson, London, 1899, 320 pp., in Jan. At least three other houses in England issued it in 1899, including George Routledge, London (1899), 312 pp., 0/6 sewed, 1/0 cloth, in Apr.; and Frederick Warne, London, Cr 8vo, 1/6 sewed, 2/0 cloth, probably in Mar. 1899.

2408 CHARLES M. SHELDON *Robert Hardy's Seven Days.* Illustrated. 0/6 sewed, 1/0 cloth, 1/6 cloth   Apr. 1 (*Acad*)

Sheldon Library No. 7. This is 1899, with 394305 pp. For descriptions and other Ward, Lock issues see Jan. above. The first edition was issued by the Congregational Sunday-School and Publishing Society, Chicago and Boston (1893), 238 pp., listed in *Public Opinion* on July 29 and in *PW* on Aug. 5, at $.90. The first English edition was probably issued by either J. Clarke & Co., London, or H. R. Allenson, London. The former was (1899), 201 pp., in Jan.; and the latter was 1899, 238 pp., in Jan. It was issued by at least four other English houses in 1899, including George Routledge, London (1899), 208 pp., 0/6 sewed, 1/0 cloth, in Feb.; and Frederick Warne, London, Cr 8vo, 1/6 sewed, 2/0 cloth, probably in Mar. 1899.

2409 RICHARD MARSH *The Crime and the Criminal.* p 8vo. Illustrated. 2/0 boards Apr. (*Bks*)

2/0 Copyright Novels No. 2. This is my copy, no date, 18.3 cm., 346 pp., with a frontispiece and a full-page illustration. It is in pictorial lithographed boards in red, brown, green, blue, and black, with a red cloth spine and plain white endpapers. There is an ad on the back cover. The first

edition was issued by Ward, Lock & Co., Ltd. (1897), 19 cm., 346 pp., illustrated, 3/6 cloth, listed in the *Ath* on Sept. 11 and *PC* on Sept. 18. The second edition at 3/6 cloth, illustrated, was advertised in the *Spect* on Nov. 27, 1897. It was issued in New York by the Amsterdam Book Co. in 1901, in their *Red Letter Series*, in paper, mentioned in editorial matter in the *New York Times Book Review* on Feb. 9.
Also 1901, 03

2410 COULSON KERNAHAN
Captain Shannon. Second Edition.
p 8vo. Illustrated. 2/o boards
Apr. (*Bks*)

2/o Copyright Novels No. 3. This is my copy, 1897, 18.1 cm., 258 pp., in pictorial, lithographed boards in brown, blue, green, and black, with a red cloth spine and plain white endpapers. It has a frontispiece and 13 full-page illustrations, with 6 pp. of ads at the back, and an ad on the back cover. Apparently the first edition title page was used and overprinted with "Second edition" or the second edition title page of 1897 was used. This ran in the *Windsor Magazine* of Ward, Lock, beginning in July 1896, illustrated. It ran monthly through Nov. 1896. The first edition was issued by Dodd, Mead & Co., New York, 1896, 19.5 cm., 296 pp., $1.25 cloth, listed in the *Nation* on Oct. 15, *PW* on Oct. 17, and the *Ind* on Oct. 29. The first English edition was issued by Ward, Lock, 1897, 258 pp., illustrated, 3/6 cloth, listed in *PC* on Apr. 24.
Also 1900

2411 ARTHUR MORRISON **Chronicles of Martin Hewitt.** Cr 8vo. Illustrated. 2/o boards   Apr. (*Bks*)

2/o Copyright Novels No. 4. This is my copy, no date, 19 cm., 322 pp., with a frontispiece, and 18 full-page illustrations and 5 textual illustrations. It is bound in pictorial lithographed boards in red, blue, brown, green, and black, with a red cloth spine and plain white endpapers. This

ran in Ward, Lock's *Windsor Magazine*, beginning in Jan. 1895, illustrated, in the first issue of the magazine, running monthly through June 1895. The first edition was issued by Ward, Lock, 1895, 19.5 cm., 322 pp., illustrated, 5/o cloth, listed in the *Ath* on Nov. 2, 1895. The first American edition was issued by D. Appleton & Co., New York, 1896, 18 cm., 267 pp., $.50 paper and $1.00 cloth, *Town and Country Library* No. 191. It was listed in *PW* on Apr. 25 and advertised in the *New-York Times* on Apr. 18 and listed Apr. 26.
Also 1901

2412 HEADON HILL (FRANCIS GRAINGER)
The Queen of Night. Frontispiece. 2/o boards   May (*Bks*)

2/o Copyright Novels No. 5. This is my copy, no date, 19 cm., 252 pp., in pictorial lithographed boards, in blue, tan, yellow, white, and black, with plain white endpapers. There are 4 pp. of publisher's ads at the back and an ad on the back cover. The first edition was issued by Ward, Lock, 1896, 19.5 cm., 252 pp., with a frontispiece, 3/6 cloth, listed in the *Ath* on Oct. 24. It was issued by the New York branch, 252 pp., at $1.00 cloth, listed in *PW* on Dec. 12, 1896, but not received.
Also 1900, 04

2413 MRS. EUPHANS STRAIN **A Man's Foes.** p 8vo. Illustrated. 2/o boards
May (*Bks*)

2/o Copyright Novels No. 6. This is my copy, no date, 18.5 cm., 467 pp., a frontispiece and one full-page illustration, pictorial lithographed boards in yellow, red, blue, green, and black, with a red cloth spine and plain white endpapers. It has 2 pp. of ads at the back and an ad on the back cover. The first edition was issued by Ward, Lock in 3 vols., 1895, Cr 8vo, at 15/o, listed in the *Ath* on Sept. 14. The second edition in 3 vols. was advertised in the *Times Weekly Edition* on Nov. 1, 1895, as "Now ready." It was issued in 1 vol., 1896,

467 pp., illustrated, at 6/0, listed in the *Times Weekly Edition* on May 8, and advertised in the *Spect* on May 9 as "Just ready." The fifth edition at 6/0 was advertised in the *Spect* on Aug. 29, 1896, as "Now ready." It was issued by the New York branch, 1896, 19 cm., 467 pp., at $1.25 cloth, listed in the *Ind* on Dec. 5, 1895, the *Nation* on Dec. 12, and *PW* on Dec. 14. It was listed by *PW* on Apr. 11, 1896, 467 pp., $.50 paper, but not received. It was issued by the New Amsterdam Book Co., New York, 1900, 12mo, 467 pp., $.50 paper, $1.50 cloth, listed in the *New York Times Book Review* on Sept. 1, illustrated, *Red Letter Series* No. 14. It was also issued by M. J. Ivers, New York, listed in the *Nation* on Feb. 23, 1896.

2414 COULSON KERNAHAN *A Dead Man's Diary.* Cr 8vo. Frontispiece (portrait). 0/6 sewed   May (*Bks*)

Sixpenny Novels and Popular Books. This is my copy, no date, 18.9 cm., 218 pp., with a preface and a preface to the third edition by G. T. Bettany, and with an inscribed date of 1899. It is in white wrappers cut flush and printed in black, with 6 pp. of ads at the back, an ad on the back cover, but with plain white endpapers. The first edition was issued by Ward, Lock, 1890, 19 cm., anonymous, 218 pp., at 3/6 cloth, with an introduction by Bettany. It has more chapters than the serial in *Lippincott's Magazine.* It was listed in the *Spect* on July 5 and advertised in the *Times Weekly Edition* on July 18 as "Just ready." The second edition was advertised there, the same, on Oct. 17, as "Now ready" and in the *Spect* on Sept. 27, as "Now ready." The fourth edition in the *Warwick House Library*, 1892, 19.5 cm., 218 pp., with the frontispiece, at 3/6 cloth, was issued as No. 4 in July. The fourth edition, the same, was also advertised in the *Times Weekly Edition* on Nov. 3, 1893, as "Now ready." This ran in *Lippincott's Magazine*, with chapters 1–4 in the Feb. 1890 issue. The first

American edition was issued by W. D. Rowland, New York, anonymous, listed in the *Nation* on Aug. 6, 1891. The New York branch of Ward, Lock issued the fifth edition at $1.00, advertised in the *Ind* on Apr. 11, 1895.

2415 COULSON KERNAHAN *God and the Ant.* 0/1 sewed   May (*Bks*)

This has 32 pp.
Also 1895, 96

2416 R. H. LYTTELTON, W. J. FORD, ET AL. *Giants of the Game.* Cr 8vo. 1/0   June 17 (*Acad*)

This is the first edition (1899), 19 cm., 192 pp.

2417 WILLIAM LE QUEUX *A Secret Service Being Strange Tales of a Nihilist.* Second Edition. Cr 8vo. Frontispiece. 2/0 boards   June (*Bks*)

2/0 *Copyright Novels* No. 7. This is my copy, 1896, 18.8 cm., 320 pp., in pictorial lithographed boards in yellow, red, green, blue, and black, with a red cloth spine and plain white endpapers. There is an ad on the back cover.
Also 1903. See *Strange Tales of a Nihilist,* 1892

2418 BERTRAM MITFORD *A Veldt Official.* p 8vo. Illustrated. 2/0 boards   July (*Bks*)

2/0 *Copyright Novels* No. 8. This is my copy, 1898, 18.5 cm., 324 pp., with a frontispiece and one full-page illustration, in pictorial lithographed boards in red, yellow, blue, white, and black, with a red cloth spine and plain white endpapers. There are ads on pp. 1–4 at the back and an ad on the back cover. This was complete in the *Windsor Magazine* of Ward, Lock in the Nov. 1895 issue. The first edition was issued by Ward, Lock, 1895, Cr 8vo, 324 pp., illustrated, at 3/6 cloth, listed in the *Ath* on May 11. It was reissued, 1896 and 1898, the same. It was issued in 1903,

Cr 8vo, at 6/o cloth, listed in the *Spect* on Aug. 29. It was issued by the New York branch, 324 pp., at $1.00 cloth, listed in *PW* on Nov. 2, 1895.

2419 DINAH M. MULOCK, later CRAIK **John Halifax, Gentleman.** Illustrated. o/6 sewed, 1/o cloth, 1/6 cloth   July (*Bks*)
Sheldon Library No. 9. The o/6 issue was Cr 8vo, with a frontispiece, in tinted art wrappers; the 1/o issue was Cr 8vo, in cloth; and the 1/6 issue was large Cr 8vo, illustrated, in cloth. This was also issued about this time in the new *Lily Series* at 1/6 cloth and in the *Pansy Series* at 1/o cloth. The first edition was issued by Hurst & Blackett, London, 3 vols., 1856, 20 cm., anonymous, 31/6, listed in the *Ath* on Apr. 19. It was issued in 1 vol. at 10/6 in 1857, a new edition, anonymous, advertised in the *Spect* on Apr. 4 as "Just ready." The first American edition was issued by Harper & Bros., New York, 1856, anonymous, $.50 paper, advertised in the *New York Daily Times* on June 26 as "On June 28," and listed in *APC&LG* on July 5. They issued a new edition at $.50 paper, advertised in the *New York Daily Times* on Nov. 28, 1856. They reissued it as *Library of Select Novels* No. 201, 1857, 24.5 cm., anonymous, 170 pp.; and reissued it in 1859, the library edition, 12mo, anonymous, 485 pp., illustrated, at $1.00, listed in the *Knickerbocker* for Aug. 1859. There were at least six English editions in 1898, the copyright having expired. Ward, Lock issued it in 1898 at 1/6, 2/o, in Nov.

2420 JOHN BUNYAN **The Holy War.** Illustrated. o/6 sewed, 1/o cloth, 1/6 cloth July?
Sheldon Library No. 8. This was also issued in the *Rainbow Series* at 1/o and in the *Youth's Library* at 1/6 about this time. The first edition was issued by Dorman Newman & Benjamin Alsop, London, 1682, 16.5 cm., 397 pp., illustrated. The first American edition was probably issued by

T. Fleet, Boston, 1736, 14.5 cm., 301 pp., with a frontispiece. Ward, Lock issued it as *Sixpenny Standard Novels and Popular Books* No. 202 in 1903 or 1904.

2421 HENRY HERMAN **Woman, the Mystery.** Illustrated. 2/o boards Aug. (*Bks*)
2/o Copyright Novels No. 9. The first edition was issued by Ward, Lock, 1894, *Warwick House Library* No. 25, Cr 8vo, 368 pp., illustrated, 3/6 cloth, listed in the *Spect* on July 14, with 4 full-page illustrations.

2422 ELLEN P. WOOD (MRS. HENRY WOOD) **Danesbury House.** Illustrated. o/6 sewed, 1/o cloth, 1/6 cloth   Sept. 16 (*Acad*)
Sheldon Library No. 10. This is 1899, with 317 pp. For descriptions and other Ward, Lock issues see *John Halifax, Gentleman* above. The first edition was a prize story, issued by the Scottish Temperance League, Glasgow; etc., 1860, 16 cm., 347 pp. They issued it at 1/o sewed, 2/o cloth, advertised in the *Spect* on Jan. 3, 1863. The first American edition was issued by Harper & Bros., New York, 1860, 20 cm., 282 pp., $.60 muslin ($.75?), listed in the *Ind* on June 14, and advertised in the *New-York Times* on June 8 as "This day."

2423 ARTHUR MORRISON **Martin Hewitt, Investigator.** Second Edition. p 8vo. Illustrated. 2/o boards   Sept. (*Bks*)
2/o Copyright Novels No. 10. This is my copy, 1895, 18.5 cm., 324 pp., in pictorial lithographed boards in red, blue, green, yellow, and black, with a blue cloth spine and plain white endpapers. There are 4 pp. of ads at the back but with a plain back cover. It has a frontispiece and 15 full-page illustrations and 35 textual illustrations. The first English edition was issued by Ward, Lock, 1894, 19.5 cm., 324 pp., illustrated, 5/o cloth, listed in the *Ath* on Dec. 22, 1894. The second edition, the

same, was issued, 1895. These stories first appeared in the *Strand Magazine*, No. 3 in May 1894, and No. 7 in Sept. The first American edition was issued by Harper & Bros., New York, 1894, 21 cm., 216 pp., illustrated, $.50 paper, *Franklin Square Library* No. 755. It was listed in the *Nation* and the *Ind* on Nov. 22. Rand McNally, Chicago and New York, also issued it, in paper, listed in the *Nation* and the *Ind* on Mar. 14, 1895.

Also 1901, 02 *See color photo section*

2424 MATTHIAS M. BODKIN *A Stolen Life.* Illustrated. 2/o boards   Sept. (*Bks*)

2/o Copyright Novels No. 11. The first edition was issued by Ward, Lock (1898), Cr 8vo, 320 pp., with a frontispiece, at 6/0, advertised in the *Ath* on Apr. 9 as "Just ready."

2425 ELIZABETH P. TRAIN *A Social Highwayman. A Professional Beauty.* p 8vo. Illustrated. 2/o boards   Sept. (*Bks*)

2/o Copyright Novels No. 12. This is my copy, no date, 18.4 cm., 161 pp., (165)–352 pp., with a frontispiece and 4 full-page illustrations. It is in pictorial lithographed boards in red, blue, green, brown, and black, with a red cloth spine and plain white endpapers, and with an ad on the back cover. It was issued at 3/6 cloth, listed in the *Times Weekly Edition* on Sept. 16, 1898.

Also 1896, 1903, 05

2426 ARTHUR C. DOYLE *A Study in Scarlet.* Demy 8vo. Illustrated. o/6 sewed   Oct. (*Bks*)

Sixpenny Novels.

Also 1887, 88, 1902

2427 RICHARD MARSH *The Datchet Diamonds.* Cr 8vo. Illustrated. 2/o boards   Oct. (*Bks*)

2/o Copyright Novels No. 13. This is my copy, no date, 18.8 cm., 302 pp., with a frontispiece and a full-page illustration. It is in pictorial lithographed boards in red, green, brown, blue, and black, with a red cloth spine and plain white endpapers. There are ads paged (1)–12 at the back and an ad on the back cover. The first edition was issued by Ward, Lock (1898), 19 cm., 302 pp., illustrated, listed in the *Ath* on Apr. 2 at 3/6 cloth. In the United States it was issued by the New Amsterdam Book Co., New York, 12mo, 302 pp., illustrated, $1.50, listed in the *New York Times Book Review* on Nov. 11, 1899.

Also 1900

2428 ADA CAMBRIDGE, later CROSS *At Midnight and Other Stories.* Cr 8vo. Illustrated. 2/o boards   Oct. (*Bks*)

2/o Copyright Novels No. 14. The first edition was issued by Ward, Lock, 1897, 19.5 cm., 305 pp., illustrated, 3/6 cloth, listed in the *Ath* and *PC* on Nov. 13, 1897.

2429 MARIA CHARLESWORTH *Ministering Children.* Illustrated. o/6 sewed, 1/o cloth, 1/6 cloth   Oct.?

Sheldon Library No. 11. The o/6 issue was Cr 8vo with a frontispiece, in a tinted art wrapper. The 1/o issue was Cr 8vo with a frontispiece, in cloth; and the 1/6 issue was large Cr 8vo, illustrated, in cloth. It was also issued in the *Pansy Series* at 1/o cloth and in the new *Lily Series* at 1/6 cloth about this time. The first edition was probably issued by Seeley, London, 1854, anonymous. A seventh thousand was issued by Seeley in 1855, 18 cm., anonymous, 426 pp., with a frontispiece, at 5/0, listed by *PC* as published July 14–30. The second edition was issued by Seeley, the same, listed by *PC* as published Jan. 31–Feb. 14, 1855. Ward, Lock issued it as *Sixpenny Standard Novels and Popular Books* No. 201 in 1903 or 1904. In the United States it was issued by Riker, Thorne & Co., New York, 12mo, anonymous, at $1.00 cloth, advertised in the *New York Daily Times* on July 22, 1854, as "This day."

2430 HENRY HERMAN **Lady Turpin.**
p 8vo. Illustrated. 2/o boards   Nov. (*Bks*)

2/o Copyright Novels No. 15. This is my
copy, 1897, 18.5 cm., 255 pp., with a frontispiece and 6 full-page illustrations. It is
in pictorial lithographed boards in white,
pink, blue, and black, with a blue cloth
spine and plain white endpapers. There
are many textual illustrations and an ad
on the back cover. Ward, Lock issued it,
1897, 18.5 cm., 255 pp., illustrated, 3/6
cloth, listed in *PC* on Apr. 17.
Also 1895, 1903, 05

2431 ARTHUR MORRISON **Adventures of
Martin Hewitt.** p 8vo. Illustrated. 2/o
boards   Nov. (*Bks*)

2/o Copyright Novels No. 16. This is my
copy, no date, 18.6 cm., 333 pp., with a
frontispiece, 18 full-page and many textual illustrations. It is in pictorial lithographed boards, in red, blue, green,
white, yellow, and black, with a red cloth
spine and plain white endpapers. There
are 10 pp. of ads at the back and an ad on
the back cover. It contains six stories.
These ran in the *Windsor Magazine* of
Ward, Lock, certainly in Mar. and June
1896, but not in July. The first book edition was issued by Ward, Lock, 1896, 19
cm., 333 pp., illustrated, 5/o, in decorated
blue buckram, listed in the *Ath* on Oct. 10.
Also 1902

2432 HAWLEY SMART **From Post to
Finish.** o/6 sewed   Nov. (*Bks*)
Also 1885, 91, 1904

2433 STEPHANIE WOHL **Sham Gold.**
1/o sewed   Nov. (*Bks*)

The first English edition was issued by
Ward & Downey, London, 1890, Cr 8vo,
316 pp., at 6/o, translated from the Hun-
garian by S. L. Simeon, issued in Sept.
They reissued it in July 1896, a new edition, at 3/6.

Ward, Lock & Co., Ltd.
London, New York, and Melbourne
1900

2434 MAX ADELER (CHARLES H. CLARK) *Out of the Hurly Burly.* o/6 sewed Jan. 20 (*Acad*)
Also 1874, 78, 82, 83

2435 BERTRAM MITFORD *The Expiation of Wynne Palliser.* Cr 8vo. Frontispiece. 2/0 boards Feb. (*Bks*)

2/0 *Copyright Novels* No. 17. This is my copy, no date, 18.8 cm., 343 pp., in pictorial lithographed boards in red, blue, brown, green, and black, with a blue cloth spine and plain white endpapers, and an ad on the back cover. The first edition was issued by Ward, Lock in 1896, 19 cm., 343 pp., illustrated, 3/6 cloth, listed in the *Ath* on May 2. It was issued by the New York branch in 1896, 343 pp., at $1.00 cloth, listed in the *PW* on June 6 but not received.

2436 FLORENCE WARDEN (FLORENCE PRICE, later JAMES) *A Sensational Case.* Second Edition. Cr 8vo. Illustrated. 2/0 boards Mar. (*Bks*)

2/0 *Copyright Novels* No. 18. This is my copy, 1898, 18.8 cm., 351 pp., with a frontispiece and 3 full-page illustrations, in pictorial lithographed boards in red, green, blue, white, and black, with a blue cloth spine and plain white endpapers, and an ad on the back cover. The first English edition was issued by Ward, Lock, 1898, 20 cm., 351 pp., illustrated, 3/6 cloth, listed in the *Ath* on Aug. 27. Glover

and Greene give this as the first edition. The *U Cat* gives the International News Co., New York (copyright 1894), 19.5 cm., 311 pp., located in just one library. I think the supposed date of 1894 is incorrect.
Also 1901

2437 ARTHUR MORRISON *The Dorrington Deed-Box.* Cr 8vo. Illustrated. 2/0 boards Mar. (*Bks*)

2/0 *Copyright Novels* No. 19. This is my copy, no date, 18.8 cm., 308 pp., with a frontispiece and 15 full-page illustrations, in pictorial lithographed boards in red, blue, yellow, white, and black, with a red cloth spine and plain white endpapers. There are 4 pp. of ads at the back and an ad on the back cover. It contains six stories. The first edition was issued by Ward, Lock (1897), Cr 8vo, 308 pp., illustrated, 5/0 cloth, listed in the *Ath* on Sept. 25 and *PC* on Oct. 16.
Also 1901

2438 MRS. EDWARD KENNARD (MARY KENNARD) *The Right Sort.* Cr 8vo. Illustrated. 2/0 boards Apr. (*Bks*)

2/0 *Copyright Novels* No. 20. This is my copy, no date, 19.1 cm., 446 pp., with a frontispiece and 7 full-page illustrations, in pictorial lithographed boards in red, green, brown, black, and white, with a blue cloth spine and plain white endpapers. There are 10 pp. of ads at the back and an ad on the back cover.
Also 1886, 1902

2439 CHARLES KINGSLEY **Westward Ho!**
0/6 sewed   May 19 (*Acad*)

Sixpenny Novels and Popular Books. The first
edition was issued by Macmillan & Co.,
Cambridge; etc., 3 vols., 1855, 19 cm., at
31/6, listed in the *Ath* on Mar. 24 and advertised there on Mar. 10 as "On Mar. 20."
The second edition in 3 vols. was issued in
1855, listed by *PC* as published May 14–
31. They issued the third edition, 1857,
Cr 8vo, 519 pp., 7/6, advertised in *Notes &
Queries* on May 16, 1857, as "Just ready."
They issued it at 6/0 cloth in 1859, Cr 8vo,
listed by *PC* as published Sept. 30–Oct.
14, a new edition; and they issued it at 6/0
with 519 pp., at least 12 times from 1861
to 1880; and there were many later issues,
1889, 1890, 1891, 1895, 1897, and 1902.
The first American edition was issued by
Ticknor & Fields, Boston, 1855, 20.5 cm,
588 pp., $1.25 cloth, in an edition of 3,000
copies, advertised as in advance of its issue
in England. It was advertised in the *New
York Daily Times* on Mar. 27, as "On Mar.
31."

2440 GUY N. BOOTHBY **A Bid for Fortune.**
Illustrated. 0/6 sewed   June (*Bks*)

*Sixpenny Lithographic Series of Copyright Nov-
els* No. 1. This is 1900, large Cr 8vo, 156
pp. This begins a new series with the same
colorful lithographed covers as appear on
the *2/0 Copyright Novels.* This ran in the
Windsor Magazine of Ward, Lock beginning with the first issue of the magazine in
Jan. 1895. The first book edition was issued by D. Appleton & Co., New York,
1895, 301 pp., $.50 paper, $1.00 cloth,
Town and Country Library No. 179. It was
listed in *PW* on Oct. 19, the *Nation* on Oct.
31, and the *Ind* on Oct. 24. The first English book edition was issued by Ward,
Lock, 1895, Cr 8vo, 344 pp., illustrated,
5/0 cloth, listed in the *Ath* on Nov. 9, and in
the *Times Weekly Edition* on Nov. 8. They issued the fourth edition, the same, advertised in the *Spect* on Nov. 27, 1897.

2441 HEADON HILL (FRANCIS GRAINGER)
Beacon Fires. Cr 8vo. Illustrated. 2/0
boards   June (*Bks*)

2/0 Copyright Novels No. 21. The first edition was issued by Ward, Lock, 1897, Cr
8vo, 304 pp., illustrated, 3/6 cloth, listed
in the *Ath* on Oct. 23.

2442 BERTRAM MITFORD **Fordham's
Feud.** Cr 8vo. Illustrated. 2/0 boards
June (*Bks*)

2/0 Copyright Novels No. 22. The first edition was issued by Ward, Lock, 1897, 19
cm., 342 pp., illustrated, 3/6 cloth, listed
in the *Ath* on May 1 and in *PC* on May 22.
It was issued by the New York branch, 342
pp., $1.00 cloth, listed in *PW* on June 12,
1897, not received (no list on May 29).

2443 FERGUS HUME **The Dwarf's
Chamber and Other Stories.** Cr 8vo.
Illustrated. 2/0 boards   June (*Bks*)

2/0 Copyright Novels No. 23. The first edition was issued by Ward, Lock, 1896, 20
cm., 386 pp., illustrated, 3/6 cloth, listed
in the *Ath* on May 23. it was listed in the
Times Weekly Edition on Oct. 16, 1897, at
3/6, possibly a new edition. It was issued
by the New York branch at $1.00 cloth,
listed in *PW* on June 6 and the *Ind* on June
11, 1896. It was issued by the Amsterdam
Book Co., New York, 1901, illustrated,
$.50 paper, advertised in the *New York
Times Book Review* on July 6.

2444 MAX PEMBERTON **Jewel Mysteries
I Have Known.** Large Cr 8vo. 0/6 sewed
July (*Bks*)

Sixpenny Lithographic Series No. 2. This has
no date and 251 pp. The first edition was
issued by Ward, Lock, 1894, 21.5 cm., 269
pp., illustrated, 5/0 cloth, listed in the *Ath*
on Nov. 10, 1894, and the *Spect* on Nov. 3.
It was issued by the New York branch, 269
pp. $1.50 cloth, listed in *PW* on Nov. 2,
1895.

2445 WILLIAM C. DAWE *The Voyage of the "Pula Way."* Cr 8vo. Illustrated. 2/o boards   July?

2/o Copyright Novels No. 24. This is my copy, no date, 18.6 cm., 312 pp., with 3 full-page illustrations, in pictorial litho-graphed boards in red, blue, yellow, brown, and black, with a blue cloth spine and plain white endpapers. There is an ad on the back cover. The first edition was is-sued by Ward, Lock (1898), Cr 8vo, 312 pp., illustrated, 3/6 cloth, listed in the *Ath* on Sept. 3. The first American edition was issued by R. F. Fenno & Co., New York; Ward, Lock, London (1899), 19 cm., 312 pp., illustrated, $1.25 cloth, listed in the *Nation* and the *Ind* on Aug. 31, and *PW* on Sept. 2.

2446 MATTHIAS M. BODKIN *Lord Edward Fitzgerald.* Cr 8vo. Illustrated. 2/o boards Aug. 4 (*Spect*)

2/o Copyright Novels No. 25. This has no date, 19 cm., 415 pp. The first edition was issued by Chapman & Hall, London, 1896, 18.5 cm., 415 pp., illustrated, 6/o cloth.

2447 ORME AGNUS (JOHN HIGGINBOTHAM) *Countess Petrovski.* o/6 sewed   Aug. (*Bks*)

Also 1898

2448 HAWLEY SMART *Bound to Win.* Large Cr 8vo. o/6 sewed   Aug. (*Bks*)

Sixpenny Lithographic Series No. 3. This is 1900, with 189 pp. The first edition was is-sued by Chapman & Hall, London, 3 vols., 1877, 20 cm., 31/6, about Feb. 3, adver-tised in the *Times Weekly Edition* on Mar. 9. A second edition was advertised there, 3 vols., on May 25. They issued it as *Select Li-brary of Fiction* No. 361, at 2/o boards, about June 2, 1877.

2449 HENRY KINGSLEY *The Recollections of Geoffrey Hamlyn.* o/6 sewed   Aug. (*Bks*)

Sixpenny Lithographic Series No. 4. Also 1891

2450 RICHARD MARSH *The Mystery of Philip Bennion's Death.* o/6 sewed Aug. (*Bks*)

Ward, Lock issued this at 3/6 in 1899, listed in the *Times Weekly Edition* on June 16.

Also 1897, 1904

2451 LAWRENCE L. LYNCH (EMMA MURDOCH, later VAN DEVENTER) *The Unseen Hand.* Cr 8vo. Illustrated. 2/o boards   Sept. (*Bks*)

2/o Copyright Novels No. 26. The first edi-tion was issued by Laird & Lee, Chicago, 12mo, $.50, listed in *PW* and the *New York Times Book Review* on Feb. 19, 1898. The first English edition was issued by Ward, Lock (1899), Cr 8vo, 416 pp., illustrated, 3/6 cloth, listed in the *Spect* on Feb. 4. It was not listed in the *Ath* until Sept. 9 and was reviewed there on Dec. 2, 1899. It is possible that the latter was a new edition, although unlikely since it got a review.

Also 1902

2452 HEADON HILL *The Rajah's Second Wife, etc.* Illustrated. 1/o sewed   Sept. (*Bks*)

The first edition was issued by Ward, Lock, 1894, *Warwick House Library* No. 24, Cr 8vo, 312 pp., with 2 full-page illustra-tions, at 3/6 cloth, listed in the *Spect* on Aug. 4.

2453 FERGUS HUME *Madam Midas.* o/6 sewed   Sept. (*Bks*)

Sixpenny Novels. This has no date, 222 pp., in white glazed wrappers, decorated in blue and lettered in red, with an ad on the back cover and on 3 leaves at the back. The first edition was issued by the Hanson Cab Publishing Co., London, 1888, 19 cm., 222 pp. Wolff's copy is the 158th thousand, 1888, at 1/o, in white stiff wrap-pers cut flush, decorated and printed in black, with ads on the inside covers, the versos of the half-title, title page, both content pp., and the dedication page. It has a leaf of ads at the front and back. It was also issued as the 185th thousand, 1888, at 1/0; and Sadleir's copy is the 100th thousand, the same, 1888. The first American edition was issued by M.J. Ivers, New York (1888), 248 pp., listed in *PW* on Sept. 8. It was also issued by George Munro, New York (1888), *Seaside Library Pocket Edition* No. 1127, 19.5 cm., 253 pp., in wrappers, listed in *PW* on Oct. 20.

2454 WILLIAM PETT RIDGE *An Important Man and Others.* 0/6 sewed Sept. (*Bks*)
Sixpenny Novels.
Also 1896

2455 HENRY HERMAN *The Crime of a Christmas Toy.* Cr 8vo. Illustrated. 2/0 boards Sept. (*Bks*)
2/0 Copyright Novels No. 27. This is my copy, no date, 18.5 cm., 251 pp., with a frontispiece, 8 full-page illustrations and many textual illustrations, in pictorial lithographic boards in red, brown, white, olive, and black, with a blue cloth spine and plain white endpapers. There is an ad on the back cover. It was issued, 1895, with the same imprint as the present edition, 251 pp., illustrated, in cloth. It was issued by the New York branch, 251 pp., $1.00 cloth, listed in *PW* on Nov. 2, 1895. Also 1893

2456 GEORGE J. WHYTE MELVILLE *Katerfelto.* Illustrated. 0/6 sewed Sept (*Bks*)
Sixpenny Lithographic Series No. 5. Ward, Lock issued this in 1898, listed in the *Times Weekly Edition* on Nov. 18, no price given. Also 1889. See 1901

2457 J. SWINDELLS BARLOW *The Great Afrikander Conspiracy.* Illustrated. 1/0 sewed Sept. (*Bks*)
This is the first edition, 1900, 18.5 cm., 188 pp., with 1 plate.

2458 ETHEL TURNER, later CURLEWIS *The Story of a Baby.* 16mo. 0/6 sewed Sept. (*Eng Cat*)
The first edition was from Ward, Lock & Bowden, Ltd., 1895, 12mo, 160 pp., illustrated, 2/6 cloth, listed in the *Times Weekly Edition* on Sept. 13 and in the *Spect* on Sept. 7, *Nautilus Series* No. 1. The *U Cat* gives also 1896, 17 cm., 160 pp., frontispiece. This series consisted of Nos. 1–6, issued in 1895 and 1896.

2459 CHARLES DICKENS *David Copperfield.* Illustrated. 0/6 sewed Oct. (*Bks*)
Sixpenny Novels.
Also 1892

2460 JOSEPH F. FLETCHER *Pasquinado.* 1/0 sewed Oct. (*Bks*)
The first edition was issued by Ward, Lock (1898), 20 cm., 265 pp., with a frontispiece. It consists of tales.

2461 HEADON HILL *The Queen of Night.* 8vo. Illustrated. 0/6 sewed Oct. (*Bks*)
Sixpenny Standard Novels and Popular Books No. 104. This is my copy, no date, 21.6 cm., 127 pp., with a frontispiece and a full-page illustration, double columns. It is in very dark blue wrappers cut flush, printed on the front in green, with ads on the inside covers and on the back cover in green.
Also 1899, 1904

2462 RICHARD MARSH *The Datchet Diamonds.* Large Cr 8vo. Illustrated. 0/6 sewed Oct. (*Bks*)
Sixpenny Lithographic Series No. 6.
Also 1899

2463 MRS. L. T. MEADE, later SMITH & ROBERT EUSTACE (EUSTACE ROBERT BARTON) *The Brotherhood of the Seven Kings.* Cr 8vo. Illustrated. 2/0 boards Oct. (*Bks*)
2/0 Copyright Novels No. 28. This is my copy, 1900, 18.7 cm., 373 pp., with 12 full-

page illustrations by Sidney Paget, in pictorial lithographic boards in brown, black, yellow, and white, printed in red, with a red cloth spine and plain white endpapers. There are 10 pp. of publisher's ads at the back and a commercial ad on the back cover. The first edition was issued by Ward, Lock, 1899, Cr 8vo, 373 pp., with 16 full-page illustrations, 5/0 cloth. It was listed in the *Ath* on Apr. 15.
Also 1903

2464 ALICE M. MEADOWS *Out from the Night.* Cr 8vo. Illustrated. 2/0 boards Oct. (*Bks*)
2/0 Copyright Novels No. 29. This has no date, 19 cm., 314 pp. The first edition was issued by Ward, Lock (1899), Cr 8vo, 314 pp., illustrated, 3/6 cloth, listed in the *Spect* on Apr. 29 and the *Ath* on May 6.
Also 1902

2465 HARRIET L. CHILDE-PEMBERTON *Dead Letters and Other Narrative and Dramatic Pieces.* 0/6 sewed Oct.?
Also 1897

2466 GUY N. BOOTHBY *The Fascination of the King.* Large Cr 8vo. Illustrated. 0/6 sewed Nov. (*Eng Cat*)
Sixpenny Lithographic Series No. 7. This ran in *Chambers' Journal* from Sept. 1896 to Jan. 1897. The first English edition was issued by Ward, Lock, 1897, Cr 8vo, 286 pp., illustrated, 5/0 cloth, listed in the *Ath*

on July 31 and *PC* on Aug. 7. They issued the fourth edition, the same, advertised in the *Spect* on Nov. 27, 1897. The first edition was issued by Rand, McNally & Co., New York and Chicago, 1897, 12mo, 288 pp., at $1.25 cloth, listed in the *Nation* on Apr. 1, *PW* on Apr. 3, and *Lit World* on Apr. 17 (no list on Apr. 3).

2467 MATTHIAS M. BODKIN *The Rebels.* Cr 8vo. Illustrated. 1/0 boards Nov. (*Eng Cat*)
2/0 Copyright Novels No. 30. The first edition was issued by Ward, Lock, 1899, 18.5 cm., 358 pp., with 1 plate, 6/0 cloth. It was listed in the *Spect* on Apr. 15 and the *Times Weekly Edition* on Apr. 14. It is a sequel to *Lord Edward Fitzgerald* above.

2468 HAWLEY SMART *Broken Bonds.* 0/6 sewed. Nov. (*Eng Cat*)
Also 1886, 1902

2469 COULSON KERNAHAN *Captain Shannon.* Large Cr 8vo. Illustrated. 0/6 sewed Dec. (*Eng Cat*)
Sixpenny Lithographic Series No. 8.
Also 1899

2470 MAX ADELER (CHARLES H. CLARK) *Random Shots.* Large Cr 8vo. Illustrated. 0/6 sewed Dec. (*Eng Cat*)
Sixpenny Lithographic Series No. 9.
Also 1879, 83, 89

Ward, Lock & Co., Ltd.
London, New York, and Melbourne
1901

2471 HAWLEY SMART **At Fault.**
o/6 sewed   Jan. (*Eng Cat*)
Also 1883, 97, 1902

2472 ARTHUR MORRISON **Martin Hewitt,
Investigator.** o/6 sewed   Jan. (*Eng Cat*)
Also 1899, 1902

2473 LAWRENCE L. LYNCH
(EMMA MURDOCH, later VAN DEVENTER)
The Last Stroke. Cr 8vo. 2/o boards
Jan. (*Eng Cat*)
2/o Copyright Novels No. 31.
Also 1897, 1902

2474 E. P. OPPENHEIM **Mysterious
Mr. Sabin.** o/6 sewed   Feb. (*Eng Cat*)
The first edition was issued by Ward, Lock
(1898), 19.5 cm., 397 pp., illustrated, 3/6
cloth, listed in the *Ath* on Oct. 8. It was issued as a supplement to the *Windsor Magazine* of Ward, Lock in Dec. 1899, 24.5
cm., 127 pp., with the illustrations. In the
United States it was issued by Little,
Brown & Co., Boston, 1905, 20 cm., 397
pp., illustrated, $1.50 cloth, from advance
sheets, listed in the *New York Times Book Review* on Jan. 28, 1905. A second edition
was listed Feb. 4, and a third edition was
advertised on Feb. 11. It was also issued by
R. F. Fenno, New York, no date, 427 pp.
Also 1905

2475 RICHARD MARSH **The Crime and
the Criminal.** Large Cr 8vo. Illustrated.
o/6 sewed   Feb. (*Eng Cat*)
Sixpenny Lithographic Series No. 10.
Also 1899, 1903

2476 ROBERT M. BALLANTYNE **The Coral
Island.** o/6 sewed   Feb. (*Eng Cat*)
Sixpenny Standard Novels and Popular Books
No. 108. This was also issued at 1/o, 1/6,
2/o, all in cloth. The 1/o was in the *Rainbow
Series* (1901) and before 1909 was *Royal Series* No. 26, Cr 8vo, with a frontispiece.
Also before 1909 the 1/6 cloth was *Youth's
Library* No. 27, Cr 8vo, with 4 full-page illustrations. The present edition has no
date. One of the present issues was 19 cm.,
372 pp., with a frontispiece. The first edition was issued by Thomas Nelson & Sons,
Edinburgh, 1858 (1857), 19 cm., 438 pp.,
with a frontispiece and 7 colored page
plates, 6/o, in sage green cloth. It had a
preface by Ralph Rover (Edinburgh,
1857). Ballantyne received £90 in full payment for it, one of the most popular boy's
books of the 19th century. Nelson issued it
in 1867 at 3/o cloth, listed in the *Spect* on
Oct. 12; and issued it in 1878, a new edition, Cr 8vo, at 3/6 cloth. Nelson, Walter
Scott, and Nisbet all issued editions in
1901. The first American edition was issued by Phillips, Sampson & Co., Boston,
1859, listed in *APC&LG* on Dec. 10, 1859.

2477 ROBERT M. BALLANTYNE
Martin Rattler. o/6 sewed   Feb. (*Eng Cat*)
Sixpenny Standard Novels and Popular Books
No. 109. This was also issued at 1/o, 1/6,
2/o, all in cloth. The 1/o issue was in the
Rainbow Series (1901), 306 pp. It was also
issued before 1909 as *Royal Series* No. 27,
Cr 8vo, with a frontispiece, at 1/o cloth.
The 1/6 cloth was also issued before 1909
as *Youth's Library* No. 28, Cr 8vo, with 4 full-

page illustrations. The first edition was is-sued by Thomas Nelson & Sons, London, Edinburgh, and New York, 1858, 17 cm., 330 pp., with a frontispiece and 3 plates, in red cloth, decorated in blind with a gilt vignette. Eric Quayle in *Early Children's Books* shows a picture of the title page with 1858 as the date. I mention this as Sadleir thought the first edition was 1859. It was listed in the *Spect* on Dec. 4, 1858. Nelson dated all of their title pages but gave no in-dication of edition. Nelson issued it in 1878, a new edition, Cr 8vo, at 3/6 cloth; and in 1867 at 3/0 cloth, both listed in the *Spect*, the former on Aug. 10 and the latter on Oct. 12.

2478 ROBERT M. BALLANTYNE *Ungava.* 0/6 sewed   Feb. (*Eng Cat*)

Sixpenny Standard Novels and Popular Books No. 110. This was also issued at 1/0, 1/6, 2/0, all in cloth. The 1/0 was in the *Rainbow Series* (1901), 367 pp. It was also issued be-fore 1909 as *Royal Series* No. 44, Cr 8vo, with a frontispiece, at 1/0 cloth. The 1/6 cloth was also issued before 1909 as *Youth's Library* No. 29, Cr 8vo, with 4 plates. The first edition was issued by Thomas Nelson & Sons, Edinburgh, 1858 (1857), 509 pp., illustrated. They reissued it in 1867, at 3/0 cloth, listed in the *Spect* on Oct. 12; and reissued it (1901), 19 cm., 272 pp., illus-trated, at 2/6, about Mar. 23. The first American edition was issued by Phillips, Sampson & Co., Boston, 1859, 17.5 cm., 406 pp., with a plate, listed in *APC&LG* on Dec. 10, 1859.

2479 MAX PEMBERTON *A Gentleman's Gentleman.* Large Cr 8vo. Illustrated. 0/6 sewed   Mar. (*Eng Cat*)

Sixpenny Lithographic Series No. 11. The first edition was issued by A. D. Innes & Co., London, 1896, Cr 8vo, 344 pp., illus-trated, 6/0, listed in the *Ath* on Mar. 7, ed-ited (or rather written) by Pemberton. Ward, Lock bought the Innes Co. in 1900. The first American edition was issued by

Harper & Bros., New York, 1896, 19 cm., 245 pp., at $1.25, listed in *PW* on Apr. 25, the *Ind* on Apr. 30, and the *Nation* on May 7.

2480 MRS. L. T. MEADE, later SMITH & ROBERT EUSTACE (EUSTACE ROBERT BARTON) *A Master of Mysteries.* Cr 8vo. Illustrated. 2/0 boards   Mar. (*Eng Cat*)

2/0 Copyright Novels No. 32. This has no date, 19.5 cm., 279 pp. The first edition was issued by Ward, Lock (1898), Cr 8vo, 279 pp., illustrated, 5/0 cloth, listed in the *Ath* on Sept. 24. It is a book of short stories.

2481 ALICE M. MEADOWS *The Eye of Fate.* Cr 8vo. Illustrated. 2/0 boards   Mar. (*Eng Cat*)

2/0 Copyright Novels No. 33. The first edi-tion was issued by Ward, Lock (1899), Cr 8vo, 311 pp., 3/6 cloth, listed in the *Spect* on Dec. 2, 1899.

2482 MATTHIAS M. BODKIN *A Bear Squeeze.* Cr 8vo. Illustrated. 2/0 boards Mar. (*Eng Cat*)

2/0 Copyright Novels No. 34. This is proba-bly the first edition, 1901, 237 pp.

2483 EDWIN L. ARNOLD *Phra the Phoenician.* Roy 8vo. Illustrated. 0/6 sewed   Mar. (*Eng Cat*)

This is my copy, no date, 24.5 cm., 156 pp., with a frontispiece and 14 plates, double columns. It is in pictorial wrappers in pink, blue, white, yellow, and green, cut flush, with the author's name on the title page only, 2 leaves of ads and a 4-page re-duced size insert at the front, and 2 leaves of ads at the back. The ad on the back cover is in blue, brown, and white. It was first published in 26 installments in the latter half of 1890 in the *Illustrated London News*. Ward, Lock issued it as a supple-ment to the *Windsor Magazine* (1898), 156 pp., illustrated. The first English book edition was issued by Chatto & Windus, London, 3 vols., 1891, 19 cm., illustrated, 31/6, listed in the *Ath* on Jan. 10, 1891. They issued a second edition, 3 vols., 1891, advertised in the *Spect* on Mar. 7; and issued it in 1891, with 12 illustrations, at 3/6, listed in the *Spect* on May 23. They issued it in 1893, my copy, a new edition, 18 cm., 347 pp., a 2/0 yellowback, with a 32-page catalog (Mar. 1893) and endpaper ads (Nov. 1892), listed in *PC* on Apr. 22. They reissued it as late as 1936. The first American edition was issued by Harper & Bros., New York, 1890, *Franklin Square Library* No. 686, 21.5 cm., 329 pp., illustrated, advertised in the *New-York Times* on Dec. 12, 1890, $.50 paper, as "This day," and listed in *Public Opinion* on Jan. 3, 1891. It was reissued, the same, advertised in the *Times* on Apr. 7, 1891.

2484 ANTHONY HOPE (SIR ANTHONY HOPE HAWKINS) *Mr. Witt's Widow.* Large Cr 8vo. Illustrated. 0/6 sewed Mar. (*Eng Cat*)

Sixpenny Lithographic Series No. 12. The first edition was issued by A. D. Innes & Co., London, 1892, 20 cm., 243 pp., at 6/0 cloth, listed in the *Ath* on Apr. 9. Ward, Lock acquired Innes in 1900. The first American edition was issued by the United States Book Co., New York (1892), 18.5 cm., 243 pp., at $.50 paper and $1.25 cloth, in the *Strathmore Series*. It was listed in the *Ind* on Oct. 6 and in *PW* on Oct. 8.

2485 GUY N. BOOTHBY *Pharos the Egyptian.* Large Cr 8vo. Illustrated. 0/6 sewed Apr. (*Eng Cat*)

Sixpenny Lithographic Series No. 13. This is my copy, no date, 21.2 cm., 153 pp., double columns, with a frontispiece and a plate. It is in pictorial lithographic wrappers, in red, blue, yellow, gray, and black. There are 6 pp. of ads at the back, ads on the inside covers, and an ad on the back cover in red, blue, and green on white. The ads at the back indicate an issue date

of 1904, and there is an inscribed date (Sept. 8, 1904). This began in Ward, Lock's *Windsor Magazine* in June 1898. The first book edition was issued by Ward, Lock, 1899, 20 cm., 376 pp., illustrated, 5/0 cloth, advertised in the *Ath* on Mar. 18 as "On Mar. 13" and listed on Mar. 18, and listed in the *Spect* on Mar. 11. The first American edition was issued by D. Appleton & Co., New York, my copy, 1899, 18.5 cm., 328 pp., $.50 paper and $1.00 cloth, *Town and Country Library* No. 261, listed in *PW* on Apr. 8 and in the *Nation* on Apr. 13. *See color photo section*

2486 HAWLEY SMART *Saddle and Sabre.* Large Cr 8vo. Illustrated. 0/6 sewed Apr. (*Eng Cat*)

Sixpenny Lithographic Series No. 14. Also 1888, 91

2487 RICHARD MARSH *The House of Mystery.* Large Cr 8vo. Illustrated. 0/6 sewed May (*Eng Cat*)

Sixpenny Lithographic Series No. 15. The first edition was issued by F. V. White, London, 1898, Cr 8vo, 312 pp., 6/0 cloth, listed in the *Ath* on Feb. 26 and the *Times Weekly Edition* on Mar. 4.

2488 ARTHUR MORRISON *The Dorrington Deed-Box.* Large Cr 8vo. Illustrated. 0/6 sewed May (*Eng Cat*)

Sixpenny Lithographic Series No. 16. This was issued in New York by the Amsterdam Book Co., 1901, $.50 paper, $1.25 cloth, advertised in the *New York Times Book Review* on Apr. 27. Also 1900

2489 H. BURFORD DELANNOY *Nineteen Thousand Pounds.* Cr 8vo. Illustrated. 2/0 boards May (*Eng Cat*)

2/0 Copyright Novels No. 35. This is the first edition (1901), 309 pp. The first American edition was issued by R. F. Fenno & Co., New York; Ward, Lock, London

(1901), 12mo, 297 pp., $1.25 cloth, listed in the *Nation* on July 11 and in *PW* on July 20.

Also 1902, 05

2490 ROBERT M. BALLANTYNE *The Young Fur-Traders.* o/6 sewed   May (*Eng Cat*)

Sixpenny Standard Novels and Popular Books No. 111. This was also issued in the *Rainbow Series* at 1/o cloth, probably in 1901; and as *Royal Series* No. 45, before 1909, Cr 8vo, with a frontispiece, at 1/o cloth. It was also issued as *Youth's Library* No. 30, probably in 1909, my copy, 19.2 cm., 376 pp., with 4 plates, 1/6 cloth. It is in dark blue cloth with matching endpapers, the front cover elaborately stamped in blind and the spine in gilt, with a preface (1856) and an inscribed date of 1909, and there are 8 pp. of ads at the back. I think the *Rainbow Series* title was *Snowflakes and Sunbeams*, with 376 pp., and the present issue is titled as I've given it. The first edition was issued by Thomas Nelson & Sons, London, New York, etc., 1856, 18.5 cm., 429 pp., illustrated, *Snowflakes and Sunbeams; or, The Young Fur Traders*, with *The Young Fur Traders* on the cover, listed in *PC* as published Sept 30–Oct. 14, Cr 8vo, at 5/o illustrated, and listed as published Oct. 30–Nov. 14, p 8vo, at 5/o, without illustrations apparently. This was the author's first book and after a few editions the first part of the title was dropped. Nelson issued it in New York, 1856, 12mo, 429 pp., illustrated, $1.25 cloth, advertised in the *New York Daily Times* on Oct. 6 as "Just published," and listed in *APC&LG* on Oct. 11. Nelson issued it in England in 1878, Cr 8vo, 3/6 cloth, listed in the *Spect* on July 27. The first edition set up in America was issued by Phillips, Sampson & Co., Boston, 1859, 16mo, 432 pp., illustrated, entitled *Snowflakes and Sunbeams*. It was listed in *APC&LG* on Dec. 10, 1859. Both Nelson and Nisbet in London issued it in 1901.

2491 GEORGE J. WHYTE MELVILLE *Market Harborough.* Large Cr 8vo. Illustrated. o/6 sewed   June (*Eng Cat*)

Sixpenny Lithographic Series No. 17. Also 1894, 1903

2492 E. P OPPENHEIM *A Monk of Cruta.* Large Cr 8vo. Illustrated. o/6 sewed June (*Eng Cat*)

Sixpenny Lithographic Series No. 18. This was also issued 1899, 19.5 cm., 317 pp., illustrated, 3/6, listed in the *Ath* on July 15, and reviewed on July 29, although the first edition was issued in 1894!

Also 1894

2493 MAX PEMBERTON *Christine of the Hills.* Large Cr 8vo. Illustrated. o/6 sewed   June (*Eng Cat*)

Sixpenny Lithographic Series No. 21. This has no date, 119 pp., with a preface (1897). The first edition was issued by A. D. Innes & Co., London, 1897, 20 cm., 312 pp., 6/o, listed in the *Ath* on Feb. 20. Innes was acquired by Ward, Lock in 1900. The first American edition was issued by Dodd, Mead & Co., New York, 1897, 18 cm., 281 pp., with a frontispiece (portrait), $1.25 cloth, advertised in the *New York Times Book Review* on Apr. 10 as "Now ready," and listed in *PW* on Apr. 17, and the *Ind* on Apr. 22.

2494 HAWLEY SMART *The Great Tontine.* Large Cr 8vo. Illustrated. o/6 sewed July (*Eng Cat*)

Sixpenny Lithographic Series No. 22. Also 1882

2495 E. P. OPPPENHEIM *The Man and His Kingdom.* Cr 8vo. Illustrated. 2/o boards July (*Eng Cat*) See color photo section

2/o Copyright Novels No. 37. This is my copy, no date, 18.6 cm., 325 pp., with a frontispiece and 3 plates, in pictorial lithographic boards in red, brown, blue, green, yellow, and black, with a red cloth

spine and plain white endpapers. There is a leaf of ads at the back and an ad on the back cover. The first edition was issued by Ward, Lock (1899), 20 cm., 325 pp., illustrated, 3/6 cloth, listed in the *Ath* on May 6. The first American edition was issued by J. B. Lippincott & Co., Philadelphia, 1900 (1899), 12mo, $.50 paper and $1.00 cloth, in *Lippincott's Series of Select Novels*. It was listed in *Public Opinion* on Nov. 23, 1899, and in *PW* on Dec. 2.
Also 1902

2496   MAX ADELER (CHARLES H. CLARK) *An Old Fogey*. Large Cr 8vo. Illustrated. o/6 sewed   Aug. (*Eng Cat*)
Sixpenny Lithographic Series No. 23.
Also 1881, 83, 89, 1905

2497   GUY N. BOOTHBY *A Maker of Nations*. Large Cr 8vo. Illustrated. o/6 sewed   Aug. (*Eng Cat*)
Sixpenny Lithographic Series No. 24. The first English edition was issued by Ward, Lock, 1900, Cr 8vo, 342 pp., illustrated, 5/0 cloth, listed in the *Ath* on Mar. 17 and the *Spect* on Mar. 10. The first American edition was issued by D. Appleton & Co., New York, 1900 (copyright 1899), 18 cm., 350 pp., $.50 paper and $1.00 cloth, *Town and Country Library* No. 280, listed in the *Nation* on Mar. 8 and *PW* on Mar. 10.

2498   E. P. OPPENHEIM *A Daughter of the Marionis*. Large Cr 8vo. Illustrated. o/6 sewed   Sept. (*Eng Cat*)
Sixpenny Lithographic Series No. 26. Ward, Lock also issued this in 1900, 255 pp., illustrated, 3/6 cloth, advertised in the *Spect* on Apr. 14, and reviewed in the *Ath* on Feb. 17, although not the first edition! The first edition was issued by Ward & Downey, London, 1895, 312 pp., 6/0 cloth, listed in the *Ath* on Aug. 31.

2499   FLORENCE WARDEN (FLORENCE PRICE, later JAMES) *A Sensational Case*. Large Cr 8vo. Illustrated. o/6 sewed Sept. (*Eng Cat*)
Sixpenny Lithographic Series No. 27.
Also 1900

2500   H. BURFORD DELANNOY *Between the Lines*. Cr 8vo. Illustrated. 2/0 boards   Oct. 12 (*Ath* ad)
2/0 Copyright Novels No. 39. This is the first edition, 1901, 311 pp., with a frontispiece and plates.
Also 1902

2501   HAWLEY SMART *Hard Lines*. Large Cr 8vo. Illustrated. o/6 sewed Oct. (*Eng Cat*)
Sixpenny Lithographic Series No. 28.
Also 1884

2502   JOHN C. SNAITH *Mistress Dorothy Marvin*. Roy 8vo. Illustrated. o/6 sewed Oct. (*Eng Cat*)   See color photo section
This is my copy, no date, 24.5 cm., 191 pp., with a frontispiece and 6 plates, double columns. It is in a pictorial lithographic cover in dark brown, green, white, and black, with a leaf of ads at the front, on 1 p. at the back, and on the inside covers. The ad on the back cover is in brown and black on white. This is a reissue of a supplement to Ward, Lock's *Windsor Magazine* (1900), 24 cm., 191 pp., issued in Dec. 1900. The first edition was issued by A. D. Innes & Co., London, 1895, Cr 8vo, 430 pp., illustrated, 6/0, listed in the *Ath* on Nov. 2, edited by J. C. Snaith. The first American edition was issued by D. Appleton & Co., New York, 1896, 18.5 cm., 419 pp., $.50 paper and $1.00 cloth, *Town and Country Library* No. 188, listed in *PW* on Mar. 21, and the *Nation* and the *Ind* on Mar. 26, edited by Snaith.

2503 GEORGE J. WHYTE MELVILLE
Sarchedon. Cr 8vo. Illustrated.
2/o boards   1901?

2/o *Copyright Novels* No. 53. This is my copy, no date, 19.1 cm., 435 pp., with a frontispiece and 3 plates, in pictorial lithographic boards in red, green, white, brown, blue, and yellow, with a red cloth spine and plain white endpapers. There is a dedication (June 1871), ads paged (1)–12 at the back, and an ad on the back cover in brown and white. The first edition was issued by Chapman & Hall, London, 3 vols., 1871, 20 cm., 31/6, advertised in the *Ath* on July 1 as "This day," and listed on July 8. They issued a new edition, 1872, 387 pp., 2/o boards, listed in the *Ath* on June 8; and reissued it in the fall of 1879 at 2/o boards, *Select Library of Fiction* No. 396. Ward, Lock issued it as a yellowback, no date but before 1892, 387 pp. The first American edition was issued by D. Appleton & Co., New York, 1871, 8vo, 195 pp., $.60 paper, advertised in the *New-York Times* on Aug. 4 as "This day," and listed in *ALG&PC* (fortnightly) on Aug. 15.
Also 1903

2504 GEORGE J. WHYTE MELVILLE
Black but Comely. Cr 8vo. Illustrated.
2/o boards   1901?

2/o *Copyright Novels* No. 56. My copy is *Sixpenny Lithographic Series* No. 32, no date, 21.6 cm., 192 pp., double columns, with an inscribed date (Nov. 8, 1902), issued in Dec. 1901. It is in pictorial, lithographic wrappers in red, brown, yellow, green, and black, with a frontispiece and a plate. There are ads on the inside covers and an ad on the back cover in red, black, blue, green, and yellow on white.
Also 1881

2505 GEORGE J. WHYTE MELVILLE
Rosine and Sister Louise. Cr 8vo. Illustrated. 2/o boards   1901?

2/o *Copyright Novels* No. 58. This is my copy, no date, 19.2 cm., 439 pp., with a frontispiece and 3 plates, in pictorial lithographic boards in red, blue, yellow, brown, and black, with a red cloth spine and plain white endpapers. There is an ad on the back cover in brown on white. Ward, Lock issued it in 1899 at 3/6 cloth, listed in the *Times Weekly Edition* on June 23. The first edition of the first title was issued by Chapman & Hall, London, 1877 (1876), Demy 8vo, 266 pp., illustrated, 16/o, listed in the *Ath* on Dec. 2, 1876. They issued it in a new edition, no date, my copy in boards, at 2/o boards, 2/6 cloth, listed in the *Ath* on Apr. 6, 1878. They issued it in the fall of 1879 and in Nov. 1880 as *Select Library of Fiction* No. 400, 2/o boards. The first American edition was issued by Lovell, Adam, Wesson & Co., New York, 1877, 114 pp., double columns, listed in *PW* on Mar. 31. It was issued by George Munro, New York, in the *Seaside Library*, in the fall of 1877, 32.5 cm., illustrated with 33 pp., paper. For the second title see 1889. *See color photo section*

2506 GEORGE J. WHYTE MELVILLE
Kate Coventry. Cr 8vo. Illustrated.
2/o boards   Nov. (*Eng Cat*)

2/o *Copyright Novels* No. 60. The first English edition was issued by John W. Parker & Son, London, 1856, edited (or rather written) by Melville, 20 cm., 322 pp., 7/6, listed in the *Spect* on Oct. 11. It had appeared in *Fraser's Magazine*, anonymous, from Jan. to June 1856. Parker issued the second edition at 7/6, advertised in the *Spect* on Dec. 6, 1856; issued a cheap edition at 5/o, advertised in the *Spect* on Oct. 2, 1858; and issued the fourth edition, Cr 8vo, at 5/o, advertised in the *Spect* on Aug. 2, 1862, as "This day." Longmans, London, issued it (1871), a new edition, 12mo, 316 pp., at 2/o boards, 2/6 cloth, listed in the *Ath* on July 8; at 1/o boards, 1/o cloth, with no date, 18.5 cm., about July 11, 1885; and at o/6 sewed, 1882, 4to, 64 pp., about Feb. 4. They issued a new edition, 1891, 18 cm., 316 pp. The first American edition was issued by J. P. Jewett & Co., Boston, 1856, 87 pp. It first appeared in the United States in *Littell's Living Age*.

2507 RICHARD MARSH *In Full Cry.*
Large Cr 8vo. Illustrated. o/6 sewed Nov. (*Eng Cat*)

Sixpenny Lithographic Series No. 25. The first edition was issued by F. V. White, London, 1899, 20 cm., 6/o, listed in the *Times Weekly Edition* on Aug. 4.

2508 HAWLEY SMART *Social Sinners.*
Large Cr 8vo. Illustrated. o/6 sewed Nov. (*Eng Cat*)

Sixpenny Lithographic Series No. 30.
Also 1881

2509 ARTHUR MORRISON *The Chronicles of Martin Hewitt.* Large Cr 8vo. Illustrated. o/6 sewed   Dec. (*Eng Cat*)

Sixpenny Lithographic Series No. 31.
Also 1899

**2510 ARCHIBALD C. GUNTER
*The Princess of Copper.*** o/6 sewed Dec. (*Eng Cat*)

Sixpenny Standard Novels and Popular Books No. 92. The first edition was issued by the Home Publishing Co., New York (1900), 19.5 cm., 283 pp., illustrated, with *Welcome Series* No. 57 on the front cover, and listed in *PW* on Aug. 11 but not received. The first English edition was issued by F. V. White & Co., London, 1900, Cr 8vo, 283 pp., 6/o cloth, listed in the *Ath* on Sept. 8.
Also 1905

**2511 GEORGE J. WHYTE MELVILLE
*Riding Recollections.*** Cr 8vo. Illustrated. 2/o boards   Dec. (*Eng Cat*)

2/o Copyright Novels No. 61. Ward, Lock also issued this in 1899 at 3/6 cloth, listed in the *Times Weekly Edition* on Sept. 15.
Also 1885

2512 CLARENCE ROOK *A Lesson for Life.*
Frontispiece. 1/o sewed   1901 (*BM*)

This is the first edition (1901), 185 pp., a tale.
Also 1902

**2513 GEORGE J. WHYTE MELVILLE
*Katerfelto.*** Cr 8vo. Illustrated. 2/o boards 1901?

2/o Copyright Novels No. 51. The *Eng Cat* gives a 1/6 issue in the New Standard Library, Cr 8vo, in Nov. 1901.
Also 1889, 1900

**2514 GEORGE J. WHYTE MELVILLE
*Cerise.*** Cr 8vo. Illustrated. 2/o boards 1901?

2/o Copyright Novels No. 52. The first edition was issued by Chapman & Hall, London, 3 vols., 1866, 19.7 cm., 31/6, listed in the *Ath* on Mar. 17. They issued the sixth edition, 1871, my copy, 441 pp., 2/o boards, listed in the *Ath* on May 20. They issued it as *Select Library of Fiction* No. 390 at 2/o boards, in the fall of 1879; and issued a new edition, 1881, my copy, in the same series, 441 pp., 2/o boards, with printer's date (Oct. 22, 1880). Sadleir had a copy in pictorial boards, in the *Library of Select Authors*, a new edition, no date, issued by Ward, Lock, with an inscribed date of 1881. The first American edition was issued by J. B. Lippincott & Co., Philadelphia; Chapman & Hall, London, 1866, 12mo, $1.75 cloth, printed in London, listed in the *Nation* on June 5 and the *Ind* on Apr. 19. This practice of Chapman & Hall of sending copies to Lippincott was roundly condemned by Anthony Trollope in a letter to Chapman & Hall of Dec. 20, 1865, their having done so with his *Belton Estate*.

**2515 GEORGE J. WHYTE MELVILLE
*Roy's Wife.*** Cr 8vo. Illustrated. 2/o boards   1901?

2/o Copyright Novels No. 57.
Also 1883

2516 GEORGE J. WHYTE MELVILLE
The Gladiators. Cr 8vo. Illustrated.
2/o boards   1901?

2/o Copyright Novels No. 59. The *Eng Cat*
gives also a 1/6 issue by Ward, Lock in the
New Standard Library, in Nov. 1901. The
first edition was issued by Longmans,
London, 3 vols., 1863, 19.7 cm., 31/6,
listed in the *Ath* on Nov. 21. They issued it
in 1870, no date, 12mo, 418 pp., 2/o
boards, 2/6 cloth, listed in the *Ath* on May
14; and issued a new edition in 1878, my
copy, no date, 418 pp., 2/o boards. They
issued it in 1864, Cr 8vo, 481 pp., with a
frontispiece, 5/o cloth, advertised in the
Spect on Feb. 27 as "On Mar. 14." They issued a new edition in 1885, no date, 18.5
cm., 418 pp., 1/o boards, 1/6 cloth, about
July 11; and issued editions in 1890 and
1892. The first American edition was
probably D. Appleton & Co., New York,
1872, 8vo, 174 pp., $.60 paper, advertised
in the *New-York Times* on Nov. 18, 1871, as
"This day," and noticed in the *Ind* on Nov.
30.

2517 GEORGE J. WHYTE MELVILLE
The Brookes of Bridlemere. Cr 8vo.
Illustrated. 2/o boards   1901?

2/o Copyright Novels No. 62. Ward, Lock issued this also in 1899, listed in the *Times
Weekly Edition* on Nov. 3 but with no price
given.
Also 1894, 1903

2518 ROBERT M. BALLANTYNE
The World of Ice. o/6 sewed   1901?

Sixpenny Standard Novels and Popular Books
No. 112. Ward, Lock also issued this as
Youth's Library No. 35, Cr 8vo, 4 plates, 1/6
cloth, before 1909; and issued it as *Royal
Series* No. 28, Cr 8vo, with a frontispiece,
1/o cloth, before 1909. The first edition
was issued by Thomas Nelson & Sons,
London, 1860 (1859), 19 cm., 315 pp., illustrated, 3/6 cloth, listed in the *Spect* on
Dec. 10, 1859. They reissued it with 232
pp. in 1902 and 1904.

2519 RICHARD DOWLING *Tempest Driven.*
o/6 sewed   Feb. (*Eng Cat*)

The first edition was issued by Tinsley
Bros., London, 3 vols., 1886, 20 cm., advertised in the *Ath* on Mar. 20 as "This
day," and reviewed on May 22. The first
American edition was issued by D. Appleton & Co., New York, 1887, 18 cm., 358
pp., listed in the *Nation* on June 16.

2520 GUY N. BOOTHBY *Love Made
Manifest.* Large Cr 8vo. Illustrated.
o/6 sewed   Feb. (*Eng Cat*)

Sixpenny Lithographic Series No. 33. The
first edition was issued by Ward, Lock
(1899), 20 cm., 376 pp., illustrated, 5/o,
listed in the *Ath* on Aug. 5 and in the *Times
Weekly Edition* on July 28. The first American edition was issued by H. S. Stone, Chicago and New York, 1899, 20 cm., 380
pp., illustrated, $1.50 cloth, listed in the
Nation on Dec. 7, 1899, and *PW* in Dec. 23.

2521 HAWLEY SMART *A False Start.*
Large Cr 8vo. Illustrated. o/6 sewed
Feb. (*Eng Cat*)

Sixpenny Lithographic Series No. 34.
Also 1888, 91

2522 HAWLEY SMART *Broken Bonds.*
Large Cr 8vo. Illustrated. o/6 sewed
Mar.?

Sixpenny Lithographic Series No. 35.
Also 1886, 1901

2523 ARTHUR MORRISON *Martin Hewitt,
Investigator.* Large Cr 8vo. Illustrated.
o/6 sewed   Mar.?

Sixpenny Lithographic Series No. 36.
Also 1899, 1901

2524 HAWLEY SMART *At Fault.* Large Cr
8vo. Illustrated. o/6 sewed   Mar.?

Sixpenny Lithographic Series No. 37.
Also 1883, 97, 1901

2525 E. P. OPPENHEIM *The World's
Great Snare.* Large Cr 8vo. Illustrated.
o/6 sewed   Mar. (*Eng Cat*)

Sixpenny Lithographic Series No. 38. The
first edition was issued by Ward & Downey, London, 1896, Cr 8vo, 316 pp., illustrated, 6/o cloth, listed in the *Ath* on June
27. Ward, Lock issued it (1900), 19 cm.,
256 pp., 3/6 cloth, listed in the *Spect* on
Oct. 13 and the *Times Weekly Edition* on
Oct. 19. The first American edition was issued by J. B. Lippincott & Co., Philadelphia, 1896, listed in *PW* on Nov. 7 and
Public Opinion on Nov. 12.

2526 GEORGE J. WHYTE MELVILLE
Satanella. Cr 8vo. Illustrated. 2/o boards
Mar. (*Eng Cat*)

2/o Copyright Novels No. 63. This was issued as *Sixpenny Lithographic Series* No. 50,
illustrated, in Oct. 1902. The present edition has no date and 310 pp. The first edition was issued by Chapman & Hall, London, 2 vols., 1872, 19 cm., illustrated,

21/0, listed in the *Ath* on June 22. It ran in the *Gentleman's Magazine*, Dec. 1871–July 1872. Chapman & Hall issued it at 2/0 boards, 2/6 cloth, my copy, 1873, a new edition, 307 pp., listed in the *Ath* on Mar. 29; and issued the 11th thousand at 2/0 boards about May 10, 1873. They issued it as *Select Library of Fiction* No. 397 in the fall of 1879; reissued in Nov. 1880; and issued again, the 17th thousand, as a yellowback with no date. The first American edition was issued by J. B. Lippincott & Co., Philadelphia, 1872, copyright edition, 19 cm., 311 pp., probably issued jointly with A. Asher, Berlin. It was listed in the *Nation* on July 18 and *PW* on July 25.

2527 F. MARION CRAWFORD *To Leeward.*
Large Cr 8vo. Illustrated. 0/6 sewed Apr. 25

Sixpenny Lithographic Series No. 39. This was listed in the *Times Literary Supplement* on Apr. 25. It is 21.5 cm. in size, with 156 pp. and 2 illustrations.
Also 1886

2528 GEORGE J. WHYTE MELVILLE *Holmby House.* Cr 8vo. Illustrated.
2/0 boards Apr. (*Eng Cat*)

2/0 *Copyright Novels* No. 64. This ran in *Fraser's Magazine*, Jan. 1859–May 1860. The first book edition was issued by John W. Parker & Son, London, 2 vols., 1860, 20 cm., illustrated, 16/0, listed in the *Ath* on Feb. 18. The second edition, the same, advertised in the *Spect* on Apr. 21, 1860, as "This day," and also on Mar. 7, 1863, the same, second edition. Longmans, London, issued a new edition in 1864, 395 pp., 5/0 cloth, listed in the *Reader* on May 7. They issued it, 1870, a new edition, 18.5 cm., 395 pp., 2/0 boards, 2/6 cloth, with a 32-page catalog (July 1870), listed in the *Ath* on July 2. The yellowback was reissued (1882), my copy; and it was issued at 1/0 boards, 1/6 cloth, a new edition, 395 pp., about July 11, 1885; and there were editions issued in 1890 and 1893 by Long-

mans. The first American edition was issued by Ticknor & Fields, Boston, 1860 (author's edition), 24 cm., 224 pp., advertised in the *Ind* (weekly) on Mar. 1 as "Just published," and listed in *APC&LG* (weekly) on Mar. 3. It was advertised in the *New-York Times* on Feb. 24, $.50 paper, "Just published."
Also 1903

2529 MARY KENNARD (MRS. EDWARD KENNARD) *The Right Sort.* Large Cr 8vo. Illustrated. 0/6 sewed May (*Eng Cat*)

Sixpenny Lithographic Series No. 40.
Also 1886, 1900

2530 ANNA K. GREEN, later ROHLFS *Agatha Webb.* Large Cr 8vo. Illustrated. 0/6 sewed May (*Eng Cat*)

Sixpenny Lithographic Series No. 41. The spring catalog of Ward, Lock for 1906 listed this as *Copyright Novels* No. 44. The first edition was issued by G. P. Putnam's Sons, New York and London, 1899, 18 cm., 360 pp., $1.25 cloth, listed in the *Nation* on July 13, *PW* on July 15, and the *Ind* on July 20. It was advertised in the *New York Times Book Review* on July 29, 1899, as published July 1 and now in the sixth thousand. Editorial matter there on Feb. 3, 1900, stated that it had passed through eight editions and was about to be issued in paper; and it was advertised there on May 25, 1901, $.50 paper, in the *Hudson Library*, as new and forthcoming. The first English edition was issued by Ward, Lock, 1900, 20 cm., 370 pp., illustrated, 3/6 cloth, listed in the *Ath* on July 28.

2531 H. BURFORD DELANNOY *The Margate Murder Mystery.* Cr 8vo. Illustrated. 2/0 boards May 30

2/0 *Copyright Novels* No. 43. This was listed in the *Times Literary Supplement* on May 30. It is the first English edition, 1902, 19 cm., 316 pp. The first edition was issued by Brentano's, New York, 1901, 12mo, 309

pp., *The Margate Mystery*, listed in *PW* on
Dec. 7, 1901, and the *New York Times Book
Review* on Nov. 16.
Also 1903, 05

2532 LAWRENCE L. LYNCH
(EMMA MURDOCH, later VAN DEVENTER)
No Proof. Large Cr 8vo. Illustrated.
o/6 sewed   June (*Eng Cat*)
Sixpenny Detective and Adventure Series No.
301. This new series starts with No. 301.
Also 1896

2533 GEORGE J. WHYTE MELVILLE
The White Rose. Cr 8vo. Illustrated.
2/o boards   June (*Eng Cat*)
2/o Copyright Novels No. 65. This ran in the
Fortnightly Review, Jan. 1867–Feb 1868.
The first book edition was issued by Chapman & Hall, London, 3 vols., Cr 8vo, 31/6,
listed in the *Ath* on Jan. 18, 1868. They issued it 1868, Cr 8vo, 5/o cloth, listed in the
Spect on Dec. 12; and issued it, 1871, my
copy in boards, a new edition, 357 pp., at
2/o boards, 2/6 cloth, listed in the *Ath* on
Aug. 12. They issued it as *Select Library of
Fiction* No. 389, at 2/o boards, in the fall of
1879. I have a copy, no date, a new edition, 357 pp., 2/o boards, with No. 389 on
the front cover, and publisher's ads at the
back dated 1880. The first American edition was issued by J. B. Lippincott & Co.,
Philadelphia, 1868, 12mo, $1.50 cloth,
printed in England, listed in *Godey's Lady's
Book* for Apr. 1868 as Chapman & Hall,
London; J. B. Lippincott & Co., Philadelphia, and thus probably issued in Jan. or
Feb. It was advertised in the *New-York
Times* on Mar. 28, 1868, at $1.50 cloth.
Lippincott issued it, 1869, 18 cm., 357
pp., $.75 paper, listed in *ALG&PC* (fort-
nightly) on May 15 and the *Nation* on May
20.

2534 GEORGE J. WHYTE MELVILLE
Tilbury Nogo. Cr 8vo. Illustrated.
2/o boards   June (*Eng Cat*)
2/o Copyright Novels No. 66.
Also 1882, 1904

2535 RICHARD H. SAVAGE
Captain Landon. Large Cr 8vo.
Illustrated. o/6 sewed   June (*Eng Cat*)
Sixpenny Lithographic Series No. 42. Ward,
Lock issued this, Cr 8vo, 6/o cloth, listed in
the *Ath* on June 22, 1901; and they issued
it as *2/o Copyright Novels* No. 45, given in
the spring 1906 Ward, Lock catalog. The
first English edition was issued by F. V.
White & Co., London, 1899, 391 pp. The
first American edition was issued by
Rand, McNally, New York and Chicago
(1899), 12mo, 391 pp., with 1 plate, $1.00,
listed in the *Nation* on Jan. 25, 1900, and
Lit World (fortnightly) on Feb. 3 (no list on
Jan. 27).

2536 HAWLEY SMART *Tie and Trick.*
Large Cr 8vo. Illustrated. o/6 sewed
July (*Eng Cat*)
Sixpenny Lithographic Series No. 43. This
has no date, 21 cm., 181 pp., with a
frontispiece.
Also 1886

2537 COULSON KERNAHAN *Scoundrels
and Co.* Large Cr 8vo. Illustrated. o/6
sewed   July (*Eng Cat*)
Sixpenny Lithographic Series No. 44. The
first edition was issued by Herbert Stone
& Co., Chicago and New York, 1899,
16mo, 320 pp., $1.25, from advance
sheets, listed in the *Nation* on Nov. 30,
1899, and the *New York Times Book Review*
on Dec. 2. The first English edition was issued by Ward, Lock (1901), Cr 8vo, 292
pp., illustrated, 3/6 cloth, listed in the *Ath*
on Mar. 2.

2538 H. BURFORD DELANNOY
Nineteen Thousand Pounds. Demy 8vo.
Illustrated. o/6 sewed   July (*Eng Cat*)
Detective and Adventure Series No. 302.
Also 1901, 05

2539 GEORGE J. WHYTE MELVILLE
Uncle John. Cr 8vo. Illustrated.
2/o boards   July (*Eng Cat*)
2/o Copyright Novels No. 67. This ran in
Temple Bar, Oct. 1873–Aug. 1874. The

first book edition was issued by Chapman & Hall, London, 3 vols., 1874, 20 cm., 31/6, listed in the *Ath* on July 4. They issued it in 1874, 10/6, listed in the *Spect* on Oct. 31; and issued it in 1875, a new edition, 2/0 boards, 2/6 cloth, listed in the *Ath* on Apr. 10. I have a yellowback, no date, a new edition, with endpaper ads of 1876. A new edition was issued, 1878; and it was issued as *Select Library of Fiction* No. 388 in the fall of 1879, 329 pp. The first American edition was issued by D. Appleton & Co., New York, 1874, 18.5 cm., 329 pp., listed in the *Nation* on Sept. 17 and *PW* on Sept. 12.
Also 1904

2540 GEORGE J. WHYTE MELVILLE
Contraband. Cr 8vo. Illustrated.
2/0 boards July (*Eng Cat*)
2/0 Copyright Novels No. 68.
Also 1894

2541 GEORGE ELIOT (MARIAN EVANS, later CROSS) *The Mill on the Floss.*
Large Cr 8vo. Illustrated. 0/6 sewed
Aug. 2 (*Acad*)
Sixpenny Standard Novels and Popular Books No. 1. A few in this series were issued in large Cr 8vo, illustrated, and numbered separately. The first edition was issued by William Blackwood & Sons, Edinburgh and London, 3 vols., 1860, 20.5 cm., 31/6, listed in the *Ath* on Mar. 31. They issued it in 2 vols., 1860, Fcp 8vo, 12/0, advertised in the *Spect* on Nov. 24. They issued the fifth edition, 1862, 19 cm., 486 pp., 6/0, advertised in the *Spect* on Dec. 6 as "This day"; and they issued a new edition in 1867, Cr 8vo, 3/6 cloth, listed in the *Spect* on Nov. 2. In 1901, they issued it at 0/6 sewed, 8vo; and also in a copyright edition, 19 cm., at 1/0 sewed, 2/0 cloth. The American editions were issued by Harper & Bros., New York; and G. G. Evans, Philadelphia. The former is 1860, 20 cm., 464 pp., in cloth, and 23.5 cm., 189 pp., at $1.00 muslin and paper, respectively. The

cloth was advertised in *Harper's Weekly* on Apr. 21 as "Just published" and listed in *APC&LG* on Apr. 28. The Evans was given by the *U Cat* as 1860, 20 cm., 464 pp. Harpers issued the $1.00 muslin edition first, advertised in the *New-York Times* on Apr. 25 as "On Apr. 26"; and they issued the paper at $.50, advertised there on Aug. 11, 1860, *Library of Select Novels* No. 215, 8vo.

2542 E. P. OPPENHEIM *The Man and His Kingdom.* Large Cr 8vo. Illustrated.
0/6 sewed Aug. (*Eng Cat*)
Sixpenny Lithographic Series No. 45.
Also 1901

2543 GUY N. BOOTHBY *A Prince of Swindlers.* Large Cr 8vo. Illustrated.
0/6 sewed Aug. (*Eng Cat*)
Sixpenny Lithographic Series No. 46. The first edition was issued by Ward, Lock (1900), 20 cm., 292 pp., illustrated, 5/0 cloth, listed in the *Spect* on July 21.

2544 ARTHUR MORRISON *Adventures of Martin Hewitt.* Large Cr 8vo. Illustrated.
0/6 sewed Aug. (*Eng Cat*)
Sixpenny Lithographic Series No. 47.
Also 1899

2545 ALICE M. MEADOWS *Out from the Night.* Demy 8vo. Illustrated. 0/6 sewed
Aug. (*Eng Cat*)
Detective and Adventure Series No. 303.
Also 1900

2546 LAWRENCE L. LYNCH
(EMMA MURDOCH, later VAN DEVENTER)
The Unseen Hand. Large Cr 8vo.
Illustrated. 0/6 sewed Sept. (*Eng Cat*)
Sixpenny Lithographic Series No. 48.
Also 1900

2547 ANNA K. GREEN, later ROHLFS
The Circular Study. Demy 8vo.
Illustrated. 0/6 sewed Sept. (*Eng Cat*)
Detective and Adventure Series No. 304. The first edition was issued by McClure, Phil-

lips & Co., New York, 1900, 19 cm., 298 pp., with diagrams, $1.25 cloth, listed in the *Nation* on Oct. 4, the *New York Times Book Review* on Oct. 20, and in *Lit World* (monthly) on Nov. 1. The first English edition was issued by Ward, Lock, 1902, 19.7 cm., 265 pp., 3/6 cloth, listed in the *Ath* on June 7 and the *Times Literary Supplement* on June 20.

2548   HAWLEY SMART   **A Race for a Wife.** Large Cr 8vo. Illustrated. 0/6 sewed Sept. (*Eng Cat*)

Sixpenny Lithographic Series No. 49.
Also 1885

2549   GEORGE J. WHYTE MELVILLE **M. or N.** Cr 8vo. Illustrated. 2/0 boards Sept. (*Eng Cat*)

2/0 Copyright Novels No. 69.
Also 1881

2550   GEORGE J. WHYTE MELVILLE **The Queen's Maries.** Cr 8vo. Illustrated. 2/0 boards   Sept. (*Eng Cat*)

2/0 Copyright Novels No. 70. This has no date, 427 pp. The first edition was issued by Parker, Son & Bourn, London, 2 vols., 1862, 20 cm., 16/0, listed in the *Ath* on July 5. They issued the second edition at 6/0, advertised in the *Spect* on Dec. 13, 1862, as "In a few days"; and the third edition at 6/0, advertised on Mar. 7, 1863. Longmans, London, issued the third edition, Cr 8vo, 451 pp., 6/0, listed in the *Reader* on Jan. 30, 1864; and they issued a new edition (1862), 19 cm., 380 pp. They issued it, no date, 380 pp., 2/0 boards, 2/6 cloth, listed in the *Ath* on Jan. 7, 1871; and reissued the yellowback, no date, in 1879; and issued it, no date, a new edition, 380 pp., 1/0 boards, 1/6 cloth, in 1885; and issued editions in 1890 and 1892.

2551   HEADON HILL (FRANCIS GRAINGER) **Caged!** Demy 8vo. Illustrated. 0/6 sewed Sept. 27 (*Acad*)

Detective and Adventure Series No. 305. The first edition was issued by Ward, Lock,

1900, 20 cm., 336 pp., illustrated, 6/0 cloth, listed in the *Ath* on June 30. They issued the second edition at 6/0, advertised in the *Spect* on Aug. 4, 1900.

2552   ARTHUR C. DOYLE   **A Study in Scarlet.** Demy 8vo. Illustrated. 0/6 sewed Oct. (*Eng Cat*)

Detective and Adventure Series No. 306. This is my copy, no date, 21.2 cm., 96 pp., with a frontispiece and 1 plate by George Hutchinson, in white wrappers cut flush, pictorially printed on the front in dark green and brown. The text is in double columns, and there are ads on the inside covers and on the back cover in dark green. There is a publisher's note on p. 7 and a preface entitled "Mr. Sherlock Holmes" on pp. 8–11.
Also 1887, 88, 99

2553   LAWRENCE L. LYNCH (EMMA MURDOCH, later VAN DEVENTER) **High Stakes.** Demy 8vo. Illustrated. 0/6 sewed   Oct. (*Eng Cat*)

Detective and Adventure Series No. 307. This is my copy, 1902, 21.2 cm., 192 pp., with a frontispiece and 1 plate, double columns, white pictorial wrappers, printed in light blue and black. There are ads on the inside covers and on the back cover in the light blue. There is an inscribed date (Oct. 1902), and the series title appears only in an ad. The first edition was issued by Laird & Lee, Chicago (1900, copyright 1899), 18.5 cm., 368 pp., illustrated, with "Pinkerton Detective Series No. 42" on the front cover. It was listed in *PW* on Feb. 24, 1900. It was listed in the *New York Times Book Review* at $.75, on Mar. 3, 1900. The first English edition was issued by Ward, Lock, 1901, 424 pp., illustrated, 3/6 cloth, listed in the *Times Weekly Edition* on July 5, 1901.

2554 H. BURFORD DELANNOY **Between the Lines.** Demy 8vo. Illustrated. o/6 sewed Oct. (*Eng Cat*)

Detective and Adventure Series No. 308.

Also 1901

2555 GEORGE J. WHYTE MELVILLE **General Bounce.** Cr 8vo. Illustrated.

2/0 boards Oct. (*Eng Cat*)

2/0 Copyright Novels No. 71. This has no date, 384 pp. It ran in *Fraser's Magazine*, Jan.–Dec. 1854. The first book edition was issued by John W. Parker & Son, London, 2 vols., 1855, 20 cm., 15/0, listed by *PC* as published Dec. 15–30, 1854. They issued the second edition, 1860, 19.5 cm., 347 pp. Longmans, London, issued it (1873), a new edition, 18.5 cm., 379 pp., 2/0 boards, 2/6 cloth, listed in the *Ath* on July 12; and they issued a new edition, no date, 18.5 cm., 379 pp., 1/0 boards, 1/6 cloth, about July 11, 1885. They issued a new edition, 1891, 17.5 cm., 379 pp.

2556 GEORGE J. WHYTE MELVILLE **Digby Grand.** Cr 8vo. Illustrated.

2/0 boards Oct. (*Eng Cat*)

2/0 Copyright Novels No. 72. This ran in *Fraser's Magazine*, Nov. 1851–Dec. 1852. The first book edition was *Digby Grand: An Autobiography*, issued by John W. Parker & Son, London, 2 vols., 1853, 21 cm., 18/0, listed in the *Spect* on Feb. 5, and advertised in *Notes & Queries* on Feb. 3. It is in red cloth with yellow endpapers and has ads paged 1–4 at the back of vol. 2. They issued the second edition, 1857, 19 cm., 334 pp., 5/0, advertised in *Notes & Queries* on May 2 as "This day." Longmans, London, issued a new edition (1872), 383 pp., 2/0 boards, 2/6 cloth, listed in the *Ath* on July 13; and a new edition (1878), my copy, 12mo, 383 pp., at 2/0 boards, with an advertisement by the author for the first edition (Feb. 1, 1853). Longmans issued it (1885), a new edition, 18.5 cm., 383 pp., 1/0 boards, 1/6 cloth, about July 11.

2557 WILLIAM T. LE QUEUX **The Temptress.** Large Cr 8vo.

Illustrated. o/6 sewed Oct. 25 (*Acad*)

Sixpenny Lithographic Series No. 51. This is my copy, no date, 21.3 cm., 154 pp., with a frontispiece and 1 plate, double columns, in pictorial, lithographed wrappers, in red, green, brown, black, and white, cut flush. There are ads on the inside covers and on 6 pp. at the back, and there is an ad in red, green, and black on a cream ground on the back. The first edition was issued by the Tower Publishing Co., London, Cr 8vo, 346 pp., 6/0, listed in *PC* on Nov. 23, 1895, and listed in the *Ath* and the *Spect* on Oct. 26. The first American edition was issued by F. A. Stokes Co., New York and London (1896), copyright 1895), 19.5 cm., 333 pp., listed in *PW* on Mar. 21, 1896. Ward, Lock issued it, 1901, 20 cm., 345 pp., illustrated, 3/6 cloth, advertised in the *Times Weekly Edition* on Sept. 20, and reviewed in the *Ath* as a new novel on Sept. 28. In a letter to the *Ath* on Oct. 5, Le Queux stated that he had noticed the review giving it as a new book but that it had been published eight years ago and that Ward, Lock had now issued it in a new guise without his knowledge or consent. Ward, Lock answered on Oct. 19 that they had purchased from Le Queux his interest in the book only four months ago! *See color photo section*

2558 E. P. OPPENHEIM **False Evidence.** Demy 8vo. Illustrated. o/6 sewed Nov. (*Eng Cat*)

Detective and Adventure Series No. 309.

Also 1896, 97

2559 CLARENCE ROOK **A Lesson for Life.** o/6 sewed Nov. (*Eng Cat*)

Also 1901

2560 MAX ADELER (CHARLES H. CLARK) **Elbow Room.** Large Cr 8vo. Illustrated. o/6 sewed Nov. (*Eng Cat*)

Sixpenny Lithographic Series No. 52.

Also 1876, 82, 83

2561 GEORGE J. WHYTE MELVILLE
The Interpreter. Cr 8vo. Illustrated.
2/0 boards   Nov. (*Eng Cat*)

2/0 *Copyright Novels* No. 73. This ran in
Fraser's Magazine, Jan.–Dec. 1857. The
first book edition was issued by John W.
Parker & Son, London, 1858, 20 cm., 431
pp., 10/6, advertised in the *Ath* on Jan. 9,
1858, as "Now ready," and advertised in
Notes & Queries on Dec. 19, 1857, as "This
day." The second edition was issued in
1858, 10/6, advertised in *Notes & Queries*
on Oct. 23, 1858, as "This day." Longmans, London, issued it, 1870, 12mo, 346
pp., 2/0 boards, 2/6 cloth, listed in the *Ath*
on July 2; and they issued a new edition,
1883, 4to, 80 pp., 0/6 sewed, *Sunbeam Series* No. 6, in Mar. They issued a new edition, no date, 18.5 cm., 346 pp., 1/0
boards, 1/6 cloth, about July 11, 1885; and
issued a new edition, 1894, 18 cm., 346
pp. They issued a new edition, 346 pp.,
5/0 cloth, advertised in the *Spect* on Apr.
23, 1864. The first American edition was
issued by Standford & Delisser, New York,
1858, listed in *APC&LG* on May 1. They
advertised the fourth edition, 8vo, $.50
paper, in the *New-York Times* on Oct. 11,
1858, as "Now ready."

2562 HAWLEY SMART **False Cards.**
Large Cr 8vo. Illustrated. 0/6 sewed
Dec. 13 (*Acad*)
Sixpenny Lithographic Series No. 53.
Also 1894

2563 E. P. OPPENHEIM **A Millionaire of
Yesterday.** Large Cr 8vo. Illustrated.
0/6 sewed   Dec. 13 (*Acad*)
Sixpenny Lithographic Series No. 54. The
first English edition was issued by Ward,
Lock (1900), Cr 8vo, 315 pp., 6/0 cloth,
listed in the *Spect* on June 30 and the *Ath*
on July 7. They issued a second edition at
6/0, advertised in the *Spect* on Aug. 4. The
first American edition was issued by J. B.
Lippincott & Co., Philadelphia, 1900,

$.50 paper, $1.00 cloth, in their *Series of
Select Novels*. It was listed in *PW* on July 7
and *Lit World* (monthly) on Aug. 1.

2564 ANNA K. GREEN, later ROHLFS
The Leavenworth Case. Demy 8vo.
Illustrated. 0/6 sewed   Dec. 13 (*Acad*)
Detective and Adventure Series No. 310.
Also 1894

2565 LAWRENCE L. LYNCH
(EMMA MURDOCH, later VAN DEVENTER)
The Last Stroke. Demy 8vo.
Illustrated. 0/6 sewed   Dec. (*Eng Cat*)
Detective and Adventure Series No. 311.
Also 1897, 1901

2566 GEORGE E. WALSH **The Mysterious
Burglar.** Demy 8vo. Illustrated.
0/6 sewed   Dec. (*Eng Cat*)
Detective and Adventure Series No. 312. The
first edition was issued by F. M. Buckles &
Co., New York, 1901, 12mo, 247 pp.,
$1.25, listed in the *New York Times Book Re-
view* on June 15. They issued a second edition, the same, 1901. The first English
edition was the present title, 1903, 94 pp.

2567 FREDERICK MARRYAT
Jacob Faithful. 0/6 sewed   1902 (*BM*)
This is a reissue of the 1881 edition
(1902), 116 pp.
Also 1881, 83

2568 GUY M. BOOTHBY **The Red Rat's
Daughter.** Large Cr 8vo. Illustrated.
0/6 sewed   1902?
Sixpenny Lithographic Series No. 55. The
first edition was issued by Ward, Lock,
1899, 20 cm., 384 pp., illustrated, 5/0,
listed in the *Spect* on Nov. 4. It was issued
in Canada by the Copp, Clark Co., Toronto, 1899, 384 pp.; and in New York by
the New Amsterdam Book Co., 1900, 19
cm., 384 pp., illustrated, $1.25 cloth, ad-
vertised in the *New York Times Book Review*
on June 16, 1900.

2569 HAMILTON DRUMMOND *For the Religion.* Large Cr 8vo. Illustrated. 0/6 sewed Jan. (*Eng Cat*)

Sixpenny Lithographic Series No. 56. Ward, Lock also issued this at 3/6 cloth in 1900. The first edition was issued by Smith, Elder & Co., London, 1898, 19.1 cm., 344 pp., 6/0 cloth, in Feb. The first American edition was issued by Brentano's, New York, 1901, 318 pp.

2570 THOMAS W. HANSHEW *The World's Finger.* Demy 8vo. Illustrated. 0/6 sewed Jan. (*Eng Cat*)

Detective and Adventure Series No. 313. The first English edition was issued by Ward, Lock, 1901, 19.1 cm., 318 pp., illustrated, 3/6 cloth, listed in the *Times Weekly Edition* on June 28 and the *Ath* on July 6. The first American edition was issued by C. E. Irwin & Co., New York (1901), 12mo, 283 pp., with a frontispiece.

2571 ROBERT M. BALLANTYNE *The Dog Crusoe.* Large Cr 8vo. 0/6 sewed Feb. (*Eng Cat*)

Sixpenny Standard Novels and Popular Books No. 113. Ward, Lock also issued this as *Royal Series* No. 49, large Cr 8vo, with a frontispiece, 1/0 cloth, before 1909; and as *Youth's Library* No. 37, large Cr 8vo, with 4 plates, 1/6 cloth, before 1909. The first edition was issued by Thomas Nelson & Sons, London, 1861 (1860), Cr 8vo, 356 pp., illustrated, 3/6 cloth, listed in the *Spect* on Dec. 29, 1860. Sadleir's copy was in pictorial violet cloth, blocked in gold and blind, with an inscribed date (May 31, 1861). Nelson issued it in 1878, Cr 8vo,

3/6 cloth, listed in the *Spect* on Oct. 19. It was issued in the United States by Crosby & Nichols, Boston, 381 pp., illustrated, probably dated 1862, listed in *APC&LG* (monthly) on Nov. 1, 1862.

2572 HAWLEY SMART *Play or Pay.* Large Cr 8vo. Illustrated. 0/6 sewed Feb. (*Eng Cat*)

Sixpenny Lithographic Series No. 57. Also 1886, 89

2573 GEORGE J. WHYTE MELVILLE *The Brookes of Bridlemere.* Large Cr 8vo. Illustrated. 0/6 sewed Feb. (*Eng Cat*)

Sixpenny Lithographic Series No. 58. Also 1894. See 1901

2574 HAWLEY SMART *Cecile.* Large Cr 8vo. Illustrated. 0/6 sewed Feb.?

Sixpenny Lithographic Series No. 59. The first edition was issued by Bentley, London, 3 vols., 1871, 20 cm., 31/6, listed in the *Ath* on Nov. 11. Chapman & Hall, London, issued it as *Select Library of Fiction* No. 364 (1877), a new edition, 393 pp., 2/0 boards, listed in the *Spect* on Nov. 3; and they reissued it at 2/0 boards in Sept. 1878; and in 1881, the latter in the illuminated decorative boards style of the series but with Ward, Lock on the spine, Sadleir's copy, 1881.

2575 E. P. OPPENHEIM *The Mystery of Mr. Bernard Brown.* Large Cr 8vo. Illustrated. 0/6 sewed Feb. (*Eng Cat*)

Sixpenny Lithographic Series No. 61. Ward, Lock also issued this, 1901, 19.5 cm., 351

pp., illustrated, 3/6 cloth, listed in the *Ath* on July 13. The first edition was issued by Bentley & Son, London, 1896, 19 cm., 372 pp., 6/o cloth, listed in the *Ath* on Feb. 15.

2576 MRS. L. T. MEADE, later SMITH & ROBERT EUSTACE (EUSTACE ROBERT BARTON) *The Brotherhood of the Seven Kings.* Demy 8vo. Illustrated. o/6 sewed Feb. (*Eng Cat*)

Detective and Adventure Series No. 314. Also 1900

2577 H. BURFORD DELANNOY *The Margate Murdery Mystery.* Demy 8vo. Illustrated. o/6 sewed Feb. (*Eng Cat*)

Detective and Adventure Series No. 315. Also 1902, 05

2578 GEORGE J. WHYTE MELVILLE *Market Harborough and Inside the Bar.* Cr 8vo. Illustrated. 2/o boards Feb. (*Eng Cat*)

2/o Copyright Novels No. 55. Also 1894, 1901

2579 GEORGE J. WHYTE MELVILLE *Songs and Verses and The True Cross.* Cr 8vo. Illustrated. 2/o boards Mar. 21 (*Spect*)

2/o Copyright Novels No. 54.

For the first title see also 1882, 83; and for the second title see also 1882

2580 GUY N. BOOTHBY *"Long Live the King."* Large Cr 8vo. Illustrated. o/6 sewed Mar. (*Eng Cat*)

Sixpenny Lithographic Series No. 60. This is 1903. The first edition was issued by Ward, Lock, 1900, 19.5 cm., 384 pp., illustrated, 5/o, in blue cloth, listed in the *Ath* on Oct. 27. The first American edition was issued by Herbert S. Stone, Chicago and New York, 1900, 19.5 cm., 408 pp., listed in the *Nation* on Nov. 22 and by *PW* on Dec. 5.

2581 LAWRENCE L. LYNCH (EMMA MURDOCH, later VAN DEVENTER) *Against Odds.* Demy 8vo. Illustrated. o/6 sewed Mar. (*Eng Cat*)

Detective and Adventure Series No. 316. Also 1895

2582 HENRY HERMAN *Lady Turpin.* Demy 8vo. Illustrated. o/6 sewed Mar. (*Eng Cat*)

Detective and Adventure Series No. 319. Also 1895, 99, 1905

2583 MORICE GERARD (JOHN J. TEAGUE) *For England.* Demy 8vo. Illustrated. o/6 sewed Apr. (*Eng Cat*)

Detective and Adventure Series No. 317. The first edition was issued by Ward, Lock (1902), 20 cm., 309 pp., illustrated, 6/o cloth, listed in the *Ath* on Feb. 22 and the *Times Literary Supplement* (London) on Feb. 14.

2584 FLORENCE WARDEN (FLORENCE PRICE, later JAMES) *The Fog Princess.* Demy 8vo. Illustrated. o/6 sewed Apr. (*Eng Cat*)

Detective and Adventure Series No. 318. The first edition was issued by Ward & Downey, London, 1889, 156 pp., 1/o sewed, 1/6 cloth, advertised in the *Spect* on May 25. They issued the second edition, 1889, the same. In the United States it was issued by Frank F. Lovell, New York (1889), 19 cm., 214 pp., *International Series* No. 18, which words were on the cover. It was listed in the *Nation* on June 6 and *PW* on June 8. It was also issued by George Munro, New York (1889), *Seaside Library Pocket Edition* No. 1193, 19.5 cm., 216 pp., in wrappers, listed in *PW* on June 1.

2585 GEORGE J. WHYTE MELVILLE *Holmby House.* Large Cr 8vo. Illustrated. o/6 sewed Apr. (*Eng Cat*)

Sixpenny Lithographic Series No. 62. Also 1902

2586 MAYNE LINDSAY *The Whirligig.* Large Cr 8vo. Illustrated. 0/6 sewed Apr. (*Eng Cat*)

Sixpenny Lithographic Series No. 63. The first edition was issued by Ward, Lock, 1901, 19.5 cm., 312 pp., illustrated, 6/0 cloth, listed in the *Spect* on May 18. In the United States it was issued by Longmans, New York, 1901, 19 cm., 285 pp., with 8 plates, $1.25, listed in the *New York Times Book Review* on Aug. 3.

2587 GEORGE J. WHYTE MELVILLE *Good for Nothing.* Cr 8vo. Illustrated. 2/0 boards Apr. (*Eng Cat*)

2/0 Copyright Novels No. 74. This ran in *Fraser's Magazine*, Jan. 1861–Dec. 1861. The first book edition was issued by Parker, Son & Bourn, London, 2 vols., 1861, 20 cm., 16/0, listed in the *Ath* on Dec. 7, 1862. They issued a second edition, 1862, 440 pp., 6/0 cloth, advertised in the *Spect* on Apr. 2; and they issued the third edition at 6/0 cloth in 1862, advertised in the *Spect* on Oct. 25. Longmans, London, issued a new edition (1871), 18.5 cm., 371 pp., 2/0 boards, 2/6 cloth, listed in the *Ath* on Jan. 7, 1871; and reissued it at 2/0 boards, my copy (1878), a new edition, 371 pp. They issued it (1885), 18.5 cm., 371 pp., 1/0 boards, 1/6 cloth, about July 11; and issued a new edition, 1890, 371 pp. The first American edition was issued by D. Appleton & Co., New York, 1871, 8vo, 210 pp., $.60 paper, advertised in the *New-York Times* on May 6 as "This day," and listed in the *Nation* on May 18. Ward, Lock issued it at 3/6 cloth, illustrated, listed in the *Times Weekly Edition* on Jan. 11, 1901.

2588 GEORGE J. WHYTE MELVILLE *Bones and I.* Cr 8vo. Illustrated. 2/0 boards Apr. (*Eng Cat*)

2/0 Copyright Novels No. 75. Also 1884

2589 WILLIAM LE QUEUX *A Secret Service.* Demy 8vo. Illustrated. 0/6 sewed May (*Eng Cat*)

Detective and Adventure Series No. 320. Also 1892, 99

2590 ELIZABETH P. TRAIN *A Social Highwayman.* Demy 8vo. Illustrated. 0/6 sewed May (*Eng Cat*)

Detective and Adventure Series No. 321. Also 1896, 99, 1905

2591 LAWRENCE L. LYNCH (EMMA MURDOCH, later VAN DEVENTER) *Under Fate's Wheel.* Demy 8vo. Illustrated. 0/6 sewed May (*Eng Cat*)

Detective and Adventure Series No. 322. This was also issued as *2/0 Copyright Novels* No. 42, listed in the *Eng Cat* as published in Nov. 1903. The first edition was issued by Ward, Lock (1900), 20 cm., 336 pp., illustrated, 3/6 cloth, listed in the *Ath* on Aug. 25. The first American edition was issued by Laird & Lee, Chicago (1901, copyright 1900), 18.5 cm., 373 pp., illustrated, with "Pinkerton Detective Series No. 46" on the cover, and listed in *PW* on Feb. 9, 1901.

2592 ARCHIBALD C. GUNTER *Mr. Barnes of New York.* 0/6 sewed May (*Eng Cat*) Also 1888

2593 ORME AGNUS (JOHN HIGGINBOTHAM) *Jan Oxber.* Large Cr 8vo. Illustrated. 0/6 sewed May (*Eng Cat*)

Sixpenny Lithographic Series No. 64. The first edition was issued by Ward, Lock (1900), 20 cm., 320 pp., illustrated, 3/6 cloth, listed in the *Ath* on June 16. The first American edition was *Jan Oxber and Love in a Village*, 2 vols., issued by the L. C. Page & Co., Boston, 1901, 19.7 cm., $2.00 cloth, listed in the *New York Times Book Review* on Aug. 24, and reviewed on Aug. 31. They also issued it, 1902 (1901), 20 cm., 159 pp., illustrated, listed in *Lit World* (monthly) on Sept. 1, 1901, and *PW* on Sept. 14. Ward, Lock issued a second edition at 3/6 cloth, advertised in the *Spect* on Aug. 4, 1900.

2594   WILLIAM LE QUEUX   **Stolen Souls.** Large Cr 8vo. Illustrated. o/6 sewed May (*Eng Cat*)

Sixpenny Lithographic Series No. 65. This is 1903, 120 pp. Ward, Lock also issued it, 1902, 317 pp., 3/6 cloth, advertised in the *Spect* on Apr. 26. The first edition was issued by the Tower Publishing Co., London, 1895, 20 cm., 317 pp., with a portrait, 6/o cloth, listed in *PC* on June 29. The first American edition was issued by F. A. Stokes Co., New York and London (1895), 19.5 cm., 305 pp., illustrated, $1.00, listed in *Public Opinion* on Oct. 31 and *PW* on Nov. 2.

2595   EDGAR ALLAN POE   **Murders in the Rue Morgue.** o/6 sewed   May (*Eng Cat*)

I think this was also issued by Ward, Lock in 1890 at o/6. The story was first issued in *The Prose Romances*, by William H. Graham, Philadelphia, 1843. They were issued in a uniform serial edition, each No. complete in itself. The present title was No. 1, 23 cm., 48 pp., $.12½, in a printed pale tan wrapper.

2596   HAWLEY SMART   **Two Kisses.** Large Cr 8vo. Illustrated. o/6 sewed June (*Eng Cat*)

Sixpenny Lithographic Series No. 66. The first edition was issued by Bentley, London, 3 vols., 1875, 19 cm., 31/6, listed in the *Ath* on May 20, 1876. The first American edition was issued by A. K. Loring, Boston (1877), 17 cm., 254 pp., in their *Tales of the Day*, listed in *PW* on Aug. 11 and the *Ind* on Aug. 16.

2597   ESTHER MILLER   **Should She Have Spoken.** Demy 8vo. Illustrated. o/6 sewed June (*Eng Cat*)

Detective and Adventure Series No. 323. The first edition was issued by Ward, Lock (1900), 20 cm., 292 pp., 3/6 cloth, in June.

2598   MRS. L. T. MEADE, later SMITH & ROBERT EUSTACE (EUSTACE ROBERT BARTON)   **The Sanctuary Club.** Demy 8vo. Illustrated. o/6 sewed   June (*Eng Cat*)

Detective and Adventure Series No. 324. This first appeared in the *Strand Magazine* in 1899. The first book edition was issued by Ward, Lock, 1900, 20 cm., 297 pp., illustrated, 5/o cloth, listed in the *Ath* on May 19.

2599   SIR WILLIAM MAGNAY   **The Red Chancellor.** Large Cr 8vo. Illustrated. o/6 sewed   June (*Eng Cat*)

Sixpenny Lithographic Series No. 67. The first English edition was issued by Ward, Lock, 1901, 20.4 cm., 315 pp., illustrated, 6/o, listed in the *Ath* on June 1. The first American edition was issued by Brentano's, New York, 1901, 19.5 cm., 303 pp., listed in the *New York Times Book Review* on Oct. 19 and the *Nation* on Oct. 3.

2600   HENRY KINGSLEY   **Ravenshoe.** Large Cr 8vo. Illustrated. o/6 sewed July (*Eng Cat*)

Sixpenny Lithographic Series No. 68. Also 1892

2601   HAWLEY SMART   **Sunshine and Snow.** Large Cr 8vo. Illustrated. o/6 sewed   July (*Eng Cat*)

Sixpenny Lithographic Series No. 69. The first edition was issued by Chapman & Hall, London, 3 vols., 1878, 20 cm., 31/6, about July 13. They issued it as *Select Library of Fiction* No. 382, 2/o boards, about Nov. 23, 1878; and issued a new edition,

1880, my copy, at 2/0 boards, with a printer's date (Oct. 24, 1879), in Jan. 1880.

2602 GERTRUDE WARDEN, later JONES
Beyond the Law. Demy 8vo. Illustrated.
o/6 sewed   July (*Eng Cat*)

Detective and Adventure Series No. 325. The first edition was issued by Ward, Lock, 1902, 20.4 cm., 314 pp., illustrated, 3/6 cloth, listed in the *Ath* on Aug. 9.

2603 MORICE GERARD (JOHN J. TEAGUE)
The Man of the Moment. Demy 8vo.
Illustrated. o/6 sewed   July (*Eng Cat*)

Detective and Adventure Series No. 326. The first edition was issued by Ward, Lock (1900), 20.4 cm., 342 pp., illustrated, 3/6 cloth, listed in the *Ath* on Sept. 8.
Also 1905

2604 MRS. K. F. HILL **A Mysterious Case.**
o/6 sewed   July (*Eng Cat*)

Sixpenny Standard Novels and Popular Books No. 102.
Also 1890

2605 GUY N. BOOTHBY **My Indian Queen.**
Large Cr 8vo. Illustrated. o/6 sewed
Aug. (*Eng Cat*)

Sixpenny Lithographic Series No. 70. The first edition was issued by D. Appleton & Co., New York, 1901 (1900), 18.5 cm., 322 pp., $.50 paper, $1.00 cloth, *Town and Country Library* No. 294. It was listed in *PW* on Dec. 9, 1900, and the *Nation* on Dec. 13. The first English edition was issued by Ward, Lock, 1901, 19.7 cm., 319 pp., illustrated, 5/0 cloth, listed in the *Spect* on Mar. 9, 1901, and reviewed in the *Ath* on Apr. 13.

2606 WILLIAM LE QUEUX **Zoraida.**
Large Cr 8vo. Illustrated. o/6 sewed
Aug. (*Eng Cat*)

Sixpenny Lithographic Series No. 71. Ward, Lock also issued this in 1902, Cr 8vo, 3/6

cloth, listed in the *Spect* on Sept. 6. The first edition was issued by the Tower Publishing Co., London, 1895, 444 pp., illustrated, 6/0 cloth, listed in the *Ath* on Apr. 20 and *PC* on May 11. It was issued by F. V. White, London, 1897, the seventh edition, 22 cm., 444 pp., illustrated, 3/6 cloth, in June. The first American edition was issued by Frederick A. Stokes Co., New York (1895), 19 cm., 434 pp., illustrated, $1.50. It was listed in *Public Opinion* on Sept. 17, the *Ind* on Sept. 19, and *PW* on Oct. 4 (no lists on Sept. 21 or 28).

2607 HUAN MEE **The Jewel of Death.**
Demy 8vo. Illustrated. o/6 sewed
Aug. (*Eng Cat*)

Detective and Adventure Series No. 328. The first edition was issued by Ward, Lock, 1902, 19.7 cm., 330 pp., 3/6 cloth, listed in the *Times Literary Supplement* (London) on Feb. 14 and the *Ath* on Feb. 15.

2608 CLARKE LITTLE **"Outlaws."**
Demy 8vo. Illustrated. o/6 sewed
Aug. (*Eng Cat*)

Detective and Adventure Series No. 329. The first edition was issued by Ward, Lock, 1902, 291 pp., 3/6 cloth, and reviewed in the *Ath* on Oct. 25.

2609 E. P. OPPENHEIM **As a Man Lives.**
Large Cr 8vo. Illustrated. o/6 sewed
Sept. (*Eng Cat*)

Sixpenny Lithographic Series No. 72. The first edition was issued by Ward, Lock (1898), 20 cm., 304 pp., illustrated, 3/6 cloth, listed in the *Ath* on May 21.

2610 HAWLEY SMART **Belles and Ringers.**
Large Cr 8vo. Illustrated. o/6 sewed
Sept. (*Eng Cat*)

Sixpenny Lithographic Series No. 73. This is 1903, with 96 pp. The first edition was issued by Chapman & Hall, London, 1880, 20 cm., 226 pp., 10/6, listed in the *Ath* on Aug. 14. They issued it as *Select Library of Fiction* No. 418, a new edition, 226 pp., 2/0 boards, in May 1881, with 1881 on the title page. They issued it in 1880, a new edition, Cr 8vo, 2/6, listed in the *Spect* on Dec. 11. The first American edition was issued by J. B. Lippincott & Co., Philadelphia, 1881, 12mo, 226 pp., listed in the *Nation* on Feb. 3, *PW* on Feb. 12, and the *Ind* on Feb. 24. It was also issued by George Munro, New York, 1881, *Seaside Library* No. 937, 32.5 cm., 30 pp., in paper, listed in *PW* on Mar. 5.

2611 LAWRENCE L. LYNCH
(EMMA MURDOCH, later VAN DEVENTER)
Moina. Demy 8vo. Illustrated.
0/6 sewed   Sept. (*Eng Cat*)
Detective and Adventure Series No. 327.
Also 1891, 92

2612 JOYCE E. MUDDOCK, later PRESTON-
MUDDOCK **Stormlight.** Demy 8vo.
Illustrated. 0/6 sewed   Sept. (*Eng Cat*)
Detective and Adventure Series No. 330.
Also 1888, 93

2613 FLORENCE WARDEN (FLORENCE
PRICE, later JAMES) **A Prince of Darkness.**
Demy 8vo. Illustrated. 0/6 sewed
Oct. (*Eng Cat*)
Detective and Adventure Series No. 331. The first English edition was issued by Ward & Downey, London, 3 vols., 1885, 31/6, advertised in the *Ath* on Aug. 8 as "Next week," and on Aug. 15 as "This day." They issued the fourth edition, 1886, 207 pp., 1/0, in decorative cream wrappers; and issued the fifth edition, 1886, 19 cm., 207 pp., 1/0 sewed, 1/6 cloth, listed in the *Spect* on Apr. 10. The first American edition was issued by D. Appleton & Co., New

York, 1885, 12mo, 293 pp., an authorized edition at $.25 paper. It was advertised in the *Ind* on Aug. 20 as "Published on Aug. 14," and listed in the *Nation* on Sept. 17 and *PW* on Aug. 22. It was also issued by George Munro, New York (1885), *Seaside Library Pocket Edition* No. 556, 18.5 cm., 336 pp., in wrappers, listed in *PW* on Sept. 5, 1885. It was issued by Cassell & Co., Ltd., New York, 1886, in the *Rainbow Series*, $.25 paper, advertised in the *Christian Union* on Apr. 29.

2614 MRS. L. T. MEADE, later SMITH &
CLIFFORD HALIFAX (EDGAR BEAUMONT)
A Race with the Sun. Demy 8vo.
Illustrated. 0/6 sewed   Oct. (*Eng Cat*)
Detective and Adventure Series No. 332. The first edition was issued by Ward, Lock, 1901, 20.4 cm., 307 pp., illustrated, 5/0 cloth, listed in the *Ath* on Apr. 27.

2615 GEORGE J. WHYTE MELVILLE
Sarchedon. Large Cr 8vo. Illustrated.
0/6 sewed   Oct. (*Eng Cat*)
Sixpenny Lithographic Series No. 74.
Also 1901

2616 ARCHIBALD C. GUNTER
The Fighting Troubadour. Cr 8vo.
Illustrated. 2/0 boards   Nov. (*Eng Cat*)
2/0 Copyright Novels No. 46. This is my copy, no date, 19.4 cm., 271 pp., with a frontispiece and 1 plate, in pictorial lithographed boards in red, white, blue, yellow, and black, with a red cloth spine and plain white endpapers. There is an ad on the back cover in brown and white. The first edition was issued by the Home Publishing Co., New York (1899), 19.5 cm., 271 pp., with "Welcome Series No. 50" on the cover. It was issued about Dec. 23, 1899. The *BM* gives F. Routledge [sic!], 1899, but aside from the incorrect publisher's imprint, I've found no evidence of this. It was issued by Ward, Lock, 1901,

20.4 cm., 271 pp., illustrated, 6/0 cloth, listed in the *Ath* on Sept. 14.
Also 1904

2617 JOHN R. CARLING *The Shadow of the Czar.* Large Cr 8vo. Illustrated.
o/6 sewed   Nov. (*Eng Cat*)

Sixpenny Lithographic Series No. 75. The first edition was issued by Ward, Lock (1902), Cr 8vo, 373 pp., 6/0 cloth, listed in the *Spect* on Sept. 6 and the *Ath* on Sept. 13. The first American edition was issued by Little, Brown & Co., Boston, 1902, 20.5 cm., 419 pp., illustrated, $1.50 cloth, listed in the *New York Times Book Review* on Oct. 4. The second edition was advertised there on the same date. It was reissued, 1903.

2618 ANTHONY HOPE (ANTHONY HOPE HAWKINS) *Half a Hero.* Large Cr 8vo. Illustrated. o/6 sewed   Nov. (*Eng Cat*)

Sixpenny Lithographic Series No. 76. This is 1903, with 122 pp. The first edition was issued by Harper & Bros., New York, 1893, *Franklin Square Library* No. 738, 21.5 cm., 314 pp., $.60 paper, listed in the *Ind* on Sept. 7, *PW* on Sept. 9, and the *Nation* on Sept. 14. The first English edition was issued by A. D. Innes & Co., London, 2 vols., 1893, 19.5 cm., 21/0, listed in the *Times Weekly Edition* (London) on Sept. 29 and the *Ath* on Oct. 14. They issued the third edition, 1894, 304 pp. Ward, Lock acquired Innes in 1900 and issued this title, 1901, 18.5 cm., 304 pp.

2619 CLIFFORD ASHDOWN (RICHARD FREEMAN) *The Adventures of Romney Pringle.* Demy 8vo. Illustrated. o/6 sewed Nov. (*Eng Cat*)

Detective and Adventure Series No. 334. The first edition was issued by Ward, Lock, 1902, 19.7 cm., 198 pp., 3/6 cloth, listed in the *Times Weekly Edition* on Nov. 7, 1902.

2620 LOUIS TRACY *A Fatal Legacy.*
Demy 8vo. Illustrated. o/6 sewed
Nov. (*Eng Cat*)

Detective and Adventure Series No. 335. This is my copy, 1903, 21.6 cm., 124 pp., with a frontispiece and 1 plate, double columns. It is clothed in white wrappers cut flush, bordered in green, printed in black, and with a picture in brown. There is an ad on the back cover in brown, ads on the inside covers, and on 4 pp. at the back. The first edition was issued by Ward, Lock (1903), Cr 8vo, 20.2 cm., 336 pp., 6/0 cloth, listed in the *Ath* on Feb. 28. The second edition was advertised there on Mar. 14 as "Now ready."
Also 1905

2621 ELLEN WOOD (MRS. HENRY WOOD) *East Lynne.* o/6 sewed   Nov. (*Eng Cat*)

Sixpenny Standard Novels and Popular Books No. 119. This was also put in the *Prize Library* at 2/0 cloth, 2/6, and in the *Lily Series* at 1/6 cloth. It first appeared in *Colburn's New Monthly Magazine* from Jan. 1860 to Aug. 1861. The first book edition was issued by Bentley, London, 3 vols., 1861, 19.5 cm., 31/6, listed in the *Ath* on Sept. 21. He issued a new edition in 3 vols., advertised in the *Spect* on Nov. 16, 1861, as "Now ready." He issued the fourth edition in 3 vols., advertised in the *Spect* as "On Feb. 25, 1862"; and issued it in 1 vol., 6/0, advertised in the *Spect* on May 10, 1862, as "Just ready." He issued the 200th thousand, 1888, 471 pp.; and issued the 350th thousand, 471 pp., 2/0 green cloth, 2/6 red cloth, as No. 1 of a new issue of Mrs. Wood's novels, advertised in the *Spect* on Jan. 12, 1895, as "On Jan. 16." Macmillan & Co., Ltd., London, issued it, 1901, 471 pp., as they had purchased Bentley about Aug. 20, 1898. They issued it, 1902, my copy, the 660th thousand, 21.2 cm., 260 pp., o/6 sewed, double columns, in June; and reissued it at 1/0 in Aug. The first American edition was issued by Dick &

Fitzgerald, New York (1861), 24 cm., 201 pp., $.50 paper, listed in *APC&LG* (monthly) on Nov. 15 and *Godey's Lady's Book* for Jan. 1862, and thus probably issued in Oct. or Nov. 1861.

2622 GUY N. BOOTHBY *Across the World for a Wife.* Cr 8vo. Illustrated. o/6 sewed Dec. (*Eng Cat*)

Sixpenny Lithographic Series No. 77. The first edition was issued by Ward, Lock, 1898, 20 cm., 379 pp., with illustrations, 5/0 cloth, listed in the *Ath* on Oct. 22.

2623 GERTRUDE WARDEN & ROBERT EUSTACE *The Stolen Pearl.* Demy 8vo. Illustrated. o/6 sewed   Dec. (*Eng Cat*)

Detective and Adventure Series No. 336. The first edition was issued by Ward, Lock (1903), 20.4 cm., 338 pp., with a frontispiece, 3/6 cloth, listed in the *Ath* on Feb. 14 and the *Times Weekly Edition* on Feb. 27.

2624 ALFRED WILSON-BARRETT
The French Master. Demy 8vo.
Illustrated.
o/6 sewed   Jan. (*Eng Cat*)
Detective and Adventure Series No. 337. The
first edition was issued by Ward, Lock
(1903), 251 pp., 3/6 cloth, issued in Mar.

2625 ANNA K. GREEN, later ROHLFS
The Sword of Damocles. o/5 sewed
Jan. (*Eng Cat*)
Also 1884

2626 HAWLEY SMART **Courtship in 1720,
in 1860.** Large Cr 8vo. Illustrated. o/6
sewed   Jan. (*Eng Cat*)
Sixpenny Lithographic Series No. 78. The
first edition was issued by Chapman &
Hall, London, 2 vols., 1876, 20 cm., 21/0,
listed in the *Ath* on Nov. 11. They issued it
as *Select Library of Fiction* No. 359, 2/0
boards, listed in the *Ath* on May 19, 1877.
The first American edition was issued by
J. B. Lippincott & Co., Philadelphia, 1877,
Star Series No. 1, 16mo, 251 pp., $1.00
cloth, listed in *PW* on Jan. 6, 1877, and the
Nation and the *Ind* on Feb. 1. The *Star Series* (Tourist's Edition) was advertised in
the *New-York Times* on Sept. 19, 1878,
16mo, $.50 stiff paper covers, as "Just
published."

2627 ROBERT M. BALLANTYNE
The Gorilla Hunters. o/6, 1/0, 1/6
Feb. (*Eng Cat*)
Sixpenny Standard Novels and Popular Books
No. 120. This was also put in the *Royal Se-
ries* at 1/0 cloth, the *Youth's Library* at 1/6

cloth, and the *Captain's Library* at 2/0 cloth,
2/6, all issued before 1909. The first edition was issued by Thomas Nelson, London, in 1861, 18 cm., 422 pp., with a frontispiece, pictorial title page, and 5
illustrations, noticed in the *Spect* on Dec.
28, 1861. They issued it in 1868, 12mo,
3/0, listed in the *Spect* on June 6. The first
American edition was probably Crosby &
Nichols, Boston, 17.5 cm., 408 pp., illustrated, which the *U Cat* gives as 1863 and
which was listed in *APC&LG* (monthly) on
Nov. 1, 1862.

2628 GEORGE J. WHYTE MELVILLE
Tilbury Nogo. Large Cr 8vo. Illustrated.
o/6 sewed   Feb. (*Eng Cat*)
Sixpenny Lithographic Series No. 79.
Also 1882, 1902

2629 ARCHIBALD C. GUNTER
The Fighting Troubadour.
Large Cr 8vo. Illustrated.
o/6 sewed   Feb. (*Eng Cat*)
Sixpenny Lithographic Series No. 80.
Also 1903

2630 ANNA K. GREEN, later ROHLFS
Hand and Ring. o/6 sewed   Feb.
(*Eng Cat*)
Also 1884

2631 H. BURFORD DELANNOY **M.R.C.S.**
Cr 8vo. 2/0 boards   Feb. (*Eng Cat*)
2/0 Copyright Novels No. 47. The first edition was issued by Ward, Lock (1903), 19.5
cm., 413 pp., illustrated, 3/6 cloth, listed
in the *Times Literary Supplement* (London)

on May 29 and the *Spect* on May 30. It was also issued as *Detective and Adventure Series* No. 353, illustrated, o/6 sewed, listed in the *Eng Cat* as published in Nov. 1904.

2632 LAWRENCE L. LYNCH (EMMA MURDOCH, later VAN DEVENTER) *A Slender Clue.* Demy 8vo. Illustrated. o/6 sewed   Feb. (*Eng Cat*) *Detective and Adventure Series* No. 338. Also 1892, 93

2633 MRS. L. T. MEADE, later SMITH *The Sorceress of the Strand.* Demy 8vo. Illustrated. o/6 sewed   Feb. (*Eng Cat*) *Detective and Adventure Series* No. 339. The first edition was issued by Ward, Lock, 1903, 19.7 cm., 312 pp., illustrated, 5/o cloth, listed in the *Ath* on June 20. The present edition is 1904, 23 cm., 95 pp.

2634 LAWRENCE L. LYNCH (EMMA MURDOCH, later VAN DEVENTER) *The Detective's Daughter.* o/6 sewed   Feb. (*Eng Cat*) Also 1887

2635 ALICK MUNRO *A Woman of Wiles.* Large Cr 8vo. Illustrated. o/6 sewed Mar. (*Eng Cat*) *Sixpenny Lithographic Series* No. 81. The first edition was issued by Ward, Lock, 1902, 20.3 cm., 304 pp., illustrated, 6/o cloth, listed in the *Ath* on June 21.

2636 GUY N. BOOTHBY *A Sailor's Bride.* Large Cr 8vo. Illustrated. o/6 sewed Mar. (*Eng Cat*) *Sixpenny Lithographic Series* No. 82. The first edition was issued by F. V. White & Co., London, 1899, 19.5 cm., 235 pp., illustrated, 5/o cloth, listed in the *Ath* on Sept. 30. They issued it at o/6 sewed, 8vo, 128 pp., in Apr. 1900.

2637 ANNA K. GREEN, later ROHLFS *A Strange Disappearance.* Demy 8vo. Illustrated. o/6 sewed   Mar. (*Eng Cat*) *Detective and Adventure Series* No. 340. Also 1884

2638 HEADON HILL *The Queen of Night.* Demy 8vo. Illustrated. o/6 sewed   Mar.? *Detective and Adventure Series* No. 341. Also 1899, 1900

2639 ÉMILE GABORIAU *In Deadly Peril.* o/6 sewed   Mar. (*Eng Cat*) Also 1888

2640 EDGAR ALLAN POE *The Fall of the House of Usher.* Demy 8vo. Illustrated. o/6 sewed   Mar. (*Eng Cat*) *Detective and Adventure Series* No. 345. This probably had other stories as well. The title story was first printed in the *Gentleman's Magazine and American Monthly Review*, Philadelphia, in Sept. 1839, on pp. 145–152. It was in *Tales of the Grotesque and Arabesque*, issued by Lea & Blanchard, Philadelphia, 2 vols., 1840, Poe's first collection of fiction. It was issued in 750 copies in purple muslin with printed spine labels. It was in *Tales*, issued by Wiley & Putnam, London, 1845, 288 pp.

2641 JOHN C. SNAITH *Lady Barbarity.* Large Cr 8vo. Illustrated. o/6 sewed Apr. (*Eng Cat*) *Sixpenny Lithographic Series* No. 83. The first edition was issued by D. Appleton & Co., New York, 1899, my copy in paper, 17.8 cm., 332 pp., $.50 paper, $1.00 cloth, in terra-cotta paper printed in black, with "Town and Country Library No. 271" on the front and on the half-title. There are publisher's ads on the back, the inside covers, and 14 pp. at the back. It was listed in the *Nation* on Sept. 7 and *PW* on Sept. 9 and is dated Sept. 1, 1899, on the front cover. The first English edition was issued by Ward, Lock, 1899, Cr 8vo, 319 pp., illustrated, 6/o cloth. It was listed in the *Spect* on Sept. 30 and the *Ath* on Oct. 14. The Canadian copyright edition was issued by Copp, Clark & Co., Toronto, 1899, 319 pp.

2642 GEORGE J. WHYTE MELVILLE
Uncle John. Large Cr 8vo. Illustrated.
o/6 sewed   Apr. (*Eng Cat*)
Sixpenny Lithographic Series No. 84.
Also 1902

2643 E. P. OPPENHEIM *The Survivor.*
Large Cr 8vo. Illustrated. o/6 sewed
Apr. (*Eng Cat*)
Sixpenny Lithographic Series No. 87. This is
1904, 21.5 cm., 123 pp. The first English
edition was issued by Ward, Lock, 1901,
Cr 8vo, 310 pp., 6/o cloth, listed in the *Ath*
on Feb. 23. I suspect the first American
edition was issued by Little, Brown & Co.,
Boston, as they issued a new edition, 1913,
12mo, 310 pp., illustrated. However, the
U Cat gives New York, 1901. Ward, Lock
issued a second edition at 6/o cloth, advertised in the *Spect* on Apr. 27, 1901, as
"Now ready."

2644 RODRIGUES OTTOLENGUI
A Conflict of Evidence. Demy 8vo.
Illustrated. o/6 sewed   Apr. (*Eng Cat*)
Detective and Adventure Series No. 342. This
is 1904, 128 pp., the first English edition
set up in England. The first edition was is-
sued by G. P. Putnam's Sons, New York
(1893), 18 cm., 347 pp., $.50 paper, $1.00
cloth. It was listed in the *New-York Times* on
June 10 as "On June 14," in the *Ind* on
June 22, and in *PW* on June 24. The au-
thor was a New York dentist. Putnam's,
London, issued it, Cr 8vo, 2/o, listed in the
Spect on July 15, 1893.

2645 ARCHIBALD C. GUNTER *The Empty
Hotel.* Large Cr 8vo. Illustrated. o/6
sewed   May (*Eng Cat*)
Sixpenny Lithographic Series No. 85. The
first American edition was *The Surprises of
an Empty Hotel*, issued by the Home Publishing Co., New York (1902), 19.5 cm.,
292 pp., illustrated. The first English edition was issued by Ward, Lock, with the
present title, 1902, 20.2 cm., 292 pp., 6/o
cloth, listed in the *Ath* on Sept. 27.

2646 SIR WILLIAM MAGNAY *The Man
of the Hour.* Large Cr 8vo. Illustrated.
o/6 sewed   May (*Eng Cat*)
Sixpenny Lithographic Series No. 86. The
first edition was issued by Ward, Lock
(1902), 19.7 cm., 288 pp., illustrated,
listed in the *Ath* on Sept. 20 and the *Times
Literary Supplement* on Sept. 19.

2647 ÉMILE GABORIAU *The Champdoce
Mystery.* o/6 sewed   May (*Eng Cat*)
Also 1889

2648 ANNA K. GREEN, later ROHLFS
Marked "Personal." Demy 8vo.
Illustrated. o/6 sewed. May (*Eng Cat*)
Detective and Adventure Series No. 343. This
is 1904, with 160 pp. The first edition was
issued by G. P. Putnam's Sons, New York,
1893, 17.5 cm., 415 pp., $.50 paper, $1.00
cloth, listed in the *Nation* on May 18 and
PW on June 2 (no list on May 27). They issued it in their *Hudson Library* in 1901,
$.50 paper, advertised in the *New York
Times Book Review* on May 25 as "Recent."
They issued it in London (1893), 19.5 cm.,
415 pp., advertised in the *Spect* on May 20,
at 2/o boards, 2/6 cloth, and listed in the
Ath on May 27 at 2/o boards. They issued
the 14th thousand at 2/o boards, 2/6 cloth,
advertised in the *Ath* on June 3, 1893.

2649 EDGAR ALLAN POE *Arthur Gordon
Pym.* Demy 8vo. Illustrated. o/6 sewed
May (*Eng Cat*)
Detective and Adventure Series No. 344. The
first edition was issued by Harper & Bros.,
New York, 1838, *The Narrative of Arthur
Gordon Pym*, 19 cm., anonymous, 201 pp.,
with a leaf of ads at the front (May 1838),
and 14 pp. at the back. It was probably issued in July, as it was reviewed in the *New-
Yorker* for Aug. 4 as "Just published," and
listed in the *North American Review* for Oct.
It was issued in various colored cloths, including green, black, and blue, with a
printed paper label on the spine. It was is-

sued in England with the same title, by Wiley & Putnam, etc., etc., London, 1838, 21 cm., anonymous, 252 pp., the first Poe book to appear in England. It was advertised in *PC* on Oct. 1 as "On Oct. 10" and listed Nov. 1, and listed in the *Literary Gazette* on Oct. 20. It has seven additional lines in the second preface, and the text varies from the American first printing and omits the diary entry of Mar. 22 at the end. The first two installments appeared in the *Messenger* in Jan. and Feb. 1838.

2650 RICHARD MARSH **The Mystery of Philip Bennion's Death.** Demy 8vo. Illustrated. o/6 sewed   June (*Eng Cat*)
Detective and Adventure Series No. 346.
Also 1897, 1900

2651 LAWRENCE L. LYNCH (EMMA MURDOCH, later VAN DEVENTER) **A Mountain Mystery.** o/6 sewed
June (*Eng Cat*)
Also 1888

2652 MRS. L. T. MEADE, later SMITH & ROBERT EUSTACE (EUSTACE ROBERT BARTON) **The Lost Square.** Demy 8vo. Illustrated. o/6 sewed   July (*Eng Cat*)
Detective and Adventure Series No. 347. The first edition was issued by Ward, Lock (1902), 19.7 cm., 264 pp., 5/o cloth, listed in the *Ath* on Apr. 19 and the *Times Literary Supplement* on Apr. 18.

2653 ELLEN WOOD (MRS. HENRY WOOD) **The Channings.** Large Cr 8vo. Illustrated. o/6 sewed   July (*Eng Cat*)
Sixpenny Lithographic Series No. 89. This was also issued in the *Lily Series* at 1/6 cloth and in the *Prize Library* at 2/o cloth, 2/6. The first edition was issued by Bentley, London, 3 vols, 1862, 19.5 cm., 31/6, listed in the *Ath* on Apr. 19. He issued it, 1862, 480 pp.; and issued the 140th thousand, 1895, 19.5 cm., 454 pp., at 2/o can-

vas, 2/6 cloth. Macmillan & Co., London, issued it, 1899, 454 pp.; and reissued it, 1902; and issued it at o/6 sewed in Oct. 1903. The first American edition was issued by T. B. Peterson & Bros., Philadelphia (1862), 24 cm., 302 pp., in both paper and cloth, listed in the *Ind* and *APC&LG* (monthly) on May 1.

2654 HAWLEY SMART **From Post to Finish.** Large Cr 8vo. Illustrated. o/6 sewed Aug. (*Eng Cat*)
Sixpenny Lithographic Series No. 88.
Also 1885, 91, 99

2655 BERTRAM MITFORD **The Induna's Wife.** Large Cr 8vo. Illustrated. o/6 sewed   Aug. (*Eng Cat*)
Sixpenny Lithographic Series No. 90. This is 1904, with 126 pp. The first edition was issued by F. V. White & Co., London, 1898, 19.5 cm., 300 pp., illustrated, 3/6 cloth, listed in the *Ath* on Mar. 12. They issued it, 8vo, at o/6 sewed, in Mar. 1900.

2656 RODRIGUES OTTOLENGUI **A Modern Wizard.** Demy 8vo. Illustrated. o/6 sewed   Aug. (*Eng Cat*)
Detective and Adventure Series No. 348. The first edition was issued by G. P. Putnam's Sons, New York and London, 1894, 18 cm., 434 pp., $.50 paper, $1.00 cloth, listed in the *Nation* on Apr. 19, and advertised in the *New-York Times* on Apr. 21 as "Now ready." It was issued in England by Putnam at 2/o boards, 2/6 cloth, advertised in the *Ath* on June 16, 1894, as "Just published."

2657 GUY N. BOOTHBY **Sheilah McLeod.** Large Cr 8vo. Illustrated. o/6 sewed Aug.?
Sixpenny Lithographic Series No. 91. This is my copy, no date, 21.1 cm., 123 pp., with a frontispiece and 1 plate, double columns. It is in pictorial lithographed wrappers

cut flush, in red, green, blue, brown, and black, with the series title appearing only in the ads. The ads are on the inside covers, on 4 pp. at the back, and on the back in brown and red. There is an inscribed date (Sept. 1905). The first American edition was issued by Frederick A. Stokes Co., New York (1897), 17 cm., 255 pp., illustrated, $.75 cloth, listed in the *Nation* and the *Ind* on Sept. 30, and advertised in the *New-York Times* on Sept. 18 as "Just published." The first English edition was issued by Skeffington & Son, London, 1897, 19 cm., 311 pp., with a frontispiece, 6/o cloth, advertised in the *Ath* on Sept. 4 as "On Sept. 23," and listed on Sept. 18

2658 E. P. OPPENHEIM *The Great Awakening.* Large Cr 8vo. Illustrated. 0/6 sewed Sept. (*Eng Cat*)

Sixpenny Lithographic Series No. 92. The first edition was issued by Ward, Lock, 1902, 20.4 cm., 320 pp., illustrated, 6/o cloth, listed in the *Ath* on June 14 and the *Times Literary Supplement* on June 20. They issued a second impression, 1902, the same, advertised in the *Spect* on Aug. 2, as "Now ready."

2659 FERGUS W. HUME *The Indian Bangle.* Demy 8vo. Illustrated. 0/6 sewed Sept. (*Eng Cat*)

Detective and Adventure Series No. 349. This is 1904, with 160 pp. The first edition was issued by Sampson Low, London, 1899, Cr 8vo, 309 pp., 3/6 pictorial cloth, listed in the *Ath* on Sept. 23.

2660 ANNA K. GREEN, later ROHLFS *Cynthia Wakeham's Money.* Demy 8vo. Illustrated. 0/6 sewed Sept. (*Eng Cat*)

Detective and Adventure Series No. 350. This is 1904, 124 pp., with a frontispiece and a plate. The first edition in both England and America was issued by G. P. Putnam's Sons, New York and London, 1892, 16mo, 336 pp., with a frontispiece. In the United States it was issued at $.50 paper, $1.00 cloth, listed in the *Ind* on July 21 and *PW* on July 23 (no list on July 16). In England it was issued at 2/o boards, 2/6 cloth, advertised in the *Spect* on Oct. 1, and advertised in the *Ath* on Sept. 26 as "Ready." The 2/6 was listed in the *Ath* on Aug. 27, and the 2/o was listed on Sept. 24.

2661 ANONYMOUS *The Wonder Book.* Cr 4to. Illustrated. 3/6 picture boards, 5/o cloth Oct. 15 (*Spect* ad)

This is the first issue of a new annual, a picture annual for boys and girls, edited by Harry Golding. It was issued annually, 1904–1927, but not in 1919. It has 8 colored plates, and illustrations. The second issue was in 1905, advertised in the *Spect* on Oct. 21, 1905.

2662 ARCHIBALD C. GUNTER *The Spy Company.* Large Cr 8vo. Illustrated. 0/6 sewed Oct. (*Eng Cat*)

Sixpenny Lithographic Series No. 93. The first edition was issued by the Home Publishing Co., New York (1902), 19.5 cm., 295 pp., with a colored frontispiece and 1 plate. The *BM* gives both Samuel French, London, 1903, 295 pp.; and Ward, Lock, 1903, 19.6 cm., 295 pp., at 6/o cloth. The latter was listed in the *Ath* on June 6 and the *Times Literary Supplement* on June 12.

2663 BERTRAM MITFORD *The Ruby Sword.* Large Cr 8vo. Illustrated. 0/6 sewed Oct. (*Eng Cat*)

Sixpenny Lithographic Series No. 94. The first edition was issued by F. V White & Co., London, 1899 (1898), 19.5 cm., 336 pp., illustrated, 3/6 cloth, listed in the *Ath* on Nov. 5, 1898. They issued it, 1900, my copy, 22 cm., 127 pp., 0/6 sewed, double columns, in café-au-lait wrappers cut flush, pictorially printed in the front in black.

2664 HEADON HILL *The Perils of the Red Box.* Demy 8vo. Illustrated. o/6 sewed Oct. (*Eng Cat*)

Detective and Adventure Series No. 351. The first edition was issued by Ward, Lock, 1903, *Seaward for the Foe*, containing two tales, one of which was the present title, 20 cm., 378 pp., illustrated, 3/6 cloth, listed in the *Ath* on Mar. 7.

2665 MRS. L. T. MEADE, later SMITH & ROBERT EUSTACE (EUSTACE ROBERT BARTON) *A Master of Mysteries.* Demy 8vo. Illustrated. o/6 sewed Oct. (*Eng Cat*)

Detective and Adventure Series No. 352. Also 1901

2666 GUY N. BOOTHBY *The Marriage of Esther.* Large Cr 8vo. Illustrated. o/6 sewed Oct. (*Eng Cat*)

Sixpenny Lithographic Series No. 95. The first edition was issued by Ward, Lock, 1895, 20 cm., 260 pp., illustrated, 5/o cloth, listed in the *Ath* on Feb. 23. They issued the fourth edition, Cr 8vo, illustrated, 5/o, advertised in the *Spect* on Nov. 27, 1897. The first American edition was issued by D. Appleton & Co., New York, 1895, 19.5 cm., 254 pp., $.50 paper, $1.00 cloth, *Town and Country Library* No. 166. It was listed in *PW* on Apr. 27 and the *New-York Times* on Apr. 28.

2667 LOUIS TRACY *Rainbow Island.* Large Cr 8vo. Illustrated. o/6 sewed Nov. (*Eng Cat*)

The first edition was issued by Ward, Lock (1903), 19.7 cm., 355 pp., illustrated, 6/o cloth, listed in the *Ath* on Sept. 19. They issued the second edition in 1903, at 6/o, advertised in the *Spect* on Oct. 17. The present edition is *Sixpenny Lithographic Series* No. 96.

2668 FERGUS W. HUME *The Fever of Life.* Demy 8vo. Illustrated. o/6 sewed Nov. (*Eng Cat*)

Detective and Adventure Series No. 354. The first English edition was issued by Sampson Low, London, 2 vols., 1893, Cr 8vo, 21/o, advertised in the *Times Weekly Edition* on Oct. 14. A new edition, Cr 8vo, 6/o, was advertised there on Oct. 20, 1893, and I think it was 20 cm., 417 pp., and dated 1893. In the United States it was issued by Tait, Sons & Co., New York (1892), copyright 1891, 12mo, 381 pp., $.50 paper, $1.00 cloth, in their *Holyrood Series*, advertised in the *New-York Times* on Dec. 3, 1892, listed in *PW* on Dec. 3 (no lists on Nov. 19 or 26), and in the *Nation* on Dec. 1. The *U Cat* gives John W. Lovell, New York (copyright 1891), 19 cm., 381 pp., and this would be in wrappers in the *Seaside Library Pocket Edition*.

Ward, Lock & Co., Ltd.
London, New York, and Melbourne
1905

2669 ELLEN WOOD (MRS. HENRY WOOD)
Mrs. Halliburton's Troubles. Large Cr 8vo.
Illustrated. o/6 sewed   Feb. (*Eng Cat*)

Sixpenny Lithographic Series No. 97. This
was also put in the *Lily Series* at 1/6 cloth
and in the *Prize Library* at 2/0 cloth, 2/6. It
first appeared in *The Quiver* of Cassell, Petter & Galpin, London, complete in vols. 1
and 2. The first English book edition was
issued by Bentley, London, 3 vols., 1862,
20 cm., 31/6, listed in the *Ath* on Nov. 15,
1862. The third thousand was advertised
in the *Spect* on Nov. 29, 1862. He issued a
new edition in 1863, Cr 8vo, 474 pp., with
2 illustrations, 6/0 cloth, listed in the
Reader on May 30. He issued the 120th
thousand, 1895, 19.5 cm., 461 pp., at 2/0
canvas, 2/6 cloth. Macmillan & Co., London, issued it, 1902, 461 pp.; and issued it,
8vo, o/6 sewed, in Mar. 1904. In the
United States it was issued by Dick & Fitzgerald, New York (1863), 23 cm., 251 pp.,
$.50 paper, $.75 cloth, advertised in the
New-York Times on Dec. 17, 1862, from advance sheets, and noticed in *Godey's Lady's
Book* for Mar. 1863, and thus probably issued in Dec. 1862 or Jan. 1863. It was also
issued by T. B. Peterson & Bros., Philadelphia, listed in *APC&LG* (fortnightly) on
Jan. 15, 1863.

2670 GUY N. BOOTHBY ***In Strange
Company.*** Large Cr 8vo. Illustrated.
o/6 sewed   Feb. (*Eng Cat*)

Sixpenny Lithographic Series No. 98. The
first English edition was issued by Ward,

Lock & Bowden, Ltd., London, New
York, and Melbourne, 1894, Cr 8vo, 300
pp., with 6 plates, 5/0 cloth, listed in the
Spect on July 14. They issued the fifth edition, the same, advertised in the *Spect* on
Nov. 27, 1897. They issued it as a supplement to the *Windsor Magazine*, for the
Christmas number, 1896, 23.5 cm., 80
pp., illustrated. The first American edition was issued by F. T. Neely, Chicago,
1894, 20 cm., 300 pp., in *Neely's International Library*, listed in the *Nation* on Nov.
15, 1894, and *PW* on Dec. 8.

2671 ANNA K. GREEN, later ROHLFS
One of My Sons. Demy 8vo. Illustrated.
o/6 sewed   Feb. (*Eng Cat*)

Detective and Adventure Series No. 355. The
first edition was issued by G. P. Putnam's
Sons, New York and London, 1901, 19.5
cm., 366 pp., with a frontispiece and 1
plate, $1.50, listed in *PW* on Nov. 23,
1901, and *Lit World* (monthly) on Jan. 1,
1902. The first English edition was issued
by Ward, Lock, 1904, 19.7 cm., 366 pp.,
cloth, listed in the *Ath* on Apr. 9 and the
Times Literary Supplement on Apr. 1.

2672 ARCHIBALD C. GUNTER ***The Sword
in the Air.*** Large Cr 8vo. Illustrated.
o/6 sewed   Mar. (*Eng Cat*)

Sixpenny Lithographic Series No. 99. The
first edition was *Adrienne de Portalis*, issued
by the Home Publishing Co., New York,
about Apr. 21, 1900. The first English edi-

tion was with the present title, issued by Ward, Lock, 1904, 19.7 cm., 309 pp., illustrated, 6/0 cloth, listed in the *Ath* on Apr. 2 and the *Spect* on Mar. 19.

2673 E. P. OPPENHEIM **The Mysterious Mr. Sabin.** Large Cr 8vo. Illustrated. o/6 sewed   Mar. (*Eng Cat*)
Sixpenny Lithographic Series No. 100.
Also 1901

2674 ARCHIBALD C. GUNTER **The Princess of Copper.** o/6 sewed Mar. (*Eng Cat*)
Also 1901

2675 MORICE GERARD (JOHN J. TEAGUE) **The Man with the White Face.** Demy 8vo. Illustrated. o/7 sewed   Mar. (*Eng Cat*)
Detective and Adventure Series No. 356. The first edition was issued by Ward, Lock, 1903, 19.7 cm., 270 pp., illustrated, 3/6 cloth, listed in the *Times Literary Supplement* on Feb. 20 and the *Ath* on Feb. 21.

2676 ARCHIBALD EYRE **The Trifler.** Large Cr 8vo. Illustrated. o/6 sewed Apr. (*Eng Cat*)
Sixpenny Lithographic Series No. 101. The first edition was issued by Ward, Lock, 1903, Cr 8vo, 319 pp., 6/0 cloth, listed in the *Ath* on June 27. The first American edition was issued by the Smart Set Publishing Co., New York and London, 1903, 19.5 cm., 334 pp., illustrated, $1.50 cloth, listed in the *New York Times Book Review* on Oct. 24.

2677 HEADON HILL (FRANCIS GRAINGER) **A Race with Ruin.** Large Cr 8vo. Illustrated. o/6 sewed   Apr. (*Eng Cat*)
Sixpenny Lithographic Series No. 102. The first English edition was issued by Ward, Lock, 1904, Cr 8vo, 318 pp., 6/0 cloth, listed in the *Ath* on Apr. 23. The first Canadian edition was issued by Langton & Hall, Toronto, 1904, 12mo, 318 pp.

2678 ORME AGNUS (JOHN HIGGINBOTHAM) **Sarah Tulden.** Large Cr 8vo. Illustrated. o/6 sewed   Apr. (*Eng Cat*)
Sixpenny Lithographic Series No. 104. The first English edition was issued by Ward, Lock, 1903, 19.7 cm., 372 pp., illustrated, 6/0 cloth, listed in the *Spect* on June 27 and the *Times Literary Supplement* on July 3. They issued the third edition at 6/0, advertised in the *Spect* on Oct. 17 as "Ready." The first American edition was issued by Little, Brown & Co., Boston, 1903, 20.4 cm., 363 pp., illustrated, $1.50, listed in the *New York Times Book Review* on May 16 and *Outlook* on June 27.

2679 GUY N. BOOTHBY **The Kidnapped President.** Large Cr 8vo. Illustrated. o/6 sewed   May (*Eng Cat*)
Sixpenny Lithographic Series No. 103. The first English edition was issued by Ward, Lock, 1902, 20.4 cm., 308 pp., 5/0 cloth, listed in the *Ath* on Aug. 30 and the *Times Literary Supplement* on Aug. 22. In the United States it was issued by George Munro's Sons, New York, copyright 1902, 18.5 cm., 191 pp., as *Laurel Library* No. 122.

2680 LOUIS TRACY **The Albert Gate Affair.** Large Cr 8vo. Illustrated. o/6 sewed   May (*Eng Cat*)
Sixpenny Lithographic Series No. 106. This is my copy, 1905, 21.5 cm., 127 pp., with a frontispiece and a plate, double columns. There are ads on the inside covers and an ad on the back in brown and red on white, printed in black. The front is a pictorial lithograph in red, green, blue, yellow, black, and white. The first edition was issued by Ward, Lock, 1904, 19.7 cm., 309 pp., illustrated, 6/0 cloth, listed in the *Ath* on Apr. 16 and the *Times Literary Supplement* on Apr. 1. The first American edition was issued by R. F. Fenno & Co., New York, 1904, 20 cm., 309 pp., *The Albert*

Gate Mystery, with a colored frontispiece and illustrations partly colored. It was listed in the *New York Times Book Review* on Oct. 22, $1.50 cloth.

2681 ARCHIBALD C. GUNTER *The City of Mystery*. Large Cr 8vo. Illustrated. 0/6 sewed June (*Eng Cat*)

Sixpenny Lithographic Series No. 105. The first edition was issued by the Home Publishing Co., New York (1902), 20 cm., 276 pp. It was issued by Ward, Lock, 1904, Cr 8vo, 275 pp., 6/0, listed in the *Ath* on July 23. The *BM* gives also Samuel French, London, 1902, 276 pp.

2682 HENRY HERMAN *Lady Turpin*. Large Cr 8vo. Illustrated. 0/6 sewed June (*Eng Cat*)

Sixpenny Lithographic Series No. 110. Also 1895, 99, 1903

2683 H. BURFORD DELANNOY *The Margate Murder Mystery*. Large Cr 8vo. Illustrated. 0/6 sewed June (*Eng Cat*)

Sixpenny Lithographic Series No. 111. Also 1902, 03

2684 JOHN R. CARLING *The Viking's Skull*. 0/6 sewed June (*Eng Cat*)

The first edition was issued by Little, Brown & Co., Boston, 1903, 22.5 cm., 349 pp., $1.50 cloth. I take this from the *U Cat* but cannot confirm the 1903 date. It was issued, 1904, the same, 20 cm., 349 pp., illustrated, $1.50 cloth, listed in the *New York Times Book Review* on Mar. 26, and advertised then also. The first English edition was issued by Ward, Lock, 1904, 19.7 cm., 352 pp., 6/0 cloth, listed in the *Times Literary Supplement* on Sept. 23 and the *Ath* on Oct. 1.

2685 WALTER HAWES *The Mystery Man*. Cr 8vo. Frontispiece. 1/0 sewed. June 23

This is the first edition, 1905, 18.4 cm., 191 pp., listed in the *Times Literary Supple-ment* on June 23 and by the *Eng Cat* as published in June.

2686 RICHARD HOWTON *Divine Healing and Demon Possession*. Cr 8vo. 1/0 June 30

This is the first edition, 1905, 19 cm., 136 pp. It was listed in the *Times Literary Supplement* on June 30 and by the *Eng Cat* as published in June. They issued the second edition, 1909, 137 pp., illustrated.

2687 LOUIS TRACY *A Fatal Legacy*. Large Cr 8vo. Illustrated. 0/6 sewed June?

Sixpenny Lithographic Series No. 107. Also 1903

2688 MORICE GERARD (JOHN J. TEAGUE) *The Man of the Moment*. Large Cr 8vo. Illustrated. 0/6 sewed June?

Sixpenny Lithographic Series No. 108. Also 1903

2689 ELIZABETH P. TRAIN *A Social Highwayman*. Large Cr 8vo. Illustrated. 0/6 sewed June?

Sixpenny Lithographic Series No. 109. Also 1896, 99, 1903

2690 GUY N. BOOTHBY *My Strangest Case*. Large Cr 8vo. Illustrated. 0/6 sewed July (*Eng Cat*)

Sixpenny Lithographic Series No. 112. The first edition was issued by L. C. Page & Co., Boston, 1901, 19 cm., 300 pp., with a frontispiece, $1.50 cloth, listed in *PW* on Sept. 14 and the *New York Times Book Review* on Oct. 12. The first English edition was issued by Ward, Lock, 1902, 20.3 cm., 315 pp., illustrated, 5/0 cloth, listed in the *Ath* on Apr. 5, the *Spect* on Mar. 22, and the *Times Literary Supplement* on Mar. 28. The *BM* and *U Cat* give this Ward, Lock edition as 1902 only, and the only listing in the *Ath* was the 1902 listing. Thus it is perplexing to see it listed in the *Spect* on Sept. 7, 1901, Cr 8vo, 5/0! I can explain this only as a mistaken entry in the *Spect*.

2691 H. BURFORD DELANNOY
Nineteen Thousand Pounds.
o/6 sewed   July (*Eng Cat*)
Also 1901, 02

2692 MAX ADELER (CHARLES H. CLARK)
An Old Fogey, etc. o/6 sewed   July
(*Eng Cat*)
Also 1881, 83, 89, 1901

2693 ANTHONY HOPE (ANTHONY HOPE
HAWKINS) *Comedies of Courtship.*
Large Cr 8vo. Illustrated. o/6 sewed
Aug. (*Eng Cat*)
Sixpenny Lithographic Series No. 113. The
first edition was issued by A. D. Innes &
Co., London, 1896, Cr 8vo, 346 pp., 6/o
cloth, listed in the *Ath* on Jan. 18, 1896. It
contains six stories. Ward, Lock issued it,
1901, 346 pp. The first American edition
was issued by Charles Scribner's Sons,
New York, 1896, copyright 1894, 1895,
and 1897, 19.5 cm., 377 pp., with a frontispiece, $1.50 cloth, listed in the *Nation*
and the *Ind* on Mar. 5, and *PW* on Mar. 7.
The latter noted that two of the stories
were printed in New York for the first
time in book form and four others had appeared in the United States in a small vol.,
unauthorized and without the author's
knowledge, with the titles changed beyond recognition!

2694 JOHN C. SNAITH *The Wayfarers.*
Large Cr 8vo. Illustrated. o/6 sewed
Sept. (*Eng Cat*)
Sixpenny Lithographic Series No. 114. The
first edition was issued by Ward, Lock,
1902, 20.3 cm., 303 pp., with a frontis-
piece and 1 plate, 6/o cloth, listed in the
Ath on Sept. 13.

2695 GUY N. BOOTHBY *Connie Burt.*
Large Cr 8vo. Illustrated. o/6 sewed
Sept. (*Eng Cat*)
Sixpenny Lithographic Series No. 115. The
first edition was issued by Ward, Lock
(1903), 19.7 cm., 317 pp., illustrated, 5/o
cloth, listed in the *Ath* on Mar. 28 and the
Times Literary Supplement on Mar. 13.

2696 ARCHIBALD EYRE *The Custodian.*
Large Cr 8vo. Illustrated. o/6 sewed
Sept. (*Eng Cat*)
Sixpenny Lithographic Series No. 118. The
first English edition was issued by Ward,
Lock, 1904, Cr 8vo, 314 pp., 6/o cloth,
listed in the *Ath* on Sept. 10. The first
American edition was issued by Henry
Holt & Co., New York, 1904, 19.5 cm.,
359 pp., illustrated, $1.50 cloth, listed in
the *New York Times Book Review* on Oct. 29.

2697 E. P. OPPENHEIM *The Traitors.*
Large Cr 8vo. Illustrated. o/6 sewed
Oct. (*Eng Cat*)
Sixpenny Lithographic Series No. 116. The
first edition was issued by Ward, Lock,
1902, 20.3 cm., 304 pp., with 2 illustrations, 6/o cloth, listed in the *Ath* on Oct. 18
and the *Times Literary Supplement* on Oct.
10. They issued the second edition at 6/o,
advertised in the *Spect* on Jan. 10, 1903, as
"Now ready." The first American edition
was issued by Dodd, Mead & Co., New
York, 1903, 19.5 cm., 344 pp., illustrated,
$1.50 cloth, listed in the *New York Times
Book Review* on Mar. 28.

Ward, Lock continued to issue the *Sixpenny Lithographic Series* for several more
years, each with illustrations and a lithographed picture in many colors on the
front. More than 200 titles had been issued by 1909.

Name Index

(Page numbers appear in boldface throughout Name Index.)

Title Index